Global Perspectives on Small and Medium Enterprises and Strategic Information Systems:
International Approaches

Pratyush Bharati
University of Massachusetts, USA

In Lee
Western Illinois University, USA

Abhijit Chaudhury
Bryant University, USA

BUSINESS SCIENCE REFERENCE

Hershey · New York

Director of Editorial Content:	Kristin Klinger
Director of Book Publications:	Julia Mosemann
Acquisitions Editor:	Lindsay Johnston
Development Editor:	Dave DeRicco
Publishing Assistant:	Keith Glazewski
Typesetter:	Keith Glazewski
Production Editor:	Jamie Snavely
Cover Design:	Lisa Tosheff
Printed at:	Yurchak Printing Inc.

Published in the United States of America by
Business Science Reference (an imprint of IGI Global)
701 E. Chocolate Avenue
Hershey PA 17033
Tel: 717-533-8845
Fax: 717-533-8661
E-mail: cust@igi-global.com
Web site: http://www.igi-global.com/reference

Library of Congress Cataloging-in-Publication Data

Global perspectives on small and medium enterprises and strategic information systems : international approaches / Pratyush Bharati, In Lee and Abhijit Chaudhury, editors.
     p. cm.
 Includes bibliographical references and index.
 Summary: "This book highlights the challenges faced by SMEs and how they are coping with the adverse environment through skillful use of IT and technologies such as Web 2.0, Enterprise Resource Planning (ERP), e-commerce, open source software, Business Process Digitization (BPD), and other emerging technologies"--Provided by publisher.
 ISBN 978-1-61520-627-8 (hbk.) -- ISBN 978-1-61520-628-5 (ebook) 1. Small business--Management. 2. Small business--Information technology. 3. Information technology--Management. I. Bharati, Pratyush, 1970- II. Lee, In, 1958- III. Chaudhury, Abhijit, 1958- IV. Title.
 HD62.7.G56 2010
 658.4'038011--dc22

2009052561

British Cataloguing in Publication Data
A Cataloguing in Publication record for this book is available from the British Library.

All work contributed to this book is new, previously-unpublished material. The views expressed in this book are those of the authors, but not necessarily of the publisher.

Table of Contents

Preface xii

Acknowledgment xv

Section 1
Practical Information System Challenges

Chapter 1
Connecting Small and Medium Enterprises to the New Consumer:
The Web 2.0 as Marketing Tool 1
    Efthymios Constantinides, University of Twente, The Netherlands

Chapter 2
Leveraging University Research to Assist SMEs in Legacy Industrial Era Regions:
The Case of I-99 Corridor 22
    Arvind Karunakaran, The Pennsylvania State University, USA
    Sandeep Purao, The Pennsylvania State University, USA
    Brian Cameron, The Pennsylvania State University, USA

Chapter 3
IT and the Transmission of the SME Culture of Nonprofit Theatres 41
    Julie E. Kendall, Rutgers University, USA
    Kenneth E. Kendall, Rutgers University, USA

Chapter 4
ERP System Selection Criteria: SMEs' Perceptions 57
    Andreja Pucihar, University of Maribor, Slovenia
    Gregor Lenart, University of Maribor, Slovenia
    Frantisek Sudzina, Copenhagen Business School, Denmark

Chapter 5
Managing Impressions of SME Legitimacy: Valuing Information and Communications
Technologies as Signals and Symbols 81
    Susan J. Winter, National Science Foundation, USA
    Connie Marie Gaglio, San Francisco State University, USA
    Hari K. Rajagopalan, Francis Marion University, USA

Section 2
Innovation and Information Technology Assimilation

Chapter 6
A Comparative Study of Small- and Medium-Sized Enterprises in Australia
and Singapore: Overall Satisfaction of Electronic Commerce Implementation 109
    Sandy Chong, Curtin University of Technology, Australia

Chapter 7
Australian SMEs' E-Commerce Adoption: Newer Perspectives 132
    Ada Scupola, Roskilde University, Denmark

Chapter 8
The Perception of Barriers to E-Commerce Adoption by SMEs:
A Comparison of Three Countries 145
    Robert C. MacGregor, University of Wollongong, Australia
    Deborah Bunker, University of Sydney, Australia
    Mira Kartiwi, University of Wollongong, Australia

Chapter 9
The Role of Organizational Slack in Technology Innovation Adoption for SMEs 169
    Jaume Franquesa, Kent State University, USA
    Alan Brandyberry, Kent State University, USA

Section 3
Strategy and Information Systems

Chapter 10
The Dual Lens Method: A Practical Approach to Information Systems Strategy in SMEs 195
    Peter Marshall, University of Tasmania, Australia
    Phyl Willson, University of Tasmania, Australia
    Judy Young, University of Tasmania, Australia
    Kristy de Salas, University of Tasmania, Australia

Chapter 11
The Alignment of Business Strategy with Agile Software Development within SMEs 215
    Pattama Kanavittaya, Murdoch University, Australia
    Jocelyn Armarego, Murdoch University, Australia
    Paula Goulding, Murdoch University, Australia

Chapter 12
Supporting SMEs Towards E-Business Success: Exploring the Importance of Training,
Competence and Stimulation 234
    Tom R. Eiekbrokk, University of Agder, Norway
    Dag H. Olsen, University of Agder, Norway

Chapter 13
Deploying the Internet for Leveraging Strategic Assets 265
    Frank Schlemmer, Optik Schlemmer, Germany
    Brian Webb, Queen's University Belfast, UK

Chapter 14
Business Process Digitalization and New Product Development: An Empirical Study
of Small and Medium-Sized Manufacturers 290
    Jun Li, University of New Hampshire, USA
    Michael Merenda, University of New Hampshire, USA
    A.R. (Venky) Venkatachalam, University of New Hampshire, USA

Chapter 15
Information Technology Interventions for Growth and Competitiveness
in Micro-Enterprises 306
    Sajda Qureshi, University of Nebraska at Omaha, USA
    Mehruz Kamal, University of Nebraska at Omaha, USA
    Peter Wolcott, University of Nebraska at Omaha, USA

Compilation of References 330

About the Contributors 380

Index 388

Detailed Table of Contents

Preface xii

Acknowledgment..xv

Section 1
Practical Information System Challenges

Chapter 1
Connecting Small and Medium Enterprises to the New Consumer:
The Web 2.0 as Marketing Tool.. 1
Efthymios Constantinides, University of Twente, The Netherlands

Chapter One presents the nature, effects, and position of social media or Web 2.0. This chapter identifies the main approaches corporations follow in engaging Web 2.0 applications in order to support, complement, or improve their traditional and online marketing activities. These approaches aim at using the social Internet as a source of marketing intelligence and for communicating with customers. The authors propose a classification of the main social media applications and identify the options for SMEs willing to utilize Web 2.0 technologies.

Chapter 2
Leveraging University Research to Assist SMEs in Legacy Industrial Era Regions:
The Case of I-99 Corridor...22
Arvind Karunakaran,The Pennsylvania State University, USA
Sandeep Purao, The Pennsylvania State University, USA
Brian Cameron, The Pennsylvania State University, USA

Chapter Two highlights the challenges faced by SMEs in legacy industrial era regions by focusing on the specific case of the I-99 corridor in the state of Pennsylvania. It discusses a structured approach toward enabling the SMEs in this region to access extended and powerful knowledge networks through a joint effort working toward regional economic development. The chapter describes the LAIR (Leveraging Advanced IT Research) project, which is aimed at understanding the risks that SMEs in the I-99 corridor are likely to face as they grow, with a specific focus on risks associated with upgrading, implementing, and integrating their information systems.

Chapter 3

IT and the Transmission of the SME Culture of Nonprofit Theatres...41
    Julie E. Kendall, Rutgers University, USA
    Kenneth E. Kendall, Rutgers University, USA

Chapter Three uses the framework provided by the metaphor of the third space as proposed by Bhabha (1994 and 1996). It elaborates on the diffusion of Broadway production business practices to small and medium-sized nonprofit theaters. The authors discover that both groups possess unique cultural competencies that open the door to using Web 2.0 technologies for staging and promoting productions and building relationships with theater patrons. They also discuss other management issues where expertise can be mutually exchanged.

Chapter 4

ERP System Selection Criteria: SMEs' Perceptions...57
    Andreja Pucihar, University of Maribor, Slovenia
    Gregor Lenart, University of Maribor, Slovenia
    Frantisek Sudzina, Copenhagen Business School, Denmark

Chapter Four presents the importance of ERP system selection criteria among SMEs in Slovenia. The investigated criteria were grouped into ERP benefits criteria, system quality criteria, vendor-related criteria, and ERP package criteria. System reliability, system functionality, vendor support, business process improvement, and improved service levels were perceived as the important ERP system selection criteria for small and medium-sized companies in Slovenia.

Chapter 5

Managing Impressions of SME Legitimacy: Valuing Information and Communications
Technologies as Signals and Symbols 81
    Susan J. Winter, National Science Foundation, USA
    Connie Marie Gaglio, San Francisco State University, USA
    Hari K. Rajagopalan, Francis Marion University, USA

Chapter Five advises SMEs to create legitimacy by mimicking the cues that signal credibility to potential stakeholders interacting with the firm. The authors examine the role of information and communications technology (ICT) in legitimacy-building from the perspectives of SME founders and potential customers.

Section 2
Innovation and Information Technology Assimilation

Chapter 6

A Comparative Study of Small- and Medium-Sized Enterprises in Australia
and Singapore: Overall Satisfaction of Electronic Commerce Implementation................................109
    Sandy Chong, Curtin University of Technology, Australia

Chapter Six examines the differences in electronic commerce (EC) implementation of SMEs in Australia and Singapore. The results show that respondents' perceptions of EC are predominantly positive. The analysis of Australian firms shows that five factors—observability, communication channel, customer pressure, supplier pressure, and perceived governmental support—make a significant contribution to the implementation of EC. In contrast, for firms in Singapore only three factors—firm size, perceived readiness, and observability—have significant impact. The author provides useful insights to adopters of EC initiatives in both countries.

Chapter 7
Australian SMEs' E-Commerce Adoption: Newer Perspectives 132
    Ada Scupola, Roskilde University, Denmark

Chapter Seven studies the factors affecting adoption of electronic commerce in small and medium enterprises in Australia. The author uses the Tornatsky and Fleischer (1990) model to investigate the impacts of environmental, organizational, and technological factors, and finds that the external environment has an influence mainly through customers' requirements and availability of IT services. The results of this study are contrary to other studies, which found that government and public administration play a significant role.

Chapter 8
The Perception of Barriers to E-Commerce Adoption by SMEs:
A Comparison of Three Countries 145
    Robert C. MacGregor, University of Wollongong, Australia
    Deborah Bunker, University of Sydney, Australia
    Mira Kartiwi, University of Wollongong, Australia

Chapter Eight examines the barriers to e-commerce perceived by SME owners and managers in the developing country of Indonesia. It then compares these perceived barriers with those in two developed economies, Sweden and Australia. The study highlights the differences in barriers to e-commerce adoption among the three countries.

Chapter 9
The Role of Organizational Slack in Technology Innovation Adoption for SMEs 169
    Jaume Franquesa, Kent State University, USA
    Alan Brandyberry, Kent State University, USA

Chapter Nine investigates the impact of organizational slack in US small and medium-sized enterprises (SMEs) on the adoption of information technology (IT) innovations. The authors find that the slack-innovation relationship, previously described for large firms, does not hold for SMEs. Their results show that potential slack is a strong predictor of technology adoption, whereas available slack is not a significant factor in SME innovation adoption. The authors argue that, in some cases, innovation adoption may represent a form of "bricolage" by resource-constrained SMEs.

Section 3
Strategy and Information Systems

Chapter 10

The Dual Lens Method: A Practical Approach to Information Systems Strategy in SMEs 195

Peter Marshall, University of Tasmania, Australia

Phyl Willson, University of Tasmania, Australia

Judy Young, University of Tasmania, Australia

Kristy de Salas, University of Tasmania, Australia

Chapter Ten presents a method of IS strategy formulation in SMEs. The method draws on the work of Levy and Powell (1999, 2000). A case study describes their experience with this method. The method is comprised of two complementary analyses: an externally focused strategic analysis and an internally focused business process analysis. The authors emphasize the importance of relevance and practicality in selecting the method in practice.

Chapter 11

The Alignment of Business Strategy with Agile Software Development within SMEs 215

Pattama Kanavittaya, Murdoch University, Australia

Jocelyn Armarego, Murdoch University, Australia

Paula Goulding, Murdoch University, Australia

Chapter Eleven studies the challenge of aligning business strategy and information technology (IT) strategy. The authors examine the adoption of agile methods by SMEs in developing software products and suggest that agile methods may facilitate the alignment of business and IT strategy. Models of strategic alignment developed for large enterprises are also validated for SMEs.

Chapter 12

Supporting SMEs Towards E-Business Success: Exploring the Importance of Training,
Competence and Stimulation 234

Tom R. Eiekbrokk, University of Agder, Norway

Dag H. Olsen, University of Agder, Norway

Chapter Twelve examines the relationship between training and performance in SMEs and discusses practical implications. They find a positive relationship between training, competence, and performance. The authors show that training explains variances in e-business competences and performance in terms of efficiency, complementarities, lock-in, and novelty. The study has practical implications for public policy makers, training suppliers, and SME managers.

Chapter 13

Deploying the Internet for Leveraging Strategic Assets 265

Frank Schlemmer, Optik Schlemmer, Germany

Brian Webb, Queen's University Belfast, UK

Chapter Thirteen investigates how a firm can use the Internet to leverage its strategic assets. They propose a theoretical framework with variables such as business resources, dynamic capabilities, and IT assets, and suggest that firm managers create competitive advantage by identifying strategic assets that complement the Internet. They also warn against the threat of overinvestment in IT assets at SMEs.

Chapter 14

Business Process Digitalization and New Product Development: An Empirical Study
of Small and Medium-Sized Manufacturers 290

Jun Li, University of New Hampshire, USA
Michael Merenda, University of New Hampshire, USA
A.R. (Venky) Venkatachalam, University of New Hampshire, USA

Chapter Fourteen examines the relationship between the extensiveness of business process digitalization (BPD) and new product development (NPD). The authors find that NPD is positively related to the extensive use of BPD, and the relationship between NPD and the extensiveness of BPD is stronger in more mature firms than in younger firms. They conclude that SME innovation strategies are positively associated with the strategic use of BPD and span spatial, temporal, organizational, and industry boundaries, thus aiding SME global competitiveness.

Chapter 15

Information Technology Interventions for Growth and Competitiveness
in Micro-Enterprises 306

Sajda Qureshi, University of Nebraska at Omaha, USA
Mehruz Kamal, University of Nebraska at Omaha, USA
Peter Wolcott, University of Nebraska at Omaha, USA

Chapter Fifteen studies the challenges faced by micro-enterprises in implementing ICT technology. They find that very few micro-enterprise entrepreneurs possess the technical skills necessary to achieve the benefits that streamline their business operations and help them compete and expand into new markets. The authors employ a focus-dominance model to investigate trends in incorporating and adopting ICTs. They demonstrate how IS combined with context-sensitive IT assistance increases awareness of information systems and predicts future usage of IT.

Compilation of References 330

About the Contributors 380

Index 388

Preface

Small and medium-sized enterprises (SMEs) play a critical role in rejuvenating and sustaining the modern economy. They generate substantial employment and serve as important innovation engines for the world economy. In the US, which is known for large multinational corporations (MNCs), SMEs are still considered indispensable. According to the Small Business Administration (SBA), they employ half of all private-sector employees, pay more than 45% of total US private payroll, have generated 60-80% of net new jobs annually over the last decade, and currently employ 40% of high-technology workers such as scientists, engineers, and computer workers. SMEs should be an important subject for IS academic researchers to study. Unfortunately, only a few papers on the subject have been published in the top IS journals worldwide. This book attempts to fill this void.

This book aims to spread research conducted on SMEs internationally and place it at the disposal of academics, practitioners, consultants, the vendor community, and policymakers. The goal of this book is to highlight the challenges faced by SMEs and how they are coping with the adverse environment through skillful use of IT and technologies such as Web 2.0, Enterprise Resource Planning (ERP), e-commerce, open source software, Business Process Digitization (BPD), and other emerging technologies. The book covers SME-relevant IS topics such as IT strategy, IT diffusion and implementation, business and IT alignment, leveraging of IT assets, knowledge networks, IT innovation, training and performance, and legitimacy building through IT. Each chapter comprises original and cutting-edge research, grounded in field studies by international researchers, with both theory and practice implications for SMEs. In total, the book has three sections and fifteen chapters.

The first section consists of chapters that focus on practical challenges faced by SMEs regarding analysis, implementation, and effective use of IT. The second section focuses on barriers to adoption of information technology innovations. The third section comprises chapters on strategy formulation, IT and business alignment, the dynamic capabilities of an SME, and SME innovation strategies.

SECTION ONE: PRACTICAL INFORMATION SYSTEM CHALLENGES

Chapter One, by Efthymios Constantinides, presents the nature, effects, and position of social media or Web 2.0. This chapter identifies the main approaches corporations follow in engaging Web 2.0 applications in order to support, complement, or improve their traditional and online marketing activities. These approaches aim at using the social Internet as a source of marketing intelligence and for communicating with customers. The authors propose a classification of the main social media applications and identify the options for SMEs willing to utilize Web 2.0 technologies.

Chapter Two, by Arvind Karunakaran, Sandeep Purao, and Brian Cameron, highlights the challenges faced by SMEs in legacy industrial era regions by focusing on the specific case of the I-99 corridor in the state of Pennsylvania. It discusses a structured approach toward enabling the SMEs in this region to access extended and powerful knowledge networks through a joint effort working toward regional economic development. The chapter describes the LAIR (Leveraging Advanced IT Research) project, which is aimed at understanding the risks that SMEs in the I-99 corridor are likely to face as they grow, with a specific focus on risks associated with upgrading, implementing, and integrating their information systems.

Chapter Three, by Julie E. Kendall and Kenneth E. Kendall, uses the framework provided by the metaphor of the third space as proposed by Bhabha (1994 and 1996). It elaborates on the diffusion of Broadway production business practices to small and medium-sized nonprofit theaters. The authors discover that both groups possess unique cultural competencies that open the door to using Web 2.0 technologies for staging and promoting productions and building relationships with theater patrons. They also discuss other management issues where expertise can be mutually exchanged.

Chapter Four, by Andreja Pucihar, Gregor Lenart, and Frantisek Sudzina, presents the importance of ERP system selection criteria among SMEs in Slovenia. The investigated criteria were grouped into ERP benefits criteria, system quality criteria, vendor-related criteria, and ERP package criteria. System reliability, system functionality, vendor support, business process improvement, and improved service levels were perceived as the important ERP system selection criteria for small and medium-sized companies in Slovenia.

Chapter Five, by Susan Winter, Connie Gaglio, and Hari Rajagopalan, advises SMEs to create legitimacy by mimicking the cues that signal credibility to potential stakeholders interacting with the firm. The authors examine the role of information and communications technology (ICT) in legitimacy-building from the perspectives of SME founders and potential customers.

SECTION TWO: INNOVATION AND INFORMATION TECHNOLOGY ASSIMILATION

Chapter Six, by Sandy Chong, examines the differences in electronic commerce (EC) implementation of SMEs in Australia and Singapore. The results show that respondents' perceptions of EC are predominantly positive. The analysis of Australian firms shows that five factors—observability, communication channel, customer pressure, supplier pressure, and perceived governmental support—make a significant contribution to the implementation of EC. In contrast, for firms in Singapore only three factors—firm size, perceived readiness, and observability—have significant impact. The author provides useful insights to adopters of EC initiatives in both countries.

Chapter Seven, by Ada Scupola, studies the factors affecting adoption of electronic commerce in small and medium enterprises in Australia. The author uses the Tornatsky and Fleischer (1990) model to investigate the impacts of environmental, organizational, and technological factors, and finds that the external environment has an influence mainly through customers' requirements and availability of IT services. The results of this study are contrary to other studies, which found that government and public administration play a significant role.

Chapter Eight, by Robert MacGregor, Deborah Bunker, and Mira Kartiwi, examines the barriers to e-commerce perceived by SME owners and managers in the developing country of Indonesia. It then compares these perceived barriers with those in two developed economies, Sweden and Australia. The study highlights the differences in barriers to e-commerce adoption among the three countries.

Chapter Nine, by Jaume Franquesa and Alan Brandyberry, investigates the impact of organizational slack in US small and medium-sized enterprises (SMEs) on the adoption of information technology (IT) innovations. The authors find that the slack-innovation relationship, previously described for large firms, does not hold for SMEs. Their results show that potential slack is a strong predictor of technology adoption, whereas available slack is not a significant factor in SME innovation adoption. The authors argue that, in some cases, innovation adoption may represent a form of "bricolage" by resource-constrained SMEs.

SECTION THREE: STRATEGY AND INFORMATION SYSTEMS

Chapter Ten, by Peter Marshall, Phyl Willson, Judy Young, and Kristy de Salas, presents a method of IS strategy formulation in SMEs. The method draws on the work of Levy and Powell (1999, 2000). A case study describes their experience with this method. The method is comprised of two complementary analyses: an externally focused strategic analysis and an internally focused business process analysis. The authors emphasize the importance of relevance and practicality in selecting the method in practice.

Chapter Eleven, by Pattama Kanavittaya, Jocelyn Armarego, and Paula Goulding, studies the challenge of aligning business strategy and information technology (IT) strategy. The authors examine the adoption of agile methods by SMEs in developing software products and suggest that agile methods may facilitate the alignment of business and IT strategy. Models of strategic alignment developed for large enterprises are also validated for SMEs.

Chapter Twelve, by Dag Olsen and Tom R. Eiekbrokk, examines the relationship between training and performance in SMEs and discusses practical implications. They find a positive relationship between training, competence, and performance. The authors show that training explains variances in e-business competences and performance in terms of efficiency, complementarities, lock-in, and novelty. The study has practical implications for public policy makers, training suppliers, and SME managers.

Chapter Thirteen, by Frank Schlemmer and Brian Webb, investigates how a firm can use the Internet to leverage its strategic assets. They propose a theoretical framework with variables such as business resources, dynamic capabilities, and IT assets, and suggest that firm managers create competitive advantage by identifying strategic assets that complement the Internet. They also warn against the threat of overinvestment in IT assets at SMEs.

Chapter Fourteen, by Jun Li, Michael Merenda, and A.R. Venkatachalam, examines the relationship between the extensiveness of business process digitalization (BPD) and new product development (NPD). The authors find that NPD is positively related to the extensive use of BPD, and the relationship between NPD and the extensiveness of BPD is stronger in more mature firms than in younger firms. They conclude that SME innovation strategies are positively associated with the strategic use of BPD and span spatial, temporal, organizational, and industry boundaries, thus aiding SME global competitiveness.

Chapter Fifteen, by Sajda Qureshi, Mehruz Kamal, and Peter Wolcott, studies the challenges faced by micro-enterprises in implementing ICT technology. They find that very few micro-enterprise entrepreneurs possess the technical skills necessary to achieve the benefits that streamline their business operations and help them compete and expand into new markets. The authors employ a focus-dominance model to investigate trends in incorporating and adopting ICTs. They demonstrate how IS combined with context-sensitive IT assistance increases awareness of information systems and predicts future usage of IT.

Acknowledgment

We would like to express our gratitude to the thirty-six authors for their invaluable contributions. Their dedication to the subject of SME research is reflected in the quality of papers published in the book. We would also like to acknowledge the help of the sixteen expert reviewers involved in the double-blind review process for the fifteen chapters of the book, without whose support it could not have been completed.

We sincerely thank Christine Bufton, Kristin M. Klinger, Julia Mosemann, Jan Travers, Mehdi Khosrow-Pour, and other members of IGI Global, whose contributions throughout the process from the inception of the initial idea to the final publication have been invaluable.

Professor Pratyush Bharati acknowledges the love and encouragement of his spouse Padma, his mother, and his in-laws. Professor In Lee would like to thank his wife, Hwa Lee, for her support. Professor Abhijit Chaudhury is thankful to his wife Banani and his immediate family, Sidhartha, Monisha, Rupsa, and Aurelia, for their patience and support.

Pratyush Bharati
University of Massachusetts, USA

In Lee
Western Illinois University, USA

Abhijit Chaudhury
Bryant University, USA

Section 1
Practical Information System Challenges

Chapter 1

Connecting Small and Medium Enterprises to the New Consumer:
The Web 2.0 as Marketing Tool

Efthymios Constantinides
University of Twente, The Netherlands

ABSTRACT

This chapter explains the nature, effects and current standing of the new generation of Internet applications, commonly known as Social Media or Web 2.0, reviews their role as marketing instruments and identifies opportunities for SMEs for engaging them as part of their marketing strategy. The chapter defines and analyses the Social Media phenomenon, identifying the main approaches corporations follow in engaging Web 2.0-based applications in order to that support, complement or improve their traditional and online marketing activities. These approaches aim at using the social Internet as source of market intelligence, communicating with customers, efficiently develop-, market- and distribute products and also improve customer relations and retention. The chapter proposes a classification of the main Social Media -based applications and their roles as passive or active marketing instruments. Based on the experience of pioneering firms the chapter identifies the main conditions and options for SMEs willing to utilize the Web 2.0 as commercial tool in order to advance their marketing operations and connect to the new consumer in the virtual and physical marketplace. While field experience so far indicates that large corporations rather than SMEs are more likely to engage in Social Media marketing the low cost, potential and apparent popularity of Social Media among customers make the domain extremely attractive for SMEs.

INTRODUCTION

Information and Communication Technologies and the Internet in particular have opened new frontiers of opportunity to corporations and consumers by revolutionizing business practices and social relationships. Having gone through the dot.com boom of the 90s and the economic debacle at the beginning of the 20th century, the Internet is viewed today as a mainstream business platform, as integral part of

DOI: 10.4018/978-1-61520-627-8.ch001

the commercial and social landscape (Birdsall, 2007; Beer and Burrows, 2007). There is plenty of evidence about the increasing importance of the Internet as communication and promotion medium at the cost of traditional mass media (TV, Radio, press); at the same time the declining power and effectiveness of traditional marketing approaches has been extensively debated in the academic circles (Dixon and Blois 1983; Kotler, 1989; Peppers and Rogers, 1995; Coviello and Brodie, 2001; Bakos, 1998; Chaffey et. al., 2000; Constantinides, 2006; Karin and Eiferman, 2006; Thomas, 2007; Eikelmann et al., 2008).

Next to becoming a major information and communication channel the Web is widely seen as a mainstream element of the marketing strategy and the corporate communication mix. It has been suggested that by 2011 the Internet will become the US leading advertising medium surpassing newspaper advertising (Gillin, 2009), a development that will mark major shift of advertising budgets from traditional to online channels worldwide; some predictions even suggest that "television advertising in 2010 will be only 35% as effective as it was in 1990"[1].

The public has adopted the Internet as a valuable business asset: according to a Zogby 2008 survey[2] the web is already the main - if often not the only - source of information for a large portion of its approximately 1.5 billion Internet users. A Newsweek article[3] emphasizes that "the web has replaced phone books, and is in the process of replacing phones. It's the place that answers our questions in four tenths of a second.....it's the main news source ...a megaphone for those who make their own media...". The Web is also a popular channel for commercial transactions: 85% of the online consumers shop online[4].

During the first half of the present decade the Internet entered a new evolutionary stage commonly referred to as Web 2.0 (this term will be used interchangeably with the term Social Media in this chapter). This stage is characterized by the emergence and fast expansion of online Peer-to-

Peer applications (Blogs, online forums, social networks, online communities and other types of User Generated Media) allowing the direct connectivity and interaction between individuals and the easy publication and editing of online content. Such applications have contributed to an unprecedented growth of information volume, new forms of networking, many new shopping alternatives and customer empowerment (Rogers et al., 1997 [47]; Wind and Mahajan, 2001 [55]; Varadarajan and Yadav, 2002 [54], Rha et al, 2002; Urban, 2005; Constantinides and Fountain, 2008). Allowing customers to talk online about shopping and product experiences, publish product reviews and exchange shopping advices the Social Media harness the collective knowledge and further undercut the impact of traditional media. Interestingly product reviews and recommendations contributed by consumers are perceived as more credible than company communication or even product reviews written by industry experts[5]; the trust on peer opinion rather than expert opinion is based on the perception that peer-created content reflects genuine feelings and unbiased product experiences.

The Social Media and the increasing customer empowerment have been for some time a source of concern for marketers, advertisers and recently subject of academic research. Fading customer trust in corporate messages, declining customer loyalty and growing doubts about the role of contemporary marketing[6] are worryingly followed by marketers.

Such fears are not ungrounded: Empowered customers have devised new tactics in searching, evaluating, choosing and buying goods and services. Anecdotal and empirical evidence point to growing customer desire for customized products, active participation in product decisions, willingness for co-creation and interaction; these developments mark a trend towards increasing customer control over the commercial process.

The wide public acceptance of the Social Media (Bernoff and Li, 2008; Gillin, 2009) and their increasing importance as marketing parameters are facts that make them an interesting strategic option for Small and Medium Enterprises (SMEs). There are several tangible advantages of engaging the Social Media as marketing tools:

- Cost advantages: reduced communication costs[7], R&D costs (Brabham, 2008; Kohler et al., 2009) and advertising costs (Berthon et al., 2008)
- Enhanced customer loyalty (Auh et al., 2007, Nambisan and Nambisan, 2008)
- Efficient innovation and reduced risk of new product development (von Hippel, 2004Ogawa and Piller, 2006) leading to new forms of collaborative value creation (Prahalad and Ramaswamy, 2004, Franke and Piller, 2004, McAfee, 2006; Ueda et al, 2008).

The advantages of Social Media marketing are clear to many players in the field: a recent survey by Stelzner (2009) on the status of Social Media marketing reports the following findings among marketers who were asked on the main benefits of this type of marketing: 81% indicated that it has generated exposure for their business, 61% that it has increased their traffic/subscribers and opt-in lists, 56% that it has resulted in new business partnerships, 45% found that it reduced their overall marketing expenses and 35% that it helped them close business.

Another recent survey published by the Aberdeen Group (2009) found that for 70% of the participating companies (what they call Best-in-Class and Industry Average performers) the engagement of Social Media as Marketing strategy increased the Return on Marketing Investment in 49% up to 87% of the companies, improved the likelihood of customers recommending their products in 36% until 95% and improved the customer acquisition rate in 68% up to 95% of the cases. Such findings combined with the low

cost involved in using such media make them an attractive alternative for SMEs.

The purpose of this chapter is to examine the Social Media phenomenon and advice SME marketers willing to engage Web 2.0 -based applications as part of their marketing toolbox. Based on the experience of large corporations, for all intents and purposes the pioneers in this field, the chapter proposes that Social Media as marketing tools is an attractive, effective and low cost option for SMEs. It discusses the main approaches in the adoption of the Social Media as sources of value and low cost marketing tools and discusses the main issues and limitations of this process. The chapter aims at helping SME marketers to understand the dimensions and possibilities of the Social Media marketing and make well-informed choices.

ADOPTION OF INFORMATION SYSTEMS, INTERNET AND WEB 2.0

The process of SME adoption of Information Systems and particularly of the Internet technology has been the subject of academic research although limited attention has been paid to this issue in leading IS journals. Regarding the factors influencing the adoption of the Internet as commercial tool by SMEs, Zheng et al. (2004) argue that the process of the web adoption as commercial tool by SMEs is different than by large organizations while Webb and Sayer (1998) argue that the Internet is not properly utilized by SMEs. Mehrtens et al., (2001) found that perceived benefits, organizational readiness and external pressure are the main motivators for SME adoption of E-Commerce; Grandon and Pearson, 2004 added to these two more factors, the perceived ease of use and perceived usefulness as important antecedents of Internet adoption by SMEs. The role of the owners is also identified as a key factor for the Internet adoption by SMEs (Levy and Powell, 2003, Montazemi, 2006) yet the priority behind IS adoption for this category of firms is as a rule focused on streamlining core operational activities rather than marketing-related processes (Bharati and Chaudhury, 2006).

Regarding the adoption of Web 2.0 technologies evidence suggests that pioneers in this field are the large corporations rather than the SMEs. A review of the literature on Social Media adoption indicates that scholars are focused mainly on the impact of the Web 2.0 -based applications on corporate processes (Yakel, 2006; Craig, 2007), the importance of online communities for corporations (Du and Wagner, 2006; Korica et al., 2006; Swaine, 2007) and the effects of these new technologies on business (Karger and Quan, 2004Biever, 2006; Deshpande and Jadad, 2006; Boll, 2007).

One area where the effects of the Social Media on marketing have been extensively investigated is the field of customer-generated innovation and co-production (von Hippel, 2004 commonly called co-creation or "crowdsourcing" (Brabham, 2008). Researchers agree that engaging the customer as innovator and co-producer becomes an increasingly important source of value creation (Franke and Piller, 2004; Prahalad and Ramaswamy, 2004; Auh et al., 2007; Potts et al., 2008, Zhang and Chen, 2008; Brabham, 2008), reducing the risks involved in new product development (Ogawa and Piller, 2006).

Non-academic (DeFelice, 2006) as well as scholarly studies provide evidence as to how corporations integrate the Web 2.0 -based applications into their operations suggesting that corporate interest on the Web 2.0 domain keeps growing and more and more firms are introducing different forms of Social Media into their daily business routines (Cymfony, 2006). In a global survey conducted in 2007 McKinsey found that the popularity of Web 2.0 -based applications is raising among businesses; while most companies surveyed have so far integrated a limited number of these applications into their business strategies the large majority think that "investing in them is important for maintaining the company's market position, either to provide a competitive edge or to match the competition and address customer demand"(McKinsey Survey on Internet Technologies, 2007). This study concludes that the Web 2.0 -based applications affect a wide spectrum of marketing activities from building product or brand awareness to sales services. Another area that increasingly attracts interest is the role of the social media as PR tools and their aptitude for damage control (Gillin 2007, 2009).

Looking to the actual experiences from the field one could argue that the Social Media issue has indeed attracted a good deal of attention in the corporate world; CEOs seem increasingly willing to invest in social media applications and integrate them into their strategic marketing arsenal at accelerating rate. (McKinsey, 2007; Forrester, 2007). A recent McKinsey (2008a) survey indicates that "a growing number of companies remain committed to capturing the collaborative benefits of Web 2.0" while according to Forrester Research (2009) the investments in Social Media are expected to grow by more than 15 percent annually over the next five years (from the level of $1 billion today) despite the current recession. A survey conducted by Prospero Technologies among firms engaging Social Media in 2007 found that "59 percent of respondents reported that Social Media performance in 2007 met or exceeded their marketing objectives, boosting future spending expectations – with 31 percent planning to spend significantly more on social media applications in 2008". Despite the popularity of the social media as marketing tools there is evidence that small businesses are a distinct minority[8] in using these applications as marketing tools. According to a recent study of American Express less than 5% of businesses with less than 100 employees have a blog.

From the above it is easy to conclude that despite the novelty of the issue and the lack of comprehensive metrics on the potential of the Social Media as marketing tools the willingness of businesses to engage them is high. The most likely reason for this is the fact that in increasing number the managers are themselves Social Media users. On the other hand marketers realize that failing to engage such tools prevents them from exercising some control on the increasing User Generated Content (UGC) domain, depriving them from networking possibilities that will help them forge better relationships with customers and the opportunity to better understand the customer needs. In order to help businesses to utilize the experience of the pioneering firms this chapter proposes a basic classification of the Social Media -based applications as elements of the marketing strategy with particular focus on the options and opportunities for SMEs.

WHAT IS WEB 2.0 / SOCIAL MEDIA?

The term Web 2.0 has been introduced by O'Reilly (2005) and was quickly embraced by Silicon Valley circles as well as by practitioners and the press. The original definition by O'Reilly is based on common elements characterizing the new generation of web applications: (Web 2.0 is)… "The Web as a platform, Harnessing of the Collective Intelligence, Data is the Next Intel Inside, End of the Software Release Cycle, Lightweight Programming Models, Rich User Experiences". A year later Musser and O'Reilly (2006) made a new attempt proposing the following definition: "Web 2.0 is a set of economic, social, and technology trends that collectively form the basis for the next generation of the Internet—a more mature, distinctive medium characterized by user participation, openness, and network effects". A flaw of this definition is its focus on trends, a vague notion by itself. So far there no definition seems to be widely accepted and the issue is presently open to discussion. A simple Google search query of this term produces more than 3 mil results and there are several definitions already proposed. In the academic literature there is also no agreement as

to the definition of the term; several researchers describe the phenomenon or its applications as a first step towards a comprehensive definition (Needleman, 2007; Coyle, 2007; Anderson, 2007, Swisher, 2007). A more comprehensive definition is proposed by Constantinides and Fountain (2008):

Web 2.0 is a collection of open source, interactive and user-controlled online applications expanding the experiences, knowledge and market power of the users as participants in business and social processes. Web 2.0-based applications support the creation of informal users' networks facilitating the flow of ideas and knowledge by allowing the efficient generation, dissemination, sharing and editing/refining of content.

On the basis of this definition the Web 2.0 can be described along three main dimensions: The Application Types, the Social Effects and the Enabling Technologies. These dimensions are illustrated in the following picture (Figure 1). Detailed descriptions are found in the appendix.

THE SOCIAL MEDIA AS MARKETING PARAMETER

For some observers the Web 2.0 is a controversial issue. Keen (2007), Keegan (2007) and Wilson (2007) question the moral foundations of the Social Media arguing that the fundamental element of it namely the User Generated Content (UGC), poses a serious threat to established business and cultural values.

According to critics the Web 2.0 movement endorses and promotes low quality amateur content at the cost of mainstream artistic products, threatens intellectual property rights and confuses people by blurring the boundaries between fact and fiction, between original content and advertising. Objections about the Social Media movement have also to do with issues of privacy

Figure 1. The three dimensions of Web 2.0 (Source: Constantinides et al., 2008)

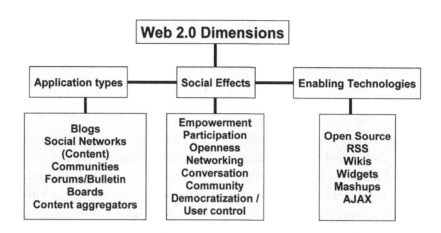

and the lack of editing responsibility for what is published on line. On the other hand Johnson (2006), Gillin (2007), O'Reilly (2005) and others argue that in fact the Social Media is a healthy phenomenon, promoting the ideas of free expression and democratization and becoming the new source of consumer influence and empowerment. Such views seem to increasingly find advocates and support even among the mainstream journalism. In 2005 The Economist published an article titled "Crowned at last" referring to the consumer as the powerful party in the marketing equation and the TIME magazine, breaking a tradition of almost forty years, assigned the title of the 2006 Man of the Year not to any particular personality but to the virtual consumer. The underlying theme of both publications – and many others that regularly appear in traditional media - was the effect of the Web 2.0 phenomenon in shaping a new class of consumers; both articles describe how Web 2.0 is affecting the way people communicate, make decisions, socialize, learn, entertain themselves, interact with each other or even do their shopping.

For an increasing number of academics and practitioners it is clear the Web 2.0 next to transforming peoples' individual and group behavior has also redefined the marketplace dynamics by causing a substantial migration of market power from producers or vendors towards web users / online customers. The customer empowerment is visible in different ways: people have more access to information, unbiased criticism, product reviews and peer recommendations and almost unlimited alternative choices.

Next to the "passive" forms of customer empowerment, stemming from ample information and choice, the customer is increasingly moving towards more active types of empowerment. On February 2007 the BusinessWeek[9] magazine published an article titled "The Latest Research Trend: Customers Behind the Wheel" revealing that the young consumers, what they call the "Collaboration Generation", are keen to participate in the product creation process as co-developers.

Such developments make strategists and marketers feel uneasy but a deeper analysis of these trends would suggest that Web 2.0 should be better seen as a marketing challenge rather than a threat; a challenge that properly addressed could open new opportunities in reaching and winning the 21st century consumer.

The positive attitude towards Social Media is already visible in the field. Marketers and firms becoming familiar with Web 2.0 increasingly engage this concept as part of their marketing strategy (Korica et al., 2006; McKinsey, 2007; Hitwise 2007[10], Forrester, 2007; Parise and Guinan, 2008).

From the academic perspective the subject is challenging and worth of further study. On fundamental level it poses some interesting questions: What is Web 2.0, what are its dimensions and possible consequences on the marketing practice? What are its effects on consumer behavior? What are the lessons already learned from the experience of the pioneers in this field? How can businesses and in particular SMEs effectively adopt Web 2.0 technologies as part of their marketing strategies and what are the expected benefits?

Attempting to address these questions we explain the basic principles of Web 2.0 and look to different ways these technologies are utilized by larger firms. Based on the field experience the chapter makes some basic recommendations on approaches that smaller enterprises should consider in embedding the Web 2.0 concepts as part of their (direct) marketing strategies.

A CLASSIFICATION OF SOCIAL MEDIA AS MARKETING TOOLS

Understanding the nature, possibilities and effects of Web 2.0 -based applications could allow marketers to reduce the treats of the Social Media as an uncontrollable terrain and utilize the domain to their advantage. The newness of the subject and lack of systematic research means that more often than not engaging Social Media as marketing communication tools is a trial-and-error process for business organizations. This process is obviously requiring new thinking and new approaches as traditional push marketing methods becomes increasingly ineffective in pursuing marketing goals in typical Web 2.0 terrains like social networking sites (Forrester, 2007). In this respect there is a considerable knowledge gap on the nature of Web 2.0 and its added value for marketing strategy. Information and knowledge

about the role of Web 2.0 -based applications as marketing tools is so far primarily based on anecdotal evidence. This evidence suggests that the vast majority of firms engaging Web 2.0 as a marketing tool are large corporations.

Based on the available field experience we can categorize the different ways marketers attempt to extract value from the Web 2.0 domain in two main approaches: The Passive and the Active way. (Figure 2)

1. The Passive Way or Listening-In: Using the Web 2.0 as an Intelligence Source i.e. as Source of Customer Voice and Market Information

Individuals talk on line exchanging reviews, experiences, problems and ideas about brands, products or services. This happens mainly in Social Media platforms like the web logs (or blogs), forums and communities. Next to written content individuals often contribute in the online dialog with video, audio or other types rich media. Product reviews, comments, recommendations, news or information posted online represents high quality market information and unbiased customer voice at no cost. The online customer voice is sometimes so powerful that crosses over to the mainstream media and reaches the general public: a online video showing a Dell laptop computer spontaneously combusting a few years ago created an enormous online and offline buzz forcing Dell to recall millions of laptops with a faulty battery. A web log with complaints of customers about a Land Rover model[11] came into the list of the 50 more influential web logs and a recorded conversation of a customer with an America On Line (AOL) sales rep revealing the company's high-pressure tactics towards subscribers trying to terminate their subscription are some of the classic examples of online stories that became first page news forcing corporations to recall products or adjust their practices.

Figure 2. Passive and active ways for engaging the social media as Marketing tools

Web 2.0 Applications as Marketing Tools					
	Passive	Active			
MARKETING OBJECTIVE	Listening In	PR and Direct Marketing	Reaching the New Influencers	Personalizing customer Experience	Tapping customer creativity
APPLICATION TYPE					
Web logs	XXX	XXX	XXX		
(Content) Communities	XXX	X		XXX	XXX
Social Networks	X	XX		XX	XX
Forums / Bulletin Boards	XXX	X	XXX		
Content Aggregators		XXX	X		

XXX: very suitable, XX: moderately suitable, X: less suitable, Blank: not suitable

Capturing the customer voice is of paramount significance and marketers are well aware of the value of it. Customer voice reveals needs, experiences, complaints, expectations and market trends (Gillin, 2007); it is vital for the effective communication with the target markets and crucial for successful product and services development. Traditionally marketers tap the consumer voice using surveys, focus groups, data mining and several other conventional market research methods. Such methods can be costly and the information accuracy can be influenced by several factors. Often the collection and processing of data requires lengthy trajectories limiting their actual value, mainly in the case of highly competitive, fast changing markets. Marketers are able today to access the "live" customer voice on a continuous basis by listening-in or even participating in the online conversation. This requires locating and monitoring what people discuss or publish in the Social Media space (blogs, podcasts, forums and online communities).

Many options are available for tapping the customer's voice ranging from simple and free-of-charge tools like Google Alerts to expert agents collecting and sorting information relevant to the a specific brand, products or competitors. There are also several specialized web tools and search engines that can be used in locating and gathering this content. Nielsen Buzz Metrics, a commercial service monitoring several millions of blogs, can provide a lot of information as to what is discussed online and even what is said about the company or its products. Specialized classification tools like Technorati, CollectiveIntellect.com, buzzcapture.com and blog search engines like BlogPulse or the "index aggregator" TalkDigger are also easy to use and low cost alternative solutions.

Most suitable Web 2.0 -based applications for listening in: Blogs, online communities and forums.

2. The Active Way: Using Web 2.0 -Based Applications as PR, Direct Marketing and Customer Influence tool as well as a Means for Personalizing the Customer Experience, Customizing Products and Tapping Customer Creativity

a. Using Web 2.0-Based Application as PR and Direct Marketing Tools

Marketers can tap on the online dialog taking place in web logs, online forums and user communities as we explained earlier; yet this dialog takes place without any active participation of businesses let alone control from them. Providing facilities for such dialog as part of the corporate online presence allows corporate executives to attract part of the online conversation in their own quarters and directly discuss or interact with their customers. There are already many examples of firms taking steps to initiate Web 2.0 – based interaction with the customer, reflected in the impressive growth of corporate blogs: in the Inc. 500 index 20% more firms were using corporate blogs in 2008 compared to 2007. Business executives like Jonathan Swartz, CEO of Sun Microsystems, Steve Jobs, CEO of Apple Computers, Alan Meckler of Jupiter Media, GM Vice Chairman Bob Lutz and McDonalds Vice President Bob Langert post regularly in their corporate blogs, encouraging customers to interact and freely express their feelings, ideas, suggestions or remarks. Most politicians have also already understood the power of blogs as channels of direct communication with their constituencies.

Not only top executives are blogging. A widely applied variant, pioneered by Microsoft back in 2003, is to encourage company employees to initiate their own blogs and forums. This approach requires openness and trust on employees' capabilities and discreetness but often drafting a number of guidelines helps avoiding problems and misunderstandings between the firm and employees.

Next to company-sponsored blogs a simple and low-cost way to engage the Social Media as PR tool is to utilize content communities - like the video sharing sites YouTube, GoogleVideo and others - as communication / advertising channels of corporate promotional material. Commercials uploaded to these sites have the potential to be viewed by thousands or even millions of viewers at practically no cost, although still the reach of video exchange sites is high only among certain population segments. This form of publicity often reaches very respectable numbers of viewers. A YouTube commercial of Unilever's Dove Real Beauty campaign was viewed more than ten million times and videos of candidates of the 2007-2008 of the American primaries and 2008 elections posted online have been downloaded and watched by several millions of viewers. The victory of Barack Obama in the presidential elections is attributed to a great extend to the innovative way of engaging Internet technologies and particularly the Social Media as part of his fund-raising effort and his campaign in general (Quelch, 2008; Baldoni, 2009)

Special interest blogs, online communities or publicly wiki-based edited environments like Wikipedia, Citizendium and Wikitravel can be also effectively used as low cost message-delivery platforms. An additional advantage of publishing in wiki-based online communities is that these in general reach high rankings in search engine queries.

Social Media-based applications can be also used as promotional media; "traditional" online advertising tools like videos, links or banners placed in special interest blogs, communities or forums enable marketers to effectively reach special interest publics. This type of publicity can be realized at a fraction of the costs required by traditional mass-media.

Finally firms can keep their customers informed about their products or services by adding at no cost RSS (Rich Site Summary) capability to the company's web site; marketers can access with such permission-based and renewable content technologies many millions of Internet users who filter the online content they receive by subscribing to RSS readers like google.com/reader, MyYahoo.com, newsgator.com and bloglines.com.

Most suitable Web 2.0-based applications for online PR: Blogs, forums and content aggregators.

b. Engaging Web 2.0 Personalities for Customer Influence

Publicity and promotion by engaging the specialized press, opinion leaders and industry experts has been traditionally part of the process of new product introduction. Such channels are important in ensuring that the message would reach the early adopters and consequently the critical mass of potential customers. Today more and more marketers understand that next to traditional influencers it is important to engage the online opinion leaders and personalities (mostly contributors of high traffic, influential blogs or forums) as a means of attracting customer attention. Such a strategy requires identifying, reaching and informing the "New Influencers" (Gillin, 2007) about the firm, its brands and new market offerings. An increasing segment of the public prefers to get informed by these channels because they are usually faster than the press or other traditional communication channels. Blogs like techcrunch.com, gizmodo.com, engadget.com and other attract daily millions of readers interested in new product information and reviews. The endorsement of product innovations by such online influencers is decisive for the adoption of products by mainstream customers. The objective of marketers should be to establish ties and working relationships with leading blogs or user forums so that they are willing to review, discuss, comment on or even recommend the usage of the firm's new products. Finding the proper channels is possible by using instru-

ments and services already available: Technorati.com, Nielsen BuzzMetrics and other specialized services measure the influence of blogs providing rankings and relevant information for better targeting.

Most suitable Web 2.0 -based applications: Blogs, forums.

c. Engaging Social Media for Personalizing the Customer's Online Experience or Customizing Products to Individual Needs (Mass Customization)

This category of approaches can positively influence customer loyalty by offering individuals the possibility to personalize their online experience or customize products they buy. Firms like about.com, MySpace.com, Nike, Disney, Coca Cola, Heineken and many others have been experimenting with Web 2.0-based tools allowing customers to modify parts of their web sites to their specific needs or preferences. Next to customizing the web site many firms have developed interactive online applications and tools commonly referred to as "Configurators"[12] allowing customers to partly or fully shape physical products they buy online.

This is the essence of the marketing approach often labeled as Mass Customization (Feitzinger and Lee, 1997; Da Silveira et.al., 2001, Cheng and Piller, 2003). The customization strategy addresses the increasing customer need for individual rather than mass products and can contribute to higher customer retention and efficient customer focused branding. The practice is becoming popular in several industries (apparel, automotive, construction, footwear, electronics etc.). Well known names active in this area are Kleenex, allowing customers to design the packaging of the product (myklenextissue.com), photostamps.com allowing consumers to create their own US Postal Service approved stamps, Heinz (myheinz.com) inviting customers to create their own personalized labels of their ketchup bottle, M&M (nymms.com) that makes possible for customers to select their favorite candy colors and print a personalized message on it and recently Heineken (designyourheineken.com) allowing individuals to design their own bottle and order online. In many cases customer designed products become available to all customers; Pepsi Co provides online design tools and invites fans to design their soft drink cans in the Design Our Pepsi Can Contest (designourpepsican.com) with the best idea adopted as the new look of the product in regular intervals. Producers of sport accessories like NIKE and Converse offer similar tools to customers allowing them to customize articles ordered online. The popular furniture chain IKEA recently launched an online campaign called "Everyone is Designer" encouraging customers to create their ideal living space using IKEA furniture (iedereenisdesigner.nl/) and publish their ideas in the IKEA site.

Most suitable Web 2.0 -based applications: Web 2.0-enabled company web site in the form of sponsored online forums and social networks.

d. Engaging the Customer as Contributor of Promotional Concepts and Innovator / Co-Creator. (Participatory Marketing and Crowdsourcing)

As mentioned earlier (Figure 1) Participation is one of the Social Effects of Web 2.0. Harnessing the collective intelligence (O'Reilly, 2005; Bernoff and Li, 2008) often referred as "Crouwdsourcing"[13] or Participatory Marketing is one of the tenets of the Social Media. Using customers as co-creators makes sense: there is evidence (Gillin, 2007) that product reviews, recommendations but also commercials and even products created by customers are perceived as better than those made by experts: customers seem to trust more the creations and opinions of their peers. While the academic attention on this issue is still limited practitioners seem to be enthusiastic about crowdsourcing.

The first variant of this option is based on using creative individuals as creators of advertising concepts. Web sites like Current.com offer corporations the possibility to recruit talented amateurs who create TV commercials that are often of professional quality[14]. Companies like SONY, Frito-Lay's, Sunkist, Coca-Cola and many other are indicative examples of a growing number of corporations partnering with talented amateurs who generate low cost advertising concepts or even TV commercials for them.

Opening the innovation process to final customers is a new variant of the Open Innovation (Chesbrough H., 2003) the approach advocating for the participation of business partners in the innovation process. The Social Media – based variant where the final customer is involved has been labeled as Distributed Co-Creation (McKinsey 2008b). This approach goes a step further than the Open Innovation in the sense that customers / end users can now become co-creators, taking actively part in innovation processes.

The customer as innovator can fulfill a number of different roles; product conceptualizer, product designer, product tester, product support specialist and product marketer (Nambisan and Nambisan, 2008). Shorter development trajectories, better products, low innovation costs and flexibility are important advantages of Distributed Co-Creation.

Applying the Distributed Co-Creation approach requires creating Virtual Customer Environments (Nambisan and Nambisan, 2008) i.e. Web 2.0-based applications allowing customers to participate in the firm's innovation processes in different ways.

There are several examples of Distributed Co-Creation; a firm in the greeting card and gift business that has been successfully using a customer community to verify and explore ideas under development by their product development department[15]. This innovation approach is popular among companies in the ICT domain: in most cases the participating individuals have access to tools, information and capabilities previously accessible only to R&D staff. SAP, HP, NOKIA and AMD invite developers to join their developers support communities, Sun Microsystems operates a developers' community called Sun Developer Network while the telecom firm NOKIA operates a complete online platform dedicated to its developer community with a discussion forum, blogs and a wiki application. In the same way LEGO, the toy-brick market leader, has engaged an enthusiastic community of customers to design, test and improve new products.

There is no shortage of individuals willing to co-create: According to a recent report McKinsey, (2008a), one in ten of the participants in the online community Second Life is already involved in co-creating with companies in different ways (testing prototypes or participating in design of new products); 60% of the participants of this community say that they are willing to experiment with co-creation. The French automaker Peugeot organizes every year the Peugeot Design Contest inviting online participants to submit original design ideas for Peugeot cars. The winners of the contest are selected by the online public. One of the previous contests attracted 4 mil submissions and resulted in a concept shown in trade shows that became also a racing model in a popular video game.

In some cases customer co-creation makes the R&D department redundant; it can be profitable not only for corporations but also for the participating customers themselves. Such collaborations create new business models with customers becoming business partners. The online t-shirt retailer Threadless invites creative Internet users to submit their own T-shirt designs; then submissions are evaluated by site visitors and the best ones become part of the online shop assortment while the designer wins 2.500 $US in cash and merchandise as award. The firm recently launched its first physical shop in Chicago.

Most suitable Web 2.0 -based applications: Corporate web sites offering social networks and online communities functionality.

WEB 2.0 ADOPTION BY SMES AND ITS POTENTIAL VALUE

From the previous discussion, field studies and examples it is easy to conclude that at present mostly large corporations explore and utilize the Social Media as marketing tools. The fact that SMEs are not pioneering in this terrain can be explained by the fact that they face a number of inhibiting parameters: Money, expertise, time are the most important ones. This is consistent with earlier research findings; with regard to Information and Communication Technologies (ICTs) previous research indicates that firm size is an important determinant of a firm's involvement and decision process in acquiring ICTs (Dholakia et al., 1993, van der Veen, 2004). Large corporations are traditionally the early adopters of new and often untested technologies; most of the large enterprises have large marketing budgets and access to expertise; they often operate globally and such technologies have the potential to provide substantial economies of scale. On the other hand the wide availability of financial and human resources and the competitive imperative to adopt new ICTs make the risk of exploring unknown terrains more acceptable for large corporations (Clemons and McFarlan, 1986).

SMEs and mainly the smallest ones are often struggling to keep up with even the more traditional online web activities like creating and maintaining a presentable and functional web site; lack of financial and human resources and lack of time are usually serious barriers for such parties in adopting online technologies (van der Veen, 2004). Yet investing in Web 2.0-based marketing activities can be potentially rewarding for this category of firms. The payoff could be more efficient and less costly marketing as well as the way to gain access to the new generation of customers who have adopted the Social Internet as part of their daily life. This section will examine the main issues applying in the case of SMEs willing to engage the Web 2.0 as marketing tool.

a. A Basic Condition: Willingness to Invest in Organizational Transformation and Human Resources

While the cost of Social Media based marketing activities is in principle lower compared to the traditional approaches (involving experts, traditional marketing research tools and mass media) engaging Web 2.0-based applications as marketing tools requires a basic investment, in organizational transformation and human resources development. Most of Web 2.0-based marketing activities require the creation of internal mechanisms efficiently utilizing and disseminating incoming data, maintaining intelligence networks and retaining contacts with the markets. Furthermore the Internet and the Social Media in particular require interaction with customers, often in real time; for many businesses this means that organizational processes must become flexible and highly responsive. SMEs willing to engage the Social Media as marketing tools must be prepared to allocate the necessary financial resources for implementing organizational changes and assigning a number of employees to the new activities. In many cases SMEs must be also willing to review and improve their more "traditional" online presence. This could mean that they have to re-design their web site improving the usability, aesthetics, interactivity i.e. the main elements of the customer online experience (Constantinides, 2004): A well-designed and usable web site is necessary not only as the company interface to the online market but also as a Social Media platform that will actively support Web 2.0 – type applications and crowdsourcing activities.

b. Reviewing Priorities and Options

The second step of adopting Social Media as part of the Marketing program is to review the company strategic and tactical marketing priorities and options and decide in what way the Social Media can help addressing these priorities. For example firms focused on continuous innovation as their main strategic competitive advantage will most likely focus their attention on creating a Social Media infrastructure promoting customer participation in the Innovation process (Distributed Co-Creation) with the aim of lower R&D and testing costs and shorter time to market. A company facing a deep in the sales of one of its brands or products will most probably be interested to find out why customers do not prefer the brand or product and what they think about the competition. In this case listening to the customer voice, described earlier as a passive approach, is the right option. A firm interested in improving customer satisfaction and retention most probably should create a CEO blog and motivate its customers to comment or complain. In other words SME marketers must decide on the right combination of Social Media tools and approaches creating a portfolio of Social Media tools and practices that better addresses their needs, priorities and available budgets. A stages approach will provide valuable experience and better results in consequent steps.

c. Engaging Social Media as Passive Marketing Tools: When and How

Looking to the two general approaches described (Passive or Active) previously (Figure 2) and the potential efficacy of each category in reaching specific marketing objectives it can be argued that for many SMEs the passive form of engaging the Social Media as marketing tools is not easily applicable in all its forms. For small size and limited market coverage SMEs there is little chance that they will be able to catch any substantial online customer talk about their products. Listening-in to the customer's voice makes sense if the company is known enough to the market as product leader, innovator or has reached a level of customer numbers that produces enough buzz and content regarding the company products. What most SMEs can do though is to listen to the voice of their target markets in general rather than trying to find what they say about their company. In that sense a company intelligence system will use the Internet (with emphasis on Web 2.0 environments) in order to identify what customers write on line and discuss about competitors, competitive products or product usage. The intelligence must be also focused on online sources providing information revealing new market trends, the need for new products, product substitutes, innovations etc. and act accordingly. The main sources of such information are outlined in the Figure 2 web logs and online forums are the most important potential sources followed by the content communities and social networks. There are several tools already available making the tapping of the online customer voice easy and accessible to lower budgets.

The investment required for engaging in such an activity is relatively limited. A well trained and experience person could identify the sources and collect / evaluate the online information; some attention must be also given to the organizational issues related to the distribution and efficient utilization of such data. Funds should also be made available for subscribing to commercial organizations that can provide assistance in locating and even analyzing the customer voice.

The advantage of using the Social Media as passive marketing tool is the limited need for organizational transformation and the quick, relatively low cost access to market information that normally requires conducting traditional market research.

d. Engage Social Media as Active Marketing Tools

The degree that an SME will engage the Social Media as active marketing tools depends as in the previous case on the company size, market coverage and of course its marketing objectives. In principle all four categories of objectives (using Web 2.0 as PR and Direct Marketing tools, reaching the new Influencers, personalizing customer experience and tapping customer creativity) are presenting very interesting options to SMEs from the cost perspective. The way of engaging the Social Media is similar to the way large corporations do that and described earlier. There are several examples of such practices and marketer's creativity can deliver very nice results. In Figure 2 the different applications and their suitability for each objective are illustrated. Compared to the Passive ones the Active approaches require in principle a higher level of firm commitment in the form of financial means and human resources and probably some degree of organizational transformation: Firms have to invest in content creation and in the design / implementation of facilities allowing the active customer interaction and involvement. For example personalizing the customer experience means that the firm must create and make available online tools that will allow users to customize their experience. Tapping consumer creativity also means actively reaching the customer and offering tools that will allow customers to express their creativity either in advertising copies or design of new products. Next to this the firm must follow-up customer product customization requests by evaluating the content generated by customers; in cases of interesting ideas the firm must evaluate them and integrate them into the mainstream marketing program.

The active engagement of Social Media is therefore depended on the management commitment and ambition and also on the capacity of the firm to create the organizational infrastructure necessary for utilizing these technologies in the proper way. As to the most likely candidates to make use of such media among SMEs, the size and market position / reputation of the firm are important criteria for this. A costs - benefits analysis is necessary in order to assess the value of the Social Media versus traditional marketing tools for achieving the above mentioned objectives. The newness of the subject means however that there is still not enough knowledge or reliable metrics of the effects of Web 2.0 -based applications as marketing tools versus traditional marketing tactics.

CONCLUSION

The Social Media, the second generation of Internet applications, has become part of the social and professional life of an even growing segment of the online population. The popularity of the Social Media can be attributed to the fact that consumers experience these as sources of empowerment and part of their social environment: a social environment addressing their need to share knowledge, information and creativity and also fulfilling a variety of other personal objectives.

The emergence of the Web 2.0 or Social Media domain presents corporations, large and small, with dilemmas and opportunities. The most important dilemma is how to reach the new, increasingly virtual customer; the opportunities are to utilize these media in order to improve their marketing strategies in novel and effective ways as well as influence the new customer's attitudes.

Large corporations are so far the pioneers in adopting the Social Media as marketing tools. This means engaging different types of Web 2.0 -based applications like Web Logs, Online Communities, Social Networks, Forums/Bulletin Boards and Content Aggregators in order to listen to the customer voice (the Passive Approach) and\ or as marketing tools (the Active Approach): For PR and Direct Marketing, for reaching the new market influencers, for offering to their customers a personalized experience and for utilizing their customers' creativity and willingness to co-create.

Although the results of such activities have not yet been properly measured and evaluated, there are compelling signals that these methods work. SMEs can learn from the experience of the large corporations pioneering in this field and engage selectively the Social Media as part of their marketing strategies.

Engaging the Social Media offers businesses the potential of low cost access to large numbers of customers and access to niches and specific audiences. SMEs pioneering in this field can count on the first mover's advantages as the experience of large corporations indicates. Managerial commitment and willingness to invest are necessary conditions for successful engagement of the Social Media as marketing strategy. Equally important is that the managers eager to do that realize that openness, honesty and sincere willingness to build up relations must underpin any effort in this direction. For many SMEs such an approach requires a substantial organizational and cultural transformation and often an extensive process reengineering.

Finally from the academic point of view more research is needed in order to better analyze this new phenomenon and understand its various effects on customer behavior. This requires research focused on the new Web 2.0 demographics, culture and the roles Social Media can play as marketing instruments and influencers of the decision-making processes. Efforts must be also made in the direction of measurement of the Social Media effects that will provide a clear picture as to the advantages of Web 2.0 as marketing tool versus the traditional marketing approaches.

REFERENCES

Aberdeen Group. (2009). *The ROI of Social Media Marketing: Why it pays to drive word of Mouth.* Retrieved from http://www.adberdeen.com

Anderson, P. (2007 February). What is Web 2.0? Ideas, technologies and implications for education. *JISC Technology and Standards Watch,* 1-64.

Auh, S., Bell, S., McLeod, C., & Shih, E. (2007). co-Production and customer loyalty in financial services. *Journal of Retailing, 83*(3), 359–370. doi:10.1016/j.jretai.2007.03.001

Bakos, Y. (1998 August). The Emerging Role of Electronic Marketplaces on the Internet. *Communications of the ACM.*

Baldoni, J. (2009). What executives can learn from Obama's BlackBerry. *Harvard Business Publishing.* Retrieved from http://blogs.harvardbusiness. org/baldoni/2009/01/a_virtual_leadership_les-son_ob.html?loomia_ow=t0:a38:g26:r2:c0.031 242:b20799989

Beer, D., & Burrows, R. (2007). Sociology and, of and in Web 2.0: some initial considerations. *Sociological Research, 12*(5). Retrieved from http://www.socresonline.org.uk/12/5/17.html

Bernoff, J., & Li, C. (2008). Harnessing the Power of the Oh-So-Social Web. *MIT Sloan Management Review, 49*(3), 36–42.

Berthon, P., Pitt, L. F., & Campbell, C. (2008). Ad Lib: When customers create an ad. *California Management Review, 50*(4), 6–30.

Bharati, P., & Chaudhury, A. (2006). Current Status of Technology Adoption: Micro, Small and Medium Manufacturing Firms in Boston. *Communications of the ACM, 49*(10), 88–93. doi:10.1145/1164394.1164400

Biever, C. (2006, December 23). Web 2.0 is all about the feel-good factor. *New Scientist, 192*, 30.

Birdsall, W. F. (2007). Web 2.0 as a social movement. *Webology, 4*(2). Retrieved from http://www. webology.ir/2007/v4n2/a40.html

Boll, S. (2007). MultiTube—Where Web 2.0 and Multimedia Could Meet. *IEEE MultiMedia, 14*(1), 9–13. doi:10.1109/MMUL.2007.17

Brabham, D. (2008). Crowdsourcing as a model for problem solving: an introduction and cases. *Convergence.* Retrieved from http://con.sagepub. com/cgi/content/abstract/14/1/75

Chaffey, D., Mayer, R., Johnston, K., & Ellis-Chadwick, F. (2000). Internet Marketing, Strategy, Implementation and Practice. Reading, MA: FT/ Pretnice Hall.

Chesbrough, H. (2003). The Era of Open Innovation. *MIT Sloan Management Review, 44*(3), 45–41.

Clemons, E. K., & McFarlan, F. W. (1986). Telecom: Hook Up Or Lose Out. *Harvard Business Review, 64*, 91–97.

Constantinides, E. (2004). Influencing The Online Consumer's Behaviour: The Web Experience. *Journal of Internet Research, 14*(2), 111–126. doi:10.1108/10662240410530835

Constantinides, E. (2006). The Marketing Mix Revisited: Towards the 21st Century Marketing. *Journal of Marketing Management, 22*(3 -4), 407 – 438.

Constantinides, E., & Fountain, S. (2008). Web 2.0: Conceptual Foundations and Marketing Issues. *Journal of Direct, Data and Digital Marketing Practice, 9*(3).

Constantinides, E., Lorenzo, C., & Gómez, M.A. (2008). Social Media: A new frontier for retailers? *European Retail Research, 22*(1).

Coviello, N. E., & Brodie, R. J. (2001). Contemporary Marketing practices of consumer and business-to-business firms: how different are they? *Journal of Business and Industrial Marketing, 16*(5), 382–400. doi:10.1108/08858620110400223

Coyle, K. (2007). The Library Catalog in a 2.0 World. *Journal of Academic Librarianship, 33*(2), 289–291. doi:10.1016/j.acalib.2007.02.003

Craig, E. (2007). Changing paradigms: managed learning environments and Web 2.0. *Campus-Wide Information Systems, 24*(3), 152–161. doi:10.1108/10650740710762185

Cymfony. (2006). *Making the case for a Social MediaStrategy* [White paper]. Retrieved from http://www.cymfony.com

Da Silveira, G., Borenstein, D., & Fogliatto, F. S. (2001). Mass customization: Literature review and research directions. *International Journal of Production Economics, 72*(1), 1–13. doi:10.1016/S0925-5273(00)00079-7

DeFelice, A. (2006, January 1). A new Marketing Medium. *CRM.com.*

Deshpande, A., & Jadad, A. (2006). Web 2.0: Could it help move the health system into the 21st century? *Journal of Men's Health & Gender, 3*(4), 332–336. doi:10.1016/j.jmhg.2006.09.004

Dholakia, R., Johnson, J., Della Bitta, A., & Dholakia, N. (1993). Decision-making Time in Organizational Buying Behavior: An Investigation of Its Antecedents. *Journal of the Academy of Marketing Science, 21*(4), 281–292. doi:10.1007/BF02894521

Dixon, D. F., & Blois, K. J. (1983). Some Limitations of the 4 P's as a Paradigm for Marketing. In *Back to Basics, Proceedings of the Marketing Education Group,* Cranfield School of Management (pp. 92-107).

Du, H., & Wagner, C. (2006). Weblog success: Exploring the role of Technology. *International Journal of Human-Computer Studies, 64,* 789–798. doi:10.1016/j.ijhcs.2006.04.002

E-Commerce Times. (2008). *B2B in a Web 2.0 World, Part 2: Social Media Marketing.* Retrieved from http://www.ecommercetimes.com/story/B2B-in-a-Web-20-World-Part-2-Social-Media-Marketing-62988.html

Eikelmann, S., Hajj, J., & Peterson, M. (2008). Opinion piece: Web 2.0: Profiting from the threat. *Journal of Direct. Data and Digital Marketing Practice, 9,* 293–295. doi:10.1057/palgrave.dddmp.4350094

Feitzinger, E., & Lee, H. L. (1997). Mass Customization at Hewlett-Packard, The Power of Postponement. *Harvard Business Review,* (January –February): 116–121.

Franke, N., & Piller, F. (2004). Value creation by toolkits for user innovation and design: the case of the watch market. *Journal of Product Innovation Management, 21,* 401–415. doi:10.1111/j.0737-6782.2004.00094.x

Gillin, P. (2007). The New Influencers, a marketer's guide to the New Social media. Fresno, CA: Quill Driver Books.

Gillin, P. (2009). Secrets of the Social Media Marketing. Fresno, CA: Quill Driver Books.

Grandon, E., & Pearson, J. M. (2004). Electronic commerce adoption: an empirical study of small and medium US business. *Information & Management, 42,* 197–216.

Hitwise, U. S. (n.d.). *Research note: Measuring Web 2.0 consumer participation.*

Johnson, S. (2007, January 1). It's all about us. *Time,* 55.

Karger, D., & Quan, D. (2004). What Would It Mean to Blog on the Semantic Web? Berlin Heidelberg: Springer.

Karin, I., & Eiferman, R. (2006). Technology-Based Marketing (TBM), A new competitive approach for High-Tech Industries. *International Journal of Global Business and Competitiveness, 2*(1), 19–25.

Keegan, V. (2007, July 5). Amateurs can be good and bad news. *The Guardian.*

Keen, A. (2007). The Cult of the Amateur: How today's Internet is killing our culture. New York: Doubleday / Random House.

Kohler, T., Matzler, K., & Fuller, J. (2009). Avatar-based innovation: Using virtual worlds for real-world innovation. *Technovation, 29*, 395–407. doi:10.1016/j.technovation.2008.11.004

Korica, P., Mauer, H., & Schinagl, W. (2006). The growing importance of E-Communities on the Web. In *Proceedings IADIS International Conference, Web Based Communities 2006,* Spain.

Levy, M., & Powell, P. (2003). Exploring SME Internet Adoption: Towards a Contingent Model. *Electronic Markets, 13*(2), 173–181. doi:10.1080/1019678032000067163

Li, C., Bernoff, J., Feffer, K. A., & Pflaum, C. N. (2007). Marketing On Social Sites. *Forrester.* Retrieved from http://www.forrester.com/Research/Document/Excerpt/0,7211,41662,00.html

McAfee, A. (2006). Enterprise 2.0: The Dawn of Emergent Collaboration. *MIT Sloan Management Review, 47*(3), 21–28.

McKinsey. (2007). How businesses are using Web 2.0: A McKinsey global survey. The McKinsey Quarterly.

McKinsey. (2008a, July). Building the Web 2.0 Enterprise: McKinsey Global Survey Results. *The McKinsey Quarterly.*

McKinsey. (2008b, June). The next step in Open Innovation. *The McKinsey Quarterly.*

Mehrtens, J., Cragg, P., & Mills, A. (2001). A model of Internet adoption by SMEs. *Information & Management, 39*, 165–176. doi:10.1016/S0378-7206(01)00086-6

Montazemi, A. R. (2006). How they manage IT: SMEs in Canada and the U.S. *Communications of the ACM, 49*(12), 109–112. doi:10.1145/1183236.1183240

Musser, J., & O'Reilly, T. (2006). Web 2.0 principles and Best Practices. *O'Reilly Radar Report.*

Nambisan, S., & Nambisan, P. (2008). How to Profit From a Better 'Virtual Customer Environment. *MIT Sloan Management Review, 49*(3), 53–61.

Needleman, M. (2007). Web 2.0/Lib 2.0—What Is It? (If It's Anything at All). *Serials Review, 33*(3), 202–203. doi:10.1016/j.serrev.2007.05.001

O'Reilly, T. (2005). *What is Web 2.0?* Retrieved from http://www.oreillynet.com/pub/a/oreilly/tim/news/2005/09/30/what-is-web-20.html

Ogawa, S., & Piller, F. (2006). Reducing the risks of new product development. *MIT Sloan Management Review, 47*(2), 65–71.

Parise, S., & Guinan, P. J. (2008). Marketing using Web 2.0. In *Proceedings of the 41st Hawaii International Conference on System Sciences.*

Peppers, D., & Rogers, M. (1995). A new Marketing paradigm: share of customer, not market share. *Managing Service Quality, 5*(3), 48–51. doi:10.1108/09604529510796412

Potts, J., Hartley, J., Banks, J., Burgess, J., Cobcroft, R., Cunningham, S., & Montgomery, L. (2008). Consumer co-creation and situated creativity. *Industry and Innovation, 15*(5), 459–474. doi:10.1080/13662710802373783

Prahalad, C. K., & Ramaswamy, V. (2004). Co-Creation experiences: the next practice in value creation. *Journal of Interactive Marketing, 18*(3), 5–14. doi:10.1002/dir.20015

Prospero Technologies, L. L. C. (2007). *Social MediaSurvey.* Retrieved from http://www.prospero.com/about_press_release_071016.asp

Quelch, J. (2008). How Better Marketing Elected Barack Obama. *Harvard Business Publishing.* Retrieved from http://blogs.harvardbusiness. org/quelch/2008/11/how_better_marketing_ elected_b.html

Rha, J.-Y., Widdows, R., Hooker, N. H., & Montalto, C. P. (2002). E-consumerism as a tool for empowerment. *Journal of Consumer Education, 19*(20), 61–69.

Rogers, E. S., Chamberlin, J., Ellison, M. L., & Crean, T. (1997). A consumer-constructed scale to measure empowerment among users of mental health services. *Psychiatric Services (Washington, D.C.), 48*(8), 1041–1047.

Stelzner, M. (2009). *How marketers are using social Media to grow their business.* Social Media Marketing Industry Report. Retrieved from http:// www.Whitepapersource.com

Swaine, M. (2007). Web 2.0 and the engineering of trust. *Dr. Dobb's Journal, 32*(1), 16–18.

Swisher, P. S. (2007). The managed web: A look at the impact of Web 2.0 on media asset management for the enterprise. *Journal of Digital Asset Management, 3*(1), 32–42. doi:10.1057/palgrave. dam.3650061

Thomas, A. R. (2007). The end of mass Marketing: or, why all successful Marketing is now direct Marketing. *Direct Marketing: An International Journal, 1*(1), 6–16. doi:10.1108/17505930710734107

Ueda, K., Takenaka, T., & Fujita, K. (2008). Toward value co-creation in manufacturing and servicing. *CIRP Journal of Manufacturing Science and Technology, 1*, 53–58. doi:10.1016/j. cirpj.2008.06.007

Urban, G. (2005). Don't Just Relate - Advocate!: A Blueprint for Profit in the Era of Customer Power. Philadelphia, PA: Wharton School Publishing.

van der Veen, M. (2004). *Explaining E-Business adoption, Innovation and Entrepreneurship in Dutch SMEs.* Doctoral Thesis, University of Twente.

Varadarajan, R., & Yadav, M. (2002). Marketing Strategy and the Internet: An Organizing Framework. *Journal of the Academy of Marketing Science, 30*(4), 296–312. doi:10.1177/009207002236907

von Hippel, E. (2004). Democratizing innovation: the evolving phenomenon of user innovation. *Journal für Betriebswirtschaft, 55*(1), 63–78. doi:10.1007/s11301-004-0002-8

Webb, B., & Sayer, R. (1998). Benchmarking small companies on the Internet. *Long Range Planning, 31*(6), 815–827. doi:10.1016/S0024-6301(98)80018-6

Wilson, A. N. (2007, June 8). The Internet is destroying the world as we know it. *Daily Mail Online.*

Wind, J., & Mahajan, V. (2001). The Challenge of Digital Marketing. In J. Wind & V. Mahajan (Eds.), Digital Marketing: Global Strategies from the world's leading experts (pp. 3-25). New York: John Wiley & Sons.

Yakel, E. (2006). Inviting the user into the virtual archives. *OCLC Systems & Services, 22*(3), 159–163. doi:10.1108/10650750610686207

Young, G. O., et al. (2009, January 6). Can enterprise Web 2.0 survive the recession? *Forrester.*

Zhang, X., & Chen, R. (2008). Examining the mechanism of the value co-creation with customers. *International Journal of Production Economics, 116*, 242–250. doi:10.1016/j. ijpe.2008.09.004

ENDNOTES

[1] McKinsey Quarterly (2005), Boosting returns on Marketing investment, nr 2.http://www.mckinseyquarterly.com/Marketing/Strategy/Boosting_returns_on_marketing_investment_1602_abstract

[2] Zogby Poll, 27 February 2008, http://www.zogby.com/news/ReadNews.dbm?ID=1454

[3] Newsweek, 2007 The New Wisdom of the Web, http://www.newsweek.com/id/45976/page/2

[4] Nielsen Online, 2008, Over 875 Million Consumers Have Shopped Online -- The Number of Internet Shoppers Up 40% in Two Years, http://www.nielsen.com/media/2008/pr_080128b.html

[5] BizReport.com, June 5, 2007

[6] Kumar N., (2004), Marketing as Strategy, Understanding the CEOs agenda for driving growth and innovation, Harvard Business School Press

[7] According to Oracle's senior vice-president and chief marketing officer, using social news releases has halved Oracle's PR budget, enabling it to save about US$4.6 million over the past year

[8] http://www.nytimes.com:80/2007/12/27/business/smallbusiness/27sbiz.html

[9] BusinessWeek Magazine, February 25, 2007

[10] HitWise.com in a study published in April 2007 calculates the participation of Web 2.0 to the top participatory web sites to 12,28%, an 668% increase compared to 2 years ago

[11] http://www.haveyoursay.com/

[12] Many examples of configurators are available in the web site Configurator Database www.configurator-database.com

[13] http://www.wired.com/wired/archive/14.06/crowds.html

[14] http://current.com/items/76314302/sony_v_cam_transformation.htm

[15] Conversations among community members ranged from discussing colors and designs that should be utilized on a greeting card to selecting what gifts and price ranges were more appropriate for a high school graduation. Community members were also asked to keep a virtual journal where they recorded and ranked marketing materials that they received from the company. Additionally, the company used the online community to learn more about the customers themselves. Members were able to upload and share their pictures and provide insights about their lifestyles, hobbies, and needs. This resulted in the company gaining valuable insights into consumer behavior, reactions to new products and ideas, as well as the effectiveness of the company's marketing materials, all at a very low cost and effort.

APPENDIX

- **Application Types:** There is a wide variety of application types fulfilling the criteria of the above-mentioned definition. In order to simplify the issue the application can be classified in five many categories.
    1. **Blogs:** Short for web logs: online journals, the most known and fastest growing category of Web 2.0 -based applications (Du and Wagner, 2006). Blogs are often combined with Podcasts i.e. digital audio or video that can be streamed or downloaded to portable devices. Examples: http://gizmodo.com, http://www.boingboing.net, http://www.huffingtonpost.com
    2. **Social Networks:** allow users to build personal websites accessible to other users for exchange of personal content and communication. Examples: http://www.myspace.com, http://www.facebook.com, www.hyves.nl, http://www.ning.com/
    3. **(Content) Communities:** Web sites organizing and sharing particular types of content. Examples are applications of Video sharing: http://video.google.com, www.youtube.com, http://etsylove.ning.com, Photos sharing: http://www.flickr.com, Social Bookmarking www.digg.com, http://del.icio.us and publicly edited Encyclopedias www.wikipedia.org, http://en.citizendium.org/wiki/Main_Page
    4. **Forums / Bulletin Boards:** sites for exchanging ideas and information usually around special interests Examples: www.epinions.com, www.personaldemocracy.com, http://www.python.org.
    5. **Content aggregators:** applications allowing users to fully customize the web content they wish to access. These sites make use of a technique known as Real Simple Syndication (RSS). Examples http://uk.my.yahoo.com/, http://www.google.com/ig, http://www.netvibes.com/

The main difference of the above applications compared to the older generation of Internet applications is the fact that in the Web 2.0 the user is a vital factor not only as consumer but also as content contributor. The term User Generated Content (UGC) is often used to underline this special attribute of all above Web 2.0 application categories.

- **Social Effects:** Enabling easy interaction, seamless generation of information and easy access to it are key advantages of Web 2.0 -based applications; the active participation and the unlimited possibilities of contacting peers allows the creation of online communities formed around special interests (Beer and Barrows, 2007; Birdsall, 2007). Generating content, copying, sharing, editing, syndicating, reproducing and re-mixing information are common practices in the Web 2.0 domain. Such practices lead to democratization of technology, information and knowledge, facilitating the active participation of the user as contributor, reviewer and reporter. Users create communities of special interests and share experiences and knowledge but also engage in a transparent conversation with the industry and politicians. The result is, as earlier mentioned, a unique form of customer empowerment allowing customers to make their voice heard as never before forcing corporations to increasingly dismiss older communication models based on the control of the mass media. This is one of the main factors likely to shape the nature and form of future marketing. The social effects of the Web 2.0 are by and large a fascinating research area and a field most likely to shape the future consumer or even human behavior.

Chapter 2
Leveraging University Research to Assist SMEs in Legacy Industrial Era Regions:
The Case of I-99 Corridor

Arvind Karunakaran
The Pennsylvania State University, USA

Sandeep Purao
The Pennsylvania State University, USA

Brian Cameron
The Pennsylvania State University, USA

ABSTRACT

Small and Medium Enterprises (SMEs) in legacy industrial era regions face unique challenges that vary from the challenges faced by SMEs in other regions. Especially, SMEs in legacy industrial regions face problems with respect to the access to knowledge networks. The authors discuss an approach that focuses on enabling the SMEs in legacy regions towards accessing these knowledge networks. The authors base their discussion upon the ongoing debate within the IS community regarding 'rigor-relevance' gap, and they take the specific case of SME's in I-99 corridor to illustrate this. The chapter highlights the challenges faced by SMEs in legacy industrial era regions, and briefly describe the ongoing research project called LAIR (Leveraging Advanced IT Research), aimed at understanding the risks that SMEs in the I-99 Corridor are likely to face as they grow, with a specific focus on risks associated with upgrading, implementing and integrating their existing and new Information Systems.

INTRODUCTION

An enduring debate within the Information Systems (IS) community focuses on the 'rigor' of research, in terms of the methodological strength and sound- ness, versus its 'relevance' to practice. Oftentimes, there have been many concerns raised about the minor impact IS research has towards guiding practice (Baskerville & Myers, 2004; Benbasat & Zmud, 1999; Davenport & Markus, 1999; Lyytinen & King, 2004). Benbasat and Zmud argue that the

DOI: 10.4018/978-1-61520-627-8.ch002

field of IS became irrelevant to practice since they emulated other academic fields within the business school - which placed a great deal of emphasis on rigor – but failed to emulate the cumulative research tradition of those fields. They conclude that there should be greater consensus within the IS community about its core theoretical concepts and the best way to facilitate increased relevance is to conduct applied theoretical research (Benbasat & Zmud, 1999).

On the other hand, Davenport and Markus argue that other academic disciplines within the business schools are wrong role models for IS, since a cumulative research tradition, instead of bridging the gap between academic rigor and practical relevance, would prevent the discipline in keeping up with the rapid changes in the business environment and the associated changes happening within the technological environment (Davenport & Markus, 1999). They argue towards emulating fields like medicine and law, which attempt to find a balance between rigor and relevance. To facilitate this, they propose 'evaluation research' and 'policy research' as alternatives to the 'applied theory research' put forth by Benbasat and Zmud (Benbasat & Zmud, 1999; Davenport & Markus, 1999).

This long-standing debate exists not only within the IS community but also within other academic disciplines within the business schools. While some propose a combined effort of researchers and practitioners using "engaged scholarship" (Van de Ven, 2007; Van De Ven & Johnson, 2006) to bridge the gap between research rigor and practical relevance, others have proposed a "relational scholarship of integration" (Bartunek, 2007) and "action research" (Baskerville & Myers, 2004) as alternatives towards bridging this gap. There are also counter-arguments that show how practitioners find little value in academic research and how practitioner and academic knowledge may be unrelated to each other (McKelvey, 2006; Nyden & Wiewel, 1992). To quote (McKelvey, 2006),

Practitioners keep looking for T-bone steaks, but what keeps flowing are turkeys. I don't quite see how any amount of engaged scholarship, paradigm pluralism, arbitrage, conflict resolution, big questions, and so forth is going to turn turkeys into T-bones, even if the flow from the left is renewed.

While we acknowledge the importance of this debate, we argue that the only way to appraise the strengths and weaknesses of any model of scholarship – be it 'engaged' or 'relational' - is by indulging in more research studies of this nature. Further, most debates arise within a disciplinary context and largely ignore the value that research universities as a whole could bring-in to the practitioner community by leveraging and combining specialized, and sometimes, esoteric knowledge across disciplines.

Drawing upon Pasteur's quadrant from Stokes' taxonomy (Stokes, 1997; Tushman & O'Reilly, 2007), we argue that both the academic and practitioner community could be better served if the research-in-context is more grounded in the phenomena. Instead of looking for an ideal model of scholarship to bridge the 'rigor' and 'relevance' gap, we suggest a focus on designing and conducting studies, and fostering relationships that would let the practitioners leverage knowledge that research universities generate as a whole, in essence, letting them find the T-bone steaks they need amidst the disciplinary turkeys (a la (McKelvey, 2006)). Through this interactive process, researchers could identify issues of communication and other barriers which hinder collaboration between the academic and the practitioner communities. Techniques to understand these can include self-reflexive analyses and/or by using a separate team of researchers to observe the interaction between the academic and practitioner communities in order to improve the understanding of those barriers.

This chapter provides the specific case of SME's in I-99 corridor to take the above discussion forward, and it talks about how a structured approach can be created towards enabling these SMEs to access the knowledge networks, through a joint effort between universities and other entities which are working towards regional economic development. It bring forth a perspective that talks about how duplication of efforts within universities could be avoided by "Co-solving" of complex problems, which further leads towards leveraging the value that research universities *as a whole* could bring-in to SMEs, as compared to the limited value that 'silos' operating in isolation could impart. The above discussion is grounded within the context of an ongoing project called LAIR (Leveraging Advanced IT Research), which is part of a larger study titled "Leveraging Advanced Research University Knowledge for Innovation in Legacy Industrial Era Regions: Pennsylvania's I-99 Corridor". The focus of the larger study is about finding ways and means towards leveraging research intensive universities for the revitalization of legacy industrial era regions (like the I-99 Corridor), which are now adjusting to post-industrial society. The specific focus of the LAIR project is to understand the risks that SMEs (Small and Medium Enterprises) in the I-99 Corridor are likely to face as they grow, with a particular emphasis on risks associated with upgrading, implementing and integrating their existing and new IT systems. The ongoing project is being conducted with a unique collaboration between the Economic Development associations and the Small and Medium Businesses in I-99 corridor and researchers from the College of Information Sciences & Technology and Materials Research Institute at The Pennsylvania State University, University Park.

BACKGROUND

Legacy Industrial Era Regions

Legacy Industrial era regions are those regions which are still undergoing a transition in adjusting to the post-industrial society (Bell, 1973; Masuda, 1980). Economic activity in these regions forms a significant portion of the heavy industry and manufacturing sectors of the U.S. economy (Faberman, 2002). Sometimes referred to as "Rust Belt", these regions signify the steep decline of the manufacturing industry throughout the late 1960s and 1970s, which lead to significant loss of jobs in those regions (Kahn, 1999). Various reasons, including increased foreign competition and lower demand for products such as steel, were attributed to the decline of these regions (Bell, 1973; Faberman, 2002; Kahn, 1999).

As a consequence, employment growth in those regions lagged behind the national average for a long period of time. Between 1969 and 1996, when the manufacturing employment of the country grew by 1.4%, manufacturing employment in the Rust Belt fell by 32.9% (Kahn, 1999). The rate of employment growth in those regions came closer to the national average only during the late 1980s. Even during the 1990s, when rapid economic expansion was taking place throughout the country, these regions failed to catch up with the rest of the United States (Faberman, 2002; Kahn, 1999). Also, when the nation as a whole has shifted toward a service economy, these regions failed to catch up with the changes that were happening around them and are still in the process of undergoing the transition to post-industrial society (Bell, 1973) (See Figure 1).

SMEs in Legacy Industrial Regions

Small and Medium Enterprises (SMEs) are considered the engines of growth and innovation of the modern economy (SBA, 1998, 2004d). According to U.S Small Business Administration, SMBs

Figure 1. Legacy industrial era regions, comparison statistics

Economic Diversity	National	New York	Illionois	Ohio	Michigan	Wisconsin	Pennsylvania	Indiana	West Virginia	Pittsburgh	Detroit	Milwaukee
Government	n/a	n/a	n/a	n/a	n/a	n/a	n/a	n/a	n/a	11%	12%	11%
Services	41%	32%	31%	28%	31%	23%	29%	26%	24%	36%	35%	34%
Trade, Transportation, and Utilities	22%	20%	22%	21%	20%	22%	22%	22%	23%	21%	19%	18%
Manufacturing	5%	8%	13%	17%	17%	20%	13%	21%	12%	9%	15%	16%
Construction	12%	4%	5%	5%	4%	5%	5%	5%	5%	5%	4%	n/a
Other*	20%	35%	22%	28%	28%	30%	31%	26%	36%	18%	13%	21%

*With the exception of I-99 Corridor, government is included in "other" but not specified

*Agriculture is omitted

Education*	National	New York	Illionois	Ohio	Michigan	Wisconsin	Pennsylvania	Indiana	West Virginia	Pittsburgh	Detroit	Milwaukee
High School Diploma (2000)	84.60%	79.06%	81.43%	82.97%	83.41%	85.09%	81.90%	82.13%	75.21%	85.06%	82.05%	84.50%
College Degree (2000)	52.50%	34.54%	32.11%	27.02%	28.74%	29.92%	28.50%	25.19%	19.70%	30.88%	29.34%	33.72%
Bachelor's Degree (2000)	27.20%	27.37%	26.06%	21.09%	21.76%	22.42%	22.35%	19.40%	14.84%	23.83%	22.76%	26.94%

*Based on adults 25 years of age or older

represent 99.7 percent of all employer firms and pay nearly 45 percent of total U.S. private payroll (SBA, 1998, 2004c, 2004d). A historical analysis shows that they have generated 60 to 80 percent of net new jobs annually over the last decade, and created more than half of non-farm private gross domestic product (SBA, 2004b). Further, SMEs hire as many as 40 percent of high tech workers such as scientists, engineers, and computer workers (SBA, 1998, 2004b, 2004c, 2004d).

According to Office of Advocacy estimates, there were 27.2 million businesses in the United States; of these, 99.9% are small firms with fewer than 500 employees (SBA, 2004c). However, two-thirds of these small businesses survive two years, 44 percent survive for four years, and 31 percent survive for seven years (SBA, 2004b). The reasons for failure can include institutional environment, financial crisis, owner/manager motivation, risk-taking propensity, competition, market conditions etc (Miner & Raju, 2004).

SMEs in legacy industrial era regions face few issues which are unique to the characteristic of the region. For example, in these regions, the percentage of people with a College degree or above is very low (See Figure. 1) as compared to the national average. As a result, the service sector in these regions is relatively weak and thereby, the SMEs in these regions seldom have access to quality service providers who would aid them in a variety of ways which would facilitate business growth (Levy, Powell, & Yetton, 2002)

IT Risks for SMEs in Legacy Industrial Era Regions

Research on SMEs within the IS (Information Systems) community initially started with studies on *adoption* of technology and the *motivators/inhibitors* that influence the adoption (Cragg & King, 1993; Iacovou, Benbasat & Dexter, 1995). However, 'SME and IS' research is expanding beyond the initial focus of IS adoption (Bharati & Chaudary, 2009), and we are seeing a relative increase in the number of studies published on the various aspects of 'SMEs and IS'(Bharati & Chaudary, 2008; Bharati & Chaudary, 2002; Caldeira & Ward, 2003; Desouza & Awazu, 2006; Garg, Goyal & Lather, 2008; Levy, Loebbecke & Powell, 2003; Woznica & Healy, 2009).

The volume of IT spending from these Small to Medium Enterprises tends to be comparable to that of Large Enterprises. The SMEs form the so-called 'Long Tail' (Anderson & Andersson, 2006) of IT spending. Together, they represent 49% of the overall IT spending, making it a lucrative market for the IT Service providers (Speyer, Pohlmann, & Brown, 2006). However, these SMEs seldom have access to *knowledge networks* that provide them the necessary information to understand their *existing* and *future* IT needs and to gain access to *quality* IT service providers, who could help them with their day-to-day IT operations. Anecdotal evidence suggests that the IT providers are often too mired in technology details and solutions (e.g. 'my router is not working'), and rarely, if ever, consider aiding the business owners to find business-IT synergies or in using IT towards facilitating business growth (e.g. 'moving to strategic uses of IT with new software functionalities'). On the other hand, these SMEs do not have the internal resources to forecast their future Information Systems (Ballantine & Levy, 1998; Levy, Powell, & Yetton, 1998) and are not able to forecast, plan and mitigate risks related to the evolution of their information systems platforms.

Due to the above reasons, SME Owner/Managers in these regions are satisfied with bandaged, ad-hoc solutions that solve an immediate problem, instead of planning for their long-term IT needs (Ballantine & Levy, 1998; Levy & Powell, 2000; Levy, Powell, & Galliers, 1999). As a result, they are often confronted with scalability and integration issues. But they keep moving on with the current systems, until the existing infrastructure hits a threshold. Once they reach a threshold, most SMEs are confronted with questions such as the one's listed below:

- Should we buy faster computers?
- Can we modify/enhance what we have?
- If not, what system do we select?
- What are the real costs involved?
- Do we need outside help and can we afford it?
- How might this type of upgrade disrupt our business?
- How long will the implementation & integration realistically take?
- Will we need additional people to maintain the system?
- What are the on-going maintenance costs of a new system?

- What other risks are involved and how can we identify and mitigate the risks?

However, there has been limited research which focuses on "risk management" from a SME perspective. The reasons for this are listed below:

- Treating SMEs as 'little big businesses' (Agell, 2004) and thereby, lack of research studies about the role of Information Systems within a SME context. Only one paper was published in the past six years in this area (Street & Meister, 2004) in top three IS journals in the US (MISQ, ISR, and JMIS).
- Even the studies which distinguish SMEs from large enterprises within the IS literature focus more about SME IS adoption and rarely tend to focus on other aspects like Risk Management. (Though there is a change of focus in recent times (Bharati & Chaudhury, 2009)).
- The phenomenon of 'Managing Risks within SMEs' is largely overlooked, since traditional studies on 'Risk Management' and 'Information Systems' focus on large enterprises[See, for example, (Alter & Sherer, 2004; Stoneburner, Feringa, & Goguen, 2002)].

Ambiguity in Size Standards and Definition

In addition to the above stated reasons, there is a also a lack of consensus regarding the definition on what constitutes a small to medium enterprise (Churchill & Lewis, 2000; Cummings, 2003; Levy, et al., 1998; O'Farrell & Hitchens, 1988; SBA, 2004a; Storey, 1998), which makes it difficult for researchers to identify appropriate organizations. IS researchers within United States tends to adopt the popular U.S. SBA's (Small Business Administration) definition(SBA, 2004a). However, SBA did not incorporate any 'Information Systems' component to distinguish between SMEs and Large Enterprises. Since the focus of our research study is on SMEs and their Information systems, it becomes important for us to come up with a hybrid definition which includes information systems as a part of the definition. In this section, we will look at the historical ambiguities in size standards and definitions. At the end, we will also disclose our working definition of a SME.

The term "Small to Medium Enterprise" (SME) is frequently used in the European Union and other international organizations like UN, World Bank, WTO, while the term "Small to Medium Business" (SMB) is prevalent in USA. Other variations like "Micro, Small and Medium Enterprises" (MSME) and "Small, Medium and Micro Enterprises" (SMME) are used in Africa (SBA, 2004a, 2004b; Storey, 1998). For the sake of consistency, we use the term "Small to Medium Enterprise" (SME) throughout the book chapter. Also, there is a historical lack of consensuses regarding the "size standards" on what constitutes a SME. Some of the variances range from 'less than 200 employees' to 'less than 20 employees and a minimum of 8 years in operation', from 'less then 50 employees and annual sales < three million dollars and sole ownership', to 'between 5 to 500 employees, and minimum of five years in operation' (Churchill & Lewis, 2000; Hanks, Watson, Jansen, & Chandler, 1993; Horton, 1991; Storey, 1998). These variations depend on different factors like "geography" and "industry segment" (Churchill & Lewis, 2000; Hanks, et al., 1993; Horton, 1991). Various parameters have been laid out which could be used to assess the size standards for a SME. Some of these parameters include:

- Staff Count
- Turnover
- No. of years in operation
- Balance Sheet total
- Workstations
- Limited operations catering only to local markets etc.

However, according to the current norms in the U.S, any firm with less than 100 employees is generally considered to be a Small Business and any firm with more than 100 employees and less than 500 employees is generally considered to be a Medium Business. In the European Union, any firm with less than 50 employees is considered to be a Small Business and any firm with more than 100 employees and less than 200 employees is considered to be a Medium Business. In Australia, any firm with 1 to 19 employees is considered to be a Small Business and any firm with 20 to 200 employees is considered to be a Medium Business (SBA, 2004a, 2004b) (See Table 1).

Since larger organizations used these generic definitions to their advantage, U.S Small Business Administration (SBA), came with a new and enhanced definition. According to the U.S SBA (SBA, 2004b), a Small Business is one that:

- is organized for profit;
- has a place of business in the United States;
- Makes a significant contribution to the U.S. economy by paying taxes or using American products, materials or labor; and,
- Does not exceed the numerical size standard for its industry.

Table 1. Current norms (based on staff count)

Type	USA	EU	Australia
Small	<100	<50	<20
Medium	<500	<250	<200

It could be a:

- Sole proprietorship
- Partnership
- Corporation
- Or any other legal form

Also, U.S. SBA had come up with a detailed table as per the industry segment and the corresponding size standard for that particular industry. The North American Industrial Classification System (NAICS) (SBA, 2004a) is used for this purpose. However, SBA did not incorporate any 'Information Systems' component in its definition.

Microsoft™ used "number of workstations" as the main criteria to come up with its definition for a SME(Microsoft, 2006). Though this definition is useful in number of ways for IS researchers, it ignores other organizational specific features like the firm size and also overlooks the differences across industry segments (See Table 2).

Hybrid Working Definition of 'SME' for IS Researchers

In order to overcome the limitations of both the SBA's as well as Microsoft's definition(Microsoft, 2006; SBA, 2004a), we came up with a hybrid definition of SME by combining U.S. SBA's definition with Microsoft's definition. This hybrid definition will be helpful during the time of 'theoretical sampling'.

- "A *'Small Business'* is an *'independently owned and operated'* organization which is *not dominant* in the industry it is operating in and *complies* with the *industry-specific* size *standard* defined by the U.S. Small Business Administration and its operating environment should *use* a minimum of 1 and a maximum of 49 workstations"
- A *'Medium Business'* is an *'independently owned and operated'* organization which is *not* a *'small business'* and is *not dominant* in the industry it is operating in and its operating environment should *use* a minimum of 50 and a maximum of 499 workstations"

Here, the term 'independently owned & operated' refers to a firm which is not a subsidiary of a larger organization. But, the firm could have multiple owners. 'Workstations in the operating environment' refers to the workstations which are active i.e. workstations located in the offices in which the organization conducts business plus workstations in their corporate office (if any). Workstations could be owned, leased or remote.

LEVERAGING UNIVERSITY RESEARCH TO ASSIST SMES

Research on 'University-Industry Collaboration' and 'University-Industry Knowledge Transfer' could be broadly categorized into four streams (Agrawal, 2001), based on whether the focus of research is on the

Table 2. The Microsoft™ definition (based on number of desktops)

Business	Segment	Minimum Number of Desktops	Maximum Number of Desktops
Small Business		**1**	**50**
	Lower Small Segment	1	4
	Core Small Segment	5	24
	Upper Small Segment	25	49

1. Firm Characteristics
2. University Characteristics
3. Geography and localized knowledge spill-overs or
4. the Channels of knowledge transfer

Research in the 'Firm Characteristics' stream focuses on issues like the internal structure of the organization, including its formal/informal structure, partnership networks and resource allocation and talks about concepts like 'absorptive capacity' of the firm(Cohen & Levinthal, 1990), 'connectedness'(Cockburn & Henderson, 1998), etc. Research in the 'University Characteristics' stream focuses on issues such as intellectual property rights, equity and licensing strategies, patents and incentive structures etc. largely ignoring the firm characteristics (Feldman, Feller, Bercovitz, & Burton, 2002; Henderson & Smith, 2002; Sampat, Mowery, & Ziedonis, 2003; Thursby, Jensen, & Thursby, 2001). Most of the literature in this stream focuses on the Bayh-Dole Act of 1980, which granted universities the 'right to license' those inventions from the projects that were federally funded(Henderson & Smith, 2002; Sampat, et al., 2003). Studies focused on the quality of university patents since the inception of Bayh-Doyle Act. 'Geography and Localized Knowledge Spillover' stream of research pays attention to the spatial relationship between the university and the firm and its relation to effective collaboration and knowledge transfer success (Audretsch & Feldman, 1996; Jaffe, Trajtenberg, & Henderson, 1993). This stream of research specifically focused on 'tacit' and 'explicit' dimensions of knowledge and the difficulty in codifying 'tacit knowledge' which could be transferred across contexts (Nonaka & Takeuchi, 1995). Finally, literature on 'Channels of Knowledge Transfer' concentrates on the various different pathways available – like research publications, practitioner conferences, patents and consulting –that would facilitate collaboration and knowledge transfer

between universities and firms (Agrawal & Henderson, 2002; Colyvas, et al., 2002).

These studies describe several factors which hinder 'University-SME Collaboration' (Hadjimanolis, 2006; Izushi, 2003; Woolgar, Vaux, Gomes, Ezingeard, & Grieve, 1998). Among them, the perception that SMEs have about *'university research'* - **as something that is not directly applicable to their specific problem** - is stated as one of the main factors which hinders collaboration (Woolgar, et al., 1998). The differences in the background and motivation of SME owner/managers from that of academic researchers pose a major challenge – in terms of the communication, collaboration and knowledge transfer (Izushi, 2003). Risk Attitudes of SME Owners play an important role in this (Izushi, 2003). Also, the inability to strike a balance between opposing priorities with respect to the expected outcome of the collaboration often adds up to the barrier (Drejer & Jørgensen, 2002). Thus, the current system is unable to fulfil the unique needs of the many different entrants into the system, since there is no "co-solving" of the complex problems, resulting in duplication of efforts (Dytche & Warren, 2007b). A structured approach towards accessing these "extended and powerful knowledge networks" (Dytche & Warren, 2007b; Warren, et al., 2008) is lacking. A recent study on 'university-industry collaboration' interviewed a number of the existing offices and confirms that the resources which are available to foster this collaboration operate largely in isolation, with little interchange of information, and sub-optimal cooperation (Dytche & Warren, 2007b).

On the other hand, SMEs have limited internal resources especially with respect to research and development (R&D) and they need to complement them with other external resources like partnership networks, collaboration with universities etc. (Hanks, et al., 1993; Levy, et al., 2002; Storey, 1998). Thus, research studies needs to be designed in a manner which could bring together the independent resources which are operating largely as silos. This could be accomplished as a joint effort between different entities like the economic development units, chambers of commerce and the industry outreach units. Also, in order to strike a balance between opposing priorities of the SME Owner/Managers and the Academic Researchers, the research-in-context should be more grounded in the phenomena. According to Stokes' taxonomy, conventional academic disciplines operate in Bohr's quadrant, and they are typically about a quest for understanding i.e. rigor without the relevance criteria, while consulting firms and other research units associated with economic development entities operate in Edison's quadrant i.e. relevance without the rigor criteria (Stokes, 1997). Stokes argue that in order to strike a balance between the two, one should pursue fundamental understanding of phenomena with the goal of tackling major real-world problems and develop communities that jointly value the quest for fundamental understanding and

considerations of use i.e. they should operate in the Pasteur's Quadrant with a dual quest for basic understanding (rigor) and with considerations of use (relevance) (Stokes, 1997; Tushman & O'Reilly, 2007) (See Figure 2).

Our research study titled "Leveraging Advanced Research University Knowledge for Innovation in Legacy Industrial Era Regions: Pennsylvania's I-99 Corridor" focuses on striking a balance between 'basic understanding' and 'considerations of use' and about finding ways and means towards leveraging research intensive universities for the revitalization of legacy industrial era regions (like the I-99 Corridor) which are now adjusting to post-industrial society. This is accomplished by a collaborative effort between different entities both within and outside the university, including the economic development associations and chambers of commerce in I-99 Corridor, thereby creating a structured approach towards enabling the SMEs in the region to ac-

Figure 2. Rigor vs. relevance (adapted from Stokes quadrants)

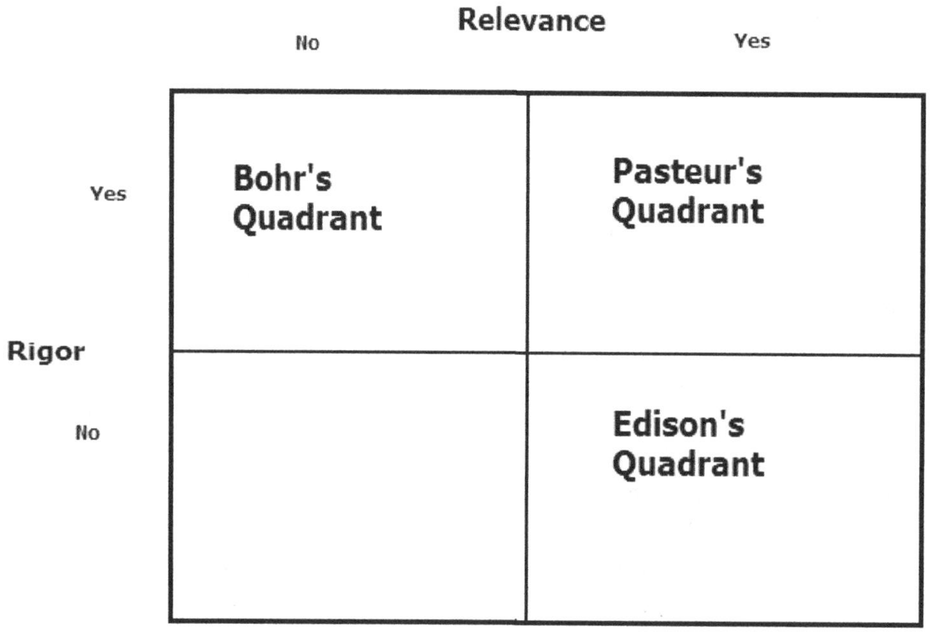

cess these "extended and powerful knowledge networks" (Dytche & Warren, 2007b), and by preventing existing available resources to operate in isolation. "Co-solving" of the complex problems is the norm and thus, duplication of efforts is largely avoided (Dytche & Warren, 2007b; Warren, et al., 2008). In addition to all these, a separate research team observes the interaction between the academic and practitioner communities in order to improve the understanding of barriers towards leveraging research intensive universities for revitalization of legacy industrial era regions which are adjusting to post-industrial society. They focus on improving the understanding of those barriers which would be detrimental to 'University-SME Collaboration' and will closely examine issues of communication between the academic and the business communities as well as diversity issues and how they impact the attraction and retention of talented people to the region.

THE I-99 CORRIDOR AS A LEGACY INDUSTRIAL ERA REGION

The I-99 Corridor (Interstate-99) is a partially-completed intrastate interstate highway (i.e. interstate highway located within a single state) in Central Pennsylvania, linking other cross-state corridors like I-80 and I-76. The current southern terminus is at the north of Bedford, while the northern terminus is near Bellefonte (Interstate 80). It also passes through Altoona and State College (home of The Pennsylvania State University). The full route of the corridor is part of "Corridor O" under the Appalachian Development Highway System, which runs from Interstate 68 near Cumberland in Maryland onto Bedford in Pennsylvania.

The Corridor is home to large number of towns whose economies are fairly fragile, which could be classified as "legacy industrial era regions". I-99 Corridor share some distinct characteristics with other similar 'legacy industrial era regions'. The percentage of population who has a Bachelor's degree is extremely low. Also, the region has not yet made a stride into the service economy, while the majority of its organizations belong to the Manufacturing, Construction and the Trade, Transportation & Utilities sector (Figure 3).

Recent research suggests that due to the geographical remoteness of the region and the lack of tangible as well as intangible infrastructures, the region is at an inherent disadvantage with respect to technology transfer and new business development (Dytche & Warren, 2007b; Warren, Hanke, & Trotzer, 2008). The tangible and intangible infrastructure available to this region is relatively low as compared to other highly developed regions. One of the metrics which a recent report used for measuring the strength of such infrastructures was the value of Venture Capital (VC) investments within a fifty mile radius. Density of VC investments tended to be high within 50 mile radii of the large research universities. Regions around California and along the East Coast had higher densities due to concentration of a number of large research universities (Dytche & Warren, 2007a, 2007b). However, the I-99 Corridor, despite having The Pennsylvania State University, one of the top research universities, within its radii, the density of VC investments tended to be much lower(Dytche & Warren, 2007b).

The resources which were available to support economic development of SMEs in this region worked independent of each other and oftentimes, viewed themselves as competitive rather than collaborative, which in turn reduced their effectiveness in its ability to attract new businesses as well as in supporting existing businesses(Dytche & Warren, 2007b; Warren, et al., 2008). Organizational barriers which undermines effective collaboration in this region is attributed not only due to the lack of effective knowledge transfer and the social capital needed to facilitate effective knowledge transfer, but also due to the fact that

Figure 3. I-99 corridor: comparison statistics

Economic Diversity	I-99 Corridor	National
Government	24%	n/a
Services	23%	41%
Trade, Transportation, and Utilities	28%	22%
Manufacturing	18%	5%
Construction	4%	12%
Other*	3%	20%

Population Growth	I-99 Corridor	National
Population Estimate (1980)	296,165	226,545,805
Population Estimate (2000)	314,796	281,421,905
Percent Change	6.3%+	24.2%+

Education**	I-99 Corridor	National
High School Diploma (2000)	85%	84.60%
College Degree (2000)	22%	52.50%
Bachelor's Degree (2000)	3%	27.20%

*,*Based on adults 25 years of age or older

*Agriculture is omitted

systems for effective collaboration is also not in place(Dytche & Warren, 2007b; Lee, 1996; Warren, et al., 2008). The region lacked a network of relationships built on top of high trust-levels and as a result, interrelated groups failed to share knowledge, operating "largely in isolation, with little interchange of information, and sub-optimal cooperation" (Dytche & Warren, 2007b). Thus, any small to medium enterprise owner/manager who approaches this network finds it difficult to get the information they are looking for and as a result, they get frustrated with the whole process.

Thus, most of the SMEs in regions like I-99 Corridor are mired in procedures and IT support that is often ad hoc and not well integrated. Even if they are interested in growth, a significant obstacle to their growth is their ability to sustain efficiency of operations in the face of these "bandaged" IT operations and procedures. In effect, the fragmentation of operations and lack of IT support may hold them back. This situation often presents a dilemma to the business owners and managers: they cannot invest a large amount in the IT infrastructure in anticipation of growth; neither can their current IT infrastructure provide them the necessary platform to grow and sustain their growth. More importantly, they seldom have access to resources which would aid them in assessing their IT risks and making critical decisions, such as "When to make a switch and move to the next level with respect to my Information Systems?" And how? Whom should I approach for this? etc."

Keystone Innovation Zones (KIZ)

On the other hand, the I-99 Innovation Corridor offers Pennsylvania's largest concentration of Keystone Innovation Zones (KIZ). These are designated zones established in regions around institutions of higher education to link technology-based companies with university faculty and research support (Dytche & Warren, 2007b). So far, ten KIZ's have been established along the I-99 Innovation Corridor to foster innovation by creating entrepreneurial opportunities and by creating a network of support systems through the form of coalitions or partnerships with organizations that are available to assist the business community.

This helps in creating a "knowledge neighbourhood", in which Pennsylvania State University, economic development associations, businesses, capital sources and other community leaders can get in touch with one another, creating a network of support and providing resources to the business community within the I-99 corridor. The business community will benefit by having access to facilities and incubator spaces. Also, there is a greater opportunity to develop research relationships with universities by taking advantage of the proximity to Penn State University, which provides greater access to students, internships, and resources related to workforce development, training, and process improvement(Dytche & Warren, 2007b; Warren, et al., 2008).

Thus, by leveraging the research intensive universities support, it is indeed possible for the SMEs in the legacy industrial era regions to gain access to the resources which would help them in making critical decisions with respect to their Information Systems and which would aid them in assessing their IT risks. The SMEs within the I-99 corridor can greatly benefit through this arrangement, wherein they can leverage the advanced research universities knowledge to address various issues which they are confronted with. Universities knowledge can be used to override the problem faced by these SMEs who have little access to quality service providers. SMEs can leverage research universities knowledge in understanding and forecasting their future needs better, than getting satisfied with ad-hoc, turnkey solutions. This could mutually benefit the universities as well, as this engagement would enable them to come up with a thicker description on the origins and causes of the various issues faced by SMEs.

However, easier said than done, SME-University collaboration often tends to be complicated and is hindered by various barriers(Hadjimanolis, 2006; Hendry, Brown, & Defillippi, 2000), including the social context of cooperative relationships (Ring & Van de Ven, 1994), culture and institutional factors, as well as the role of government policies (Nakamura, Vertinsky, & Zietsma, 1997).

LAIR PROJECT

LAIR (Leveraging Advanced IT Research) is a sub-project under the larger grant which is designed to understand the risks that SMEs in the I-99 Corridor are likely to face as they grow, with a specific focus on risks associated with upgrading, implementing and integrating their existing and new IT systems. The purpose of this research study is to develop an understanding about the information systems integration risks faced by the small and medium enterprises. Based on this understanding about the risks specific to the small and medium enterprises, we would propose a mitigation strategy which could help the small and medium businesses in assessing and tackling these risks. The goal of the research project is to understand barriers to growth for SMEs in the I-99 corridor (Bedford, Blair and Centre County). The main aim of our project is to

- Understand the various risks related to business growth and Information systems growth (Workstations, Networks, Software, IT personnel, Users) faced by

Small and Medium Businesses in the I-99 corridor and

- To develop approaches which would help the SMEs to assess and mitigate the risks that they are likely to face as they grow.

Some of the broad research questions which we focus on are listed below:

- What are the dominant theories of 'risks' and 'risk management'? Are these theories applicable to small and medium enterprises?
- Do existing risk management frameworks address the issues faced by Small and Medium Businesses? Are there any unique risks which are specific to the small and medium enterprises?
- Are there any unique risks are specific to the small and medium enterprises in "legacy industrial era regions" like I-99 corridor, as compared to other regions?
- What are the risks faced by the SMEs when they plan to upgrade their Information systems? How does these risks, when left unattended, impact the overall business growth?
- How do SME Owner/Managers perceive these risks? Do they sense most of these risks? What are their intended plans of action to mitigate these risks?

METHODOLOGY

As a first step towards answering some of the above questions, we analyzed the risk items and IT risk management frameworks that were developed for the traditional larger enterprises, and we examined its relevance to SMEs (Ballantine & Levy, 1998). Also, a simple comparative analysis of I-99 corridor is done to position it with other industrial regions (See Figure 1 & 3). However, analysis of such secondary data alone would

not provide key insights, or concrete answers to the above questions. Real-world observation of social phenomena could alone provide us a better understanding about these problem areas. Thereby, we used Grounded theory (Strauss and Corbin, 1998), and the data that was obtained henceforth was from real-world observations and interviews. Grounded theory does not employ any specific theoretical perspective, and its strength lies in the interaction between the data collection and the coding process. Coding is considered to be a continual process, and themes that emerge during this process are subjected to continuous modifications, based on subsequent collection and analysis of data.

We used "Snowball Sampling" (Biernacki & Waldorf, 1981) and the initial contacts with SMEs were established with the help of the economic development associations in the I-99 corridor. A meeting was arranged by the economic development association to connect the team of researchers with the SME Owner/Managers of the region. Researchers presented the intent of their study to the SME Owner/Managers and feedback was obtained from the SMEs to get a broad sense of the IT issues which they are confronted with. Once this was accomplished, a template was developed which could be used to understand the IT Infrastructure within the individual SMEs. After the initial contacts were established, a pilot study was conducted by a student consulting team - aided by senior faculty members and a graduate research assistant – with few SMEs. The team did a thorough assessment of their existing information systems. They did this through a mixture of face-to-face meetings and multiple qualitative, semi-structured, telephonic interviews. The interviews were designed to understand the current and future business and IT needs of those companies. The existing IT infrastructure of those companies was assessed, in order to understand the gaps between the current and future needs. Based on the preliminary analysis of the initial interview, further interview questions were developed to understand how the perception of the usefulness of information systems differed among SMEs which are at different stages of growth. A risk-item, specific to the organizational IT, was developed and the severities of those risks were assessed.

INITIAL FINDINGS AND CONTRIBUTION

From the conducted pilot study, we observed that risks related to SMEs Information Systems vary to a significant extent from the risks related to Large Enterprise's Information Systems (Ballantine & Levy, 1998). Also, even within SMEs, there are different stages of risks and the nature of those risks is proportionate to the stage of growth an SME is at (Agell, 2004; Ballantine & Levy, 1998; Churchill & Lewis, 2000). We also observed that the perception about Information Systems and its usefulness to business growth widely differs among the owner/manager's of SMEs at different stages of growth (Ballantine & Levy, 1998; Cragg & King, 1993; Cummings, 2003) and it is important to conceptualize the different levels of growth and maturity within SMEs, and not to envision them as unitary entities. Also, we integrated several definitions of SMEs, and came up with a hybrid definition that would be helpful to IS researchers during their sampling phase.

In addition to the findings from the research study, we described some of the barriers which are detrimental to 'University-SME Collaboration'. We also illustrated the first few steps on how a structured approach can be created towards enabling the SMEs in legacy region to access the "knowledge networks" (Dytche & Warren, 2007b; Warren, et al., 2008) through a joint effort between the university and different entities which are working towards regional economic development. We found out that SMEs derived more value from studies when the research university *as a whole* – through multiple inter-departmental collaborations - participated in multiple integrated projects,

as opposed to the usual 'silo' approach (Dytche & Warren, 2007b; Warren, et al., 2008). Through this way, duplication of efforts was avoided by "Co-solving" of complex problems.

However, during the course of this study as well, some of the anticipated meetings with the SMEs did not materialize as expected. Some of the meetings with other units which are involved in economic development activities took longer than expected. Upon reflection, the factors which we listed in previous sections contributed to the roadblocks that we continue to face on the LAIR project. But, by being self-reflective about the entire process, and by sharing the roadblocks we faced with the separate research team who observes the interaction between the academic and practitioner communities, we aim to continually improve upon the communication and co-ordination mechanisms and gain a better understanding about the barriers towards leveraging research intensive universities for revitalization of legacy industrial era regions.

Also, by grounding research-in-context in the phenomena i.e. "managing IT risks", we managed to strike a balance between opposing priorities of the stakeholders and operated in the Pasteur's Quadrant with a dual quest for basic understanding (rigor) and with considerations of use (relevance) (Stokes, 1997; Tushman & O'Reilly, 2007). Thus, we argue that instead of theorizing about the ideal model of scholarship to bridge the 'rigor' and 'relevance' gap and connect SMEs with Universities, we should focus on designing and conducting more studies in a manner that would let the SMEs leverage research available at the university through a well-defined point of access to the knowledge networks surrounding SMEs. Through this process, researchers could identify issues of communication and other barriers which hinder collaboration between the academic and the practitioner communities. This could be accomplished by either being actively self-reflexive about the process and/or by using a separate team of researchers to observe the interaction between the academic and practitioner communities in order to improve the understanding of those barriers.

FUTURE RESEARCH

Future research aims at examining the applicability of the current risk theories and risk management frameworks to small and medium enterprises in legacy industrial era regions, with a particular focus on identifying risks related to information systems upgrade and integration. We are planning to accomplish this through a dual process of identifying IS risks which are specific to SMEs and identifying IS risks which are specific to the small and medium enterprises in legacy industrial era regions like I-99 corridor. A risk assessment and mitigation strategy, which could be of a significant benefit to the small and medium enterprises around the I-99 Corridor, and a methodology to assist SMEs in prioritizing the risks involved with respect to their Information Systems is also being developed.

We aim to understand how applicable the current risk theories and risk management frameworks are to the small and medium enterprises (Alter & Sherer, 2004; Stoneburner, et al., 2002). Also, the Small Business Development Center (SDBC) at Penn State could leverage our findings, which might foster the growth of small businesses in and around State College. Potential outcomes of the project include an inventory of risks in this area, survey of approaches to mitigate risks, and developing a methodology and toolsets to assist SMEs in legacy industrial era regions. The developed methodology would help the SMEs to identify and analyze the risks involved in upgrading or expanding their current IT systems, and help them prioritize challenges and issues that should be considered.

ACKNOWLEDGMENT

The work reported has been funded by the National Science Foundation's PFI grant under award number 0650124. Any opinions, findings and conclusions or recommendations expressed in this material are those of the author(s) and do not necessarily reflect the views of the National Science Foundation (NSF).

REFERENCES

Agell, J. (2004). Why are small firms different? Managers' views. *The Scandinavian Journal of Economics*, *106*(3), 437–452. doi:10.1111/j.0347-0520.2004.00371.x

Agrawal, A. (2001). University-to-industry knowledge transfer: literature review and unanswered questions. *International Journal of Management Reviews*, *3*, 285–302. doi:10.1111/1468-2370.00069

Agrawal, A., & Henderson, R. (2002). Putting patents in context: Exploring knowledge transfer from MIT. *Management Science*, 48(1), 44–60. doi:10.1287/mnsc.48.1.44.14279

Alter, S., & Sherer, S. A. (2004). A General, But Readily Adaptable Model Of Information System Risk. *Communications of AIS, 2004*(14), 1-28.

Anderson, C., & Andersson, M. (2006). The long tail: Hyperion New York.

Audretsch, D., & Feldman, M. (1996). R&D Spillovers and the Geography of Innovation and Production. *The American Economic Review*, 630–640.

Ballantine, J., & Levy, M. (1998). Evaluating information systems in small and medium-sized enterprises: issues and evidence. *European Journal of Information Systems*, *7*(4), 241. doi:10.1057/palgrave.ejis.3000307

Bartunek, J. M. (2007). Academic-Practitioner Collaboration Need Not Require Joint Or Relevant Research: Toward A Relational Scholarship Of Integration. *Academy of Management Journal, 50*(6), 1323–1333.

Baskerville, R., & Myers, M. D. (2004). Special Issue On Action Research In Information Systems: Making Is Research Relevant To Practice--Foreword. *MIS Quarterly, 28*(3), 329–335.

Bell, D. (1973). The Coming of Post-Industrial Society. *Business & Society Review/Innovation*(5).

Benbasat, I., & Zmud, R. W. (1999). Empirical Research In Information Systems: The Practice Of Relevance. *MIS Quarterly, 23*(1), 3–16. doi:10.2307/249403

Bharati, P., & Chaudary, A. (2009). SMEs and Competitiveness: The Role of Information Systems. *International Journal of E-Business Research, 5*(1).

Bharati, P., & Chaudhury, A. (2002). Assimilation of Internet-based technologies in small and medium sized manufacturers. Proceedings of 2002 IRMA International Conference.

Bharati, P., & Chaudhury, A. (2006). Studying the current status of technology adoption. *Communications of the ACM, 49*(10), 88–93. doi:10.1145/1164394.1164400

Bharati, P., & Chaudhury, A. (2008). IT Outsourcing Adoption by Small and Medium Enterprises: A Diffusion Innovation Approach. In *Proceedings of the Americas Conference on Information Systems (AMCIS)*, August 14-17.

Biernacki, P., & Waldorf, D. (1981). Snowball sampling: Problems and techniques of chain referral sampling. *Sociological Methods & Research, 10*(2), 141–163.

Caldeira, M., & Ward, J. (2003). Using resource-based theory to interpret the successful adoption and use of information systems and technology in manufacturing small and medium-sized enterprises. *European Journal of Information Systems, 12*(2), 127–141. doi:10.1057/palgrave.ejis.3000454

Churchill, N., & Lewis, V. (2000). The five stages of small business growth. *Small Business: Critical Perspectives on Business and Management*, 291.

Cockburn, I., & Henderson, R. (1998). Absorptive capacity, coauthoring behavior, and the organization of research in drug discovery. *The Journal of Industrial Economics*, 157–182.

Cohen, W., & Levinthal, D. (1990). Absorptive capacity: a new perspective on learning and innovation. *Administrative Science Quarterly*, 128–152. doi:10.2307/2393553

Colyvas, J., Crow, M., Gelijns, A., Mazzoleni, R., Nelson, R., & Rosenberg, N. (2002). How do university inventions get into practice? *Management Science, 48*(1), 61–72. doi:10.1287/mnsc.48.1.61.14272

Cragg, P. B., & King, M. (1993). Small-Firm Computing: Motivators and Inhibitors. *MIS Quarterly, 17*(1), 47–60. doi:10.2307/249509

Cummings, M. F. (2003). Understanding Enterprise, Entrepreneurship and Small Business (Book). *Irish Journal of Management, 24*(1), 229–230.

Davenport, T. H., & Markus, M. L. (1999). Rigor Vs. Relevance Revisited: Response To Benbasat And Zmud. *MIS Quarterly, 23*(1), 19–23. doi:10.2307/249405

Desouza, K., & Awazu, Y. (2006). Knowledge management at SMEs: five peculiarities. *Journal of Knowledge Management, 10*(1), 32-43. doi:10.1108/13673270610650085

Drejer, I., & Jørgensen, B. (2002). The generation and application of knowledge in public-private collaborations. Knowledge Creation and the Learning Economy.

Dytche, J., & Warren, A. (2007a). I99 Corridor Innovation Portal – Summary. Farrell Center for Corporate Innovation and Entrepreneurship, Smeal College of Business, The Pennsylvania State University.

Dytche, J., & Warren, A. (2007b). Penn State KIZ Innovation Grant Team I-99 Innovation Network Portal. Farrell Center for Corporate Innovation and Entrepreneurship, Smeal College of Business, The Pennsylvania State University.

Faberman, R. (2002). Job flows and labor dynamics in the US Rust Belt. *Monthly Labor Review, 125*(9), 3–10.

Feldman, M., Feller, I., Bercovitz, J., & Burton, R. (2002). Equity and the technology transfer strategies of American research universities. *Management Science, 48*(1), 105–121. doi:10.1287/mnsc.48.1.105.14276

Garg, A., Goyal, D., & Lather, A. (2008). Information systems success factors in software SMEs: a research agenda. *International Journal of Business Information Systems, 3*(4), 410–430. doi:10.1504/IJBIS.2008.018041

Hadjimanolis, A. (2006). A case study of SME-university research collaboration in the context of a small peripheral country (Cyprus). *International Journal of Innovation Management, 10*(1), 65. doi:10.1142/S1363919606001405

Hanks, S. H., Watson, C. J., Jansen, E., & Chandler, G. N. (1993). Tightening the Life-Cycle Construct: A Taxonomic Study of Growth Stage Configurations in High-Technology Organizations. *Entrepreneurship: Theory & Practice, 18*(2), 5–30.

Henderson, J., & Smith, J. (2002). *Academia, Industry, and the Bayh-Dole Act: An Implied Duty to Commercialize.* Center for the Integration of Medicine and Innovative Technology (CIMIT), Cambridge, MA. Retrieved from http://www.cimit.org/coi_part3.pdf

Hendry, C., Brown, J., & Defillippi, R. (2000). Understanding Relationships between Universities and SMEs in Emerging High Technology Industries: The Case of Opto-Electronics. *International Journal of Innovation Management, 4*(1), 51.

Horton, R. B. (1991). The Corporation of the 1990s: Information Technology and Organizational Transformation. *Sloan Management Review, 32*(4), 85–86.

Iacovou, C. L., Benbasat, I., & Dexter, A. S. (1995). Electronic Data Interchange and Small Organizations: Adoption and Impact of Technology. *MIS Quarterly, 19*(4), 465–485. doi:10.2307/249629

Izushi, H. (2003). Impact of the length of relationships upon the use of research institutes by SMEs. *Research Policy, 32*(5), 771–788. doi:10.1016/S0048-7333(02)00085-9

Jaffe, A., Trajtenberg, M., & Henderson, R. (1993). Geographic localization of knowledge spillovers as evidenced by patent citations. *The Quarterly Journal of Economics*, 577–598. doi:10.2307/2118401

Kahn, M. (1999). The silver lining of Rust Belt manufacturing decline. *Journal of Urban Economics, 46*(3), 360–376. doi:10.1006/juec.1998.2127

Lee, Y. (1996). 'Technology transfer' and the research university: a search for the boundaries of university-industry collaboration. *Research Policy, 25*(6), 843–863. doi:10.1016/0048-7333-(95)00857-8

Levy, M., Loebbecke, C., & Powell, P. (2003). SMEs, co-opetition and knowledge sharing: the role of information systems. *European Journal of Information Systems, 12*(1), 3–17. doi:10.1057/palgrave.ejis.3000439

Levy, M., & Powell, P. (2000). Information systems strategy for small and medium sized enterprises: an organisational perspective. *The Journal of Strategic Information Systems, 9*(1), 63–84. doi:10.1016/S0963-8687(00)00028-7

Levy, M., Powell, P., & Galliers, R. (1999). Assessing information systems strategy development frameworks in SMEs. *Information & Management, 36*(5), 247–261. doi:10.1016/S0378-7206-(99)00020-8

Levy, M., Powell, P., & Yetton, P. (1998). *SMEs and the gains from IS: from cost reduction to value added.*

Levy, M., Powell, P., & Yetton, P. (2002). The dynamics of SME information systems. *Small Business Economics, 19*(4), 341–354. doi:10.1023/A:1019654030019

Lyytinen, K., & King, J. L. (2004). Nothing At The Center?: Academic Legitimacy in the Information Systems Field 12. *Journal of the Association for Information Systems, 5*(6), 220–246.

Masuda, Y. (1980). The information society as post-industrial society, *The information society as post-industrial society.*

McKelvey, B. (2006). Response - Van de Ven and Johnson's engaged scholarship: Nice try, but. *Academy of Management Review, 31*(4), 822–829.

Microsoft. (2006). *Microsoft's Definition of Small and Medium Business.* Retrieved September 20, 2008, from http://www.microsoft.com/technet/solutionaccelerators/smbiz/smbprgovw/progovrw_1.mspx#ETAAC

Miner, J. B., & Raju, N. S. (2004). Risk Propensity Differences Between Managers and Entrepreneurs and Between Low- and High-Growth Entrepreneurs: A Reply in a More Conservative Vein. *The Journal of Applied Psychology, 89*(1), 3–13. doi:10.1037/0021-9010.89.1.3

Nakamura, M., Vertinsky, I., & Zietsma, C. (1997). Does culture matter in inter-firm cooperation? Research consortia in Japan and the USA. *Managerial and Decision Economics, 18*(2).

Nonaka, I., & Takeuchi, H. (1995). The knowledge-creating company: How Japanese companies create the dynamics of innovation. New York: Oxford University Press.

Nyden, P., & Wiewel, W. (1992). Collaborative research: Harnessing the tensions between researcher and practitioner. *The American Sociologist, 23*(4), 43–55. doi:10.1007/BF02691930

O'Farrell, P., & Hitchens, D. (1988). Alternative theories of small-firm growth: a critical review. *Environment and Planning, 20*(10), 1365–1383. doi:10.1068/a201365

Ring, P., & Van de Ven, A. (1994). Developmental processes of cooperative interorganizational relationships. *Academy of Management Review,* 90–118. doi:10.2307/258836

Sampat, B., Mowery, D., & Ziedonis, A. (2003). Changes in university patent quality after the Bayh–Dole act: a re-examination. *International Journal of Industrial Organization, 21*(9), 1371–1390. doi:10.1016/S0167-7187(03)00087-0

SBA. (1998). The New American Evolution: The Role and Impact of Small Firms. *Small Business Research Report.* Retrieved September 12, 2008, from http://www.sba.gov/advo/

SBA. (2004a). Office of Size Standards. *Starting Your Business.* Retrieved September 12, 2008, from http://www.sba.gov

SBA. (2004b). *Small Business Resources for Faculty, Student, and Researchers*. Retrieved September 12, 2008, from http://www.sba.gov/advo/

SBA. (2004c). *Small Firms and Technology: Acquisitions, Inventor Movement, and Technology Transfer*. Small Business Research Summary No. 233. Retrieved September 12, 2008, from http://www.sba.gov/advo/

SBA. (2004d). *Top Ten Reasons to Love Small Business*. Small Business Administration News Release, SBA 04-06 ADVO. Retrieved September 12, 2008, from http://www.sba.gov/advo/

Speyer, M., Pohlmann, T., & Brown, K. (2006). IT spending in the SMB sector. Cambridge, MA: Forrester Research.

Stokes, D. (1997). Pasteur's quadrant: Basic science and technological innovation: Washington, DC: Brookings Institution Press.

Stoneburner, G., Feringa, A., & Goguen, A. (2002). Risk management guide for information technology systems. Washington, DC: US Gov. Print. Off.

Storey, D. (1998). Understanding the small business sector. Stamford, CT: International Thomson Business Press.

Strauss, A., & Corbin, J. (1998). Basics of Qualitative Research: Techniques and Procedures for Developing Grounded Theory (2nd ed.). Thousand Oaks, CA: Sage.

Street, C. T., & Meister, D. B. (2004). Small Business Growth And Internal Transparency: The Role Of Information Systems. *MIS Quarterly*, *28*(3), 473–506.

Thursby, J., Jensen, R., & Thursby, M. (2001). Objectives, characteristics and outcomes of university licensing: A survey of major US universities. *The Journal of Technology Transfer*, *26*(1/2), 59–72. doi:10.1023/A:1007884111883

Tushman, M., & O'Reilly, C. (2007). Research and relevance: implications of Pasteur's quadrant for doctoral programs and faculty development. [AMJ]. *Academy of Management Journal*, *50*(4), 769–774.

Van de Ven, A. H. (2007). Engaged scholarship: a guide for organizational and social research. Oxford, UK: Oxford University Press.

Van De Ven, A. H., & Johnson, P. E. (2006). Nice Try, Bill, But... There You Go Again. *Academy of Management Review*, *31*(4), 830–832.

Warren, A., Hanke, R., & Trotzer, D. (2008). Models for university technology transfer: resolving conflicts between mission and methods and the dependency on geographic location. *Cambridge Journal of Regions. Economy and Society*, *1*(2), 219.

Woolgar, S., Vaux, J., Gomes, P., Ezingeard, J., & Grieve, R. (1998). Abilities and competencies required, particularly by small firms, to identify and acquire new technology. *Technovation*, *18*(8-9), 575–592. doi:10.1016/S0166-4972(98)00049-2

Woznica, J., & Healy, K. (2009). The level of information systems integration in SMEs in Irish manufacturing sector. *Journal of Small Business and Enterprise Development*, *16*(1), 115–130. doi:10.1108/14626000910932917

Chapter 3
IT and the Transmission of the SME Culture of Nonprofit Theatres

Julie E. Kendall
Rutgers University, USA

Kenneth E. Kendall
Rutgers University, USA

ABSTRACT

It is often assumed in the MIS literature and in practice that only large organizations are capable of transmitting culture and information technology (IT) to small and medium enterprises (SMEs). The authors use the framework provided by the metaphor of the third space as proposed by Bhabha (1994 and 1996) to gain insights that refute these popular misconceptions, by demonstrating that dominant powers and former colonies exchange cultural artifacts such as information and communication technologies (ICTs) and best management practices in mutually influential ways. The authors' research furthers their understanding of the initial relationships (termed mimicry) between small and medium-sized nonprofit theatres and commercial productions (symbolized by Broadway productions) as well as their current and future exchanges facilitated by hybridity in the third space. The authors discover that both groups possess unique cultural competencies that open the door to using Web 2.0 technologies for staging and promoting productions, building relationships with theatre patrons; and numerous other management issues where their expertise can be usefully exchanged.

INTRODUCTION

In this chapter we use the epistemology of the third space developed by Bhabha (1994) and extended by Frenkel (2008) along with Bhabha's idea of mimicry (1994) to examine the past relationship of

DOI: 10.4018/978-1-61520-627-8.ch003

dominant commercial productions and native nonprofit theatres. Although both Bhabha and Frenkel were discussing knowledge transfer, we use their conceptualizations to characterize and explore more deeply the transfer process of culture (and thereby IT, useful management practices, and worthwhile lessons) from small, professional, nonprofit theaters to large commercial productions.

Since the inception of the community theatre movement in the US, vaguely dated to have begun between 1850 to the mid-1870s, there has been a noticeable amount of communication between the large commercial productions and small theatres. Development of nonprofit regional theatres dates from around the turn of the last century (Conte, and Langley, 2007, pp. 114-119.)

The intent of this chapter is to examine the MIS research pertaining to SMEs, and to characterize the theatre literature regarding large commercial productions in relationship to small nonprofit theatres. We then use Bhabha's (1994 and 1996) framework on power relationships characterizing colonial and post colonial relationships as encounters of mimicry, whereby hybridity of cultures emerges, as well as the third space of in between to identify the problems of colonial powers, seen as large commercial productions, and small nonprofit theatres, the dominated, as they exchange cultural artifacts such as ICTs (information communication technologies), and actively use them to promote and stage theatre productions, build relationships with theatre patrons, and share many other strategic management practices. In addition, we provide specific recommendations for IT practitioners and managers, and suggest future research directions.

The objectives of this chapter therefore are to:

1. Examine the MIS research pertaining to SMEs and characterize the theatre literature regarding large commercial productions in relationship to small, professional nonprofit theatres.
2. Use Bhabha's (1994 and 1996) framework of power relationships between colonial and post colonial relationships to understand the relationship of large commercial productions (symbolized by Broadway) and small, professional, nonprofit theatres embodied in Off-Broadway theatres.

3. Discuss the findings of our Bhabhaian analysis in order to identify and illuminate mimicry, hybridity, and the third space of nonprofit Off-Broadway and commercial productions of Broadway where exchanges of cultural artifacts such as ICTs, promotion and staging of theatre productions, building relationships with theatre patrons, and sharing other strategic management practices take place.
4. Provide specific recommendations for IT practitioners and managers. and
5. Suggest future research directions in the possible exchanges of IT innovations between SME theatres and large commercial productions.

Bharati and Chaudhury (2009) present a framework for SME and IS research. Our research about the transmission and sharing of IT advances in the theatre industry fits well into their relationship link 2. They aptly point out that Levy et al. (2002) concluded that SMEs were moving towards a wider set of goals that included innovation and collaboration. The difference in our research is that we observe collaboration not only among small nonprofit theatres. We also observed mimicking, sharing, and collaboration between small nonprofits with large commercial productions.

Bharati and Chaudhury also point out that a number of researchers have concluded that factors such as reduced operating costs, improved service to customers, improved market intelligence, and even enhanced relationships with partners encouraged Internet adoption by SMEs. We observed that there were many additional factors pushing SMEs to adopt IT, including pressure to conform with government and granting agency requirements, the interests in technology of the nonprofit's patrons, competition, and cooperation.

BACKGROUND

In this section, we present some basic definitions of the terms we will be using throughout the chapter; introduce Bhabha's (1994 and 1996) conceptualization of the third space; provide a brief overview of the history of the theatre, and review the relevant MIS literature in order to focus on SME research that helps inform our research questions about how small to medium nonprofit theatres and large commercial productions influence each other.

Several terms used frequently throughout the chapter may be unfamiliar to the reader so we briefly introduce them here. Key definitions include SME and SMB.

Small and Medium Enterprises (SME)

Surprisingly, attempting to define small-to-medium enterprises and small and medium businesses is often fraught with controversy (Street and Meister, 2004). We will offer the standard definitions from both the European Union (EU) and the U.S. Small Business Administration; with caveats that IS researchers working in these areas often depart significantly from these standards, and frequently develop their own definitions.

The acronym SME refers to small and medium enterprises, and it is a term that is primarily defined and used internationally and particularly by the European Union (EU) (European Union Web site ec.europa.eu last accessed March, 2009) in order to categorize medium-sized, small, and micro enterprises. The definition (revised in 2003), acknowledges SMEs for their contribution to the economies of the EU (they comprise 99 percent of all enterprises in the EU and provide 65 million jobs), and tries to redress "particular difficulties" that SMEs face by "granting various advantages to SMEs." There is special care taken so that small parts of larger organizations are *not* granted the special advantages of SMEs in legislative support.

The general guidelines for determination of whether an organization is to be classified as a SME take into consideration factors such as headcount and inventory turnover, or balance sheet total. *Medium*-sized enterprises according to the EU should have less than a 250-person headcount. By definition, *small* enterprises employ less than 50 people.

Small and Medium Businesses (SMB)

By contrast to European designation of organizations as SMEs, in the United States, the more common term for these enterprises is "small and medium business," also known as SMBs. Researchers (Street and Meister, 2004, p. 475) adopt a simple but useful definition, stating, "Like many authors, we have adopted a commonly used definition form the U.S. Small Business Administration: a small business is independently owned and operated and not dominant in its field of operation." The U.S. Small Business Administration (Small Business Administration Web site found at web.sba.gov, March, 2009) notes that it has established a "size standard" for most industries that relate to the dollar size of the business or the number of employees it has, adjusted for industry, so the figure is about 500 employees for most manufacturing and mining industries and 100 employees for all wholesale trade industries. The upshot is that in the US, it depends heavily on what industry one is in as to how it is classified, and even with that said, about a quarter of the industries have sizes that are different than the levels cited.

In the US as well as Europe, classification of an organization as a SME or SMB plays an important role in eligibility to apply for grants, loans, and other types of government funding. Many of the nonprofit theatre companies we consider here fit well within the EU definition of small enterprises in terms of headcount and budget, and they would be considered small businesses according to the

US definition as well in terms of the number of people employed and their budgets.

Next we will take up the definitions of mimicry, hybridity, and the third space of in between as identified by Bhabha (1994 and 1996) and elaborated by Frenkel (2008).

Bhabha's Conceptualization of Mimicry, Hybridity, and the Third Space

The author Homi Bhabha (1994 and 1996) writes compellingly of the power relationships between those who are dominant powers (or colonizers) and those who are the natives (the colonized). While each camp harbors certain expectations as to how relationships between colonies and the colonizers will unfold, Bhabha leads us to the insight that even as the relationship is forming, it is never a one-way street.

At the outset of colonization there is what Bhabha would characterize as "mimicry." The colonial power (dominant) tries to impose their culture on the colonists (the dominated), and to actually change the identity of the colonists at its very core (Bhabha, 1994). Laws, culture, language, even ways of behaving and technological preferences are all subject to this influence. But even in the mimicry phase, the imposition is never quite seamless, the mimicry never flawless.

Bhabha (1994, p. 86) asserts, "In order to be effective mimicry must continually produce its slippage, its excesses, its difference." Frenkel (2008, p. 927) notes that this disruption is a way for the colonized world to express resistance. This turns out to be incredibly important, as this ruptured relationship fraught with tensions between the colonies and the colonizers wishing to impose their culture results in something Bhabha labels "hybridity."

In this idea, "hybridity" is seen as "narrative" (Bhabha, 1994) constructions that are an ongoing process resulting in interpretation and

reinterpretations. (Frenkel, 2008. P. 927). Frenkel continues:

Proponents of a Bhabhaian perspective would ask how the introduction of practices or technologies contributes to the reformulation of national identities and cultural beliefs...". Bhabha emphasizes that individuals' characteristics are not limited to ethnic heritage, but, rather, are subject to change and modification through experience, including the experience of coping with an imposed body of foreign knowledge (2008, pp. 927 & 928).

Bhabha's (1994) conceptualization of the third space is the space around these exchanges, confrontations, and unexpected meetings between the former colonists and the colonizers. It is neither the old culture nor the entirely new, but something constantly emerging from participants' exchanges. (See Kendall and Kendall (2009) for further elaboration of Bhabha and Frenkel, as well as a comparison of Nonaka and Konno's (1991) concept of ba with the third space.) While this research uses the metaphor of colonial powers and their colonies to illuminate the power relationships between commercial productions and small and medium nonprofit professional theatres, it is not our purpose to put forth a political cause, or study world politics. We believe that using the filter of colonialism permits us to analyze and interpret business relationships and how IT is used in the third space in mutually advantageous exchanges.

Nonprofit Theatres in Relationship to Commercial Broadway Productions

The history of nonprofit theatres can be viewed as a struggle for an identity independent of commercial productions, symbolized by the Broadway theatre. The origin of nonprofit commercial theatres dates to around the turn of the last century. Their number has grown to about 1,800 currently in the US. Nonprofit professional theatres were begun by innovators in large cities and smaller towns who possessed theatre skills, but also developed a sense of what a homegrown theatre could contribute to the life of a city that a pale imitation of Broadway could not. Many of the earliest founders of nonprofit theatres were those who left the dominant New York City and Broadway culture to explore the idea of a native theatre.

At the turn of the 20th century, most Broadway theatres were located on Broadway, the street, in Manhattan, but today only four of the Broadway designated theatres are actually on Broadway the street.

Professional theatre in the North America began in Williamsburg, Virginia in 1752, and moved to New York one year later. "Broadway" moved from Downtown to Union Square around 1870, then up to Madison Square by the 1890s, then moved again to Times Square in the early 1900s.

The beginnings of modern business practices of Broadway theatre can be traced to the toppling of the Theatrical Syndicate, who had absolute control over all of the theatre bookings in the U.S. and (according to Conte and Langley, 2007) were "less interested in standards of production than in making large profits." The Shubert Brothers were successful because they demanded open door policies for both booking and casting and convinced everyone that they were the saviors of theatre.

Soon everyone began to realize that the Shuberts themselves were becoming powerful, but this time the organization itself actually owned the theatres. Commercial productions would be booked into a theatre owned by the Shubert Organization, which owns 17 theatres or one of the other organizations: the Nederlander Organization (9 theatres) or Jujamcyn (5 theatres).

Viagas (1998) explains the difference in Broadway and Off-Broadway depends mainly on the way trade union contracts are written:

People who work in big theatres generally get paid more because there are more tickets to sell. So the distinction generally has to do with theatre size (but not 100 percent of the time). Theatres with up to 99 seats generally are considered Off-Off-Broadway; 99-499 seats generally denote Off-Broadway; and 499 and larger generally denote Broadway. There are many exceptions, however, and some overlap. The real key is what sort of contract the production has.

The culture of Broadway theatres is mainly profit-oriented. Off-Broadway theatre can be commercial or nonprofit. In this chapter, we are interested in nonprofits, which takes a completely different approach to theatre productions. According to Conte and Langley (2007), the birth of the nonprofit theatre movement occurred in the years from 1950 to 1960. The New York Shakespeare Workshop was founded in 1954. The workshop later became known as the Public Theater.

In order for a production (or an actor, director, costume designer within a production and so on) to be eligible for a Tony Award, the production must be mounted in a Broadway theatre.

The Drama League Awards, which predates the Tony Awards by 12 years, include both Broadway and Off-Broadway productions. We have served as official nominators for the Drama League and have evaluated a multitude of productions. At the end of a theatre season (typically late April), after four to eight shows are nominated in each category, the entire membership of the Drama League votes on which productions will receive awards.

Commercial productions, symbolized by shows on Broadway are viewed as the epitome of professionalism, artistic accomplishment, and scenic craft (Conte and Langley, 2007; Volz, 2004; & Webb, 2004). The standards set by the dominant commercial productions were and continue to be very high. The nonprofits were enmeshed in the desire to emulate (or mimic) what they could not in actuality accomplish. Specifically, Broadway productions set the tone with well-trained actors, well-staffed box offices, scripts and script adaptations that featured evocative narrative that resonated with the theatre-going public and scenic and stage effects that transported audiences.

For many decades, the nonprofit professional theatres attempted to conform to and mimic Broadway productions. This was an unachievable goal. Eventually many respected theatre people broke away from Broadway because of a desire to realize artistic goals only achievable in a nonprofit setting. During the beginning years of 1912-1847, Conte and Langley (2007) recognize the importance of the National Theatre Conference, "as a collection of theatre people…who sought to reduce the dominance of commercial Broadway theatre and encourage artistically challenging work, not tied to the profit motive," (p.115). And as the founders of the nonprofessional theatres of the 1940s pushed away from the colonial power of Broadway commercial productions, they forged a separate identity that had as its goal the transmission of culture, rather than being an anemic, underfunded colony of the commercial Broadway productions, which focused on attaining financial success.

In the 1950s and 1960s, nonprofit professional theatres grew in their recognition across the country as the first of many foundation and government grants explicitly made to nonprofit theatres was made (Conte and Langley, 2007). This seed money helped solidify the identity of the nonprofits (commercial theatres were not eligible for the grants), moved theatre arts into the same respected artistic realm as music and dance, pushed the performing arts to more standardization in their business practices, and helped them identify and collaborate with their peers. As a result, nonprofit professional theatre was less about mimicry of the dominant Broadway culture, and more about trying to find a way to express a variety of cultures, viewpoints, and practices that would help transmit culture through active engagement with the theatre audience.

Nonprofit professional theatres were moving out from under the artistic and commercial dominance of Broadway, and away from their colonial oppressors to champion artistic expression. In doing so they were escaping pressures of skyrocketing production costs and a mainstream mindset that hampered artistic risk-taking. They could invent new types of theatre. New plays were written from a variety of viewpoints; actors who played in nonprofit theatres were hired by commercial productions. Entire productions were moved from nonprofit theatres to Broadway houses. Broadway was exchanging actors, scripts, directors, even entire productions, with professional nonprofit theatres.

LITERATURE REVIEW OF SMES IN MIS RESEARCH

The topic of small to medium enterprises and their strategic use of IT to meet business goals is a growing source of interest for IT researchers and practitioners alike. Over the last two decades, a panoply of questions has been raised including: exploring factors influencing IT adoption and adoption success in small businesses (Bharati and Chaudry, 2008; Cragg and King, 1993; Harrison, Mykytyn, Jr and Rimenschneider, 1997; Raymond, 1985; Yeung, Shim, and Lai, 2003); how to evaluate IT performance in SMEs (Ballantine, Levy, and Powell, 1998; and Iacovou, Benbasat, and Dexter, 1995); examining the determinants of success for use of computers in small business (Delone, 1988; and Igbaria, Zinatelli, and Cavaye, 1998); the evolution of IS in SMEs (Cragg and Zinatelli, 1995); owner's attitudes toward implementation (Winston and Dologite, 2002); strategic alignment of IT in small businesses (Hussin, King, and Cragg, 2002; and Levy, Powell, and Yetton, 2001); SMEs that are encountering rapid growth as they change into larger organizations (Barringer, Jones, and Lewis, 1998; Street and Meister, 2004); dangers of overinvesting in IT for small and medium enterprises (Schlemmer, 2009), pursuit and success of ecommerce for SMEs with lesser financial resources (Al-Qirim, 2004 and Franquesa and Brandyberry, 2009) and a host of other topics, many of which are also found in the IS literature investigating IT in larger organizations.

Other researchers have compared the use of IT in the US and other countries, specifically, Canada (Montazemi, 2006). He notes that manufacturing SMEs in the US do a better job of managing the implementation of IT and also of using IT for improving profitability compared with Canada. He encourages expanded exchanges between SMEs in the two countries in order to expedite the adoption of best practices for the management of IT resources.

Other authors have fruitfully considered the topic of knowledge management in SMEs (Chan & Chao, 2008; Panyasorn, Panteli, & Powell, 2009), often noting the importance of retaining the unique organizational properties of SMEs (flat structure, few employees, cross-training) as aspects usefully modeled in knowledge management systems those SMEs create or adopt.

Although there are lively debates surrounding issues of SMEs and IT, many IT researchers still labor under a fundamental misunderstanding of the SME phenomenon. Even though the last two decades or more have established the differences between large organizations and SMEs, IT researchers often fall back on approaches that are better suited to the study of large organizations. In those cases, their work seems to be influenced by the mistaken notion that SMES are "just like" larger organizations, only smaller. This is akin to the now-discredited approach of depicting children as miniature adults, who are "just like" the grownups they will become, just smaller. This approach is no longer acceptable in childhood studies, nor, eventually will it be in studying information technology and SMEs, as noted by Bharati and Chadhury, (2009, p. vii). The similarities and the differences, as well as the unique aspects ascribable only to SMEs and SMBs are worthy of research that is not just a "one-off" from studying large corporations. In

fact, it is interesting to note that many SMEs do not harbor growing into a larger organization as one of their goals.

Differences in research of small to medium enterprises and IT also present contrasts between US researchers and those in countries which compose the European Union. Often in business schools in the US, the small business development center is a separate entity from the rest of the school. Their focus may be more applied than that of researchers in other units, and the ability to gain government grants for research or for seed money for small to medium businesses is also present. Every few years, a special issue of an IS journal is devoted to IT research and SMEs (Bharati and Chaudhury, 2009.) Recently, a new journal, on technology in small and medium enterprises (Mirza, forthcoming 2011) was announced to commence publication in 2011.

The European approach differs somewhat in that for the last half dozen years, special programs to fund SMEs as well as research into appropriate SME policies and hold conferences dedicated to SMES is integrated into the business school and the curriculum, and it is also seen as a legitimate topic of research in its own right.

HOW SME CULTURE AND IT INTERACT IN THE THIRD SPACE

The Practice of Mimicry

The analysis of encounters between the dominant and the dominated reveals how nonprofit theatres and commercial productions performed in the practice of Bhabhaian mimicry. When you examine Figure 1, you will see the depiction of commercial Broadway productions imposing their IT and management practices of small nonprofit theatre companies. For their part, the small nonprofit theatres attempt to copy the "colonizers" practices, sometimes to tragic effect, sometimes to comical ends.

Five of the important ways that commercial Broadway productions attempted to impose their culture on the nonprofits was 1) the setting of geographical boundaries for where a play could be produced physically and still be counted as being on Broadway; 2) altering audience expectations; 3) stipulating to the size of the house in order to characterize it as a Broadway production or not; 4) the length of the run; and 5) preserving dominance and enforcing mediocrity because of their ability to attract well known actors because of higher pay scales.

Figure 1 depicts specific examples of the behaviors of commercial Broadway productions (the colonizer) and the colonist (nonprofit professional theatres) during the mimicry phase Bhabha elucidates in his framework (1994 and 1996). The downward arrows indicate the direction of the practices instituted by the colonizer flowing downward such as electronic box offices, payroll systems, links to actors' databases, patron mailing lists, email industry communication and so on. The downward arrows in the lower left hand corner depict the practices from the colonizer, which the

Figure 1. Mimicry as it exists between the Broadway commercial productions and the SME nonprofit theatre companies

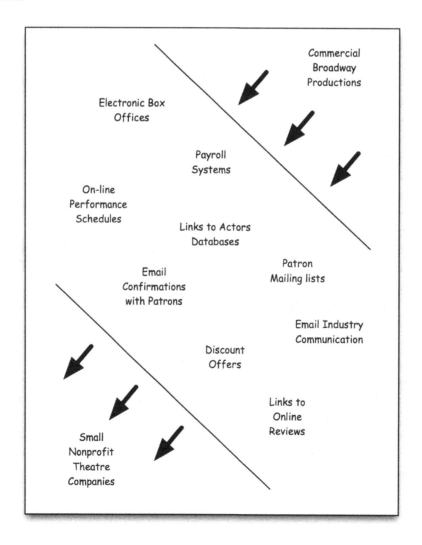

colonists are trying to imitate. During mimicry, some strange or unexpected results can appear, since the mimicked behavior is not rooted in the culture of the colonist. There is always a "slip" or some untoward twist in the way the practice or behavior is imitated.

Many specific examples of these colonizer and colonist behaviors are visible here. For example, electronic box offices make ticket sales more efficient and small nonprofit theatres try to copy them. However, early results of this copying were inadequate, since small theatre companies would put up a Web page, but still required patrons to complete the sale by printing out a form and faxing it back, or, once a patron viewed the production dates on the Web site, required them to phone the box office.

Encounters in the Third Space

In Figure 2, the concept of the third space is evident. The arrows point both up and down, showing transmission of culture through Web 2.0 technologies. The third space opens up the possibilities of nonprofit theatres developing and sharing their own cultures and how they use IT to develop their culture using Web 2.0 technologies.

Web 2.0 technologies refers to the multitude of new ways that the Internet is being used as a platform for developing and hosting software applications and developing and exchanging content development and exchanging by both information systems developers and users.

New uses of the Web that will likely have meaningful and enduring impacts on the way that humans interact and the way businesses operate include social networking Web sites, and other sites where user-generated content is the basis of exchanges over the Web, such as enabling sharing of video files, the use of Wikis, the posting of blogs, and the combining of Web resources to create mashup (defined as dynamic combinations of Web sources resulting in a new application

on the Web). Tim O'Reilly popularized the term by holding a conference devoted to the topic in 2004.

European researchers (Lindermann, Valcárcel, Schaarschmidt and von Kortzfleisch, 2009) are currently examining the use of Web 2.0 as a pathway to what is termed "open innovation" in a regional network of SMEs in northern Germany. They have coined the apropos term of "SME 2.0," (p. 30.) and they are interested in using SME 2.0 as a way to get small to medium-sized businesses to collaborate on creating innovations to solve common work life problems. The authors go on to explain open innovation by stating that, "At its core, it is the increasing usage of external sources for creating and developing new ideas which lead to innovation. In contrast to a closed innovation paradigm, firms try to include customers, users, universities and even competitors in different stage of their new product development processes," (Lindermann, et al., p. 32). It is clear that open innovation and the idea of using Web 2.0 technologies to facilitate exchanges among a network of SMEs is a promising proposal. In our work, the use of Web 2.0 technologies can be informed by the possibilities of mutually influential exchanges expressed by Lindermann et al. (2009).

In the third space, the original culture of nonprofits is evident in original scripts harkening to an original narrative voice. Given the right resources, small nonprofit theatres can be edgier, and riskier in their productions. The exchanges in the third space opens the door for nonprofits to do more, to take more risks, to develop in hybridity and learn from one another. Interestingly, commercial productions benefit as well from the sharing of culture that goes on in the third space. Many productions that originate in nonprofit theatres are finding their way onto Broadway stages. As interactions accelerate, nonprofit professional theatres are involved in workshopping (creating and refining) original plays and musicals for eventual production on Broadway (Kendall, Kendall and Lee, 2005; and

Figure 2. Hybridity as it ideally exists between commercial productions and SME nonprofit theatres through the use of Web 2.0 technologies

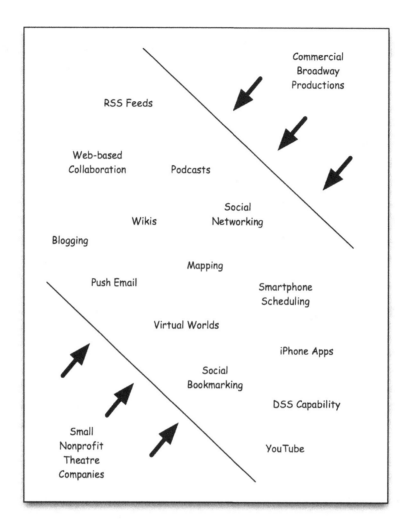

Martin, 2007). Similarly, many actors who once would remain unknown in nonprofit theatres now work in both cultures, and are well regarded in both cultures, as well.

In the third space, an air of experimentation can exist. This includes the adoption, and inclusion and perfecting of information technology such as Web 2.0 technologies. These include RSS Feeds, podcasts, social networking sites, Smartphone schedule, iPhone Apps, DSS Capability, Web-base collaboration, creation of Wikis, mapping to provide a strategic planning view as

well as parking directions for patrons, blogging to involve patrons, fans, critics and artistic talent in the planning and creative process, and both cultures in communications, push emails to inform each culture about what the other is doing, virtual worlds to meet, rehearse, and exchange creative ideas, an social bookmarking, and YouTube to raise the awareness of the topology of different cultures in many different social circles.

There are many best IT practices and lessons learned from small to medium sized nonprofit theatres and we subsequently explore how they can be picked up and shaped in a useful way by large, for-profit commercial productions. The examples include the use of CRM (customer relationship management systems), the centralization of ticketing, patron, and marketing databases, and the role of organizational memory aided by IT. (Cortés and Rafter, 2007) provide a revealing look at IT in nonprofits in their readings collection.

There are numerous ways that culture (including ICTs and management practices) is transmitted in the third space. In unexpected ways, IT functions as both the medium and the message (McLuhan, 1964) for cultural transmission. Of most interest to us here, however, is to answer the question of what sort of information technologies facilitate exchanges in the third space.

The intended effect of IT adoption is typically to improve communication, efficiency, effectiveness, speed, and accuracy of decision-making; cooperation and the building of infrastructure (K. Kendall, 1999). IT tools make an even exchange among equals possible. Colonizers and the formerly dominated alike experience a level playing field of the third space with the use of IT. Power relationships are no longer one way with the dominant pushing culture onto the dominated. Rather, when both SMEs and large organizations possess enabling IT, their creation of the third space becomes ever more participative and democratic.

The wide array of information technologies that further harmony in the third space include RSS feeds, Web based collaboration (Pflughoeft, Ramamurthy, Soofi, Ehsan, Yasai-Ardekani, and Zahedi, 2003), Podcasts, Social networking, Wikis, mapping, smartphone scheduling, blogging, push email (Kendall and Kendall, 1999), virtual worlds, iPhone apps, social bookmarking, DSS capability, and YouTube.

There are numerous examples of the mutual impacts of small professional, nonprofit theatres on large commercial productions, as well as the opposite, as revealed by our analysis using the framework of the third space.

For example, the Atlantic Theater in New York, a small, nonprofit professional Off-Broadway theatre that was founded by the American playwright David Mamet and actor William H. Macy, just recently added several Web 2.0 technologies to its Web site. They are all displayed prominently on the Web site's home page, and include the social networking site *Facebook*; *twitter*, the social networking/micro-blogging site that allows users to send 140-character messages that can be received via the *twitter* Web site, via SMS (short message service) or other applications to which the user might subscribe; and *tumblr.* which is an easy to use blogging Web site that even permits the user to call in audio posts to their blog.

While the Atlantic does not have Webisodes (short, often professionally produced videos including interviews and show clips that detail the artistic process of creating the show), the lavish new musical *Shrek* on Broadway prominently displays 10 Webisodes on its Web site. They also feature old-style, communication and information technologies such as television appearances, in-store appearances, and radio interviews.

In contrasting the use of Web 2.0 technologies between the nonprofit, small theatre the Atlantic and the commercial Broadway production of *Shrek* the Atlantic site documents that the Atlantic launched their first tweet on *twitter* on March 3, 2009. Tellingly, the *Shrek* production adopted *twitter* on May 28, 2009. In Internet time, those 2 and a half months represent a lengthy lull. And interestingly it is not the main characters or artistic staff that is tweeting, it is the minor character of *Gingy*, the wise-cracking, politically incorrect gingerbread man. There is clearly an exchange between the colonizer and colonists in this instance, where the former colonizer is learning from and adopting the Web 2.0 technology of the former colonists.

RECOMMENDATIONS FOR IT PRACTITIONERS AND MANAGERS

This part of the chapter relies on our own consulting work, and IT research with numerous nonprofit, Off-Broadway, and regional performing arts groups (Abuhamdieh, Kendall & Kendall, 2002 and 2007; Kendall, 2008, Te'eni and Kendall, 2004). We are grateful to the nonprofit theatre companies in New York City and Philadelphia for providing access to the administrative and artistic staff, actors, and directors as well as the producers of Broadway productions who enabled us to gather the knowledge and data for this chapter. The Drama League also deserves thanks for its ongoing help and support.

Achieving success with IT in a nonprofit, noncommercial setting, and then communicating that success to larger organizations will alter the power relationships established over a long period of time.

For their part, small nonprofit theatres can benefit from altered power relationships by taking some practical steps to use the interactions afforded by the third space. Much of the work of establishing good interactions begins with the theatre itself. Strategic plans and mission statements need to be reviewed and rewritten if necessary with an eye to identifying what makes the theatre company stand apart as unique. In their relationships with commercial productions, small nonprofit theatres need to be able to communicate the uniqueness of their approach. Using Web 2.0 technologies is a sound approach, since most small nonprofit theatres do not possess large IT staffs, but they still need to communicate. Using the Web as a platform for exchange in the third space can be highly effective. Using free or low-cost open source software and joining an alliance that donates their IT services to nonprofit theatres are two ways to minimize cost while maximizing utilization of these tools.

Large, commercial productions need to be alert and proactive in seeking out success stories of the nonprofit theatres. They need to actively cultivate exchanges in the third space. Once again, using IT to exchange artistic commentaries, artists via interactive video sessions as auditions; establishing virtual worlds where actors and others can interact; reaching out to a youthful set of artists, designers, directors and so on via social networking, and creating a lively presence on YouTube are available to facilitate and equalize relationships in the third space.

FUTURE RESEARCH DIRECTIONS

There are many possible avenues for research revealed by our work, which has identified, analyzed, and described the third space of Bhabha (1994 and 1996) and the exchanges possible between SMEs and larger organizations in the theatre industry.

An applied research question that arises directly out of our work is whether small-to-medium businesses and large organizations should work to formalize the third space of interaction in a systematic way. Certainly, our research reveals the usefulness of the exchanges taking place on an ad hoc or serendipitous basis between small nonprofit theatres and commercial productions. Would this exist as an even more powerful relationship if it were formally recognized and nurtured? Researching the third space in other industries that have experienced shifts in power relationships presents great potential. For example what learning and exchanges occur in the relationship between the Hollywood film industry and independent or foreign filmmakers when the latter produce low budget films that become mainstream box office hits? The power relationships and the learning in both industries are changing. Research can help us find out how each industry is shaping and influencing the other.

One interesting line of inquiry is to examine the possibility of scaling up SME IT activities and management practices to work in larger organizations. What are the possibilities? What are the limitations? Is it feasible to scale up the IT used in SMEs? Is it desirable from a strategic point of view? What are the limitations of creating more complex realizations of IT that have worked for SMEs?

The opposite also holds a potentially fruitful line of investigation. What IT policies, hardware, and software can successfully be scaled down from large installations to work in SMEs? The benefits and drawbacks of scaling down IT and strategic management activities should be weighed as well.

CONCLUSION

We examined the metaphor of the third space as proposed by Bhabha (1994), as a way to critique the discourse (both verbal and physical) that encompasses IT, strategic management, and other exchanges between small nonprofit theatres and the large, commercial productions emblematic of the Broadway theatre. We achieved three main objectives. The first is that we deepened our understanding of the relationship between small and medium-sized nonprofit theatre and commercial productions in their use of IT in the mimicry phase of their relationship. Specific applications of internal information systems such as payroll systems, links to actors' databases, patron mailing lists, electronic box offices, are copied from the best practices of commercial productions. Later on, online performance schedules, email confirmations for patrons, email industry-wide communication, discount offers and links to online reviews are mimicked by the small nonprofit theatres in efforts to meet the industry standards imposed by commercial productions.

Secondly, we asserted that in order to understand how ICTs and strategic management are transmitted between these two entities, it is important to use a framework such as Bhabha's (1994 and 1996) conceptualization of the third

space where hybridity of cultures takes place. In the third space there is a cultural exchange by dominant powers and former "colonies" wherein they are both shaped and influenced in their practices. Both learn from each other. This insight runs counter to many of the widespread assumptions that culture (in this case, ICTs and strategic management) can only change through imposition of an imperial or dominant culture onto the colonized one.

Finally, we discovered that nonprofit theatres and commercial productions, can use their unique cultural competencies with the help of Web 2.0 technologies such as RSS feeds, Podcasts, Web-based collaboration, Wikis, social networking, blogging, Smartphone scheduling, push email, virtual worlds, YouTube, social bookmarking, and DSS capability to open the door to exchanging explicit cultural competencies when handling productions, theatre patrons, and management issues where their expertise can be usefully communicated to one another.

REFERENCES

Abuhamdieh, A., Kendall, J. E., & Kendall, K. E. (2002). An Evaluation of the Web presence of a nonprofit organization: Using the balanced scorecard approach in ecommerce. In R. Traunmüller (Ed.), Information systems: The e-business challenge (pp. 210-222). Boston: Kluwer Academic Publishers.

Abuhamdieh, A., Kendall, J.E., & Kendall, K.E. (2007). E-commerce Opportunities in the Nonprofit Sector: The case of New York Theatre Group. *International journal of cases on electronic commerce, 3*(1), 29-48.

Al-Qirim, N. A. Y. (2004). Electronic commerce in small to medium-sized enterprise: Frameworks, issues, and implications. Hershey, PA: Idea Group Publishing.

Ballantine, J., Levy, M., Powell, P. (1998). Evaluating information systems in small and medium-sized enterprises: Issues and evidence. *European journal of information, 7(4)*, 241 – 251.

Bhabha, H. K. (1996). Cultures in between. In S. Hall & P. du Gay (Eds.), Questions of cultural identity (pp. 53-60). London & Thousand Oaks, CA, Sage.

Bhabha, H. K. (2008). The Location of culture. New York: Routledge Classics. (Original work published in 1994.).

Bharati, P., & Chaudhury, A. (2006). Studying the current status: Examining the extent and nature of adoption of technologies by micro, small, and medium-sized manufacturing firms in the greater Boston area. *Communications of the ACM, 49*(10), 88–93. doi:10.1145/1164394.1164400

Bharati, P., & Chaudhury, A. (2009). SMEs and competitiveness: The role of information systems. *International journal of e-business research, 5*(1), 1-9.

Chan, I., & Chao, C. (2008). Knowledge management in small and medium-sized enterprises. *Communications of the ACM, 51*(4), 83–88. doi:10.1145/1330311.1330328

Conte, D. M., & Langley, S. (2007). Theatre management: Producing and managing the performing arts. Hollywood, CA: Entertainment Pro.

Cortés, M., & Rafter, K. M. (2007). Nonprofits & Technology. Chicago: Lyceum Books, Inc.

Cragg, P. B., & King, M. (1993). Small-Firm computing: Motivators and inhibitors. *MIS Quarterly, 17*(1), 47–60. doi:10.2307/249509

Cragg, P. B., & Zinatelli, N. (1995). The Evolution of information systems in small firms. *Information & Management, 29*(1), 1–8. doi:10.1016/0378-7206(95)00012-L

DeLone, W. H. (1988). Determinants of success for computer usage in small business. *MIS Quarterly, 12*(1), 51–61. doi:10.2307/248803

European Commission. (n.d.). *Definition of SME.* Retrieved March 31, 2009 from http://ec.europa.eu/enterprise/enterprise_policy/SME_definition/index_en.htm

Franquesa, J., & Brandyberry. Organizational slack and information technology innovation adoption in SMEs. *International journal of e-business research, 5*(1), 25-48.

Frenkel, M. (2008). The multinational corporation as a third space: Rethinking international management discourse on knowledge transfer through Homi Bhaba. *Academy of Management Review, 33*(4), 924–942.

Harrison, D. A., Mykytyn, P. P. Jr, & Rimenschneider, C. K. (1997). Executive decisions about the adoption of information technology in small business: Theory and empirical tests. *Information Systems Research*, 8(2), 171–195. doi:10.1287/isre.8.2.171

Hussin, H., King, M., & Cragg, P. (2002). IT alignment in small firms. *European Journal of Information Systems, 11*(2), 108–127. doi:10.1057/palgrave/ejis/3000422

Iacovou, C. L., Benbasat, I., & Dexter, A. S. (1995). Electronic data interchange and small organizations: Adoption and impact of technology. *MIS Quarterly, 19*(4), 465–485. doi:10.2307/249629

Igbaria, M., Zinatelli, N., Cragg, P., & Cavaye, A. L. M. (1997). Personal computing acceptance factors in small firms: a structural equation model. *MIS Quarterly, 21*(3), 279–305. doi:10.2307/249498

Kendall, J. E. (2008). Metaphors for e-collaboration: A study of nonprofit theatre Web presence. In N. Kock (Ed.), E-collaboration in modern organizations: Initiating and managing distributed projects (pp. 14-30). Hershey, PA: Information Science Reference.

Kendall, J. E., & Kendall, K. E. (1999). Web pull and push technologies: The emergence and future of information delivery systems. In K. E. Kendall, (Ed.), Emerging information technologies: Improving decisions, cooperation, and infrastructure (pp.265-288). Thousand Oaks, CA: SAGE Publications, Inc.

Kendall, J. E., & Kendall, K. E. (2009). SMEs, IT, and the third space: Colonization and creativity in the theatre industry. In G. Dhillon, B.C. Stahl, and R. Baskerville (Eds.), CreativeSME2009, Advances in information and communication technology, 301 (pp. 10-27). Berlin: Springer.

Kendall, J. E., & Kendall, K. E. (2009). SMEs, IT, and the third space: Colonization and creativity in the theatre industry. In B. Stahl, G. Dhillon, & R. Baskerville, (Eds.), The role of IS in leveraging the intelligence and creativity of SMEs. New York: Springer.

Kendall, K. E. (1999). Emerging information technologies. In K. E. Kendall (Ed.), Emerging information technologies: Improving decisions, cooperation, and infrastructure (pp. 1-18). Thousand Oaks, CA: SAGE Publications, Inc.

Kendall, K. E. (1999). Emerging information technologies. In K. E. Kendall (Ed.), Emerging information technologies: Improving decisions, cooperation, and infrastructure (pp. 1-18). Thousand Oaks, CA: SAGE Publications, Inc.

Kendall, K. E., Kendall, J. E., & Lee, K. C. (2005). Understanding disaster recovery planning through a theatre metaphor: Rehearsing for a show that might never open. *Communications of AIS, 16,* 1001–1012.

Levy, M., Powell, P., & Yetton, P. (2001). SMEs: Aligning IS and the Strategic Context. *Journal of Information Technology, 16*(2), 133–144. doi:10.1080/02683960110063672

Lindermann, N., & Valcárel, S. Schaarschmidt, & von Kortzfleisch, H. (2009). SME 2.0: Roadmap towards Web 2.0-based open innovation in SME-Networks—A case study based research framework. In G. Dhillon, B.C. Stahl, and R. Baskerville (Eds.), CreativeSME2009, IFIP Advances in information and communication technology, 301 (pp. 28-41). Berlin: Springer.

Martin, J. SJ. (2007). A Jesuit Off-Broadway. Chicago, IL: Loyola Press.

McLuhan, M. (1994). Understanding media: The extensions of man. New York, NY: Mentor. (Original work published in 1964). Reissued in 1994. Cambridge, MA: MIT Press.

Mirza, A. A. (in press). *International journal of technology in small and medium enterprises (IJTSME)*. Announcement available at http://www.igi-global.com/journals/. Last accessed on April 7, 2009.

Montazemi, A. R. (2006). How they manage IT: SMEs in Canada and the U.S. *Communications of the ACM, 49*(12), 109–112. doi:10.1145/1183236.1183240

Nonaka, I., & Konno, N. (1998). The concept of ba: Building a foundation for knowledge creation. *California Management Review, 40*(3), 40–54.

Panyasorn, J., Panteli, N., & Powell, P. (2009). Knowledge management in small firms. In G. Dhillon, B.C. Stahl, and R. Baskerville (Eds.), CreativeSME2009, Advances in information and communication technology, 301 (pp. 192-210). Berlin: Springer.

Pflughoeft, K. A., & Ramamurthy, K., Soofi, Ehsan, Yasai-Ardekani, M., & Zahedi, F. (2003). Multiple conceptualizations of small business Web use and benefit. *Decision Sciences*, *34*(3), 467–512. doi:10.1111/j.1540-5414.2003.02539.x

Raymond, L. (1985). Organizational characteristics and MIS success in the context of small business. *MIS Quarterly*, *9*(1), 37–52. doi:10.2307/249272

Schlemmer, F. (2009). The Internet as a complementary resource for SMEs: The interaction effect of strategic assets and the Internet. *International journal of e-business research issue, 5*(1), 1-25.

Street, C. T., & Meister, D. B. (2004, September). Small business growth and internal transparency: The role of information systems. *MIS Quarterly*, *28*(3), 473–506.

Te'eni, D., & Kendall, J. E. (2004). Internet commerce and fundraising. In D.R. Young (Ed.), *Effective economic decision-making by nonprofit organizations* (pp. 167-189). New York, NY: The Foundation Center. *U.S. Small Business Administration*. (n.d.). Retrieved March 31, 2009, from http://web.sba.gov/faqs/faqIndexAll.cfm?areaid=15

Viagas, R. (1998). *How To Tell Broadway from Off-Broadway*. Retrieved July 31, 2009, from http://www.playbill.com/features/article/76751-How_To_Tell_Broadway_from_Off-Broadway_from_._._.

Volz, J. (2004). How to run a theater. New York: Back Stage Books.

Webb, D. M. (2004). Running theaters: Best practices for leaders and managers. New York: Allworth Press.

Winston, E. R., & Dologite, D. (2002). How does attitude impact IT implementation: A study of small business owners. *Journal of End User Computing, 14*(2), 16–29.

Yeung, J. H. Y., Shim, J. P., & Lai, A. Y. K. (2003). Current progress of e-commerce adoption: Small and medium enterprises in Hong Kong. *Communications of the ACM, 46*(9), 226–232. doi:10.1145/903893.903941

Zinatelli, N., Cragg, P. B., & Cavaye, A. L. M. (1996). End user computing sophistication and success in small firms. *European Journal of Information Systems, 5*(3), 172–181. doi:10.1057/ejis.1996.23

Chapter 4

ERP System Selection Criteria:
SMEs' Perceptions

Andreja Pucihar
University of Maribor, Slovenia

Gregor Lenart
University of Maribor, Slovenia

Frantisek Sudzina
Copenhagen Business School, Denmark

ABSTRACT

This chapter presents the importance of ERP system selection criteria for SMEs. Altogether, 28 ERP selection criteria were investigated. The criteria were grouped into the ERP benefits criteria, ERP system quality criteria, ERP vendor-related criteria and ERP package criteria. The main purpose of the study was to identify the current situation of ERP usage in SMEs in Slovenia and to measure how important the identified ERP selection criteria are in the process of acquisition of ERP systems. Beside the importance of ERP selection criteria for SMEs, the impact of companies' factors (company size, representation of the IT department on the board level in the company, implemented information strategy in the company, ERP implementation stage and turnover growth) on ERP system selection criteria was also investigated. The findings are useful for companies considering ERP system implementation and for ERP system vendors to better understand different customers' needs and expectations.

1 INTRODUCTION

Companies face a rapidly changing business environment with raised customer expectations in expanded markets with increased competition. This increases the pressure on companies to change their existing business practices and procedures to achieve lower total costs of operation in the entire supply chain, to shorten throughput times, to drastically reduce inventories, to expand product choice, to provide more reliable delivery dates and better customer service, to improve quality, and to efficiently coordinate global demand, supply, and production (Umble et al., 2003; Jafari et al., 2006). From the information systems perspective, coordination of the individual elements of the overall set of business processes can be supported by enterprise resource planning (ERP) systems.

DOI: 10.4018/978-1-61520-627-8.ch004

ERP systems can be considered the most important development in the corporate use of information technology and are beginning to become the backbone of companies. Also referred to as "enterprise-wide systems" due to their enterprise-wide scope, they provide seamless integration of all the information flows and business processes across functional areas within a company, including finance, human resources, manufacturing, logistics, sales, distribution and purchasing (Davenport, 1998; Markus & Tanis, 2000; Law & Ngai, 2007; Bernroider, 2008). Thus, ERP systems aim to integrate business processes and information and communication technologies (ICT) into a synchronized suite of procedures, applications and metrics that cross companies' boundaries (Wier et al., 2007).

Due to their nature (complexity and high implementation costs), ERP systems used to be mostly in the domain of large companies. However, in recent years ERP vendors have faced challenges in also providing ERP systems to the SMEs (Malie et al., 2008). The reasons for this trend could be the saturation of the market (as most large companies have already implemented an ERP system), increasing possibilities and need for the integration of systems between companies (mostly pressures of large companies) and the availability of relatively inexpensive hardware (Gable & Stewart, 1999; Esteves, 2009). Furthermore the importance of SMEs in the global economy is opening new markets for ERP vendors and, as such, presents an enormous market opportunity for them.

Across the EU, there are approximately 23 million SMEs; i.e. 99% of all enterprises (Eleftheriadou, 2008; European Commission, 2008; European Commission, 2002); they account for about 75 million jobs. Moreover, in some key industries, such as textiles, construction and furniture-making, they account for as many as 80% of all jobs. They are, therefore, the generators of dynamic and economic growth (Eleftheriadou,

2008; European Commission, DG Enterprise and Industry 2008).

In Slovenia, a country with just two million citizens, 96.2% of enterprises are micro- or small enterprises in which 45.0% of employees are employed. In the less than 1% of Slovenian enterprises that are ranked among large enterprises; one third of employees are employed (SURS – Statistični urad Republike Slovenije 2007).

Although SMEs are generally considered to be flexible, adaptive and innovative (Rao, et al., 2003), and thus have more ability to respond to the new opportunities and innovations than larger enterprises (Lomerson et al., 2004), various studies have reported that SMEs are generally lagging behind large organizations with regards to the adoption and usage of new ICT (Eleftheriadou, 2008; Kartiwi & MacGregor, 2007; Levy et. al., 2005; Levenburg, 2005; Chitura, 2008; Riquelme, 2002). This is becoming a serious issue since SMEs are the backbone of the European economy.

SMEs are not simply scaled-down large businesses. They have their own distinct and special characteristics. Although size is a major distinguishing factor, SMEs also differ from large companies in important ways affecting their ICT adoption (Bouanno et al., 2005, Ramdani & Kawalek, 2009). The adoption of information systems innovations in SMEs cannot be perceived as a miniaturised version of that in larger companies (Ramdani & Kawalek, 2009).

Many SMEs report practical difficulties in ICT adoption. SMEs often lack of adequate levels of technical expertise, managerial resources, financial resources for ICT investments, and awareness about the possible benefits of ICT usage (Pucihar et al., 2009; Kartiwi & MacGregor, 2007; MacGregor & Vrazalic, 2005; Cragg/King, 1993). Many SMEs also consider a lack of trust and confidence as barriers to their engagement in B2B e-business (European Commission, DG Enterprise and Industry, 2008). In contrast, the perceived benefits, organisational readiness, and external pressure seem to be major drivers for ICT adoption (Mehrtens et al., 2001). Past experience has indicated that, currently, obstacles or incentives for the broader use of e-business are especially dependent on standard commercial practices, the business environment as well as the state examples and incentives.

In this challenging race of competitiveness and excellence, where new technologies and innovation play a central role, SMEs cannot afford to be left behind (Eleftheriadou, 2008).

ERP systems provide SMEs with opportunities that are largely unexploited (Ramdani & Kawalek, 2009). ERP systems are a strategic information technology tool that helps companies to gain competitive advantage by integrating business processes and optimizing the resources available, resulting in higher efficiency, effectiveness, as well as better quality of services and minimisation of costs (Metaxiotis, 2009).

Recently, an increasing number of SMEs have been adapting or upgrading their legacy systems to ERP systems (Esteves, 2009). Due to the large potential of the SME market, ERP vendors are increasingly focusing on providing solutions tailored to the needs of SMEs (Costa & Gianecchhini, 2006; Morabito et al, 2005).

The ERP market consists of many different products, services and methodologies, not all of them applicable to different companies (Malie et al, 2008). While selecting their ERP system, companies need to consider different criteria related to ERP systems. Knowing the importance of these criteria could help companies to select a more suitable ERP system and to avoid mistakes and the high costs of failed implementations.

Due to the important role of SMEs in the global economy, environmental changes, market challenges and the need for SMEs to be globally competitive, an interesting research question arises: What are the ERP system selection criteria that should be considered in the decision making process of SMEs when acquiring ERP systems? As Bharati and Chaudbury (2009) point out in

proposed research framework there is a need to research an information systems assets adoption impact on SMEs performance.

In this chapter, we present the criteria that SMEs consider to be important in the phase of ERP system acquisition. The importance of criteria is presented on the basis of research done in small and medium-sized companies in Slovenia. The findings are useful for companies considering ERP system implementation and for ERP system vendors to better understand different customers' needs and expectations.

2 LITERATURE REVIEW

Much research in recent years investigated ERP adoption (Laukkanen et al, 2007, Raymond & Sylvestre, 2007). However, most of it has examined ERP adoption in large companies and less in SMEs (Hitt et al, 2002, Adam & O'Doherty, 2000, van Everdingen et al, 2000, Kumar & van Hillegersberg, 2000).

Van Everdingen et al (2000) investigated ERP systems adoption in medium-sized companies. In this research, the relative importance of factors of information system selection was investigated. The three most important factors were fit, flexibility and costs. Bernroider & Koch (2001) compared ERP systems selection process in medium-sized and large organizations. The criteria for selection of a particular ERP system showed different priorities, e.g. an increasing organizational flexibility, extra-organizational ties with customers and suppliers and internationality are less of an issue for smaller companies compared to costs and adaptability of software. Baki & Cakar (2005) identified 17 main selection criteria for the ERP selection process. Fit with parent/allied organizational system, cross module integration, compatibility with other systems were identified as the most important selection criteria.

The ERP selection criteria investigated in this research were mainly adopted from Bernroider &

Koch (2001) and supported by other research results in the field of ERP systems selection criteria. Although the evaluation of information systems investments began in the 1960s (Frielink, 1961; Joslin 1968), very little has been written recently about packaged software selection criteria in academic journals (Keil & Tiwana, 2006). The ERP systems selection criteria identified by prior research are summarized in the Tables 1 to 4. ERP systems criteria are grouped into the ERP systems benefits criteria, system quality criteria, vendor-related criteria, ERP package criteria.

3 RESEARCH METHODOLOGY

The main purpose of this study was to identify the current situation of ERP usage in small and medium-sized companies in Slovenia and to measure how important the identified ERP selection criteria are in the process of acquisition of ERP solution in these companies. For that purpose, a questionnaire was developed to gather the data from the companies.

The hard copy of questionnaires with introduction letters, explaining the purpose of the study, with self-addressed return envelopes, were sent to 300 medium-sized companies (50-249 employees) and 600 small companies (10-49 employees) in Slovenia in 2007. The number of questionnaires mailed to small companies was double the number of medium-sized companies because small companies constitute the highest proportion of companies – 96.2% of enterprises are micro or small enterprises (SURS – Statistični urad Republike Slovenije 2007) – and, based on experience from previous research in Slovenia, they are less likely to respond.

Lists of addresses and information about the number of employees and turnover were retrieved from the Statistical Office of Republic in Slovenia. Three hundred medium-sized companies and 600 small companies with the highest turnover in 2006 were selected. The reason companies with higher turnover were selected is the assumption that the usage of ICT in these companies is on a higher level than in other companies. With this, we also wanted to assure a higher response rate of the questionnaire from the companies, since it was expected that they have better understanding of the impact of ICT on business operation.

Although Bala and Venkatesh (2007) claimed that the fact whether the company is dominant or not also may matter, we limited our research to investigating companies based only on the size of the company and turnover. Self-evaluation of the companies could result in being likely biased.

Table 1. ERP system benefits criteria

ERP benefits criteria	Author(s)
Enhanced decision making	Bernroider (2008); Nah & Delgado (2004)
Reduced cycle times	Bernroider (2008); Bernroider & Leseure (2005);
Business process improvement	Bernroider (2008); Bernroider & Leseure (2005); Kumar et al. (2002, 2003), Nah & Delgado (2004); Bernroider & Koch (2001)
Enabler for desired business processes	Bernroider (2008); Bernroider & Leseure (2005); Kumar et al. (2002, 2003)
Integrated and better quality of information	Bernroider (2008); Bernroider & Leseure (2005); Nah & Delgado (2004)
Increased organizational flexibility	Bernroider (2008); Umble et al (2003); Bernroider & Koch (2001)
Increased customer satisfaction	Bernroider & Koch (2001); Bernroider & Leseure (2005)
Improved innovation capabilities	Bernroider (2008); Bernroider & Leseure (2005); Bernroider & Koch (2001)
Improved service levels/quality	Bernroider (2008); Bernroider & Leseure (2005); Wei et. al (2005)

Table 2. System quality criteria

System Quality Criteria	Author(s)
System flexibility	Bernroider (2008); Malie et. Al (2008); Bernroider & Leseure (2005); Kumar et al. (2002, 2003); Wei, et al (2005); Verville & Halingten (2003); Bernroider & Koch (2001); Bernroider (2008);
System functionality	Bernroider (2008); Malie et. Al (2008); Bernroider & Leseure (2005); Botta-Genoulaz et. Al (2005); Kumar et al. (2002, 2003); Wei, et al (2005), Han (2004); Liao et al. (2007); Lall & Teyarachakul (2006); Verville & Halingten (2003); Bernroider & Koch (2001)
System usability	Bernroider (2008)
System interoperability	Bernroider (2008); Kumar et al. (2002, 2003); Verville & Halingten (2003); Bernroider (2008);
Internationality of system	Bernroider (2008); Bernroider & Leseure (2005); Verville & Halingten (2003); Bernroider & Koch (2001)
System reliability	Bernroider (2008); Malie et. Al (2008); Bernroider & Leseure (2005); Kumar et al. (2002, 2003); Wei, et al (2005);
Operating system independence	Bernroider & Leseure (2005); Bernroider & Koch (2001)

The questionnaire survey was mainly based on criteria identified by Bernroider and Koch (2001) and other criteria, identified later from literature review and field study. The research was part of a multi-country study, previously conducted in Austria and United Kingdom and later in Denmark, Slovakia and Slovenia. The questionnaire was tested in all countries with selected representatives from the companies to assure clear understanding of it. In this chapter, the results from research in Slovenia are presented.

The criteria were grouped into the ERP benefits criteria, system quality criteria, vendor-related criteria and ERP package criteria.

The ERP benefits criteria group consists of enhanced decision making, improved service levels/quality, reduced cycle times, business process improvement, enabler for desired busi-ness processes, integrated and better quality of information, increased organizational flexibility, increased customer satisfaction, improved innovation capabilities.

The system quality criteria group consists of system flexibility, system functionality, system usability, system interoperability, internationality of system, system reliability and operating system independence.

The vendor-related criteria group consists of vendor support, vendor reputation and market position of vendor.

The ERP package criteria group includes short implementation time, software costs (licenses, maintenance), e-business enablement, organizational fit of system, connectivity (intra/extranet, mobile, etc.), advanced technology, incorporation of business best practice, availability of an indus-

Table 3. Vendor-related criteria

Vendor-related criteria	Author(s)
Vendor support	Malie et. al (2008); Bernroider & Leseure (2005); Kumar et al. (2002, 2003), Wei, et al (2005); Liao et al. (2007); Umble et al. (2003); Rao (2000); Fisher et al. (2004); Lall & Teyarachakul (2006); Verville & Halingten (2003)
Vendor reputation / Market position of vendor	Malie et. Al (2008); Malie et. Al (2008); Kumar et al. (2002, 2003); Wei et al (2005); Han (2004); Liao, et al. (2007); Lall & Teyarachakul (2006); Verville & Halingten (2003); Bernroider & Koch (2001)

Table 4. ERP package criteria

ERP package criteria	Author(s)
Short implementation time	Malie et. al (2008); Wei et al (2005); Umble et al (2003); Fisher et al. (2004); Lall & Teyarachakul (2006); Verville & Halingten (2003); Bernroider & Koch (2001)
Software costs (licenses, maintenance, etc.)	Bernroider (2008); Bernroider & Leseure (2005); Kumar, et al. (2002, 2003); Wei, et al (2005); Umble et al. (2003); Fisher et al. (2004); Lall & Teyarachakul (2006)
E-business enablement	Bernroider & Leseure (2005)
Organizational fit of system	Malie et. al. (2008); Botta-Genoulaz et al. (2005); Kumar et al. (2002, 2003); Nah & Delgado (2006); Umble et al (2003); Lall & Teyarachakul (2006)
Connectivity (Intra/Extranet, Mobile computers, etc.)	Bernroider & Leseure (2005)
Advanced technology	Bernroider & Leseure (2005); Kumar et al. (2002, 2003); Liao, et al. (2007); Rao (2000)
Incorporation of business best practice	Bernroider & Leseure (2005); Kumar et al. (2002, 2003)
Availability of an industry focused solution	Malie et. Al 2008); Bernroider & Leseure (2005)
Enabling technology for CRM, SCM, etc.	Bernroider & Leseure (2005); Botta-Genoulaz et. al (2005); Kumar et al. (2002, 2003)

try focused solution and enabling technology for CRM, SCM, etc.

These dependent variables were measured on a five-point Likert scale, where 1 is of very little importance and 5 is of very high importance. Although there are some drawbacks to it, such as that it prevents exposing the model's constructs to a robust test of their measure and relationships to each other, (their nomological validity) and this use leaves researchers unsure about whether or not they have selected an efficient way, in terms of survey completion time, to assess these constructs (Chin et al., 2008), nearly all prior studies on TAM used Likert scales (Chin et al., 2008).

Au, Ngai and Cheng (2008) discussed psychological issues related to user satisfaction. In relation to this research, we have used one criterion – ease of use – in a means of expectations of usage satisfaction that we may investigate before purchasing an actual ERP system. A significant positive relationship between perceived ERP usability and perceived usability of ERP documentation was also confirmed by Scott (2008).

The data about the company and the importance of ERP selection criteria were analyzed. In addition to company size (Sudzina, 2007), representation of the IT department on the board level (chief information officer position - CIO) and information strategy, ERP stage and turnover growth were also used as independent variables. The impact of these independent variables on ERP system selection criteria was measured with an ANOVA multivariate analysis with a confidence level of $\alpha = 0,05$. In order to discover between what instances of independent variables there are significant differences, a Tukey-Kramer multiple-comparison test is used. The research model is presented in Figure 1.

"Information strategy" refers to the formal information strategy adopted on the company level. Possible impact of alignment of business and information strategy was identified by Oh and Pinsonneault (2007). "Presentation of the IT department on the board level" means that there is a CIO (Chief information officer) or similar director-level position for IT in the company. Companies with adopted information strategy and with a formal position of IT or CIO director were expected to be more advanced in their understanding of the impact of ICT on business performance. Thus, the purpose of the study was to discover if there are some significant differences in ERP selection criteria importance between those companies and companies without an implemented

Figure 1. Research model

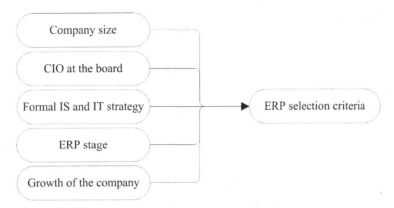

information strategy and represented CIO on the board level.

Common understanding between a company's IT department and line managers on how IT can enhance specific business processes was investigated by Ray et al. (2007). In our research, information strategy and IT department/CIO on the board level were only investigated as independent variables as a means of measuring the differences of ERP selection criteria importance between the companies with or without IS strategy and CIO on the board. Common understanding of how IT can enhance specific business processes would require a more detailed investigation of each company, which was not the purpose of this research.

ERP stages range from (1) ERP system is being considered, (2) ERP system is being evaluated for the selection of a specific solution, (3) ERP system is being configured and implemented, (4) an ERP system was recently implemented and is now being stabilised, (5) an ERP system is being used and maintained, to (6) the first ERP system was replaced with a new one. In the study, it was investigated if there are some significant differences in ERP selection criteria importance between companies being in different stage of ERP adoption (stage).

Growth of the company was measured with achieved turnover in the previous year (2006) and was divided into (1) reduction in turnover,

(2) stable turnover, (3) growth of turnover from 0-5%, (4) growth of turnover from 5-10% and (5) growth of turnover higher than 10%. The purpose of the study was to identify if there are some significant differences in ERP selection criteria importance between companies with different levels of turnover.

In the next chapter, we present empirical results from the perspectives of companies' profile data, the importance of ERP system selection criteria and companies' factors (company size, representation of the IT department/CIO on the board level, information strategy, ERP stage and turnover) impact on the importance of ERP system selection criteria.

4 EMPIRICAL RESULTS

4.1 Companies Profile Data

Number of Respondents

Altogether, 36 (12%) medium-sized companies and 27 (4.5%) small companies responded to the questionnaires. In most cases, the respondents were chief executive officers (35.5%) and chief information officers (15.9%), followed by accountants and IT managers (7.9%), chief financial officers, chief operational officers, project managers and quality executives (2%).

Industry Profile

Most of the respondents from medium-sized companies came from manufacturing (41.7%), trade (22.2%), services (8.3%) and building and construction (8.3%) industry sector. In the case of small companies, most respondents came from trade (22.2%), IT services (18.5%), building and construction (11.1%), manufacturing (14.8%) and transport (7.4%) industry sector.

Revenue Data

Altogether, 29.4% of medium-sized companies had higher revenue growth than 10%; 26.5% had revenue growth from 5-10%; 29.4% from 0-5% of growth; 8.8% had stable revenue, and 5.9% had reduction of turnover in the previous year of the research study. A total of 23.1% of small companies had higher revenue growth than 10%; 26.9% had revenue growth from 5-10%; 11.5% from 0-5% of growth; 30.8% had stable revenue, and 7.7% had reduction of turnover in the previous year of the research study.

Representation of IT Department/CIO on the Board

Half of the medium-sized companies and only 33% of small companies reported that they have a CIO represented at the board level in the company. Half of the medium-sized companies and only 15% of small companies reported that they have formal IS/IT strategy implemented.

Usage of ERP Software

The results have shown that 66.7% of medium-sized and 37% of small companies, which participated in research, already use an ERP system. Among medium-sized companies, the Perftech Largo solution from a Slovene provider was most popular (17%), following by localized versions from the ERP system providers SAP and MS Dynamics NAV (each with 12%). This is followed by solutions from Slovene providers e.g. Datalab Pantheon and RCL (each with 8%). Only 4% of medium-sized companies reported using an in-house developed ERP system. In small companies, the most commonly used ERP system was MS Dynamics NAV (30%), followed by Datalab Pantheon and in-house developed ERP solutions (both 20%).

Due to the small number of respondents from small companies using ERP solutions, these data are not representative and present the situation only for companies participating in this research. Data from other sources show that only 10% of small and 50% of medium-sized companies in Slovenia use ERP systems (Sulčič, 2008).

Implementation Time

Medium-sized companies in most cases have recently implemented ERP solutions (48.6%). Altogether, 25.7% of medium-sized companies have had stable use of ERP solution for some years. Most small companies have only recently implemented an ERP solution (40%), while 32% of small companies are in the stage of considering ERP solution implementation.

The most frequently implemented ERP modules in small and medium-sized companies are finance and controlling, following with sales and distribution, manufacturing, logistics and human resources modules.

Implementation Type

In most cases, small (54%) and medium (43%) sized companies used the so-called big bang implementation strategy of all modules at the same time. A pilot project implementation strategy of one module followed by all other modules in one step was used in 25% of medium-sized and 31% of small companies. A slow-phased implementation approach, i.e. one module at a time, was used in 15% of small companies and 32% of medium-sized companies.

Implementation Costs

A total of 67% of small companies and 52% of medium-sized companies reported that implementation cost were equal to those estimated, while 41% of medium-sized and 25% of small companies reported that implementation costs were higher than estimated.

4.2 Importance of ERP System Selection Criteria

In the Tables 5 to 8, the importance of ERP system selection criteria is presented by mean values, ordered from very high importance to very little. The importance of ERP system selection criteria was investigated by five-point Likert scale, where 1 is of very little importance and 5 is of very high importance. The data are analyzed and presented for small and medium-sized companies together as the company size impact on importance of ERP system selection criteria was separately investigated by ANOVA multivariate approach. ANOVA analysis results are presented later in Section 4.3.

With regard to expectations of gained benefits from ERP system adoption, the most important

Table 5. Importance of ERP benefits criteria

ERP benefits criteria	N	Mean	Std. Deviation
Integrated and better quality of information	56	4.48	0.738
Improved service levels/quality	56	4.34	0.721
Business process improvement	55	4.18	0.748
Increased organizational flexibility	56	4.11	0.779
Reduced cycle times	57	4.09	0.808
Increased customer satisfaction	56	4.05	0.942
Enhanced decision making	57	4.00	0.945
Enabler for desired business processes	56	3.84	0.804
Improved innovation capabilities	56	3.36	0.980

Table 6. Importance of ERP system quality criteria

System quality criteria	N	Mean	Std. Deviation
System reliability	56	4.55	0.601
System flexibility	56	4.32	0.765
System functionality	56	4.30	0.685
System usability	55	4.20	0.890
System interoperability	56	4.00	0.894
Operating system independence	55	3.62	0.991
Internationality of software	56	3.32	1.208

Table 7. Importance of ERP vendor-related criteria

Vendor-related criteria	N	Mean	Std. Deviation
Vendor support	56	4.32	0.855
Vendor reputation	56	3.45	0.989
Market position of vendor	55	3.42	0.896

criteria perceived by SMEs are integrated and better quality of information, improved service levels/quality, business process improvement, increased organization flexibility, reduced cycle times, increased customer satisfaction and enhanced decision making.

The expectations of small and medium-sized companies regarding the ERP system quality criteria are system reliability, system flexibility, system functionality, system usability and system interoperability.

The most important expectation for small and medium-sized companies from ERP vendors is vendor support.

Small and medium-sized companies' most important expectations from ERP package criteria are e-business enablement, organizational fit of the ERP system, connectivity of the ERP system and ERP software costs.

4.3 Companies' Factors Impacting on Single ERP Selection Criteria

The impact of independent variables – company size, representation of the IT department/CIO on the board level, implemented information strategy, ERP stage and turnover on importance of ERP system selection criteria – was measured with an ANOVA multivariate analysis. In order to discover between what instances of an independent variable there are significant differences, a Tukey-Kramer multiple-comparison test is used.

Significant differences were identified for the following selection criteria: reduced cycle times and improved innovation capabilities (ERP system benefits criteria), system reliability, system usability and operating system independence (system quality criteria) and organizational fit of the system and advanced technology criteria (ERP package criteria). There was no significant impact of companies' factors on the importance of vendor-related criteria.

Table 8. Importance of ERP package criteria

ERP package criteria	N	Mean	Std. Deviation
E-business enablement	56	4.39	0.705
Organizational fit of system	56	4.25	0.879
Connectivity (intranet/extranet, mobile, etc.)	53	4.04	0.898
Software costs (licenses, maintenance, etc.)	56	4.00	0.739
Short implementation time	56	3.91	0.769
Advanced technology	56	3.91	0.668
Incorporation of business best practice	56	3.79	0.803
Availability of an industry focused solution	56	3.70	0.807
Enabling technology for CRM, SCM, etc.	56	3.55	1.094

The results reflect a confidence level of $\alpha = 0.05$. The research model is presented in Figure 1 in the methodology section. The results are presented in Tables 9 to 15).

4.3.1 ERP Benefits Criteria

Reduced Cycle Times

The analysis of the impact of company size, the representation of the IT department on the board level (CIO), information strategy, ERP stage and growth on reduced cycle times criteria are presented in Table 9. The importance of the reduced cycle time criterion depends on the company size. The importance of these criteria is higher in medium-sized companies (4) than in small companies (3.4).

Improved Innovation Capabilities

The analysis of the impact of company size, representation of the IT department on the board level (CIO), information strategy, ERP stage and growth on improved innovation capabilities criteria is presented in Table 10. The importance of improved innovation capabilities criteria depends on the ERP stage in the companies. The importance of improved innovation capabilities criteria is higher in companies where an ERP system has

been in use and maintained for some years (4.1) than in companies where ERP system is being just considered (2.7).

4.3.2 System Quality Criteria

System Reliability Criteria

The analysis of the impact of company size, representation of the IT department on the board level (CIO), information strategy, ERP stage and growth on system reliability is presented in Table 11. The importance of system reliability criteria depends on company size. The importance of this criteria is higher in medium-sized companies (4.6) than in small companies (4.1).

System Usability Criteria

The analysis of the impact of company size, representation of the IT department on the board level (CIO), information strategy, ERP stage and growth on system usability criteria is presented in Table 12. The importance of system usability criteria depends on the IT department being present on the board (CIO). The importance of these criteria is higher in companies where the CIO is not present on the board (4.3) than in companies where the CIO is present on the board (3.6).

Table 9. Analysis of variance table for reduced cycle criteria

Factor	DF	Sum of Squares	Mean Square	F-ratio	P-value	Power (Alpha=0.05)
Company size	1	3.249468	3.249468	4.79	0.034740*	0.569009
CIO	1	0.0151583	0.0151583	0.02	0.881986	0.052438
Information strategy	1	0.2145384	0.2145384	0.32	0.577224	0.085108
ERP stage	5	2.76072	0.5521439	0.81	0.547444	0.259968
Growth	4	1.889213	0.4723033	0.70	0.599495	0.205209
S	39	26.47589	0.6788689			
Total (Adjusted)	51	34.82692				
Total	52					

* Term significant at alpha = 0.05

Table 10. Analysis of variance table for improved innovation capabilities criteria

Factor	DF	Sum of Squares	Mean Square	F-ratio	P-value	Power (Alpha=0.05)
Company size	1	2.193201	2.193201	2.91	0.096265	0.383167
CIO	1	0.03498056	0.03498056	0.05	0.830616	0.055067
Information strategy	1	0.2225927	0.2225927	0.30	0.590074	0.082717
ERP stage	5	10.49043	2.098087	2.78	0.030850*	0.770869
Growth	4	2.492381	0.6230953	0.83	0.516683	0.238743
S	38	28.65246	0.7540121			
Total (Adjusted)	50	44.15686				
Total	51					

* Term significant at alpha = 0.05

Operating System Independence

The analysis of the impact of company size, the representation of the IT department on the board level (CIO), information strategy, ERP stage and growth on operating system independence criteria is presented in Table 13. The importance of the operating system independence criteria depends on company size and the ERP stage in the companies. The importance these criteria is higher in small companies (3.6) than in medium-sized companies (2.9).

The importance of these criteria is also higher in the companies where an ERP system was recently implemented and is now being stabilized (3.5), where the ERP system is being configured and implemented (3.8), where an ERP system is being used and maintained (4) and where an ERP system is being evaluated for the selection of a specific solution (4.5) than in companies where an ERP system has been replaced with a new one (0.4).

4.3.3 ERP Package Criteria

Organizational Fit of the System Criteria

The analysis of the impact of company size, the representation of the IT department on the board level (CIO), information strategy, ERP stage and growth on the organizational fit of the system is presented in Table 14. The importance of these

Table 11. Analysis of variance table for system reliability criteria

Factor	DF	Sum of Squares	Mean Square	F-ratio	P-value	Power (Alpha=0.05)
Company size	1	1.95603	1.95603	5.10	0.029811*	0.594913
CIO	1	0.005490579	0.00590579	0.02	0.901937	0.051677
Information strategy	1	0.2515228	0.2515228	0.66	0.423272	0.123831
ERP stage	5	0.9101833	0.1820367	0.47	0.793082	0.160912
Growth	4	2.271598	0.5678996	1.48	0.227591	0.413958
S	38	14.586	0.3838421			
Total (Adjusted)	50	18.70588				
Total	51					

* Term significant at alpha = 0.05

Table 12. Analysis of variance table for system usability criteria

Factor	DF	Sum of Squares	Mean Square	F-ratio	P-value	Power (Alpha=0.05)
Company size	1	0.519492	0.519492	0.64	0.430607	0.121390
CIO	1	4.595949	4.595949	5.62	0.023101*	0.636246
Information strategy	1	0.3423079	0.3423079	0.42	0.521716	0.096597
ERP stage	5	2.481358	0.4962717	0.61	0.695231	0.197400
Growth	4	2.524913	0.6312281	0.77	0.550668	0.223707
S	37	30.26904	0.8180821			
Total (Adjusted)	49	40.02				
Total	50					

* Term significant at alpha = 0.05

criteria depends on the IT department being present on the board (CIO). The importance of these criteria is higher in the companies without a CIO present on the board (4.3) than in companies with one (3.5).

Advanced Technology

The analysis of the impact of company size, the representation of the IT department on the board level (CIO), information strategy, and ERP stage and growth on advanced technology criteria is presented in Table 15. The importance these criteria depends on the IT department being present on the board (CIO). The importance of these criteria is higher in companies where the CIO is present

on the board (4.1) than in companies, where the CIO is not present on the board (3.6).

4.3.4 Companies' Factors Impacting on all ERP Selection Criteria

The analysis of the impact of company size, representation of the IT department on the board level (CIO), information strategy, ERP stage and growth on all ERP selection criteria is presented in Table 16. The importance of all these criteria depends on the representation of the IT department on the board level (CIO), ERP stage, turnover growth, and on which criterion it is. The latter was the main reason for this analysis. The importance

Table 13. Analysis of variance table for operating system independence criteria

Factor	DF	Sum of Squares	Mean Square	F-ratio	P-value	Power (Alpha=0.05)
Company size	1	4.059023	4.059023	4.66	0.037460*	0.556549
CIO	1	0.08351625	0.08351625	0.10	0.758605	0.060487
Information strategy	1	0.01884852	0.01884852	0.02	0.883869	0.052356
ERP stage	5	13.58727	2.717454	3.12	0.018993*	0.821539
Growth	4	2.081295	0.5203237	0.60	0.666947	0.179170
S	37	32.2391	0.871327			
Total (Adjusted)	49	49.78				
Total	50					

* Term significant at alpha = 0.05

Table 14. Analysis of variance table for organizational fit of the system criteria

Factor	DF	Sum of Squares	Mean Square	F-ratio	P-value	Power (Alpha=0.05)
Company size	1	1.374061	1.374061	1.70	0.199779	0.246362
CIO	1	6.558371	6.558371	8.13	0.007011*	0.793361
Information strategy	1	0.02955463	0.02955463	0.04	0.849252	0.053998
ERP stage	5	3.314304	0.6628608	0.82	0.542201	0.261558
Growth	4	1.693667	0.4234167	0.52	0.718162	0.161717
S	38	30.66508	0.8069757			
Total (Adjusted)	50	40.03922				
Total	51					

* Term significant at alpha = 0.05

of all criteria is lower in companies with a CIO (3.8) than in companies without one (3.9). It is lower in companies in ERP Stage 1 (3.5) than in companies in Stages 2 (4.0), 4 (4.1), 5 (4.0), and it is lower in companies in ERP Stage 3 (3.7) than in companies in Stages 4 (4.1). It is lower in companies with reduction in turnover in previous three years (3.7) than in companies with turnover growth of 5-10% (4.0).

The differences between criteria are illustrated in Table 17. The theoretical average values (estimated by the model, not the actual averages presented in Tables 5-8) are in the second row and in the second column. The inequality signs should be read as the importance of the criterion in row i is significantly smaller or higher than the importance of the criterion in column j. (Despite the signs, the test is conservatively two-, not one-sided.)

Accounting for the impact of all factors on criteria, there is no significant difference between systems reliability and integrated and better quality of information, e-business enablement, system flexibility, improved service levels/quality, functionality of the system, vendor support, organizational fit of system, business process improvement, system usability, increased organizational flexibility, reduced cycle times, connectivity (intra/extranet, mobile comp., etc.), enhanced decision making, software costs (licenses, maintenance,

Table 15. Analysis of variance table for advanced technology criteria

Factor	DF	Sum of Squares	Mean Square	F-ratio	P-value	Power (Alpha=0.05)
Company size	1	0.332086	0.332086	0.82	0.371136	0.142840
CIO	1	2.105346	2.105346	5.19	0.028383*	0.602982
Information strategy	1	0.2118356	0.2118356	0.52	0.474194	0.108550
ERP stage	5	0.9370106	0.1874021	0.46	0.801773	0.157650
Growth	4	2.230817	0.5577043	1.38	0.260613	0.386349
S	38	15.40559	0.4054103			
Total (Adjusted)	50	22.5098				
Total	51					

* Term significant at alpha = 0.05

Table 16. Analysis of variance table for all criteria

Factor	DF	Sum of Squares	Mean Square	F-ratio	P-value	Power (Alpha=0.05)
Company size	1	0.05369971	0.05369971	0.08	0.782520	0.058765
CIO	1	3.576168	3.576168	5.08	0.024414*	0.614685
Information strategy	1	0.008805531	0.008805531	0.01	0.910998	0.051431
ERP stage	5	33.94508	6.789015	9.64	0.000000*	0.999970
Growth	4	6.894649	1.723662	2.45	0.044690*	0.703593
Criterion	27	162.1903	6.007047	8.53	0.000000*	1.000000
S	1355	954.5634	0.7044748			
Total (Adjusted)	1394	1171.419				
Total	1395					

* Term significant at alpha = 0.05

etc.), system interoperability, increased customer satisfaction. Therefore, all the 17 criteria should be treated as a most important.

4. 4 Known Limitations

Although the response rate of 12% for medium-sized companies and 4.5% for small companies is somewhat low, Armstrong and Overton (1977) illustrate that even a response rate of 80% may lead to biased estimates. In contrast, as Newman (2009) points out, statistical power depends on the number of responses rather than on the response rate *per se*. Extrapolation methods assume that subjects who responded less readily are more like non-respondents (Pace 1939). "Less readily" means answering later, or requiring more prodding to answer. Since in this research we did not remind or urge respondents to reply, our less ready respondents are only late respondents. We compared early and late responders to see if there is a significant difference between them. Altogether, we consider the first 49 responses (who answered by the time we requested) to be early responses, the remaining 14 responses are considered to be late. There is not any significant difference in early and late respondents with regards to distribution of independent variables

(company size, CIO, information strategy, ERP stage, growth) and averages/medians of dependent variables (criteria). Test values and p-values for the former are presented in Table 18. Regarding the latter, Table 19 presents the test values and p-values of normality tests, of equal variance tests, and of ANOVA or of Kruskal-Wallis tests (depending on normality test results). Although it does not prove that the non-respondents would give the same answers, at least it does not suggest that they would differ significantly.

6 DISCUSSION

This chapter examines the importance of ERP system selection criteria also studied by Bernroider & Koch (2001) and Bernroider & Leseure (2005). Altogether, 28 ERP selection criteria were identified and investigated in the research. The investigated criteria were grouped into the ERP benefits criteria, the ERP system quality criteria, the ERP vendor-related criteria and the ERP package criteria.

Out of 28 investigated selection criteria, 17 are the most important in a means of expectations of SMEs from ERP system adoption. These criteria are the following:

Table 17. Comparison of criteria

Criteria		3.17	3.17	3.33	3.35	**3.43**	3.50	3.57	3.63	3.73	3.75	**3.79**	3.87	3.87	3.89	3.90	3.91	**3.94**	3.97	4.04	4.06	4.09	4.17	**4.17**	4.19	4.19	4.27	4.35	4.43
Improved innovation capabilities	3.17												<	<	<	<	<	<	<	<	<	<	<	<	<	<	<	<	<
Internationality of software	3.17												<	<	<	<	<	<	<	<	<	<	<	<	<	<	<	<	<
Market position of vendor	3.33																		<	<	<	<	<	<	<	<	<	<	<
Vendor reputation	3.35																			<	<	<	<	<	<	<	<	<	<
Enabling technology for CRM, SCM, etc.	3.43																					<	<	<	<	<	<	<	<
Operating system independence	3.50																							<	<	<	<	<	<
Availability of an industry focused solution	3.57																										<	<	<
Incorporation of business best practices	3.63																										<	<	<
Enabler for desired business processes	3.73																												<
Short implementation time	3.75																												<
Advanced technology	3.79																												<
Increased customer satisfaction	3.87	>	>																										
System interoperability	3.87	>	>																										
Software costs (licenses, maintenance, etc.)	3.89	>	>																										
Enhanced decision making	3.90	>	>																										
Connectivity (intra/extranet, mobile comp., etc.)	3.91	>	>																										
Reduced cycle times	3.94	>	>																										
Increased organizational flexibility	3.97	>	>	>																									
System usability	4.04	>	>	>	>																								
Business process improvement	4.06	>	>	>	>																								
Organizational fit of system	4.09	>	>	>	>	>																							
Functionality of the system	4.17	>	>	>	>	>																							
Vendor support	4.17	>	>	>	>	>	>																						
Improved service levels/quality	4.19	>	>	>	>	>	>																						
System flexibility	4.19	>	>	>	>	>	>																						
E-business enablement	4.27	>	>	>	>	>	>	>	>																				
Integrated and better quality of information	4.35	>	>	>	>	>	>	>	>																				
Systems reliability	4.43	>	>	>	>	>	>	>	>	>	>	>																	

- The most expected benefits gained from ERP system adoption perceived by SMEs are integrated and better quality of information, improved service levels and quality, business process improvement, increased organization flexibility, reduced cycle times, increased customer satisfaction and enhanced decision making. These are the ERP selection criteria that were ranked as of highest importance in the group of ERP benefits criteria.

- The highest expectations of SMEs regarding the ERP system quality criteria are system reliability, system flexibility, system functionality, system usability and system interoperability. These criteria were of highest importance for SMEs in the group of ERP system quality criteria.

- The most important expectation of SMEs from ERP vendors is vendor support. Vendor reputation and market position of the vendor were less important criteria for

Table 18. Comparison of early and late respondents in independent variables

Factor	Chi-square	P-value
Company size	3.375000	0.066193
CIO	0.000000	1.000000
Information strategy	2.930224	0.086935
ERP stage	6.877090	0.229943
Growth	4.044213	0.400055

the SMEs in the group of ERP vendors-related criteria.

- SMEs' most important expectations from the ERP package criteria are e-business enablement, the organizational fit of the ERP system, the connectivity of the ERP system and ERP software costs. These ERP package criteria were ranked as of highest importance for SMEs.

All of these criteria are the most sensitive for SMEs in the phase of ERP system acquisition and its usage. ERP vendors are strongly recommended considering these criteria to meet SMEs' expectations in a most efficient way.

In addition to the importance of ERP selection criteria for SMEs, the impact of companies' factors (company size, representation of the IT department on the board level (CIO) and information strategy, ERP stage and turnover growth) on ERP system selection criteria was also investigated. The analysis has shown that company size affects reduced cycle times criteria. The importance is higher in medium-sized companies (4.0) than in small companies (3.4). This could be explained by the complexity of business processes, practices and procedures, which seems to be more complex in medium-sized companies than in small companies. In the ERP system acquisition phase, the medium-sized companies will devote more attention to the ability of an ERP system to reduce the cycle times of business operation.

Company size also has an impact on the system reliability of the ERP system selection criterion, where importance is higher for medium-sized companies (4.6) than for small companies (4.1). The higher importance of this factor in medium-sized companies could be again explained by the complexity of business processes, which are more complex in medium-sized companies, where more people are cooperating in the same business processes and thus greater system reliability is needed. It is expected that in the ERP system acquisition phase the medium-sized companies will have higher expectations regarding the reliability of ERP system.

Another criterion depended on company size is operating system independence. The importance of this criterion is higher for small companies (3.6) than for medium-sized companies (2.9). This is related to fewer resources being available for ICT investments in small companies. Small companies are most likely to use less complex, cheaper, affordable solutions, including open source solutions. In a phase of ERP system acquisition, small companies will be more sensitive regarding the ERP system independence from operating system.

The importance of operating system independence criteria is also higher in the companies where: an ERP system was recently implemented and is now being stabilized (3.5), an ERP system is being configured and implemented (3.8), an ERP system is being used and maintained (4) and an ERP system is being evaluated for the selection of a specific solution (4.5) than in companies where ERP system has been replaced with a new one (0.4).

Table 19. Comparison of early and late respondents in dependent variables

Criterion	Omnibus Normality of Residuals		Modified-Levene Equal-Variance Test		Test	Test Value (Chi-square or F-ratio)	P-value
	Test Value	P-value	Test Value	P-value			
Reduced cycle times	3.5783	0.167106	0.0850	0.771765	ANOVA	0.52	0.472481
Enhanced decision making	6.5870	0.037123	0.3169	0.575769	KW	0.002525443	0.959920
Improved service levels/quality	5.4241	0.066400	1.9728	0.165874	ANOVA	1.12	0.293788
Incorporation of business best practices	2.2114	0.330985	0.2304	0.633190	ANOVA	0.09	0.759803
Business process improvement	2.6177	0.270124	0.2837	0.596519	ANOVA	1.01	0.320179
Integrated and better quality of information	22.8894	0.000011	0.9442	0.335531	KW	0.4332644	0.510391
E-business enablement	6.7093	0.034921	0.2435	0.623706	KW	0.06663448	0.796302
Increased organizational flexibility	2.5801	0.275254	0.0633	0.802303	ANOVA	3.32	0.073896
Increased customer satisfaction	4.8320	0.089277	2.3288	0.132833	ANOVA	0.05	0.817495
Improved innovation capabilities	0.2692	0.874078	0.2982	0.587250	ANOVA	1.39	0.243039
Enabler for desired business processes	1.6341	0.441724	0.0355	0.851259	ANOVA	2.43	0.124738
Organizational fit of system	8.8798	0.011797	1.1723	0.283736	KW	0.02071229	0.885566
Software costs (licenses, maintenance, etc.)	10.7018	0.004744	0.0925	0.762234	KW	0	1.000000
Functionality of the system	8.3319	0.015515	0.1816	0.671684	KW	0.01111084	0.916052
System flexibility	13.2401	0.001333	0.0000	1.000000	KW	0.4465376	0.503984
Systems reliability	9.6058	0.008206	1.3450	0.251253	KW	1.958306	0.161695
Advanced technology	1.7622	0.414328	0.2098	0.648727	ANOVA	1.08	0.302974
Operating system independence	9.1048	0.010542	0.0246	0.875949	KW	1.746138	0.186363
System interoperability	8.7463	0.012612	0.3354	0.564903	KW	0.06736971	0.795206
Internationality of software	3.1257	0.209540	0.6791	0.413531	ANOVA	0.02	0.899710
System usability	15.8097	0.000369	0.0878	0.768133	KW	0.1113296	0.738635
Vendor reputation	2.9613	0.227491	0.0085	0.927039	ANOVA	0.05	0.817480
Vendor support	25.0967	0.000004	0.5347	0.467818	KW	0.07362872	0.786125
Market position of vendor	2.9455	0.229294	0.3244	0.571371	ANOVA	0.97	0.328819
Availability of an industry focused solution	11.3725	0.003392	0.6131	0.437056	KW	1.215256	0.270294
Short implementation time	1.3136	0.518507	0.5121	0.477297	ANOVA	0.49	0.487733
Enabling technology for CRM, SCM, etc.	5.9481	0.051097	0.0080	0.928882	ANOVA	0.60	0.442996
Connectivity (intra/extranet, mobile comp., etc.)	3.6834	0.158547	0.4086	0.525525	ANOVA	0.28	0.596365

Legend: KW – Kruskal-Wallis test; test value is F-ratio for ANOVA, chi-square for Kruskal-Wallis test

The representation of the IT department within executive board impacts the ERP system usability criterion. The importance of this criterion is higher in companies where the CIO is not present on the board (4.3) than in companies where the CIO is present on the board (3.6). The reason for this could be explained by the fact that executives have higher expectations for ERP system usability compared to CIO's expectations. Executives perceived ERP system usability from a business perspective, while CIOs usually take into account more technological than business perspectives of system usability.

The importance of the advanced technology criterion depends on the representation of the IT department on the board level (it is lower in companies without a CIO or similar (3.73) than in companies with one (4.17)) and on information strategy (it is lower in companies without a formal information strategy (3.79) than in companies with one (4.11)). Companies with a CIO on the board level and an implemented information strategy have greater understandings at a higher management level of the importance of advanced technology usage for achieving lower costs of business operation and higher efficiency.

The importance of the improved innovation capabilities criterion depends on the ERP stage in the companies. The importance of improved innovation capabilities criteria is higher in companies where an ERP system has been used and maintained for some years (4.1) than in companies where an ERP system is being just considered (2.7). This difference seems to be very logical. Companies with already implemented ERP systems are more familiar with their functionalities and opportunities that are still unexploited. Nowadays, customers' expectations are very high. Companies are faced daily with new competitors entering global markets. Thus, innovation is a key driver for every company to survive and gain an important competitive advantage in global markets.

The importance of the organizational fit of the system criterion depends on the IT department being present on the board (CIO). The importance of this criterion is higher in the companies without a CIO present on the board (4.3) than in companies with a CIO (3.5). A CIO has greater understanding of ERP system functionalities and capabilities. Thus, the organizational fit of the system criterion

was more important in the companies without a CIO present on the board.

Compared to other research (Bernroider & Koch, 2001; Bernroider & Leseure, 2005), the importance of the following ERP criteria was confirmed: system reliability, vendor support, functionality of the system, business process improvement, improved service levels, and integrated and better quality of information. All of these criteria were also perceived as most important ERP system selection criteria in our research. Compared to the investigation of van Everdingen et al (2000) on ERP systems adoption in medium-sized companies, the importance of following factors was confirmed: the organizational fit of the system, the flexibility of the system and the costs of the system. Compared to Baki and Cakar (2005), the investigation of ERP package selection criteria in Turkish manufacturing companies, the organizational fit of the ERP system was confirmed to be important an ERP selection criteria.

According to the study of Bernroider & Leseure (2005), we have also identified differences of the importance of e-business enablement of ERP selection criterion, which was a more important ERP selection criterion in our case than in the previously mentioned research study. E-business enablement is becoming an increasing important ERP system selection criteria as the need for better business integration, supported by ICT of all partners in supply chain is urgent to achieve competitive advantage in the market.

Although the results of our research have shown that 66.7% of medium-sized and 37% of small companies that participated in research already use an ERP system, the overall situation is much worse. Data from other sources show that only 10% of small and 50% of medium-sized companies in Slovenia use ERP systems (Sulčič, 2008). However, we can observe the recent trend that a higher proportion of SMEs have recently adopted ERP systems. Many of them are still planning to adopt an ERP system in the near future. They are searching for the most suitable solutions for their needs.

Currently, the SME ERP market offers many opportunities for ERP providers. In recent years, ERP system providers, previously mainly specialized for large organizations (e.g. SAP and Oracle), have also started to provide packages especially tailored for SMEs. However, it seems that in Slovenia local providers have greater potential in this market.

Many SMEs in Slovenia already use ERP systems from Slovene providers. It is expected that local providers will also have a very important role in the near future. Local providers offer ERP systems focused and tailored especially for SMEs' needs. The knowhow of business operations integrated in these ERP systems is very important for SMEs. These ERP systems integrate standardized operations, based on national business practices, law and regulations, including automated calculation for taxations, customs, payments procedures, salaries calculation, etc. Most of the ERP systems from national providers also integrate XML schemes for basic business documents (order, order confirmation, dispatch advice and invoice) based on the eSLOG national standard. This enables SMEs to adopt not just an ERP system but also e-commerce, which is the only way to stay competitive and efficiently operate in the local and global markets.

REFERENCES

Adam, F., & O'Doherty, P. (2000). Lessons from Enterprise Resource Planning Implementations in Ireland - Towards Smaller and Shorter ERP projects. *Journal of Information Technology, 15*(4), 305–316. doi:10.1080/02683960010008953

Armstrong, J. S., & Overton, T. S. (1977). Estimating Nonresponse Bias in Mail Surveys. *JMR, Journal of Marketing Research, 14*(3), 396–402. doi:10.2307/3150783

Au, N., Ngai, E. W. T., & Cheng, T. C. E. (2008). Extending the Understanding of End User Information Systems Satisfaction Formation: An Equitable Needs Fulfillment Model Approach. *MIS Quarterly, 32*(1), 43–66.

Baki, B., & Çakar, K. (2005). Determining the ERP package-selecting criteria: The case of Turkish manufacturing companies. *Business Process Management Journal, 11*(1), 75–86. doi:10.1108/14637150510578746

Bala, H., & Venkatesh, V. (2007). Assimilation of Interorganizational Business Process Standards. *Information Systems Research, 18*(3), 340–362. doi:10.1287/isre.1070.0134

Bernroider, E. (2008). IT governance for enterprise resource planning supported by the DeLone-McLean model of information system success. *Information & Management, 45*(5), 257–269. doi:10.1016/j.im.2007.11.004

Bernroider, E., & Koch, S. (2001). ERP selection process in midsize and large organizations. *Business Process Management Journal, 7*(3), 251–257. doi:10.1108/14637150110392746

Bernroider, E. W. N., & Leseure, M. J. (2005). *Enterprise resource planning (ERP) diffusion and characteristics according to the system's lifecycle: A comparative view of small-to-medium-sized and large enterprises.* Working papers on information processing and Information Management. Wien, Austria: Vienna University of Economics and Business Administration, Institute of Information Processing and Information Management.

Bharati, P., & Chaudhury, A. (2009). SMEs and competitiveness - The role of information systems. *International Journal of E-Business Research, 5*(1), 1–9.

Botta-Genoulaz, V., Millet, P.-A., & Grabot, B. (2005). A survey on the recent reserach literature on ERP systems. *Computers in Industry, 56*(6), 510–522. doi:10.1016/j.compind.2005.02.004

Buonanno, G., Faverio, P., Pigni, F., & Ravarini, A. (2005). Factors affecting ERP system adoption: A comparative analysis between SMEs and large companies. *Journal of Enterprise Information Management*, *18*(4), 384–426. doi:10.1108/17410390510609572

Chin, W. W., Johnson, M., & Schwarz, A. (2008). A Fast Form Approach to Measuring Technology Acceptance and Other Constructs. *MIS Quarterly*, *32*(4), 687–703.

Chitura, T., Mupemhi, S., Dube, T., & Bolongkikit, J. (2008). Barriers to Electronic Commerce Adoption in Small and Medium Enterprises: A Critical Literature Review. *Journal of Internet Banking and Commerce*, *13*(2), 1–13.

Costa, G., & Gianecchini, M. (2006). *Tecnologia, cambiamento organizzativo e competitività. Il ruolo dei sistemi informativi integrati.* Paper presented at the workshop WOA 2006: Organizzazione, Regolazione e Competitività, Fisciano, Salerno.

Cragg, P. B., & King, M. (1993). Small-firm computing: Motivators and inhibitors. *MIS Quarterly*, *17*(1), 47–59. doi:10.2307/249509

Davenport, T. (1998). Putting the Enterprise into the Enterprise System. *Harvard Business Review*, *76*(4), 121–131.

Eleftheriadou, D. (2008). *Small- and Medium-Sized Enterprises Hold the Key to European Competitiveness: How to Help Them Innovate through ICT and E-business. The Global Information Technology Report 2007-2008.* World Economic Forum.

Esteves, J. (2009). A benefits realization roadmap framework for ERP usage in small and medium-sized enterprises. *Journal of Enterprise Information Management*, *22*(1/2), 25–35. doi:10.1108/17410390910922804

European Commission. (2002). Benchmarking National and Regional E-business Policies for SMEs. Final report of the E-business Policy Group of the European Union, Brussels.

European Commission. (2008). The European e-Business Report 2008. The impact of ICT and e-business on firms, sectors and the economy. 6th Synthesis Report of the Sectoral e-Business Watch.

European Commission, & DG Enterprise and Industry. (2008). *A comprehensive policy to support SMEs.* Retrieved April 18, 2009, from http://ec.europa.eu/enterprise/entrepreneurship/sme_policy.htm

Fisher, D. M., Fisher, S. A., & Kiang, M. Y. (2004). Evaluating mid-level ERP software. *Journal of Computer Information Systems*, *45*(1), 38–46.

Frielink, A. B. (1961). Auditing Automatic Data Processing. Amsterdam, Netherlands: Elsevier.

Gable, G., & Stewart, G. (1999). SAP R/3 implementation issues for small to medium enterprises. *Americas Conference on Information Systems*. Milwaukee, WI: Association for Information Systems, 779-781.

Han, S. W. (2004). ERP - Enterprise resource planning: A cost-based business case and implementation assessment. *Human Factors and Ergonomics in Manufacturing*, *14*(3), 239–256. doi:10.1002/hfm.10066

Hitt, L. M., Wu, D. J., & Zhou, X. (2002). Investment in enterprise resource planning: business impact and productivity measures. *Journal of Management Information Systems*, *19*(1), 71–98. doi:10.1201/1078/43199.19.1.20020101/31479.10

Jafari, S. M., Osman, M. R., Yusuff, R. M., & Tang, S. H. (2006). ERP Systems Implementation in Malaysia: The Importance of Critical Success Factors. *International Journal of Engineering and Technology, 3*(1), 125–131.

Joslin, E. O. (1968). Computer Selection. London: Addison-Wesley.

Kartiwi, M., & MacGregor, R. C. (2007). Electronic Commerce Adoption Barriers in Small to Medium-Sized Enterprises (SMEs) in Developed and Developing Countries: A Cross-Country Comparison. *Journal of Electronic Commerce in Organizations, 5*(3), 35–51.

Keil, M., & Tiwana, A. (2006). Relative importance of evaluation criteria for enterprise systems: a conjoint study. *Information Systems Journal, 16*(3), 237–262. doi:10.1111/j.1365-2575.2006.00218.x

Kumar, K., & Hillegersberg, J. V. (2000). ERP experiences and evolution. *Communications of the ACM, 43*(4), 22–26. doi:10.1145/332051.332063

Kumar, V., Maheshwari, B., & Kumar, U. (2002). Enterprise resource planning systems adoption process: a survey of Canadian organizations. *International Journal of Production Research, 40*(3), 509–523. doi:10.1080/00207540110092414

Kumar, V., Maheshwari, B., & Kumar, U. (2003). An investigation of critical management issues in ERP implementation: empirical evidence from Canadian organizations. *Technovation, 23*(10), 793–807. doi:10.1016/S0166-4972(02)00015-9

Lall, V., & Teyarachakul, S. (2006). Enterprise Resource Planning (ERP) System selection: A Data Envelopment Analysis (DEA) approach. *Journal of Computer Information Systems, 47*(1), 123–127.

Laukkanen, S., Sarpola, S., & Hallikainen, P. (2007). Enterprise size matters: objectives and constraints of ERP adoption. *Journal of Enterprise Information Management, 20*(3), 319–334. doi:10.1108/17410390710740763

Law, C. C. H., & Ngai, E. W. T. (2007). ERP system adoption: An exploratory study of the organizational factors and impacts of ERP success. *Information & Management, 44*(4), 418–432. doi:10.1016/j.im.2007.03.004

Levenburg, N. M., Schwarz, T. V., & Motwani, J. (2005). Understanding adoption of internet technologies among SMEs. *Journal of Small Business Strategy, 16*(1), 51–69.

Levy, M., Powell, P., & Worrall, L. (2005). Strategic Intent and E-Business in SMEs: Enablers and Inhibitors. *Information Resources Management Journal, 18*(4), 1–20.

Liao, X. W., Li, Y., & Lu, B. (2007). A model for selecting an ERP system based on linguistic information processing. *Information Systems, 32*(7), 1005–1017. doi:10.1016/j.is.2006.10.005

Lomerson, W. L., McGrath, L. C., & Schwager, P. H. (2004). An examination of the benefits of e-business to small and medium size businesses. In *Proceedings of the 7th Annual conference of the Southern Association for Information System,* Southern Association for Information Systems.

Mac Gregor, R., & Vrazalic, L. (2005). The Role of Small Business Clusters in Prioritising Barriers to E-commerce Adoption: A Study of Swedish Regional SMEs. CRIC Cluster conference. Beyond Cluster-Current Practices & Future Strategies, Ballarat, Victoria.

Malie, M., Duffy, N., & van Rensburg, A. C. J. (2008). Enterprise resource planning solution selection criteria in medium-sized South African companies. *South African Journal of Industrial Engineering, 19*(1), 17–41.

Markus, M. L., & Tanis, C. (2000). The Enterprise System Experience: From Adoption to Success. In R. W. Zmud (Ed.), Framing the Domains of IT Management: Projecting the Future through the Past (pp. 173-207). Cincinnati, OH: Pinnaflex Educational Resources Inc.

Mehrtens, J., Cragg, P. B., & Mills, A. M. (2001). A model of Internet adoption by SMEs. *Information & Management, 39*(3), 165–176. doi:10.1016/S0378-7206(01)00086-6

Metaxiotis, K. (2009). Exploring the rationales for ERP and knowledge management integration in SMEs. *Journal of Enterprise Information Management., 22*(1/2), 51–62. doi:10.1108/17410390910922822

Morabito, V., Pace, S., & Previtali, P. (2005). ERP Marketing and Italian SMEs. *European Management Journal, 23*(5), 590–598. doi:10.1016/j.emj.2005.09.014

Nah, F. F. H., & Delgado, S. (2006). Critical success factors for enterprise resource planning implementation and upgrade. *Journal of Computer Information Systems, 46*(SI), 99-113.

Newman, D. A. (2009). Missing data techniques and low response rates: the role of systematic nonresponse parameters. In C. E. Lance & R. J. Vandenberg (Eds.) Statistical and methodological myths and urban legends (pp. 7-36). New York: Routledge.

Oh, W., & Pinsonneault, A. (2007). On the Assessment of the Strategic Value of Information Technologies: Conceptual and Analytical Approaches. *MIS Quarterly, 31*(2), 239–265.

Pace, C. R. (1939). Factors Influencing Questionnaire Returns from Former University Students. *The Journal of Applied Psychology, 23*(3), 388–397. doi:10.1037/h0063286

Pucihar, A., Bogataj, K., & Lenart, G. (2009). Increasing SMEs' efficiency through the single European electronic market as a new business model. In B Paape, & D. Vuk (Ed.), Synthesized organization (pp. 347-368). Frankfurt am Main: P. Lang.

Ramdani, B., & Kawalek, P. (2009). Predicting SMEs' adoption of enterprise systems. *Journal of Enterprise Information Management, 22*(1/2), 10–24. doi:10.1108/17410390910922796

Rao, S. S. (2000). Enterprise resource planning: business needs and technologies. *Industrial Management & Data Systems, 100*(2), 81–88. doi:10.1108/02635570010286078

Ray, G., Muhanna, W. A., & Barney, J. B. (2007). Competing With IT: The Role of Shared IT-Business Understanding. *Communications of the ACM, 50*(12), 87–91. doi:10.1145/1323688.1323700

Raymond, L., & Sylvestre, U. (2007). A profile of ERP adoption in manufacturing SMEs. *Journal of Enterprise Information Management, 20*(4), 487–502. doi:10.1108/17410390710772731

Riquelme, H. (2002). Commercial Internet Adoption in China: Comparing the experiences of small, medium and large businesses. *Internet Research: Electronic Networking Applications and Policy, 12*(3), 276–286. doi:10.1108/10662240210430946

Scott, J. E. (2008). Technology Acceptance and ERP Documentation Usability. *Communications of the ACM, 51*(11), 121–124. doi:10.1145/1400214.1400239

Sudzina, F. (2007). Importance of EPR selection criteria in Slovak companies. *Manažment v teórii a praxi, 3*(4), 4-20.

Sulčič, V. (2008). E-poslovanje v Slovenskih malih in srednje velikih podjetjih. *Management, 3*(3), 347–361.

SURS – Statistični urad RS. (2007). *Uporaba informacijsko-komunikacijske tehnologije v podjetjih z 10 in več zaposlenimi osebami*. 1. Četrtletje 2007. Retrieved February 17, 2008, from http://www.stat.si/novica_prikazi.aspx?id=1284

Umble, E. J., Haft, R. R., & Umble, M. M. (2003). Enterprise resource planning: implementation procedures and critical success factors. *European Journal of Operational Research, 146*(2), 241–257. doi:10.1016/S0377-2217(02)00547-7

Van Everdingen, Y., van Hillegersberg, J., & Waarts, E. (2000). ERP adoption by European mid-size companies. *Communications of the ACM, 43*(4), 27–31. doi:10.1145/332051.332064

Verville, J., & Halingten, A. (2003). A six-stage model of the buying process for ERP software. *Industrial Marketing Management, 32*(7), 585–594. doi:10.1016/S0019-8501(03)00007-5

Wei, C. C., Chien, C. F., & Wang, M. J. J. (2005). An AHP-based approach to ERP system selection. *International Journal of Production Economics, 96*(1), 47–62. doi:10.1016/j.ijpe.2004.03.004

Wier, B., & Hunton, J., & HassabElnaby, H. R. (2007). Enterprise resource planning systems and non-financial performance incentives: The joint impact on corporate performance. *International Journal of Accounting Information Systems, 8*(3), 165–190. doi:10.1016/j.accinf.2007.05.001

Chapter 5

Managing Impressions
of SME Legitimacy:
Valuing Information and Communications Technologies as Signals and Symbols

Susan J. Winter[1]
National Science Foundation, USA

Connie Marie Gaglio
San Francisco State University, USA

Hari K. Rajagopalan
Francis Marion University, USA

ABSTRACT

To succeed, SMEs must create legitimacy by mimicking the cues that signal credibility to convince potential stakeholders that something stands behind their promises. This research examines the role of information and communications technology (ICT) in legitimacy-building from the perspective of both SME founders and potential customers. Small and medium-sized enterprises (SMEs) face more serious challenges to their survival than do larger firms. To succeed, SMEs must establish and maintain credibility in the marketplace to attract the resources required for survival. Most borrow legitimacy by mimicking the cues that signal credibility to convince potential stakeholders that something stands behind their promises. This research examines the role of information and communications technology (ICT) in legitimacy creation from the perspective of both SME founders and customers. In-depth, semi-structured interviews were conducted in a variety of industries to determine whether the ICT-related legitimacy schema from the customers' perspective differs substantially from that of firm founders. Results indicate that customers compare the ICT information provided in SME's sales pitches to pre-existing ICT expectations about the nature of desirable sales transactions. We describe the relationship between violations of ICT expectations, legitimacy, and purchase decisions. Implications for theory and practice are discussed.

DOI: 10.4018/978-1-61520-627-8.ch005

INTRODUCTION

Small and expanding firms generate 50 percent of all innovations and 95 percent of all radical innovations in the U.S. (Timmons, 1999; Vesper, 1996). Great opportunities cannot be realized unless innovative firms can attract the resources and support required for their survival and growth (Pfeffer & Salanick, 1978; Starr & MacMillan, 1990; Stinchcombe, 1968). Research on the business value of information and communication technologies (ICT) for small and medium sized enterprises (SMEs) emphasizes its substantive performance role in garnering resources by efficiently managing internal operations and supply chain activities to improve productivity and profitability (Levy & Powell, 2005). While this narrative has value, reliance on a single paradigm limits our understanding of any IS phenomenon (Orlikowski & Iacono, 2001). We explore the business value of ICT using a nontraditional approach that draws upon commonly accepted traditions in non-IS business research and explores the value of ICT in SME legitimacy and competitiveness.

As new ICTs are developed, researchers have attempted to understand their adoption and use by SMEs. This work has determined that many of the resources developed for larger firms to guide strategic IS planning, alignment and the evaluation of ICT investments are often inappropriate for SMEs (Bharati & Chaudhury, 2006; Blili & Raymond, 1993; Dandridge, 1979; Senn & Gibson, 1981; Wainwright, et al., 2005; Welsh & White, 1981). Previously identified barriers to ICT adoption by SMEs include negative attitudes and the financial and knowledge constraints faced by many smaller firms (Parker & Castleman, 2007). Investments in ICT are usually justified based on demonstrating its substantive business value as a complementary asset in the efficient and effective handling of information to improve the efficiency of transactions and other routine operations, enabling better analysis and strategic decision making (Gregor, et al. 2006; Melville et al. 2004; Murphy & Simon 2002, Peppard, et al. 2007).

However, the organizational literature has long recognized that operational efficiency and productivity are not the only prerequisites for organizational success (Meyer & Rowan, 1977; Scott, 2001). Although SME success is related to internal operational efficiency and effectiveness, it also requires access to external resources such as labor, financing, and most importantly, a steady stream of income from sales (Harrison, Dibben, & Mason, 1997). Attracting the resources and support required for SME survival and growth requires that firms also establish that they are credible players in the marketplace; this process is referred to as gaining legitimacy (Pfeffer & Salancik, 1978; Suchman, 1995).

Previous research (Gaglio, Cecchini & Winter, 1998) regarding SME founders' beliefs about creating legitimacy revealed a surprising uniformity about the characteristics of a legitimate new firm. In most cases, new firms have borrowed or co-opted legitimacy (Starr & MacMillan, 1990) by garnering endorsements and associations and by mimicking the standards, practices, and cues of their relevant industries (Heugens & Lander, 2009). This paper investigates whether these mimicked standards include expectations regarding the use of ICT and whether ICT acts as a signal and symbol of legitimacy among potential customers.

This approach extends the literature on SMEs and IS in an important way. The IS field has long recognized the symbolic meaning of ICT and its use as a signal by various stakeholders (Feldman & March, 1981; Kling & Iacono, 1988). Research on the computerization of work has explored what ICT symbolizes to employees, shareholders and developers or special interest groups (e.g. Jackson, Poole & Kuhn, 2002; Prasad, 1993; Ranganathan & Brown, 2006; Swanson & Ramiller, 1997). Missing from this research is a systematic exploration of the link between an SME's ICT, the customers' image of the firm, and the likelihood of purchase, a central concern for managers and researchers.

This work also extends the organizational theory literature in two important ways. First, it focuses on establishing legitimacy whereas the existing literature focuses on its maintenance and repair (Suchman, 1995). Secondly, we examine both how SMEs convey impressions and what potential customers expect to hear whereas the existing literature usually examines only one or the other (e.g., Arnold, Handelman & Tigert, 1996; Harrison et al., 1997).

If potential customers form impressions of an SME based on its use of ICT and these impressions are positively related to purchase behavior, managers who want to attract and retain customers may want to consider adopting ICT as a signal, not just for its productivity-related business value. If these impressions are negatively related to purchase behavior, SMEs may consider avoiding the ICT, or at least obscuring its use. Thus, the customers' perceptions of the symbolic meaning of ICT forms an important component of its total business value, which may include both improvements in internal operational efficiency and its ability to act as a signal and affect purchase behavior among external stakeholders (Heugens & Lander, 2009).

The first two related research questions addressed here are: Do prospective SME customers infer legitimacy from the presence of ICT? Does this perceived legitimacy affect the likelihood that customers will make a purchase? To answer these questions, we investigate 1) whether these symbol meanings are tacit or explicit; 2) whether customers' and SME founders' views of ICT's symbolic meanings are sufficiently similar to one another to enable accurate signaling; 3) whether SME founders are aware of the customers' perspective and could purposefully manipulate their firm's images through their choice of ICT; and 4) attributions about SMEs drawn from the use of ICT emphasizing customer expectations and the

implications when these are violated. The third research question addressed is: Why and how does ICT act as a symbol of legitimacy?

We begin by briefly describing the existing corporate image literature with particular attention to identifying the potential role of ICT in assessing firm legitimacy. This is followed by an in-depth presentation of an inductive investigation of why ICT signals legitimacy by investigating the importance of matching customer expectations. Although it is generated from the more specific results, the findings from this phase begin with the presentation of the abstract theoretical frame or paradigm model (as recommended by Strauss & Corbin, 1998), highlighting the importance of schemas and mental models in creating a corporate image and the symbolic role of ICT in judging legitimacy. Each element of the model is then described with supporting evidence and comparisons between the findings and existing legitimacy theory to identify areas of confirmation or contradiction, allowing the generation of an integrative, general and particularistic theory of the symbolic role of ICT in a corporate image of legitimacy (Martin & Turner, 1986). Finally, implications of this model for managers and directions for future theory and research are discussed.

BACKGROUND AND HYPOTHESES

Corporate Image

No existing theory has looked specifically at the role of an SME's ICT use in creating legitimacy and encouraging customers to make purchases. The ICT and SME literature has focused on the role of ICT in improving substantive performance through operational efficiency and overcoming barriers to adoption (Parker & Castleman, 2007). The ICT literature has investigated how ICT adoption and use have affected the views of various organizational stakeholders (e.g. Fichman, 2000; Orlikowski & Iacono, 2000), but has not focused on customers' views of a firm. The organizational literature has investigated how firms are perceived by stakeholders and the effects of these views on organizational members (Gioia, Schultz, and Corley, 2000), but has not considered the role of ICT and the customer perspective.

How a firm is perceived has been termed its corporate image and definitions of corporate identity and image[2] have been extensively debated. Briefly, corporate identity is a firm's personality or the essence of what the firm is (Albert & Whetten, 1985; Balmer, 1998). It is reflective of the firm-level mission, values, history, philosophy, culture, and behavior (Ind, 1992; van Riel, 1997). Recent work in corporate brand management supports an inclusive and multidimensional conceptualization of corporate identity including the expression of a firm's: 1) corporate culture; 2) brand and organizational structure; 3) industry identity; and 4) strategic positioning; through 5) the behavior of the corporation, its employees, and managers; 6) corporate communication; and 7) corporate design, which includes corporate visual identity elements such as buildings, clothes, and graphics (Melewar & Karaosmanoglu, 2006).

Definitions of corporate image vary depending upon whose view of the corporation is emphasized. Consistent with the work of Berg (1985), our interest is in the views of customers. The perception of customers is the firm's corporate image (Melewar & Karaosmanoglu, 2006) and the importance of establishing a corporate image has long been accepted (Christian, 1959; Easton, 1966; Hatch & Schultz, 1997; Meyer & Rowan, 1977; Pfeffer & Salancik, 1978; Spector, 1961). The literature provides broad guidance on the dimensions of an SME that play a role in creating a corporate image but does not provide information about the detailed particularistic meanings of specific cues such as ICT.

Institutional Theory and Firm Image

From a more macro perspective, institutional theory focuses on the social structure of the environment and its effects on organizational decision making. Researchers have found that managers' choices, such as those involving adoption of ICT, often represent attempts to manage external images of the firm held by stakeholders such as customers (DiMaggio & Powell, 1983; Pfeffer & Salancik, 1978). A firm may differentiate itself in the marketplace by creating a distinct identity, managing its image by leveraging the symbolic and physical resources institutionalized in its business environment. However, firms are constrained in their differentiation and must be careful to remain within a range of acceptability. Managers manipulate symbols, but must be careful to convey the impression that the firm adheres to customer expectations and codes of conduct, which have been identified as central to corporate identity (Pfeffer & Salancik, 1978). Success depends on whether the manager knows and understands customer expectations and which symbols convey the "right" impression (Feldman & March, 1981). However, previous investigations of ICT adoption and use by SMEs have not considered their effects on customer's images of the firm and the pressures these exert on organizational decision-makers. If SMEs are aware of their customers' assumptions, they can adopt and use ICT to create a desirable corporate image that appeals to their target markets (Dutton & Dukerich, 1991).

Legitimacy

Creating and managing the stakeholder's impressions of the firm to gain access to external resources are crucial to the survival of the firm (Elsbach, et al., 1998; Pfeffer & Salancik, 1978, Starr & MacMillan, 1990; Stinchcombe, 1968). Successful resource acquisition depends on far more than merely locating useful sources; agents must also persuade resource owners to sell, lease or lend needed resources to the firm on favorable terms (Heugens & Lander, 2009). When resource owners evaluate the utility of providing resources, they evaluate tradeoffs across several issues: the possible return on investment; the attractiveness of that return versus alternative investment options; the consequences for their own strategic competitive positioning; legal and social implications, and so on (Gaglio, Cecchini & Winter, 1998). Not least among resource owners' considerations is the likelihood that they will indeed realize a positive return on investment and that there will be minimal, if any, negative consequences: in other words, how much risk and uncertainty is involved? If deemed too risky, resource owners will deny access. However, perceptions that the requesting firm has a credible track record of keeping commitments and performing as promised allows a resource owner to reframe the transaction's uncertainty into a calculated risk. Therefore, a central factor in a resource owner's tradeoffs and evaluation is his or her perceptions of the requesting firm's credibility and legitimacy.

While firm legitimacy is generally conceptualized as a complex belief that develops over time based on many of the firm's attributes, particularly performance (Arnold, Handelman & Tigert, 1996; Elsbach & Sutton, 1992; Suchman, 1995), it is also true that most potential supporters make quick assessments and judgments about a firm's legitimacy and the agent's credibility during surprisingly brief interactions (Gaglio, Cecchini & Winter, 1998). Nevertheless, these decisions can have important consequences. Positive decisions provide the opportunity for performance-based perceptions of legitimacy to develop through continued interactions over time. Negative decisions usually preclude any further interactions and so diminish the likelihood that the firm can establish credibility and legitimacy. Therefore, a firm's survival depends in large part upon its agents'

abilities to create and maintain impressions of the firm's credibility and legitimacy among resource owners and other stakeholders.

Threats to a firm's legitimacy can have profound consequences ranging from diverting resources to aggressively attack the threat (e.g., Ford Motor and Firestone coping with rollovers); to retiring the brand name and re-launching under another name (e.g., Hooker Chemicals after the Love Canal incident); to riding the demise of an industry (e.g., Philip Morris or RJR tobacco companies); to being driven out of business (e.g., Valuejet). Many small and young firms fail to build and maintain legitimacy and so die in the process of birth because they are unable to attract needed resources such as customers, capital and employees (Stinchcombe, 1965).

Given the importance of firm legitimacy and credibility, it is not surprising that the topic has attracted considerable scholarly attention. Despite the substantial body of literature, there is an important gap. The empirical literature tends to examine the strategies and tactics used to maintain or repair perceptions of firm legitimacy (Aldrich & Fiol, 1994; Allen & Caillouet, 1994; Elsbach, 1994); obviously, maintenance and repair require that perceptions already exist. There is little empirical evidence about how perceptions of firm legitimacy and credibility are established in the first place. Consequently, it is difficult to infer what kinds of criteria and heuristics stakeholders actually use to decide that a firm is legitimate enough to be worthy of support. Also, it is difficult to infer the role legitimacy truly plays in stakeholders' decisions to provide support; is legitimacy a necessary and sufficient condition?

Two routes for attaining legitimacy have been identified (Starr & MacMillan, 1990). The most compelling and credible route is to build a track record of performance and, ultimately, all firms must do this or fail. However, at birth, new firms or existing SMEs pursuing innovative ideas are caught in a "catch-22:" they cannot build a track record until at least one potential supplier, customer, or investor provides some indication of support, but none of these stakeholders will do so without at least the perception of legitimacy. Therefore, most SMEs rely on the second route and co-opt or borrow legitimacy by garnering endorsements and associations and by mimicking the standards, practices and cues that signal credibility and legitimacy in the industry (Heugens & Lander, 2009).

Before a track record has been established, innovative SMEs must give stakeholders permission to believe that there is something more behind the firm than just enthusiasm and good ideas. Legitimacy must be achieved and maintained because it allows a firm to attract employees, financing, supplier contracts and, most importantly, customers. Information has been shown to play a powerful role and to act as a signal and symbol of desirable organizational qualities. Simple possession of information in organizations can produce benefits irrespective of actual use (Feldman, 1989). Similarly, the long-recognized, socially interpreted properties of ICT (cf., Orlikowski 1991; Robey & Azevedo 1994) have been found to generate business value by acting as a symbol of legitimacy in large organizations (Noir & Walsham, 2007). It is possible that ICTs can also create and maintain legitimacy in SMEs.

For SMEs, most sales are made to other businesses (Levy & Powell, 2005) and success depends on the firm persuading potential customers to actually make purchases, a decision that hinges on perceptions of the firm's legitimacy (Suchman, 1995; Zimmerman, 1997, Zimmerman & Zeitz, 2002). Legitimacy is especially important for new firm survival (most begin as SMEs) because smaller and newer firms fail at a higher rate (Hannan & Freeman, 1984, Singh et al. 1986, Stinchcombe 1965) which suggests that obtaining access to resources may be more difficult (Singh, Tucker & Meinhard, 1991). However, little research on ICT use by SMEs has explicitly

considered its role in perceptions of legitimacy and purchase decisions.

Entrepreneurship lore is replete with anecdotes relating how founders deliberately manage perceptions of legitimacy (e.g., Darwell, Sahlman & Roberts, 1998). The entrepreneurs' initial job is to supply appropriate and sufficient symbols and cues regarding the new firm's legitimacy so that potential stakeholders are willing to accept the presence of an unseen organization and the resources required to provide the products or services described by the founder, to fill in any missing details, and to move on to considering the merits of the offering. To do this, entrepreneurs attempt to actively manage stakeholders' initial impressions regarding the new venture. The popular press offers numerous anecdotes about how startup firms use addresses, answering services, and so on, to convey the proper impression that attracts the right kind of customer or investor support (INC, 1995).

These stories also suggest that stakeholders make decisions with incomplete information. For example, the interactions often take place in the offices of customers, suppliers, retailers, bankers, and so on, or in neutral sites such as trade shows. Even those that take place on the firm's premises are limited to the on-stage areas of the firm with the backstage area normally unavailable for inspection (Grove & Fisk, 1989). This practice effectively limits stakeholders to only indirect information about the firm's capabilities and facilities. Similarly, potential stakeholders may ask for client references, but will likely be directed only to satisfied customers and may not even actually contact them. This limits stakeholders' knowledge about the firm's interaction style and performance record. Few stakeholders perform an exhaustive audit of the firm's financial, organizational or policy books before making decisions unless governmental regulations require it (Gaglio, Cecchini & Winter, 1998).

The anecdotes indicate that, in most cases, new and innovative firms co-opt legitimacy (Starr &

MacMillan, 1990) by obtaining endorsements and associations, and by mimicking the standards and practices of their relevant industries (Heugens & Lander, 2009; Pfeffer, 1981). Colorful stories are interesting and memorable but are not necessarily evidence, nor do they facilitate understanding how and why these kinds of tactics work. Nevertheless, the existence of such anecdotes indicates that firm founders and their potential stakeholders are consciously aware of and actively wrestling with the issue of firm legitimacy. Consequently, they may be able to speak feelingly and knowingly about the problems encountered and about the resolution or accommodation processes.

Thus, legitimacy is central to the process of survival of new organizations (Hannan & Freeman, 1984). By gaining legitimacy among its stakeholders a firm finds it easier to obtain access to resources, to respond to competition (Baum & Oliver, 1994) and attract customers (Wiewel & Hunter, 1985). Newer, smaller, and more innovative firms face a higher mortality risk due to a lack of external legitimacy (Singh et. al. 1986). In the absence of a track record of performance and in the face of potential customers who lack knowledge and understanding of the firm and its offerings (Aldrich & Fiol, 1994, Hannan & Carroll, 1992, Shepherd & Zacharakis, 2003), legitimacy is often conferred upon an SME when it is endorsed by influential external actors (Stinchcombe 1968) and strong relationships are developed with external constituencies (Singh et. al 1986).

One important task of SME founders is to create and maintain an image that attracts resources such as customers (Elsbach, Sutton & Principe, 1998; Meyer & Rowan, 1977; Starr & MacMillan, 1990). Legitimacy is a universally desirable corporate image that is judged based upon conformity to social norms and beliefs and is linked to purchasing and repeat business (Suchman, 1995; Zimmerman & Zeitz, 2002). Legitimacy is defined as a "generalized perception or assumption that the actions of an entity are desirable, proper, or appropriate within some socially constructed sys-

tem of norms, beliefs, and definitions" (Suchman, 1995, pg. 574). It is a quality of the firm, but is conferred by observers (who refer to a firm that is credible or real (Human & Provan, 2000)). For example, industry size is an indication of legitimacy (Hannan & Carroll, 1992; Ranger – Moore et al. 1991). Customers' assumptions about the appropriateness of adoption and use of ICT by an SME should affect their judgment of the SME as legitimate and desirable as an exchange partner (Dutton & Dukerich, 1991; Feldman & March, 1981) and influence the likelihood that they will make a purchase.

ICT and a Firm Image of Legitimacy

When examining the role of ICT in creating an image of a firm as legitimate, one is asking how SMEs can use ICT in ways that meet customer expectations. In order to solve the mystery of SME legitimacy, it appears that SMEs and customers activate schema about doing business in their industry, about doing business in general, and about new businesses. Schemas are mental models that reflect an individual's knowledge and beliefs about how the physical and social worlds work and are used to define reality and to guide understanding and action (Gioia, 1986). Schemas reflect an actor's understanding and feelings about the kinds of elements (events, people and objects) relevant to the current situation; the types of possible relationships among these elements; the typical rules governing the forming of such relationships; the types of possible causal sequences; and the types of actions that are permissible, sanctioned, and were previously successful or misguided (Fiske & Taylor, 1991; Markus & Zajonc, 1985).

Cognitive psychology assumes that information processing begins with the individual's classification of stimuli (firm, person, situation, media) based on matching the attributes of the stimuli with those of pre-existing schema categories. This perspective emphasizes a theory-driven or top-down approach. Given the complex nature of social worlds such as business and organizations, it is almost inconceivable that actors participate without the benefit of some learned mental structures to help organize and direct their experiences so this assumption is not unwarranted.

In this conceptualization, schema act as perceptual filters and interpretative frames; as such they do not need to be objectively accurate, just good enough to guide action and feeling (Weick, 1983). However, inconsistent information or stimuli are not always categorically rejected. When actors are motivated to be accurate, they will attend to incongruent or disconfirming stimuli and engage in additional cognitive processing. This additional effort improves the precision and scope of their existing schemas. Similarly, if the stimuli are not too incongruent, then regardless of motivation, actors will process the stimuli rather than simply discard it. These efforts, which indicate the dynamic nature of schema, ensure that they remain useful mental guides for information processing and action.

Presumably, SMEs' agents would call their schemas to mind as they create and manage impressions about their firms and stakeholders would call their mental models to mind as they listen to and evaluate the sales pitch or other information about an SME. The schema activated reflects an SME's agent and potential customers' knowledge and experiences with previous vendors or with other business people; activating these schema bring to mind a set of expectations, standards, and norms about good and bad business transactions. These schema blend together into a cognitive map against which customers then evaluate the specific SME in order to estimate the firm's legitimacy and to determine whether an order should be placed (Gaglio, Cecchini & Winter, 1998).

Schematic processing appears to be a very efficient method for handling what would otherwise prove to be overwhelming amounts of information (Bargh, 1984). Additional communication efficiencies are achieved when symbols are employed (Gioia, 1986). Indeed, since symbols

are broadly defined as signs that represent an entity, concept, or object that is significant for the perceiver, it appears that any verbal or nonverbal cues that activate a schema, must, by definition, be functioning as symbols.

Symbols

Symbols can include visual images, actions or non-actions (which may involve ICT, and metaphors (Morgan, Frost & Pondy, 1983). However, the communicative power of a symbol lies in the meaning attached to it and a symbol can have different connotations in different situations or to different social groups because a symbol has no meaning until it is socially constructed. Therefore, a symbol's connotations, like schema expectations, are context specific. While using symbols that have developed agreed upon significance acts as a sort of shorthand method of communication, it is important to remember that it is the meaning of a symbol, not the symbol itself, that guides subsequent behavior and influences beliefs and values.

In order to have meaning, symbols must express concepts in relation to other concepts that are already understood. When a potential symbol is encountered, it is compared to existing knowledge to generate meaning (Gioia, 1986). Understanding occurs when a current symbol is associated with one of these structured symbolic networks developed over time and stored in memory. Thus, symbols and schemas work together to produce "good-enough" meaning or understanding which guides interpretation and action in ambiguous or uncertain situations. Relative to the issue of establishing perceptions of SME legitimacy, social cognition theorists would frame the issue in terms of the founder's ability to match the attributes or symbols that stakeholders have in their business legitimacy schemas.

The literature does not provide guidance regarding the content of these schemas. This study develops a particularistic account of the symbols that ordinary people use to convey and evaluate images of legitimacy, focusing specifically on the role of ICTs as a cue and their meaning. These results are then related to existing theories identifying areas in which the data confirm or contradict existing explanations (Martin & Turner, 1986), integrating the inductively derived concepts with abstract theory and providing analytic generalization (Yin, 1989).

METHOD AND RESULTS

An inductive grounded methodology (Eisenhardt, 1989; Glaser & Strauss, 1967; Martin & Turner, 1986; Strauss & Corbin, 1998) was used to discover the role of ICT in communicating image and triggering a sale. Inductive grounded techniques are particularly appropriate for investigating relationships among context (including customer expectations) and actors, providing particularistic details to elaborate abstract substantive theories (Eisenhardt, 1989; Martin & Turner, 1986). Semi-structured in-depth interviews enabled a greater depth of understanding than could be developed with a questionnaire. Inductive methods allowed identification of the dimensions and language that are meaningful to the informants with legitimacy and customer expectations acting as sensitizing concepts (van den Hoonaard, 1997).

Procedures

To control for issues unrelated to the use of ICT that could affect an SME's image (e.g. a previous track record) we focused on sales pitches of new firms. Sales pitches of new firms are particularly appropriate for studying the process of creating legitimacy and acquiring customers. Founders often recount how they managed impressions of their firms when making their first sales, so the phenomena should be familiar to them (Darwell, et al., 1998) and attempts to establish perceptions all begin at the sales pitch to which each party

brings a set of assumptions, so it should be easier to identify participants' ICT assumptions. However, the meaning of ICT and the legitimacy images created are not expected to vary by firm age.

Informants: Two kinds of samples were drawn. SME founders and prospective customers (experienced buyers who have purchased from new firms). This allowed cross-checking and substantiation of the resulting constructs (Martin & Turner, 1986; Strauss & Corbin, 1998). The goal was to map the diversity of responses and generate theory applicable to various contexts, so the sample was constructed to include variety rather than statistical representation. This practice (called theoretical sampling (Denzin, 1989)) precludes drawing inferences about the norms in specific industries. When new interviews failed to yield novel responses, dimensions, or relationships, data collection ended. Two rounds of data collection allowed refinement of the questions and expansion of the sample (Denzin, 1989).

SME Founders: Samples were drawn using the Dun and Bradstreet database[3]. The first round included 15 founders in the San Francisco Bay Area; the second included 18 founders in South Florida (in total, a 27% participation rate). Founders often work in excess of 12 hours a day and many were too busy to participate.

Potential Customers: The second round included purchasers of 14 businesses in South Florida (a response rate of 15%) who received sales calls from a variety of vendors, and had recently used at least one new firm. To avoid inflating the degree of agreement, we included three buyers who had done business with a new firm in our sample and eleven who had not[4]. The firms represented various sectors, scopes and sizes (see Winter, Rajagopalan & Gaglio, 2009 for details). Purchase decisions also were diverse and ranged from purchasing office supplies, business services, raw materials and finished goods for resale through sub-contracting portions of the firm's activities.

Procedures: Sessions were conducted at the participants' places of business, lasted 45 to 90 minutes, were tape-recorded and later transcribed. The first round was performed by a trained master's student, the second by one of the authors.

First Iteration

Data Collection: The first round included only founders; open-ended questions encouraged respondents to talk about the issues that they considered important in convincing their first customers to place an order. Informants described the work their firm performs, their products, customers, competitors and the content of their first sales pitches. Probes asked about the most effective cues or tactics, including the role of ICT.

Data Analysis: The analysis proceeded iteratively; moving between the data, emerging theory and existing literature (Eisenhardt, 1989; Glaser & Strauss, 1967) allowing discrepancies to be reconciled, leading toward closure (Denzin, 1989). In open coding, categories were identified and microscopic data examination generated initial categories, recognized taken-for-granted

assumptions, and identified other cases for theoretical sampling (Strauss & Corbin, 1998). Theoretical comparisons were made between the images created by visual identity symbols such as furnishings and wardrobe and those created by ICT. Data were coded for the importance of violations of expectations, a sensitizing construct linked to legitimacy. Concepts were organized by recurring themes, forming stable and common categories during axial coding (Martin & Turner, 1986; Strauss & Corbin, 1998) yielding broad categories and associated concepts that described the participants' understanding of the symbolic information transmitted by ICT and its role in the purchase decision.

Findings[5]: The first step in determining whether prospective legitimacy is inferred from the presence of ICT was to determine whether the signaling function of ICT was tacit or explicit. As shown in Table 1, 85% of founders in the first round of interviews indicated that ICT improved operations, mentioning this aspect a total of 32 times. Some denied that ICT had any symbolic value and insisted that its only value was its functionality, although many were forthcoming

Table 1. Percent of 1st round SME founders (n=13) who discussed a category. Results of Fisher's exact test of the difference between 1st and 2nd round founders also shown

Element	%
Substantive Performance (Functionality Improves Operational Efficiency, Productivity, or Effectiveness)	85
Legitimacy	38*
Prototype Expectations	85
Taken-for-granted	77
Novel-Neutral	8*
Novel-Positive	23
Novel-Negative	0*
Support Decision	46
Positive	31
Negative	0
Neutral	15

* p < .05

about the symbolic role of office attire, location, and office furnishings.

Proposal Development and Presentation Training: The technology is essential ... but it is simply the tool... The thing that gives us an edge is not the technology but the office space.

About a third (38%) said that ICT symbolized their firm's legitimacy (e.g. seriousness, professionalism, size, or financial strength).

These results reflect the norm of rationality in the U.S. and an emphasis on the functional value of ICT in improving SME operations (Feldman & March, 1981; Hirschheim & Newman 1991; Kling & Iacono, 1984; Levy & Powell, 2005; Winter, 1996). They are consistent with literature suggesting that the symbolic meaning of an artifact such as ICT is unlikely to be elicited through direct questioning because meanings are often deeply connected with assumptions about the way the world works (Schein 1985).

This raised questions about whether symbolism works differently for ICT than it does for other artifacts, whether SME founders are unaware of ICT's symbolic value to customers or whether the symbolic meaning is tacit and so cannot be readily articulated. Consistent with Strauss and Corbin (1998), we hypothesized that our results reflected a taken-for-granted assumption about ICT and collected additional data to better understand the symbolism of ICT.

Second Iteration

Data Collection: Consistent with Denzin (1989) the second round of data collection included both SME founders and potential customers and the data collection methods were changed to surface taken-for-granted assumptions (see Winter, Rajagopalan & Gaglio, 2009 for details).

Data Analysis: Analysis of the second round proceeded much like that of the first with inductive open coding that included legitimacy, expectations and violations as sensitizing concepts (Martin & Turner, 1986). One author read the founder interview transcripts; the other read those of customers. Each created a preliminary inclusive framework representing the features of the data and the distinctions made by the informants (Martin & Turner, 1986; Strauss & Corbin, 1998). Comments were coded based on apparent category membership and axial coding was used to organize concepts (Martin & Turner, 1986; Strauss & Corbin, 1998). The data gathered from founders and customers were compared to identify their degree of overlap and a single integrative framework was created when it became clear that they included similar concepts. Comparing the data to the emerging model and discussing disagreements about the elements allowed continued refinement of the typology. These networks of categories were used to create theoretical constructs and associated maps of causal elements that were constructed into a theory of the role of ICT in firm legitimacy and purchase decisions. A model of the important elements, their cues and interrelationships was developed. The resulting framework derives empirical validity from accounting for the data and provides a general pattern across the data sources (Martin & Turner, 1986).

Transcripts were then coded for each element by the third author who counted the number of participants who mentioned a category and the number of times a category was mentioned. Fisher's Exact [6] tests were performed to determine whether the responses of second round founders differed from first round founders or from customers.

Findings – Theoretical Frame: Although developed later as an aggregation of the more detailed results, the abstract theoretical frame (paradigm model) that summarizes the theory is presented first (Strauss & Corbin, 1998). It shows how the elements of the constructs are connected and acts as a map to steer through the detailed results, which are presented after the model. At the highest level of abstraction, the purchase decision process (shown in Figure 1) resembles

Figure 1. Model of ICT, customer expectations, firm legitimacy and purchase

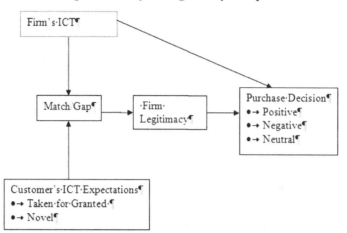

schema theory (Fiske & Taylor, 1991) and is influenced by the prototypes and mental models held by the prospective customer who infers SME legitimacy from the symbolic information provided by firm's ICT.

The SME founders and potential customers have formed mental models about various kinds of firms and their activities. A mental model consists of sets of interconnected information elements (including ICTs) and a prototype is a typical set of elements for a category. This mental model includes possible firm categories represented as prototypes, some of which are more likely to result in a positive transaction experience than others. The firm may be a legitimate, serious, professional, adequately capitalized company or an illegitimate company, a category that includes both inexperienced undercapitalized hobbyists trying to become professionals and firms of dubious legality sometimes called fly-by-night.

SMEs use ICTs in providing their products or services including both office technologies (e.g. inventory management systems, cell phones) and production technologies (e.g. CAD/CAM, robotics). A firm's representative contacts a potential customer and makes a sales pitch describing the company and its products or services and may describe their ICTs or provide indirect evidence of them. During a sales pitch, the potential cus-

tomer tries to learn what kind of firm he or she is dealing with to determine the likelihood that placing an order would result in a positive transaction. Potential customers match the firm's ICT to those expected in each prototype and categorize a firm as legitimate or illegitimate based on the characteristics shared. Some ICTs will be taken-for-granted or assumed to be in use, others may be novel or optional in that they may or may not be present. Once a firm has been categorized, it is assumed to have other characteristics of the category (honesty, trustworthiness, etc.) based on the interconnected information elements in the mental model, even if the potential customer has not experienced them directly. These inferred characteristics of the firm then influence the likelihood that a potential customer will actually place an order. In addition to corporate image effects, ICT has a direct effect on purchase decisions if customers find them more convenient.

In the following section, these concepts and their interactions are discussed in detail.

Findings – Model Elements: Participants were clearly more comfortable discussing the functionality of ICT than its symbolic meaning, suggesting that functionality is explicit and symbolic meaning is more tacit. However, we found four patterns linking ICT to corporate image. First, customers' symbolic meanings and those of founders were very similar suggesting that accurate signaling can occur and that the latter could purposefully manipulate their ICT use to create desired corporate images. Further, founders were aware of the customers' perspective and those meanings were instrumental in their ICT adoption decisions. Second, firm legitimacy characteristics are inferred from ICT and linked to decisions to support the firm. Third, three distinct patterns link violations of expectations about a firm's ICT to its image. A firm could be missing an ICT whose presence had been taken-for-granted, include a novel ICT that detracts from a firm's image, or include a novel ICT that enhances its image. Each of these areas is described in more detail below.

Functionality vs. Symbolic Meaning

Institutional theory has shown that organizational choices can simultaneously enhance both a firm's substantive performance and social judgments of its symbolic performance through conformity with stakeholder expectations (Heugens & Lander,

2009). As shown in Table 2, an overwhelming majority of second round participants (97%) mentioned the substantive performance value of ICT 126 times in total. However, the use of focus group techniques yielded much more information about the symbolic meaning of ICT than was uncovered in the first round of interviews. As shown in Tables 1 and 2, the percentage of first and second round founders linking ICT to social judgments of legitimacy increased significantly (1st round: 38%; 2nd round 87%; Fisher's Exact $p<.05$) and 90% of the second round participants linked ICT and legitimacy.

Similarity between Founder and Customer Views

In the second round of interviews, participants articulated a consistent set of issues surrounding legitimacy, ICT and purchase decisions. Both founders and customers reported similar views of each of the ten elements of the model, but four of these elements appear to be more salient

Table 2. Percent of 2nd found respondents who discussed a category broken down by SME founder vs. customer. Results of Fisher's exact test of the difference between 2nd round founders and customers also shown

	Founders n=15	Customers n =14	Founders & Customers n=29	
Element	**%**	**%**	**%**	**No. of Times Mentioned**
Substantive Performance (Functional Improves Operational Efficiency, Productivity, or Effectiveness)	93	100	97	126
Legitimacy	87	93	90	92
Prototype Expectations	100	100	100	433
Taken-for-granted	93	86	90	254
Novel-Neutral	67	71	69	93
Novel-Positive	47	86*	66	72
Novel-Negative	40	36	38	14
Support Decision	60	100*	79	125
Positive	33	79*	55	61
Negative	20	7	14	5
Neutral	47	93*	69	59

* $p < .05$

to customers than to founders. Customers were significantly more likely to identify ICTs that were novel and helped form a positive image of the firm (mentioned 16 times by 47% of founders vs. 56 times by 86% of customers), to link ICT directly to support (mentioned 26 times by 60% of founders vs. 99 times by 100% of customers), to discuss a positive link between ICT and making a purchase (mentioned 29 times by 33% of founders vs. 49 times by 79% of customers), and to identify ICTs that would have no effect on their decision to make a purchase (mentioned 10 times by 47% of founders vs. 49 times by 93% of customers).

Founders also indicated that they were aware of the customer's perspective and that ICT adoption decisions were influenced by the desire to create a particular corporate image.

Medical Lab: I think that to be in the business world you need a Web page and people do judge you ... whether they be potential clients or whoever, and they'll look at your Web page and ... there's a better feel for us as a company when they see our Web page.

This strong overlap between the views of founders and customers is not surprising. Shared meanings, communication, and organized action are reciprocally interdependent (Donnellon, Gray, & Bougon, 1986) and would be required for an SME founder to successfully create an image of legitimacy.

Legitimacy Inferred From ICT

There was no statistically significant difference between the percentage of founders (87%) and the percentage of customers (93%) who reported inferring an SME's legitimacy from its ICT. ICT acts as a cue symbolizing dimensions of legitimacy (Suchman, 1995), which was mentioned by the overwhelming majority (90%) of the participants a total of 92 times. Participants agree that legitimacy

influences the firm's ability to attract customers, and often mention legitimacy elements (size, seriousness, professionalism, capitalization) and support together.

Apparel Catalog: It's the little things that make you aware of what type of company you're dealing with. Again, if they don't have voice mail, if they don't have a cell phone, if they don't have fax capabilities, e-mail capabilities, these are the signs. This is what you sense. This is how you know that this isn't a real big company. If they make the commitment to have a fax machine, to have everything in place before they start up then they are a little more serious and maybe you'll take the chance and take the risk of putting the product in the book... You know that they're not financed if they don't even have a fax machine

Although conceptually distinct, the elements of legitimacy are mentioned together and cued by the same symbol, suggesting that they co-occur in participants' mental models of legitimate and illegitimate firms. This is consistent with the retrieval of prototype characteristics as outlined in the earlier paradigm model (Fiske & Taylor, 1991). Large, serious, professional firms are often contrasted with "hobbyists" or "fly-by-night" firms, suggesting that these represent common firm prototypes. Consistent with previous research on legitimacy, no participants wanted to work with "hobbyists" or "fly-by-night" firms.

Our results suggest that the adoption and use of ICT is a form of behavior linked to judgments that a firm is legitimate, an image that is universally desirable and is central to a firm's success (Zimmerman & Zeitz, 2002). Customers' assumptions about the appropriate adoption and use of ICT affect their judgment of the firm as legitimate. If decision-makers adopt and use ICT in ways that are consistent with customers' assumptions about what is appropriate, they can create an image of legitimacy, avoid being labeled "fly-by-night", and improve the likelihood that they will receive customer orders (Dutton & Dukerich, 1991).

Creating and maintaining a corporate image requires SMEs to choose behavioral, verbal and non-verbal symbols to convey the impression that the firm adheres to the stakeholders' expectations and codes of conduct identified by institutionalism (Pfeffer & Salancik, 1978). These codes of conduct reflect the system of meaning that underlies the social construction of reality (Berger & Luckmann, 1967; Feldman & March, 1981; Schein, 1985) and allows actors to make sense of their world by interpreting symbols (Gioia, 1986). This paper provides evidence that ICT is one of those symbols and that these expectations form accepted standards for ICT use (DiMaggio & Powell, 1983) informed by customers' mental models and SME prototypes. Legitimacy influences purchase decisions, a crucial determinant of SME survival.

ICT Linked To Purchase Decisions

An SME's ICT can make purchase decisions more likely or less likely, often depending on the ICTs involved (although sometimes they have no effect). However, some participants linked support with specific ICTs, while others linked it to an SME being "high tech" reflecting the influence of a constellation of ICTs.

As previously mentioned and shown in Table 2, support issues were more salient to customers than to founders, but overall 79% of participants mentioned a link (positive, negative or neutral) between ICT and support 125 times. More specifically, 55% mentioned 61 times that some ICTs could increase the probability of support (often, this was stated in the negative in that they would not make a purchase from a firm that did not have an ICT, implying that having the ICT is positively related to support).

System Integrator: I can't imagine that they would want to do business with somebody that didn't use email.

Promotional Products: If a company now doesn't have a fax machine, I probably wouldn't do business with them

About two-thirds (69%) of participants mentioned 59 times that that having or not having some forms or ICT would have no effect on purchase decisions.

Spa and Beauty Supply: I don't expect it (fax machine, computer, beepers, cell phones) and I would not stop doing business with somebody because of it. Nor would I necessarily consider not doing business with them because of that.

A small percentage of respondents (14%) mentioned 5 times that some ICTs would decrease the likelihood of a sale.

Community Association Manager: I prefer a company that does not have voicemail, but they're hard to find.

Thus, ICT is among the elements considered by customers in deciding whether or not to place an order with an SME, an example of what the legitimacy literature calls providing active support (Suchman, 1995). Although conceptually distinct, many authors treat legitimacy and support of a firm as overlapping constructs and some indicators of legitimacy (e.g. certification) are also indicators of support (Suchman, 1995). The use of ICT may allow SMEs to create an image of legitimacy (Pfeffer & Salancik, 1978) through trait-based, frequency-based, or outcome-based imitation (Heugens & Lander, 2009), and provide a survival advantage because ICT's symbolic meanings increase the likelihood that an SME will attract customers.

Mismatches and their Effects on Corporate Image of Legitimacy

Creating an image of legitimacy requires conformity with customer expectations (Heugens & Lander, 2009; Meyer & Rowan, 1977; Pfeffer & Salancik, 1978; Suchman, 1995; Scott, 2001; Zimmerman & Zeitz, 2002). So, we examined the effects of mismatches between the use of ICT and customers' expectations, one of our sensitizing concepts. We found three different kinds of mismatches that affected legitimacy and purchase decisions. A firm could be missing an ICT that customers had taken-for-granted; include an ICT that is novel in that it is not taken-for-granted, but enhances the firm's image; or it could include an ICT that is novel and detracts from the firm's image.

Table 2 shows that both SME founders and customers had expectations about the kinds of ICT firms should have (mentioned 433 times by 100% of participants). Three distinct patterns link violations of expectations about firm's ICT to its image. First, 90% of participants indicated 254 times that some kinds of ICT are taken-for-granted.

Environmental Clean-up Consulting: [Didn't have e-mail?] 'Wow! Where have you been?' You know, it's like they should have it. Even if it's at hotmail. com ... That's just, I expect it.

Systems Integrator: I can't imagine a company existing without pagers. I mean, we use pagers so you can send a message. I just can't imagine.

This is consistent with what Saga and Zmud (1994) have called the routinization stage of ICT implementation, and with schema theory, the use of mental models, and prototypes (Fiske & Taylor, 1991). Some ICTs have been so completely integrated into the business world that customers' SME prototypes invariably include this element.

When a mental model of legitimate firms is accessed, these ICTs are among the characteristics assumed to be present, even if they have not been observed. SMEs that do not have them are less likely to be seen as legitimate. Their absence violates expectations and raises legitimacy concerns because of the symbolic meaning attached to the technology.

But, contrary to legitimacy theory, mismatches do not always lead to judgments that a firm is not legitimate and may not even reflect positively on the firm if the ICT is novel rather than taken-for-granted. About two-thirds (66%) of participants indicated 72 times that the symbolic meaning of a novel ICT is also considered and can lead customers to infer that a firm shares their values, and that they should place an order.

Wireless Services Provider: E-mail, yes. They don't have to have it but it's a one up, it's a plus if they do.

General Contractor: [Vendors who bring in results of computer runs] Gives us a comfort level as opposed to the one that's scratched out on a piece of paper.

Of course, the converse is also true. Customers use the symbolic meaning of novel ICT to infer that a SME's actions will be undesirable, although it may not reflect upon the firm's legitimacy. For example, customers often encounter automated call routing to answer incoming calls, so the presence of this ICT cannot be considered a violation of expectations. However, many infer that firms using call routing are large, uncaring and will treat them impersonally. Overall, 38% of participants indicated 14 times that a novel ICT can be considered detrimental to a firm's image without affecting its legitimacy.

Community Association Manager: [Automated call routing indicates a firm is] too big. Unpersonal [sic]. Yeah, I don't like it. I hate it.

The determining factors are whether this deviation from expectations is within the range of acceptability and whether the underlying symbolic meaning ascribed to the novel technology is consistent with the customer's values and ideas about desirable firms. For example, if industry leadership is considered desirable, an ICT that signals this enhances a firm's image. If large, uncaring firms are considered undesirable, automated call routing ICT that signals this detracts from a firm's image. Thus, consistent with Saga and Zmud's (1994) implementation phases, ICT that is accepted, but not taken-for-granted, is viewed as novel.

Schema theory would suggest that these technologies are not elements of all SME prototypes, so their presence or absence is used in classifying firms according to their desirability as exchange partners (Fiske & Taylor, 1991). In contrast, legitimacy theory asserts that the presence of a novel ICT violates expectations, so the probability of a purchase should always be diminished (Suchman, 1995). Our data contradicts legitimacy theory by providing evidence that these mismatches can be positive, enhancing an SME's image, and increasing the likelihood of a sale depending upon the inferences that customers draw about the firm's values and the desirability of its actions based on the symbolic meaning underlying a novel ICT. When these are positive, the firm's image is enhanced. When they are negative, it is diminished. In contrast, violating expectations regarding a taken-for-granted ICT always diminishes a firm's image. This relationship is shown in Table 3.

How and Why ICT Acts as a Symbol

Information about SMEs is stored as mental models comprising multiple elements (Gaglio, Cecchini & Winter, 1998). Pre-existing categories of firms form prototypes that reflect particular constellations of elements, including ICT artifacts which act as cues from which a firm's legitimacy dimensions (e.g. size, professionalism, seriousness, and capitalization) are inferred. These dimensions are bundled together in the mental model, along with additional details that are filled in (inferred). As the SME founder makes a sales pitch, customers glean information about the firm's ICT and compare it to their expectations regarding each ICT mental model element. The observed and inferred characteristics are used to categorize firms by comparison with existing firm prototypes (e.g. legitimate vs. hobbyists or fly-by-night). SMEs that share a large number of traits or characteristics with the prototype for a legitimate and desirable exchange partner will be considered legitimate and be preferred by customers. When customers and founders attribute similar meanings to ICT, the SME can better control the image communicated through apparent trait-based imitation of legitimate firms (Heugens & Lander, 2009).

This process resembles schematic processing of symbols, which can include artifacts such as ICT and actions such as their use (Bargh, 1984; Gioia, 1986; Morgan, Frost & Pondy, 1983). Information processing begins with the classi-

Table 3. Relationship between ICT novelty, presence, and corporate Image of legitimacy

ICT	Taken-for-granted	Novel	
		Positive	Negative
Present	Legitimate	Positive Image	Negative Image
Absent	Not Legitimate	Neutral Image	Neutral Image

fication of stimuli based on matching attributes with those of pre-existing categories stored in schemas. Once categorized, missing pieces are filled in with category-consistent information. When a potential symbol is encountered, it is compared to existing schemas to generate meaning (Gioia, 1986). When a symbol is associated with a schema, understanding occurs that guides interpretation and action in ambiguous or uncertain situations. The communicative power of symbols lies in the meaning attached to them, which, like schemas, varies in different situations or social groups (Berger & Luckman, 1967).

In the absence of prior interaction with an SME, potential customers generate meaning by scrutinizing available signals, such as ICT (Snyder & Stukas, 1999), compare this information to their schemas for the use of ICT by legitimate firms, classify the firm into an appropriate category, fill in missing information, and make inferences about the desirability of the SME as an exchange partner. Quite simply, legitimacy is judged based partly upon ICT whose meaning has been stored in schemas reflecting social institutions (Barley & Tolbert, 1997). The ICT acts as a symbol of conformity to the expectations and values of the perceiver for legitimate firms. To be judged desirable, a firm should match customers' schemas for desirable firms or violate them in a manner that indicates pursuit of goals that conform to market segment values (Heugens & Lander, 2009). Thus, an ICT can affect a firm's substantive performance, but its symbolic meaning simultaneously affects the firm's image and influences purchase decisions that determine survival.

Contributions and Limitations

We developed a general and particularistic model of the issues surrounding the symbolic value of ICT, legitimacy, and customers' purchase behavior. This study extends our understanding of the creation of legitimacy, mental models, and schemas to identify the language, behavior and symbols

that ordinary people use to convey and evaluate images, focusing specifically on the role of ICT as a signal, the firm characteristics that are linked to legitimacy, and how ICTs carry meaning. In addition, it clarifies that mismatches between audience expectations about an SME's ICT are not always negative.

DISCUSSION

Our results show that ICT does signal legitimacy. When asked directly, participants suggest a purely functional explanation for ICT adoption, reflecting the norm of rationality and social desirability (Feldman & March, 1981; Kling & Iacono, 1984; Winter, 1996). However, less salient dimensions were elicited using focus group techniques. Most of our respondents when asked about adopting technology argued for the rational and functional view of ICT yet when it came to behaving as a customer they were also affected by its symbolic aspects. Participants may be unaware of or unable to articulate the symbolic nature of ICT, but be influenced by its symbolic aspects and its ability to create SME legitimacy.

The ultimate purpose of a sales pitch is to make a sale, but a proximal purpose is the display of symbols such as ICT that create a positive image of the firm. Potential customers clearly use ICT to infer legitimacy and fill in unknown details from existing prototypes. They seek to categorize the firm in terms of its type, based in part on a comparison of its ICT capabilities with those that were expected. Classification into the preferred exchange partner category is crucial to the survival of SMEs because they seldom have the resources to overcome a poor corporate image. This study extends the literature on the symbolic meaning of ICT by considering the customer's view of SMEs and the effects of ICT on purchase behavior and extends the literature on corporate image to include the effects of ICT.

Implications for Managers

Purchase decisions are influenced by potential customers' images of the firm. Decisions about the use of ICT in SMEs should consider image issues and symbolic meaning in addition to operational efficiency and effectiveness concerns and executives must be familiar with their stakeholders' expectations regarding an ICT. As institutional theory predicts, an SME that fails to adopt an ICT that has become taken-for-granted will find it more difficult to make the sales required to survive. As schema theory predicts (especially for ICT that is novel), executives must understand the symbolic meaning underlying ICT use to ensure a positive interpretation. For example, voice mail call routing may enhance one firm's image of efficiency, but may be incompatible with another's efforts to be seen as providing excellent personalized customer service. Unlike larger corporations, managing corporate image through the use of ICT is critically important for SMEs. SMEs do not have well established brand images based on corporate reputation or a proven track record of performance. They must create an image of legitimacy before they have established a reputation based on performance, created a large customer base or been able to mount a broad marketing campaign. SMEs must rely most heavily on signals and symbols and should include both the symbolic and the productivity dimension in any calculation of the business value of ICT.

Implications for Theory

This study found a strong relationship between the symbolic meaning of an ICT, a corporate image of legitimacy, and purchase behavior. SMEs that wish to attract customers should consider the benefits of choosing ICT that creates a corporate image of legitimacy, even if the ICT yields limited improvement in substantive performance. To be most effective, an SME's ICT choices should be guided by both customer expectations and productivity concerns.

Customers are motivated tacticians actively working to decide whether the SME is the kind of firm that they want to support. They take an active role in perceiving, organizing and drawing inferences based on the limited information provided by the objects and events they encounter. The meanings that customers derive from these symbols act as clues in the support puzzle. Missing data is filled in, inferences are drawn and firms are rapidly categorized (as, for example, hobbyist, competent, etc.). Perhaps the most plausible account of these data is schema-based.

The psychological literature on social cognition describes the individual level process of decision-making by detailing the cognitive structures, called schema, that drive how information is perceived, stored and used to form judgments (Fiske & Taylor, 1991). These concepts have not previously been applied to the decision to provide support for an SME, but institutional theory rests on concepts that are central to social cognition such as schemas and scripts (Barley & Tolbert, 1997; Powell & DiMaggio, 1991). The legitimacy elements and process described by Suchman (1995) can be reconciled with theories of social cognition.

A Social Cognitive View of SME Legitimacy and Support

Schemas are organized knowledge bases about a given area that actively guide the information perceived, the information retrieved from memory, the inferences that are drawn, and the action plans considered (Fiske & Taylor, 1991; Johnston & Dark, 1986). Every individual has hundreds of schemas stored in memory, including those used to sort people and firms into groups based on an abstract set of features typically associated with that category (a prototype). Something is judged to be a member of a category if it shared a sufficient number of features with the category's prototype. Once it is categorized, the perceiver fills in missing pieces or gaps with category consistent information. When actors are concerned about accurate classification, information that is not consistent with the prototype will be noticed and undergo further processing to discount the information or change the schema.

A social cognitive explanation of SME support rests on the assumption that existing schemas and expectations shape the perception process. They affect what we notice about a firm's form and activities and how we interpret what we perceive. These driving schemas can be considered the system of shared norms, values, beliefs and definitions that play a central role in institutionalism and legitimacy. Cognitive psychologists (Fiske & Taylor, 1991; Johnston & Dark, 1986; Lord & Foti, 1986) would argue that, when entering into the sales pitch, both the SME's agents and prospective customers activate their respective schemas regarding a sales pitch and other associated topics, including various prototypical organizations (e.g. mom-and-pop, fly-by-night, established). Customers listen to the sales pitch and compare its cues and symbols (such as ICT) to their mental models. As suggested by schema theory, minor mismatches or violations are ignored; major violations are considered inconsistencies in the story and prompt a search for more information. Missing information may go undetected because the customer fills in the details based on the activated mental models.

Certainly, our data show evidence of pattern matching, which appears to support the hypothesized cognitive dynamics. Customers use ICT as a cue to categorize SMEs based on how well they match prototypes of legitimate firms. The limited information provided during the sales pitches is compared to the schema elements for prototypes of various kinds of firms and checked for consistency. Customers pay particular attention to features that appear in one prototype but not another, because they are diagnostic of category membership, and additional category consistent information is filled in.

Cues and symbols inform the customer about the firm's form and activities. Driven by relevant schemas, firms' ICT characteristics can be perceived, assumed or inferred. The meaning underlying cues and symbols will be particularly important to customers' support behavior when no track record of performance is available. Firms that share many elements with an appropriate prototype are deemed a good enough match to receive provisional support. Firm support, then, depends on two kinds of congruence. First, the firm's perceived form and activities must be congruent with those of a recognizable prototype. Second, that prototype must match the customer's preferences for a business partner. For example, some customers preferred to work with suppliers that were small, but others preferred large firms.

Legitimacy and Support

A social cognitive view of SME support also suggests a helpful distinction between legitimacy and support. The behavioral decision making literature distinguishes between a judgment, which reflects a psychological appraisal and can result in a decision, which involves a behavioral component (Stevenson, et al., 1990). From this perspective, legitimacy is a judgment because it is defined as a perception or assumption (Suchman, 1995). Passive support that is limited to a psychological appraisal (such as forming a positive attitude) would also be a judgment. Positive judgments may lead to support behavior, which would be a decision. By definition, active support involves a change in behavior and so represents a decision. This distinction could help guide future research on SME legitimacy and help disentangle it from SME support.

In sum, social cognition highlights the role of perception and schemas in the judgment process. An SME is judged to be a desirable partner when its perceived behavior is congruent with shared norms, beliefs and values stored in memory as schemas. SME survival depends on positive judgments leading to decisions to provide support. Consistent with social cognition, congruence implies a matching process such as that found in schema theory, the resulting categorization of an SME reflects a form of judgment and supporting the firm represents a decision.

Social cognition does not provide guidance about the different dimensions on which SMEs are judged or the firm characteristics that would predict support. Its contribution is to clarify the judgment processes mediating between perceived information and the support behavior (Fiske & Taylor, 1991). The definitions of legitimacy found in the organizational institutionalism literature provide some guidance on which perceptions are relevant, what kinds of legitimacy are judged and what kinds of support can be provided, but these do not consistently match the implicit theories guiding SME and customer behavior and shown in Figure 1. These results also contribute to our understanding of the relationship between symbolic meaning and action. Organizational cognition suggest that the symbolic meaning of an ICT will dominate diffusion before its productivity effects have been documented and may continue thereafter as the presence of an ICT innovation becomes an institutionalized norm. Corporate image forms a valuable link between the symbolic meaning of ICT and its diffusion. Integrating these fields clarifies how an ICT acquires symbolic meaning allowing it to be used by SMEs to create and maintain corporate images. Social cognition and the role of schemas in interpreting an ICT as a cue are central to the creation of perceptions that a firm is legitimate, is a desirable exchange partner and is more likely to be supported.

CONCLUSION

SMEs face particularly difficult survival challenges with success dependent upon persuading potential customers to actually make purchases, a decision that hinges on perceptions regarding the firm's legitimacy (Suchman, 1995; Zimmerman & Zeitz, 2002). Consequently, SME survival depends in large part on creating and maintaining impressions of the firm's legitimacy among external stakeholders (Darwell, et al. 1998). This study has shown that potential customers make snap judgments about a firm's legitimacy based on expectations regarding the use of ICT due to its symbolic meaning and has begun to explore the processes by which ICT acts as a symbol. Future research should consider other valued organizational outcomes related to the symbolic meaning of ICT for external stakeholders, such as attracting valued employees, financing and accreditation or licensure. In addition, the meanings of ICT and mediating concepts of corporate image will likely differ by industry, time period and culture. To provide additional value in guiding practice, considerably more work is needed to map the meanings of particular ICTs to different contexts. Understanding the complex multidimensional costs and benefits of ICT will allow us to develop a more complete view of its business value for SMEs.

REFERENCES

Albert, S., & Whetten, D. (1985). Organizational identity. In L.L. Cummings & B. Staw (Eds.), Research in organizational behavior, 7 (pp. 263-295). Greenwich, CT: JAI Press.

Aldrich, H. E., & Fiol, C. M. (1994). Fools rush in? The institutional context of industry creation. *Academy of Management Review*, *19*(4), 645–670. doi:10.2307/258740

Allen, M. W., & Caillouet, R. H. (1994). Legitimation endeavors: Impression management strategies used by an organization in crisis. *Communication Monographs*, *61*, 44–62. doi:10.1080/03637759409376322

Arnold, S. J., Handelman, J., & Tigert, D. J. (1996). Organizational legitimacy and retail store patronage. *Journal of Business Research, 35*, 229–239. doi:10.1016/0148-2963(95)00128-X

Balmer, J. M. T. (1998). Corporate identity and advent of corporate marketing. *Journal of Marketing Management, 14*, 963–996. doi:10.1362/026725798784867536

Bargh, J. A. 1984. Automatic and conscious processing of social information. In R.S. Wyer, Jr., & T.K. Srull (Eds.), Handbook of social cognition (pp. 1-43). Hillsdale, NJ: Erlbaum.

Barley, S. R., & Tolbert, P. S. (1997). Institutionalization and structuration: Studying the links between action and institution. *Organization Studies, 18*(1), 93–117. doi:10.1177/017084069701800106

Baum, J. A., & Oliver, C. (1991). Institutional linkages and organizational mortality. *Administrative Science Quarterly, 36*(2), 187–219. doi:10.2307/2393353

Berg, P. O. (1985). Organization change as a symbolic transformation process. In P. Frost, L. Moore, M.R. Louis, C. Lundberg, & J. Martin (Eds.), Reframing organizational culture (pp. 281-300). Beverly Hills, CA: Sage.

Berger, P. L., & Luckmann, T. (1967). The social construction of reality. NY: Anchor Books.

Bharati, P., & Chaudhury, A. (2006). Current status of technology adoption: Micro, small and medium manufacturing firms in Boston. *Communications of the ACM, 49*(10), 88–93. doi:10.1145/1164394.1164400

Blili, S., & Raymond, L. (1993). Information technology: Threats and opportunities for small and medium sized enterprises. *International Journal of Information Management, 13*(6), 439–448. doi:10.1016/0268-4012(93)90060-H

Christian, R. C. (1959). Industrial marketing. *Journal of Marketing*, 79–80. doi:10.2307/1248856

Dandridge, J. C. (1979). Children are not small grown ups – Small businesses need their own organizational theory. *Journal of Small Business Management, 17*(2), 53–57.

Darwell, C., Sahlman, W. A., & Roberts, M. J. (1998). DigitalThink: Startup (Case # 9-898-186). Cambridge, MA: Harvard Business School Publishing.

Denzin, N. K. (1989). The research act: A theoretical introduction to sociological methods. Englewood Cliffs, NJ: Prentice Hall.

DiMaggio, P. J., & Powell, W. W. (1983). The iron cage revisited: Institutional isomorphism and collective rationality in organizational fields. *American Sociological Review, 48*, 147–160. doi:10.2307/2095101

Donnellon, A., Gray, B., & Bougon, M. G. (1986). Communication, meaning, and organized action. *Administrative Science Quarterly, 31*(1), 43–55. doi:10.2307/2392765

Dutton, J., & Dukerich, J. (1991). Keeping an eye on the mirror: Image and identity in organizational adaptation. *Academy of Management Review, 34*, 517–554. doi:10.2307/256405

Easton, A. (1966). Corporate style versus corporate image. *JMR, Journal of Marketing Research, 3*, 68–174. doi:10.2307/3150206

Eisenhardt, K. M. (1989). Building theories from case study research. *Academy of Management Review, 14*(4), 532–550. doi:10.2307/258557

Elsbach, K. D. (1994). Managing organizational legitimacy in the California cattle industry: The construction and effectiveness of verbal accounts. *Administrative Science Quarterly, 39*, 57–88. doi:10.2307/2393494

Elsbach, K. D., & Sutton, R. I. (1992). Acquiring organizational legitimacy through illegitimate actions: A marriage of institutional and impression management theories. *Academy of Management Journal, 35*(4), 699–738. doi:10.2307/256313

Elsbach, K. D., Sutton, R. I., & Principe, K. E. (1998). Averting expected challenges through anticipatory impression management: A Study of hospital billing. *Organization Science, 9*(1), 68–86. doi:10.1287/orsc.9.1.68

Feldman, M. S. (1989). Order without design: Information production and policy making. Stanford, CA: Stanford University Press.

Feldman, M. S., & March, J. G. (1981). Information in organizations as signal and symbol. *Administrative Science Quarterly, 26*(2), 171–186. doi:10.2307/2392467

Fichman, R. (2000). The diffusion and assimilation of information technology innovations. In R. Zmud (Ed.), Framing the Domains of IT Management: Projecting the Future Through the Past (pp. 105-104). Cincinnati, OH: R. Pinnaflex Educational Resources.

Fiske, S. T., & Taylor, S. E. (1991). Social cognition (2nd ed.). New York: McGraw Hill.

Gaglio, C. M., Cecchini, M., & Winter, S. (1998). Gaining legitimacy: The symbolic use of technology by new ventures. In Frontiers of Entrepreneurship Research (pp. 208-215). Wellesley, MA: Babson College.

Gioia, D. A. (1986). Symbols, scripts, and sensemaking: creating meaning in the organizational experience. In H.P. Sims, Jr., & D.A. Gioia (Eds.), The thinking organization: Dynamics of organization cognition (pp. 49-74). San Francisco: Jossey Bass.

Gioia, D. A., Shultz, M., & Corley, K. G. (2000). Organizational identity, image, and adaptive instability. *Academy of Management Review, 25*(1), 63–81. doi:10.2307/259263

Glaser, B. G., & Strauss, A. L. (1967). The discovery of grounded theory. Chicago, IL: Aldine.

Gregor, S., Martin, M., Fernandez, W., Stern, S., & Vitale, M. (2006). The transformational dimension in the realization of business value from information technology. *The Journal of Strategic Information Systems, 15*, 249–270. doi:10.1016/j.jsis.2006.04.001

Grove, S. J., & Fisk, R. P. (1989). Impression management in services marketing: A dramaturgical perspective. In R.A. Giacalone and P. Rosenfeld (Eds.), Impression management in the organization (pp. 427-438). Hillsdale, NJ: Lawrence Erlbaum.

Hannan, M. T., & Carroll, G. R. (1992). Dynamics of organizational populations: Density, legitimation, and competition. New York: Oxford University Press.

Hannan, M. T., & Freeman, J. (1984). Structural inertia and organizational change. *American Sociological Review, 49*(2), 149–164. doi:10.2307/2095567

Harrison, R. T., Dibben, M. R., & Mason, C. M. (1997). The role of trust in the informal investor's investment decision: An exploratory analysis. *Entrepreneurship Theory and Practice, 21*(4), 63–81.

Hatch, M. J., & Schultz, M. (1997). Relations between organizational culture, identity, and image. *European Journal of Marketing, 5*(6), 356–365.

Heugens, P. P. M. A. R., & Lander, M. W. (2009). Structure! Agency! (and other quarrels), A meta-analysis of institutional theories of organization. *Academy of Management Journal, 52*(1), 61–85.

Hirschheim, R., & Newman, R. (1991). Symbolism and information systems development: Myth, metaphor and magic. *Information Systems Research, 2,* 29–62. doi:10.1287/isre.2.1.29

Human, S. E., & Provan, K. G. (2000). Legitimacy building in the evolution of small firm multilateral networks: A comparative study of success and demise. *Administrative Science Quarterly, 45,* 327–365. doi:10.2307/2667074

Ind, N. (1992). The corporate image. London: Kogan Page.

Jackson, M. H., Poole, M. S., & Kuhn, T. (2002). The social construction of technology in studies of the workplace. In L. Lievrouw & S. Livingstone (Eds.), Handbook of new media: Social shaping and consequences of ICTs (pp. 236-253).

Johnston, W. A., & Dark, V. J. (1986). Selective attention. *Annual Review of Psychology, 37,* 43–75. doi:10.1146/annurev.ps.37.020186.000355

Kling, R., & Iacono, S. (1984). The control of information systems after implementation. *Communications of the ACM, 27*(12), 1218–1226. doi:10.1145/2135.358307

Kling, R., & Iacono, S. (1988). The mobilization of support for computerization: the role of computerization movements. *Social Problems, 35*(3), 226–243. doi:10.1525/sp.1988.35.3.03a00030

Levy, M., & Powell, P. (2005). Strategies for growth in SMEs: The role of information and information systems. Amsterdam: Elsevier.

Lord, R. G., & Foti, R. J. (1986). Schema theories, information processing and organizational behavior. In H.P. Sims, Jr., & D.A. Gioia (Eds.), The thinking organization: Dynamics of organization cognition (pp. 20-48). San Francisco: Jossey Bass.

INC. Magazine. (1995 August). *Started with $1,000 or less.* 27-38.

Markus, H., & Zajonc, R. B. (1985). The cognitive perspective in social psychology. In G. Lindzey & E. Aronson (Eds.), Handbook of social psychology (Vol. 1, 3rd ed., pp. 137-230). New York: Random House.

Martin, P. Y., & Turner, B. A. (1986). Grounded theory and organizational research. *The Journal of Applied Behavioral Science, 22*(2), 141–157. doi:10.1177/002188638602200207

Melewar, T. C., & Karaosmanoglu, E. (2006). Seven dimensions of corporate identity: A categorisation from the practitioners' perspectives. *European Journal of Marketing, 40*(7/8), 846–869. doi:10.1108/03090560610670025

Melville, N., Kraemer, K. L., & Gurbaxani, V. (2004). Information technology and organizational performance: An integrative model of IT business value. *MIS Quarterly, 28*(2), 283–322.

Meyer, J., & Rowan, B. (1977). Institutionalized organizations: Formal structure as myth and ceremony. *American Journal of Sociology, 83,* 340–363. doi:10.1086/226550

Morgan, G., Frost, P. J., & Pondy, L. R. (1983). Organizational symbolism. In L.R. Pondy, P.G. Frost, G. Morgan & T.C. Dandridge (Eds.), Organizational symbolism. Greenwich, CT: JAI Press.

Murphy, K. E., & Simon, S. J. (2002). Intangible benefits valuation in ERP projects. *Information Systems Journal, 12,* 301–320. doi:10.1046/j.1365-2575.2002.00131.x

Noir, C., & Walsham, G. (2007). The great legitimizer: ICT as myth and ceremony in the Indian healthcare sector. *Information Technology & People, 20*(4), 313–333. doi:10.1108/09593840710839770

Orlikowski, W. J. (1991). Integrated information environment or matrix of control? The contradictory implications of information technology. *Accounting. Management and Information Technologies, 1*, 9–42. doi:10.1016/0959-8022(91)90011-3

Orlikowski, W. J., & Iacono, C. S. (2000). The truth is not out there: an enacted view of the 'digital economy. In E. Brynjolfsson & B. Kahin (Eds.), Understanding the Digital Economy: Data, Tools, and Research. Cambridge, MA: MIT Press.

Orlikowski, W. J., & Iacono, C. S. (2001). Research Commentary: Desperately seeking the IT in IT research – A call to theorizing the IT artifact. *Information Systems Research, 12*(2), 121–134. doi:10.1287/isre.12.2.121.9700

Parker, C. M., & Castleman, T. (2007). New directions for research on SME-ebusiness: Insights from an analysis of journal articles from 2003-2006. *Journal of Information Systems and Small Business, 1*(1-2), 21–40.

Peppard, J., Ward, J., & Daniel, E. (2007). Managing the realization of business benefits from IT investments. *MISQ Executive, 6*(1), 1–11.

Pfeffer, J. (1981). Management as symbolic action: The creation and maintenance of organizational paradigms. In L.L. Cummings & B.M. Staw (Eds.), Research in organizational behavior (Vol. 13, pp. 1-52). Greenwich, CT: JAI Press.

Pfeffer, J., & Salancik, G. R. (1978). The external control of organizations: A resource dependence perspective. New York: Harper and Row.

Powell, W. W., & DiMaggio, P. J. (1991) Introduction. In W.W. Powell & P.J. DiMaggio (Eds.), The new institutionalism in organizational analysis. London: University of Chicago Press.

Prasad, P. (1993). Symbolic processes in the implementation of technological change: A symbolic interactionist study of work computerization. *Academy of Management Journal, 36*, 1400–1429. doi:10.2307/256817

Ranganathan, C., & Brown, C. V. (2006). ERP investments and the market value of firms: toward an understanding of influential ERP project variables. *Information Systems Research, 17*(2), 145–161. doi:10.1287/isre.1060.0084

Ranger-Moore, J., Banaszak-Holland, J., & Hannan, M. T. (1991). Density-dependent dynamics in regulated industries: Founding rates of banks and life insurance companies. *Administrative Science Quarterly, 36*(1), 36–65. doi:10.2307/2393429

Robey, D., & Azevedo, A. (1994). Cultural analysis of the organizational consequences of information technology. *Accounting, Management, and Information Technologies, 4*, 23–37. doi:10.1016/0959-8022(94)90011-6

Saga, V. L., & Zmud, R. W. (1994). The nature and determinants of IT acceptance, routinization and infusion. In L. Levine (Ed.), Diffusion, transfer and implementation of information technology (pp. 67-86). North Holland: Elsevier Science.

Schein, E. H. (1985). Organizational culture and leadership. San Francisco, CA: Jossey-Bass.

Scott, W. R. (2001). Institutions and organizations (2nd ed.). Thousand Oaks, CA: Sage.

Senn, J. A., & Gibson, V. R. (1981). Risks of investment in microcomputers for small business management. *Journal of Small Business Management, 19*(3), 24–32.

Shepherd, D. A., & Zacharakis, A. (2003). A new venture's cognitive legitimacy: An assessment by customers. *Journal of Small Business Management, 41*(2), 148–167. doi:10.1111/1540-627X.00073

Singh, J. V., Tucker, D., & Meinhard, A. G. (1991). Institutional change and ecological dynamics. In W.W. Powell & P.J. DiMaggio (Eds.), The new institutionalism in organizational analysis (pp. 390-422). Chicago, IL: University of Chicago Press.

Singh, J. V., Tucker, D. J., & House, R. J. (1986). Organizational legitimacy and the liability of newness. *Administrative Science Quarterly*, *31*(2), 171–193. doi:10.2307/2392787

Snyder, M., & Stukas, A. (1999). Interpersonal processes: The interplay of cognitive, motivational and behavioral activities in social interaction. *Annual Review of Psychology*, *50*, 273–303. doi:10.1146/annurev.psych.50.1.273

Spector, A. (1961). Basic dimensions of the corporate image. *Journal of Marketing*, 47–51. doi:10.2307/1248513

Starr, J. A., & MacMillan, I. C. (1990). Resource co-optation via social contracting: Resource acquisition strategies for new ventures. *Strategic Management Journal*, *11*, 79–92. doi:10.1002/smj.4250110107

Stevenson, M. K., Busemeyer, J. R., & Naylor, J. C. (1990). Judgment and decision-making theory. In M.D. Dunnette & L.M. Hough (Eds.) Handbook of industrial and organizational psychology (Vol. 1, pp. 283-374). Palo Alto, CA: Consulting Psychologists Press.

Stewart, D. W., & Shamdasani, P. N. (1990). Focus groups: Theory and practice. Newbury Park, CA: Sage.

Stinchcombe, A. (1965). Social structure and organizations. In J.G. March (Ed.) Handbook of organizations (pp. 142 – 193). Chicago, IL: Rand McNally.

Stinchcombe, A. (1968). Constructing social theories. New York: Harcourt Brace.

Strauss, A. L., & Corbin, J. (1998). Basics of qualitative research: Technique and procedure for developing grounded theory. Thousand Oaks, CA: Sage.

Suchman, M. C. (1995). Managing legitimacy: Strategic and institutional approaches. *Academy of Management Review*, *20*(3), 571–610. doi:10.2307/258788

Swanson, E. B., & Ramiller, N. C. (1997). The organizing vision in information systems innovation. *Organization Science*, *8*(5), 458–474. doi:10.1287/orsc.8.5.458

Timmons, J. (1999). New venture creation: Entrepreneurship for the 21st century. Boston, MA: Irwin McGraw-Hill.

van den Hoonaard, W. C. (1997). Working with sensitizing concepts: Analytical field research. Thousand Oaks, CA: Sage.

van Riel, C. B. M. (1997). Research in corporate communications: An overview of an emerging field. *Management Communication Quarterly*, *11*(2), 288–309. doi:10.1177/0893318997112005

Vesper, K. H. (1996). New venture experience. Seattle, WA: Vector Books.

Wainwright, D., Green, G., Mitchell, E., & Yarrow, D. (2005). Towards a framework for benchmarking ICT practice, competence and performance in small firms. *Performance Measurement and Metrics*, *6*(1), 39–52. doi:10.1108/14678040510588580

Weick, K. E. (1983). Managerial thought in the context of action. In S. Srivasta & Associates (Eds.), The executive mind (pp. 221-242). San Francisco, CA: Jossey-Bass.

Welsh, J. A., & White, J. F. (1981). A small business is not a little big business. *Harvard Business Review*, *59*(4), 18–32.

Wiewel, W., & Hunter, A. (1985). The interorganizational network as a resource: A comparative case study on organizational genesis. *Administrative Science Quarterly*, *30*(4), 482–499. doi:10.2307/2392693

Winter, S. J. (1996). The symbolic value of computers: Expanding analyses of organizational computing. In J.W. Beard (Ed.), Impression management and information technology (pp. 21-38). Westport, CT: Quorum Books.

Winter, S. J., Gaglio, C. M., & Rajagopalan, H. K. (2009). The value of information systems to small and medium-sized enterprises: Information and communications technology as signal and symbol of legitimacy and competitiveness. *International Journal of Electronic Business Research*, *5*(1), 65–91.

Yin, R. K. (1989). Case study research: Design and methods. Beverly Hills, CA: Sage.

Zimmerman, M. A. (1997). *New venture legitimacy—A review*. Paper presented at the annual meeting of the Academy of Management, Boston, MA.

Zimmerman, M.A., & Zeitz, G.J. (2002). Beyond survival: Achieving new venture growth by building legitimacy. *Academy of Management Review*, *27*(3), 414–431. doi:10.2307/4134387

ENDNOTES

[1] Any opinions, findings, and conclusions or recommendations expressed in this material are those of the author and do not necessarily reflect the views of the National Science Foundation.

[2] The term "corporate image" is widely accepted in the marketing literature, but is not meant to exclude not-for-profit, volunteer, or governmental organizations.

[3] Firms were 2 - 5 years old and experienced a rapid growth rate (annual sales of at least 25%). The focus on purchase decisions dictated that firms be at least 2 years old since they are likely generating income from sales.

[4] A list of potential customers was developed through referrals from SME founders and the local telephone book. Many would not knowingly support a new firm or were unwilling to make the time commitment.

[5] Percentages and counts suggest the extent to which perceptions were shared among the respondents, but do not represent population values or an issue's importance. Quotes provide a sense of the spirit of the responses.

[6] Differences in the percentage of participants mentioning a category could not be tested with Chi-Square because the relatively small sample sizes and uneven distribution of responses yielded a high number of cells with expected values smaller than five. Under these conditions Chi-Square values become unstable; Fisher's Exact test is preferred

Section 2
Innovation and Information Technology Assimilation

Chapter 6
A Comparative Study of Small- and Medium-Sized Enterprises in Australia and Singapore:
Overall Satisfaction of Electronic Commerce Implementation

Sandy Chong
Curtin University of Technology, Australia

ABSTRACT

Since July 2003, Australia demonstrated the promotion of EC outside the country by forming an international EC partnership with Singapore. While both countries want to increase their international competitiveness by entering this as part of the bilateral free trade agreement, cultural barriers in EC implementation have to be considered and championed. The findings of the study seek to help companies that are embarking upon cross border activities by illustrating the differences in EC implementation in different countries. Results of preliminary interviews of small businesses in both countries show that respondents' perceptions of EC are pre-dominantly positive. A regression analysis was carried out and 5 out of 19 influencing factors were found to make a significant contribution to the implementation of EC in Australia – observability, communication channel, customer pressure, supplier pressure, and perceived governmental support; while only 3 factors – firm size, perceived readiness, observability have significant impact in Singapore.

1 INTRODUCTION

Electronic Commerce (EC) has changed and is still changing the way business is conducted around the world. The commercialization of the Internet and World Wide Web (WWW) has driven EC to become one of the most promising channels for

inter-organizational business processes. Despite the economic downturn and the burst of the "dot-com" bubble, EC is expected to continue its significant growth. EC has emerged as a whole of business strategy that enables organisations to improve business processes and communication, both within the firm and with trading partners. In the US alone, the second decade of EC would boost online sales from $172 billion in 2005 to $329 billion in 2010

DOI: 10.4018/978-1-61520-627-8.ch006

(Forrester Research, 2005), while Asia Pacific's B2B EC is forecasted to grow rapidly at a Compound Annual Growth Rate (CAGR) of fifty-nine percent (IDC, 2004). Specifically in Australia, EC is estimated to be worth $11.3 billion dollars annually (Australian Government Information Management Office, 2005). Singapore also began its nationwide internet journey in the 1990's with the launch of Singnet, its first commercial Internet service, in 1994. Currently, Singapore is ranked 12th in the world for Internet penetration, with a penetration rate of 60 percent (Internet World Stats, 2004) and it is predicted that this will continue to rise as Singapore's e-commerce revenue is forecast to hit some US$43 million in 2008.

EC has helped opened up the market, particularly on the supply- and demand-side for **SMEs**. Small firms are now able to compete in the same global arena that has previously only been the exclusive territory of multinationals corporations. This massive change for SME's has resulted in a number of studies being undertaken by EC researchers worldwide. The strong interest is driven by two clear facts: (1) SMEs play a significant role in most countries' economies, and (2) EC can provide SMEs with an unprecedented range of benefits, including a relatively inexpensive means of accessing global markets using a low cost communication medium (Al-Qirim & Corbitt, 2004; Chau.& Turner, 2002,). However, despite its obvious advantages, Australia and Singapore have been relatively slow in implementing EC in comparison with other countries (Department of Communications, Information Technology and Arts, 2004; Thong, 2001; Sensis, 2005; Singapore Enterprise, 2001). Prior research in Australia showed that most SMEs perceive the challenge of integrating EC into their business operations as risky, complex, time-consuming, and an expensive initiative (NOIE, 2002). In Singapore, it was indicated that merchants were uncertain about the business potential of the Internet as a medium for trading and payment (Lee et. al., 1997).

1.1 Significance of the Study

The major contribution of this study is to address the limitation of the current literature by looking beyond adoption-decision. As highlighted by Parker and Castleman (2009) between 2003 to 2008, there has been extensive research on SMEs' adoption of EC, many of which explores the factors that influence SME owner-manager adoption decisions (Chong, 2005; Gibbs, et.al., 207; Gilmore, et.al., 2007; Quaddus & Hofmeyer, 2007; Robers & Toleman, 2007; Simmons, et.al., 2008). While adoption factors based studies are useful, it was argued that SME EC research community has reached a point where progress is needed beyond factors that influence adoption decision. This study aims to help SMEs understand the continuity of adoption and affective reasons which would prompt the further width and depth of EC usage.

It has also been observed and verified in many studies that SMEs have been actively looking for suitable solutions and methods of adopting and integrating EC into their business process (Benbasat, Bergeron & Dexter, 1993; Cragg & King, 1993; Dos Santos & Peffers, 1998; Massey, 1986). Although there is a growing body of literature dedicated to the analysis of the technical and operational aspects of EC, there is little empirical research to date that examines the success of EC deployments in organisations once the technology has been adopted. If the EC or IT implementation is successful, potential benefits to small businesses can include increased sales, improved profitability, increased productivity, reduced costs associated with inventories, procurement and distribution, improved quality of service, and secured competitive positions (see Al-Qirim, 2005; Chong, 2006; Dholakia & Kshetri, 2004; Grandon & Michael, 2004; Rivard, et.al., 2006; Stockdale & Standing, 2004; Whiteley, 2000). On the other hand, if EC implementations are unsuccessful, it will have severe repercussions on small businesses with their limited resources. This paper aims to identify which factors are important in the successful implementation of EC for SMEs.

Another major contribution is the cross-cultural comparison which this study undertook. According to a recent meta-analyses study done across all SME-EC journal articles, only 9 out of 120 journals between 2003 and 2007 covered cross-country comparisons (Parker & Castleman, 2007). This study bridges the gap in which the scholars proposed as opportunity to shed light on possible national or cultural contexts. While the joint trade approach between Australia and Singapore in promoting EC has clear economic benefits, one factor that must also be considered is that past studies have shown that an innovation (such as EC) diffuses differently in different cultures depending on the socio-cultural environment (Daghfous & Petrof, 1999; Parker & Castleman, 2009). SMEs that hope to operate successfully in a global environment would not only consider in adopting EC but also be able to adapt to foreign EC business practices. Given that possessing cross-country awareness is a critical factor to succeed in any international business interaction, this study may help companies embarking upon cross border activities by illustrating the differences in EC adoption in different countries. For Australia and Singapore, this study is useful for both governments and their respective local enterprises, as it provides a close examination of the inhibiting and facilitating factors which can affect EC adoption success. This knowledge may eventually prove to be the key for a successful partnership between these two Asia-Pacific nations.

Based on case studies and surveys, a number of potential factors have been identified in the literature of IS and IT as critical to implementation success in small business (Cragg & King, 1993; Delone, 1988; Gable, 1991; Gunasekaran & Cecille, 1998; Lees, 1987; Montazemi, 1988; Raymond, 1985; Sohal, 1999; Yap, *et al.*, 1992). However, limited IS, IT and EC literature have investigated the relative importance of the identified factors of implementation success. Without knowing the relative importance of these factors, SMEs may be expending their limited resources and energy on less important factors which have limited contribution to EC implementation success. Thus, there is a need to identify the more important factors so that implications and guidelines can be drawn for effective EC implementation in SMEs. Although adoption and implementation processes may vary from industry to industry, the findings of this study should be broadly applicable. It is therefore the intention of this research to develop general conclusions free of industry bias.

1.2 Research Objectives

The purpose of the paper is twofold. Firstly, to develop a model of EC **implementation success** for SMEs, and secondly, to present outcomes of a comparative study between two countries to reflect the differences in the adoption strategies and explore reasons behind such variations. In this study, the assessment of implementation success is represented by **Overall Satisfaction** which is a strong and subjective component used extensively in previous IS/IT adoption studies. In attempting to determine the success of the overall EC effort, the study measures the overall satisfaction of the owner or top management of SMEs.

1.3 Scope of Study

The study focuses solely on SMEs mainly because they are the backbone of the Australian and Singaporean economies[1]. In Australia, SMEs constitute 95% of the total market and employ more than half of those Australians working in the private sector. Similarly, half of Singapore's workforce is employed in the SME sector. EC as defined in this study principally includes, but is not limited to, Internet-based EC. The scope of EC applications is limited to the utilisation of the Internet as the technological infrastructure to communicate, distribute and conduct information exchange and transactions with business partners.

This study is purposely focused on organisations that use business-to-business EC to carry out transactions and interactions that affect existing business relationships or preexisting contractual relations between trading partners.

2 THEORETICAL PERSPECTIVE OF THE STUDY

It should be noted that this study has been informed by a substantial variety of previous research on adoption, implementation, and innovation diffusion theories applied to technology in general: Information Systems (IS), Information Technology (IT), Electronic Data Interchange (EDI), Inter-Organisational System (IOS), and Management of Information Systems (MIS). Clearly, EC is not identical with any of them. It necessarily involves IT which it shares with IS and MIS and at more sophisticated levels is likely to enable EDI. It is also undeniably 'Inteorganisational'. It may therefore be argued that any factor that has been shown to influence the adoption and implementation of technology or application in general is worthy of consideration as a potential explanatory variable with respect to EC. The reader is reminded that in this regard, due to the lack of previous EC specific research within this area, the current study is essentially exploratory. This will encourage an "open mind" to be in effect with regard to what variables (if any) will be related to a particular factor. To ensure thoroughness, wherever previous research or reasoning suggested a relationship between a factor and one of the variables, its possible influence on the focal variables will also be hypothesised. Innovation diffusion theories have been particularly useful for understanding the facilitators and inhibitors of EC, because they provide insight into the factors that influence the adoption of innovation. After a critical analysis of existing models, their influencing factors, stages, and process, the theoretical framework is extended to incorporate important organisational and contextual aspects of adoption in the development of a research model.

2.1: The Measure of EC Adoption and Implementation

As defined in Rogers innovation diffusion theory (1995), *adoption* is a decision to make full use of an innovation as the best course of action. In this study, we are only looking at the factors that influence the *extent* of adoption and not the adoption *process*. It is argued that EC adoption is essentially a continuum involving a range of progressive developments and a broadening variety of applications. For several reasons, there is rarely any clear separation between adoption and implementation in EC. In other words, EC is not "one simple or single innovation" that a firm either does or does not adopt, but should be considered as consisting of a number of combinations of innovations of varying complexity and sophistication on a continuum requiring lesser to greater levels of commitment. While conceptually distinct, there is no temporal dividing line between all the dependent variables in this study as they tend to merge into one another (i.e. *State of Adoption, Extent of Deployment, Level of Usage,* and *Overall Satisfaction*). Rather, their hierarchy is logical in that each is a necessary condition for the next: whilst one feature is becoming more utilised, another is being explored and a third is being considered or enabled.

Implementation Success of EC has technical components, similar to other IT innovations. However, EC is also a special case of innovation that also encompasses inter-organisational elements, and this distinguishes it from other types. Perhaps the most obvious, intellectually appealing, and arguably the most commercially appropriate measure of success for any given state of EC adoption would be the change in profitability that is attributable to it. However, to arrive at a valid measurement for this within the rubric of a rapidly changing business world is almost impossible, as it would be extremely difficult to separate the profit that is engendered by EC from what is generated by a myriad of other powerful influences. Hence it is rarely practical to conduct controlled experiments in the commercial world. Clearly, other more easily observable measures of success must be used. This study employs three conceptually distinct but naturally related measures: *Extent of Deployment, Level of Usage,* and *Overall Satisfaction.* The first two are observable outcomes of adoption and as such are specified by the researcher. Neither of these, however, will necessarily cover the issues most important to the individual firm. Therefore, there also exists a need for a criterion that incorporates the values held by individual firms as far as possible. A measure of success that reflects this range of values is *Overall Satisfaction.* No attempt will be made to combine these three into a single measure as each provides a useful perspective in its own right and, taken separately, reveal a richer and more complete picture of some of the dimensions of success.

The following section will focus on discussing the significance of *Overall Satisfaction* as a measure of implementation success. The other three dependent variables are beyond the scope of this paper.

Overall Satisfaction

Although many variables may be considered for constituting the indicator for success of an Internet-based EC undertaking, *Overall Satisfaction* has been chosen for the current report. Perceived satisfaction naturally has an element of volatility due to the influence the respondents' personalities and personal opinions. Even with no substantial change from week to week, small irregular frustrations are likely to influence the level of the *Overall Satisfaction.* However, there is an implicit assumption that a person who rates themselves higher than another person is more satisfied.

User satisfaction or user information satisfaction is probably the most widely used single measure of IS success. In small business research, satisfaction has often been used as the dependent variable (Lees, 1987; Montazemi, 1988; Raymond, 1990; DeLone & McLean, 1992). The reasons for this are at least threefold. Firstly, "satisfaction" has a high degree of face validity. It is hard to deny the success of a system in which users voluntarily indicate their satisfaction levels. Secondly, the development of the Bailey & Pearson (1983) instrument and its derivatives has provided a reliable set of tools for measuring satisfaction and for making comparisons among studies. The third reason for the appeal of satisfaction as a success measure is that most of the other indexes are not of sufficient standard; being either conceptually weak or empirically difficult to obtain (DeLone & McLean, 1992).

Despite the fact that "satisfaction" is somewhat subjective construct, it is utilised in the current report because no better objective measure has yet been devised. Moreover, alternative indexes of success are either inappropriate or unquantifiable. When the use of EC is required, the successful interaction with the system by management can be measured in terms of *Overall Satisfaction.* The key issue is whose satisfaction should be quantified. In attempting to determine the success of the overall EC effort, this study measures the satisfaction of the owner or the top management of SMEs.

A more comprehensive set of potential determinants that are important in both the adoption and subsequent implementation of EC will be addressed in future study. At present, the purpose of the current paper is to direct its discussion towards the identification of factors that exert an influence on the implementation success of EC; and this will be achieved by utilising the findings of the survey. To this end, the current report has been structured as follows: 1. a model of EC implementation success and the outline of the influencing factors; 2. a brief description of the data collection, measurement of the variables, and instrument validation; and finally 3. a discussion of the findings of the study, encompassing the implications that are likely to be of importance in assisting SMEs and public policy makers achieve a better understanding of EC adoption and implementation.

3 RESEARCH MODEL

In this report, it is proposed that several factors influence the satisfaction level of EC implementation. In the absence of empirical studies to assist in the selection of the most significant variables for EC adoption, a number of possible relevant factors have been identified, and grouped into broad categories of *internal* and *external environmental factors*. The distinction between internal and external environmental factors is made to separate organisation-specific (and organisation-determined) factors from those that are imposed (and determined) from outside the organisation. Figure 1 presents the research model in which the relationship between the influencing factors and the *Overall Satisfaction* was examined.

In terms of describing relationship between the variables, the following proposition was stated in a non-directional manner.

Study Proposition: *Organisational factors, innovation factors, communication factors, industry factors and national factors are related to the **Overall Satisfaction** for EC implementation.*

For the sake of thoroughness and this being an exploratory study, the decision was taken to test all the above-mentioned factors on the dependent variable.

3.1 Influencing Factors of EC Implementation

Internal Environmental Factors

Despite the advantages of EC, SMEs around the world are not adopting it as rapidly as originally anticipated (Dholakia & Kshetri, 2004; Grandon & Pearson, 2003; McCole & Ramsey, 2005; Mirchandani & Motwani, 2001; Rao, Metts & Monge, 2003; The Age, 2002; Van Beveren &

Figure 1. Conceptual model of factors that influence implementation success of EC

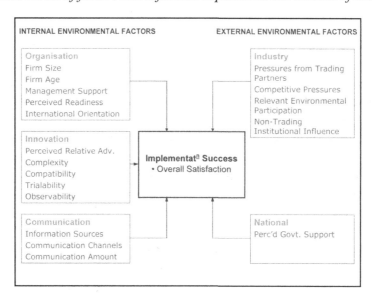

Thomson, 2002; Wagner, Fillis & Johansson, 2003). Several **organisational factors** that inhibit IT and EC adoption were identified after conducting preliminary interviews and an extensive literature search. Among these were the cost of technology, a lack of managerial and technological skills, a lack of system integration and a lack of financial resources (Cragg & King, 1993; Iacovou, Benbasat & Dexter, 1995; McCole & Ramsey, 2005; Nilankanta & Scamell, 1990; Stockdale & Standing, 2004). These inhibitors are expected to play a major role in the context of small organisations, where resources and the level of computer sophistication are limited (Dholakia & Kshetri, 2004; Grandon & Michael, 2004; Lertwongsatien & Wongpinunwatana, 2003; Riemenschneider & McKinney, 2001-2002, Stockdale & Standing, 2004; Tan, et.al., 2007; Van Beveren & Thomson, 2002; Zhu, Kraemer & Xu, 2003), thus *firm size* and *perceived readiness* are included in the category of internal environmental factors. Another recurrent observation is that EC adoption seems to be more of a management issue than a technical one (Corbitt, Behrendorf & Brown-Parker, 1997). Many researchers have found that if there is a lack of support amongst top executives, technology cannot be successfully adopted (Cooper & Zmud, 1990; Grandon & Pearson, 2003; Lertwongsatien & Wongpinunwantana, 2003; Premkumar & Ramamurthy, 1995). It is therefore reasonable to assume that *management support* is a critical factor to the successful adoption of EC. Previous scholars also anticipated that the *age of the firm* could either foster or impede technology adoption in terms of resistance to change, a track record of successfully overcoming hurdles, and experience in adopting prior technological advances (Germain, Droge & Daugherty, 1994). The *international orientation* of the company is also examined in this study, as previous research within the area of Internet adoption demonstrates that firms that are operating in the international markets tend are more likely to conduct EC through portals than those that do not have foreign collaborations (see Daniel

& Grimshaw, 2002; Lal, 2002; Wagner, Fillis & Johansson, 2003).

Although the most well known have been developed by Rogers (1995), these **innovation factors** have also been the key feature of several other IT adoption studies (Iacovou, et al., 1995; Kwon & Zmud, 1987; Moore & Benbasat, 1991; Sharif, 1994; Tornatzky & Klein, 1982) and EC studies (Kendall, Tung, Chua, Ng, & Tan, 2001; Lertwongsatien & Wongpinunwatana, 2003; McCole & Ramsey, 2005; Van Slyke, Belanger, & Comunale, 2004; Wagner, *et. al.*, 2003). In this study, they are adapted for the current report as follows: *perceived relative advantage* (i.e. the perceived EC benefits and impact relative to its existing practice or system), *compatibility* (how well EC fits in both technical and organisational processes), *trialability* (the degree to which EC can be pilot tested or experimented without high start-up costs), *complexity* (ease of use or the ease with which EC can be learned) and *observability* (the extent to which EC advantages or gains are visible to firms).

According to the findings of preliminary interviews and an extensive literature search, there is a lack of reliable sources of information that SMEs can exploit in order to gain knowledge of EC. This may serve to hinder the smooth adoption of EC in many cases. Moreover, following the work of Rogers (1995), other scholars argue that the adoption of a new technology is influenced by *communication channel types* (mass media vs. interpersonal channels), *information source* (external source vs. internal source) and *communication amount* (Brancheau & Wetherbe, 1990; Nilankantan & Scamell, 1990). Hence **communication factors** were added to the EC adoption model.

External Environmental Factors

SMEs are usually characterised by a high level of environmental uncertainty that includes fluctuations in interest rates, reliability of supply, and competition. Related to this factor, the use of IT and EC is often imposed on SMEs by major customers or suppliers. Such pressure from trading partners plays a critical role in encouraging small firms to adopt IT and EC, as evidenced in previous studies (Daniel & Grimshaw, 2002; Grandon & Pearson, 2003; Iacovou et al., 1995; McCole & Ramsey, 2005; Stockdale & Standing, 2004; Thong, 1999; Wagner, *et. al.*, 2003; Zhu, *et. al.*, 2003). In addition, the competitive pressure that firms face within the industry also has an influence on the company's decision to adopt IT or EC (Grandon & Pearson, 2003, Iacovou et al., 1995; McCole & Ramsey, 2005; Wagner, *et. al.*, 2003; Zhu, *et. al.*, 2003). As more competitors adopt EC, small firms are more inclined to follow suit in order to maintain their own competitive positions. Even though it should also be noted that the influence of non-trading institutions such as industry associations, government, financial institutions, the media and universities may not be as strong as that of the entities the firm trades with, they may still influence the adoption of EC to a certain extent. Thus, the aforementioned justifications lead to the inclusion of *trading partner's pressure*, *competitive pressure* and *non-trading institutional influence* under the category of **industry factors**. *Relevant environmental participation* is also an important factor for any firm that is trying to employ new technology or systems to their fullest potential. Without the wide acceptance of applications or systems, current or potential customers may resist the adoption of EC because of the lack of infrastructure, suitable platform, or compatible technological standards (Lertwongsatien & Wongpinunwatana, 2003; McCole & Ramsey, 2005; Wagner, *et. al.*, 2003). It should be noted that although relevant environmental participation recognizes the existence of a possible critical mass, it is not synonymous with that term. While the concept of critical mass may be appropriate to studying the movement of a single innovation through a large social system, its usefulness when applied to innovations that lie on a continuum

(such as EC in SMEs) is limited.

Finally, the **national factor** is included in the adoption model in order to provide a macro country-level view of EC, its adoption behaviour and the business environment. This study demonstrates that in addition to the private sector, the governmental sector can also act as a crucial catalyst in stimulating a successful adoption experience for the SMEs (see Grandon & Pearson, 2003; Wagner, *et. al.*, 2003). Previous studies have illustrated that governmental support in funding infrastructure projects, adoption schemes and initiatives have provided direct and indirect stimulation to the supply of information which – as a consequence – produces faster technology diffusion (Kettinger, 1994; Tan, 1998). Governmental subsidy and supports have been demonstrated to have a positive impact on the uptake of IT use and innovative business practice by organisations, especially SMEs (Payton & Ginzberg, 2001; Tung & Rieck, 2005; Wagner, *et. al.*, 2003). Institutional regulations that promote electronic interactions and transactions may also encourage EC or future IT adoption in small businesses (King, Gurbaxani & Kraemer, 1994; Rao, *et. al.*, 2003). In this study, we examine the influence of *governmental support* and its propensity to shape the push for EC in SMEs.

4 RESEARCH METHODOLOGY

A positivist approach was undertaken in order to develop a research model rather than confirming an existing one. This model is operationalised on the basis of correlational hypothesis testing, as opposed to the determination of a definitive cause and effect relationship. The desired result testing the model is the identification of variables that are *associated* with the *Overall Satisfaction* of EC adoption. Due to the exploratory nature of this study, a cross sectional approach was undertaken to measure firms' responses with regard to the adoption of EC.

4.1 Data Collection

The current study was conducted in three phases: 1. preliminary investigation, 2. pilot study and 3. questionnaire survey. Preliminary interviews with five Australian and Singaporean SMEs[2] were conducted. These were supported by an extensive literature review; all of which combined to provide some direction as to what adoption factors are imperative to SMEs. A survey instrument with questions and multiple-item scales was developed and pilot-tested to capture the information reflecting the perceptions and practice of those adopting EC, specifically what internal or external environmental factors affect the adoption of EC and the degree of influence. In order to focus on SMEs, assistance was sought from governmental and research institutions in both countries to develop a database of such businesses and contact details of target respondents. As the survey was intended to apply to a wide geographical area, the chosen method of delivery was a combination of email, web, and mail survey techniques. 780 survey questionnaires were personally disseminated and addressed to the director or owner of the respective firms. In order to improve response rate, reminders were sent out to target respondents two weeks after the commencement of the first and second-waves of mail-outs. A total of 115 usable responses were collected in Australia and 42 in Singapore.

4.2 Measurement of Variables

Some of the indicators were developed by the researcher, whilst some were adopted or modified from previous scholars. For cases in which previous measures were adequate and instructive, the current researcher has adopted or adapted them; and due credit was given for these items. In other cases, new indicators were added and compared to previous measures according to the suggestions made by Neuman (1997) in coming up with a new index. Table 1 below depicts a comprehensive list of the variables used in the current report. These variables were presented with the corresponding indicators, the types of scales utilised, and an indication of whether they were researcher-defined or adapted and/or adopted from other sources (as indicated in the appropriate column). Some variables were based on many multiple-item scales, as incorporating several items results in a more realistic and comprehensive indicator (Neuman, 1999). To ensure the validity of the dependent measure, this study also incorporates a single rating scale so as to provide a comparison of results.

4.3 Non-Response Bias Assessment

In order to encourage SMEs' participation in the study, more than two mailings of the questionnaire were conducted. To further increase the response rate, each of the covering letters accompanying the questionnaire was personally addressed to the Director or Chief Executive Officer (where such

Table 1. Original construct measurement

DEPENDENT VARIABLES			
Variables	**Indicators**	**Measurement**	**Adopted /Adapted Sources**
Implementation Success			
Overall Satisfaction	Perceived overall satisfaction of the EC adoption and implementation	Likert Scale	DeLone & McLean, 1992; Raymond, 1985

information was available). For those businesses for which no details were supplied, the covering letter was addressed to the position title of Director or Chief Executive Officer. A reply paid envelope was also issued and this was an effort to encourage responses even further. A copy of summary findings was yet another incentive offered to ensure a high response rate. To arrive at the estimate of total non-response error, a comparison of the data obtained from the two mailing rounds was conducted. The basic assumption behind this approach is that subjects that respond only after further prompting were potential non-respondents. Analyses from the first round of respondents are compared with results from later rounds. If no statistically significant difference between the two groups is found, then it is reasonable to assume that non-response error is not present and that the remaining non-respondents exhibit similar characteristics to the respondents (Churchill, 1991).

In summary, the two-step response assessment process that was utilised, together with the personally addressed covering letters, reply paid facility, and an offer of summary findings, were put into practice in order to counteract the disadvantages normally associated with a mail survey: namely, low response rates and the problem of non-response error. It was therefore safe to make the assumption that the data obtained from the respondents was representative of the sample and that, as a consequence, any findings derived from this data were generalisable to the sample frame in its entirety.

4.4 Instrument Development

The questionnaire used in this study was design to measure variables in the theoretical model illustrated previously. Some of the indicators were developed by the researcher, while some were adopted or modified from previous scholars. In some cases in which a previous measure is adequate, sources and proper credit were cited. In other cases, new indicators were added and compared with the previous measures to help improve the explanatory power of the research model. Slight modifications of the wordings were made to reflect the business-to-business EC nature of the study and any further changes to the instrument were retested and then included in the final survey.

4.5 Instrument Validation

As recommended by Nunnally (1978), the reliability and validity of the measures for this study were tested to ascertain the suitability and rigour of the study instrument. The Cronbach's (1951) coefficient alpha has been used in the present research to examine the internal consistency of the scales relating to all the independent variables of this study. This reliability measure of two or more construct indicators produces values between 0 and 1. Higher values indicate greater reliability among the indicators (Hair, *et al.*, 1998:618). The amount of scale reliability could have been improved by repeating or requesting the same essential question in a disguised or re-oriented form in another part of the questionnaire. However, this would have substantially lengthened the questionnaire and very likely decreased the response rate. The following are the practical considerations and principles (Neuman, 1999) that were taken to ensure the reliability of the current study:

- Clarity of most constructs was carefully examined. Most of which have already been established in previous literature.
- Pre-tests and pilot studies were used.
- The most precise level of measurement was used in each question within the constraints of meaningful discernibility of values. A 5-point scale is used in the questionnaire.
- Multiple indicators were used where any possibility of ambiguity existed on the part of the respondents.

It should be noted that methods of testing the stability of any measurement becomes relatively meaningless and unnecessary when a concept or construct has defined the essential components, each of which is measured using an appropriate item (Jacob, 2000). Here, the items are not expected to be homogenous, nor are they selected at random.

A test of internal consistency amongst each set of items representing the Internal and External Environmental Factors was conducted. These tests reveal that the *Innovation Factors – Perceived Relative Advantage* (0.73), *Compatibility* (0.77) and *Complexity* (0.72) and *Observability* (0.79), all had Cronbach Alpha values greater than the 0.7 benchmark suggested by Nunnally (1978). The value for *Trialability* (0.56) was marginally below the cut off value of 0.6, acceptable in the early stages of research (Tan & Teo, 2000). The reliability coefficient for the new variables, *Management Support* (0.94), and *Non-Trading Institutional Influence* (0.98) all exceeded 0.7. Thus, overall the results appeared robust enough to carry out further analysis. It must be acknowledged however, that since the items comprising some of these scales were not heterogeneous collections drawn from a large number of possible candidates but specifically designed to cover distinct components, the appropriateness of equivalence reliability measures such as Cronbach Alpha may be debated. The lists of items for the variables concerned are not created by a large sample of possible phenomena. They are almost an exhaustive list but not a complete one. The applicability of the standard reliability score (0.70) by Cronbach Alpha is limited for the following reasons:

1. The list does not consist of a small heterogeneous collection of items drawn from a large number of potential candidates.
2. However, for those who insist on Cronbach Alpha, the results are presented above. The Cronbach Alpha indicates that the list of items is internally homogeneous.

3. These methods of reliability analysis are of limited ability. However, in each case Cronbach Alpha does at least indicate a satisfactory level of internal consistency.

The issue of face validity in the case of previously recognized concepts is taken as established. The researcher-defined concepts naturally awaits general acceptance. Content validity is achieved during the planning and construction stages of the scale and not when the scale is completed, hence procedures that are used to develop the instrument are the key to content validity (Churchill, 1991). The key issues to be addressed in this study regarding content validity include: 1. Whether the full set of items being measured covers all the relevant variables 2. Whether each specific set of items cover the intended range of components in a given variable. Various indexes such as the *Management Support, Organisational Readiness, Innovation Factors* and the *Communication Factors* have already been tested, as many of these measures contain items or components that have been borrowed or adopted from previous studies.

Criterion-related validity is an important issue where latent variables are involved. No variable in this study can be regarded as truly latent. Whilst several measures involve subjective perceptions on part of the respondents, it is the actual perception which is the focal variable and not the latent reality behind it. One such variable is the *Perceived Readiness*. The perception of one's own readiness is a potential influencing factor related to, but nonetheless distinct from, the actual readiness; and has an influence on decisions in its own right. To assess whether the various indicators of the concept operate in a consistent manner, construct validity was tested. Very few variables in this study fall into the category of abstract concepts that possess serious ambiguity. Those that did, namely, the *Innovation Factors*, were extensively investigated. The issue of construct validity was addressed in the pilot study and resulted in the removal or modification or some potentially ambiguous items which further ensures clear measurement and consistency.

Despite all endeavour to ensure the validity of each measure in this study, it should be noted that it is not possible to achieve it in an absolute sense, as constructs are abstract ideas while indicators are concrete observations. As argued by Bohrnstedt (1992), validity is a matter of degree and is a part of a dynamic process that grows by accumulating evidence over time, and without it all measurement becomes meaningless.

5 RESULTS

5.1 Sample Profile

The profiles of the Australian and the Singaporean samples are shown in Table 2 below. Information pertaining to the profile of the company and the respondent were collected and covered in the various sections of the questionnaire. This information is critical to understanding the arena in which this study was conducted. The values in the table indicate that the respondents are distributed across various business types, industry sectors and turnover levels. These data were compared with the data reported by the Australian Bureau Statistics and the Singapore Productivity Board to gauge the representation of the sample in this study. The comparison showed that no groups or category were seriously under or over represented. Other sample profile such as the title of respondent, serves as an indicator of the credibility of infor-

mation provided by the key informant. The most dominant group has been presented in bold.

5.2 Categories of EC Adopters

Figure 2 indicated that the responding firms had a wide range of experience with EC adoption and implementation. Some firms were relatively new to the EC mode of operations (19.1 percent had less than 6 months EC experience), as well as firms who had used it for many years (23.5 percent had 5 years experience of using EC). A sufficient range of adopters from early to late adopters is represented in the sample. The high percentage of late adopters is consistent with the natural expectation from a relatively new and growing business practice of EC. The largest proportion of respondents that have been using EC applications (42.6 percent had 2 years EC experience) in their business can be regarded as the majority in the adoption curve. Of those who indicated, "Did not adopt" (5.2 percent), this may imply that the responding firm hasn't adopted EC at the time of the study.

Figure 3 indicated that the responding firms in Singapore also had a wide range of experience with EC adoption and implementation. The most dominant group of respondents that have been using EC applications (52.4 percent had less than 6 months EC experience) in their business can be regarded as late adopters in the adoption curve. There are firms who were relatively new to the EC mode of operations (26.2 percent had 2 years EC experience), as well as firms who had

Table 2. Sample profile

1. Firm's Size – Number of Employees	Australian Sample		Singaporean Sample	
	Frequency	Percentage %	Frequency	Frequency
Less than 50 employees	**83**	**72.2**	**23**	**54.8**
Between 50 to 100 employees	18	15.7	12	28.6
Between 101 to 150 employees	4	3.5	4	9.5
More than 151 employees	10	8.7	3	7.1

Figure 2. Categories of Adopters in Australia

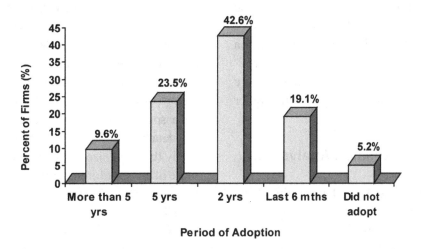

used it for many years (14.3 percent had 5 years or more experience of using EC). A sufficient range of adopters from early to late adopters is represented in the sample. The high percentage of late adopters is expected from a relatively new and growing business practice of EC.

It is evident by comparing results of the adopters' category between responding firms from the two countries – the distribution of the Australian adopters category can be described as symmetrical

(see Figure 2), while the one of Singaporean SMEs (see Figure 3 above) is distinctively negatively skewed. This suggests that Singaporean SMEs evidently were relatively behind the Australian SMEs in terms of EC adoption at the time of the study.

In summary, profiles of the respondents clearly show that firms that employed less than 50 employees are the dominant group amongst firms participating in this study. Majority of the

Figure 3. Categories of Adopters in Singapore

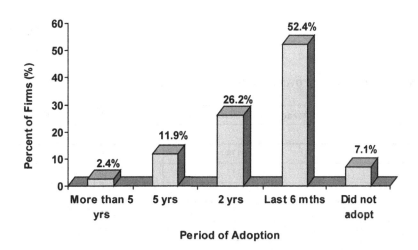

SMEs fall into the business structure of proprietary limited and most of them came under the manufacturing industry. While the turnover of these responding firms differs between Australia and Singapore, the collected information is reliable as the majority of the questionnaires were completed by either the Managing Director or the CEO of the firm.

5.3 Multiple Regression Analysis

Table 3 represents the Australian results of the stepwise-backward elimination, whereby factors that are statistically significant in the model for **Overall Satisfaction** are retained. These reveal an expected moderate reduction in R-squared and an increase in adjusted R-squared value from 0.397 to 0.407. There is also an improvement in the overall significance of F-value from 0.001 to 0.000.

Since the F-value is significant at the 1 percent level, it can be asserted that there is strong evidence to support that the overall model is significant and the independent variables retained are related to the *Overall Satisfaction*. As illustrated in Table 3, the adjusted R-squared value indicates that 40.7 percent of the variation in Overall Satisfaction by Australian SMEs is explained by the corresponding variations in *Observability*, *Variety of Communication Channels*, *Customer Pressure*, *Supplier Pressure*, and *Perceived Governmental Support*. All variables are significant at the 0.05 level or better.

As for the Singaporean data, the regression model explained 60.6 percent of *Overall Satisfaction*. Of all the three factors, *Observability* was the only significant variable at the 0.01 level for the Singaporean SMEs. This result is consistent with the Australian findings. Both organisational factors, *Size of the Firm* and *Perceived Readiness*, are associated with significance in the Singaporean data but not in the Australian data. This may imply that firm size and perceived readiness are more of an issue for the implementation of EC in Singaporean firms than for companies in Australia (See Table 4).

Figure 4 depicts the factors that are supported by significant evidence in both countries.

6 RESULTS

Size of Firm: For Singaporean SMEs, *Size of Firm* was found to have a probable relationship to their Overall Satisfaction, indicating that the perceived level of satisfaction with EC implementation was more likely to be high when respondents are derived from a larger company. The emergence of *Size of Firm* as a significant variable in influencing adoption success is in line with existing literature, in which it was found that firms that have large operations are comparatively better off than other firms where investment in new technologies is concerned (Pavitt, Robson, & Townsend, 1987; Siddharthan, 1992). Moreover,

Table 3. Final model estimation for overall satisfaction (Australian data)

Influencing Factors	Standardised Coefficient (beta)	t-value	Significance
(Constant)		1.600	0.115
OBSERVA	0.478	4.391	0.000
COMM.CHAN	0.315	2.865	0.006
CUST.PRES	-0.312	-2.228	0.030
SUPP.PRES	0.263	1.915	0.061
PCD.GOV.SUP	0.216	2.132	0.038

$R^2 = 0.457$ Adjusted $R^2 = 0.407$ F-significance = 0.000 Observations = 115

Table 4. Final model estimation for overall satisfaction (Singaporean data)

Influencing Factors	Standardised Coefficient (beta)	t-value	Significance
(Constant)		-1.146	0.260
SIZE. FIRM	0.190	1.814	0.078
PCD.RDNS	0.537	4.988	0.000
OBSERV	0.387	3.684	0.001

R^2 = 0.637 Adjusted R^2 = 0.606 F-significance = 0.000 Observations = 42

large firms are in a better position to appropriate the benefits of new innovation. Sound financial positions and appropriate conditions have strong bearings on the adoption of the latest technologies and investing in innovative activities. Larger firms have the other advantage of employing a more skilled workforce in aggregate, which may be necessary for the utilisation of new technologies at a certain level of efficiency and efficacy. This would presumably lead to a higher degree of satisfaction in the adoption and implementation of such technologies.

Perceived Readiness:*Perceived Readiness* is found to be the most significant factor relating to the Overall Satisfaction of EC adoption in the Singaporean SMEs. This finding supports the notion that organisational resources increase the likelihood of IS implementation success for small businesses (Thong, 2001). As SMEs often lack financial and technological resources, insufficient funds may be allocated for the implementation of EC. An inadequate resource base may place constraints on the implementation effort and this may lead to partial ineffectiveness and thus dissatisfaction with EC. On the other hand, firms with adequate resources can contribute more effectively to the EC implementation through their involvement during the requirements and design phases. This involvement may also encourage more realistic expectations from EC and more comfortable participating in the implementation

Figure 4. Factors related to overall satisfaction (Australian and singaporean data)

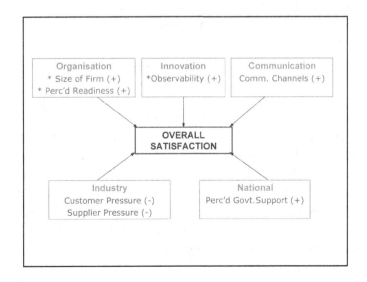

process which leads to a more satisfying experience for the adopting firms.

Observability: *Observability* appears to be a significant factor related to the Overall Satisfaction with EC adoption in both Australian and Singaporean data. The degree to which the results of EC are more visible to SMEs leads to higher satisfaction in its implementation. In the ability to observe the benefits of EC, SMEs may have already observed success in the initiatives taken by other companies, be it trading partners or competitors. With the constant media exposure about EC, SMEs would have now believed EC to be highly valued and that most firms would adopt EC in the near future. With such confidence and belief, it is very likely that this would naturally be transformed into satisfaction with what the firm is pursuing in the adoption of EC. In the case of doing business online, effects such as quicker access and dissemination of information, and savings in costs (e.g. printing, advertising, communication and overhead costs) are more immediate and easier to acknowledge from trading partners or associates. These easily demonstrated benefits (short-term, but visible effects) might help promote continued adoption of the long-term goals of EC, which inevitably lead to higher level of success of implementation for the adopting firms.

Despite its significance, the validity of the *Observability* items when transferred into the context of Overall Satisfaction of EC implementation may be questionable. The components of the *Observability* variable are in fact a combination of confidence, optimism, observed outside success and inevitability (i.e. the inevitable progress of EC in the future). The explanation for the existence of this relationship therefore requires a psychological approach. For future reference, this variable has to be treated with slight caution, as the benefits of EC or any kind of technological adoption have to be observable to be satisfying.

Variety of Communication Channels: In Australia, Overall Satisfaction was found positively related to the *Variety of Communication*

Channels used by firms to disseminate EC-related information or strategy. The use of a greater variety of communication channels to communicate EC information may help to encourage the firms' trading partners to adopt EC, thus increasing the business links, and leading to higher levels of satisfaction with adoption. Expanding the variety of communication channels to increase the awareness and knowledge about EC also helps in improving the level of confidence in users, which increase the level of adoption, and eventually improves the level of use and satisfaction with EC. Thus, SMEs should consider adopting multiple channels as part of the influence strategy to encourage their employees and trading partners to adopt EC.

The descriptive findings of this study suggested that EC initiators (e.g. early adopters, vendors, consultants) could actively communicate the benefits of EC through promotional seminars, presentations, and on-site visits or demonstrations. Internally, on-the-job-training is the most popular communication channels utilised by firms to disseminate EC-related information within the company as hands-on experience is considered to be more effective than mass training. In terms of interorganisational communication channel, it has been found that the most effective means of influencing trading partners is to set the example by using electronic means themselves to communicate with their partners.

Customer Pressure: *Customer Pressure* was negatively related to Overall Satisfaction for Australian SMEs, suggesting that the more pressure the customers placed on the firm, the less satisfied they might be with the current adoption. On the other hand, it can be interpreted as once the firms attained the desired outcome of adoption and are satisfied with the performance, they may perceive lower pressure from their customers. This perhaps implies that firms that adopt and use EC on their own initiative tend to be less affected by their customers.

If firms feel easily pressured by their customers, then it is possible that their EC system is not working well enough. A firm will tend to feel pressure from a source whenever it is vulnerable and its performance in relation to that source is less than adequate. In relation to customers, the firm must necessarily be sensitive to clients' needs and demands. If the potential client controls the relationship, then the fate of the firm is in the client's hands. When the customer is satisfied (exerting little pressure), the firm is likely to see its own systems (including its EC status) as being satisfactory. Hence the inverse relationship between perceived *Customer Pressure* and Overall Satisfaction.

Supplier Pressure: For Australian SMEs, *Supplier Pressure* was found to have a probable relationship to the Overall Satisfaction, indicating that the perceived level of satisfaction with EC adoption was more likely to be higher when respondents perceived the pressure imposed by their suppliers to be high. The relationship with suppliers is different in one important respect: the firm is now much less vulnerable as it controls the relationship. The supplier is unlikely to try to exert pressure on an unimportant client to modify his business practice (i.e. adopt EC) unless there are substantial benefits to the supplier (due to lower costs and increased efficiency). When they do so, this increases with the volume of business transacted. However, the greater the volume ordered from the supplier, the more thriving the business of the client firm is likely to be, and the greater the overall satisfaction the client would have with his current state of business practice (of which EC is a part). This results in a direct positive relationship between *Suppliers Pressure* and Overall Satisfaction.

Being a customer, the positive link between *Supplier Pressure* and Overall Satisfaction shows that supplier pressure ought not to be resisted. Needless to say, suppliers would have to provide their customers with the necessary educational support and incentive in order to achieve mutually beneficial gains through the implementation of EC. This support may be critical especially for customers that do not have the expertise to implement EC. It is imperative that firms and their trading partners work together to build trust and a supportive operational relation or environment and share the potential benefits waiting to be unleashed from EC.

Perceived Level of Governmental Support: The *Perceived Level of Governmental Support* was related to the Overall Satisfaction of EC implementation for Australian SMEs. Although many responding firms consider the level of governmental support to be disappointing (Chong, 2004), those firms that think favourably of the assistance tend to be satisfied with the EC experience. In this case, it is reasonable to suggest that when the government improve the support, adopters are likely to experience higher level of satisfaction. Another assumption may also be true that when a firm is satisfied with the adoption, it naturally holds higher regard to the governmental support that was given to the firm at that point of time.

In any case, increasing governmental support would not be futile and it could lead to a greater satisfaction in adoption and implementation for SMEs. As revealed in the descriptive findings, even though educational support was found to be the most used form of support at the time of the survey, SMEs have high expectations that governmental assistance would come in the form of advisory support. In other words, governmental support is expected to be more advisory-oriented than anything else. Success in this area would tend to be seen as success in governmental support.

7 FUTURE RESEARCH DIRECTIONS

This paper has developed and tested a proposed model of EC implementation success for SMEs by conceptualising the theoretical framework from established IS research on adoption, innovation, implementation and diffusion. The study focuses on theory development rather than theory confirmation. This, with the cross sectional nature of data also limits the ability of this study to draw causal implications in the findings. In making generalisation from the research sample, one has to take into consideration the context of Australia and Singapore. The findings may not be universally true, but they are likely to be applicable in similar cultural contexts.

The exploratory nature of the research has also helped identify associations between variables from which more confirmatory or causally directional hypotheses can be generated in the future. Progress towards the formulation of a more comprehensive causal model may be achieved in future research. Here the technique of Structural Equation Modelling may be usefully applied. It would also be insightful to conduct longitudinal studies to confirm the direction and to help clarify causality and test for feedback effects of adoption decisions. In this study, no attempt was made to control for industry type. The models may be tested more intensively in a chosen or a specific industry. Comparison of the research model can also be conducted over several countries, particularly from different geographic regions. The contrasting contexts may provide some interesting results. Lastly, having established the soundness of the theoretical framework of implementation success for SMEs, other researchers may investigate its applicability to a wider range of business communication technologies and further innovations in the future.

8 FURTHER RESEARCH

In this paper, *Overall Satisfaction* is the more subjective measure of success that complements the other components of implementation success in the broader study (i.e. *Extent of Deployment* and the *Level of Usage*). According to the results

of this study, firms in Singapore that are *larger*, possess higher sense of *readiness*, have higher confidence and *observability* in the value and benefits that EC would bring them, tend to be more satisfied with the implementation of EC. In Australia, apart from possessing positive attitude towards future gains of EC, those that use a greater variety of *communication channels* to disseminate EC-related information tend to have greater overall satisfaction with the adoption. *Supplier pressure* should not be resisted by SMEs and it should be viewed as an opportunity to seek support from supplying firms to improve its EC capability. In contrast, when higher *customer pressure* is experienced, the overall satisfaction tends to be lower for the adopters. Interestingly, the factors that were found to be unique to the SMEs in Singapore are Internal Environment-related (*size of firm, perceived readiness*), while factors that are exclusive to the Australian experience are External Environment-related (*supplier pressure, customer pressure,* and *perceived governmental support*). This further confirms the view that SMEs in both countries adopt a different attitude towards adoption and implementation of EC. In Singapore, SMEs adopts an *inward*-looking attitude towards adoption and implementation when the knowledge of sufficient resources seemed to improve the *Overall Satisfaction*. On the other hand, firms in Australia are more *outwardly*-oriented when the *Overall Satisfaction* of the adoption involves adequately managing or controlling the pressure that was exerted by their trading partners, and attaining assistance from the government. Then again, the *perceived readiness* amongst Singaporean SMEs may also be due to the extensive effort put in by the Singapore government in establishing electronic-infrastructure services and setting (Garelli, 2001)[3].

REFERENCES

Australian Government Information Management Office. (2005). *E-Government: Australia's Approach*. Keynote Address, Special Minister of State Senator The Hon Eric Abetz, Commonwealth of Australia, Nikkei Fifth Strategic Conference on e-Government, 28th – 29th July, Tokyo, Japan.

Bailey, J. E., & Pearson, S. W. (1983). Development of a tool for measuring and analysing *computer* user satisfaction. *Management Science*, *29*(5), 530–545. doi:10.1287/mnsc.29.5.530

Benbasat, I., Bergeron, M., & Dexter, A. (1993). Development and Adoption of Electronic Data Interchange Systems: A Case Study of the Liquor Distribution Branch of British Columbia. In *Proceedings of Administrative Science Association of Canada Twenty First Annual Conference*, Lake Louise, Alberta, Canada, May (pp.153-163).

Boston Consulting Group. (1999). E-tail of the Tiger: Retail E-Commerce in the Asia Pacific. Boston, MA: Boston Consulting Group.

Brancheau, J., & Wetherbe, J. (1990). The Adoption of Spreadsheet Software: Testing Innovation Diffusion Theory in the Context of End-User Computing. *Information Systems Res*earch, 1&2, 115 - 143.

Chong, S. (2005). Electronic Commerce adoption by Small- and Medium-sized Enterprises in Australia: An Empirical Study of Influencing Factors. *Journal of Contemporary Issues in Business and Government*, *11*(1), 49–70.

Chong, S. (2006, August). An Empirical Study of Factors that Influence the Extent of Deployment of Electronic Commerce for Small- and Medium-sized Enterprises in Australia. *Journal of Theoretical and Applied Electronic Commerce Research*, *1*(2), 45–57.

Churchill, G. A. (1991). Marketing research: Methodological foundations (5th Ed.). Chicago: Dryden Press.

Cooper, R., & Zmud, R. (1990). Information technology implementation research: A technological diffusion approach. *Management Science*, *36*(2), 123–139. doi:10.1287/mnsc.36.2.123

Corbitt, B., Behrendorf, G., & Brown-Parker, J. (1997). SMEs and Electronic Commerce. *The Australian Institute of Management*, *14*, 204–222.

Cragg, P., & King, M. (1993). Small-firm computing: motivators and inhibitors. *MIS Quarterly*, *17*(1), 47–60. doi:10.2307/249509

Cronbach, L. J. (1951, September). Coefficient alpha and internal structure of tests. *Psychometrika*, *16*, 297–334. doi:10.1007/BF02310555

Damanpour, F. (1991). Organizational innovation: A meta-analysis of effects of determinants and moderators. *Academy of Management Journal*, *34*(3), 555–590. doi:10.2307/256406

Daniel, E. M., & Grimshaw, D. J. (2002). An exploratory comparison of electronic commerce adoption in large and small enterprises. *Journal of Information Technology*, *17*(3), 133–147. doi:10.1080/0268396022000018409

Davis, D. (1996). Business Research for Decision Making (4th Ed.). Pacific Grove, CA: Duxbury Press.

DeLone, W. H., & McLean, E. R. (1992). Information Systems success: The quest for the dependent variable. *Information Systems Research*, *3*(1), 60–95. doi:10.1287/isre.3.1.60

Dholakia, R. R., & Kshetri. (2004). Factors Impacting the Adoption of the Internet among SMEs. *Small Business Economics*, *23*(4), 311–322. doi:10.1023/B:SBEJ.0000032036.90353.1f

Dos Santos, B., & Peffers, K. (1998). Competitor and vendor influence on the adoption of innovative applications of electronic commerce. *Information & Management, 34*, 175–184. doi:10.1016/S0378-7206(98)00053-6

Forrester Research. (2002). *E-Commerce Next Wave: Productivity and Innovation*. Presented by J. Meringer in a seminar on Revenue Implications of E-commerce: Trends in E-commerce, WTO Committee on Trade and Development, April.

Forrester Research. (2005, September 14). *US eCommerce Forecast: Online Retail Sales To Reach $329 Billion By 2010*. Forrester Research Inc. Retrieved September 2005, from http://www.forrester.com/Research/Document/Excerpt/0,7211,37626,00.html

Garelli, S. (2001 June). *The World Competitiveness Yearbook 2001*. International Institute for Management Development.

Gatignon, H., & Robertson, T. (1989). Technology Diffusion: An Empirical Test of Competitive Effects. *Journal of Marketing, 53*(1), 35–49. doi:10.2307/1251523

Germain, R., Droge, C., & Daugherty, P. (1994). A Cost and Impact Typology of Logistics Technology and the Effect of its Adoption on Organisational Practice. *Journal of Business Logistics, 15*(2), 227–248.

Gibbs, J., Kraemer, L., & Dedrick, J. (2003). Environment and Policy Factors Shaping Global E-commerce Diffusion: A Cross-Country Comparison, *The Information Society. Special Issue: Globalization of Electronic Commerce, 19*(1), 5–18.

Grandon, E., & Michael, J. (2004). Electronic commerce adoption an empirical study of small and medium US business. *Information & Management, 42*, 197–216.

Grandon, E., & Pearson, J. M. (2003). Strategic Value and Adoption of Electronic Commerce: An Empirical Study of Chilean Small and Medium Businesses. *Journal of Global Information Technology Management, 6*(3), 22–43.

Hair, J. F., Anderson, R. E., Tatham, R. L., & Black, W. C. (1998). Multivariate Data Analysis with Readings (5th Ed.). Englewood Cliffs, NJ: Prentice-Hall.

Iacovou, C., Benbasat, I., & Dexter, A. (1995). Electronic Data Interchange and small organisations: Adoption and impact of technology. *MIS Quarterly, 19*(4), 465–485. doi:10.2307/249629

IDC. (2004, August 6). *IDC Predicts Double Digit Growth of Asia/Pacific Internet Buyers from 2003 to 2008*. IDC Australia. Retrieved September 2005, from http://www.idc.com.au/newsletters/idcpulse/detail.asp?intID=43

Jacob, C. (2000). Advanced Data Analysis. Lecture Series, Curtin University of Technology, Western Australia.

Kendall, J., Tung, L., Chua, K. H., Ng, C. H., & Tan, S. M. (2001). Receptivity of Singapore's SMEs to electronic commerce adoption. *The Journal of Strategic Information Systems, 10*(3), 223–242. doi:10.1016/S0963-8687(01)00048-8

Kettinger, W. J. (1994). National infrastructure diffusion and the U.S. information super highway. *Information & Management, 27*(6), 357–368. doi:10.1016/0378-7206(94)90016-7

King, J., Gurbaxani, V., & Kraemer, K. (1994). The institutional factors in Information Technology innovation. *Information Systems Research, 5*(2), 139–169. doi:10.1287/isre.5.2.139

Kwon, T., & Zmud, R. (1987). Unifying the fragmented models of Information System implementation. In R. Boland and R. Hirschheim (Eds.), Critical Issues in Information System Research. New York: John Wiley.

Lal, K. (2002). E-business and manufacturing sector: A study of small and medium-sized enterprises in India. *Research Policy, 31*, 1199–1211. doi:10.1016/S0048-7333(01)00191-3

Lees, J. D. (1987). Successful development of small business information systems. *Journal of Systems Management, 25*(3), 32–39.

Lertwongsatien, C., & Wongpinunwatana, N. (2003). E-commerce adoption in Thailand: An empirical study of Small and Medium Enterprises (SMEs). *Journal of Global Information Technology Management, 6*(3), 67–83.

Massey, T. (1986). Computers in Small Business: A Case of Under-Utilisation. *American Journal of Small Business, 11*(2), 51–60.

McCole, P., & Ramsey, E. (2005). A Profile of Adopters and Non-adopters of eCommerce in SME Professional Service Firms. *Australasian Marketing Journal, 13*(1), 36–48.

Mirchandani, D. A., & Motwani, J. (2001). Understanding Small Business Electronic Commerce Adoption: An Empirical Analysis. *Journal of Computer Information Systems, 41*(3), 70–73.

Mohr, J., Fisher, R., & Nevin, J. (1996, July). Collaborative communication in interfirm relationships: Moderating effects of integration and control. *Journal of Marketing, 60*, 349–370. doi:10.2307/1251844

Montazemi, A. R. (1988). Factors affecting information satisfaction in the context of the small business environment. *MIS Quarterly, 12*(2), 239–256. doi:10.2307/248849

Moore, G., & Benbasat, J. (1991). Development of an instrument to measure the perceptions of adopting an Information Technology innovation. *Information Systems Research, 2*(3), 192–222. doi:10.1287/isre.2.3.192

Neuman, L. W. (1999). Social research methods: Qualitative and Quantitative Approaches (4th Ed.). Upper Saddle River, NJ: Allyn & Bacon, U.S.A.

Nilakanta, S., & Scamell, R. (1990). The effect of information sources and communication channels on the diffusion of innovation in a data base development environment. *Management Science, 36*(1), 24–40. doi:10.1287/mnsc.36.1.24

Parker, C., & Castleman, T. (2007). New directions for research on SME-eBusiness: Insights from an analysis of journal articles from 2003-2006. *Journal of Information Systems & Small Business, 1*(2), 21–40.

Pavitt, K., Robson, M., & Townsend, J. (1987). The size of distribution of innovating firms in the UK: 1945-1983. *The Journal of Industrial Economics, 35*, 297–316. doi:10.2307/2098636

Payton, F., & Ginzberg, M. (2001). Interorganisational health care systems Implementations: An exploratory study of early Electronic Commerce initiatives. *Health Care Management Review, 26*(2), 20–32.

Premkumar, G., & Roberts, M. (1998). Adoption of new Information Technologies in rural small businesses. *The International Journal of Management Science, 27*, 467–484.

Rao, S. S., Metts, G., & Monge, C. A. M. (2003). Electronic commerce development in small and medium sized enterprises. *Business Process Management Journal, 9*(1), 11–32. doi:10.1108/14637150310461378

Raymond, L. (1990). End-User computing in the small business context - Foundations and directions for research. *Database, 20*(4), 20–26.

Riemenschneider, C. K., & McKinney, V. R. (2002). Assessing belief differences in small business adopters and non-adopters of web-based e-commerce. *Journal of Computer Information Systems*, *42*(2), 101–107.

Rogers, E. M. (1995). Diffusion of Innovations (4th Ed.). New York: The Free Press.

Sharif, N. (1994). Technology change management: Imperatives for developing economies. *Technological Forecasting and Social Change*, *47*, 103–114. doi:10.1016/0040-1625(94)90043-4

Siddharthan, N. (1992). Transaction costs, technological transfer and in-house R&D: A study of the Indian private corporate sector. *Journal of Economic Behavior & Organization*, *18*, 265–271. doi:10.1016/0167-2681(92)90031-6

Soh, C., Mah, Q. Y., Gan, F. Y., Chew, D., & Reid, E. (1997). The use of the Internet for business: The experience of early adopters in Singapore. *Internet Research*, *7*(3), 217–228. doi:10.1108/10662249710171869

Stockdale, R., & Standing, C. (2004). Benefits and barriers of electronic marketplace participation: an SME perspective. *Journal of Enterprise Information Management*, *17*(4), 301–311. doi:10.1108/17410390410548715

Tan, J., Tyler, K., & Manica, A. (2007). Business-to-Business Adoption of eCommerce in China. *Information & Management*, *44*, 332–351. doi:10.1016/j.im.2007.04.001

Tan, M. (1998). Creating the digital economy: perspectives from Singapore, Electronic Commerce in the Information Society. In *Proceedings from the 11ᵗʰ International Bled Electronic Commerce Conference*, Bled, Slovenia, June 8 – 10.

Tan, M., & Teo, T. S. H. (2000). Factors Influencing the Adoption of Internet Banking. *Journal of the AIS*, *1*(5), 1–42.

Thong, J. (2001). Resource constraints and information systems implementation in Singaporean small businesses. *OMEGA International Journal of Management Science*, *29*, 143–156. doi:10.1016/S0305-0483(00)00035-9

Tornatzky, L., & Klein, K. (1982). Innovation characteristics and innovation adoption-implementation: A meta analysis of findings. *IEEE Transactions on Engineering Management*, *29*(11), 28–45.

Tung, L., & Rieck, O. (2005). Adoption of electronic government services among business organizations in Singapore. *The Journal of Strategic Information Systems*, *14*, 417–440. doi:10.1016/j.jsis.2005.06.001

Van Beveren, J. V., & Thomson, H. (2002). The use of electronic commerce by SMEs in Victoria, Australia. *Journal of Small Business Management*, *40*(3), 250–253. doi:10.1111/1540-627X.00054

Wagner, B. A., Fillis, I., & Johansson, U. (2003). E-business and e-supply strategy in small and medium sized businesses (SMEs). *Supply Chain Management*, *8*(4), 343–354. doi:10.1108/13598540310490107

Whiteley, D. (2000). E-Commerce - Strategy, Technologies and Applications. Berkshire, UK: McGraw-Hill Publishing Company.

Zhu, K., Kraemer, K., & Xu, S. (2003). E-Business adoption by European firms: A cross-country assessment of the facilitators and inhibitors. *European Journal of Information Systems*, *12*(4), 251–268. doi:10.1057/palgrave.ejis.3000475

ENDNOTES

[1] Australian SMEs are typically organizations with an annual turnover of less than $20 million and a staff of less than 200 employees (Australian Bureau Statistics,

2004). As for Singapore, the Productivity Board of Singapore (PSB) defines a SME as a company employing less than 200 people with an annual turnover not exceeding $15 million.(Productivity and Standards Board, 2004).

[2] Definition of Small- and Medium-sized Enterprises (SMEs) differ between Australia and Singapore. According to the Australian Bureau Statistics (ABS), small business is any business employing less than 20 people; and 20 or more but less than 200 people for medium business. As for Singapore, the Productivity Board of Singapore (PSB) defines a SME as a company employing less than 200 people with an annual turnover not exceeding $15 million. (For further definitions of SMEs, please refer to http://sbdc. gov.au and http://psb.gov.sg).

[3] Global research has shown that Singapore has done reasonably well in their transformation efforts. Singapore was rated 1st in Asia and 5th worldwide for its EC infrastructure in the World Competitiveness Yearbook 2001(Garelli, 2001). The Boston Consulting Group (1999) places Singapore as one of the top 10 companies in the Asia Pacific for online consumer spending and the Economic Intelligence Unit (2001) ranks Singapore as the 1st in Asia and 7th internationally for E-Business readiness.

Chapter 7
Australian SMEs and
E-Commerce Adoption:
Newer Perspectives

Ada Scupola
Roskilde University, Denmark

ABSTRACT

This chapter presents the results of a study on factors affecting adoption of e-commerce in small and medium size enterprises in Australia. The Tornatsky and Fleischer (1990) model is used in the investigation therefore the main group of factors taken into consideration are environmental, organizational and technological. Top managers employed in five companies located in the area of Brisbane, Queensland have been interviewed. The results are partially in line with similar studies on e-commerce adoption in SMEs. However many differences are also found. For example this study found that the external environment has an influence mainly through customers' requirements and pressure and availability of IT services, contrary to other studies that found that government and public administration have a big role. The organizational and technological contexts have also much relevance and include factors such as employees and CEO attitude.

INTRODUCTION

Small and medium size enterprises (SMEs) are an important sector of the economy and in some countries constitute more than 90% of businesses (OECD, 2002). The management issues, problems and opportunities faced by SMEs are very different from those faced by large corporations, therefore the need to focus specifically on this segment. In this paper the Australian Bureau of Statistics (ABS) definition of SMEs is adopted according to which a small and medium size business is any business employing less than 200 employees (www.abs.gov. au). By drawing on Zwass (1996) e-commerce is here defined as the sharing of business information, maintaining business relationships, and conducting business transactions by means of telecommunications networks. The literature on SMEs' e-commerce adoption is extensive and addresses different aspects among which technological characteristics such as

DOI: 10.4018/978-1-61520-627-8.ch007

barriers and benefits, predictors and determinants (e.g. Saffu et al., 2008; Chitura et al. 2008; Sabherwal et al. 2006; Jeyaraj et al., 2006; Walczuch et al., 2000).

The purpose of this chapter is to present the results of a study on adoption and implementation of e-commerce in Australian SMEs. There have been a number of studies investigating factors affecting SMEs' adoption of e-commerce both in Australia (e.g. Marshall et al., 2000; Akkeren and Cavaye 2000; Poon, 2000) and other countries (e.g. Scupola, 2003; Chen and McQueen, 2008). However, as the rate of e-commerce adoption and diffusion among SMEs increases and consequently SMEs become more acquainted and sophisticated in incorporating e-commerce in their operations it can be expected that the drivers and inhibitors of e-commerce adoption and implementation change as a result. Therefore there is the need of new studies to monitor such evolution and status quo. In addition this study distinguishes itself from previous literature on e-commerce adoption in Australia because by drawing on Tornatzky and Fleischer (1990) it mainly focuses on the organizational, technological and environmental factors.

The basic research question investigated in this paper is:"What are the factors affecting the adoption and implementation of e-commerce in small and medium size enterprises in Australia?" The study can be relevant both to academics and practicing managers interested in understanding the problems faced by SMEs in adopting e-commerce as a major business channel.

The chapter is structured as follows. The first section is the introduction and presents the motivation for the study and the research question. The second section presents a literature review of small business IT adoption frameworks with a focus on the model used in this paper and positions the study within the overall SME research landscape. The third section describes the research design and the data collection process, while a description of the companies is given in the fourth section. The following section is the main thrust of the chapter

and presents the analysis and discussion of the study results. The last two sections present future research directions and conclusions.

Factors Affecting IT Adoption: A Literature Review and a Research Model

A fundamental approach to studying the adoption of new technologies is the diffusion of innovations (Rogers, 1995). According to Rogers (1983:21), adoption is a decision to make full use of an innovation as the best course of action whereas rejection is a decision not to adopt an available innovation. In this study, adoption is defined as *the decision to make use of e-commerce to conduct business or transaction with trading partners*. There are two levels of adoption. Initially, innovation must be purchased, adopted and acquired by an organization. Subsequently, it must be accepted by the ultimate users in that organization also called implementation (Chong and Bauer, 2000; Rogers, 1995). Many studies have investigated explanatory variables for inter-organizational systems (IOS), IS and IT adoption both in small and large organizations (e.g. Saffu et al., 2008; Sabherwal et al. 2006; Jeyaraj et al., 2006; Kurnia & Johnston 2000; Chau & Tam,1997). For example, in one well known study, Iacovou et al. (1995) identified three major factors responsible for EDI adoption: 1) organizational readiness, operationalized as financial and technological resources of the firm; 2) external pressures divided into competitive pressure and imposition by trading partners and 3) perceived benefits of the technology. By investigating seven case studies of small businesses, Iacovou concluded that "a large number of small organizations tend to lack the needed high organizational readiness and perceived benefits that are required for integrated, high impact systems" and that a major reason for small companies to adopt EDI is the external pressure by trading partners. Thong (1999) developed and tested a model including CEO, IS, organizational and environmental characteristics as explanatory variables for IS adoption. His results show that the CEO characteristics have a major importance in IS adoption. In addition, Palvia and Palvia (1999) focused on businesses with very few employees and conducted a study to measure and report satisfaction among small-business users" (Palvia and Palvia, 1999, p. 128). They found that IT satisfaction is influenced by business-related factors such as type of business, size, profitability, location and by owner characteristics. Kuan and Chau (2001) conducted a study to understand factors distinguishing adopters from non adopters. The main results show that perceived direct benefits were distinguishing adopters from non adopters, while perceived indirect benefits were not a distinguishing factor. Perceived financial cost and perceived technical competence was more an obstacle for non adopters then adopter firms and adopters perceived a higher government pressure and lower industry pressure then non adopters. Finally Wymer and Regan (2005) consolidated previous factors of e-commerce and IT adoption and determined their level of influence on the adoption decision. A set of 26 factors, used as variables in various adoption models from the literature, were presented in a neutral manner, without pre-classifying them as barriers or incentives, through a survey sent to SMEs. They found that the only consistent factor across all groups was cost as perceived barrier and concluded that factors are perceived differently by adopters, intended adopters and those not intending to adopt.

In this chapter a model developed by Scupola (2009) is adopted in the investigation (Figure 1). This model is based on the Tornatzky and Fleischer's (1990) framework and is tailored to the specific context of SMEs e-commerce adoption. Tornatzky and Fleischer's (1990) framework has three main explanatory variables for technology adoption: the external environmental context, the organizational context and the technological context. The external environment is the arena in

which an organization conducts its business. By conducting a thorough literature review, Scupola (2009) finds that the significant external factors that might influence SMEs' e-commerce adoption are competitive pressures (Dholakia and Kshetri, 2004; Zhu et al., 2003), pressure from trading partners such as buyers and suppliers (Iacovou et al., 1995; Grandon and Pearson, 2003), the role of government (Kuan and Chau, 2001; Scupola, 2005), and technology support infrastructure such as access and quality of ICT consulting services (Scupola, 2003). The organizational context represents the factors internal to an organization influencing an innovation adoption and implementation (Tornatsky and Fleischer, 1990). Some of the organizational factors more cited in the literature are organizational size (Iacovou et al., 1995) and organizational structure (Jeyaraj et al., 2006). Scupola (2009) finds that CEO characteristics and top management support, employees' IS knowledge, and resource constraints are among the most important organizational factors affecting e-commerce adoption. The technological context represents the pool of technologies available to a firm for adoption. These can be both the technologies available on the market and the firms' current equipment. The decision to adopt a technology depends not only on what is available on the market, but also on how such technologies fit with the technologies that a firm already possesses (Tornatsky and Fleischer, 1990; Jeyaraj et al., 2006, Sabherwal et al. 2006; Wymer and Regan, 2005). In this chapter, the main factors considered are e-commerce relative advantage (e-commerce barriers and benefits) and e-commerce related technologies.

Bharati and Chaudhuryi (2009) in an introductory article for the special issue on "SMEs and Competitiveness—The Role of Information Systems", of the International Journal of E-Business Research provide a review of the current state of research on information systems and SMEs. In this preface they develop a framework (Figure 2 below) that illustrates where the research on IS

Figure 1. A model of e-commerce adoption in SMEs (Scupola, 2009; adapted from Tornatsky and Fleischer, 1990 and Chau and Tam, 1997)

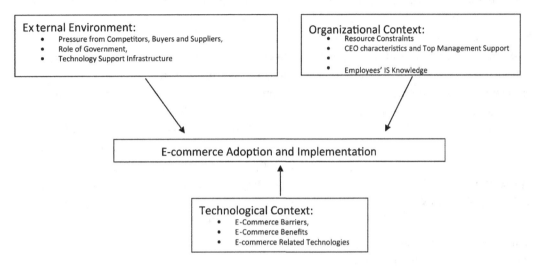

and SMEs has been concentrated and which areas are just beginning to be explored.

According to Bharati and Chaudhuryi (2009) this framework identifies the important antecedent factors such as organizational characteristics and environmental factors used in IS research for SMEs as well as the goals which have usually been adoption and nature of the IS asset. Increasingly, they also have found that firm-level

performance appear to be one of the goals to be causally explained. They identify three links between IS assets and other factors in Figure 1. Link 1 represents the relationship between organizational characteristics and IS asset adoption and utilization. With the advent of e-commerce in the world of SMEs, the research focus widened to include more antecedent factors and how IS assets related to the internet were affecting firm

Figure 2. The SME and IS research framework (source:Bharati, P., & Chaudhury, A. (2009). SMEs and competitiveness - The role of information systems. International Journal of E-Business Research, 5(1), i-ix.)

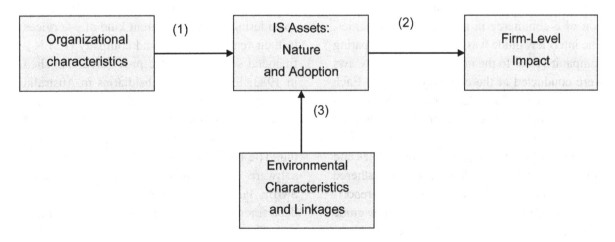

performance, which is represented with link 2 in Figure 2. Finally Bharati and Chaudhuryi (2009) argue that the relationship between environmental factors and IS assets has recently become a focus for research (link 3 in Figure 1). I would argue that the research conducted in this chapter, addressing the external environment, the organizational and the technological context can be positioned in links 1 and 2 in Figure 2.

RESEARCH APPROACH AND DATA COLLECTION

To investigate the research question a number of interviews have been conducted in different companies (Yin, 1994). To ensure that the companies chosen were subject to the same external factors, geographical proximity was defined as one criterion for selection. Another major selection criterion was that firms had to practice e-commerce. The companies participating in this study were chosen across different business sectors. Five companies in Brisbane area have been selected. They varied in regards to ownership, size and age. Due to the commercial confidentiality, names of the companies are kept undisclosed.

Face-to-face semi-structured interviews based on an open-ended questionnaire were used to collect the data. The interviews were conducted with CEOs, managers and other employees that had been involved in the adoption and implementation of e-commerce in the selected companies. The interview guide was sent to the participating companies prior to the interview. The interviews were conducted at the company location. Each interview lasted for about 1 hour. All interviews were tape-recorded and transcribed. Notes were also taken during the interviews. Each interview was transcribed in a sequential order (Miles and Huberman, 1994). Data have also been gathered from the company web sites, brochures and reports provided by the companies. The interview guide included two parts. Part one captured the back-

ground information about the respondents' gender, age, educational level, years with the organization as well as general information about e-commerce and e-commerce sophistication. In part two the questions focused on gaining information about factors affecting adoption and implementation of e-commerce with regard to the three contexts of the Tornatzky and Fleischer model as showed in Fig. 1. The data were analyzed intuitively by the author according to each context of Tornatzky and Fleischer (1990) by following Yin (1994) and Miles and Huberman (1994). The results of the study were sent to the companies to ensure external validity.

COMPANIES BACKGROUND

The age of the five firms ranged from 6 to 40 years. Firms' size varies from 2 to 140 employees. Two out of the five firms (F2 and F4) conduct international business. The degree of sophistication of the web pages varies from a static web page (F1, F4) to a web page offering the capability to download software components (F3) or offering online training and online customer support (F2). F2 has an Intranet. A summary of the companies' characteristics can be found in Table 1.

Company F1 is in the business of site and facilities management and has been founded in 1964. The company has 35 employees and has started using e-commerce in year 2000. The company is considering offering different kind of e-services to their tenants. The second company (F2) is a financial service software provider, established in 1983. F2 has three subsidiaries in Australia and serves the Australian and the New Zealand markets. The company has 140 employees and offers online customer support and online training. The third company's (F3) core business is software development. The clients are mainly SMEs, larger size companies and government departments, such as the department of education. They serve the local Brisbane market. The

Table 1. Characteristics of respective companies in the sample

Firm	Business Type	Years in Business	Number of employees	International business	Year of e-commerce adoption	Internet use
F1	Site and facilities Management	40	35	No	2000	Communication, searching information, online purchasing of office supplies, market research
F2	Financial Service Software Provider	20	140	Yes	1996	Communication, online customer support, online training, relationship management. Intranet is used for news, HR management, and internal communication.
F3	Software Development	6	3	No	1997	Communication, marketing, online promotion, offering of trial software from the web site, searching information.
F4	Manufacturing	32	80	Yes (limited)	1996	Communication, information retrieval, chasing new customers, sending invoices and purchasing orders, online purchasing of office supplies.
F5	Human Resource Consulting	15	2	No	2002	Advertising, e-banking, customer relationship management, searching information, communication.

company employees 3 people including the CEO/owner. It is possible to download some software application components from the web side for trial by the client companies, but they do not charge for it yet. The fourth company (F4) was established in 1971 and serves the national and the international market. F4 has 80 employees and manufacturers point of sale objects such as displays and illuminated signs. They have adopted e-commerce in 1996. The fifth company (F5) is a private practice in Human Resource Management, serving the local market and all Queensland. The customers are government agencies and private services. The company is 15 years old and is a family driven business.

ANALYSIS

This section is structured around the three contexts of the model of Figure 1: environmental, organizational and technological context. The factors belonging to each one of these contexts are summarized in Table 2, Table 3 and Table 4 respectively.

Environmental Context

As it can be seen from Table 2 the main external factors that have influenced adoption and implementation of e-commerce have been pressure from customers as also found by Iacovou (1995) and Scupola (2003) and quality of IT services. In fact 4 out of 5 companies state that these factors had a big influence in e-commerce adoption. Regarding the quality of IT services, small companies were generally satisfied with the consulting services, while very dissatisfied with the quality of the service provided by Internet service providers. All the companies in the sample had changed Internet service provider several times, and only recently they started being satisfied with the level of service provided.

Table 2. Analysis of the firms with respect to adoption factors within environmental context

Company / Factor	F1	F2	F3	F4	F5
Competitive Pressure	No	Yes	No	No	No
Customers' Pressure	No	Yes	Yes	Yes	Yes
Suppliers' Pressure	No	No	No	No	Yes
IT services	Yes	No	Yes	No	Yes
Government	No	No	Yes (Indirectly)	No	Yes (Indirectly)
Public Administration	Yes (Indirectly)	No	No	No	Yes (Indirectly)
Trade Associations	Yes (Indirectly)	No	Yes (Indirectly)	No	No
New Factors found in the study			Globalization/ Open Source Movement/ Big Corporations as Driving Force		

Table 3. Analysis of firms with respect to adoption factors within organizational context

Company / Factor	F1	F2	F3	F4	F5
Financial resources	Yes	Yes	No	Yes	Yes
Employees' IT knowledge/ attitude	Yes	Yes	Yes	No	No
CEO's characteristics	Yes	Yes	Yes	Yes	Yes
Other factors		Marketing Department		EDB Department (Only recently)	

Table 4. Analysis of firms with respect to adoption factors within the technological context

E-Commerce Barriers	Reduction of productivity of the employees (F1, F4); constant interruption and distraction (F1,F3); too much junk mails (C1, C3); cost (F1, F2, F4, F5); technology change and evolution (F2); lack of technology readiness for customers (F1); lack of time (F5); fear of getting lost in cyberspace (F 5); vendor lock in (F2), fear of theft of identity (F3), lack of trust in banks supporting electronic transactions (F3), lack of bandwidth and infrastructure outside the capital cities (F3); loss of sales due to unreliable service providers (F4);
E-Commerce Benefits	Fast access to information (F1, F5, F2, F3, F4); first mover advantage (F2); contribution to internationalization (F5, F3), increased company visibility (F1, F3); increased efficiency (F1, F4), increased market potential (F5, F4), increased collaboration (F5, F3), increased sales (f4), increased public media interest in the company (F1), online customer support function (F2), Online training (F2).
E-Commerce Related Technologies	Push technology e.g. the ability to stream information out to the clients (F2); videoconferencing (F3); video camera connected with PCs (F3)

As it can be seen in Table 2, competition and supplier pressures as well as the influence of government, public administration and trade association is negligible. The companies believe that government, public administration and trade associations were providing some information, organizing seminars, etc., but they were mostly directed to the private citizen. However, they all believed that becoming the private citizen more informed and more used to e-commerce would also influence the extent of adoption in SMEs. None of the companies were aware of direct government intervention such as tax breaks, pilot projects, financial incentives, etc. F3 believed that globalization, the open source movement and the adoption of e-commerce by big corporations could also affect adoption of e-commerce in small companies, at least in the software sector.

Organizational Context

The five companies in the sample had recognized the relative advantage of e-commerce and had allocated the required financial resources to its adoption. However the companies had expressed concern about further investing in e-commerce, especially due to uncertainty of the return on investment (F1, F2, F3, F4, F5). Therefore financial constraints and uncertainty of return on investment are still important factors influencing adoption of e-commerce in SMEs, even though they have been found important in earlier research as well (e.g. Wymer and Regan, 2005; Iacovou et al., 1995).

As it can be seen in Table 3, employees' IT knowledge, expertise and attitude are important in three companies, but they have importance on the way e-commerce is used only once it has been adopted. The decision to adopt and extent of implementation is still made by upper management and CEOs (F1, F2, F3, F4, F5), thus supporting the results found in other studies (e.g. Poon and Swatman, 1999; Thong 1999). However, this study shows that CEOs are starting taking into

considerations the employees' suggestions (F1, F2, F3). For example the CEO of F3 stated that he is willing to listen to employees suggestions regarding e-commerce usage and expansion. The EDB department is starting having an important role in e-commerce adoption in F4. The decision to adopt is mainly based on financial constraints, the uncertainty of return on investment, and on the knowledge of the upper management and CEO. Lack of managerial time was the reason for late adoption in F5.

Technological Context

In this study the factors of the technological context have been grouped under three main categories according to the model of Figure 1 and are summarized in Table 4. This study found that some companies believe that e-commerce leads to a productivity increase (e.g. F2); others (F1, F3) instead pointed out to a productivity decrease mainly due to the fact that employees start using e-mails for their own purposes. The amount of junk mail and e-mail is considered to be a mean of constant interruption and distraction. Other factors that have emerged as potential barriers are vendor lock-in and threat of disintermediation (F2). Furthermore F3 said that there is a lack of trust in the banks' support for electronic transactions, since the customer is not protected if anything goes wrong, and the fear of theft of identity. F4 considered loss of sales due to unreliability of the service providers as an inhibitor to further use e-commerce. Cost of adoption and implementation was still considered an important issue by all the companies, except F3 as also found by Wymer and Regan (2005).

All firms in the sample identified a number of short- and long term benefits of e-commerce that are similar to those already mentioned in the literature (e.g. Wymer and Regan, 2005; Scupola, 2003). The most important experienced short-term benefits were reduction of administrative burden (F1, F2), easy access to information or products

(F1, F2, F3, F5), increased public media interest in the company (F1). The most important long term benefit was improvement of customers relations and communications (F2, F3, F4, F5), increased market potential (F5, F4), contribution to internationalization (F5, F3). F2 considered an important benefit the possibility of being able to offer online training and online customer support.

The study also found that complementary technologies could be important facilitators of e-commerce use and adoption in line with Scupola (2003). For example, F2 said that the coming into the market of push technology, giving the possibility of streaming information out to the clients could enhance further use of e-commerce in the company. F3 said that more widespread and cheaper use of videoconferencing and video camera connected to a PC could potentially further adoption and use of e-commerce.

DISCUSSION OF FINDINGS

This study has investigated factors affecting adoption and implementation of e-commerce in small- and medium-sized enterprises in Australia. The study found that among the external factors two factors have a major importance in adoption of e-commerce: customer pressure and quality of IT services. Marshall et al. (2000) and Akkeren and Caveye (2000) also found industry-related factors as being important in e-commerce adoption, but they were identified mainly in competitors and suppliers pressure. Similarly to the study conducted by Scupola (2003) and Kuan and Chau (2001), this study has found that the influence of government, public administration and trade associations is limited to an indirect source of influence. Industry pressure is important at least in terms of customers. As far as the managers interviewed are aware of there are no financial governmental incentives directly or indirectly targeting adoption of e-commerce in SMEs. There have been some informational campaigns con-

ducted by the government and trade associations have been organizing seminars (F1), but they did not have a big influence. What could make a difference is financial incentives (F1, F2, F3, F4, F5) as also found by Scupola (2003). However, F3 did say that the government could influence the adoption of e-commerce among local SMEs by starting offering electronic tendering. This was the case in Kuan and Chau (2001). Furthermore, three companies (F1, F3, F4) perceive that governmental campaigns are mostly directed towards the private citizen, eventually impacting SMEs' e-commerce adoption in an indirect way.

Regarding access to IT related services the study shows that the companies interviewed are generally satisfied with consulting services in the area (F1, F4, F5). However they have been very dissatisfied with the quality of the Internet service providers (F1, F2, F3, F4, F5). Only recently this is getting better. This is different from the Marshall et al. (2000) results that found most dealers used an ad hoc approach to their web sites and were reluctant to use consultants.

Finally two factors have emerged in this study that had not been discussed in earlier literature: the importance of globalization and the open source movement (F3). However it is difficult from this study to say whether these factors are peculiar to the software industry. Further research is necessary to test this.

Regarding the organizational context, the CEOs characteristics appear as the most important factors with five out of five companies mentioning it as a determinant factor in the decision to adopt e-commerce. Usually the CEO's decision is based on his/her perception of return on investment, the financial resources of the firm and the perceived benefits of e-commerce. For example F4 specifically mentions that they first prioritize investments in manufacturing and then in IT, so if there is no enough money in the budget, there will be no investment in IT made that year, even though the employees feel that they need extra facilities or applications.

Employees' interest and attitude is also considered important by F1, F2 and F3 both for adoption and extent of implementation. For example the CEO of F3 said that if one of his employees goes to him and says that he would like to buy an application to do so and so, then he would normally give the permission for the acquisition. F2 said instead that the marketing department had a major role in suggesting to the CEO what to do regarding e-commerce, while F4 said that until recently it had been the CEO the only one deciding, but recently he was also opening up to the suggestions from the EDB department. So we can conclude that the results of this study are in line with other studies on IT adoption, finding that the characteristics of the CEO are determinant in adoption (e.g. Palvia and Palvia, 1999; Thong, 1999). This study also shows that the CEO is more and more basing his decisions on inputs coming from other employees within the company or consultants external to the company.

Regarding the technological context, the study has found full support for the categories of e-commerce barriers, e-commerce benefits and Internet-related technologies. Among the mentioned benefits relevant is increased media interest in the company (F1).

Among the barriers, relevant to mention are vendor lock-in and threat of disintermediation (F2). Cost is still an important factor inhibiting adoption in Australia, even though some years have passed from previous studies (e.g. Marshall et al., 2000; Poon and Swatman, 1999).

FUTURE RESEARCH DIRECTIONS

In the last decade or so the research on SMEs and IT adoption has been flourishing (e.g. Chen and McQueen, 2008; Chitura et al., 2008; Jeyaraj et al., 2006) as well as the research on IT adoption barriers and benefits (e.g. Scupola, 2003; Poon, 2000). However Bharati and Chaudhury (2009) show how research into SMEs and IS is progressing away from the limited focus on IS adoption, and moving more towards studies that investigate the relationship between environmental factors and IS assets (link 3 in Figure 2 above) and studies that investigate the impact of IS or IT assets on the performance of the company (Link 2 in Figure 2). Regarding the methodology, previous research has been positivistic, qualitative and interpretative. Interesting subjects for future research could be to study and analyze the impact that IT/e-commerce use can have on the relationships between SMEs and the business environment in which they are in (e.g. clusters or networks of companies). Some studies already exists (see for example Scupola and Steinfield, 2008; Steinfield and Scupola, 2008; Steinfield et al., 2009), but there is a need for more. Finally another interesting area could be the exploration of e-services in SMEs (see for example Scupola, 2008; Scupola, 2008a).

CONCLUSION

This chapter has presented the results of a study investigating factors affecting the adoption and extent of implementation of e-commerce in SMEs located in the area of Brisbane in Australia. To investigate the research question a qualitative approach has been used. The results are mainly in line with previous studies in SMEs e-commerce adoption located in Australia as well as in other parts of the world, showing that some factors are always the same even though time goes on such as costs and CEO's characteristics. However this chapter also finds new interesting results that are peculiar to Brisbane area. The study groups the factors into environmental, organizational and technological according to the Tornatzky and Fleischer (1990) framework, therefore positioning itself in the studies that investigate the impact of organizational and environmental factors on IT adoption (Link 1 and 3 according to Bharati and Chaudhury (2009)'s framework). In addition this chapter briefly provides some directions for future research.

Finally the study presents a number of limitations. For example, the data were collected only in the area of Brisbane. In order to generalize from these results to the whole Australia, the study needs to be replicated in other settings. In addition the study is qualitative in nature, which also limits its generalizability. Nevertheless, this research gives some insights into SMEs e-commerce adoption issues in Australia that can be of interest to researchers, SMEs owners and practicing managers.

REFERENCES

Akkeren, J. K., & Cavaye, A. L. (2000). Why Australian Car Retailers do not Adopt E-Commerce Technologies. In *Americas Conference in Information Systems (AMCIS)* (pp. 72-81).

Bharati, P., & Chaudhury, A. (2009). SMEs and competitiveness - The role of information systems. *International Journal of E-Business Research, 5*(1), 1–9.

Chau, P. Y. K., & Tam, K. Y. (1997). Factors Affecting the Adoption of Open Systems: An Exploratory Study. *MIS Quarterly, 21*(1), 1–24. doi:10.2307/249740

Chen, J., & McQueen, R. J. (2008). Factors Affecting E-Commerce Stages of Growth in Small Chinese Firms in New Zealand: An Analysis of Adoption Motivators and Inhibitors. *Journal of Global Information Management, 16*(1), 26–61.

Chitura, T., & Mupemhi, S., Dube & Bolongkikit, T. (2008). Barriers to Electronic Commerce Adoption in Small and Medium Enterprises: A Critical Literature Review. *Journal of Internet Banking and Commerce, 13*(2), 1–13.

Iacovou, C. L., Benbasat, I., & Dexter, A. S. (1995). Electronic Data Interchange and Small Organizations: Adoption and Impact of Technology. *MIS Quarterly, 19*(4), 465–485. doi:10.2307/249629

Jeyaraj, A., Rottman, J., & Lacity, M. J. (2006). A review of the predictors, linkages, and biases in IT innovation adoption research. *Journal of Information Technology, 21*(1), 1–23. doi:10.1057/palgrave.jit.2000056

Kuan, K. K., & Chau, P. Y. K. (2001). A Perception-based model for EDI adoption in small business using a technology-organization-environment framework. *Information & Management, 38*, 507–521. doi:10.1016/S0378-7206(01)00073-8

Kurnia, S., & Johnston, R. B. (2000). The need for a processual view of inter-organizational systems adoption. *The Journal of Strategic Information Systems, 9*(4), 295–319. doi:10.1016/S0963-8687(00)00050-0

Marshall, P., Sor, R., & McKay, J. (2000). The Impacts of Electronic Commerce in the Automobile Industry: An Empirical Study in Western Australia. In B. Wangler & L. Bergman (Eds.), CAiSE 2000 (pp. 509-521). Berlin Heidelberg: Springer Verlag.

Miles, M. B., & Huberman, A. M. (1994). Qualitative Data Analysis (2nd Ed.). Thousand Oaks, CA: Sage Publications.

OECD. (2002). Electronic commerce and SMEs, ICT and electronic commerce for SMEs: Progress Report. Working Party on Small and Medium-Sized Enterprises and Entrepreneurship, Geneva, DSTI/IND/PME (2002)7.

Palvia, P. C., & Palvia, S. C. (1999). An examination of the IT satisfaction of small-business users. *Information & Management, 35*(3), 127–137. doi:10.1016/S0378-7206(98)00086-X

Poon, S. (2000). Business Environment and Internet Commerce Benefit-A Small business Perspective. *European Journal of Information Systems, 9,* 72–81.

Poon, S., & Swatman, P. M. C. (1997). Small business use of Internet Findings from Australian case studies. *International Marketing Review,* 14.

Poon, S., & Swatman, P. M. C. (1999). An exploratory study of small business Internet commerce issues. *Information & Management, 35*(1), 9–18. doi:10.1016/S0378-7206(98)00079-2

Premkumar, G., & Ramamurthy, K. (1995). The Role of Interorganisational and Organizational Factors on the Decision Mode for Adoption of Interorganisational Systems. *Decision Sciences, 26*(3), 303–336. doi:10.1111/j.1540-5915.1995.tb01431.x

Rogers, E. M. (1995). Diffusion of Innovations (4th Ed.). New York: The Free Press.

Sabherwal, R., Jeyaraj, A., & Chowa, C. (2006). Information System Success: Individual and Organizational Determinants. *Management Science, 52*(12), 1849–1864. doi:10.1287/mnsc.1060.0583

Saffu, K., Walker, J. H., & Hinson, R. (2008). Strategic value and electronic commerce adoption among small and medium-sized enterprises in a transitional economy. *Journal of Business and Industrial Marketing, 23*(6), 395–404. doi:10.1108/08858620810894445

Scupola, A. (2003). The Adoption of Internet Commerce by SMEs in the South of Italy: An Environmental, Technological and Organizational Perspective. *Journal of Global Information Technology Management, 6*(1), 51–71.

Scupola, A. (2008). Conceptualizing Competences in E-Services Adoption and Assimilation in SMEs. *Journal of Electronic Commerce in Organizations, 6*(2).

Scupola, A. (2008a). E-Services: Definition, Characteristics and Taxonomy: Guest Editorial Preface, Special on E-Services. *Journal of Electronic Commerce in Organizations, 6*(2).

Scupola, A. (2009). SMEs' E-commerce Adoption: Perspectives from Denmark and Australia. *Journal of Enterprise Information Management, 22*(1-2).

Scupola, A., & Steinfield, C. (2008). The role of a network organization and Internet-based technologies in clusters-The Case of Medicon Valley. In L. Fuglsang (Ed.), Innovation and the Creative Process. Cheltenham, UK: Edward Elgar.

Steinfield, C., & Scupola, A. (2008). Understanding the Role of ICT Networks in a Biotechnology Cluster: An Exploratory Study of Medicon Valley. *The Information Society, 24*(5), 319–333. doi:10.1080/01972240802356091

Steinfield, C., Scupola, A., & Lopez-Nicolas, C. (2009). Social Capital, ICT Use and Company Performance: Findings from the Medicon Valley Biotech Cluster. In *Proceedings of the International Conference on Organizational Learning, Knowledge and Capabilities (OLKC),* Amsterdam, The Netherlands, April 26-28, 2009.

Thong, J. Y. L. (1999). An integrated model of information systems adoption in small business. *Journal of Management Information Systems, 15*(4), 187–214.

Tornatzky, L. G., & Fleischer, M. (1990). The Processes of Technological Innovation. Lanham, MD: Lexington Books.

Walczuch, R., Van Braven, G., & Lundgren, H. (2000). Internet adoption barriers for small firms in the Netherlands. *European Management Journal, 18*(5), 561–572. doi:10.1016/S0263-2373(00)00045-1

Wymer, S., & Regan, E. A. (2005). Factors Influencing e-commerce Adoption and Use by Small and Medium Businesses. *Electronic Markets*, *15*(4), 438–453. doi:10.1080/10196780500303151

Yin, R. K. (1994). *Case Study Research - Design and Methods* (2nd Ed.). Thousand Oaks, CA: Sage Publications. Retrieved from http://www.abs.gov.au

Zwass, V. (1996). Electronic Commerce: Structures and Issues. *International Journal of Electronic Commerce*, *1*(1), 3–23.

Chapter 8
The Perception of Barriers to E–Commerce Adoption by SMEs:
A Comparison of Three Countries

Robert C. MacGregor
University of Wollongong, Australia

Deborah Bunker
University of Sydney, Australia

Mira Kartiwi
University of Wollongong, Australia

ABSTRACT

Electronic commerce (e-commerce) has been utilised as a vehicle to rapidly transform the world into an information society. Yet despite the proven potential of e-commerce in the small business sector, studies have shown that it is the larger businesses that have reaped the benefits, with small/medium enterprise (SME) adoption remaining relatively low by comparison. This slow growth of e-commerce adoption by SMEs has been attributed to various adoption barriers that are faced by small business owners/ managers. While many recent studies have begun examining the relationship between the perceptions of adoption barriers in developed economies, the relationship between the perceptions of these barriers has not been fully examined in developing economies. This chapter firstly presents the authors' understanding of what defines an SME and then highlights our current understanding of the similarities and differences in barriers to e-commerce adoption by SMEs in developed and developing economies. It then describes and discusses a study which examines differences in the groupings and priorities, of barriers to adoption of e-commerce as perceived by SME owner/managers in a developing economy (Indonesia) and two developed economies (Sweden and Australia). The chapter finally describes the implications of these findings for practitioners and researchers.

DOI: 10.4018/978-1-61520-627-8.ch008

INTRODUCTION

The importance of the small to medium enterprise (SME) sector as the cornerstone of most economies is widely recognised (Abdullah and Bakar, 2000; Hall, 2002; NOIE, 2002; Bharati & Chaudhury, 2009). This is not only borne out by the number of SMEs (almost 90% of the total number of businesses across the world), but also by their significant role in creating employment opportunities (Hall, 2002). The role of SMEs is further highlighted in studies by Abdullah and Bakar (2000) and Urata (2000) that suggest that SMEs are vital to the emergence of healthy private sectors, especially in poorer countries. However, research has indicated that the SME contribution to the GDP of many nations has fallen over the past few years (Abernethy, 2002). While the reasons for this decrease are diverse, SMEs are attempting to reverse the trend by turning to global markets. This development has been enabled by the advent of electronic commerce (E-commerce) technology. E-commerce, defined as "the buying and selling of information, products, and services via computer networks" (Kalakota and Whinston, 1997) is radically changing the dynamics of the business environment and the way in which people and organizations are conducting business with one another. For SMEs, e-commerce has the potential to become a source of competitive advantage. E-commerce is a cost effective way of accessing customers globally and competing on par with large businesses. Indeed, Lee (2001) suggests that e-commerce has altered the outlook of businesses from one focused on lean manufacturing (termed as economics of scarcity) to a focus on information which he terms as economics of abundance. SMEs have started to capitalise on these benefits initially by connecting to the Internet. Indeed, according to the American City Business Journals (IEI, 2003), SMEs using the Internet have grown 46% faster than their counterparts who do not use the Internet (Bajaj and Nag, 1999; Khiang and Chye, 2002; Scupola, 2003).

Despite the proven potential of e-commerce and the continued growth of the technology, studies (Riquelme 2002, Magnusson 2001, MacGregor & Vrazalic 2005) have shown that it is the larger businesses that have reaped the benefits, with SME adoption remaining relatively low by comparison (Bharati & Chaudhury, 2009, Kim, 2008). This is particularly the case in many developing economies (Kapurubandara & Lawson 2006). Studies over the past decade have shown that the slower growth of e-commerce adoption in SMEs can been attributed to various adoption barriers that are faced by small business owners/managers. These barriers have been well documented in numerous research studies (Lockett & Brown 2006, MacGregor & Vrazalic 2007, Al Qirim 2007, Quayle 2002, Kim 2008). While most of these studies (see for example Beatty et al. 2001, Mehrtens et al. 2001) have been carried out in developed economies, a number of recent studies (Kapurubandara & Lawson 2006, Kartiwi 2006, Hermana et al. 2006, Kaewkitipong & Brown, 2008) have begun to look at developing economies. The differences between developed and developing economies (such as available infrastructure, social and cultural issues) invariably lead to the conclusion that findings derived from developed economies cannot be generalised to developing economies. Indeed, recent studies (Kaynak et al. 2007, Molla & Heeks 2007) suggest that simply transplanting findings from developed to developing economies results in conclusions that are little more than conceptual models without any rigorous empirical foundations.

The aim of this chapter is twofold: to identify the underlying factors of e-commerce barriers in developed and a developing economies; and to determine whether the underlying factors themselves differ between SMEs in developed and developing economies. The chapter begins by examining the nature of SMEs and identifying features that are unique to SMEs. A discussion of barriers to e-commerce adoption based on previous research is then presented and these barriers are mapped to unique SME features. A recent study was completed by the authors, where data has been gathered from SME owner managers in 3 countries, representing both developed and developing economies. A correlation and factor analysis is described for each country and discussion of similarities and differences between these countries is then presented and conclusions for practitioners and researchers are drawn.

BACKGROUND TO SMES

The nature of SMEs can be understood from the perspectives of how they are formally defined and the characteristics that are unique to this sector.

Defining an SME

There are a number of definitions of what constitutes an SME. Some of these definitions are based on quantitative measures, while others employ a qualitative approach. Meredith (1994) suggests that any definition of an SME must include a quantitative component that takes into account staff levels, turnover and assets together with financial and non-financial measurements, but that the description must also include a qualitative component that reflects how the business is organised and how it operates.

The lack of a formal definition of SMEs has lead to diverse definitions being adoption by governments and other organisations in different countries. In Australia in the 1960s, the Federal Government commissioned a report from a committee known as the Wiltshire Committee. This report suggested a flexible definition of an SME as (Meredith, 1994, p 31) "one in which one or two persons are required to make all of the critical decisions (such as finance, accounting, personnel, inventory, production, servicing, marketing and selling decisions) without the aid of internal (employed) specialists and with owners only having specific knowledge in one or two functional

areas of management". The Wiltshire Committee concluded that this definition could normally be expected to apply to the majority of enterprises in Australia with fewer than 100 employees. This recommendation has remained in use to the present day with the Australian Bureau of Statistics (ABS) defining a small business as an enterprise employing up to 99 people. A medium enterprise employs between 100 and 199 individuals and organisations with more than 200 employees are considered large businesses. The ABS definition has become the de-facto definition of SMEs in Australia. In 2006 1,646,344 organisations fell into this category according to the ABS (ABS 2006).

The United States bases its definition on the position of the organisation within the overall marketplace. According to the United States Small Business Administration (SBA), Section 3 of the Small Business Act of 1953 defines an SME as "one which is independently owned and operated and which is not dominant in its field of operation". The SBA defines different size standards for each industry in the USA. For example, in manufacturing the standard is 500 employees, while the standard for the services industry is defined in terms of annual receipts (US$6 million in this instance).

By comparison, the United Kingdom took a similar approach to Australia and rather than defining SMEs by industry, a common standard of having fewer than 50 employees and not being a subsidiary of any other company was laid out in the UK Companies Act (1989) to define a small business. The UK definition is in agreement with the European Commission's definition of less than 50 employees (Europa, 2003). More than 99% of all businesses in Sweden are classified as small to medium enterprises (SMEs), which means they employ less than 250 people. Of those, 94% are micro businesses with less than 10 employees.

Owing to these differences across countries, researchers have applied diverse SME definitions in their own studies, which have implications for cross-study comparisons. However, it is not simply the number of employees that sets apart an SME from a larger organisation. SMEs have their own unique characteristics.

Unique Characteristics of SMEs

Not only has the definition of SMEs been the subject of both government and academic debate, the special circumstances of the SME sector has been the topic of investigation by both government and academic researchers. Perhaps most important in the ongoing discussion of SMEs is the view, best summarised by Westhead and Storey (1996) that

... the small firm is not a scaled down' version of a large firm. In short, theories relating to SMEs must consider the motivations, constraints and uncertainties facing smaller firms and recognise that these differ from those facing large firms (Westhead & Storey, 1996, p. 18)

Indeed, there are many factors influencing enterprise scale, including economies of scale, transaction costs and market structure (Street & Meister 2004). This apparent inappropriateness of applying large firm concepts to small organisations presents the researcher with the critical question: just how do small firms differ from their larger counterparts?

Brigham and Smith (1967) found that SMEs tended to be more risky than their larger counterparts. This view was supported in later studies (Walker, 1975; DeLone, 1988) and is still in evidence today with high failure rates in the SME sector. Cochran (1981) agreed that SMEs tended to be subject to higher failure rates while Rotch (1987) suggested that they maintained inadequate records of transactions. Welsh and White (1981), in a comparison of SMEs with their larger counterparts found that they suffered from a lack of trained staff and had a short-range management perspective. They termed these traits 'resource

poverty' and suggested that their net effect was to magnify the effect of environmental impact, particularly when information systems were involved.

These early suggestions have been supported by more recent studies that have found most SMEs lack technical expertise (Barry & Milner, 2002) and adequate capital to undertake technical enhancements (Gaskill et al., 1993; Raymond, 2001), and also suffer from inadequate organisational planning (Tetteh & Burn, 2001; Miller & Besser, 2000). Many small organisations also differ from their larger counterparts in the extent of the product/service range available to customer (Reynolds et al., 1994).

A number of recent studies (Reynolds et al., 1994; Murphy, 1996; Bunker & MacGregor, 2000) have examined the differences in management style between large and small businesses. These studies have shown that among other characteristics, SMEs tend to have a smaller management teams (often one or two individuals), they are strongly influenced by the owner and the owner's personal idiosyncrasies, they have little control over their environment (this is supported by the studies of Westhead and Storey (1996) and Hill and Stewart (2000)) and they have a strong desire to remain independent (this is supported by the findings of Dennis (2000) and Drakopoulou-Dodd et al. (2002)).

Based on our review of the literature, a summary of the features unique to SMEs was derived (Table 1). An analysis of the features revealed that they could be classified as being internal or external to the business. Internal features include management, decision-making and planning processes, and the acquisition of resources, while external features are related to the market (products/services and customers) and the external environment (risk taking and uncertainty). These features have significant implications for an SME's ability, and indeed, desire, to adopt new technology (including e-commerce). Perhaps central to the characteristics distinguishing SMEs from their larger counterparts are the views of Westhead and Storey (1996) and Hill and Stewart (2000) who suggest that uncertainty is the key difference between small and large businesses. They suggest that while 'internal' uncertainty is more a characteristic of large business, it is 'external' uncertainty that characterises smaller organisations.

While some of this external uncertainty may be attributable to those factors termed external features (see Table 1), Hill and Stewart (2000) suggest that the major reason for external un-

certainty is the lack of influence over the market environment. In order to cope with the changing market place, SMEs are often obliged to operate in a regime that is far more short term. While this short term strategy may provide the advantage of flexibility of response to external changes, Hill and Stewart (2000) suggest that very often it is "like plate spinning, waiting to see which one comes down first" (p. 107). Most of the characteristics summarised in Table 1 can be viewed in this light - as opportunities or constraints. More

Table 1. A list of features unique to small to medium enterprises (SMEs) (adapted from MacGregor & Vrazalic 2004)

ID	FEATURES UNIQUE TO SMEs	REPORTED BY	
	Features Related to Management, Decision Making and Planning Processes		
INT 1	SMEs have small and centralised management with a short range perspective	Bunker & MacGregor (2000) Welsh & White (1981) Will (2008), St-Pierre & Raymond (2004) O'Regan & Ghobadian (2004) Matzler et al. (2008)	
INT 2	SMEs have poor management skills	Blili & Raymond (1993) Fuller-Love & Street (2006) Kyobe 2008	
INT 3	SMEs exhibit a strong desire for independence and avoid business ventures which impinge on their independence	Dennis (2000) Reynolds et al. (1994) Chahine & Filatotchev (2008)	
INT 4	SME Owners often withhold information from colleagues	Dennis (2000) Chahine & Filatotchev (2008)	
INT 5	The decision making process in SMEs is intuitive, rather than based on detailed planning and exhaustive study	Reynolds et al. (1994) Bunker & MacGregor (2000) Haugh & Mckee (2004)	
INT 6	The SME Owner(s) has/have a strong influence in the decision making process	Reynolds et al. (1994) Bunker & MacGregor (2000) Elliott & Boshoff (2007) Mole (2007)	INTERNAL FEATURES
INT 7	Intrusion of family values and concerns in decision making processes	Dennis (2000) Bunker & MacGregor (2000) Reynolds et al. (1994) Chirico (2008) Mole (2007)	
INT 8	SMEs have informal and inadequate planning and record keeping processes	Reynolds et al. (1994) Allred et al. (2007) Meers & Robertson (2007) Tetteh & Burn (2001) Miller & Besser (2000) Markland (1974) Rotch (1967)	

continued on following page

Table 1. continued

ID	FEATURES UNIQUE TO SMEs	REPORTED BY	
	Features Related to Resource Acquisition		**INTERNAL FEATURES**
INT 9	SMEs face difficulties obtaining finance and other resources, and as a result have fewer resources	Cragg & King (1993) Welsh & White (1981) Gaskill & Gibbs (1994) Reynolds et al. (1994) Blili & Raymond (1993) Mir & Feitelson (2007) Johnston et al. (2007)	
INT 10	SMEs are more reluctant to spend on information technology and therefore have limited use of technology	Walczuch et al. (2000) Dennis (2000) MacGregor & Bunker (1996) Poon & Swatman (1997) Abell & Limm (1996) Mir & Johnston et al. (2007) MacGregor & Vrazalic (2007) Celuch et al. (2007)	
INT 11	SMEs have a lack of technical knowledge and specialist staff and provide little IT training for staff	Martin & Matlay (2001) Cragg & King (1993) Bunker & MacGregor (2000) Reynolds et al. (1994) Welsh & White (1981) Blili & Raymond (1993) Lockett & Brown (2006)	
	Features Related to Products/Services and Markets		**EXTERNAL FEATURES**
EXT 1	SMEs have a narrow product/service range	Bunker & MacGregor (2000) Reynolds et al. (1994) Wolff & Pett (2006) Runyoan & Huddleston (2006) Barrett & Burgess (2008)	
EXT 2	SMEs have a limited share of the market (often confined towards a niche market) and therefore heavily rely on few customers	Hadjimanolis (1999) Lawrence (1997) Quayle (2002) Reynolds et al. (1994)	
EXT 3	SMEs are product oriented, while large businesses are more customer oriented	Reynolds et al. (1994) Bunker & MacGregor (2000) MacGregor et al. (1998)	
EXT 4	SMEs are not interested in large shares of the market	Reynolds et al. (1994) MacGregor et al. (1998)	
EXT 5	SMEs are unable to compete with their larger counterparts	Lawrence (1997) Lawrence (2007)	
	Features Related to Risk Taking and Dealing with Uncertainty		
EXT 6	SMEs have lower control over their external environment than larger businesses, and therefore face more uncertainty	Westhead & Storey (1996) Hill & Stewart (2000) Lawrence (2007)	
EXT 7	SMEs face more risks than large businesses because the failure rates of SMEs are higher	Brigham & Smith (1967) DeLone (1988) Cochran (1981) Will (2008)	
EXT 8	SMEs are more reluctant to take risks	Walczuch et al. (2000) Dennis (2000)	

often than not, they are constraints that limit the expansion and growth of SMEs. SMEs in regional areas are particularly susceptible to these types of constraints.

It must be noted, that these studies have been predominantly carried out in developed economies with mature markets that exhibit different economic and organisational/cultural features than those of developing economies. In order to begin to understand the possible differences in SME features within and between developed and developing economies we now review some studies of e-commerce adoption by SMEs in developing economies.

SMEs in Developing Countries

There have been a number of studies that have examined the nature of SMEs in developing economies. Many of these have shown that specific characteristics of small businesses can act as an obstacle to e-commerce adoption. Palvia & Vemuri (2002) suggest that the basis for discussing differences (developed-developing economies) needs to be twofold – economic and cultural differences. Economic features include connection costs, the availability of disposable income to allow trading and purchasing online, tariffs, currency exchange and shipping requirements. Cultural features include language, work habits and methods of organising, localisation of pricing and regulations as well as graphics and graphical components of websites. Jennex et al. (2004), while noting these earlier findings, suggest that these features cannot simply be examined from a 'global' level, but must include the cultural and economic features of the particular business. This includes perception of future growth, perception of costs and perception of how evidence of value-add is presented to customers. A number of studies have examined specific developing economies and while there are appear to be similarities between SMEs worldwide, differences can be seen specifically in developing economies with many specific

factors re-appearing within these studies. SMEs within developing economies have:

- A lack of access to hardware, software or internet infrastructure (Mukti 2000, Dedrick & Kraemer 2001, Oshikoya & Hussain 2007, Ochara et al. 2008, Thompson & Brown 2008);
- Security concerns which encompass the operation of their businesses (Jennex et al. 2004, Chiware & Dick 2008, Cloete et al. 2002);
- Payment issues which concern the ability and the where-with-all of supplier's and customer's ability to consistently meet their payment obligations (Mukti 2000, Kartiwi 2008);
- Lack of general business skills and education (Ochara et al. 2008, Thompson & Brown 2008);
- Lack of uniform accounting, regulatory and financial methods (Chepaitis 2002);
- A reluctance to share information, knowledge or data within and external to their businesses (Jennex et al. 2004);
- Informal entrepreneurship skills, relying on barter and black markets (Jennex et al. 2004, Chepaitis 2002); and
- Difficulty coping with incrementally complex application of technology (Thompson & Brown 2008).

Barriers to E-Commerce Adoption in SMEs

It has been demonstrated previously that the rate of e-commerce adoption in SMEs has been low. This slow paced uptake of e-commerce technologies has been documented and researched widely, with results indicating that SMEs face inhibitors or barriers that prevent them from implementing and fully reaping the benefits of e-commerce.

Like the unique features of SMEs, the barriers to e-commerce adoption can be classified as external or internal to the business. Hadjimanolis (1999), in a study of e-commerce adoption by SMEs in Cyprus, found that external barriers could be further categorised into supply barriers (difficulties obtaining finance and technical information), demand barriers (e-commerce not fitting with the products/services or not fitting with the way clients did business) and environmental barriers (security concerns). Internal barriers were further divided into resource barriers (lack of management and technical expertise) and system barriers (e-commerce not fitting with the current business practices). An analysis of e-commerce adoption barriers which has been mapped to the unique features of SMEs (see Table 1) is presented as Table 2. For example, one of the most commonly cited barriers to e-commerce adoption is that it is too expensive to implement, a barrier that arises from the fact that SMEs face difficulties obtaining finance, unlike their larger counterparts. If the finance was readily available to SMEs, high cost may not be a barrier to e-commerce adoption.

It must be noted once again, however that these adoption barriers and unique SME features, and their subsequent analysis to produce Table 2, have been taken from research studies predominantly conducted in developed economies. In order to better understand barriers to adoption for SMEs in developing economies we must look at studies of SMEs operating in these economies.

Barriers to E-commerce Adoption in SMEs in Developing Economies

There have been a number of recent studies focussing on the adoption of e-commerce in developing economies. Some of these studies have focussed on the role of infrastructure within the country and some have examined the role of organisational barriers, while others have examined barriers concerned with finance, technical requirements and standards.

Studies conducted by Kapurubandara & Lawson (2006), Gefen & Heart (2006), Gefen et

al. (2005), Saffu et al. (2008), Purcell & Toland (2004) and Kartiwi 2006 highlight *technical and security issues* and suggest that SMEs:

- Perceive a lack of security of e-commerce as a base technology platform for doing business;
- Have concerns regarding credit card use within the potential customer base as a result of this perceived lack of security; and
- Perceive a lack of usefulness of the technology to the organisation.

Studies conducted by Cloete et al. (2002), Kapurubandara & Lawson (2006) and MacGregor & Vrazalic (2007) all indicate that SMEs in developing economies have concerns with the *organisational factors* affecting e-commerce adoption in the way that that they do business indicating that:

- There is a lack of critical mass of customers and suppliers using e-commerce in supply chain arrangements;
- It is a problem convincing many owner/ managers of the benefits of e-commerce for buying and selling of their products and services; and
- E-commerce is not appropriate for the way these SMEs suppliers and customers are used to conducting business.

Cloete et al. (2002), Purcell & Toland (2004) and Kapurubandara & Lawson (2006), Chepaitis 2002), Saffu et al. (2008) and MacGregor & Vrazalic (2007) have found that owner/managers *lack of time, knowledge and awareness about e-commerce* which affects its adoption highlighting that owner/managers:

- Lack time to investigate options when considering e-commerce adoption;
- Have far less awareness and experience than those owner/managers in developing

Table 2. List of e-commerce adoption barriers and their relationship to the features unique to SMEs

BARRIERS TO E-COMMERCE ADOPTION	REPORTED BY	RELATED TO UNIQUE FEATURE ID
High cost of e-commerce implementation; Internet technologies too expensive to implement	Iacovou et al. (1995) Quayle (2002) Purao & Campbell (1998) Lawrence (1997) Riquelme (2002); Van Akkeren & Cavaye (1999) Carnaghan et al. (2004) Al-Qirim (2006)	INT 9
E-commerce too complex to implement	Quayle (2002) Lockett & Brown (2006) Warren (2004)	INT 11
Low level of existing hardware technology incorporated into the business	Lawrence (1997) Levenberg et al. (2005)	INT 10
SMEs need to see immediate ROI and e-commerce is a long-term investment	Lawrence (1997) Holmes et al. (2004)	INT 1
Organisational resistance to change because of the fear of new technology amongst employees	Lawrence (1997) Van Akkeren & Cavaye (1999) Archer et al. (2008) Fillis & Wagner (2005)	INT 2; INT 11
Preference for and satisfaction with traditional manual methods, such as phone, fax and face-to-face	Lawrence (1997) Venkatesan & Fink (2002) Poon & Swatman (1998) MacGregor & Vrazalic (2005, 2007)	INT 10; EXT 3
Lack of technical skills and IT knowledge amongst employees; Lack of computer literate/specialised staff	Quayle (2002) Lawrence (1997) Riquelme (2002) Van Akkeren & Cavaye (1999) Iacovou (1995) Damsgaard & Lyytinen (1998) Chau & Turner (2002) Tucker & Lafferty (2004) MacGregor & Vrazalic (2005)	INT 11
Lack of time to implement e-commerce	Walczuch et al. (2000) Lawrence (1997) Van Akkeren & Cavaye (1999) Archer et al. (2008)	INT 5; INT 2; INT 1
E-commerce is not deemed to be suited to the way the SME does business	Abell & Limm (1996) Hadjimanolis (1999) Iacovou et al. (1995) Poon & Swatman (1997) Quaddus & Hofmeyer (2007)	INT 5; INT 8; EXT 3;
E-commerce is not deemed to be suited to the products/services offered by the SME	Walczuch et al. (2000) Kendall & Kendall (2001) Hadjimanolis (1999) Quaddus & Hofmeyer (2007) Lee & Christy (2004)	EXT 1; EXT 5
E-commerce is perceived as a technology lacking direction	Lawrence (1997) MacGregor & Vrazalic (2005)	INT 1; INT 10; EXT 8
Lack of awareness about business opportunities/ benefits that e-commerce can provide	Iacovou et al. (1995) Quayle (2002)	INT 1; INT 2; INT 5; INT 8; EXT 3; EXT 4

continued on following page

Table 2. continued

BARRIERS TO E-COMMERCE ADOPTION	REPORTED BY	RELATED TO UNIQUE FEATURE ID
Lack of available information about e-commerce	Lawrence (1997) MacGregor & Vrazalic (2005)	EXT 8
Concern about security of e-commerce	Quayle (2002) Purao & Campbell (1998) Abell and Limm (1996) Riquelme (2002) Van Akkeren & Cavaye (1999) Poon & Swatman (1998) Hadjimanolis (1999) Tucker & Lafferty (2004)	EXT 6; EXT 7; EXT 8
Lack of critical mass among customers, suppliers and business partners to implement e-commerce	Abell and Limm (1996) Hadjimanolis (1999) Al-Qirim (2006) Levenbeurg et al. (2005)	EXT 2
Heavy reliance on external consultants (who are considered by SMEs to be inadequate) to provide necessary expertise	Lawrence (1997) Van Akkeren & Cavaye (1999) Chau & Turner (2002)	INT 11
Lack of e-commerce standards	Tuunainen (1998) Robertson & Gatignon (1986) MacGregor & Vrazalic (2005)	INT 11

economies.

- Lack e-commerce technical knowledge and awareness within the organisation; and
- Lack information on the possible options available for e-commerce.

Purcell & Toland (2004), Saffu et al. (2008), Cloete et al. (2002), Kapurubandara & Lawson (2006), Schmid et al. (2001), Cooray (2003 - cited in Kapurubandara & Lawson 2006) and Chepaitis (2002) all focussed on *financial issues* that many SMEs face and their studies indicate that financial barriers to e-commerce adoption by SMEs in developing economies include:

- The cost involved in setting up e-commerce-based operations within the organisation;
- Additional costs incurred by SMEs because of antiquated legal and financial systems within their economy;

- Government involvement in pricing structures which reduces the financial benefit of technology to the SME; and
- Poor transport systems which add to the cost of product distribution incurred by the SME when adopting e-commerce.

Whilst many of these barriers to e-commerce adoption by SMEs in developing economies are similar to those that are evident in developed economies, many of these barriers are exacerbated by specific economic and cultural conditions. These include the evident lack of critical infrastructure, education, technical security and financial resources (*economic*) as well as perceived lack of appropriateness of e-commerce for the supply chain arrangements (*cultural*).

A COMPARATIVE STUDY OF E-COMMERCE ADOPTION BY SMES IN DEVELOPED AND DEVELOPING ECONOMIES

In order to understand what might be driving e-commerce adoption for SMEs within both developed and developing economies we now look at a specific study conducted by the authors of this chapter. The aim of this study was twofold: to identify the underlying e-commerce barriers in developed and a developing economy; and to determine whether these barriers differ between SMEs in developed and a developing economy. Data was collect in Australia, Sweden and Indonesia and then analysed to examine the correlation and underlying factors of barriers to e-commerce as perceived by SME owner/managers in each of these countries. Australia and Sweden were selected as examples of developed countries, Indonesia as an example of a developing economy (World Bank 2006).

SMEs in Australia

SMEs account for more than 95% of companies in Australia. As such, collectively SMEs are a significant customer segment for financial services providers. Of the over 600,000 SMEs in Australia, more than 2/3 employ between 1 and 4 people with a further 180,000 employing between 5 and 19 people. For the past 7 years, SME financial deposits have been growing at approx 15.5% pa. Temperley et al. (2004) suggest that the key success factors of most SMEs are the skill, drive and vision of the CEO and as success relies on a single person there are significant benefits in sharing with the broader community. These same authors suggested that most SMEs were flexible and responsive to customer requests and change requirements; they found it onerous and difficult to apply for or gain any form of government grant; most undertook some innovation but were ambivalent towards patents; and unlike European and American SMEs, most were not part of any industry-based association.

SMEs in Sweden

The European Union views SMEs as a catalyst for regional development (Europa, 2003). SMEs have been earmarked as playing an important role in promoting growth because they are seen as a key source of jobs and employment prospects (Keniry et al., 2003; Larsson et al., 2003). For the purposes of its various support programs and measures, the European Commission has constructed a single set of definitions of SMEs (EIRO, 2006). Two major interconnected policies exist in Sweden. These are termed the SME policy and the Entrepreneurship policy. Both policies pursue several major objectives – to stimulate employment creation, to stimulate regional development, to stimulate innovation and to expand economic growth. Lundström and Stevenson (2002) suggest, amongst other things, the two policies support the creation of new firms, the delivery of education and support to newly established firms, the promotion of women as owner/manager, the spread of technology to SMEs and the streamlining of financial, organisational and exporting support for SMEs.

At a practical level, Boter and Lundström (2005) point to 2 National agencies (Almi Business Partner and Swedish Trade Council) and 2 regional agencies (the National Labour Market Board and the County Administration Board) whose tasks include the development of entrepreneurship curricula, the development of business – education partnerships, the development of community support, the administration of funding for new initiatives and the involvement the students in technical and organisational analysis of SME firms and ventures.

SMEs in Indonesia

During the last twenty years, there has been a considerable growth in terms of the number of SMEs throughout Asian economies, and Indonesia in particular. Indonesian SMEs have proven to be the most dynamic and vibrant sector, especially during the time of financial crisis in 1997 (Urata, 2000). There is no consensus on the definition of SMEs in Asia Pacific region. The definitions differ from country to country depending on the phase of economic development as well as their existing social conditions. As the focus of this study is on the Indonesian economic setting, the official definitions from two Indonesian government bodies The Central Bureau of Statistics (CBS, 2004) and the Ministry of Cooperatives and Small Medium Enterprises (DEPKOP, 2005a) will be adopted.

There are currently more than 40 million SME establishments in Indonesia. They account for 99.99% of the total number of business enterprises. Based on the latest data (DEPKOP, 2005b), the largest percentage is in the agriculture sector (58.9%), followed by trade (22%) and manufacturing (6.3%) sectors with transportation and services also significant. The significance of SMEs to the Indonesia economy is further highlighted by their contribution to national development and by the fact that, as a sector, they provide and create jobs especially during times of recession (Asian Development Bank., 2003; DEPKOP, 2005a).

RESEARCH METHODOLOGY

The 17 barriers identified from the literature describing SMEs in developed economies (see Table 2) and the additional barriers highlighted from the studies of SMEs in developing economies, were initially clustered into 10 "statements". These represented the significant reasons (or perceived barriers) as to why an owner manager of an SME might not adopt e-commerce (see Figure 1).

These statements formed the basis of 6 in-depth interviews in Australia, 6 in-depth interviews in Sweden and 8 in-depth interviews in Indonesia with SME owner/managers and consultants. The aim of the interviews was to ensure the applicability and completeness of these statements (perceived barriers) to SME owner/managers in each one of the locations. These statements were validated by interviewees in all locations and no extra statements were added.

Based on the results of these interviews a survey instrument was then developed. The survey was used to collect data from a greater number of SMEs who were non-adopters of e-commerce. SME owner/managers were asked to rate the importance of each statement to their decision not to adopt e-commerce. A standard 5 point Likert scale was used to rate the importance with 1 (very unimportant) and 5 (very important) – see Figure 1.

Surveys were conducted in regional areas of all of these countries in an attempt to "standardise" possible respondents to the survey and the types of reasons they would not adopt e-commerce i.e. similar characteristics of SMEs faced with similar problems in regional areas (independent of the country being surveyed). Issues such as isolation from mainstream markets, less effective and available e-commerce infrastructure, lack of resources and access to information and education would be familiar to all respondents in this regard.

Phone surveys were conducted in Australian in the Illawarra, Hunter and Western Sydney areas as being representative of regional locations in Australia. Printed surveys were distributed by post in four regional areas of Sweden: Karlstad, Filipstad, Saffle and Arvika. Postal surveys were also distributed to three regional provinces in Indonesia: West Java (Bandung, Sukabumi, Tasikmalaya); Bali (Denpasar, Kuta, Gianyar) and DKI Jakarta.

Figure 1. Question about barriers to e-commerce adoption used in survey

Please indicate why your organisation is not using e-commerce. Below is a list of statements indicating possible reasons. Based on your opinion, please rank each statement on a scale of 1 to 5 to indicate how important it was to your decision NOT to use e-commerce, as follows:

1 = the reason was very unimportant to your decision not to use e-commerce
2 = the reason was unimportant to your decision not to use e-commerce
3 = the reason was neither unimportant nor important to your decision not to use e-commerce
4 = the reason was important to your decision not to use e-commerce
5 = the reason was very important to your decision not to use e-commerce

Our organisation does not use e-commerce because:	Rating				
E-commerce is not suited to our products/ services.	1	2	3	4	5
E-commerce is not suited to our way of doing business.	1	2	3	4	5
E-commerce is not suited to the ways our clients (customers and/or suppliers) do business.	1	2	3	4	5
E-commerce does not offer any advantages to our organisation.	1	2	3	4	5
We do not have the technical knowledge in the organisation to implement e-commerce.	1	2	3	4	5
E-commerce is too complicated to implement.	1	2	3	4	5
E-commerce is not secure.	1	2	3	4	5
The financial investment required to implement e-commerce is too high for us.	1	2	3	4	5
We do not have time to implement e-commerce.	1	2	3	4	5
It is difficult to choose the most suitable e-commerce standard with so many different options available.	1	2	3	4	5

RESULTS

247 non-adopter SMEs answered the questionnaire in Australia which gave a response rate of 48%. Responses were obtained from 129 Swedish non-adopter SMEs giving a response rate of 27%. Responses were obtained from 96 Indonesian SMEs, for a response rate of 19%. A test for reliability was applied to the 3 sets of data. The Cronbach's Alpha for the Australia was .905, the Swedish data .910 and for Indonesia .780.

A factor analysis was used to examine the barriers to E-commerce for the 3 locations. The Kaiser-Meyer-Olkin MSA (905 Australia, .895 Sweden,.720 Indonesia) and Bartlett's Test for Sphericity ($\chi^2 = 1395$, p=.000 Australia, $\chi^2 = 845$, p=.000 Sweden, $\chi^2 = 448$, p=.000 Indonesia)) indicated that the data set satisfied the assumptions for factorability. Principle Components Analysis was chosen as the method of extraction in order to account for maximum variance in the data using a minimum number of factors. A two-factor solution was extracted with Eigenvalues of 4.212 and 3.586 for Australia. Again, this was supported by an inspection of the Scree Plot. These two factors accounted for 77.976% of the total variance. A two-factor solution was extracted with Eigenvalues of 5.615 and 1.556 for Sweden. This was supported by an inspection of the Scree Plot. These two factors accounted for 71.717% of the variance. A three-factor solution was extracted with Eigenvalues of 3.439, 2.586 and 1.014 for Indonesia. Again, this was supported by an inspection of the Scree Plot. These three factors accounted for 70.400% of the variance. Table 3 provides the details.

In all 3 cases the resulting components were rotated using a Varimax procedure and a simple structure was achieved as shown in Table 4.

Table 3. Total variance explained

Component	Sweden			Australia			Indonesia		
	Eigen value	% Var.	Cum. %	Eigen value	% Var.	Cum. %	Eigen value	% Var.	Cum. %
Too Difficult	5.615	56.154	56.154	4.212	42.116	42.116	2.586	25.864	60.255
Unsuitable	1.556	15.652	71.717	3.586	35.860	77.976	3.439	34.391	34.391
Time/ Choice							1.014	10.145	70.400

DISCUSSION

The aim of this study was to identify the underlying factors of e-commerce barriers in developed and a developing economy; and to determine whether the underlying factors themselves differ between SMEs in developed and a developing economy. An examination of tables 3 and 4 show a number of interesting findings. Firstly, and perhaps most obvious, is that the Indonesian respondents differed from both the Swedish and Australian respondents.

Table 3 shows that both the Swedish and Australian respondents considered that barriers to e-commerce adoption were either technical (termed too difficult) or organisational (termed unsuitable). Both considered that the most important set of barriers were the technical group (shown with the larger Eigenvalue). By comparison, the Indonesian respondents considered that there were three types of barriers, technical (again termed too difficult), organisational (again termed unsuitable), and a third set (termed time/ choice). The data also shows that the Indonesian respondents considered that the organisational barriers were the most important.

If we now examine Table 4, it can be seen that all three sets of respondents loaded four barriers onto the organisational factor. These were: "E-commerce is not suited to our products/ services"; "E-commerce is not suited to our way of doing business"; "E-commerce is not suited to the ways our clients (customers and/or suppliers) do business"; and "E-commerce does not offer any

advantages to our organisation". For the Swedish and Australian respondents, 6 barriers loaded onto the technical factor. These were: "We do not have the technical knowledge in the organisation to implement e-commerce": "E-commerce is too complicated to implement"; "E-commerce is not secure"; "The financial investment required to implement e-commerce is too high for us"; "We do not have time to implement e-commerce"; and "It is difficult to choose the most suitable e-commerce standard with so many different options available". By comparison, the Indonesian respondents loaded 2 barriers onto a separate factor. These were: "We do not have time to implement e-commerce"; and "It is difficult to choose the most suitable e-commerce standard with so many different options available". A number of studies (Cloete et al. 2002, Purcell & Toland 2004, Kapurubandra & Lawson 2006) suggest that SMEs in developing economies find lack of time and lack of information concerning choices to be much more of a barrier than those in developed economies. While it is not possible to compare these separately across the three locations, it is interesting to note that they are considered as a separate and uncorrelated group by the Indonesian respondents.

The results of this study are significant in another way. The analysis has shown that ten of the most common barriers to e-commerce adoption can be grouped in relation to two or three main factors. This gives researchers a powerful explanatory tool because it reduces the "noise" in the data. Instead of accounting for ten different

Table 4. Rotated component matrix

Barrier	Sweden		Australia		Indonesia		
	Too Difficult	Unsuitable	Too Difficult	Unsuitable	Too Difficult	Unsuitable	Time/ Choice
1		.864		.917		.876	
2		.882		.912		.926	
3		.729		.909		.863	
4		.803		.837		.671	
5	.714		.787		.874		
6	.864		.869		.722		
7	.699		.767		.596		
8	.798		.795		.648		
9	.829		.813				.782
10	.809		.802				.850

Legend

1 E-commerce is not suited to our products/ services.

2 E-commerce is not suited to our way of doing business.

3 E-commerce is not suited to the ways our clients (customers and/or suppliers) do business.

4 E-commerce does not offer any advantages to our organisation.

5 We do not have the technical knowledge in the organisation to implement e-commerce.

6 E-commerce is too complicated to implement.

7 E-commerce is not secure.

8 The financial investment required to implement e-commerce is too high for us.

9 We do not have time to implement e-commerce.

10 It is difficult to choose the most suitable e-commerce standard with so many different options available.

barriers, the inhibitors to e-commerce adoption can be explained as a result of one of three factors: e-commerce is either too difficult, unsuitable to the business or there is an evident problem with time and choice. The Rotated Component Matrix also enables the prediction of the scores of each individual barrier based on the score of the two or three factors and vice versa, for an SME. This has implications for research into e-commerce barriers. Whereas before researchers identified various barriers (such as the ones listed in Table 3), this is the first time a study has shown that certain barriers are correlated and can be logically grouped according to two or three factors. This makes it simpler not only to explain, but also predict barriers to e-commerce adoption in SMEs in both developed and developing economies.

The fact that Australian and Swedish SMEs grouped all of the barriers into 2 factors (organi-sational and technical) and the Indonesian SMEs grouped barriers into 3 factors (organisational, technical and time/choice) raises an interesting question of how SMEs in different economic and cultural contexts might perceive barriers to adoption of e-commerce. While those SMEs in the study in Australia and Sweden perceive time/ choice barriers as technical in nature, Indonesian SMEs categorised them separately. This may be indicative of the less plentiful availability of resources in a developing economies such as In-donesia (economic context) or perhaps differences in Indonesian work habits and methods of organ-ising and localisation of pricing and regulations (cultural context) may have a profound effect on the ability to choose an appropriate e-commerce solution.

These results should be investigated in more detail in order to better understand their deeper meaning. The findings of this study also have some concurrence with other studies of developing economies discussed within this chapter, that have highlighted the owner/manager's lack of knowledge regarding e-commerce *technical and security issues, organisational factors, lack of time, knowledge and awareness and financial issues.* This would suggest that further enquiry into these areas would bear fruitful and useful results.

It should also be noted that this study has several limitations. The data used for this study was drawn from 4 areas in Sweden, 3 areas in Australia and 3 provinces in Indonesia. As is apparent, while conclusions can be drawn about the barriers that these particular SME owner/managers perceive, they are not generalisable to SMEs in other locations. Also, the data for the study was collected from various industry sectors and it is not possible to make sector specific conclusions about barriers. Finally, this is a quantitative study, and further qualitative research is required to gain a better understanding of why these (and other) owner managers perceive that these are barriers to e-commerce adoption and the effect of economic and cultural context on why they group differently from developed to developing economies.

CONCLUSION

The aim of this chapter was twofold: to identify the underlying factors of e-commerce barriers in developed and a developing economies; and to determine whether the underlying factors themselves differ between SMEs in developed and a developing economies. As an example we outlined a study that was conducted by the authors in Australia, Sweden and Indonesia which showed that while the Swedish and Australian respondents were more concerned with technical and organisational issues, Indonesian respondents were also concerned with time/choice barriers to adoption.

The results of this study highlight important issues for both researchers as well as small business practitioners (including government agencies and owner/managers). While many studies over the years have suggested (or at least predicted) that E-commerce 'levels the playing field', the study we have outlined in this chapter has shown that 'a level playing field' may only be applicable at a technical and organisational level. Indeed, our example study raises a number of interesting questions as to why it is that time/choice barriers are of importance in the emerging use of e-commerce in SMEs in Indonesia. An examination of many governmental websites and brochures concerned with E-commerce adoption by SMEs suggest that they are more focussed on the technical and organisational problems that may beset a small business than time/choice concerns. Indeed, Taylor & Murphy (2004) suggest that governments are 'besotted with technology', often to the ignorance of economic and cultural limitations that many SMEs experience. The data clearly shows that, particularly for a developing economy such as Indonesia, that organisational and time/choice impacts of E-commerce appear far stronger than technical concerns. For the owner/managers surveyed in this study, the data clearly shows that it is essential to consider the organisational and time/choice impacts of E-commerce adoption, including customers, suppliers, products/services and the methods employed within the small business especially in developing economies. It would appear that time/choice factors are not considered to be technical concerns for the Indonesian SME owner/managers, unlike their Australian and Swedish counterparts, and that economic and cultural factors may be affecting their views in this regard. Contextualisation of these results through a qualitative mode of enquiry may present better opportunities to find out why these owner/managers think in this way.

The study presented in this paper is only one small part of a larger long-term project investigating the drivers and barriers to e-commerce adoption in SMEs. Further research is urgently needed to better understand how SME economic and cultural factors impact and affect the adoption of e-commerce by SMEs. Bharati and Chaudhury (2009) take up this theme in their suggested SME and IS research framework which focuses on the effect that *organisational* and *environmental* characteristics have on the *nature and adoption of IS assets* which in turn has an effect on *firm-level impacts*. In light of our analysis and findings, such a framework is worthy of further analysis and development and might form the basis for an effective research focus in this area.

REFERENCES

Abdullah, M. A., & Bakar, M. I. H. (2000). Small and medium enterprises in Asian Pacific countries. Huntington, NY: Nova Science Publishers.

Abell, W., & Lim, L. (1996). *Business use of the internet in New Zealand.* Retrieved August 2004 from http://ausweb.scu.edu.au/aw96/business/abell/index.htm

Abernethy, M. (2002). SMEs: Small World Order. *The Bulletin, 120*(34).

Al-Qirim, N. (2006). Personas of E-Commerce Adoption in Small Businesses in New Zealand. *Journal of Electronic Commerce in Organizations, 4*(3), 18–45.

Allred, A., Addams, H. L., & Chakraborty, G. (2007). Is Informal Planning the Key to the Success of the INC 500? *Journal of Small Business Strategy, 18*(1), 95–104.

Archer, N., Wang, S., & Kang, C. (2008). Barriers to the adoption of online supply chain solutions in small and medium enterprises. *Supply Chain Management, 13*(1), 73–82. doi:10.1108/13598540810850337

Asian Development Bank. (2003). *Private sector development and finance.* Asian Development Bank. Retrieved August 2009, from http://www.adb.org/PrivateSector/default.asp

Australian Bureau of Statistics. (ABS 2006). 8127.0 *Australian Small Business Operators - Findings from the 2005 and 2006 Characteristics of Small Business Surveys, 2005-06.* Retrieved June 2009 from http://www.abs.gov.au

Bajaj, K. K., & Nag, D. (1999). E-commerce: The cutting edge of business. New Delhi: Tata McGraw-Hill.

Barrett, R., & Burgess, J. (2008). Small firms and the challenge of equality, diversity and difference *Equal Opportunities International, 27*(3), 213 - 220.

Barry, H., & Milner, B. (2002). SME's and Electronic Commerce: A Departure from the Traditional Prioritisation of Training? *Journal of European Industrial Training, 26*(7), 316–326. doi:10.1108/03090590210432660

Beatty, R., Shim, J., & Jones, M. (2001). Factors Influencing Corporate Web Site Adoption: A Time-based Assessment. *Information & Management, 38*(6), 337–354. doi:10.1016/S0378-7206-(00)00064-1

Bharati, P., & Chaudhury, A. (2009). SMEs and competitiveness - The role of information systems. *International Journal of E-Business Research, 5*(1), 1–9.

Blili, S., & Raymond, L. (1993). Information Technology: Threats and opportunities for small medium-sized enterprises. *International Journal of Information Management, 13*(6), 439–448. doi:10.1016/0268-4012(93)90060-H

Boter, H., & Lundström, A. (2005). SME perspectives on business support services. *Journal of Small Business and Enterprise Development, 12*(2), 244–258. doi:10.1108/14626000510594638

Brigham, E. F., & Smith, K. V. (1967). The cost of capital to small firm. *The Engineering Economist, 13*(1), 1–26. doi:10.1080/00137916708928761

Bunker, D., & MacGregor, R. C. (2000). Successful generation of Information Technology (IT) requirements for Small/Medium Enterprises (SMEs). - Cases from regional Australia. In Proceedings of SMEs in Global Economy. Wollongong, Australia (pp. 72-84).

Carnaghan, C., Downer, P., Klassen, D., & Pittman, J. (2004). CAP Forum on E-Business: E-Commerce and Tax Planning: Canadian Experiences. *Canadian Accounting Perspectives, 3*(2), 261–287. doi:10.1506/V82X-X152-PND1-ABHE

CBS. (2004). Survey usaha terintegrasi 2004. Central Bureau of Statistics (CBS).

Celuch, K., Murphy, G. B., & Callaway, S. K. (2007). More bang for your buck: Small firms and the importance of aligned information technology capabilities and strategic flexibility. *The Journal of High Technology Management Research, 17*(2), 187–197. doi:10.1016/j.hitech.2006.11.006

Chahine, S., & Filatotev, I. (2008). The Effects of Information Disclosure and Board Independence on IPO Discount. *Journal of Small Business Management, 46*(2), 219–241. doi:10.1111/j.1540-627X.2008.00241.x

Chau, S. B., & Turner, P. (2001). A Four Phase Model of EC Business Transformation Amongst Small to Medium Sized Enterprises. In *Proceedings of the 12th Australasian Conference on Information Systems*, Coffs Harbour, Australia.

Chepaitis, E. V. (2002). E-commerce and the information environment in an emerging economy: Russia at the turn of the century. In P. C. Palvia, S. C. J. Palvia, & E. M. Roche (Eds.), Global Information Technology and Electronic Commerce: Issues for the new millennium (pp. 53 - 72).

Chirico, F. (2008). The Creation, Sharing and Transfer of Knowledge in Family Business. *Journal of Small Business and Entrepreneurship, 21*(4), 413–434.

Chiware, E. R. T., & Dick, A. L. (2008). The use of ICTs in Namibia's SME sector to access business information services. *The Electronic Library, 26*(2), 145–157. doi:10.1108/02640470810864055

Cloete, E., Courtney, S., & Fintz, J. (2002). Small Businesses' Acceptance and Adoption of E-commerce in the Western Cape Province of South Africa. *Electronic Journal of Information Systems in Developing Countries, 10*(4), 1–13.

Cochran, A. B. (1981). Small business mortality rates: A review of the literature. *Journal of Small Business Management, 19*(4), 50–59.

Cragg, P. B., & King, M. (1993). Small-firm computing: Motivators and inhibitors. *MIS Quarterly, 17*(1), 47–60. doi:10.2307/249509

Damsgaard, J., & Lyytinen, K. (1998). Contours of Diffusion of Electronic Data Interchange in Finland: Overcoming Technological Barriers and Collaborating to Make it Happen. *The Journal of Strategic Information Systems, 7*, 275–297. doi:10.1016/S0963-8687(98)00032-8

Dedrick, J., & Kraemer, K. L. (2001). China IT Report. *Electronic Journal of Information Systems in Developing Countries, 6*(2), 1–10.

DeLone, W. H. (1988). Determinants of Success for Computer Usage in Small Business. *MIS Quarterly, 12*(1), 51–61. doi:10.2307/248803

Dennis, C. (2000). Networking for marketing advantage. *Management Decision, 38*(4), 287–292. doi:10.1108/00251740010371757

DEPKOP. (2005a). *Peran Koperasi dan Usaha Kecil Menengah Dalam Pembangunan Nasional.* Kementrian Koperasi dan Usaha Kecil Menengah.

DEPKOP. (2005b). *Statistik Usaha Kecil Menengah.* 2005. Kementrian Koperasi dan Usaha Kecil Menengah.

Drakopoulou-Dodd, S., Jack, S., & Anderson, A. R. (2002). Scottish Entrepreneurial Networks in the International Context. *International Small Business Journal, 20*(2), 213–219. doi:10.1177/0266242602202005

EIRO. (2006). *Industrial relations in SMEs.* Retrieved March 2006, from http://www.eiro.eurofound.eu.int/1999/05/study/tn9905201s.html

Elliot, R., & Boshoff, C. (2007). The influence of the owner-manager of small tourism businesses on the success of internet marketing. *South African Journal of Business Management, 38*(3), 15–27.

Fillis, I., & Wagner, B. (2005). E-business Development: An Exploratory Investigation of the Small Firm. *International Small Business Journal, 23*(6), 604–634. doi:10.1177/0266242605057655

Fuller-Love, N., & Street, K. (2006). Management development in small firms. *International Journal of Management Reviews, 8*(3), 175–190. doi:10.1111/j.1468-2370.2006.00125.x

Gaskill, L. R., & Gibbs, R. M. (1994). Going away to college and wider urban job opportunities take highly educated away from rural areas. *Rural Development Perspectives, 10*(3), 35–44.

Gaskill, L. R., Van Auken, H. E., & Kim, H. (1993). The Impact of Operational Planning on Small Business Retail Performance. *Journal of Small Business Strategy, 5*(1), 21–35.

Gefen, D., & Heart, T. (2006). On the Need to Include National Culture as a Central Issue in E-commerce Trust Belief. *Journal of Global Information Management, 14*(4), 1–30.

Gefen, D., Rose, G., Warkentin, M., & Pavlou, P. (2005). Cultural Diversity and Trust in IT Adoption: A Comparison of Potential E-voter in the USA and South Africa. *Journal of Global Information Systems, 13*(1), 54–78.

Hadjimanolis, A. (1999). Barriers to Innovation for SMEs in a Small Less Developed Country (Cyprus). *Technovation, 19*(9), 561–570. doi:10.1016/S0166-4972(99)00034-6

Hall, C. (2002). Profile of SMEs and SME issues 1990-2000. Asia-Pacific Economic Cooperation, Singapore.

Haugh, H., & McKee, L. (2004). The Cultural Paradigm of the Smaller Firm. *Journal of Small Business Management, 42*(4), 377–394. doi:10.1111/j.1540-627X.2004.00118.x

Hermana, B., Sugiharto, T., & Margianti, E.S. (2006). Determinants of Internet Adoption by Indonesian Small Business Owners: Reliability and validity of Research Instrument. *E-LIS,* 1- 14

Hill, R., & Stewart, J. (2000). Human Resource Development in Small Organisations. *Journal of European Industrial Training, 24*(2/3/4), 105 - 117.

Holmes, T. P., Vlosky, R. P., & Carlson, J. (2004). An exploratory comparison of Internet use by small wood products manufacturers in the North Adirondack Region of New York and the State of Louisiana. *Forest Products Journal, 54*(12), 277–282.

Iacovou, C. L., Benbasat, I., & Dexter, A. S. (1995). Electronic Data Interchange and Small Organisations: Adoption and Impact of Technology. *MIS Quarterly, 19*(4), 465–485. doi:10.2307/249629

IEI. (2003). *Facts & Figures: The Internet and Business.* The Internet Economy Indicators. Retrieved June 4, 2003, from http://www.internetindicators.com/facts.html

Jennex, M. E., Amoroso, D., & Adelakun, O. (2004). E-Commerce Infrastructure Success Factors for Small Companies in Developing Economies. *Electronic Commerce Research, 4*(3), 263–286. doi:10.1023/B:ELEC.0000027983.36409.d4

Johnston, D. A., Wade, M., & McLean, R. (2007). Does e-Business Matter to SMEs? A Comparison of the Financial Impacts of Internet Business Solutions on European and North American SMEs. *Journal of Small Business Management, 45*(3), 354–361. doi:10.1111/j.1540-627-X.2007.00217.x

Kaewkitipong, L., & Brown, D. (2008). Adoption and Evaluation of E-business in Thai SMEs: A Process Perspective. *AMCIS 2008 Proceedings,* 1-13.

Kalakota, R., & Whinston, A. B. (1997). Electronic commerce: A manager's guide. Reading, MA: Addison-Wesley.

Kapurubandara, M., & Lawson, R. (2006). Barriers to Adopting ICT and e-commerce with SMEs in Developing Countries: An Exploratory study in Sri Lanka. *CollECTeR, 2006,* 1–13.

Kartiwi, M. (2006). Case Studies of E-commerce Adoption in Indonesian SMEs: The Evaluation of Strategic Use. *Australasian Journal of Information Systems, 14*(1), 69–80. doi:10.3127/ajis.v14i1.8

Kartiwi, M. (2008). *Electronic Commerce Adoption in Urban and Rural Indonesian SMEs.* PhD Dissertation, University of Wollongong, Australia.

Kartiwi, M., & MacGregor, R. C. (2007). Electronic Commerce Adoption Barriers in Small to Medium-sized Enterprises (SMEs) in Developed and Developing Countries: A Cross-country Comparisons. *Journal of E-commerce in Organizations, 5*(3), 35–51.

Kaynak, E., Tatoglu, E., & Kula, V. (2005). An analysis of the factors affecting the adoption of electronic commerce by SMEs: Evidence from an emerging market. *International Marketing Review, 22*(6), 623–640. doi:10.1108/02651330510630258

Kendall, J. E., & Kendall, K. E. (2001). A Paradoxically Peaceful Coexistence Between Commerce and Ecommerce. *Journal of Information Technology. Theory and Application, 3*(4), 1–6.

Keniry, J., Blums, A., Notter, E., Radford, E., & Thomson, S. (2003). *Regional business - A plan for action.* Department of Transport and Regional Services. Retrieved December 13, 2003, from http://www.rbda.gov.au/action_plan

Khiang, A. L. B., & Chye, G. N. K. (2002). Information technology and e-commerce for successful SMEs. *Malaysian Management Review, 37*(2), 5–19.

Kim, D. J. (2008). An OBTG (Organisational - Business - Technological - Governmental) E-business Adoption Model for Small and Medium Sized Enterprises. *AMCIS 2008 Proceedings,* 1-8.

Kyobe, M. (2008). The Impact of Entrepreneur Behaviours on the Quality of e-Commerce Security: A Comparison of Urban and Rural Findings. *Journal of Global Information Technology Management, 11*(2), 58–79.

Larsson, E., Hedelin, L., & Gärling, T. (2003). Influence of expert advice on expansion goals of small businesses in rural Sweden. *Journal of Small Business Management, 41*(2), 205–212. doi:10.1111/1540-627X.00076

Lawrence, K. L. (1997). Factors Inhibiting the Utilisation of Electronic Commerce Facilities in Tasmanian Small-to-Medium Sized Enterprises. In *Proceedings of 8th Australasian Conference on Information Systems* (pp. 587-597).

Lawrence, W. W. (2007). Small Business Operation Strategy: Aligning Priorities and Resources. *Journal of Small Business Strategy, 18*(2), 89–103.

Lee, C.-S. (2001). An analytical framework for evaluating e-commerce business models and strategies. *Internet Research, 11*(4), 349–359. doi:10.1108/10662240110402803

Levenburg, N. M., Schwarz, T. V., & Motwani, J. (2005). Understanding Adoption of Internet Technologies Among SMEs. *Journal of Small Business Strategy, 16*(1), 51–69.

Lockett, N., & Brown, D. H. (2006). Aggregation and the Role of Trusted Third Parties in SME E-Business Engagement. *International Small Business Journal, 24*(4), 379–404. doi:10.1177/0266242606065509

Lundström, A., & Stevenson, L. (2002). On the road to Entrepreneurship Policy: The Entrepreneurship Policy for the Future Series. In *Forum för Småföretagsforskning (FSF 2002)* (Vol. 2).

MacGregor, R. C., & Bunker, D. (1996). The effect of priorities introduced during computer acquisition on continuing success with IT in small business environments. In *Proceedings of Information Resource Management Association International Conference*, Washington (pp. 271-227).

MacGregor, R. C., Bunker, D., & Waugh, P. (1998). Electronic commerce and small/medium enterprises in Australia: An EDI pilot study. In *Proceedings of Proceedings of 11th International Bled E-commerce Conference*, 8th-10th June, Bled, Slovenia (pp. 331-345).

MacGregor, R. C., & Vrazalic, L. (2005). A Basic Model of Electronic Commerce Adoption Barriers: A Study of Regional Small Businesses in Sweden and Australia. *Journal of Small Business and Enterprise Development, 12*(4), 510–527. doi:10.1108/14626000510628199

MacGregor, R. C., & Vrazalic, L. (2007). E-commerce in Regional Small to Medium Enterprises. Hershey, PA: IGI Global.

Magnusson, M. (2001). E-commerce in small businesses - focusing on adoption and implementation. In *Proceedings of Proceedings of the 1st Nordic Workshop on Electronic Commerce*, May 28-29, Halmstad, Sweden.

Markland, R. E. (1974). The role of the computer in small business management. *Journal of Small Business Management, 12*(1), 21–26.

Martin, L., & Matlay, H. (2001). 'Blanket approaches to promoting ICT in small firms: some lessons from DTI ladder adoption model in the UK'. *Internet Research: Electronic Networking Applications and Policy, 11*(5), 399–410. doi:10.1108/EUM0000000006118

Matzler, K., Schwarz, E., Deutlinger, N., & Harms, R. (2008). The Relation between Transformational Leadership, Product Innovation and Performance in SMEs. *Journal of Small Business and Entrepreneurship, 21*(2), 139–152.

Meers, K. A., & Robertson, C. (2007). Strategic Planning Practices in Profitable Small Firms in the United States. *Business Review (Federal Reserve Bank of Philadelphia), 7*(1), 302–307.

Mehrtens, J., & Cragg, P.B., & Mills. (2001). A Model of Internet Adoption by SMEs. *Information & Management, 39*, 165–176. doi:10.1016/S0378-7206(01)00086-6

Meredith, G. G. (1994). Small Business Management in Australia (4th Ed.). New York: McGraw Hill.

Miller, N. J., & Besser, T. L. (2000). The importance of community values in small business strategy formation: Evidence from rural Iowa. *Journal of Small Business Management, 38*(1), 68–85.

Mir, D. F., & Feitelson, E. (2007). Factors Affecting Environmental Behavior in Micro-enterprises. *International Small Business Journal, 25*(4), 383–415. doi:10.1177/0266242607078583

Mole, K. F. (2007). Tacit knowledge, heuristics, consistency and error signals, How do business advisers diagnose their SME clients? *Journal of Small Business and Enterprise Development, 14*(4), 582–601. doi:10.1108/14626000710832712

Molla, A., & Heeks, R. (2007). Exploring E-commerce Benefits for Businesses in a Developing Country. *The Information Society, 23*, 95–108. doi:10.1080/01972240701224028

Mukti, N. A. (2000). Barriers to putting businesses on the Internet in Malaysia. *Electronic Journal of Information Systems in Developing Countries, 2*(6), 1–6.

Murphy, J. (1996). Small Business Management. London: Pitman.

NOIE. (2002). *e-Business for Small Business.* The National Office of Information Economy. Retrieved May 25, 2003, from http://www.noie.gov.au/projects/ebusiness/Advancing/SME/

O'Regan, N., & Ghobadian, A. (2004). Short- and long-term performance in manufacturing SMEs: Different targets, different drivers. *International Journal of Productivity and Performance Management, 53*(5), 405–424. doi:10.1108/17410400410545888

Ochara, N. M., Van Belle, J., & Brown, I. (2008). Global Diffusion of the Internet XIII: Internet Diffusion in Kenya and Its Determinants - A Longitudinal Analysis. *CAIS, 23*(7), 123-150.

Oshikoya, T. W., & Hussain, M. N. (2007). Information technology and the challenge of economic development in Africa. In A. Opoku-mensah & M. M. A. Salih (Eds.), African E-markets: Information and Economic Development. Copenhagen: CODI.

Palvia, S. C. J., & Vemuri, V. K. (2002). Global E-commerce: An Examination of Issues Related to Advertising and Intermediation. In P.C. Palvia, S.C.J. Palvia, & E.M. Roche (Eds.), Global Information Technology and Electronic Commerce: Issues for the new millennium (pp. 215 - 254).

Poon, S., & Swatman, P. M. C. (1997). Small business use of the Internet: Findings from Australian case studies. *International Marketing Review, 14*(5), 8.1-8.15.

Poon, S., & Swatman, P. M. C. (1998). Small Business Internet Commerce Experiences: A Longitudinal Study. In *Proceedings of Proceedings of the 11th International Bled Electronic Commerce Conference,* June 8-10. Bled, Slovenia (pp. 295-309).

Purao, S., & Campbell, B. (1998). Critical Concerns for Small Business Electronic Commerce: Some Reflections Based on Interviews of Small Business Owners. In *Proceedings of the Association for Information Systems Americas Conference,* Baltimore, MD, 14 – 16 August (pp. 325 - 327).

Purcell, F., & Toland, J. (2004). Electronic Commerce for the South Pacific: A Review of E-Readiness. *Electronic Commerce Research, 4*, 241–262. doi:10.1023/B:ELEC.0000027982.96505.c6

Quaddus, M., & Hofmeyer, G. (2007). An investigation into the factors influencing the adoption of B2B trading exchanges in small businesses. *European Journal of Information Systems, 16*(3), 202–215. doi:10.1057/palgrave.ejis.3000671

Quayle, M. (2002). E-commerce: The challenge for UK SMEs in the twenty-first century. *International Journal of Operations & Production Management, 22*(10), 1148–1161. doi:10.1108/01443570210446351

Raymond, L. (2001). Determinants of Web Site Implementation in Small Business. *Internet Research: Electronic Network Applications and Policy, 11*(5), 411–422. doi:10.1108/10662240110410363

Reynolds, J., Savage, W., & Williams, A. (1994). Your own business: A practical, guide to success. ITP.

Riquelme, H. (2002). Commercial internet adoption in China: Comparing the experiences of small, medium and large businesses. *Internet Research: Electronic Networking Applications and Policy, 12*(3), 276–286. doi:10.1108/10662240210430946

Robertson, T., & Gatignon, H. (1986). Competitive Effects on Technology Diffusion. *Journal of Marketing, 50*(3), 1–12. doi:10.2307/1251581

Rotch, W. (1967). Management of small enterprises: Cases and readings. Richmond, VA: University of Virginia Press.

Runyan, R. C., & Huddleston, P. (2006). Getting customers downtown: the role of branding in achieving success for central business districts. *Journal of Product and Brand Management, 15*(1), 48–63. doi:10.1108/10610420610650873

Saffu, K., Walker, J. H., & Hinson, R. (2008). Strategic Value and Electronic Commerce Adoption Among Small and Medium-Sized Enterprises in a Transitional Economy. *Journal of Business and Industrial Marketing, 23*(6), 395–404. doi:10.1108/08858620810894445

Schmid, B., Stanoevska-Slabeva, K., & Tschammer, V. (2001). Towards the E-society: E-commerce, E-business, E-government. Amsterdam: Kluwer Academic Publishers.

Scupola, A. (2003). The adoption of Internet commerce by SMEs in the south of Italy: An environmental, technological and organizational perspective. *Journal of Global Information Technology Management, 6*(1), 52–71.

St-Pierre, J., & Raymond, L. (2004). Short-term effects of benchmarking on the manufacturing practices and performance of SMEs. *International Journal of Productivity and Performance Management, 53*(8), 681–699. doi:10.1108/17410400410569107

Street, C. T., & Meister, D. B. (2004). Small Business Growth and Internal Transparency: The Role of Information Systems. *MIS Quarterly, 28*(3), 473–506.

Taylor, M., & Murphy, A. (2004). SMEs and e-business. *Journal of Small Business and Enterprise Development, 11*(3), 280–289. doi:10.1108/14626000410551546

Templerley, N. C., Galloway, J., & Liston, J. (2004). SMEs in Australia's Higher technology Sector: Challenges and Opportunities. AEEMA.

Tetteh, E., & Burn, J. M. (2001). Global strategies for SMe-business: applying the SMALL framework. *Logistics Information Management, 14*(1/2), 171–180. doi:10.1108/09576050110363202

Thompson, S., & Brown, D. (2008). Change Agents Intervention in E-business Adoption by SMEs: Evidence from a Developing Country. *AMCIS 2008 Proceedings*, 1-7.

Tucker, D., & Lafferty, A. (2004). Implementing Electronic Commerce in SMEs: Processes and Barriers. *Journal of Electronic Commerce in Organizations, 2*(4), 20–29.

Tuunainen, V. K. (1998). Opportunities of Effective Integration of EDI for Small Businesses in the Automotive Industry. *Information & Management, 34*(6), 361–375. doi:10.1016/S0378-7206(98)00070-6

Urata, S. (2000). *Outline of Tentative Policy Recommendation for SME Promotion in Indonesia.* JICA. Retrieved November 2003, from http://www.jica.or.id/FOCI_urata.html

Van Akkeren, J., & Cavaye, A. L. M. (1999). Factors Affecting Entry-Level Internet Technology Adoption by Small Business in Australia: An Empirical Study. In *Proceedings of Proceedings of the 10th Australasian Conference on Information Systems,* 1-3 December. Wellington, New Zealand.

Venkatesan, V. S., & Fink, D. (2002). Adoption of Internet Technologies and E-Commerce by Small and Medium Enterprises (SMEs) in Western Australia. In *Proceedings of the Information Resource Management Association International Conference* (pp. 1136-1137).

Walczuch, R., Van Braven, G., & Lundgren, H. (2000). Internet adoption barriers for small firms in The Netherlands. *European Management Journal, 18*(5), 561–572. doi:10.1016/S0263-2373(00)00045-1

Walker, E. W. (1975). Investment and Capital Structure Decision Making in Small Business. In E.W. Walker (Ed.), The Dynamic Small Firm: Selected Readings. Austin, TX: Austin Press.

Warren, M. (2004). Farmers online: drivers and impediments in adoption of Internet in UK agricultural businesses. *Journal of Small Business and Enterprise Development, 11*(3), 371–381. doi:10.1108/14626000410551627

Welsh, J. A., & White, J. F. (1981). A Small Business Is Not a Little Big Business. *Harvard Business Review, 59*(4), 18–32.

Westhead, P., & Storey, D. J. (1996). Management Training and Small Firm Performance: Why is the Link so Weak? *International Small Business Journal, 14*(4), 13–24. doi:10.1177/0266242696144001

Will, M. (2008). Talking about the future within an SME? Corporate foresight and the potential contributions to sustainable development. *Management of Environmental Quality, 19*(2), 234–242. doi:10.1108/14777830810856618

Wolff, J. A., & Pett, T. L. (2006). Small-Firm Performance: Modelling the Role of Product and Process Improvements. *Journal of Small Business Management, 44*(2), 268–284. doi:10.1111/j.1540-627X.2006.00167.x

World Bank Group. (2006). *Country groups.* Retrieved March 2006 from http://web.worldbank.org/

Chapter 9
The Role of Organizational Slack in Technology Innovation Adoption for SMEs

Jaume Franquesa
Kent State University, USA

Alan Brandyberry
Kent State University, USA

ABSTRACT

This study explores the relevant dimensions of organizational slack in small and medium enterprises (SMEs) and investigates their impact on adoption of different types of information technology (IT) innovations. Using recent data from a representative sample of 2,296 U.S. SMEs, the authors find that the slack-innovation relationships previously described in larger firms do not hold well for SMEs. Their results show potential slack (measured as access to external credit) to be a strong predictor of technology adoption in SMEs. By contrast, available slack appeared not to be a significant factor in SME innovation adoption. Moreover, the direction of the effects of potential slack was moderated by the capital-intensity of the innovation. In particular, e-commerce, which required lesser financial resources for SME adoption, was found to be pursued by those with lesser potential slack. The authors argue that, in some cases, innovation adoption may represent a form of "bricolage" by resource constrained SMEs.

INTRODUCTION

Organizations must strike a balance between stability and innovation–i.e., between exploitation of their current business model and processes and exploration and adoption of alternative solutions (March, 1991). Accordingly, understanding the processes by which organizations adjust their propensity to innovate, as well as the conditions most likely to foster innovation in a firm, is an important endeavor that has motivated a large innovation literature in management (see Daniel et al., 2004; Damanpour, 1991; Drazin & Schoonhoven, 1996; and Fiol, 1996, for reviews of this literature).

DOI: 10.4018/978-1-61520-627-8.ch009

Prior theory predicting innovation rates highlights the role of organizational slack as an important condition that facilitates exploration and, thus, contributes to a firm's innovativeness (Cyert & March, 1963; Greeve, 2003). On the other hand, slack is also argued to be related to inefficiencies in the use of resources (Bourgeois, 1981) and to less disciplined investment (Jensen, 1986), which may be detrimental to innovation. Given these competing arguments, Nohria and Gulati (1996) argued and found support for an inverted U-shaped relationship between slack and innovation. Their findings suggest that greater levels of slack increase the rate of adoption of technical and administrative innovations, but only up to a point. Beyond this point, excess slack appears to be counterproductive and results in reduced innovation rates.

Subsequent research by Geiger and Cashen (2002) extended Nohria and Gulati's (1996) work by examining the shape of the slack-innovation relationship for different dimensions of slack. Prior studies had distinguished among available slack, recoverable slack, and potential slack (Bourgeois & Singh, 1983; Bromiley, 1991). Geiger and Cashen (2002) found available and recoverable slack to have a curvilinear, inverted-U shaped, relationship with innovation, while potential slack had a linear positive relationship to innovation.

An important limitation of the prior organizational slack literature is that it has overwhelmingly focused on large, publicly traded firms[1]. With regard to the slack-innovation relationship, the technology adoption literature in information systems (IS) has shown a greater interest in small and medium enterprises (SMEs) and, thus, can be seen as filling some of the void left by the broader literature. In particular, a number of studies have explored the role of financial resources as an antecedent to SME adoption of specific IT innovations (e.g., Iacovou, Benbasat, & Dexter, 1995; Kuan & Chau, 2001; Mirchandani & Motwani, 2001). To date, however, this literature can offer only limited

and tentative insights regarding slack-innovation relationships: First, most prior SME technology adoption studies undertake a superficial treatment (at best) of financial resource considerations as one of the many factors in the typical technology adoption model. Also, the definition and measurement of financial resource variables differs widely across studies and often deviates form the concept of financial slack. Moreover, in the few cases where financial drivers are operationalized as financial slack (i.e., Grandon & Pearson, 2004; Wang & Cheung, 2004), the reliance on relatively small samples and the focus on a single technological innovation limits the generalizability of findings and prohibits a comparative analysis of the characteristics of the innovation as a possible moderator of the slack-adoption relationship. In sum, there is limited evidence regarding the role of organizational slack on SME innovation adoption. Also, no prior study has investigated how different dimensions of organizational slack may influence innovation in SMEs. Furthermore, the presence of curvilinear relationships between slack and SME adoption has yet to be explored.

Given the importance of SMEs to the U.S. economy (e.g., Bharati & Choudhury, 2006; Small Business Administration, 2006), as well as the expectation that prior findings using samples of large firms will not generalize to the SME context (Dandridge, 1979; Thong, 1999), the lack of in-depth study of the role of organizational slack in the context of small firms represents an important gap in our understanding of slack-innovation relationships. SMEs represent 99.7 percent of all U.S. employers, are responsible for about half of the private sector jobs, and generate about half of the private GDP (Small Business Administration, 2006). Moreover, SMEs play a critical role in industrial innovation and renewal of economic sectors (Baumol, 2002; Small Business Administration, 2003) and, thus, are major contributors to the competitiveness of the economy. At the same time, there are fundamental differences between

SMEs and large businesses (Dandridge, 1979; Welsh & White, 1981; Thong, 1999) which suggest that both the levels and types of slack, as well as the mechanisms by which slack influences innovation, may vary across contexts. In particular, SMEs are usually severely resource constrained (Oviatt & NcDougall, 1994; Baker & Nelson, 2005). Also, they exhibit high mortality rates that result from their double *liabilities of smallness and newness* (Freeman, Caroll, & Hannan, 1983), which affects their willingness to take risks.

The purpose of the present research is to extend prior slack-innovation studies (i.e., Geiger & Cashen, 2002; Nohria & Gulati, 1996) by developing the concept and dimensions of organizational slack in the context of SMEs, and investigating how different types of slack relate to innovation adoption in these firms. Our study is based on a representative sample of 2,296 U.S. SMEs. In an attempt to explore how characteristics of the innovation itself may moderate the slack-innovation relationship, we study SMEs' adoption of two specific information technologies that represent opposite minimum requirements in terms of their capital intensity and complexity: e-commerce and computerized core process technologies.

The remainder of the paper is organized as follows. First we define and discuss organizational innovation and present previous research on IT innovation adoption in SMEs. We then discuss organizational slack as well as the multidimensional aspects of slack and its relationship with innovation. This is followed by a discussion of how the distinctive environment of SMEs is likely to affect both the relevant dimensions of organizational slack and their relationship to innovation adoption. This section concludes with our hypotheses. Next, data and measures are presented followed by methods and results. Finally, we offer a discussion of results, directions for future research, and limitations of the present study.

ORGANIZATIONAL INNOVATION

Organizational innovation research has been approached from many diverse perspectives and has been extensively researched over the past half century. If Rogers (1962) did not originate the field, his work is often given credit for popularizing it. Several distinctions can be made concerning the different research streams in this area. One important distinction (Damanpour & Wischnevsky, 2006) is whether the focus is on internal innovation concerning the development of innovations within an organization (e.g., Cormican & O'Sullivan, 2004; Dougherty & Hardy, 1996; Kivimaki & Lansisalmi, 2000; Wong & Chin, 2007) or on the adoption of innovations within an organization regardless of the origin of the innovation (e.g., Brancheau & Wetherbe, 1990; Compeau, Higgins, & Huff, 1999; Davis, 1989; Kishore & McLean, 2007; Moch & Morse, 1977; Moore & Benbasat, 1991; Venkatesh, Morris, Davis, & Davis, 2003; Yang, Lee, & Lee, 2007). In this research we focus on the later form of adoption of external innovations.

In this context, it is important to define specifically what is meant by an innovation. Although competing definitions exist, most research has adopted a definition similar to that of Damanpour (1991, p. 556), "innovation is defined as adoption of an internally generated or purchased device, system, policy, program, process, product, or service that is new to the adopting organization." This definition provides sufficient specificity as to what is considered an innovation and removes the problem of subjectively determining the level of innovativeness represented by the technology. It simply requires that the technology be new to the adopting organization. Many other distinctions may be made to differentiate between types of innovations. Innovations may be considered technical or administrative, radical or incremental, and product or process. These and other distinctions are discussed in detail in the extant literature (Damanpour, Szabat, & Evan, 1989; Damanpour, 1991; Swanson, 1994).

The two specific innovations chosen for this research are *electronic commerce* adoption and what we will term *computerized core* adoption. E-commerce adoption is present when a firm engages in any level of sales of products and/or services via the Internet. In the general population such adoption can vary immensely in scope. As we discuss more fully in our measurement section, the type of adoption we expect our sample to engage in is supplementary rather than primary. Computerized core adoption relates to the adoption of computer systems that contribute directly to the firm's primary business activity. As explained below, the differences represented in these two innovations will allow us to explore the extent to which slack-innovation relationships may be moderated by characteristics of the innovation itself.

IT INNOVATION ADOPTION IN SMEs

A substantial amount of research in the information systems literature has been devoted to studying predictors of adoption of new information technologies by SMEs (see Premkumar, 2003; Parker & Castleman, 2007 for reviews of some of this literature). Much of the most recent research in this area is fairly limited in scope or context (Corrocher & Fontana, 2008; Oh, Cruickshank, & Anderson, 2009; Ramsey, Ibbotson, & McCole, 2008; Saffu, Walker, & Hinson, 2008; Sharma, 2009; Spanos & Voudouris, 2009). However, organizational slack has received relatively little attention in this research.

The Technology Acceptance Model (TAM) introduced by Davis (1989) is adapted in a number of SME technology adoption studies (e.g., Igbaria et al., 1997; Riemenschneider, Harrison, & Mykytyn, 2003). Others (e.g., Riemenschneider & McKinney, 2001) employ the Theory of Planned Behavior (TPB) which Ajzen (1991) adapted

from the Theory of Reasoned Action (Fishbein & Ajzen, 1975). Both of these approaches focus on the perceived characteristics of the particular technology as the key driver of adoption. Hence, this has been termed the "technological" perspective. Others extend this perspective to include characteristics of the organization and of its external environment as further predictors of adoption. This is commonly referred to as the Technology-Organization-Environment (TOE) framework (Tornatzky & Fleischer, 1990; Premkumar & Roberts, 1999; Kuan & Chau, 2001).

The TOE model has been applied to SME adoption of specific technological innovations. Iacovou et al. (1995) developed a model of adoption of Electronic Data Interchange (EDI) by SMEs that proposes *perceived benefits* of the innovation (i.e., the technological context), *organizational readiness* (organizational context) and *external pressure* (environmental context) as the key determinants of the decision to adopt. Of particular interest to the present study is the organizational readiness factor, which is composed of two sub-dimensions: the extent to which the SME possesses the (i) technological resources and (ii) the financial resources necessary to adopt e-commerce. The later may be understood as (or including) financial slack. Iacovou et al.'s (1995) model was subsequently tested by Chwelos et al. (2001) using a sample of 268 Canadian SMEs, and by Kuan and Chau (2001) using a sample of 575 small trading companies based in Hong Kong. In both cases, the financial dimension of organizational readiness (measured as financial resources in one case and as perceived financial costs of adoption in the other) was found to be an important contributor to the intent to adopt EDI.

The TOE model has also been applied to adoption of internet-based technologies in SMEs. Interestingly, financial considerations have been found to play a lesser role in this context[2]. Mehrtens, Cragg, and Mills (2001) developed a model of internet adoption by SMEs through a multi-case inductive study. Their final model was very similar to Iacovou et al.'s (1995), except that it did not include financial resources as a subcomponent of the organizational readiness factor. Subsequently, survey-based studies of internet adoption in SMEs using the TOE framework have often de-emphasized financial resources (e.g., Premkumar & Roberts, 1999; Beckinsale, Levy & Powell, 2006). Others have included this element but have found it not to be an influencing factor. In particular, in the specific context of e-commerce adoption in SMEs, both Mirchandani and Motwani (2001) and Grandon and Pearson (2004) found financial considerations not to be an important factor.

Overall, most prior SME innovation adoption studies have either paid no attention to financial resources or have modeled this as a sub-dimension of the broader construct of organizational readiness. Most important, when included, the financial component of readiness has been operationalized as something other than financial slack. For example, Chwelos et al. (2001) used a 3-item scale that includes number of employees and annual sales, so that their measure is actually capturing firm size. Similarly, others have used profit levels to proxy for financial resources (e.g., Dembla, Palvia, & Brooks, 2007). Still others have focused on the perceived financial cost of the innovation as opposed to financial resources (Kuan & Chau, 2001; Mirchandani & Motwani, 2001).

The studies by Grandon and Pearson (2004) and by Wang and Cheung (2004) provide exceptions to this and, as such, represent important precedents to the present study. Grandon and Pearson's (2004) single-item measure of financial resources was constructed by asking respondents if they thought they had the "Financial resources to adopt e-commerce" (p. 213). This appears to capture financial slack conditional on perceived costs of adoption (we also suspect this measure is rather capturing *available slack*, as defined below). As noted above, this measure was found not to be an important factor in e-commerce adoption. Wang and Cheung (2004) used a 4-item measure that captures overall (perceived) financial slack of the firm. In a sample of 137 small travel agencies in Taiwan, this measure was found to be negatively related to the intention to adopt e-commerce, but positively related to the degree of e-commerce implementation. The authors argued that the availability of funds facilitates implementation but, at the same time, greater levels of financial slack may result from better past performance and, thus, may be related to resistance to change in the first place.

In sum, taken as a whole, the prior IT innovation adoption literature provides some, but limited insight into the role of slack on innovation adoption in SMEs. We believe that further understanding of SME adoption issues will benefit from greater attention to, as well as more precise definition of, organizational slack.

ORGANIZATIONAL SLACK

Organizational slack is defined as resources in excess of what an organization requires to maintain its standard operations (Cyert & March, 1963). Cyert and March (1963) argued that slack is crucial to resolving political conflicts emanating from goal expectations of different coalitions within organizations. Slack has long been held to have a positive effect on various aspects of performance within a firm. Bourgeois (1981) discusses four often cited functions of slack within an organization: as motivation for organizational participants to remain; as a source of resolving conflicts; as workflow buffers; and to aid in the facilitation of creative or innovative processes within the organization. With regard to the latter, it has been suggested that slack allows (i) the exploration of new ideas before they are actually needed, (ii) the purchase of innovations, (iii) the funding of innovation implementation costs, and (iv) the absorption of failure (Rosner, 1968).

Types of Organizational Slack

Singh (1986) suggested two different types of organizational slack. *Absorbed* (or recoverable) slack relates to administrative resources beyond what is necessary for the normal operation of the organization –i.e., excessive organizational overhead. This creates a "cushion" of resources that can be made available either by eliminating costs that are not required or by deploying underutilized staff, facilities, or other assets. By contrast, *unabsorbed* slack is resources that are liquid and uncommitted in the organization, like cash reserves (Singh, 1986). Singh empirically demonstrated that absorbed and unabsorbed slack have different effects on risk-taking behavior. Subsequently, Bourgeois and Singh (1983) suggested further dividing slack into three categories: available (unabsorbed) slack, recoverable (absorbed) slack, and potential slack. *Potential* slack refers to additional financial resources that may be obtained through credit, as indicated by the firm's unused borrowing capacity. Bourgeois and Singh's (1983) typology has been broadly adopted in the prior literature, which has focused on the study of large organizations (Geiger & Cashen, 2002; Greeve, 2003; Herold, Jayaraman, & Narayanaswamy, 2006).

Slack and Innovation

Slack has been argued to allow and, to some extent, promote expenditures associated with creativity and experimentation which, in turn, leads to greater organizational performance (Cyert & March, 1963; Bourgeois, 1981). Other researchers, however, argue that slack promotes wasteful use of resources and, thus, is negatively associated with firm innovation and performance (Simon, 1957; Jensen & Meckling, 1976). The divergence of opinion appears to revolve around how wisely slack resources will be allocated (Herold et al., 2006; Nohria & Gulati, 1996).

Bourgeois (1981) synthesized the competing arguments regarding the role of slack by hypothesizing "that the correlation between 'success' and slack is positive, up to a point, then negative; in other words, the relationship is curvilinear" (p. 31). There are several reasons why excessive slack may lead to inefficiencies: If the number of investment projects increases with additional slack and if projects are funded rationally, it makes sense that the most promising will be funded first and additional projects may have diminishing returns (Herold et al., 2006; Nohria & Gulati, 1996). Moreover, additional slack may lead to less disciplined management of projects in terms of their selection, support, and termination (Herold et al., 2006; Nohria & Gulati, 1996).

Nohria and Gulati (1996) extended this argument to the relationship of organizational slack and innovation (arguably a subset of Bourgeois' (1981) concept of "success"). The authors argued that the relationship between slack and innovation (measured either as total economic impact or as total number of innovations) would be inverse U-shaped, and provided empirical support for this hypothesized relationship. Subsequently, Geiger and Cashen (2002) extended Nohria and Gulati (1996) by taking a multidimensional view of slack. Specifically, they studied possible curvilinear relationships of available, recoverable, and potential slack with innovation. There are few other empirical studies utilizing a multidimensional view of slack and considering non-linear relationships but, apart from Geiger and Cashen (2002), no other study of this sort investigates slack-innovation effects[3].

ORGANIZATIONAL SLACK IN SMEs

As discussed above, the previous slack-innovation literature has focused almost exclusively on the study of larger publicly-traded firms. Only a few studies in the I.S. literature have investigated the role of organizational slack on innovation adoption by SMEs (Grandon & Pearson, 2004; Wang & Cheung, 2004). Moreover, no prior study has pursued a multidimensional view of slack within the SME context. Also, no study has explored the existence of a curvilinear relationship of slack (or dimensions of slack) with innovation in SMEs. Consequently, there is no evidence that current arguments and findings in the slack-innovation literature will hold for small firms. Indeed, there is little reason to expect that they would (Dandridge, 1979; Welsh & White, 1981).

There are fundamental differences between SMEs (defined as firms with fewer than 500 employees) and large firms. The U.S. Small Business Administration reports that the average SME has one location and 10 employees, while the average large employer had 61 locations and 3,300 employees in 2003 (SBA, 2006). Similarly, population estimates with the database used in the present study suggest that more than 80 percent of U.S. SMEs employed fewer than 10 workers in 2004, and more than 70 percent had annual sales of less than $500,000 in 2003 (Mach & Wolken, 2006). Also 59 percent of SMEs were less than 15 years old, and 94 percent were owner-managed (Mach & Wolken, 2006). In short, the large majority of SMEs are very small, rather young, owner-managed firms. There are several important implications that derive from this. First, SMEs are severely undercapitalized (Holtz-Eakin, Joulfaian, & Rosen, 1994a, 1994b) and resource constrained (Baker & Nelson, 2005; George, 2005; Oviatt & NcDougall, 1994). Second, they tend to have highly centralized structures, where the owner-manager (or owner-manager group) makes most of the firm's decisions. Third, they are afflicted by rather volatile performance (Ekanem, 2005) and high mortality rates that result from their double *liabilities of smallness and newness* (Freeman, Caroll, & Hannan, 1983), which may impact their willingness to take risks. Given these characteristics, it is reasonable to expect that the levels and types of slack, as well as the mechanisms by

which slack influences innovation, will differ in the context of SMEs as compared to the context of large and well-established firms.

Dimensions of slack that are relevant for larger firms may be immaterial in the case of SMEs (George, 2005). In particular, the concept of *absorbed* slack seems a contradiction of terms with the size, resource scarcity, and volatility and precariousness that characterize these firms. Even in the case of firms that beat the odds and have protracted periods of above-average returns, the highly centralized ownership structure characteristic of these firms makes it unlikely that surpluses will be "absorbed" throughout the organization in the form of idle or underutilized personnel and facilities. Hence, we do not believe absorbed (or recoverable) slack to be a consequential phenomenon, and thus a meaningful driver of innovativeness, in the context of SMEs.

With regard to *available* slack, it is important to understand that the financial reserves of SMEs will tend to be very limited. SMEs are often "running on fumes" and need to rely on several forms of financial bootstrapping to continue their operations (Winborg & Landstrom, 2001). Given this, the typical SME will not have funds to develop breakthrough innovations internally, and will rather adopt innovations already in existence (Baumol, 2002). Their limited funds also mean that SMEs will tend to seek simpler technologies (Bharati & Choudhury, 2006) and the lowest cost adoption of IT innovations (Thong, 1999).

Finally, in terms of *potential* slack, which refers to an organization's ability to raise external capital, it is important to recognize that since they may have little financial records or collateral, many SMEs represent high-risk borrowers and may not have access to commercial credit at all (i.e., have very little chance to obtain a bank loan), or may be credit constrained by their lenders (i.e., may receive lesser amounts of credit than their business can responsibly carry). Thus, in contrast to the prior literature which has emphasized financial leverage (i.e., debt-to-equity ratio) as the key indicator of potential slack, we believe that the most salient indicator of potential slack for SMEs is access to credit in the first place.

ORGANIZATIONAL SLACK AND INNOVATION ADOPTION IN SMEs

Available Slack

As previously discussed, past studies of larger firms have argued and found support for an inverted U-shaped relationship between available slack and innovation (Geiger & Cashen, 2002; Nohria & Gulati, 1996). Despite a tighter resource environment as well as differences in management processes and the types of innovations that will be pursued, we expect this type of slack to influence innovation in a similar way in SMEs. At low levels of available slack it is unlikely that there are resources for innovation adoption. As financial reserves increase, we expect adoption of e-commerce and computerized core processes to increase. However, for very high levels of cash reserves, which may signal a very successful business model, we expect greater inertial pressure and a lesser willingness to innovate (Wang & Cheung, 2004). Stated formally:

H1: The relationship between available slack and SME adoption of e-commerce will be inverted U-shaped (i.e., positive but declining in strength, and becoming negative beyond an intermediate optimal level).

H2: The relationship between available slack and SME adoption of computerized core will be inverted U-shaped (i.e., positive but declining in strength, and becoming negative beyond an intermediate optimal level).

Potential Slack

Geiger and Cashen (2002) argue that, unlike available and (for larger firms) recoverable slack, potential slack is unlikely to display an inverse U-shaped relationship with innovation. A high level of potential slack simply represents little or no debt rather than current resources. Since greater use of debt generates new (interest) expenses and may prompt increases in other (capital) costs, it is unlikely that greater access to external credit will lead to lesser managerial attention and a laxer use of such resources. Regardless of the level of potential slack, decisions concerning new debt cannot be made carelessly. Consistent with this, Geiger and Cashen (2002) hypothesize and empirically confirm a positive linear relationship between potential slack and innovation.

We believe that discipline in the use of debt may be even more intense in the SME context. SMEs seeking new debt are likely to receive rigorous external scrutiny by would-be creditors at any level of potential slack. Hence, we similarly expect the relationship between potential slack and SME adoption to be linear (i.e., invariant over the range of potential slack values).

In terms of direction, however, specific characteristics of the innovation being considered may moderate how adoption is affected by potential slack (Herold et al., 2006). In particular, the capital-intensity of minimum requirements to adopt a given IT innovation relative to the minimum investment required for alternative processes may determine the role of potential slack in SME contexts. In the case of e-commerce, this innovation offers a low-investment alternative to SME expansion via traditional means such as opening new locations[4]. Hence, SMEs may adopt e-commerce as a way to develop a cost-minimizing marketing channel (Santarelli & D'Altri, 2003). Indeed, for SMEs, e-commerce might be regarded as a form of *bricolage*, or utilizing 'what is at hand' (Andersen, 2008; Baker & Nelson, 2005), in order to be able to grow the business. Consistent with this, we expect firms that are more credit constrained (i.e., with lower potential slack) to be more likely to adopt this innovation. Formally:

H3: Potential slack will exhibit a linear and negative relationship with SME adoption of e-commerce.

Conversely, process-enhancing technological innovations such as computerizing core activities are likely to require substantial capital investment over and above the no-adoption alternative. Some of this investment may be derived from available slack but this type of innovation is likely to require additional financial resources. Hence, adoption of computerized core innovations is more likely to be pursued by financially healthier SMEs with greater potential slack. This leads to our final hypothesis:

H4: Potential slack will exhibit a linear and positive relationship with SME adoption of computerized core.

DATA AND MEASURES

Sample

The data used for this study were obtained from the *2003 Survey of Small Business Finances* (SSBF). The SSBF is a survey conducted every five years by the Federal Reserve Board to gather information about the use of credit and other financial services by SMEs[5]. The so-called 2003 survey was actually administered between June 2004 and January 2005 and gathered data from a nationally representative sample of 4,240 private, nonfinancial, nonfarm firms with fewer than 500 employees. Besides credit use, it contains 2003 financial statement information, as well as other details on the characteristics of these firms and their owners. Both the 1998 and 2003 editions of

the SSBF included information about computer use by SMEs. However, the 2003 survey offers greater level of detail regarding firms' adoption of different IT applications.

The sampling frame for 2003 SSBF was about 6.3 million firms listed in the Dun's Market Identifier (DMI) file as of May 2004, and which met the target population definition. The DMI file is thought to be an almost complete listing of all U.S. business establishments (Reynolds, 1994) –although it is likely to under-represent the smallest and newest firms (March & Wolken, 2006). The survey design was a stratified random sample by (i) employment size categories, (ii) broad U.S. Census regions, and (iii) metropolitan versus rural locations. Also, since mid-size firms represent a small percentage of the U.S. population of SMEs, the survey over-sampled larger firms (20-499 employees) –to ensure reliable estimators for this sub-group. As a result, in order to obtain unbiased population estimates from these data, researchers must use techniques that account for the complex structure of the survey (2003 SSBF Technical Codebook: 10-11). Response rate was about 32%.

Prior SSBF editions were released as a complete data set where all missing values (about 2% of data values sought) had been imputed. Imputation of missing data is performed by the Federal Reserve using randomized regressions that model a variable as a function of other survey variables. This practice was often regarded as problematic by prior management authors, and has been cited as a detriment to the use of SSBF data (Cox, Camp & Sexton, 2000)[6]. Interestingly, the 2003 SSBF release provides greater information regarding imputation, and thus greater flexibility in its treatment. The newest data set contains five separate versions of the fully imputed data, referred to as "implicates". This allows researchers to employ statistical techniques that combine estimates from the separate implicates to obtain adjusted standard errors that account for the additional variation due to imputation (Rubin, 1996). The

2003 release also "flags" values that have been imputed. Therefore, researchers have the option to identify and delete observations with imputed values. We conducted analyses under both alternatives and obtained similar results. For simplicity, only results with the reduced sample that contains no imputed values are presented here.

In order to provide a clear demarcation among the two types of IT application of interest, our study was limited to non-retail and non-wholesale firms (i.e., SIC codes 50, 51, 52, 53, 54, 55, 56, 57 & 59). Retailers and wholesalers may regard selling as their primary activity, so that adoption of e-commerce in these firms might be inextricable from adoption of a computerized core. There were 3,101 observations in the 2003 SSBF with non-missing values in the variables used in the present study. Of these, 2,464 observations corresponded to non-distribution firms. We also required that businesses that (i) were not corporate subsidiaries, (ii) had positive sales and positive assets, and (iii) had their three primary owners control more than 50% of the firm's ownership[7]. This resulted in a total of 2, 313 firms that could be used for our analyses. After deleting 17 observations with outlier values of accounting-based available slack (defined below), we were left with a study sample of 2,296 firms.

Dependent variables. *e-Commerce Adoption.* Respondents were asked if their firm used the computer "to sell business products and services via the internet". We coded affirmative responses as 1 and negative responses as zero. There were 711 study firms that had adopted this innovation by the end of 2004. Given their analytical survey weights, adopters are estimated to represent 27.9 percent of the U.S. population of non-retail & non-wholesale SMEs. The survey also asked where did the business primarily sell its products or services, and only two respondents (four respondents for the overall 2003 SSBF), or .08 percent of the population, reported conducting business primarily through the internet or phone.

This suggests that practically all adopters used e-commerce as a way to complement their primary sales channel.

There is reason to believe that the vast majority of e-commerce users in our sample are recent adopters. Unfortunately, a precise estimate of the growth of e-commerce adoption in this population is not available. While the 2003 questionnaire distinguished between participation in internet purchases (i.e., e-procurement) and internet sales (i.e., e-commerce), the 1998 SSBF questionnaire merely inquired if the firm used "the computer to purchase or sell business products and services via the Internet". Nevertheless, we can derive useful information from the available data. First, a comparison of the *1998 SSBF* data (collected in 1999) with the data used in the present study, shows that adoption of the internet for business transactions (either purchases or sales) exploded from 26.9% in 1999 to 66.0% of the population of non-distribution SMEs in 2004. Second, the data shows that almost all SMEs that had adopted the internet for business transactions by 2004 were using it to purchase products/services (94%). By contrast, a minority of those transacting via the internet in 2004 used it to sell their own products/services (41%). Thus, similarly, we would expect that a minority of those reporting to have adopted electronic transactions in 1999 would have been e-commerce firms. Moreover, prior research, as well as the lesser prevalence of e-commerce observed here, suggest a staged adoption of electronic processes, so that it is reasonable to assume an even lesser relative incidence of e-commerce *vis-a-vis* e-procurement in 1999 than in 2004. Prior studies have found SMEs to pass through a set of sequential adoption stages from e-mail use, to a web presence, to e-procurement, and culminating with e-commerce adoption (e.g., Daniel, Wilson, & Myers, 2002; Rao, Metts, & Monge, 2003). E-procurement may precede e-commerce adoption due to the greater involvement and greater commitment of resources needed for the latter. Also, by becoming an on-line purchaser of goods and services first, the business owner gains familiarity and experience with the internet, which may be instrumental to his/her motivation and ability to adopt an on-line store-front later on. In short, we believe that e-commerce adoption among SMEs occurred primarily and progressively in the years after 1999. Since our independent variables are measured at the end of the 2003 fiscal year, we believe to be capturing the relationships of interest at around the time of innovation adoption. Also, as discussed below, our study focuses on dimensions of financial slack that would be more static or slow to adjust after adoption, so that, even if captured several months later, they would still be reflective of conditions present at the time of adoption.

Computerized Core Adoption. Respondents were asked if their firm used computers "to directly contribute to the firm's primary business activity". We coded affirmative responses as 1 and negative responses as zero. There were 258 firms in our sample that had adopted this innovation. Given their survey weights, we estimate that 9.06 percent of the U.S. population of non-retail & non-wholesale SMEs had computerized their core processes by the end of 2004.

Independent variables. *Available slack.* In prior studies using samples of larger firms, available slack is normally measured using either the quick ratio (Herold et al., 2006; Geiger & Cashen, 2002) or current ratio (Bromiley, 1991; Cheng & Kesner, 1997). These are measures of liquidity or solvency, defined as current assets divided by current liabilities. However, using a measure of this sort proved to be problematic with the present sample of SMEs, as 32 percent of firms in our sample had zero current liabilities. Thus, we opted for using working capital instead, defined as current assets (cash, inventory, account receivables, and other assets that can be converted to cash within one year) minus current liabilities (accounts payable and other debts due within one year). Since this measure was denominated in

absolute dollar values, it was important to adjust it for the different operational resource requirements of firms (George, 2005; Greve, 2003). We decided to use working capital over sales as our final measure, as firms with greater sales need greater amounts of working capital[8]. As opposed to measures used in the prior literature that focus on more ephemeral or high-discretion dimensions of available slack (e.g., George, 2005), our measure captures aspects that are more static or slow to adjust after adoption. In particular, cash reserves, which is the more ephemeral component of current assets, are rather small for firms in our study (31% of non-retail SMEs had $2,000 or less in cash, and the median cash amount was $6,000).

Potential slack. As discussed above, we believe that the most relevant measure of potential slack for SMEs is access to commercial credit. Given recent technological developments in banking leading to broad adoption of automated underwriting technologies (i.e., credit scoring) for small business loans (Frame, Srinivasan & Woosley, 2001; Berger, Frame, & Miller, 2005), we used the firm's credit score as an indicator of its access to credit. Our measure is derived from the Dun & Bradstreet Commercial Credit Score Percentile, as provided in SSBF. The credit score percentile is a measure of credit quality. For example, as of the time of this writing, the D&B customer service website reported that firms that fall in between the 1 and 10 percentiles have an incidence of delinquency of 58.8%; by contrast, firms in the 91 to 100 percentiles have an incidence of delinquency of only 2.5%. The measure available in the SSBF database, is an ordinal index ranging from 1 (worst credit) to 6 (best credit): Firms with a credit score percentile between 1-10 are coded as 1, 11-25 percentiles are coded as 2, 26-50 percentiles are coded as 3, 51-75 percentiles are coded as 4, 76-90 are coded as 5, and firms in the 91-100 percentile are coded as 6. Firms with a high credit score have greater access to credit (i.e., are more likely to be approved for greater amounts of credit) and, thus, have greater potential slack. By contrast, firms with a low credit score will be credit constrained and, thus, have lower potential slack.

Control variables. *Owner(s)' characteristics.* Since it is often difficult to separate small business owners from their firms, we sought to control for characteristics of the owner (or owner-group) that might be related to his/her/their willingness to take risks and/or to their propensity to adopt IT applications. We controlled for *age* and *education* of the owner(s), which prior studies found to be related to computer adoption (e.g., Dickerson & Gentry, 1983). The 2003 SSBF includes demographic information for up to three (largest) owners, and our study selected only firms where three or less owners would represent a majority of ownership. Given this, our measure of owner age is the weighted average age of the dominant owner group in years, using ownership shares as weights. Our measure of owner education is also a weighted average across the dominant owner group. Education was an ordinal variable coded 1 if the person had "less than a high school degree"; 2 for "high school graduate", 3 for "some college but no degree granted", 4 for "associate degree", 5 for "trade school/vocational program", 6 for "college degree (BA, BS, AB, etc.)", and 7 for "post graduate degree". In our analyses we also controlled for the *managerial experience* of owners, which may be related to the level of understanding of business processes as well as to familiarity with business IT applications (Damanpour, 1991). This variable, however, was never significant and it was very strongly correlated with other control variables (owners' age and firm age, in particular). Thus, we decided to drop it from the regression models presented here.

Firm's characteristics. We controlled for *firm age*, which may be related to adoption and which has been found to be related to the effective use of financial slack in private firms (George, 2005). We also controlled for *firm size*, which has been related to IT adoption in SMEs (Bharati & Chaudhury, 2006; Wang & Cheung, 2004), as

well as in larger firms (e.g., Tsikriktsis, Lanzolla & Frohlich, 2004). We used the natural log of the number of employees, as well as the number of different sites or locations as proxies for firm size. Albeit related, these measures capture two slightly different aspects of size that may drive adoption. Prior studies have found *centralization* and *professionalism* to be related to innovation (e.g., Damanpour, 1991). We used the ownership share of the primary owner as our proxy for centralization. We added a dummy variable to control for *professionally managed firms* (1=yes). The firm's *legal form* has been related to risk-taking. In particular, because of limited liability, corporations and S-corporations are regarded as more inclined to take risks (e.g., Petersen & Rajan, 1994). Given this, we included a dummy variable coded 1 for corporations and S-corporations. We also added a control for prior performance, which has similarly been found to be related to risk-taking (e.g., Wiseman & Bromiley, 1996) and to innovation adoption (e.g., Greve, 2003). We used *sales growth* during the past 3 years as our measure for prior performance. This variable was coded 1 if sales had increased in comparison to the fiscal-year ended in 2000; 0 if sales were the same; and -1 if sales had declined in comparison to fiscal-year 2000. Finally, to account for possible differences in the propensity to adopt the two technical innovations of interest —over and above industry effects (see below), we controlled for different levels of *fixed asset intensity* across firms. The latter was measured as net fixed assets (i.e., book value of land plus net book value of depreciable assets) divided by sales (Kracaw, Lewellen & Woo, 1992).

Environmental drivers. We controlled for *industry* effects, using dummy variables for each two-digit SIC code that was represented by at least 1 percent of firms in the sample (e.g., Ang, Cole & Lin, 2000). Hence, the reference group for industry effects is the set of minority industries in the U.S. population of non-distribution SMEs (small firms are a lesser presence in industries that are more capital intensive). We also controlled for the firm's *urban versus rural* location of the firm's headquarters office, as this may be related to the need to seek business beyond the local market. Our variable took the value 1 if the firm was located in a Metropolitan Statistical Area (MSA) as designated by the Bureau of the Census, and 0 otherwise. Finally, since our arguments regarding potential slack are based on a firm's access to commercial credit, we decided to control for the level of *concentration in the local banking market*, as prior research with SSBF data has found firms in more concentrated markets to have less access to credit (e.g., Cavalluzzo & Wolken, 2005). The SSBF measure used is an ordinal variable, ranging from 1 to 3, based on the Herfindahl index (HI) of commercial bank deposits at the end of 2003 for the MSA or county where the firm is located. The measure takes value 1 if the local HI is between 0 and 1000; 2 if the HI is between 1000 and 1800; and 3 if the HI is above 1800, indicating high levels of concentration.

METHODS AND RESULTS

Statistical Analysis

To test our hypotheses regarding the effects of different types of financial slack on adoption of different IT applications we ran maximum-likelihood logistic regression analyses of our dependent variables. In each case, we fitted a reduced model first, with control variables only, followed by the full model that added the financial slack variables of interest and their quadratic terms. Although we did not hypothesize quadratic effects for potential slack, we included the quadratic term for this variable as well, so as to provide a thorough test of our hypothesis. In order to facilitate interpretation of the quadratic equations, slack variables were mean-centered –i.e., expressed as deviations from their means

(Aiken & West, 1991). To produce appropriate population estimates of regression parameters we used the SURVEYLOGISTIC procedure in SAS 9.1, which takes into account the stratified sample design and corrects for the sampling weight of each observation. Therefore, our regression coefficient estimates provide evidence regarding the effect of a change in independent variables on the likelihood of e-commerce (or computerized core processes) adoption by non-retail, non-wholesale U.S.-based SMEs.

Results

Figure 1 shows descriptive statistics and correlations among the variables included in the study.

Figure 2 provides the results of the logistic regression analyses. The columns labeled Model 1 and Model 3 present results for the reduced regression equations that include only control variables, for e-commerce and computerized-core adoption respectively. Both regression equations are strongly significant, due in large part to very strong industry effects. A brief comment on the contrast of these two equations seems warranted. First, in terms of industry effects, the likelihood of e-commerce adoption was found to be greater in some of the capital-intensive industries that SMEs tend to shy away from (e.g., SIC 37-Transportation Equipment; or SIC 38-Measurement and Control Instruments), as well as in hotels (SIC 70) and insurance and brokerage services (SIC 64). By contrast, computerized-core adoption was most likely among SMEs in printing and publishing (SIC 27), machinery and computer equipment (SIC 35), and engineering, accounting, research, and management services (SIC 87). Beyond industry differences, the likelihood of e-commerce adoption was found to increase for larger firms, as well as for younger firms, firms that are incorporated, and firms which have suffered performance declines in the recent past (although the latter effects were only marginally significant). In turn,

Figure 1.

Descriptive Statistics and Pearson Correlation Coefficients[a]

Variables	Mean	S.D.	1	2	3	4	5	6	7	8	9	10	11	12	13	14	15
1 . e-Commerce adoption	0.28	0.46															
2 . Computerized-core adoption	0.09	0.32	0.06														
3 . Average age of owner group	50.56	10.52	-0.03	0.01													
4 . Average education of owner group	4.68	1.88	0.05	0.06	0.09												
5 . Firm age	13.93	11.23	-0.06	0.01	0.53	-0.04											
6 . Number of employees (ln)	1.32	1.60	0.08	0.01	0.02	-0.02	0.08										
7 . Number of sites	1.21	0.98	0.07	0.03	-0.01	0.03	0.01	0.29									
8 . Ownership share of primary owner	83.07	26.09	-0.08	-0.02	-0.01	0.00	0.05	-0.30	-0.15								
9 . Professionally managed firm	0.04	0.26	0.01	-0.02	0.09	-0.04	0.05	0.17	0.03	-0.06							
10 . Legal form (incorporated)	0.46	0.49	0.11	0.07	0.00	0.04	-0.04	0.42	0.12	-0.21	0.06						
11 . Sales growth	0.36	0.86	-0.01	-0.01	-0.18	0.04	-0.26	0.08	0.07	-0.06	0.06	0.02					
12 . Fixed asset intensity	0.47	0.95	-0.02	0.02	0.02	-0.08	-0.03	-0.07	0.01	-0.08	-0.02	-0.17	-0.06				
13 . Urban location	0.79	0.41	0.07	0.05	-0.02	0.14	-0.06	0.01	-0.01	0.02	0.04	0.09	0.05	-0.06			
14 . Local banking market concentration	2.43	0.61	-0.04	-0.02	0.01	-0.06	0.02	-0.03	-0.01	-0.01	-0.02	-0.06	-0.02	0.01	-0.36		
15 . Available slack (working capital/sales)	0.25	0.51	0.04	-0.01	0.05	0.04	0.03	-0.06	-0.02	0.01	0.01	-0.06	-0.06	0.14	0.02	-0.01	
16 . Potential slack (credit rating)	3.62	1.44	-0.05	0.06	0.17	0.07	0.23	0.05	-0.02	-0.01	-0.04	0.09	-0.07	-0.04	-0.03	0.04	0.02

[a] n = 2,296. Population estimates (i.e., statistics are adjusted for sampling weights). Correlations greater than |.07| are significant at p<.001.

Figure 2.

Results of Logistic Regression Models Predicting the Likelihood of Innovation Adoption[a]

Variables	E-commerce adoption				Computerized-core adoption			
	Model 1		Model 2		Model 3		Model 4	
Owners' characteristics:								
Average age of owner group	-0.009	(0.007)	-0.008	(0.007)	-0.010	(0.011)	-0.011	(0.011)
Average education of owner group	0.027	(0.039)	0.027	(0.039)	0.112 †	(0.064)	0.108 †	(0.063)
Firm's characteristics:								
Firm age	-0.013 †	(0.008)	-0.009	(0.008)	0.018 †	(0.011)	0.014	(0.011)
Number of employees (ln)	0.173 **	(0.066)	0.192 **	(0.067)	0.118	(0.097)	0.090	(0.100)
Number of sites	0.082	(0.099)	0.082	(0.099)	0.081	(0.185)	0.086	(0.180)
Ownership share of primary owner	-0.002	(0.003)	-0.002	(0.003)	0.000	(0.004)	-0.001	(0.004)
Professionally managed firm	-0.006	(0.347)	-0.055	(0.343)	-0.347	(0.476)	-0.343	(0.493)
Legal form (incorporated)	0.248 †	(0.149)	0.303 *	(0.152)	0.354	(0.238)	0.304	(0.237)
Sales growth	-0.136 †	(0.082)	-0.150 †	(0.083)	-0.006	(0.111)	0.008	(0.112)
Fixed asset intensity	-0.121	(0.075)	-0.133 †	(0.076)	0.332 ***	(0.096)	0.352 ***	(0.099)
Environmental factors:								
Urban location	0.170	(0.177)	0.164	(0.178)	0.178	(0.288)	0.175	(0.290)
Local banking market concentration	-0.088	(0.113)	-0.072	(0.115)	0.103	(0.177)	0.089	(0.179)
Industry: 2-digit SIC code dummies	included ***		included ***		included ***		included ***	
Financial Slack:								
Available slack (working capital/sales)			0.328	(0.235)			-0.295	(0.299)
Available slack squared			-0.059	(0.077)			0.046	(0.080)
Potential slack (credit rating)			-0.164 **	(0.051)			0.177 **	(0.068)
Potential slack squared			-0.050	(0.031)			0.068	(0.042)
Intercept	0.406	(0.575)	0.293	(0.586)	-3.373 **	(1.143)	-3.243 **	(1.188)
Wald χ^2	222.29 ***		236.2829 ***		20,955.01 ***		20,652.43 ***	
d.f.	34		38		34		38	

[a] n= 2,296. Coefficient estimates and their standard errors are adjusted for sampling weights and stratification of the survey design. Standard errors are in parentheses.

Detailed industry dummy estimates not reported. † p < .10, * p < .05, ** p < .01, *** p < .001

the likelihood of adoption of computerized core processes was greater for more asset-intensive firms, as well as for older firms with more educated owners (tentatively).

Hypothesis 1 predicts an inverted U-shaped relationship between available slack and the likelihood of e-commerce adoption. Consistent with this, we expected to find a negative coefficient for the quadratic available slack term. As shown in Figure 2 (Model 2) this coefficient was negative, as expected, but was not statistically significant ($\beta = -.059$; $p=.439$). Hence, Hypothesis 1 was not supported. Indeed, we found no evidence that available slack is related to e-commerce adoption among the population of U.S. SMEs, as the linear available slack term was also non-significant.

Hypothesis 2 predicts an inverted U-shaped relationship between available slack and the likelihood of computerized-core adoption. However, the estimated regression coefficient for the quadratic available slack term in Figure 2 (Model 4) was positive (against prediction) and non-significant. Hence, Hypothesis 2 was not supported. As in the case of e-commerce, computerized-core adoption by U.S. SMEs appears not to be related to available slack as the linear effect failed to reach statistical significance as well.

Hypothesis 3 predicts an inverse relationship between potential slack and the likelihood of e-commerce adoption. Consistent with this, the regression coefficient for potential slack in Figure 2 (Model 2) was negative and significant ($\beta = -.164$; $p=.001$). Hence, Hypothesis 3 is strongly supported.

Hypothesis 4 predicts a direct relationship between potential slack and the likelihood of adoption of computerized core processes. As expected, the regression coefficient for potential slack in Figure 2 (Model 4) was positive and significant ($\beta = .177$; $p=.009$). This result provides strong support for Hypothesis 4.

DISCUSSION

This study sheds light on the relevance of different types of financial slack in SMEs, as well as on the relationships between slack and adoption of different types of IT applications. Our first contribution relates to our characterization of organizational slack in the context of SMEs. We argue that available and potential slack will be the most salient sources of financial slack in the case of SMEs, while absorbed or recoverable slack will tend to be immaterial and, thus, play a negligible role as a driver of innovation. In contrast to larger and well-established firms, SMEs are unlikely to experience lengthy surpluses in returns and cash-flows, and are unlikely to absorb those surpluses in the form of redundant or underutilized firm assets. Rather, SMEs tend to be characterized as operating under severe resource constraints (e.g., Storey, 1994). Furthermore, we argue that the salient dimension of potential slack for SMEs is not the financial leverage capacity implicit in their capital structure (and measured by the debt-to-equity ratio) as professed for larger firms, but rather their ability to access external debt in the first place. Access to commercial credit or to other sources of external financing (like venture capital) are not a given and, rather, tend to be the exception for these firms (e.g, Baker & Nelson, 2005).

Second, this is the first study to investigate relationships between different types of slack and innovation adoption in SMEs. Drawing from the prior literature, we argued for an inverted U-shaped relationship between available slack and innovation adoption in SMEs. We posited that available slack would increase innovation adoption in SMEs up to an optimal point, beyond which greater amounts of slack would provide disincentives to innovation. By contrast, and also based on the prior literature, we argued for a linear relationship between potential slack and adoption. However, as an extension to prior theory, we further espoused that in the SME context this relationship would be moderated by the capital requirements associated with implementing the innovation relative to the no-innovation scenario. We hypothesized that e-commerce would tend to be pursued by SMEs with lesser potential slack, as this innovation may allow the development of a sales channel for considerably less investment than alternative forms of distribution (Santarelli & D'Altri, 2003. By contrast, we argued that computerized-core applications will tend to be more capital intensive than alternative processes and, thus, will tend to be pursued by those with greater potential slack (i.e., greater access to credit). Our test of these hypotheses using a representative sample of non-retail and non-wholesale SMEs in the U.S. produced mixed support for our theoretical model: Hypotheses regarding potential slack were strongly supported. However, we found no support for the hypothesized inverted U-shape relationship between available slack and innovation adoption. Indeed, our findings suggest that available slack plays no meaningful role as a driver of innovation adoption in the SME context. This is in stark contrast to its role as a driver of innovation in the case of larger and better established organizations (Geiger & Cashen, 2002).

The third contribution of the study stems from its characterization of some forms of innovation as "bricolage" –i.e., "make do with what's at hand" (Baker & Nelson, 2005) or, at the very least, as alternative business models that are adopted in an attempt to economize resources when organizational slack is limited. In this view, innovation adoption may be born out of necessity, or may be motivated by a desire to preserve (as opposed to an opportunity to spend) resources. This contrasts with virtually all prior research investigating the relationship between slack and innovation, which has been built on the premise that the latter is germane to greater marginal resource expenditures. As such our work extends emerging research on the positive or 'enabling' aspects of resource constraints with regard to innovation (Katila & Shane, 2005). I also answers a recent call for research that explores how the nature of innova-

tions themselves, and in particular their relative dependency on funding from slack resources, moderates their relationship to organizational slack (Herold et al., 2006).

Consistent with our proposition that e-commerce adoption represents a form of "bricolage" by resource-constrained SMEs, we found adopters to be lesser asset-intensive firms; firms that had experienced performance declines in the recent past; and, most important, firms with lesser potential slack. By contrast, adopters of computerized-core applications were firms with greater levels of asset intensity and with greater potential slack.

Implications for Research

Our study has important implications for organizational slack research. We have filled a gap in the prior literature by investigating slack-innovation relationships in SMEs. We discuss the relevant dimensions of organizational slack in the context of SMEs, document the challenges of using established measures of financial slack in this context, and advance what we believe are sensible alternative measures for available and potential slack of small firms. We also show that available slack and potential slack play very different roles as drivers of innovation in SMEs as opposed to their roles in larger organizations (Geiger & Cashen, 2002; Nohria & Gulati, 1996). All of this, then, challenges the generalizability of received slack-innovation theory, and underscores the need for further organizational slack research using SME populations.

Indeed the present research raises many new questions that may be answered by future research. In particular, future studies might further investigate the role of available slack in SMEs. After modeling both linear and quadratic effects, the present study suggests that available slack has no influence on innovation adoption by SMEs. Given the observed low levels of working capital among U.S. SMEs, it is possible that business owners don't perceive the latter to be resources "in excess of what an organization requires to maintain its standard operations" (Cyert & March, 1963). Population frequency estimates from the 2003 SSBF indicate that 13 percent of non-distribution SMEs have zero or negative working capital, 36 percent have $5,000 or less of working capital, and the median working capital is $13,928. These marginal amounts may not be regarded as "available" resources to fund investment projects, but rather as necessary buffer to protect operations against cash-flow fluctuations during the normal course of business. Alternatively, our results might be due to a limitation of our research design whereby our measure of available slack may be captured several months after adoption (this limitation is further discussed below). Although we believe that adoption for most firms occurred around the time of the 2003 SSBF survey, and that the aspects of available slack that are more salient in this population (i.e., inventories) are slow to change, if levels of working capital were to decrease significantly after adoption (either because "excess" cash reserves were deployed with adoption, or because the innovation increased the efficiency of internal processes and, thus, reduced inventories) our study would fail to capture the true effects of available slack. Hence, further research is needed to confirm the findings of the present study.

Future research may also explore the relationship between types of slack developed here and performance of SMEs. Also, how are these relationships mediated by innovation adoption? For example, is a firm with low levels of potential slack who adopts e-commerce as a form of bricolage more or less likely to survive and increase performance?

Our study also has implications for research on adoption of new IT innovations by SMEs. First, as far as adoption of e-commerce is concerned, our findings may explain prior mixed results regarding organizational slack. Consistent with our findings, Grandon and Pearson (2004) found a single-item measure that appears to capture available slack

not to be a determinant of adoption. By contrast, Wang and Cheung (2004) found a broader measure of organization slack to be marginally significant ($p<0.10$) and negatively related to the intention to adopt e-commerce. Interestingly, Wang and Cheung's measure includes items that seem related to available slack (e.g., "sufficient slack capital"), as well as others that capture potential slack (e.g., "able to secure necessary funds"). Based on findings from the present study, we would venture that the effect observed in Wang and Cheung's study resulted from the potential slack component of their measure. Second, our study suggests that (potential) slack is an important determinant of adoption. This contrasts with the little attention given to financial slack in the prior SME innovation adoption literature. Interestingly, Wang and Cheung (2004) also found their organizational slack measure to be positively related to the degree of e-commerce implementation after adoption. Their broad measure, however, does not allow concluding if this effect was due to available or potential slack, or both. Others have also applied the TOE framework to explore the extent of implementation of new technologies as opposed to adoption (e.g., Xu, Zhu, & Gibbs, 2004). Hence, this opens an interesting avenue for future investigation as researchers may seek to explore the role of different dimensions of slack on innovation adoption as well as on subsequent implementation. In short, future studies need to include financial slack among organizational drivers of SME innovation and, most importantly, need to discriminate between available and potential slack. This can be done within the confines of the TOE framework or as part of other theoretical schemes. Finally, our review of this literature suggests that it is important to develop more consistent measurement across innovation adoption studies, and to distinguish organizational slack from other concepts like firm size, firm profitability, or perceived cost of adoption.

Implication for Practice and Policy

Using a representative sample of the U.S. population of SMEs, our study shows that the ability to obtain external credit is a strong driver of innovation adoption in this population. Indeed this is the only dimension of organizational slack that is related to SME adoption. In terms of the practical significance of our results, it is important to note the substantial magnitude of the estimated population effects. The odds ratio estimate for the effect of potential slack on e-commerce adoption is 0.849 (p=.0014), indicating that improving the firm's potential slack score from the sample mean of 3.6 to one unit above the mean (which corresponds, approximately, to an increase from the 53rd to the 75th percentiles of the Dun & Bradstreet Commercial Credit Score) decreases the likelihood of e-commerce adoption by 15.1 percent.[9] In turn, the odds ratio estimate for the effect of credit rating on computerized-core adoption is 1.194 (p=.009), which suggests that improving the firm's potential slack by one unit from the mean (i.e., increasing the firm's Credit Score from the 53rd to the 75th percentile) increases the likelihood of computerized-core adoption by 19.4 percent. Hence our results show that improving SMEs access to credit can indeed have meaningful effects in their ability to adopt capital-intensive technological innovations.

Although a firm's credit rating was used here as only a proxy for its access to external credit, credit ratings have become increasingly important for U.S. SMEs in obtaining external funding so that they may constitute an end in themselves. During the second half of the 1990's most banks (especially large banks) substituted traditional "relationship" lending (based on direct, long-term relationships between local loan officers and business owners) for automated underwriting of small business loans based on business credit scores (Frame et al., 2001; Berger et al., 2005). As credit-scored loans become the norm, the implication for practitioners is that maintenance of a good

credit score may become instrumental to be able to adopt new technological innovations.

A related implication is that the recent changes in the banking industry may make it more difficult for young firms to become adopters of capital-intensive innovations. Younger firms have less of a credit record and, as a result, tend to have lower business credit scores. For example, as shown in Figure 1, the correlation between firm age and business credit rating was r=.23 in the present study. Also, as shown in Figure 2, prior to adding credit rating to our regression model, firm age was negatively related to e-commerce adoption (Model 1) and positively related to computerized-core adoption (Model 3). As a result, capital-intensive innovation adoption by young firms may depend on the availability of relationship-based loans (Ang, 1992; Petersen & Rajan, 1994). The implication for policy makers is that support of small, independent local banks operating under the traditional relationship lending model may contribute to a healthier rate of business innovation.

Limitations

The use of the 2003 SSBF for the purpose of the present study affords the opportunity to draw from a large, representative data set and to derive population estimates of the effects of interest. This benefit, however, comes at the expense of imposing other shortcomings on our analysis.

Results from the present study must be considered in the context of the following limitations: First and foremost, we do not know the time of innovation adoption and, thus, the extent to which our independent variables reflect the organizational context at that time. This concern is most important with regard to available slack, as endogeneity could be more acute in this case. By contrast, our measure of potential slack (i.e., credit score) is both more unchanging and less likely to be affected by technology adoption. Second, while measures of financial slack derived from the SSBF data compare favorably with those used in the prior literature on technology adoption in SMEs, SSBF measures of computer adoption were rather coarse. In particular, as far as our computerized-core variable is concerned, it is not known what specific IT innovations are being adopted. Finally, another aspect that may limit comparison with prior studies is that, as the population of U.S. SMEs is overwhelmingly dominated by micro firms (<10 employees), the population statistics produced in the present study will largely reflect conditions and relationships characteristic of these firms. Our results need to be interpreted in this context.

CONCLUSION

The present study fills a gap in the prior literature by investigating how different dimensions of slack relate to innovation adoption in the SME context. It is found that both the dimensions of slack and their relationships to innovation differ in this context as compared to the case of larger and better established firms. This challenges the generalizability of extant slack-innovation theory and underscores the need for further organization-slack research using SME populations. Our study provides a valuable contribution toward this endeavor. Nevertheless, as a first multidimensional examination of slack and its effects within SMEs we leave other questions to be answered.

REFERENCES

Aiken, L. S., & West, S. G. (1991). *Multiple Regression: Testing and Interpreting Interactions*. Thousand Oaks, CA: Sage Publications.

Ajzen, I. (1991). The theory of planned behavior. *Organizational Behavior and Human Decision Processes*, *50*(2), 179–211. doi:10.1016/0749-5978(91)90020-T

Andersen, O. J. (2008). A bottom-up perspective on innovations: Mobilizing knowledge and social capital through innovative processes of bricolage. *Administration & Society*, *40*(1), 54–81. doi:10.1177/0095399707311775

Ang, J. S. (1992). On the theory of finance for privately held firms. *Journal of Small Business Finance*, *1*(3), 185–203.

Ang, J. S., Cole, R. A., & Lin, J. W. (2000). Agency costs and ownership structure. *The Journal of Finance*, *55*(1), 81–106. doi:10.1111/0022-1082.00201

Baker, T., & Nelson, R. E. (2005). Creating something from nothing: Resource construction through entrepreneurial bricolage. *Administrative Science Quarterly*, *50*(3), 329–366. doi:10.2189/asqu.2005.50.3.329

Baumol, W. J. (2002). Entrepreneruship, innovation and growth: The David-Goliath Symbiosis. *Journal of Entrepreneurial Finance and Business Ventures*, *7*(2), 1–10.

Beckinsale, M., Levy, M., & Powell, P. (2006). Exploring internet adoption drivers in SMEs. *Electronic Markets*, *16*(4), 361–370. doi:10.1080/10196780600999841

Berger, A. N., Frame, W. S., & Miller, N. H. (2005). Credit scoring and the availability, price, and risk of small business credit. *Journal of Money. Credit and Banking*, *37*(2), 191–222. doi:10.1353/mcb.2005.0019

Bharati, P., & Chaudhury, A. (2006). Studying the current status of technology adoption. *Communications of the ACM*, *49*(10), 88–93. doi:10.1145/1164394.1164400

Bourgeois, L. J. (1981). On the measurement of organizational slack. *Academy of Management Review*, *6*, 29–39. doi:10.2307/257138

Bourgeois, L. J., & Singh, J. V. (1983). Organizational slack and political behavior within top management teams. *Academy of Management Proceedings,* 43-47.

Brancheau, J. C., & Wetherbe, J. C. (1990). The adoption of spreadsheet software: Testing innovation diffusion theory in the context of end-user computing. *Information Systems Research, 1*(2), 115–143. doi:10.1287/isre.1.2.115

Bromiley, P. (1991). Testing a causal model of corporate risk taking and performance. *Academy of Management Journal, 34*(1), 37–59. doi:10.2307/256301

Cavalluzzo, K., & Wolken, J. (2005). Small business loan turndowns, personal wealth, and discrimination. *The Journal of Business, 78*(6), 2153–2177. doi:10.1086/497045

Cheng, J., & Kesner, I. (1997). Organizational slack and response to environmental shifts: The impact of resource allocation patterns. *Journal of Management, 23,* 1–18. doi:10.1177/014920639702300101

Chwelos, P., Benbasat, I., & Dexter, A. S. (2001). Research report: Empirical test of an EDI adoption model. *Information Systems Research, 12*(3), 304–321. doi:10.1287/isre.12.3.304.9708

Compeau, D. R., Higgins, C. A., & Huff, S. (1999). Social cognitive theory and individual reactions to computing technology: A longitudinal study. *MIS Quarterly, 23*(2), 145–158. doi:10.2307/249749

Cormican, K., & O'Sullivan, D. (2004). Auditing best practice for effective product innovation management. *Technovation, 24,* 819–829. doi:10.1016/S0166-4972(03)00013-0

Corrocher, N., & Fontana, R. (2008). Expectations, network effects and timing of technology adoption: Some empirical evidence from a sample of SMEs in italy. *Small Business Economics, 31*(4), 425–441. doi:10.1007/s11187-007-9062-1

Cox, L. W., Camp, S. M., & Sexton, D. L. (2000). The Kauffman Financial Statements Database. In J.A. Katz (Ed.), Databases for the Study of Entrepreneurship. Advances in Entrepreneurship Research, 4, 305-334.

Cyert, R. M., & March, J. G. (1963). A behavioral theory of the firm. Englewood Cliffs, NJ: Prentice-Hall, Inc.

Damanpour, F. (1991). Organizational innovation: A meta-analysis of effects of determinants and moderators. *Academy of Management Journal, 34*(3), 555–590. doi:10.2307/256406

Damanpour, F., Szabat, K. A., & Evan, W. M. (1989). The relationship between types of innovation and organizational performance. *Journal of Management Studies, 26*(6), 587–601. doi:10.1111/j.1467-6486.1989.tb00746.x

Damanpour, F., & Wischnevsky, J. D. (2006). Research on innovation in organizations: Distinguishing innovation-generating from innovation-adopting organizations. *Journal of Engineering and Technology Management, 23*(4), 269–291. doi:10.1016/j.jengtecman.2006.08.002

Dandridge, T. C. (1979). Children are not little grown-ups: Small business needs its own organizational theory. *Journal of Small Business Management, 17*(2), 53–57.

Daniel, E., Wilson, H., & Myers, A. (2002). Adoption of e-commerce by SMEs in the UK. *International Small Business Journal, 20*(3), 253–270. doi:10.1177/0266242602203002

Daniel, F., Lohrke, F. T., Fornaciari, C. J., & Turner, R. A. (2004). Slack resources and firm performance: a meta-analysis. *Journal of Business Research, 57,* 565–574. doi:10.1016/S0148-2963-(02)00439-3

Davis, F. D. (1989). Perceived usefulness, perceived ease of use, and user acceptance of information technology. *MIS Quarterly, 13*, 319–339. doi:10.2307/249008

Dembla, P., Palvia, P., & Brooks, L. (2007). Organizational adoption of web-enabled services for information dissemination. *Journal of Information Science and Technology, 3*(3), 24–49.

Dickerson, M. D., & Gentry, J. W. (1983). Characteristics of adopters and non-adopters of home computers. *The Journal of Consumer Research, 10*, 225–235. doi:10.1086/208961

Dougherty, D., & Hardy, C. (1996). Sustained product innovation in large, mature organizations: Overcoming innovation-to-organization problems. *Academy of Management Journal, 39*(5), 1120–1153. doi:10.2307/256994

Drazin, R., & Schoonhoven, C. B. (1996). Community, population, and organization effects on innovation: A multilevel perspective. *Academy of Management Journal, 39*(5), 1065–1083. doi:10.2307/256992

Ekanem, I. (2005). 'Bootstrapping': The investment decision-making process in small firms. *The British Accounting Review, 37*(3), 299–318. doi:10.1016/j.bar.2005.04.004

Fiol, C. M. (1996). Squeezing harder doesn't always work: Continuing the search for consistency in innovation research. *Academy of Management Review, 21*(4), 1012–1021.

Fishbein, M., & Ajzen, I. (1975). Belief, attitude, intention, and behavior: An introduction to theory and research. Reading, MA: Addison-Wesley.

Frame, W. S., Srinivasan, A., & Woosley, L. (2001). The effect of credit scoring on small-business lending. *Journal of Money. Credit & Banking, 33*(3), 813–825. doi:10.2307/2673896

Freeman, J., Caroll, G. R., & Hannan, M. T. (1983). The liability of newness: Age dependence in organizational death rates. *American Sociological Review, 48*, 692–710. doi:10.2307/2094928

Geiger, S. W., & Cashen, L. H. (2002). A multidimensional examination of slack and its impact on innovation. *Journal of Managerial Issues, 14*(1), 68–85.

George, G. (2005). Slack resources and the performance of privately held firms. *Academy of Management Journal, 48*(4), 661–676.

Grandon, E. E., & Pearson, J. M. (2004). Electronic commerce adoption: an empirical study of small and medium US businesses. *Information & Management, 42*(1), 197–216.

Greve, H. R. (2003). A behavioral theory of R&D expenditures and innovations: Evidence from shipbuilding. *Academy of Management Journal, 46*(6), 685–702.

Herold, D. M., Jayaraman, N., & Narayanaswamy, C. R. (2006). What is the relationship between organizational slack and innovation? *Journal of Managerial Issues, 18*(3), 372–392.

Hillman, A. J., Shropshire, C., & Cannella, A. A. (2007). Organizational predictors of women on corporate boards. *Academy of Management Journal, 50*(4), 941–952.

Holtz-Eakin, D., Joulfaian, D., & Rosen, H. S. (1994a). Entrepreneurial decisions and liquidity constraints. *The Rand Journal of Economics, 25*(2), 334–347. doi:10.2307/2555834

Holtz-Eakin, D., Joulfaian, D., & Rosen, H. S. (1994b). Sticking it out: Entrepreneurial survival and liquidity constraints. *The Journal of Political Economy, 102*(1), 53–75. doi:10.1086/261921

Iacovou, A. L., Benbasat, I., & Dexter, A. (1995). Electronic data interchange and small organizations: adoption and impact of technology. *MIS Quarterly, 19*(4), 465–485. doi:10.2307/249629

Igbaria, M., Zinatelli, N., Cragg, P., & Cavaye, A. (1997). Personal computing acceptance factors in small firms: a structural equation model. *MIS Quarterly, 21*(3), 279–302. doi:10.2307/249498

Jensen, M. C. (1986). Agency costs of free cash flow, corporate finance, and takeovers. *The American Economic Review, 76*, 323–329.

Jensen, M. C., & Meckling, W. H. (1976). Theory of the firm: Managerial behavior, agency costs, and ownership structure. *Journal of Financial Economics, 3*, 305–360. doi:10.1016/0304-405-X(76)90026-X

Katila, R., & Shane, S. (2005). When does lack of resources make new firms innovative? *Academy of Management Journal, 48*(5), 814–829.

Kishore, R., & McLean, E. R. (2007). Reconceptualizing innovation compatibility as organizational alignment in secondary IT adoption contexts: An investigation of software reuse infusion. *IEEE Transactions on Engineering Management, 54*(4), 756–775. doi:10.1109/TEM.2007.906849

Kivimaki, M., & Lansisalmi, H. (2000). Communication as a determinant of organizational innovation. *R & D Management, 30*(1), 33–42. doi:10.1111/1467-9310.00155

Kracaw, W. A., Lewellen, W. G., & Woo, C. Y. (1992). Corporate growth, corporate strategy, and the choice of capital structure. *Managerial and Decision Economics, 13*, 515–526. doi:10.1002/mde.4090130607

Kuan, K. K. Y., & Chau, P. Y. K. (2001). A perception-based model for EDI adoption in small businesses using a technology-organization-environment framework. *Information & Management, 38*, 507–521. doi:10.1016/S0378-7206(01)00073-8

Lee, R. P., & Grewal, R. (2004). Strategic responses to new technologies and their impact on firm performance. *Journal of Marketing, 68*, 157–171. doi:10.1509/jmkg.68.4.157.42730

Mach, T. L., & Wolken, J. D. (2006 October). Financial services used by small businesses: Evidence from the 2003 Survey of Small Business Finances. *Federal Reserve Bulletin*, A167-A195.

March, J. G. (1991). Exploration and exploitation in organizational learning. *Organization Science, 2*, 71–87. doi:10.1287/orsc.2.1.71

Mehrtens, J., Cragg, P. B., & Mills, A. M. (2001). A model of internet adoption by SMEs. *Information & Management, 39*, 165–176. doi:10.1016/S0378-7206(01)00086-6

Mirchandani, A. A., & Motwani, J. (2001). Understanding small business electronic commerce adoption: an empirical analysis. *Journal of Computer Information Systems, 41*(3), 70–73.

Moch, M. K., & Morse, E. V. (1977). Size, centralization, and organizational adoption of innovations. *American Sociological Review, 42*(5), 716–725. doi:10.2307/2094861

Moore, G. C., & Benbasat, I. (1991). Development of an instrument to measure the perceptions of adopting an information technology innovation. *Information Systems Research, 2*(3), 192–222. doi:10.1287/isre.2.3.192

Nohria, N., & Gulati, R. (1996). Is slack good or bad for innovation? *Academy of Management Journal, 39*(5), 1245–1264. doi:10.2307/256998

Oh, K., Cruickshank, D., & Anderson, A. R. (2009). The adoption of e-trade innovations by Korean small and medium sized firms. *Technovation, 29*(2), 110–121. doi:10.1016/j.technovation.2008.08.001

Oviatt, B. M., & McDougall, P. P. (1994). Toward a theory of international new ventures. *Journal of International Business Studies, 25*(1), 45–64. doi:10.1057/palgrave.jibs.8490193

Parker, C. M., & Castleman, T. (2007). New directions for research on SME-eBusiness: insights from an analysis of journal articles from 2003 to 2006. *Journal of Information Systems and Small Business, 1*(1-2), 21–40.

Petersen, M. A., & Rajan, R. G. (1994). The benefits of lending relationships: Evidence from small business data. *The Journal of Finance, 49*(1), 3–37. doi:10.2307/2329133

Premkumar, G. (2003). A meta-analysis of research on information technology implementation in small business. *Journal of Organizational Computing and Electronic Commerce, 13*(2), 91–121. doi:10.1207/S15327744JOCE1302_2

Premkumar, G., & Roberts, M. (1999). Adoption of new information technologies in rural small businesses. *OMEGA. The International Journal of Management Science, 27*(4), 467–484.

Ramsey, E., Ibbotson, P., & McCole, P. (2008). Factors that impact technology innovation adoption among irish professional service sector SMEs. *International Journal of Innovation Management, 12*(4), 629–654. doi:10.1142/S1363919608002114

Rao, S. S., Metts, G., & Monge, C. A. M. (2003). Electronic commerce development in small and medium sized enterprises: A stage model and its implications. *Business Process Management Journal, 9*(1), 11–32. doi:10.1108/14637150310461378

Reynolds, P. (1994). Autonomous firm dynamics and economic growth in the United States, 1986-1990. *Regional Studies, 28*(4), 429–442. doi:10.1080/00343409412331348376

Riemenschneider, C. K., Harrison, D. A., & Mykytyn, P. P. (2003). Understanding IT adoption decisions in small business: integrating current theories. *Information & Management, 40*(4), 269–285. doi:10.1016/S0378-7206(02)00010-1

Riemenschneider, C. K., & McKinney, V. R. (2001). Assessing belief differences in small business adopters and non-adopters of web-based e-commerce. *Journal of Computer Information Systems, 42*(2), 101–107.

Rogers, E. M. (1962). Diffusion of innovations. New York: The Free Press.

Rosner, M. (1968). Economic determinants of organizational innovation. *Administrative Science Quarterly, 12*, 614–625. doi:10.2307/2391536

Rubin, D. B. (1996). Multiple imputation after 18+ years. *Journal of the American Statistical Association, 91*, 473–489. doi:10.2307/2291635

Saffu, K., Walker, J. H., & Hinson, R. (2008). Strategic value and electronic commerce adoption among small and medium-sized enterprises in a transitional economy. *Journal of Business and Industrial Marketing, 23*(6), 395–404. doi:10.1108/08858620810894445

Santarelli, E., & D'Altri, S. (2003). The diffusion of e-commerce among SMEs: Theoretical implications and empirical evidence. *Small Business Economics, 21*, 273–283. doi:10.1023/A:1025757601345

Sharma, M. K. (2009). Receptivity of india's small and medium-sized enterprises to information system adoption. *Enterprise Information Systems, 3*(1), 95–115. doi:10.1080/17517570802317901

Simon, H. A. (1957). Administrative Behavior. New York: Free Press.

Singh, J. V. (1986). Performance, slack, and risk taking in organizational decision making. *Academy of Management Journal, 29*(3), 562–585. doi:10.2307/256224

Small Business Administration. (2003). Small Serial innovators: The small firm contribution to technical change. *Small Business Research Summary, #225*. Washington, DC. Retrieved from www.sba.gov/advo/

Small Business Administration. (2006). *The Small Business Economy: For Data Year 2005*. Washington, D.C.: www.sba.gov/advo/.

Spanos, Y. E., & Voudouris, I. (2009). Antecedents and trajectories of AMT adoption: The case of greek manufacturing SMEs. *Research Policy, 38*(1), 144–155. doi:10.1016/j.respol.2008.09.006

Stotey, D. (1994). Understanding the Small Business Sector. New York: Routledge.

Swanson, E. B. (1994). Information systems innovation among organizations. *Management Science, 40*(9), 1069–1092. doi:10.1287/mnsc.40.9.1069

Tan, J. (2003). Curvilinear relationship between organizational slack and firm performance: Evidence from Chinese state enterprises. *European Management Journal, 21*(6), 740–749. doi:10.1016/j.emj.2003.09.010

Tan, J., & Peng, M. W. (2003). Organizational slack and firm performance during economic transitions: Two studies from an emerging economy. *Strategic Management Journal, 24*(13), 1249–1263. doi:10.1002/smj.351

Thong, J. Y. L. (1999). An integrated model of information systems adoption in small businesses. *Journal of Management Information Systems, 15*(4), 187–214.

Tornatzky, L. G., & Fleischer, M. (1990). The Processes of Technological Innovation, Lexington, MA: Lexington Books.

Tsikriktsis, N., Lanzolla, G., & Frohlich, M. (2004). Adoption of e-processes by service firms: An empirical study of antecedents. *Production and Operations Management, 13*(3), 216–229.

Venkatesh, V., Morris, M. G., Davis, G. B., & Davis, F. D. (2003). User acceptance of information technology: Toward a unified view. *MIS Quarterly, 27*(3), 425–478.

Wang, S., & Cheung, W. (2004). E-business adoption by travel agencies: Prime candidates for mobile e-business. *International Journal of Electronic Commerce, 8*(3), 43–63.

Welsh, J. A., & White, J. F. (1981). A small business is not a little big business. *Harvard Business Review, 59*(4), 18–32.

Winborg, J., & Landstrom, H. (2001). Financial bootstrapping in small businesses: Examining small business managers' resource acquisition behaviors. *Journal of Business Venturing, 16*, 235–254. doi:10.1016/S0883-9026(99)00055-5

Wiseman, R. M., & Bromiley, P. (1996). Toward a model of risk in declining organizations: An empirical examination of risk, performance and decline. *Organization Science, 7*(5), 524–543. doi:10.1287/orsc.7.5.524

Wong, S., & Chin, K. (2007). Organizational innovation management: An organization-wide perspective. *Industrial Management & Data Systems, 107*(9), 1290–1315. doi:10.1108/02635570710833974

Xu, S., Zhu, K., & Gibbs, J. (2004). Global technology, local adoption: A cross-country investigation of internet adoption by companies in the United States and China. *Electronic Markets, 14*(1), 13–24. doi:10.1080/1019678042000175261

Yang, K. H., Lee, S. M., & Lee, S. (2007). Adoption of information and communication technology: Impact of technology types, organization resources and management style. *Industrial Management & Data Systems, 107*(9), 1257–1275. doi:10.1108/02635570710833956

ENDNOTES

[1] A notable exception is George (2005) which investigates the relationship between slack and performance in privately held firms.

[2] This is consistent with arguments presented later on in this paper that e-commerce is a form of innovation that allows an SME to economize in the use of financial resources as compared to other alternatives.

[3] Tan (2003) explores curvilinear effects of slack dimensions on the performance of medium to large Chinese state-operated firms, and finds that both absorbed and unabsorbed slack have an inverse U-shaped relationship with firm performance. Another study using the same population of firms found similar results (Tan & Peng, 2003).

[4] Our data shows that most SMEs adopt e-commerce as supplemental sales channels, which suggests that they invest in this innovation at the lower end of the spectrum.

[5] The 1987 and 1993 surveys were called the National Survey of Small Business Finances.

[6] Although the overall SSBF rate of missing values is rather low, missing data problems are widely divergent across variables, and are most acute for items that are financial in nature. Since the present study draws on several of these financial indicators, careful attention to this issue was important.

[7] Since the 2003 SSBF provides demographic information on up to three owners only, this screen was needed to guarantee that our owner-characteristic variables would properly depict the dominant owner group.

[8] Standardizing on the basis of sales volume was preferable here to standardizing on the basis of assets (e.g., Lee & Grewal, 2004), as the latter may change substantially for SMEs upon technology adoption – especially in the case of computerized-core adoption. It is important to note also that we ran additional analyses on the reduced sample for which current ratio could be defined (n=1534, after deleting outliers), and that regression results using either current ratio or working capital over sales were essentially the same. Results for current ratio were also essentially the same as those presented here for working capital over sales using all available data.

[9] Since variables are log-transformed for the logistic regression analysis, the magnitude of effects is nonlinear so that, here, the straightforward interpretation of odds ratios informs about effect sizes for one-unit changes around the sample mean only (Hillman, Shropshire & Cannella, 2007). Odds ratios are not reported in our results table.

Section 3
Strategy and Information Systems

Chapter 10
The Dual Lens Method:
A Practical Approach to Information Systems Strategy in SMEs

Peter Marshall
University of Tasmania, Australia

Phyl Willson
University of Tasmania, Australia

Judy Young
University of Tasmania, Australia

Kristy de Salas
University of Tasmania, Australia

ABSTRACT

This chapter describes the development and testing of a method for information systems (IS) strategy formulation in small and medium enterprises (SMEs). A case study describing a practical experience with the method is presented. Essentially the method is comprised of two complementary analyses: an externally focused strategic analysis and an internally focused business process analysis. The method draws on the work of Levy and Powell (1999, 2000). The method is simple and clearly prescribed and does not require, as does the approach of Levy and Powell (1999, 2000, 2005), the selection of approaches from a range of applicable techniques. However, before assessing IS strategy formulation approaches for SMEs, including the work of Levy and Powell (1999, 2000, 2005) the authors will seek to justify the need for an IS Strategy Formulation Method for SMEs and then reflect on the importance of relevance and practicality, as two features of the approach which are important considerations in terms of establishing the method in practice.

DOI: 10.4018/978-1-61520-627-8.ch010

INTRODUCTION

This section will justify the need for an IS strategy formulation method for SMEs and then reflect on the importance of relevance and practicality, as two features of the approach which are important considerations in terms of establishing the method in practice.

The Need for an IS Strategy Formulation Method for SMEs

A failure by SMEs, or any organisation, to effectively plan IS strategy that is well aligned with the organisation's strategic business goals can result in serious financial consequences resulting from poor ICT investment decisions. Recent research indicates that SMEs that manage their ICT strategically and in alignment with their business strategy enjoy financial benefits (Wynn, 2009). Whilst a formalised process for developing an information systems (IS) strategy is commonplace in many large organizations, the same cannot be said of IS strategy formulation in small and medium-sized enterprises (SMEs). In SMEs, reflective and considered enterprise-wide planning of IS investments is frequently lacking (Blili & Raymond, 1993; Levy & Powell 2000). The result of this can be disjointed IS portfolios that are not well aligned or integrated with the organisation's strategic goals (Ward & Peppard, 2002; Levy & Powell, 2005). Past studies have suggested that the problem is that management in these businesses generally do not understand the role, nature and importance of effective decisions regarding IS investments (Levy & Powell, 2000; Hagmann & McCahon, 1993). Further, an effective yet simple IS strategy formulation method specifically taking account of the specificity of the SME business environment has not yet been developed, published and publicized (Levy & Powell, 2000).

What is required, therefore, is a theoretical framework and practical tools that are more simple and straightforward than those used in large companies (Blili & Raymond, 1993; Levy & Powell, 2000). In an attempt to address the disproportionate focus of the information systems strategy literature in the past on large organisations, this paper describes a theoretically-informed method, specifically designed to guide small to medium business enterprises (SMEs) in developing an information systems strategy, by taking into account the special characteristics of SMEs.

It is important to note in passing that the information systems strategy formulation method presented in this paper focuses on the determination of the strategic information systems capabilities that are needed in an organisation, and not on simple IT-based utilities such as e-mail and Microsoft Office-type capabilities. Such utilities and office support are considered necessities in today's business world and below the focus of an enterprise-wide strategic information systems plan. However, if desired, such considerations could easily be included in the Information Systems strategy formulation method.

The Need for Relevance and Practicality

It has been noted (Teubner, 2007; Teubner & Mocker, 2005; Peters et al., 2002) that despite a significant outpouring of academic papers in the last three decades, the wealth of academic papers on IS strategy do not connect in any meaningful way with practice. The elaborate and, indeed even artistic sets of ideas and conceptualisations in the academic literature are, in the experience of the authors, remote from, and lacking influence in practice in business. While this is true in large organisations, it is true with much more force in small organisations given the practical and operational focus of SMEs (Beaver & Prince, 2004; Doukidis et al., 1996). In this paper the authors' focus is on developing a method for IS strategy formulation that is acceptable, workable and relevant for SME managements.

Despite some evidence pointing to small but growing tendencies for SMEs to develop strategic business and IS plans (O'Regan & Ghobadian, 2007; Hua, 2007; Giffy-Browne & Chun, 2007), it remains true that it is not uncommon for SMEs to lack both formal business and IS strategies (Blili & Raymond, 1993; Hagmann & McCahon, 1993; Levy & Powell, 2000, 2005). In an attempt to address this issue and remain relevant and aware of the realities of contemporary SMEs this research has used an Action Research (AR) approach, thus engaging with the actual issues of determining IS strategies in SMEs. The research described in this paper involved an AR case study, details of which are given later.

BACKGROUND

The definition of SME varies from country to country (de Saulles, 2007). Even within some countries there is no agreed definition (Alam & Ahsan, 2007) and for this reason it is necessary to explain what we mean when we use the term SME. This research was situated in Australia and so it seems appropriate to adopt the definition offered by the Australian Bureau of Statistics (ABS, 2000, p.2).

Under the ABS definition, the term SME covers the following:

- micro businesses — businesses employing less than five people, including non-employing businesses;
- other small businesses — businesses employing five or more people, but less than 20 people;
- small businesses — businesses employing less than 20 people;
- medium businesses— businesses employing 20 or more people, but less than 200 people…

Some researchers have argued that SMEs have characteristics that are distinctly different from those of large organisations (Beaver & Prince 2004; Riemenschneider et al., 2003). Thus, this section of the paper begins by describing the special nature of SMEs. Having established these characteristics of SMEs, the paper then deals with the issues regarding IS strategy for SMEs, including the current issues and problems, how IS strategy formulation methods for large companies are not suitable for SMEs and what is required for an effective and practical method for SMEs.

Characteristics of SMEs

Whilst it may be tempting to trivialise the contribution of SMEs, in fact they are of considerable importance and make major contributions to many economies (Burke & Jarratt, 2004; Griffy-Browne & Chun, 2007; Jocumsen; 2004; Tse & Soufani, 2003).To the extent that they are commonly considered to be key contributors to innovation and economic growth (Griffy-Browne & Chun 2007, Guimaraes 2000, Wong & Aspinwall 2004) SMEs are worthy of study in their own right.

There is a considerable body of knowledge that has supported the view that SMEs are distinctly different from large organisations (Bharati & Chaudhury 2009, Hussin et al 2002, Riemenschneider et al 2003, Beaver & Prince 2004, Culkin & Smith 2000, Dandridge 1979). The major characteristics that differentiate SMEs from large organisations are now outlined. Firstly, decision-making, planning and direction setting, and authority generally are very much under the control of owner-managers or CEOs, possibly together with a small coterie of senior executives (Beaver & Prince, 2004; Beaver & Ross, 2000; Berry, 1998; Bharati & Chaudhury, 2009; Holmes & Gibson, 2001; Lefebvre & Lefebvre, 1992; Lefebvre, Mason & Lefebvre 1997; Martin 1989; Thong, 1999, 2001; Thong, Yap, & Raman, 1996). These influential players in the SME context are much closer to the operational and marketing realities of the firm than their large firm counterparts (Beaver and Prince 2004). Secondly, there is a relative scarcity of resources in SMEs compared to large organisations. This not only includes a relative lack of physical and financial resources, but also human resources including IS and other staff professionals (Beaver & Prince, 2004; Beaver & Ross, 2000; Bharati & Chaudhury, 2009; Blili & Raymond 1993; Delone, 1981; Thong, 1999, 2001; Welsh and White 1981). Other characteristics distinguishing SMEs from large organisations include a short-term and operational focus, a low risk propensity, ad hoc and informal management practices, and a small and closed network of business and supply chain partners (Beaver & Prince, 2004; Beaver & Ross, 2000; Bharati & Chaudhury, 2009; Blili & Raymond 1993; Thong, 1999, 2001).

The above key characteristics have implications for business and IS planning. In a sense, while the absence in SMEs of challenging and diverse opinions can lower the quality of planning, the power, influence, and closeness to operational and marketing realities of a company of the small senior management team of an SME, means that planning in SMEs can be a simpler and smoother process than for large companies where agreement is required between a potentially large group of managers, each of whom is more detached from the workings of the firm than his/her SME counterparts. Further, despite the notorious time pressures on SME managers, intuitive and judgemental evaluation and decision-making can proceed effectively in the planning processes of the SME, whereas large firms need to rely more on abstract and formal analysis. However, despite these potential advantages for SME planning it is not uncommon for SMEs to fail, and, for this failure to be attributed to a lack of business planning and strategic focus (Perry 2001, Jocumsen, 2004).

SMEs and IS Strategy

Previous research on IS in SMEs has focused on adoption and implementation issues and problems (Beckinsdale, Levy, & Powell, 2006; Bharati & Chaudhury, 2006, 2009; Cragg & King, 1993; Davies & Garcia-Sierra 1999; Iacovou, Benbasat, & Dexter, 1995; Igbaria, Zinatelli, Cragg, & Cavaye, 1997; Mehrtens, Cragg, & Mills, 2001; Raymond, 1985; Riemenschneider, Harrison, & Mykytyn, 2003; Thong, 1999, 2001; Thong, Yap, & Raman, 1996). Research on information systems strategy formulation or strategic information systems planning (SISP) is limited to a small number of publications. The only work dedicated to developing and testing a SISP process or methodology specifically for SMEs is the work of Levy and Powell and their various co-authors (Levy & Powell, 1997, 2000, 2005; Levy, Powell, & Galliers, 1999; Levy, Powell, & Yetton, 2001). Other research work that ostensibly involves SISP and related concerns includes Li and Chen (2001), Proudlock, Phelps, and Gamble (1998), Doukidis, Lybereas, and Galliers (1996), Blili and Raymond (1993), Hagman and McCahon (1993), Bergeron and Raymond (1992), Kyobe (2004) and Griffy-Brown and Chun (2007).

Li and Chen (2001) describe and test a general SISP method called output-driven Information Systems Planning. The method is scalable to SMEs, but requires those utilising the method to select the outputs required and then construct the method from a set of potential methods including Application Portfolio (McFarlan, 1981), Business Systems Planning, Critical Success Factors, Strategy Set Transformation, Information Engineering, and Strategic Planning for Information Resources (King, 1988). Thus the paper does not present a SISP method that is particularly and uniquely suited to SMEs. Further, it requires of SME managements that they have particular skills regarding SISP methodology construction, or they employ experts who do.

The paper by Doukidas et al. (1996) while containing the term "information systems planning" in the title, is actually more concerned with contextual factors regarding IS adoption and growth in 26 organisations in Greece, although there are some minor observations regarding SISP. In particular, the conclusion regarding SISP was that IS growth was not planned but proceeded in an unsystematic and opportunistic way.

Proudlock et al. (1998) studied IS decision-making in small professional firms of fewer than 50 employees. The IS decision-making processes studied included SISP, risk management and product selection. Of the 9 firms studied, 5 firms carried out both business and IS planning. Unsurprisingly, those not carrying out planning were the smaller firms. No information is given by the authors regarding the planning process or its success.

The papers by Bergeron and Raymond (1992), Blili and Raymond (1993), Hagmann and Mc-Cahon (1993), Kyobe, Griffy-Browne and Chun (2007) are essentially about strategic information systems and competitive advantage. Bergeron and Raymond (1992) present a method for identifying strategic information systems and, based on 5 case studies, claim that the method is useful in identifying strategic opportunities for IT Investments. The papers by Blili and Raymond (1993), Hagmann and McCahon (1993) and Kyobe (2004) find that SMEs tend not to be strategic in their approach to the adoption and use of information systems. Blili and Raymond (1993) suggest a top-down method for SISP in SMEs, but, despite carefully distinguishing SMEs from large organisations and presenting the distinguishing characteristics of SMEs, they do not distinguish the method from SISP methods in large organisations. In contrast to the findings of Blili and Raymond (1993), Hagmann and McCahon (1993) and Kyobe (2004), the research by Griffy-Browne and Chun (2007) finds that SMEs in Japan in the 1990s and 2000s

are using IS strategically to link to and build relationships with supply chain partners and customers. However, even in these firms there is no systematic SISP process and the actual process for identifying, adopting and using strategic IS has been unsystematic and ad hoc.

Generally speaking, as indicated above, previous research has found that relatively few SMEs undertake information systems strategy formulation (Proudlock et al., 1998; Doukidas, 1996; Blili & Raymond, 1993; Hagmann & McCahon, 1993). Indeed, SME managements seem to be practically and operationally focussed on moderately short term issues and problems related to their survival, and hence are not motivated to undertake a relatively abstract exercise such as the long term planning of information systems investments (Beaver & Prince, 2004; Doukidis et al., 1996). Although the recent research by Griffy-Browne and Chun (2007) referred to above indicates that SMEs in Japan have used IS strategically, they note that these SMEs "have tended to do so in an ad hoc manner" (p.46). This lack of enthusiasm or perhaps simple neglect of information systems strategy formulation persists despite the fact that information systems deserve a longer term focus from SME managements. Information systems require substantial investment, and their potential strategic importance means that their choice should be made with strategic objectives in mind (Blili & Raymond, 1993). Despite this however, SMEs information systems selection is often focussed primarily on improving operational processes rather than achieving strategic objectives (Duhan, Levy & Powell, 2005; O'Regan & Ghobadian, 2007). Determining required information systems is often done on an informal basis by focusing on particular information systems products, resulting in information systems portfolios that are not aligned with the business goals of the organisation (Beheshti, 2004; Kyobe, 2004; Hagmann & McCahon, 1993). Furthermore, recent research has suggested that a significant number of strategic plans are written without incorporating objectives or goals (O'Regan & Ghobadian, 2007). As a result, SMEs tend to develop portfolios of information systems that are not integrated, are developed in a piecemeal manner, and neither contribute to strategic vision nor enhance organisational flexibility so as to be able to respond to market changes (Levy & Powell, 2005).

In concluding this section, it is worth noting that one of the premises or assumptions of the research reported in this paper is that strategic planning is a worthwhile and positive process that delivers business performance benefits over ad hoc, unsystematic and opportunistic decision making in both business and IS. While to some extent this premise is an article of faith, there is some evidence in the researches of Bracker and Pearson (1986, 1988) and others that the notion that planning improves business performance has some validity (Robinson & Pearce, 1984; Schwenk & Shrader, 1993; Rue & Ibrahim, 1998; Perry, 2001).

IS Strategy Formulation Methods for Large Companies

There is a need for raising the awareness of SME managements to the potential benefits of information systems strategy formulation, as well as to the potential problems that can result from neglecting such a process. The authors of this paper argue, however, that part of the problem, is the lack of an information systems strategy formulation method that is suitable for SMEs. (The very few existing methods for IS strategy formulation in SMEs will be reviewed later in the paper). The availability of such a method would go some of the way to increasing the likelihood of the adoption of information systems planning in SMEs. Surely, it might be argued, the available methods described in the literature together with the many exemplary case studies would provide suitable guidance and motivation for SME managements in this matter (Tozer, 1996; Lederer & Gardiner, 1992; Martin, 1982; Min et al., 1999; Li & Chen, 2001; Ward &

Peppard, 2002). The authors, however, along with Blili and Raymond (1993), beg to differ. Indeed, the current situation is no different in respect of information systems strategy formulation within SMEs from 1993, when Blili and Raymond (1993) wrote the following concerning strategic information systems planning methodologies:

The methodologies presently available were designed with large firms in mind, and, being quite inflexible, energy-consuming and expensive, are not at all suitable for smaller firms (page 446)

The authors of this paper argue, in this context, that while the extant methods for information systems strategy formulation are in principle and in essence what is required for SMEs, some adjustments to these methods are necessary in order to evolve or emerge a method that is appropriate for SMEs, as well as attractive and acceptable to SME managements. Thus, to some extent our position regarding available methods is somewhat less critical than Blili and Raymond (1993) in that we argue simply that some amendments to currently available methods are necessary.

In order for a method to be appropriate for SMEs, and also and in particular, acceptable and attractive to SME managements, the method needs to be simple, direct and business and problem focused, rather than abstract, laboured and data and technology focused. The strategic information systems planning methods of the 80s and 90s, which include Method/1 (Lederer & Gardiner, 1992), SP4IS (Tozer, 1996), IBM's BSP (Martin, 1982; IBM, 1984), the approach described by Ward and Peppard (2002) and others, include technical and data-processing oriented activities such as corporate or enterprise data modelling (Flynn & Arce, 1995). These approaches also include, in some cases at least, detailed considerations and plans regarding the IT department (Ward & Peppard, 2002). What is required for information systems strategy formulation in SMEs is an approach which is stripped of the data-processing and data modelling activities, and which is not concerned with the activities of a large and influential IT department.

For SMEs, an IS strategy method needs to take account of the near-term and operations-focused mindset of SME managements, and work through IS support for the improvement of pressing problem situations and IS support for taking advantage of key business opportunities. Thus a method for IS strategy formulation for SMEs needs to be problem-focused and practical in addition to providing a strategic framework within which the SME can develop and grow.

Existing Approaches to IS Strategy for SMEs

The authors agree with Levy and Powell (2000, p. 63) that "information systems strategy use is under-developed for and under-researched in, small and medium-sized enterprises". The relevant research on information systems strategy formulation methods in SMEs is largely confined to the work of Blili and Raymond (1993) and the work of Levy and Powell (2000, 2005). Blili and Raymond (1993) proposed a strategically-focused method that is similar to, although simpler than, the standard large firm methods, but they do not include an analysis of the IS support for the business processes of the company. Given the operational focus of SME managements, this could be a problem. Further, the method has the formal and abstract feel of the methods that are used in large companies, and this could also be a problem for similar reasons.

Levy and Powell (2000) proposed a framework for an IS strategy formulation method that includes what they term as strategic content, business context and business processes. The business context involves identifying the business strategy and analysing the business environment of the company. It includes looking for strategic opportunities to use IS. The business process element of the framework involves identifying the

high value-added processes and activities of the company and the information flows between them. Finally, the strategic content element or phase draws on both the business context analysis and business process analysis, using these analyses and the strategic vision of the management to assist in determining appropriate IS for the future of the company.

Although Levy and Powell's framework is quite straightforward, they suggest a large number of activities in each state or phase of the framework, and suggest a number of techniques to use, including CSFs, the Information Intensity Matrix, Balanced Scorecard, SSM and others. Of course, particular information systems strategy formulation exercises may not use all of these techniques, but even if they utilise a number of them, the approach could become abstract and complex and lose its practical focus. The authors of the current paper propose a more clearly defined problem-focused approach that is more direct and less complex and onerous. Thus, rather than suggesting a range of, in some cases, abstract methods, we propose a simple and direct approach to both the strategic and the organisational analysis. The strategic analysis proceeds via a strategic conversation among the top management team and the inward-looking organisational analysis proceeds via a simple high-level business process analysis.

A SIMPLE AND DIRECT APPROACH TO IS STRATEGY FORMULATION IN SMEs

The authors of this paper argue that an effective IS strategy formulation process for SMEs consists of two sub-processes - a strategically and externally-focused process, and an efficiency-oriented internally-focused process (see Figure 1). Both processes are designed, not only to be effective, but to be engaging and relevant to SME managements, since it is the top management teams of

Figure 1. The dual lenses: strategic perspective and business process perspective

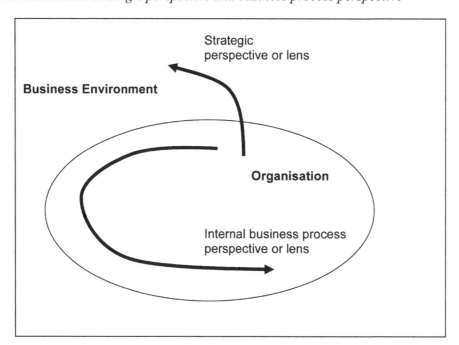

SMEs that must engage with this task. Given this, the strategy formulation method focuses on the central and important task of specifying an effective future application portfolio for the SME. Both sub-processes focus on the same problem of determining the applications portfolio, but they take complementary but different perspectives or lenses on the problem. Issues outside the determination of the applications portfolio, that may be considered in a comprehensive IS strategy formulation, such as details of data, hardware and other issues are best left, in the experience of the authors, in the case of SMEs, to an IS/IT consultant. Implementation and change management concerns are left to the various IS/IT project managers implementing the various systems. These people may also be, of course, IS/IT consultants associated with the firm. In summary, in an effort to get SME managements to feel relaxed and comfortable with the method, the IS strategy formulation method was essentially kept as focused and simple as possible. The method is briefly described below.

The alignment of information systems investments with business strategic goals is important (Bodnar 2003, Earl 1993, Luftmann 2005, van Grembergen, De Haes and Guldentops 2004, Zolkos 2005). Therefore, in IS strategy formulation, one needs an external analysis of the business environment focused on strategic issues concerning the achievement of strategic goals. In this part of the IS strategy formulation, SME managements would be determining appropriate IS support for the achievement of the business strategic goals. The focus on strategic issues or problems will give a practical and realistic edge to the process, thus engaging SME managements. An approach that works through strategic issues to evolve strategy by engaging senior management in discussion stimulated by a series of targeted questions proved to be most effective in the research example presented in this paper.

Thus this approach is a recommended approach to this part of the IS strategy formulation since it can easily be extended from determining overall business strategy to determining IS strategy (de Salas et al 2007).

Attaining IS support for the achievement of strategic goals, however, does not address the issues of business process efficiency. It is possible to address strategic concerns but still have inefficient and unproductive processes relative to other firms in the industry due to a lack of appropriate IS support. Thus it is wise to carry out, as part of the IS strategy formulation process, a business process analysis aimed at determining the IS that are needed to support the company's business processes. This has importance regarding the "look and feel" of the IS strategy formulation method since, in the experience of the authors, SME managements view IS less as a strategic investment than as a means to bring about business process efficiency. Thus the business process analysis phase emphasizes the practicality and relevance of the IS strategy formulation to immediate and practical concerns.

The above two sub-processes (the strategic analysis and business process analysis) have an external perspective or focus and an internal perspective respectively. Both sub-processes are used to determine the necessary portfolio of IS for the future. In some cases, the sub-processes will confirm that existing systems are suitable, while in other cases enhanced or new systems will be required. The complete set of systems determined by each of the sub-process are accumulated to give the future IS portfolio. That is, if the strategic view or perspective leads to systems capabilities A, B, and C being recommended and the business process view leads to systems B, C and D being determined, then the final portfolio is simply systems A, B, C and D. Because the method involved two complimentary perspectives or lenses on the problem of determining a suitable future applications portfolio, the method

was called the Dual Lens Approach to IS strategy formulation.

After the final IS portfolio has been determined, it remains to prioritize the IS and to formulate a time-phased and costed plan for the implementation of the systems (Ward and Peppard 2002). The prioritization of the systems can be carried out via a strategic conversation among the top management team of the SME. This is likely to consist of inputs from a very small number of senior managers, and so formal methods can be dispensed with in favour of the informed yet intuitive judgments of SME senior executives. A time-phased and costed plan for the strategy implementation can be worked on by one or more of the top management team assisted by some of the managers who report to them. Thus, the SME senior management team can take advantage of the efficiencies and advantages of having a small management team that is close to, and hence well informed on, the operational and marketing issues and needs of the firm. Carrying out the prioritization of the IS portfolio and determining the time-phased plan in this way is important, since the method needs to stay simple, efficient in terms of time and staff resources, and within the comfort zone of SME managements

The Dual Lens Approach was used in an action research case study that is described in the next section.

APPLYING THE DUAL LENS IN ABC

The action research case study presented in this paper took place at a regional company in Australia. For the purposes of the paper we will refer to the company as ABC. ABC provides trustee services and financial products and has over $1.2 billion in funds under management for a range of investors and approximately $750 million of trust assets under management.

ABC fits neatly within the Australian definition of a medium-sized enterprise, (ABS, 1999)

employing approximately 85 staff. Staff are located in a small number of branches and offices in major population centres. The senior management team of ABC formally consisted of four members plus the CEO. These five managers regularly met in formal senior management team meetings. However, two of the managers were considered very highly by the CEO, and the CEO used them to help him make most strategic decisions. These two managers were the CFO and the Marketing Manager.

ABC had a small IT department of three members, consisting of an IT manager and two very junior IT professionals. Generally the role of the IT department was to carry out computer and systems setup and maintenance. Thus the IT department had very little in the way of a proactive business or strategic role, and was mainly concerned with technical issues. The IT manager reported to the CFO.

Early in 2005, ABC approached the researchers to assist the company in developing an IS/IT strategy. ABC's was motivated to take this action for three reasons:

1. improving what was perceived to be "basic infrastructure
2. getting the small team of IT professionals "out of the trenches" where they were focussed on technical issues only
3. developing "a more strategic focus" for the firm's IT adoption and use..

Top-Down Review of the Strategic Business Environment

The application of the first lens of the Dual Lens Approach involves a top-down review of the strategic business environment. In completing this stage the research team interviewed the top management team at ABC. The outputs of this process were an updated business strategy and a set of reviewed, revised and expanded strategic goals for the organisation. The next step involved

challenging the managers to consider and evaluate whether their existing IS support, in terms of applications, infrastructure and expertise, was adequate to support the achievement of the newly revised and expanded goals. If the managers indicated the IS was not adequate, then they were asked to specify their requirements for adequate IS functionality or capabilities. The research team then involved the managers in a facilitated discussion in order that an agreed and negotiated position among the top management team regarding the strategic goals and the IS needed to support the attainment of those goals could be achieved. Thus, emerging and determining the IS strategy with the top management team was carried out in the following manner:

1. semi-structured interviews with five individual senior managers to elicit strategic directions and goals.
2. amalgamation of individual responses into a senior management group response by the research team.
3. the senior management group determine a list of IS needs to address the business and IS strategic directions and goals identified through step 1 of the process.

Following the above steps, the strategic goals for ABC were determined to be as follows:

*   achieve better customer service and hence improve customer retention.
*   achieve increased business process efficiency so as to lower costs thus improving customer service and achieving cost parity with competitive rivals.

In the senior management discussion regarding the information systems investments that would enable achievement of these goals, it was determined that a customer relationship management system would enable the firm to achieve better customer service, and further, would enable increased "closeness" to customers leading to market-informed management actions that would achieve increased customer retention. Secondly, an extensive update - or possibly replacement - of the extensive trust management system of ABC was seen as necessary to the achievement of business process efficiency and hence cost parity with competitors. Thirdly, the Marketing Manager had carried out customer surveys that indicated that customers of ABC viewed the company's lack of a web site with e-business functionality for customers as a lack of basic and necessary customer service. Customers wished to have the capability to do basic banking transactions online and to be able to check their investment situation online as well. Thus a company web site with electronic transaction capability and investment lookup capability was planned. In summary, then, the top-down review of the strategic business environment resulted in the planning of two new systems and one significant system update and enhancement. These systems were as follows:

- a customer relationship management system
- a e-business capability for customers enabling Internet-based lookup and transaction
- an update and enhancement of the trust management system

Bottom Up Review of the Organisation's Business Processes

At the request of the CEO and the CFO, this second lens of the Dual Lens approach was completed with the active involvement of operational level managers rather than the more senior managers interviewed in the completion of the strategic review. In SMEs the operational managers are often process owners and experts and as such they can have an extensive knowledge of the processes they manage. For this reason they were considered the best source of information regarding the organisation's processes. The CEO and CFO were to review and accept or revise the output of this phase of the Dual Lens approach.

The following steps were undertaken in the completion of this stage of review:

1. development of high-level process models through group forums with operational managers.
2. determination of more detailed process models via interviews with both managers and with employees who were working more directly on process tasks.
3. determination of process inefficiencies and opportunities via interviews with both managers and with employees who were working more directly on process tasks.
4. determination of a broad list of information systems needed to increase the operational efficiency of the organization's processes.

In step 1 above, the first high-level process map that was determined was an enterprise-wide core process map.

The core or central process model consisted of seven key processes, as follows:

- a strategy formulation process
- a trust and estate management process
- an investment management and process
- a leading management process
- a financial planning process
- marketing process
- a product sales and service process

In the financial service industry in Australia, compliance with government regulations for the industry is important. Thus, it was discussed as to whether the core process model should contain a separate process called compliance management. However, it was decided to treat compliance management as part of each of the core processes of trust and estate management, investment management, lending management

Figure 2. Value chain models for the lending management process

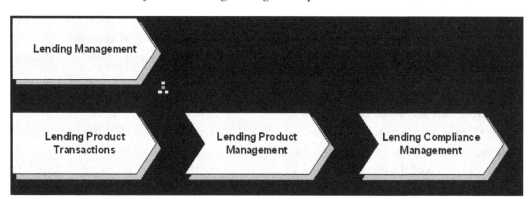

and financial planning. Similar discussions took place with respect to product sales and service, but in this case a separate process was preferred since sales persons often dealt with multiple financial products.

Broad value chain-like models of each core process were then developed. Given its successful track record in business process modeling, the ARIS modelling approach (Scheer et al. 2003) and software (Davis 2001) was chosen as a specific vehicle for supporting the analysis and modelling of ABC's business processes. Figure 2 shows the broad value chain models for the lending process.

The structure of each process was then modelled in more detail: specifically, in the ARIS terminology, '*event driven process chain*' models were developed with the objective of investigating process inefficiencies in more detail. An example of part of the event driven process chain for lending management is shown in Figure 3.

After an understanding of the process logic and the information systems support provided for a given process, group forums and one-on-one interviews were held to brainstorm and evaluate process inefficiencies and deficiencies, and in particular, to look for challenges and problems in the process due to inadequate information provision and information systems support. In the lending process, for example, it was found that there were significant process inefficiencies due

to a lack of integrated information provision. For example, lending service officers of ABC had to access several databases to compile the required information to complete standard mortgage loan initiation and review tasks. Further, there was a lack of basic information systems support for client and contact management, and at the senior management level there was a lack of adequate aggregated corporate information for decision-making regarding lending management.

As the application of this second organisation business process lens proceeded a list of IS systems and capabilities required to increase the efficiency of existing organisational business processes was identified. These included:

- a lending management system.
- an update and enhancement of the trust management system.
- an investment management system.

In particular, it is worth noting that a number of improvements to the trust management system were made in this stage that extended the enhancements suggested in the strategic review and analysis. Thus, many operational and efficiency improvements were made in this business process analysis stage that were not forthcoming at the strategic review stage.

The CEO, CFO and Marketing Manager reviewed the above business process analysis as it

Figure 3. Part of the event driven process chain for the lending management process

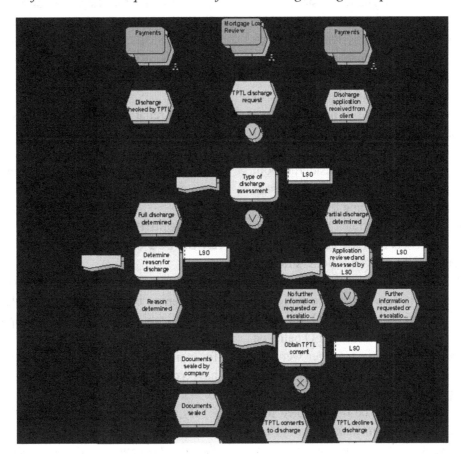

proceeded, both guiding and adapting it to their wishes. Generally speaking, they accepted the output of the middle management team working on this stage.

An IS Portfolio for ABC

The Dual Lens Approach was used within ABC in order to determine the most appropriate IT systems and applications to support the both organisation's strategic goals and directions and the firm's need for operational efficiency. The application of the two lenses, providing as they did a top-down review of the strategic business environment and a bottom-up review of the organisation's business processes, resulted in the creation of two lists

recommending information systems portfolios specially targeted at the strategic directions and the operational efficiency of ABC. These two lists were as follows:

1. Top-down Review of the Strategic Business Environment:
   ○ a customer relationship management system.
   ○ an update and enhancement of the trust management system.
   ○ an e-business capability enabling Internet-based look-up and transactions.
2. Bottom Up Review of the Organisation's Business Processes:

○ A lending management system.

○ an update and enhancement of the trust management system.

○ an investment management system.

It is evident from reviewing the two lists that the application of the two lenses resulted in two differing lists. This difference reflects the different but complementary perspectives at work within the organisation and the need for considering both the strategic direction and the business processes when organisations are planning IS investments. The example of ABC illustrates that the Dual Lens Approach can help SMEs to achieve a more complete picture of their organisations' strategic requirements for ICTs.

At this point the two lists were reviewed during several meetings by the CEO, the CFO and the Marketing Manager. (The CEO believed that the CFO and Marketing Manager were the key executives in the matter of IS investments.) The review quickly determined that the lending management system could be incorporated into the trust management system, making that system a general operational system for the business. They also prioritized the systems and developed, with the help of the firm's chief accountant and the IT manager, a time-phased and costed plan for implementing the new IS portfolio. The IS portfolio below is listed in order of the priority of implementation:

- an e-business capability enabling Internet-based look-up and transactions.
- a customer relationship management system.
- an update and enhancement of the trust management system.
- an investment management system.

DISCUSSION

As mentioned in the introduction of this paper, the purpose of this paper was to present the Dual Lens Approach for IS strategy formulation within SMEs that is simple, effective and targeted to the needs of SMEs. The Dual Lens Approach offers the following advantages for IS strategy development in SMEs:

- not reliant on a formal business strategy.
- provides an analysis of IS investment across the whole organization.
- a straightforward and easily implemented method for rapid analysis.

Not Reliant on a Formal Business Strategy

It is not necessary for an SME to have a formally documented business strategy in place prior to the application of the Dual Lens approach. This aspect of the Dual Lens Approach is important for many SMEs as it is uncommon for SMEs to have a documented business strategy (Jocumsen, 2004).

By working through the steps outlined in the sub-section *Top Down Review of the Strategic Business Environment* SMEs can determine their strategic goals and directions quickly and easily. It would be useful for SMEs to work through these steps even if their business strategy had been previously formally documented in order to review, expand and confirm their strategic directions prior to moving on to completing the bottom up review of their business process outlined in the previous sub-section *Bottom Up Review of the Organisation's Business Processes*.

Analysis of IS Investment Across the Whole Organization

SME planning of IT investment commonly occurs in response to a particular need or imperative and can be fragmentary and sporadic (Frost, 2003). The Dual Lens Approach encourages a considered and well thought-out whole of organisation approach to IS strategy formulation and the analysis of IS investments. Importantly the Dual Lens Approach supports the integration of business strategy with IS planning and investment and extends the strategic alignment and integration to include business processes and operations within the organization.

A Straightforward and Easily Implemented Method for Rapid Analysis

The objective of this paper was to present a method for IS strategy formulation within SMEs that is strategically focused and fast, simple and effective. The method does not rely on forcing SME senior managers through abstract and formal methods, but takes advantage of the small management team of SMEs, by encouraging intuitive and holistic judgments. Ideally the approach can be used by members of an SME organization without the need for outside support or assistance, although if it was necessary or desired by the SME a consultant could support the organization through the planning.

The application of the Dual Lens Approach involves a two step approach that includes a top down review of the SMEs strategic business environment and a bottom up review of the organization's business processes.

The first step - the top-down review - essentially relies on a strategic conversation between the members of the top management team. This may be managed by one of the members of the top management team or it can be managed by a suitably skilled consultant. Either way, the process is one of group and one-on-one discussions which must converge to a determination of the strategic goals of the organisation. The strategic conversation then moves to consider what information systems are required to enable the realisation of the strategic goals. In the case of ABC, this step was completed via a number of one-on-one interviews and the process was completed within one week of moderately intense deliberations.

The second step - the bottom-up review of business processes - took about six weeks of interviews and workshops with considerable time being invested in the detailed event driven process chain diagrams. However, a significant finding of our work with ABC was that the detailed business process models added very little to the process of determining appropriate information systems support for business processes. Thus, for the purposes of determining information systems needs for process support, the key inputs are broad high-level process models of the value chain level or type that simply identify the main activities of the process. If such models are combined with a good issue and problem analysis, then this is more than sufficient for determining the required information systems. This is particularly the case given that many contemporary SMEs purchase application software packages rather than building custom-built information systems, and then redesign the business processes to fit the new information systems. Thus detailed process models, we have found, are likely to be irrelevant to the organisation after implementation of the information systems strategy.

Thus, broad high-level process models together with a problem or issue analysis of each core process is what is required for the bottom-up process of the Dual Lens method. The problem or issue analysis should, given that we are determining an information systems strategy, focus on problems of information provision and information Systems support for the business process of concern. The authors believe that such process analysis could be completed in two to three weeks for an SME.

While it is suitable for small organisations, the authors do not believe that the Dual Lens method would scale easily. With large numbers of active stakeholders in the IS strategy formulation process, relying on informal processes for such steps as determining strategic goals or the prioritisation of the systems would be problematic. For larger organisations it would be necessary to have more formal evaluation processes at various points in

SIS P methods to ensure consensus and to deal with the increased complexity of large organisations.

The research described in this paper is based on one case study in a financial services organisation and hence it is difficult to generalise the results. Further studies of the efficacy of the Dual Lens approach in other SMEs, particularly those in other industry sectors would be necessary for one to be able to conclude with confidence that the approach was an efficient and effective way to determine an IS strategy for an SME.

CONCLUSION

The aim of this paper was to present an IS strategy formulation process that was simple and straightforward enough to be applied by an SME organization, yet rigorous enough to enable the identification and selection of an IS portfolio aligned with the organization's strategy and the organization's business processes. Within the limitations of a case study approach, the Dual Lens Approach fulfils these requirements. The exemplar case study has illustrated how the Dual Lens Approach can be used to develop a portfolio of IS systems and solutions that are relevant to the individual business and aligned with the strategic goals of the organization. In addition, an output of the Dual Lens Approach is to assist SMEs to develop and formalise their business strategy in order that considered decisions can be made regarding the appropriate selection and use of ICTs for strategic advantage.

FUTURE WORK

The Dual Lens Approach was developed by the authors through an action research project undertaken within the exemplar organization. The next step is to continue to test and develop the approach by multiple case studies using non-participant observation of the application of the Dual Lens Approach within a large number of SMEs.

REFERENCES

Alam, S. S., & Ahsan, N. (2007). ICT adoption in Malaysian SMEs from services sectors: Preliminary findings. *Journal of Internet Banking and Commerce, 12*(3), 1–11.

Australian Bureau of Statistics. (2000). *Small business in Australia 1999*. Retrieved from http://www.ausstats.abs.gov.au/ausstats/subscriber.nsf/0/F64FDF829D4BE50BCA2568E80004BADB/$File/13210_1999.pdf

Beaver, G., & Prince, C. (2004). Management, strategy and policy in the UK small business sector: A critical review. *Journal of Small Business and Enterprise Development, 11*, 34–49. doi:10.1108/14626000410519083

Beaver, G., & Ross, C. (2000). Enterprise in recession: The role and context of strategy. *International Journal of Entrepreneurship and Innovation, 1*(1), 23–31.

Beckinsdale, M., Levy, M., & Powell, P. (2006). Exploring Internet adoption drivers in SMEs. *Electronic Markets, 16*(4), 137–188.

Beheshti, H. M. (2004). The impact of IT on SMEs in the United States. *Information Management & Computer Security, 12*(4), 318–327. doi:10.1108/09685220410553532

Bergeron, F., & Raymond, L. (1992). Planning of information systems to gain a competitive advantage. *Journal of Small Business Management, 30*, 21–26.

Berry, M. (1998). Strategic planning in small high tech companies. *Long Range Planning, 31*(3), 455–466. doi:10.1016/S0024-6301(98)80012-5

Bharati, P., & Chaudhury, A. (2006). Current Status of Technology Adoption: Micro, Small and Medium Manufacturing Firms in Boston. *Communications of the ACM, 49*(10), 88–93. doi:10.1145/1164394.1164400

Bharati, P., & Chaudhury, A. (2009). SMEs and competitiveness: The role of information systems. *International. Journal of Business Research, 5*(1), 1–9.

Blili, S., & Raymond, L. (1993). Information Technology: Threats and opportunities for small and medium-sized enterprises. *International Journal of Information Management,* 13(6): 439–448. doi:10.1016/0268-4012(93)90060-H

Bodnar, G. H. (2003). IT governance. *Internal Auditing, 18*(3), 27–32.

Bracker, J. S., Keats, B. W., & Pearson, J. N. (1988). Planning and financial performance among small firms in a growth industry. *Strategic Management Journal, 9*(6), 591–603. doi:10.1002/smj.4250090606

Bracker, J. S., & Pearson, J. N. (1986). Planning and financial performance of small mature firms. *Strategic Management Journal, 7*(6), 503–522.

Burke, G., & Jarratt, D. (2004). The influence of information and advice on competitive strategy definition in small-and medium-sized enterprises. *Qualitative Market Research, 7,* 126–138. doi:10.1108/13522750410530039

Cragg, P. B., & King, M. (1993). Small firm computing: motivators and inhibitors. *MIS Quarterly, 17*(1), 47–60. doi:10.2307/249509

Culkin, N., & Smith, D. (2000). An emotional business: A guide to understanding the motivations of small business decision takers. *International Journal of Qualitative Marketing Research, 3*(3), 145–157. doi:10.1108/13522750010333898

Dandridge, T. C. (1979). Children are not little grown-ups: Small business needs its own Organizational Theory. *Journal of Small Business Management, 17*(April), 53–57.

Davies, A. J., & Garcia-Sierra, A. J. (1999). Implementing electronic commerce in SMEs – three case studies. *BT Technology Journal, 17*(3), 97–111. doi:10.1023/A:1009684605872

Davis, R. (2001). Business process modelling with ARIS: A practical guide. London: Springer Verlag.

De Saulles, M. (2007). Information literacy amongst UK SMEs: An information policy gap. *Aslib Proceedings: New Information Perspectives, 59*(1), 68–79.

Delone, W. H. (1981). Firm size and the characteristics of computer use. *MIS Quarterly, 5*(4), 65–77. doi:10.2307/249328

Doukidis, G. I., Lybereas, P., & Galliers, R. D. (1996). Information systems planning in small business: A stages of growth analysis. *Journal of Systems and Software, 33,* 189–201. doi:10.1016/0164-1212(95)00183-2

Duhan, S., Levy, M., & Powell, P. (2005). IS strategy in SMEs using organizational capabilities: The CPX framework. In *Thirteenth European Conference on Information Systems,* 26th to 28th May, Regensburg, Germany.

Earl, M. J. (1993). Experiences in strategic information systems planning. *MIS Quarterly, 17*(1), 1–24. doi:10.2307/249507

Flynn, D. J., & Arce, E. A. (1995). Theoretical and practical issues in the use of strategic information systems planning (SISP) approaches to integrating business and IT in organisations. *International Journal of Computer Applications in Technology, 8*(1/2), 61–68.

Frost, F. A. (2003). The Use of Strategic Tools by Small and Medium-sized Enterprises: An Australian Study. *Strategic Change, 12*, 49–62. doi:10.1002/jsc.607

Griffy-Browne, C., & Chun, M. (2007). Aligning businesses and IS resources in Japanese SMEs: A resource based view. *Journal of Global Information Technology Management, 10*(3), 28–51.

Guimaraes, T. (2000). The impact of competitive intelligence and IS support in changing small business organisations. *Logistics Information Management, 13*, 117–125. doi:10.1108/09576050010326510

Hagmann, C., & McCahon, C. S. (1993). Strategic information systems and competitiveness. *Information & Management, 25*, 183–192. doi:10.1016/0378-7206(93)90067-4

Holmes, S., & Gibson, B. (2001). Definition of small business: final report. The University of Newcastle, NSW, Australia.

Hua, G. B. (2007). Applying the strategic alignment model to business and ICT strategies of Singapore's small and medium-sized architecture, engineering and construction enterprises. *Construction Management and Economics, 25*(2), 157–169. doi:10.1080/01446190600827041

Hussin, H., King, M., & Cragg, P. (2002). IT alignment in small firms. *European Journal of Information Systems, 11*, 108–127. doi:10.1057/palgrave/ejis/3000422

Iacovou, C. L., Benbasat, I., & Dexter, A. S. (1995). Electronic data interchange and small organizations: Adoption and impact of technology. *MIS Quarterly, 19*(4), 465–485. doi:10.2307/249629

IBM. (1984). Business systems planning – information systems planning guide (4th Ed.). IBM Publication #GE20-0527-4.

Igbaria, M., Zinatelli, N., Cragg, P., & Cavaye, A. L. M. (1997). Personal computing acceptance factors in small firms: A structural equation model. *MIS Quarterly, 21*(3), 279–302. doi:10.2307/249498

Jocumsen, G. (2004). How do small Business Managers make strategic marketing decisions? *European Journal of Marketing, 38*(5/6): 659–674. doi:10.1108/03090560410529277

King, W. R. (1988). Strategic planning for information resources: The evolution of concepts and practice. *Information Resources Management Journal, 1*(4), 1–8.

Kyobe, M. E. (2004). Investigating the strategic utilization of IT resources in the small and medium-sized firms of the eastern Free State province. *International Small Business Journal, 22*(2), 131–158. doi:10.1177/0266242604041311

Lederer, A. L., & Gardiner, V. (1992). Strategic information systems planning: The method/1 approach. *Information Systems Management, 9*(3/4), 13–20. doi:10.1080/10580539208906877

Lefebvre, E., & Lefebvre, L. A. (1992). Firm innovativeness and CEO characteristics in small manufacturing firms. *Journal of Engineering and Technology Management, 9*(3), 243–277. doi:10.1016/0923-4748(92)90018-Z

Lefebvre, L. A., Mason, R., & Lefebvre, E. (1997). The influence Prism in SMEs: The power of CEOs perceptions on technology policy and its organisational impacts. *Management Science, 43*(6), 856–878. doi:10.1287/mnsc.43.6.856

Levy, M., & Powell, P. (1997). Assessing the value of information systems planning at Heath Springs. *International Journal of Technology Management, 13*(4), 426–442. doi:10.1504/IJTM.1997.001673

Levy, M., & Powell, P. (2000). Information systems strategy for small and medium sized enterprises: An organisational perspective. *Strategic Information Systems*, *9*, 63–84. doi:10.1016/S0963-8687(00)00028-7

Levy, M., & Powell, P. (2005). Strategies for growth in SMEs: The role of information and information systems. Oxford, UK: Elsevier Butterworth-Heinemann.

Levy, M., Powell, P., & Galliers, R. (1999). Assessing Information Systems Strategy Development Frameworks in SMEs. *Information & Management*, *36*, 247–261. doi:10.1016/S0378-7206(99)00020-8

Levy, M., Powell, P., & Yetton, P. (2001). SMEs: Aligning IS and the strategic context. *Journal of Information Technology*, *16*(3), 133–144. doi:10.1080/02683960110063672

Li, E. Y., & Chen, H. G. (2001). Output-driven information system planning: A case study. *Information & Management*, *38*, 185–199. doi:10.1016/S0378-7206(00)00066-5

Luftmann, J. N. (2005). Key issues for IT executives 2004. *MIS Quarterly Executive*, *4*(2), 269–285.

Marshall, P., & McKay, J. (2004). Strategic IT planning, evaluation and benefits management: The basis for effective IT governance. *Australasian Journal of Information Systems*, *11*(2), 14–26.

Martin, C. J. (1989). Information management in the smaller business: The role of the top manager. *International Journal of Information Management*, *9*(3), 187–197. doi:10.1016/0268-4012-(89)90006-6

Martin, J. (1982). Strategic Data Planning Methodologies. Upper Saddle River, NJ: Prentice Hall.

McFarlan, F. W. (1981). Portfolio approach to information systems. *Harvard Business Review*, *59*(5), 142–150.

Mehrtens, J., Cragg, P., & Mills, A. (2001). A model of Internet adoption by SMEs. *Information & Management*, *39*(3), 165–176. doi:10.1016/S0378-7206(01)00086-6

Min, S. K., Suh, E. H., & Kim, S. Y. (1999). An integrated approach toward strategic information systems planning. *The Journal of Strategic Information Systems*, *8*, 373–394. doi:10.1016/S0963-8687(00)00029-9

O'Regan, N., & Ghobadian, A. (2007). Formal strategic planning: Annual raindance or wheel of success? *Strategic Change*, *16*(1-2), 11–22. doi:10.1002/jsc.777

Perry, S. C. (2001). The relationship between written business plans and the failure of small businesses in the US. *Journal of Small Business Management*, *39*(3), 201–208. doi:10.1111/1540-627X.00019

Peters, S. C. A., Heng, M. S. H., & Vet, R. (2002). Formation of the information systems in a global financial services Company. *Information and Organization*, *12*, 19–38. doi:10.1016/S1471-7727(01)00011-2

Proudlock, M. J., Phelps, B., & Gamble, P. R. (1998). IS decision-making: A study in information-intensive firms. *Journal of Information Technology*, *13*(1), 55–66. doi:10.1080/026839698344954

Raymond, L. (1985). Organizational characteristics and MIS success in the context of small business. *MIS Quarterly*, *9*(1), 37–52. doi:10.2307/249272

Riemenschneider, C., Harrison, D., & Mykytyn, P. Jr. (2003). Understanding IT adoption decisions in small business: Integrating current theories. *Information & Management*, *40*, 269–285. doi:10.1016/S0378-7206(02)00010-1

Robinson, R. B., & Pearce, J. A. (1984). Research thrusts in small firm strategic planning. *Academy of Management Review, 9*(1), 128–137. doi:10.2307/258239

Rue, L. W., & Ibrahim, N. A. (1998). The relationship between planning sophistication and performance in small businesses. *Journal of Small Business Management, 36*(4), 24–32.

Scheer, A. W., Abolhassan, F., Jost, W., & Kirchmer, M. (Eds.). (2003). Business process change management: ARIS in Practice. Berlin: Springer.

Schwenk, C. R., & Shrader, C. B. (1993). Effects of formal strategic planning on financial performance in small firms: A meta-analysis. *Entrepreneurship Theory and Practice, 17*(3), 53–64.

Teubner, R. A. (2007). Strategic information systems planning: A case study from the financial services industry. *The Journal of Strategic Information Systems, 16*, 105–125. doi:10.1016/j.jsis.2007.01.002

Teubner, R. A., & Mocker, M. (2005). *Strategic information planning – Insights from an action research project in the financial services industry.* Working Paper No. 3, ECRIS - European Center for Information Systems.

Thong, J. Y. L. (1999). An integrated model of information systems adoption in small business. *Journal of Management Information Systems, 15*(4), 187–214.

Thong, J. Y. L. (2001). Resource constraints and information systems implementation in Singaporean small business. *Omega, 29*(2), 143–156. doi:10.1016/S0305-0483(00)00035-9

Thong, J. Y. L., Yap, C., & Raman, K. S. (1996). Top management support, external expertise and information systems implementation in small business. *Information Systems Research, 7*(2), 248–267. doi:10.1287/isre.7.2.248

Tozer, E. E. (1996). Strategic IS/IT Planning. Boston, MA: Butterworth-Heinemann.

Tse, T., & Soufani, K. (2003). Business strategies for small firms in the new economy. *Journal of Small Business and Enterprise Development, 10*, 306–320. doi:10.1108/14626000310489781

van Grembergen, W., De Haes, S., & Guldentops, E. (2004). Structures, processes and relational mechanisms for IT governance. In W. van Grembergen (Ed.), Strategies for Information Technology Governance. Hershey, PA: Idea Group Publishing.

Ward, J., & Peppard, J. (2002). Strategic Planning for Information Systems. Chichester, UK: John Wiley and Sons.

Welsh, J. A., & White, J. F. (1981). A small business is not a little big business. *Harvard Business Review, 59*(4), 18–32.

Wong, K. Y., & Aspinwall, E. (2005). An empirical study of the important factors for knowledge-management adoption in the SME sector. *Journal of Knowledge Management, 9*(3), 64–82. doi:10.1108/13673270510602773

Wynn, M. (2009). Information systems strategy development and implementation in SMEs. *Management Research News, 32*(1), 78–90. doi:10.1108/01409170910922041

Zolkos, R. (2005). Striking a balance between business and IT. *Business Insurance, 7*, 20–21.

Chapter 11
The Alignment of Business Strategy with Agile Software Development within SMEs

Pattama Kanavittaya
Murdoch University, Australia

Jocelyn Armarego
Murdoch University, Australia

Paula Goulding
Murdoch University, Australia

ABSTRACT

The alignment of business strategy and IT strategy has been recognised as a strategic weapon within organisations. Small and medium sized enterprises (SMEs) also recognise a need for new Information Technology and Information Systems (IT/IS) functions to support business strategies, and provide new services to the market. Agile methodologies support the timely and economical development of Web and Internet-based software, the technologies being exploited by organisations seeking to enhance their business performance. Based on multiple-case research, this paper explores the impact of agile software development on the alignment of business strategy with IT strategy in SMEs. Several models of strategic alignment developed for large enterprises were used to examine the SME environment. The findings suggest that agile methods are applied to provide added flexibility for organisations to create or react to new opportunities, to increase responsiveness to customer requirements not possible with traditional software development, and to gain competitive advantage. Personal interest was found to be a factor in adopting agile methodologies, in addition to IT maturity and technical IT sophistication. However, the use of agile methods in response to internal and external uncertainty may change the role of ICT in the firms, and hence impact on the alignment of business and IT/IS strategy.

DOI: 10.4018/978-1-61520-627-8.ch011

INTRODUCTION

In today's dynamic market environment, many organisations have been driven by rapid change in both technology and the global market to seek a new way of conducting business for survival and growth. The need for organisations to adapt their structures, strategies, and technology to suit the new environment is also becoming more and more critical (Nerur & Mahapatra, 2005).

In particular, SMEs recognise a need for new Information Technology and Information Systems (IT/IS) functions to support business strategies, and provide new services to the market (Papp, 1999). In this study the term SMEs is defined as business establishments having less than 250 employees (EuropeanCommision, 2005). Since the late 1980s, IT/IS has played an increasingly strategic role in changing marketing characteristics (Johnston & Carrico, 1988). ICT (Information and Communications Technologies) has also been highlighted as a strategic weapon in gaining a competitive position in the marketplace for SMEs (Hussin, King, & Cragg, 2002; Ismail & King, 2007). Throp (1998) suggests successful utilisation of ICT (and the implied close alignment of business and IT/IT strategy) can provide sustainable competitive advantage for the organisation, regardless of size. However, Levy, Powell, & Yetton (2003) suggest that the alignment process in SMEs varies from larger organisations. In addition, ICT adoption decisions in SMEs are most frequently made by the owner, who often shows little concern for IT strategic planning.

The objective of the study that underpins this chapter is to explore how agile software development impacts on the alignment of business strategy with IT strategy in both large organisations and SMEs. The aims of this chapter are to focus on the roles that can/should be played by IT/IS in supporting business strategy formulation, particularly for SMEs, and to provide some insight into the role of agile software development in the small business environment.

This chapter is outlined into five sections as follow:

- The *first* section provides the introduction and background of the research
- The *second* section presents the existing literature
- The *third* section presents the cases and describes the research methodology used in this study
- The *fourth* section reviews the case study analysis and findings
- The *last* section provides cross-case findings and a conclusion.

BACKGROUND

During the last ten years, the attention on alignment of IT/IS to business strategies has increased, and research in the areas of strategic management and IT/IS management has focused on and contributed to this subject. It has consistently been one of the top concerns in the business strategy and IT literature (Rathnam, Johnsen, & Wen, 2004/2005; Reich & Benbasat, 2000). Strategic alignment in this context refers to the matching of process and outcomes of IT/IS strategy with business strategy (Reich & Benbasat, 2000).

The concept of strategic alignment is widely believed to improve organisational performance. The literature in the area of business and IT/IS alignment abounds with documents and frameworks that examine the need to align IT/IS strategy to business strategy (Chan, Huff, Barclay, & Copeland, 1997; Das, Zahra, & Warkentin, 1991). The benefits of alignment between business strategy and IT strategy have also been recognised, with alignment described as having significant positive impact on business and organisational performance (Bleistein, Cox, Verner, & Phalp, 2006; Chan & Huff, 1993; Henderson & Venkatraman, 1993; Kearns & Lederer, 2000). Avison, Jones et al. (2004) identify additional benefits, including maximising return on IT/IS investment to organisations, helping organisations to gain competitive advantage through IT/IS, and providing direction and flexibility for organisations to react to new opportunities. However, much of these discussions tend to focus on larger organisations, with less work undertaken in SMEs.

This is an important concern, as the literature suggests findings for large organisations cannot generally be extrapolated to SMEs – they are not smaller versions of large firms (Welsh & White, 1981), and hence exhibit a different set of organisational characteristics. A review of the current published literature found few articles on strategic alignment in SMEs (these are discussed in the next section). This is supported by Bharati & Chaudhury (2009), who indicate that the space provided for research on the ICT aspects of SMEs in most standard journals has been limited. This is despite the innovative potential of SMEs as an industry growth driver (Morgan, 1997). Where research has been conducted, mostly during the 1990s, the focus has been on aspects other than alignment (eg, implementation, maturity, motivators/inhibitors, adoption or success, etc. (Cragg & King, 1993; Prananto, McKay, & Marshall, 2003)). More recently, however, the importance of business strategy (new products or markets) in driving technology adoption in SMEs has been confirmed (Levy, Powell, & Worrall, 2005), albeit tailored to the resources available to them (Edelman, Brush, & Manolova, 2005). Enhanced relationships with customers and trading partners, and improved market understanding have also been reported for more recent investment in Internet and Web-based technology (Merhrtans, Cragg, & Mills, 2001; Quale & Christiansen, 2004) within the sector.

At the same time, agile software development has emerged as a new paradigm for dealing with software development projects (Pedrycz, 2006). At a fundamental level, agile methodologies, which have evolved primarily to support the timely (Mekelburg, 2003) and economical development

of high quality software that meets customer needs, are becoming an integral and strategic part of all modern software industry and commerce. Agile methodologies have been used primarily in Internet and Web software development contexts (Meso & Jain, 2006). These are technologies being exploited by organisations seeking to enhance their business performance. As discussed in Truex, Baskerville et al. (1999) this chapter considers agile software development methods as part of the IT/IS function. The interaction between strategy development and adoption of agile methodologies within the IT infrastructure of SMEs is explored in this chapter.

Business Strategy and IT/ IS Alignment in SMEs

Prior research on business strategy has been discussed from various perspectives. Through such lenses, it is possible to identify critical issues, including the scope or boundaries of each business that satisfies customer requirements and which business units are necessary in order to achieve and maintain a competitive advantage in the market (Hofer & Schendel, 1978; Kotha, 1989; Wheelwright, 1984). Based on Chan & Huff (1992), business strategy can be described as a process of planning how a company will compete in the market in a given environment.

In order to provide a framework to underpin the discussions, this study utilises Miles and Snow's (1978) typology to examine case organisations. They propose a useful model to identify strategic choice based on the following characteristics:

Defender. This organisation focuses on a narrow range of product/market domains. It tends to prevent competition by offering high quality products and services with lower cost. This type of organisation is technology based, does not tend to search outside its market for new opportunities, and rarely makes major adjustments in structure or technology.

Prospector. An organisation with this strategy typically seeks for new product and market opportunities, with a tendency to invest heavily in research and development. This type of organisation always deals with change and uncertainty in the market. In recognition of this, it invests in leading-edge technology in order to gain advantage over competitors.

Analyser. This strategy shares characteristics of both Defender and Prospector. This type of organisation attempts to minimise risk while maximising the opportunity for growth. In delivering new products/or services, this type of organisation carefully observes the action of its competitors. At the same time, it produces a limited range of products, and does not invest in new technologies.

Reactor. This type of organisation does not have clear strategy or plan in dealing with its competitors in the market. Such organisations perceive market opportunities and change but are unable to adapt effectively.

Since the 2000s, business strategy and IT/IS alignment in SMEs has become an area of increased study, with different aspects of the alignment investigated. For example, Hussin, King et al. (2002) found that SMEs were influenced to develop alignment by three major factors: IT maturity, technical IT sophistication, and the CEO's software knowledge. The study by Kyobe (2008) examines three different modes of strategy-making that influence aspects of alignment and performance: planned mode, adaptive mode, and entrepreneurial mode. That study found that each mode of strategy-making gives different results on certain aspects of alignment.

Levy, Powell et al. (2001) state that the key inhibitor and enabler of IT/IS investment in SMEs are market position and competitiveness. Hussin, King et al. (2002) also agreed that IT/IS investment serves SMEs as a strategic weapon to maintain their competitive advantage, and that therefore SMEs should look to *developing* an IT/IS strategy. However, it has been argued that some SMEs face

difficulty due to limited resources to invest in IT/IS (Edelman et al., 2005; Fink, 1998). Boohalis (1996) and Chell, Hawarth, and Brearly (1991) indicate that informal management practices are a characteristic of SMEs, with decisions tending to be made only by the owners and top managers of small firms. Hussin, King et al. (2002)'s focus on development of IT/IS strategy suggests a continuing limitation in formal planning in this area within SMEs. In this study IT/IS strategy is defined as an outlining of the vision of how the organisation's demand for Information Systems will be supported by technology (Ward & Peppard, 2002).

In order to understand the alignment process, this study applies the strategic alignment model (SAM) developed by Henderson and Venkatraman (1993). This model, depicted in Figure 1, describes the integration of business strategy with IT strategy. One important aspect of this model is to measure the contribution of IT/IS to the business requirements. Although the body of literature on strategic alignment that applies the Henderson and Venkatraman (1993) model is extensive, little has been reported on its use in small firms.

Agile Software Development Methods

The concept of agility is outlined by the Agile Manifesto (Beck & Andres, 2005), and combines methods and techniques that share values and principles of agile software development. According to the Agile Manifesto (2001), the four values of agile methods are:

- *Individuals and interactions over processes and tools*
- *Working software over comprehensive documentation*
- *Customer collaboration over contract negotiation*
- *Responding to change over following a plan.*

Figure 1. Business and IT/IS alignment model (adapted from Henderson & Venkatraman (1993))

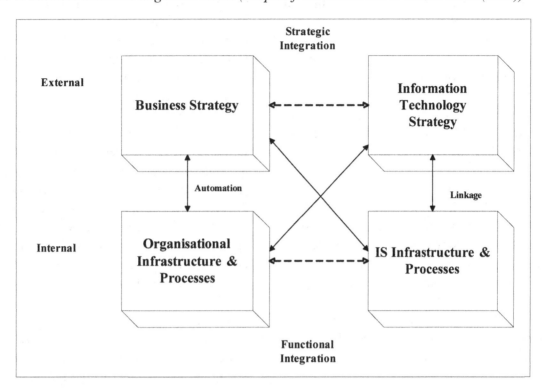

Given the concept of agile methods described above, Melnik and Maurere (2005) define agile software development methods as *"a departure from plan-driven traditional approaches, where the focus is on generating early releases of working software using collaborative techniques, code refactoring, and on-site customer involvement"* (p.197). There are a number of major types of agile methodologies currently available in the market (eg Extreme Programming (XP), Scrum, Adaptive Software Development (ASD), Crystal family, Dynamic Systems Development Method (DSDM), Feature Driven Development (FDD)) (Bauer, 2004; Highsmith, 2002), with choice of methodology generally based on the requirements of the project undertaken.

The literature on software development methods uses two terms to distinguish software development processes: *lightweight,* now called agile processes, and *heavyweight,* which refers to traditional methodologies. There is a strong emphasis on planning and processes in traditional methodologies, with numerous rules involved, whereas agile methods focus on short iteration cycles. In order to achieve a better understanding of how agile processes and traditional software processes differ, Tsui & Karam (2006) identified six different characteristics and compared these:

- *requirements* in agile processes are uncertain and will change all the time, while in traditional processes the requirements are perceived as consistent and will not change
- *design* in agile processes is informal and follows an iterative model, but in traditional software processes is formal and uses upfront design
- agile processes have *user involvement* throughout the project, whilst with traditional software processes the user is in-

volved only at the beginning and at the end of the project

- in terms of *documentation,* agile processes have minimal documentation while traditional software processes tend to be document-driven
- *processes complexity and overhead* are low in agile processes, while very high in traditional software processes.

Due to the management characteristics noted above, great benefits can be derived by SMEs from the adoption of agile methods in developing software products. However, a review of literature (e.g. Aydin, Harmsen et al. (2005); Turk, France et al. (2005); Pikkarainen and Passoja (2005)) indicates that current research focuses on the agile methods being used in larger organisation, rather than in SMEs, and on adaptability and practice, rather than on agile management in organisations.

THE CASE STUDIES

According to Yin (1989, p.23) a case study is an empirical inquiry that: "*investigates a contemporary phenomenon within its real-life context; when the boundaries between phenomenon and context are not clearly evident; and in which multiple sources of evidence are used*". In the field of IS,, case study has been used extensively among researchers (Shanks & Parr, 2003). This study is concerned with an investigation of *cases* to explore the level of alignment between business strategy and IT/IS strategy where agile software development is a component of the IT infrastructure. In order to investigate any cross-cultural aspects of the findings, both organisations based in Thailand and Australia were included. Case study research typically combined various types of data collection methods (Pare, 2004). Yin (1989) classifies six sources of evidence that work well when conducting case study research: documentation, archival records, interviews, direct observations,

participant-observation, and physical artefacts. The interview was considered as the primary data source for this study, supported by other sources including documentation, field notes, and internet sources such the company website.

This chapter reports on those cases where the organisation was identified as an SME. Organisations that practice agile software development were approached to participate in the study through in-depth interviews using both structured and semi-structured questions for triangulation of data. The semi-structure interview instrument consisted of eight open-ended questions addressing participants' understanding of business strategy and agile development and their perception of the level of alignment within their firm. The questionnaire consisted of fifteen standardised, closed questions addressing the same topics. Response to these structured questions was based on a 5-point Likert scale. Both the interview guide and survey questionnaire are written in English, and translated into Thai as required. Subsequently, the responses have been translated back into English. Interviews with participants were taped and later translated (where required) and transcribed. In each case, the Business Manager and IT Manager were identified as the most likely to be able to discuss and describe the organisation's stance on business/IT alignment. Where possible (but not in all cases), interviews were conducted with the persons who fulfilled these roles.

Case organisations were defined in terms of the work of Miles and Snow (1978). They proposed a framework for characterising business strategy traits, and describe four types of business strategy: *Defender, Prospector, Analyser* and *Reactor.* The important elements of this typology are that it includes dimensions such as product/market attitude, technology, organisational structure and management characteristics, and reflects on a complex set of environment and organisation processes (Croteau & Bergeron, 2001; Smith, Guthrie, & Chen, 1989). The typology assumes that organisations act to create their own environments through a series of choices regarding market, product and technologies (Parnell, 2002). An additional value of this model is that it has been tested extensively in SMEs (Aragon-Sanchez & Sanchez-Marin, 2005; O'Regan & Ghobadian, 2006), and has been cited as the most appropriate in the case of SMEs (O'Regan, Ghobadian, & Gallear, 2006).

The model for analysing strategic alignment applied in this study is Henderson and Venkatraman (1993) strategic alignment model (SAM). As indicated in Figure 1, the top two components refer to the *Strategic* level, looking at the relationship between business strategy and IT strategy. This is defined as having an *external positioning focus*. *Strategic Integration* addresses the capability of the IT/IS strategy to shape and/or support the business strategy. The bottom two components refer to *Functional* level, looking at the relationship between organisational infrastructure and processes and IT infrastructure and processes. This is defined as the *internal domain*. *Functional Integration* considers how choices made in the IS/IT domain impact on the business domain and vice versa, and examines the internal coherence between organisational requirements and IT/IS capability to deliver. Relationships across the external/internal domains are also examined: *Linkage* indicates the alignment between business strategy and IT/IS infrastructure, whilst *Automation* indicates the alignment between IT strategy and organisational infrastructure.

The relationships across the four domains are presented as four perspectives, categorised by whether business or ICT serves as the driving force. The first perspective is *Strategic Execution,* whereby business strategy is the organisational driver for design choices in IT/IS infrastructure, representing a classic view of strategic management. The second perspective is *Technology Transformation.* This perspective involves identifying the appropriate ICT to support business strategy, and migrating the IT/IS infrastructure in support. This perspective therefore has strong implications for the ICT domains – impacting on IT/IS strategy with subsequent changes in IT/IS infrastructure. The third and fourth perspectives view ICT as the enabler or enhancer of business strategies, with corresponding organisational implications. The *Competitive Potential* perspective involves taking advantage of emerging ICT capability to enhance new business strategy. Adaptation of business strategy is an outcome of this perspective. Finally, the *Service Level* perspective focuses on how to build IT to meet the need of IS customers. Here, business strategy provides the direction to stimulate customer demand. The SAM model is valuable in this study in that it shows, through identified relationship between the domains, how alignment can be accomplished.

IT/IS strategy is a multidimensional construct and can be defined in different ways (Hirschheim & Sabherwal, 2001). Therefore, in order to interpret the IT/IS strategy of case organisations, this study applies the profiles defined by Hirschheim & Sabherwal (2001). This model is useful for this study because it clearly defines the types of business strategy for specific organisations, and identifies the characteristics of IT/IS expected to align with the three strategy profiles. Alignment is seen to be best achieved when the business and IS strategies are considered harmonious.

As indicated in Figure 2, the IT/IS strategy alignment model identifies three different modes of how IT/IS strategy can be constructed and how an organisation can achieve alignment. In this model IT/IS strategy is defined in terms of *Role* – the manner in which the IT/IS function is viewed by senior management; *Sourcing* – the arrangements by which ICT products and services are provided, and *Structure* – which reflects the configuration of the ICT function and the locus

Figure 2. IT/IS strategic alignment profiles (adapted from Hirschheim & Sabherwal (2001))

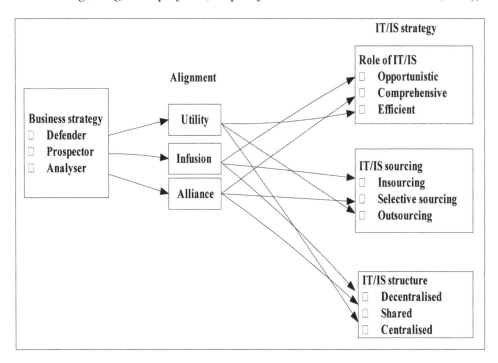

of responsibility for IT/IS management decisions. A brief description of the alternatives within each is provided below:

- Role – *efficiency* is achieved through process improvement and long-term decisions; *opportunistic* focuses on market flexibility and quick decisions, while *comprehensiveness* involves careful decisions based on knowledge of other organisations
- Sourcing – *outsourcing* requires 80% of the IT/IS budget to be allocated to third-party providers; *insourcing* assumes the same percentage provided by an internal department, while *selective sourcing* enables organisations to retain a substantial internal ICT facility as well as outsourcing a component
- Structure – *centralised* indicates IT/IS decision-making is concentrated within the corporate structure; *decentralised* has

responsibility within the business unit, and enables responsiveness to users, while a *shared* responsibility is divided between the two.

Where the business strategy is *Defender,* the *Utility* profile identifies the IT/IS strategy as focussing on low cost delivery, using outsourcing approaches, and/or has a centralised IT/IS structure. The *Infusion* profile identifies IT/IS strategy as focused on technologies that play an opportunistic role, selected insourcing approach, and/or have a decentralised IT/IS structure, where the business strategy is *Prospector*. Lastly, where the business strategy is *Analyser*, the *Alliance* profile identifies IT/IS strategy to be focused on the deployment of technologies that plays a comprehensive role, has selective sourcing approach, and/or has a shared IT/IS structure.

Company X: Defender

Company X is a small software house operating in Bangkok, Thailand. Although this organisation was used as a pilot case study, participants provided significant insight to the value of alignment. Company X has, as one of its goals, to create a long-term partnership between the company and its customers. Company X is highly focused on a small niche market. In order to keep its position in the market, company X places emphasis on cost effectiveness rather than high margins. At the same time, it maintains and improves the standard of quality of its products and services. The emphasis on quality is high as a mechanism to prevent new entrants from entering the market. In company X, agile methods were implemented to develop and customise software products, with the types of agile methods selected dependent on the characteristics of the project. Being as a small software house, the company has a flat hierarchy, with employees organised into functional groups and the managing director overseeing these. It adopts small working teams, and all employees have the flexibility to adapt to change when the circumstance or working environment has changed.

Based on the comments made during the interview, together with secondary data such as the company's information given on the Website, it can be noted that company X has the features of *Defender* with respect to Miles and Snow (1978)'s strategic model:

We focus on a strategy where we pick a niche market, our business strategy is to work closely with business partners for long term relationship, our business strategy is to focus on a large scale enterprise, our strategy is to develop our own product mind in order to create cash flow.

We do lots of small projects. In our case, we position ourselves as a niche high end consulting firm

so we focus on that as a solution, and we sell this to our customers, so we sell high margin, and low project volume because we are a very specialist group of people.

However, it should be noted that while the managing director indicated that he has a role to a *great extent* in terms of business strategy formation of company X, he was *neutral* in agreeing that company X has a well-formulated business strategy. This may, perhaps, be based on his perception of how the firm is placed, compared to other companies in the same industry. In relation to IT/IS strategic alignment profiles, the IT/IS strategy of company X would be expected to display *Utility* characteristics. Company X sought improvement in their software development processes in order to strengthen their ability to deliver quality software products and be able to compete in the market. The major focus of company X is to maintain a stable market and growth area. The IT/IS of this company seemed to play an *Efficiency* role: agile methods were selected as a major technology to improve the operation processes and were recognised as a mechanism to gain efficiency.

The interviews highlighted issues with significant implications in developing software for company X in terms of the capability to deliver quality software products based on customer need. Short software development cycles were the main driver for the implementation of agile methods. The strategic value of agile methods is identified:

Customer - agile gives a solution to what the customer wants - we deliver the solution based on the customer needs. An important aspect of agile is it improves communication. The number one failure to all software projects is communication. Agile is always testing, instead of waiting till the end to test, agile tests at a unit level, testing as it goes, seeing the outcome now, not later, refining rapidly.

Moreover, the benefit of the alignment of business strategy and IT strategy was perceived as helping the company increase their bottom line. The managing director of company X *agreed* there is a need to have agile methods addressed as part of IT/IS strategy, and aligned with business strategy.

With reference to the SAM model (Henderson & Venkatraman, 1993), company X fits into the *Competitive Potential* perspective. In this case, IT/IS strategy is the driver for choosing agile methods to enhance the software development processes. Since company X seeks to strengthen their ability to deliver software products and be able to compete in the market, a high degree of improvement in software development processes is considered an enabler. At the same time the managing director of company X has strong knowledge in agile methods, and expressed the belief that the capability of agile methods offered an opportunity for the company to become a leader in the local software industry. According to the managing director of company X:

Agile is one point in business strategy, in business strategy defined by your objective, your goals. So for us, our business strategy is to be in the marketplace with a product focus and customer development, with agile as a core concept.

Company A: Analyser

Company A is a mining consultancy service that operates in Perth, Western Australia. The vision of the organisation is to improve ICT in the mining and exploration industry. Company A has a significant market share in the Australian market. Further, in order to keep its profitability up, company A has decided to branch out and innovate in a new market off-shore. Company A sees both local and international competitors as the major threat. The organisational structure of this company is functional based. A CEO and a board of directors govern each division.

To achieve improvements in ICT within their industry, company A has invested in technologies which allow the firm not only to save on time but most importantly to better understand the needs and expectations of its customers. In company A, agile methods were adopted for building both commercial products and custom software solutions. The organisation had moved to agile to defuse issues with traditional software development. Agile methods are considered to be dynamically evolving within each software development project: in building software products, company A refuses to use one particular agile method - rather the organisation takes some aspects of agile methods such as Crystal, FDD, DSDM, and Scrum, customises them and adopts this selection as their own method.

Based on the comments made during the interview, combined with secondary data such as the company's information given on the Website, it can be noted that company A has the characteristics of *Analyser* with respect to Miles and Snow (1978)'s strategic model. The IT vision of company A is to be the world's best IS services provider to the mining sector. By mapping company A's IT vision with IT/IS strategic alignment profile, the results show that IT/IS strategy of this company should be identified as having *Alliance* characteristics. Agile methods were adopted as a core technology with a comprehensive role within the IT/IS strategy of the organisation.

The interview with participants revealed that traditional software development was regarded as an operational problem contributing to the failure of software development projects. It became apparent to the firm that the traditional way of software development was not flexible enough to handle the issues surrounding company A's projects. Poor estimation in terms of costs and schedule, and low quality software products were provided as examples of issues. Traditional software development also did not meet the future demands of business:

We basically got to the point 2 years ago that we needed to do something. We had to choose, we had no scope definition, we had a lot of issues with poor estimation, bad quality software. We had a lot of traditional issues of software development, and we decided that we needed to go with methodology or group of methodologies that we know, and people can actually recognise. Agile technique fitted with what we wanted...and also it has essentially fitted the way we work.

Despite recognition of the importance of agile software development within the business-IT/IS strategy alignment, there was not a clearly presented alignment process in company A. However, both participants felt that business strategy and IT/IS strategy should be aligned and *agreed* that agile methods has improved organisational performance.

Company A followed the *Technology Transformation* perspective of the Henderson and Venkatramann (1993) alignment model. Based on the findings of the interviews, it was recognised that, in company A, business strategy was a principal driver for the choice of agile methods for building their software products, and creating new business opportunities for the firm. As mentioned by a participant:

In terms of business strategy that is what we want to be and be seen as, without the agile techniques, we are not delivering that, so we didn't have good quality software, we were not using best practice methodologies. We were not leading in this area.

With the maturity of IT in company A in line with strategy making, agile methods appeared to fulfil and correspond to the business need, with the IT infrastructure changing in terms of the roles of employees and their skills. The IT strategy within company A was shaped around organisational objectives and goals, in order to meet the demand of the chosen business strategy.

Company B: Prospector

Company B is a food industry organisation that operates in Bangkok, Thailand. Company B has a vision of developing new products and services with high quality standards through the use of advanced technology. Company B considers itself as a strongly innovative firm where innovation is central to business success. As such, company B is driven to give greater emphasis to the development of new knowledge and expertise through IT/IS applications to enable the firm to find new opportunities for innovation in products and services. The products under development within the software house within company B included web-based knowledge, web-data and information, and web-technology. Company B has been using agile methods for two years, using Scrum exclusively. Company B is divided along functional lines. Each division is led by managing director who reports directly to the CEO.

The data gathered from the interviews and secondary sources show that company B has the features of *Prospector* with respect to Miles and Snow (1978)'s strategic model. According to participant:

Business strategy here, we focused on providing the development of new products with high quality standard through the use of advanced technology.

Company B's ICT vision is aimed at using information to enable the IT domain to be more effective and efficient. The IS strategic alignment profiles show that IT/IS strategy of this company would be expected to present *Infusion* characteristics. The adoption of agile methods focuses on flexibility and quick response to market uncertainty, to allow the firm to gain advantage over its competitors. Overall, by embedding agile methods as part of the IT strategy, it appears the IT/IS strategy of Company B plays an opportunistic role, due to the fact that agile methods support innovative IT products and services and create new opportunities for the firm.

In the interview, participants identified the issues that led to the use of agile methods: the existing software development process failed to support the management structure in terms of planning and resources. According to one participant:

Before we were using agile, we have the problem in managing the software development process. The software development process that we used before did not support our software planning process, and management of the project. Then we found that agile process can solve the problems that we have. So, that is the main driving force for us.

The IT manager and project manager acknowledged a responsibility to keep up to date with the latest technologies and any methods that provide greater versatility in developing software projects effectively. The interviews indicated that company B has not clear focus on the importance of the alignment between business strategy and IT infrastructure. One participant indicated that in many organisations, although use of agile methods can be aligned with business strategy, top management may not attempt to do this. His concern was that, as agile methods are only one component of ICT, in order to undertake alignment, management must consider the IT domain as a whole. This perspective suggests alignment across the external/internal domains is not well developed in Company B.

It is clear that company B matches the *Technology Transformation* perspective of the Henderson and Venkatramann (1993) alignment model. The business strategy appears to be the driving force for company B to determine the technologies that could support business, as pointed out by one participant:

Business cycle has changed quickly and that has already happened in many industries. When we talk about what technology can respond quickly to those changes and what technology can give good results when that change happened. I think what agile can do this, it can be adapted to whenever direction business has changed, and it does not required a plan for it.

Due to the technical maturity of company B, agile methods were implemented to support the internal operation of the IT/IS function in order for the firm to be able to adjust to changing business requirements. Looking at the use of agile methods in Company B, it was claimed that the capabilities of agile methods were the driver of change in IT infrastructure in order to meet the demand of business strategy.

CROSS-CASE FINDINGS

The findings of each case were compared in order to search for similarities and differences between them. Obvious differences (as far as their industries and location of operation are concerned) did not appear to have major impact on the perception provided by interview participants in relation to business and IT/IS strategy within their organisations.

Utilising Miles and Snow (1978)'s typology to underpin the comparison of cases, the firms described in this chapter exhibited features of each of three typology profiles. Company X aligned with a *Defender* profile, while Company A exhibited strong *Analyser* characteristics and Company B, followed a *Prospector* strategic type. In terms of the characteristics of IT/IS strategy profiles of Hirschheim & Sabherwal (2001), as a *Defender,* the IT/IS strategy of company X is characterised as *Utility.* In contrast, company A's IT/IS strategy can be classified as *Alliance,* and Company B's IT/IS strategy would be classified as *Infusion.* However, although the Role played

Figure 3. Result of strategic alignment perspectives (Adapted from Luftman (1996))

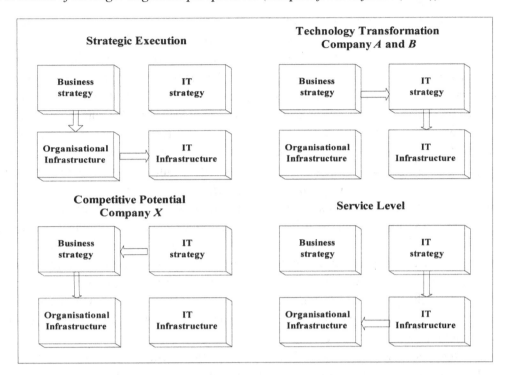

by the IT/IS function appears to align with the appropriate profile, neither the Sourcing nor the Structure of the case organisations would seem to do so. Companies X, A and B maintain strong internal ICT functions, with very little, if any, outsourcing undertaken. In addition, company X's decision-making is highly centralised, while company A appears to have shared decision-making. Decision-making in Company D, on the other hand, appears to be undertaken in a decentralised manner. This indicates the model may not apply to SMEs adopting agile methods. Further study is required to confirm this suggestion. Nevertheless, based on responses from participants, each firm appears to have a good understanding of the business environment in which they operate. The IT/IS strategy of each company was seen to be in some harmony with the chosen business strategy.

With respect to the SAM model proposed by Henderson and Venkatraman (1993), the findings indicated that two types of strategic alignment perspectives were shown by the firms (see Figure 3): company A and company B demonstrate the *Technology Transformation* perspective and company X the *Competitive Potential* profile. These results indicate that the level of alignment in company X is operations driven, while companies A and B are strategy driven. It is perhaps not surprising that a Strategic Execution perspective was not evident in these cases – representing a classic, hierarchical view of strategic management, this perspective may be exhibited more frequently in large firms.

Although companies A and B were different in terms of the choice of business strategy (*Analyser* and *Prospector*, respectively), the need for flexibility and innovation required both firms to exploit new techniques and methods that could meet their business and market need in order to achieve their goals. Agile methods served as a flexible technology that each applied to their products and services in order to improve their competitive position in the market. In addition, each case exhibited the characteristics of the appropriate IS alignment profiles as described by Hirschheim & Sabherwal (2001). Therefore companies A, B and X have the possibility of achieving a high level of alignment. Both models appear to be relevant in the SME environment.

The three organisations utilised agile methods to support or enable business strategy. However, the motivation behind the adoption of agility differed markedly. Company A suffered from such issues as failure and the limitation of traditional software development processes. Agile methods, therefore were considered a means of maximising growth opportunity while minimising risk. Company B actively searched for improved processes – agility was deemed a core mechanism for competitive advantage. Company X was concerned with the rapid pace of change in IT and the impact on the software life cycle. Agile methods were considered as methods that embraced change in order to build competitive advantage. Based on the results of the interviews, it therefore appeared that traditional software development was not the only issue that some participants encountered. Speed to market was also a factor in the choice of agile methods.

As indicated by the findings, the issues that led to the decision to apply agile methods in software development derived from two major factors: the failure in traditional software methods and search for improvement in the software development process, and speed to market. In addition, some participants agreed that they have personal interest in agile methods and recognised the benefits of agile software development. These findings were similar to the recent study by Vijayasarathy and Turk (2008) that included personal interest and the benefits of agile methods as being significant in their adoption. The findings also confirm that strategic alignment is facilitated by factors such as IT maturity, technical maturity, and managing director's software knowledge. These results are consistent with the literature (Hussin et al., 2002).

Despite a difference in motivating factors, a core similarity exists for the outcomes of agile method utilisation. For instance, *improve management of the project*, and *improve communication within the team* were common outcomes that company A, B, and X identified. *Improved customer satisfaction* was another outcome of agile methods that was seen by company B. Company X on the other hand identified *improved the quality of testing process* and *provided quick delivery software products* as the outcomes of agile methods. Study participants from each organisation perceived the importance and benefits of business strategy and IT/IS alignment in that the alignment could assist the firm in gaining competitive advantages while providing cost and time improvements. This is in accordance with the literature regarding the benefits of business strategy and IT alignment (Avison et al., 2004).

In interpreting the values and explaining the role of IT/IS manager, Henderson and Venkatraman (1993) clearly identified key roles of IT/IS manager and top management within each perspective. In the *Technology Transformation* perspective, the IT/IS manager should be involved in designing and implementing the required I/S infrastructure that is consistent with the IT vision. In the case of company B, participants play a vital role in planning, designing and implementing the business strategic plan. In company A, the role of the IT manager included a direct communication with the CEO. In the *Competitive Potential* perspective, the role of top management is to be a business visionary and the role of the IT/IS management is to be a catalyst in the whole transformation process. In company X, the managing director plays a significant role in making such changes in software processes as he has a strong view and belief that the adoption of agile methods could meet the business objective.

However, several other comments from the participants indicated that the speed and flexibility of agile methods allowed such rapid response to changes at the operational level that formalised alignment processes becomes less important. Whether this responsiveness will loosen the relationships between and across the four domains of business and IS/IT strategy, and organisational and ICT infrastructure is an area that requires further study. For company X:

Whether your company aligns to agile is [based on] whether your operation management believes there [is a] need to fix the problem. In our case, we put agile as fundamental business strategy. There is no alignment of how we do that

with the implication that business strategy would follow suit.

CONCLUSION

The purpose of this study was to explore how organisations align business strategy with IT/IS strategy where agile software development has been adopted. This research indicates that agile methods may be emerging as a core infrastructure in order to achieve the organisation's business strategy in a rapidly changing environment. The research findings suggest that agile methods have been applied successfully within the case organisations. However, while the benefits of business and IT/IS strategy alignment were recognised by participants, the narratives suggest this alignment may be more relevant at functional than at strategic level. The use of agile methods in response to internal and external uncertainty, therefore, may change the role of ICT in the firms, and hence impact on the alignment of business strategy and IT/IS strategy. Further study, such as a longitudinal study of strategic alignment pre- and post- adoption of agile methods is required, to investigate whether the agile environment underlies this perception.

REFERENCES

Agilemanifesto. (2001). *Manifesto for agile software development.* Retrieved on February 20, 2007, from http://www.agilemanifesto.org/

Aragon-Sanchez, A., & Sanchez-Marin, G. (2005). Strategic orientation, management characteristics, and performance: A study of Spanish SMEs. *Journal of Small Business Management, 43*(3), 287–308.

Avison, D., Jones, J., Powell, P., & Wilson, D. (2004). Using and validating the strategic alignment model. *The Journal of Strategic Information Systems, 13*, 223–246. doi:10.1016/j.jsis.2004.08.002

Aydin, M. N., Harmsen, F., Slooten, K. v., & Stegwee, R. A. (2005). On the adaptation of an agile information systems development method. *Journal of Database Management, 16*(4), 24–40.

Bauer, M. (2004). FDD and project management. *Cutter IT Journal, 17*(6), 38–44.

Beck, K., & Andres, C. (2005). Extreme programming explained: Embrace change (2nd ed.). Boston: Addison-Wesley.

Bharati, P., & Chaudhury, A. (2009). SMEs and competitiveness - The role of information systems. *International Journal of E-Business Research, 5*(1), 1–9.

Bleistein, S. J., Cox, K., Verner, J., & Phalp, K. T. (2006). B-SCP: A requirements analysis framework for validating strategic alignment of organisational IT based on strategy, context, and process. *Information and Software Technology, 48*, 846–868. doi:10.1016/j.infsof.2005.12.001

Boohalis, D. (1996). Enhancing the competitiveness of small and medium sized tourism enterprise at the destination level. *Electronic Markets, 6*(1).

Chan, Y. E., & Huff, S. L. (1992). Strategy: An information systems research perspective. *The Journal of Strategic Information Systems, 1*(4), 191–204. doi:10.1016/0963-8687(92)90035-U

Chan, Y. E., & Huff, S. L. (1993). Strategic information systems alignment. *Business Quarterly, 58*(1), 51–55.

Chan, Y. E., Huff, S. L., Barclay, D. W., & Copeland, D. G. (1997). Business strategic orientation, information systems strategic orientation, and strategic alignment. *Information Systems Research, 8*(2), 125–150. doi:10.1287/isre.8.2.125

Chell, E., Hawarth, J., & Brearley, S. (1991). The entrepreneurial personality. London: Routledge.

Cragg, P. B., & King, M. (1993). Small-firm computing: Motivator and inhibitors. *MIS Quarterly, 17*(1), 47–60. doi:10.2307/249509

Croteau, A.-M., & Bergeron, F. (2001). An information technology trilogy: business strategy, technological deployment and organisational performance. *The Journal of Strategic Information Systems, 10*, 77–99. doi:10.1016/S0963-8687-(01)00044-0

Das, S. R., Zahra, S. A., & Warkentin, M. E. (1991). Integrating the content and process of strategic MIS planning with competitive strategy. *Decision Sciences, 22*(5), 953–984.

Edelman, L. F., Brush, C., & Manolova, T. (2005). Co-alignment in the resource--performance relationship: Strategy as mediator. *Journal of Business Venturing, 20*(3).

EuropeanCommision. (2005). *SME definition*. Retrieved on March 25, 2008, from http://ec.europa.eu/enterprise/enterprise_policy/sme_definition/index_en.htm

Fink, D. (1998). Adoption of information technology in small and medium enterprises. *International Journal of Information Management, 18*(4), 243–253. doi:10.1016/S0268-4012(98)00013-9

Henderson, J. C., & Venkatraman, N. (1993). Strategic alignment: leveraging information technology for transforming organisations. *IBM Systems Journal, 32*(1), 4–16.

Highsmith, J. (2002). Agile software development ecosystems. Boston: Pearson Education, Inc.

Hirschheim, R., & Sabherwal, R. (2001). Detours in the Path toward strategic information systems alignment. *California Management Review, 44*(1), 87–108.

Hofer, C. W., & Schendel, D. (1978). Strategy formulation: Analytical concepts. Minneapolis, MN: West Publishing CO.

Hussin, H., King, M., & Cragg, P. (2002). IT alignment in small firms. *European Journal of Information Systems, 11*, 108–127. doi:10.1057/palgrave/ejis/3000422

Ismail, N. A., & King, M. (2007). Factors influencing the alignment of accounting information systems in small and medium sized Malaysian manufacturing firms. *Journal of Information Systems and Small Business, 1*(1-2), 1–20.

Johnston, H. R., & Carrico, S. R. (1988). Developing capabilities to use information strategically. *MIS Quarterly, 12*(1), 37–48. doi:10.2307/248801

Kearns, G. S., & Lederer, A. L. (2000). The effect of strategic alignment on the use of IS-based resources for competitive advantage. *The Journal of Strategic Information Systems, 9*(4), 265–293. doi:10.1016/S0963-8687(00)00049-4

Kotha, S. (1989). Generic manufacturing strategies: A conceptual synthesis. *Strategic Management Journal, 10*(3), 211–231. doi:10.1002/smj.4250100303

Kyobe, M. (2008). The influence of strategy-making types on IT alignment in SMEs. *Journal of Systems and Information Technology, 10*(1), 22–38. doi:10.1108/13287260810876876

Levy, M., Powell, P., & Worrall, L. (2005). Strategic intent and e-business in SMEs: Enablers and inhibitors. *Information Resources Management Journal, 18*(4), 1–20.

Levy, M., Powell, P., & Yetton, P. (2001). SMEs: aligning IS and the strategic context. *Journal of Information Technology, 16*, 133–144. doi:10.1080/02683960110063672

Levy, M., Powell, P., & Yetton, P. (2003). *IS alignment in small firms: New paths through the maze.* Paper presented at the Proceedings of the 11th European Conference on Information Systems, ECIS 2003, Naples, Italy.

Luftman, J. N. (1996). Applying the strategic alignment model. New York: Oxford University Press.

Mekelburg, D. (2003). Project Expectations: The boundaries for agile development. *Crosstalk: The Journal of Defense Software Engineering, April*, 28-30.

Merhrtans, J., Cragg, P., & Mills, A. (2001). A model of internet adoption by SMEs. *Information & Management, 39*.

Meso, P., & Jain, R. (2006). Agile software development: Adaptive systems principles and best practice. *Information Systems Management, 23*(3), 19–30. doi:10.1201/1078.10580530/46108.23.3.20060601/93704.3

Miles, R. E., & Snow, C. C. (1978). Organizational strategy, structure, and process. New York: McGraw-Hill.

Miles, R. E., Snow, C. C., Meyer, A. D., Henry, J., & Coleman, J. (1978). Organizational strategy, structure, and process. *Academy of Management Review, 3*(3), 546–562. doi:10.2307/257544

Morgan, K. (1997). The learning region: Institutions, innovations and regional renewal, regional studies. *The Journal of Regional Studies Association, 31*(5), 491–503. doi:10.1080/00343409750132289

Nerur, S., & Mahapatra, R. (2005). Challenges of migrating to agile methodologies. *Communications of the ACM, 48*(5), 72–78. doi:10.1145/1060710.1060712

O'Regan, N., & Ghobadian, A. (2005). Strategic planning - a comparison of high and low technology manufacturing small firms. *Technovation, 25*(10), 1107–1117. doi:10.1016/S0166-4972-(03)00091-9

O'Regan, N., & Ghobadian, A. (2006). Perceptions of generic strategies of small and medium sized engineering and electronics manufacturers in the UK: The applicability of the Miles and Snow typology. *Journal of Manufacturing Technology Management, 17*(5), 603–620. doi:10.1108/17410380610668540

O'Regan, N., Ghobadian, A., & Gallear, D. (2006). In search of the drivers of high growth in manufacturing SMEs. *Technovation, 26*(1), 30–41. doi:10.1016/j.technovation.2005.05.004

Papp, R. (1999). Business-IT alignment: Productivity paradox payoff? *Industrial Management & Data Systems, 99*(8), 367–373. doi:10.1108/02635579910301810

Pare, G. (2004). Investigating information systems with positivist case study research. *Communications of the Association for Information Systems, 13*, 233–264.

Parnell, J. A. (2002). A business strategy typology for the new economy: Reconceptualization and synthesis. *Journal of Behavioral and Applied Management, 3*(3), 206–229.

Pedrycz, W. (2006). Quantitative logic-based framework for agile methodologies. *Journal of Systems Architecture, 52*, 700–707. doi:10.1016/j.sysarc.2006.06.014

Pikkarainen, M., & Passoja, U. (2005). *An approach for assessing suitability of agile solutions: A case study.* Paper presented at the International conference of Extreme Programming and agile process in software engineering, UK.

Prananto, A., McKay, J., & Marshall, P. (2003). *The spectrum of e-business maturity in Australian SMEs: A multiple case study approach to the applicability of the stages of growth for e-business model.* Paper presented at the Proceeding of the 11th European conference on information systems (ECIS).

Quale, M., & Christiansen, J. (2004). Business issues in the 21st century. In N. A.-. Qirim (Ed.), Electronic commerce in small to medium-sized enterprises: Frameworks, issues and implications. Hershey, PA: Idea Group Publishing.

Rathnam, R. G., Johnsen, J., & Wen, H. J. (2004/2005). Alignment of business strategy and IT strategy: A case study of a fortune 50 financial service company. *Journal of Computer Information Systems, 45*(2), 1–8.

Reich, B. H., & Benbasat, I. (2000). Factors that influence the social dimension of alignment between business and information technology objectives. *MIS Quarterly, 24*(1), 81–113. doi:10.2307/3250980

Smith, K. G., Guthrie, J. P., & Chen, M.-J. (1989). Strategy, size and performance. *Organization Studies, 10*(1), 63–81. doi:10.1177/017084068901000104

Throp, J. (1998). The information paradox: Realizing the business benefits of information technology. Toronto: McGraw-Hill Ryerson.

Truex, D. P., Baskerville, R., & Klein, H. (1999). Growing systems in emergent organizations. *Communications of the ACM, 42*(8), 117–123. doi:10.1145/310930.310984

Tsui, F. F., & Karam, O. (2006). Essentials of software engineering. Sudbury, MA: Jones & Bartlett Publishers.

Turk, D., France, R., & Bernhard Rumpe, B. (2005). Assumptions underlying agile software-development processes. *Journal of Database Management, 16*(4), 62–87.

Vijayasarathy, L. R., & Turk, D. (2008). Agile software development: A survey of early adopters. *Journal of Information Technology Management, 19*, 1–8.

Ward, J., & Peppard, J. (2002). Strategic planning for information systems. West Sussex, UK: John Wiley & Sons.

Welsh, J. A., & White, J. F. (1981). A small business is not a little big business. *Harvard Business Review, 59*(4), 18–32.

Wheelwright, S. C. (1984). Strategy, Management, and Strategic planning approaches. *Interfaces, 14*(1), 19–33. doi:10.1287/inte.14.1.19

Yin, R. K. (1989). Case study research: Design and methods. Newbury Park, CA: SAGE Publications, Inc.

ADDITIONAL READING

Baron, A. (2002). Application management. London: The Stationery Office.

Blumentritt, T., & Danis, W. M. (2006). Business strategy types and innovative practices. *Journal of Managerial, 18*(2), 274–291.

Burn, J. M., & Szeto, C. (2000). A comparison of the views of business and IT management on success factors for strategic alignment. *Information & Management, 37*, 197–216. doi:10.1016/S0378-7206(99)00048-8

Byrd, T. A., Lewis, B. R., & Bryan, R. W. (2006). The leveraging influence of strategic alignment on IT investment: An empirical examination. *Information & Management, 43*, 308–321. doi:10.1016/j.im.2005.07.002

Grant, G. G. (2003). Strategic alignment and enterprise systems implementation: the case of Metalco. *Journal of Information Technology, 18*(3), 159–175. doi:10.1080/0268396032000122132

Henderson, J. C., & Venkatraman, N. (1989). Strategic alignment: A framework for strategic information technology management. Cambridge, MA: Center for Information Systems Research, Massachusetts Institute of Technology.

Luftman, J. N., Lewis, P. R., & Oldach, S. H. (1993). Transforming the enterprise: The alignment of business and information technology strategies. *IBM Systems Journal, 32*(1), 198–221.

Mata, F. J., Fuerst, W. L., & Barney, J. B. (1995). Information technology and sustained competitive advantage: A resource-based analysis. *MIS Quarterly, 19*(4), 487–505. doi:10.2307/249630

Morton, M. S. S. (1991). The corporation of the 1990s: Information technology and organisational transformation. New York: Oxford University Press.

Raymond, P. (2001). Strategic information technology: Opportunities for competitive advantage. Hershey, PA Idea Group Publishing.

Tan, F. B. (1995). The responsiveness of information technology to business strategy formulation: an empirical study. *Journal of Information Technology, 10*(3), 171–178. doi:10.1057/jit.1995.21

Zahra, S. A., & Covin, J. G. (1993). Business strategy, technology policy and firm performance. *Strategic Management Journal, 14*(6), 451–478. doi:10.1002/smj.4250140605

Zahra, S. A., & Pearce, J. A. (1990). Research evidence on the Miles-Snow typology. *Journal of Management, 16*(4), 751–768. doi:10.1177/014920639001600407

Chapter 12

Supporting SMEs Towards E-Business Success:
Exploring the Importance of Training, Competence and Stimulation

Tom R. Eikebrokk
University of Agder, Norway

Dag H. Olsen
University of Agder, Norway

ABSTRACT

The low e-Business implementation in small and medium-sized enterprises (SMEs) is an important issue in most countries. This chapter examines the relationship between training, competence and performance of small and medium-sized enterprises (SMEs) and discusses the implications for practice and further research. The study combined data about e-business competences and performance in 339 SMEs with data about training supply from 116 providers of e-business related training in three European countries. The authors find a positive relationship between training, competence and performance and show that training explains variances in e-business competences and performance in terms of efficiency, complementarities, lock-in and novelty. The research contributes to theoretical development by lending support to the idea that methodological issues are an important reason behind the lack of empirical support frequently reported in the literature. The study has practical implications for public policy makers, training suppliers and SME managers.

INTRODUCTION

Small and medium sized enterprises (SMEs) generate a substantial share of the GDP in industrial economies. The more than 20 million SMEs in Europe are an important source of new jobs and entrepreneurial activity (European Commission,

2002a, 2002b). Considerable funding has been granted to research programs targeting the development of SMEs in general and in specific areas such as the diffusion of e-business. It is assumed that success with e-business in the SME segment will increase a country's competitiveness in the long run, and that successful adoption and use of

DOI: 10.4018/978-1-61520-627-8.ch012

e-business technology is crucial for survival in the new economy (see Debreceny, Putterill, Tung, & Gilbert, 2002 for an overview).

Governments in most industrialized countries have implemented various stimulation programs including training to increase e-business competence. Despite these efforts, there is only scarce knowledge of how training programs influence the creation of competence and e-business performance. SMEs are reluctant to engage in training initiatives despite the existence of incentives (Maton, 1999). Organizational constraints seem to create barriers to SMEs. Lack of time and financial resources, along with ignorance to the supply of training have been found to represent such barriers (Marlow, 1998; Westhead & Storey, 1997). With better understanding of the relationship between training, e-business competence and performance in the SME segment, governments would be able to better tailor stimulation programs to target SME competence needs. Several studies indicate that development of the SME segment is challenging and that SMEs for the most part are unable to successfully adopt and use e-business technology (Debreceny et al., 2002). A number of studies has emphasized the lack of e-business competence and lack of training (Fillis, Johannsson, & Wagner, 2003; Ihlström & Nilsson, 2003; Ivis, 2001; Johnston, Shi, Dann, & Barcay, 2006; Kinkaide, 2000; Lewis & Cockrill, 2002) as the major cause for this problem. Such competence is seen as important for understanding the implications of e-business for the business domain, and for developing the distinctive capabilities needed to perform well in the e-business era (Grandon & Pearson, 2004).

This chapter investigates the relationships between training supply, e-business competence and e-business performance in SMEs. More specifically, we investigate whether the provision of training lead to more competence, and eventually, to better performance in the context of e-business. This issue has received interest from researchers in the general field of SME research, but few studies have focused on the context of e-business. There is scarce and ambiguous evidence that training leads to better performance in SMEs (Bryan, 2006; Devins & Johanson, 2003; Patton, Marlow, & Hannon, 2000; Westhead & Storey, 1996, 1997).

BACKGROUND

It is generally acknowledged that SMEs differ from large firms with respect to investing in information systems. Bharati and Chaudhury (2009) review some of the differences. Firstly, SMEs experience dis-economies of scale and limited autonomy, which constrain growth and business activities. Second, SMEs have low risk propensity. Managers are often owners with a stake in the financial success, and are therefore more risk averse than managers of large firms. Third, SMEs are centralized and have low formalism levels. Typically, decisions are taken by owners and a few top managers. Management practices are often ad hoc and informal. Fourth, SMEs experience cultural insularity and have identity-based trust relationships. Because of their small size, are SMEs usually limited to trade with partners in a small geographical area. Strong ties with a local network may close out impulses from other sources.

E-Business and SMEs

E-business and the internet have opened new arenas for competing and collaborating for SMEs, but most of them are in an early stage of their e-business. We have adopted a relatively broad definition of e-business as the conduct of business generally with the assistance of telecommunication and telecommunications-based tools (Clarke, 2003). There is not a common definition of Small and Medium sized organizations. The term Small Business is commonly used in the United States where measures as number of employees, total turnover, and industry are used to define a Small Business. The European Union (EU) uses a uniform definition of SMEs as independent companies with fewer than 250 employees, with either a turnover of less than 40 million € or total assets of less than 27 million € (European Commission, 2004). Independent companies are those that are not owned as to 25% or more of the capital or the voting rights by one enterprise, or jointly by several enterprises. We have adopted the EU definition.

Training and Performance in the Context of E-Business in SMEs

Research suggests that there are some basic differences between training activities in large companies and SMEs. A number of studies have indicated that large organizations train more than SMEs (Boulay, 2008; Forth, Bewley, & Bryson, 2006; Lynch & Black, 1998). The U.S. Dept of Education found that larger organizations provide more formal job related training (2004). There is some evidence that SMEs implement training in informal and reactive ways to a higher degree than large companies (Forth et al., 2006; Hill & Stewart, 1999; Westhead & Storey, 1996). This may suggest that SMEs generally are less systematic in their training and use less formal training. Boulay (2008) argues that SMEs may see training as an interrelated part of other job activities, and there are indications that SMEs use informal and on-the-job training (Johnson, 2002; Kitching & Blackburn, 2002; Rowden, 2002).

Westhead and Storey (1996) suggest that the differences in training between large and SME organizations can be due to differences in uncertainty. Large companies are most concerned with internal uncertainty, such as whether executive decisions are carried out at all levels. SMEs have little market power and are more concerned with external uncertainty. Westhead and Storey (1996) suggest that this may lead to short term focus, and therefore to less formal training approaches.

Storey (2004) argues that SMEs make appropriate and well-informed decisions for their training, based on the findings in a study of SMEs in six OECD countries.

Governments invest substantial resources in stimulating training suppliers to develop competence programs to the SME sector. Such programs are based on the assumption that the provision of training in terms of developing existing or introducing new skills and/or knowledge to SMEs, will improve their business performance. This assumption is general and includes the context of e-business. The demand side is also stimulated. Financial incentives encourage organizations, including SMEs, to develop training programs for their employees. Yet, there is an ongoing debate about whether a positive relationship exists between training and small business performance. We can split the debate into three components. Some studies investigate the effect of training on small business performance. Other studies divide the link into two parts: the impact of training on competence, and the impact of competence on performance.

Patton, Marlow and Hannon (2000) reviewed the status of the research on training and performance in small firms. They conclude that despite the almost axiomatic proposition that training increases business performance, very few empirical studies have been able to demonstrate the significance of this relationship. A similar review by Westhead and Storey (1996, 1997) concluded in a similar vein that there was no substantial evidence for the causal link between training and performance in SMEs. A more recent study (Fuller-Love, 2006) reviewed the literature on management development in small firms and concluded that management development programs in general are effective for small firms through the development of competence. By focusing on developing new skills in management, capabilities of management systems and techniques, team building, planning, delegation and financial management, the training programs led to reduction in failure and improvement in performance.

Troshano and Rao (2007) focused on the enabling factors behind e-business competitive advantage in the Australian financial services industry. After interviewing 12 companies in an exploratory study they argue that e-business technologies enable or stimulate organizational competences which, in turn, explain higher levels of performance. The authors do not present any empirical evidence that demonstrate the existence of the link between e-business technologies and organizational performance. Bryan (2006) conducted a study of the relationship between training and performance, taking the effect of time into consideration. By studying a random sample of 114 manufacturing SMEs in 1996 and then in 2003, Bryan concludes that external management training has a greater impact on sales growth than in-house training programs.

Patton et al (2000) propose three possible explanations for the mixed and inconclusive results and the problems of finding a casual link between training and performance: Firstly, it is possible that a causal relationship does not exist. Secondly, methodological problems associated with measuring and isolating the effects could explain the lack of evidence. Thirdly, the lack of evidence could be a result of not taking into account other possible variables that influence the relationship between training and business performance. Patton et al (2000) argue that since studies already have demonstrated that it is possible to find a significant link between training and business performance, it is less likely that a causal relationship does not exist. They find it much more likely that there are methodological explanations behind to the inability to explain the lack of clear empirical findings and to identify and separate the effects of training. They suggest that improvements in research methodology could improve the ability to detect contextual factors. In addition, improved research methodology could improve the ability to generalize the results. They

advise that future studies should explore the differences in business context and utilize research methods that triangulate qualitative field research with quantitative surveys. Future studies should also focus on characteristics of the providers of training along with the characteristics, needs and available resources of the small businesses themselves. Studies from UK (e.g. Westhead & Storey, 1996) analyzed the training supply and found that the supply rarely is based on what is demanded, thereby creating a gap between the content of the supply and the needs of the business sector.

Training and Competence Development in SMEs

It is generally recognized that SMEs are poor in resources and competencies. Harindranath et al. (2008) studied 378 ICT adoption and use in UK SMEs. They find that SMEs lack fundamental competencies about ICT technology. They conclude that SME owner/managers in most cases have weak ICT background and lack the skills necessary to evaluate potential ICT investments. Most of them are also unaware of the gamut of support programs through national and regional agencies that target SMEs. They also lack internal ICT champions. They further find that fear of technology obsolescence requiring frequent updates was an important problem. SMEs frequently encountered operational problems which lead to dependence on external consultants and vendors. This was seen as a major problem for SMEs, with their limited resources.

Harindranath et al. (2008) further found that SMEs did not perceive ICT as offering long term solutions to business sustainability. They argue that SMEs are driven by cost issues, and have a limited strategic flexibility, and their ICT investments reflect this. ICT investments were often driven by the need to comply with government regulations, rather than strategic considerations. They argue that SMEs need to think more strategically in relation to ICT, and that the agencies charged with the development of SME ICT capabilities need to address the fundamental competence gaps.

It is generally assumed that training leads to improved competence, and the development of appropriate competence and investments in staff training has been identified as central barriers to successful e-business implementation and use (Fillis et al., 2003). Several EU programs have targeted the provision of e-business training for SMEs. However obvious the assumption about the relation between training and competence may be, there is scarce empirical support. In their review, Fuller-Love (2006) identified five studies from 1992-1997 that empirically identified a link between training and performance through the development of competence. These improved competences led to reduction in failure and improvement in performance. Still, Fuller-Love concludes that the empirical evidence is limited and should be complemented by more studies focusing on both single cases and on cross-sectional data from different industries and geographical areas.

Several government initiatives in Europe have targeted the need for training and management development in small firms. The EU Commission initiated a benchmarking study in order to describe and benchmark the national and regional policies and instruments promoting e-business in SMEs (European Commission, 2002b). Based on the experiences from more than 150 initiatives in 16 countries the benchmarking study concludes that the training initiatives had varying impact on awareness and competence development. The best training initiatives were characterized by being based on solid research and data, flexible, coordinated, and tailored to the needs of the SMEs in different regions and sectors.

Competence and E-Business Performance in SMEs

The link between e-business competence and e-business performance has been found in several empirical studies. Eikebrokk and Olsen (2007) found empirical evidence in support of this link for small and medium-sized companies. Saeed, Grover and Hwang (2005) identified a positive relationship between e-business competence and subsequent e-business performance, using data from 73 companies listed among the top 500 US Internet companies. We base our identification of competence dimensions on a review of several sources including the IS field and organization science.

First, there is the dimension of strategy competence. Bharadwaj et al. (2000) and Feeny and Willcocks (1998) conceptualized this dimension as "Business IT strategic thinking". Elements of this dimension are also implicitly contained in two of the dimensions of both Peppard et al. (2000) and Basselier et al. (2001), and one of the dimensions of Sambamurthy and Zmud (1994) and Feeny and Willcocks (1998). Several empirical studies have documented the important role of strategic vision for SMEs' adoption of e-business (Grandon & Pearson, 2004; Love & Irani, 2004). This dimension can be divided into two sub-dimensions. A significant part of this dimension is the company's ability to envision the strategic potential of new e-business technology in its marketplace (Bharadwaj et al., 2000; Feeny & Willcocks, 1998). It involves understanding the concept of e-business, and it will reflect the maturity of the enterprises' understanding of the e-business domain and what new possibilities and threats e-business creates in the business domain. On the other hand, this dimension also includes the ability to understand and use strategic planning methods needed to develop an e-business strategy, which describes how e-business will be put into action (Bharadwaj et al., 2000).

Second, we have the issue of competence in IT-business process integration. The IS literature offers broad support for the notion that a company's ability to realize potential benefits of new technology is influenced by the ability to organize business processes that leverage this potential (e.g.

Hammer, 1990; Keen, 1991). More specifically, empirical studies in the area of IS economics have documented that among Fortune 500 companies productivity gains from utilizing new technologies are higher in companies that organize themselves in ways that leverage the potential of the new technology (e.g. Brynjolfsson & Hitt, 1998). In a European study of 441 Spanish SMEs, Dans (2001) found a similar correlation between IT-investments and productivity for SMEs that can partly be attributed to organizational redesign. The most fundamental challenge to SMEs may lie in changing the mindset of the organization. Several authors (Lawrence, 1997; C. S. Lee, 2001; Tetteh & Burn, 2001) have argued that the adoption of e-business fundamentally alters internal procedures within SMEs. This dimension is explicitly recognized in recent articles on IT/IS competence (Bharadwaj et al., 2000; Peppard et al., 2000), and implicitly present in the other sources. New business or IT work processes can be designed or old processes can be restructured in order to leverage the opportunities of new technology (Davenport, 1993). Regardless of which strategy is chosen, the company must have the ability to identify and implement changes in business processes in order to increase process efficiency to the level required by the business and the potential of the technology (Bharadwaj et al., 2000; Davenport, 1993). Companies need competence to organize and manage work processes in new and powerful ways. Competence is needed both in developing the new business model and in the subsequent implementation of this model in the organization.

Third, there is the dimension of IT management. It is defined as activities related to the management of the IT function, such as IS planning and design, IS application delivery, IT project management, and planning for control and standards (Bharadwaj et al., 2000; DeLone, 1988). Bharadwaj et al. (2000) demonstrates the empirical significance of IT management. SMEs generally have an ad-hoc approach to IT management, and therefore seldom have a defined IT budget or an explicit IT plan or strategy, and investments in technology are often driven by the owner, rather than by any formal cost-benefit or strategic analysis (Ballantine, Levy, & Powell, 1998; Dans, 2001).

Fourth, competence in systems and infrastructure was covered in several literature sources, including the empirical study of Bharadwaj et al. (2000). We define competence in systems and infrastructure as the knowledge of the data, network, and processing architectures that support the enterprise applications and services. Systems and infrastructure influence the gamut of business opportunities available to firms applying IT in their business strategies (Keen, 1991). Successful use of e-business technologies involves both finding technology with a strategic potential and having a technological and managerial infrastructure that can implement and support it. As a result, companies need competence on available e-business solutions as well as on the importance of having or creating internal structures that can utilize the new solutions.

Fifth, there is the issue of relationship competence. A core premise of the network economy is that business networks that effectively source and coordinate resources and capabilities will be highly competitive (Mowshowitz, 1997; Rayport & Sviokla, 1995; Timmers, 1999). Therefore effective communication and interaction internally as well as with business partners will be important to e-business performance. Our literature review identified two sub-dimensions of relationship competence, sourcing and alignment. These dimensions are present in Bharadwaj et al. (2000) where they are termed "IT-business partnerships" and "External linkages", and implicitly contained in other competence terms in all our other sources.

We define the first sub-dimension, competence in *sourcing,* as the ability to secure access to relevant competences either inside or outside of the company. MacGregor (2004) argues that electronic business has forced organizations to reassess their boundaries and focus their attention on inter-organizational issues. A study of small manufacturing firms found that inter-organizational relationships are important for performance (Golden & Dollinger, 1993). Networks, whether in the form of strategic alliances or informal linkages, are important to pool resources and talents for mutual benefit of participants (Dean, Holmes, & Smith, 1997; Premaratne, 2001; Rosenfeld, 1996). Jarratt (1998) found that competence derived through participation in networks overcame other business weaknesses. Studies on EDI adoption and Internet adoption have also highlighted the role of relationship competence (S. Lee & Lim, 2005; Mehrtens, Cragg, & Mills, 2001). Also, studies of IS outsourcing success have documented the importance of the ability to form high quality partner relationships and having the capability to learn or to acquire the needed knowledge (J.-N. Lee, 2001; Shi, Kunnathur, & Ragu-Nathan, 2005).

We define the other sub-dimension, competence in *alignment,* as the ability to combine and use available competences. For example, sourcing could take place through two different activities that either create access to competences through recruitment, training, or contractual arrangements, or outsource activities where competences are needed. When the need for and access to competences are defined by sourcing arrangements, competences in alignment will influence how well accessible competences are combined and activated in the use process. Normally, alignment is regarded in the literature as an intra-organizational activity (e.g. "IT-Business partnership" in (Bharadwaj et al., 2000)); but when companies cooperate and form alliances, alignment takes on an inter-organizational dimension. As a result, competence in alignment will have both an internal and an external perspective. Most studies point to the importance of flexible systems and IT infrastructure with key business partners without explicitly recognizing the importance of competences in managing these inter-organizational

relationships (e.g Bharadwaj et al., 2000). In the network economy, businesses that are able to form effective partnerships will be more agile (Sambamurthy, Bharadwaj, & Grover, 2003) and competitive. This ability is particularly important for small and medium-sized enterprises, which typically have scarce resources and limited ability to exploit business opportunities on their own. Sourcing and alignment competences will enable small businesses to take advantage of e-business opportunities and take part in business network partnerships.

E-Business Performance Dimensions

Amit and Zott (2001) conducted one of the most cited studies on e-business performance. They perform a thorough review of the entrepreneurship and strategic management literature. They conclude that no single economic theory can fully explain the sources of value creation of e-business. Johansson and Mollstedt (2006) argue that Amit and Zott's four dimensions of e-business success are not only relevant for understanding the drivers of value but could also be used as performance dimensions when evaluating the success of e-business.

Wade and Hulland (2004) argue that the researcher need to conceptualize resources as well as performance with a certain level of specificity, to identify the effects of resources on performance. They suggest that in choosing a dependent variable for understanding the importance of resources, the researcher needs to address three key attributes regarding the constructs ability to address: 1) performance, 2) competitive aspects, and 3) performance over time. The performance dimensions of Amit and Zott (2001) used as evaluative dimensions of e-business performance as suggested by Johansson and Mollstedt (2006), exhibit all three of these criteria. Consequently, we base our definition of e-business performance on the work of Amit and Zott (2001) who describe the potential of value creation in e-business in four interrelated dimensions: efficiency, complementarities, lock-in, and novelty. Efficiency describes possible reductions in transaction costs, whereas complementarities describe the value potential from combining products and services, technologies and activities in new and innovative ways. Lock-in describes the potential value in creating switching costs from arrangements that motivate customers and business partners to repeat and improve transactions and relationships. Novelty describes value creation resulting from innovations in the way business is conducted (e.g. web-based auctions, etc.).

RESEARCH MODEL AND HYPOTHESES

Our research model and hypotheses will test the influence of training and competence on performance in small and medium-sized enterprises by focusing on how these influences work in the context of e-business. We follow the advice put forward by Patton et al. (2000), Fuller-Love (2006) and Wade and Hulland (2004). They argue that further studies should narrow their focus on a specific setting involving a limited set of competences, industries or geographical regions. Moreover, following the advices from the benchmarking report of European training initiatives (European Commission, 2002a), we will base our inclusion of competence on previous research and focus on the relevance of competence supplied through the training offered.

We define e-business competence as the knowledge, skills and capability of SMEs to utilize the concept of e-business and e-business related technologies. The concept of training is included as a potential predictor of both e-business competence and e-business performance. Training is defined as the relevant training supply in the context of e-business and SMEs. Training will be measured by collecting information from the different training providers in the chosen industries and countries.

The providers' interest in the SME segment and the content of the training supply are important factors in defining the training supply as it appears to the SMEs. The demand for training is formed by the SMEs' awareness of the training supply and the ability to invest in the training offered.

We propose that e-business performance is influenced by both e-business competence and relevant training supply in this context. E-business performance is defined as the results of the e-business efforts in terms of the effects created in the four dimensions of efficiency, complementarities, lock-in and novelty. The research model is illustrated in Figure 1. We propose the following research hypotheses:

H1: There is a positive association between training and e-business performance in terms of a) efficiency, b) complementarities, c) lock-in and d) novelty.

H2: There is a positive association between training and e-business related competence.

H3: There is a positive association between e-business related competence and e-business performance in terms of a) efficiency, b) complementarities, c) lock-in and d) novelty.

METHODOLOGY

We conducted a cross sectional study with a sample of 339 SMEs from three industries (tourism, transportation, and food and beverages) in three European countries (Norway, Finland and Spain). A sample of 116 training providers was also drawn randomly from the same countries. Based on a random sample of SMEs, executives were phoned, and if their company used web pages, e-mail or e-commerce systems for business purposes, they were invited to take part in the survey. 339 executives accepted and were subsequently interviewed. A total sample of 130 training providers, equally shared between the

Figure 1. Research model

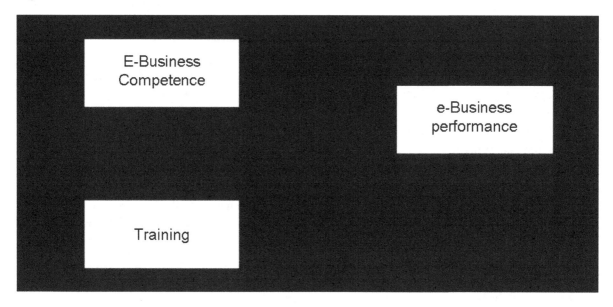

countries, were phoned and invited to take part in a sample. 116 providers accepted and were then interviewed.

We based the operationalizations of e-business competence on instruments and operationalizations previously documented (Bassellier et al., 2001; Bharadwaj et al., 2000; Feeny & Willcocks, 1998; Heijden, 2000; D. M. S. Lee, Trauth, & Farwell, 1995; Sambamurthy & Zmud, 1994). The operationalization of e-business training was based on the work of Patton et al. (2000) who identified characteristics of both the supply side and demand side as important to understand the relevance of the training supply. As a result, training supply was operationalized in four dimensions: the attractiveness of the different SME size segments to the training provider, the financial ability of SMEs of different sizes to invest in training programs, the SMEs' awareness of existing training programs, and the content of the training offered in terms of the types of competence offered. The competence dimensions characterizing the training supply were the same as in the e-business competence variable targeting the SMEs. The final measure

of training was constructed as a summed index for each country.

The supply and demand of training as a function of SME size, were added to the data set of each country. The average awareness of SMEs about the training supply in each country was coded with the average value for each SME in the respective countries. The index representing the training content in each country was coded in a similar fashion.

We constructed the final measure of training as a formative measure where training emerged as a result of the external supply and internal demand described above. The data about training represents a pooling of information from the supply side (providers) and the demand side (SMEs as customers). Training suppliers were asked to report which competences they cover for the different SME size segments. The suppliers were also used as informants on how SMEs of different size have varying demand of training as a function of their awareness and financial ability to pay for the training supply. By combining data from the SMEs and their training providers we get richer information about how the training supply appears to the SMEs in terms of content, availability and relevance, as suggested by Patton et al. (2000).

'E-business performance' was operationalized according to the dimensions described by Amit and Zott (2001). The indicators for all constructs were measured on a seven point Likert-type scale between 'totally disagree'/'not at all' and 'totally agree'/'very large extent'. The independent variables were measured as formative indicators (for a review of construct indicators and measurement model specification, see (Burke Jarvis, Mackenzie, & Podsakoff, 2003)). The dependent variable e-business performance was measured with reflective indicators of each of the four dimension of performance: efficiency, complementarities, lock-in and novelty. We then conducted open-ended interviews with eight SME managers and two related consultants as an additional reality check of our model and as a test of the relevance, wording and response format of the indicators. The outcome of this process led to the resulting questionnaires. The survey instruments are shown in appendix 2 and 3.

DATA ANALYSIS

We determined that partial least squares analysis (PLS) would be the most appropriate technique in the testing of our hypotheses along with the measurement quality of our formative and reflective indicators. PLS is a confirmatory, second-generation multivariate analysis technique (Fornell, 1982) that is well suited for highly complex predictive models (Jöreskog & Wold, 1982). PLS has several advantages that makes it well suited for this study, including the ability to handle reflective and formative indicators and robustness in relation to departure from multivariate normality, as occurred in our data. Moreover, as with multiple regression, PLS focuses on the model's ability to predict rather than explain the variability of the dependent variables. PLS is therefore most

useful in situations where the theory is still being developed (W. W. Chin, 1998) and can suggest refinements in theory by showing how substantially indicators are related to constructs and how assumed predictors are related to one or more dependent variables. In PLS, the predictive ability of constructs is optimized and the performance of the individual scale items is reported.

Descriptive Statistics

We show descriptive statistics for the two samples in appendix 1. All 339 SMEs in our sample used at least one of the eight e-business systems surveyed (Q4) in addition to e-mail. Each company had at least a web presence where individual customers or companies could find information about products and services. Appendix 1 shows the distribution of the different e-business systems (Q4a-h) in the SME sample. The second sample consisted of 116 training providers, where Norway and Finland were represented by 40 providers each and Spain by 36 suppliers. The size of the training providers varied substantially, ranging from 1 to almost 800 employees. The median size of the training providers in the sample was 37.4 employees (See Table 1).

Measurement and Measurement Quality

Formative items represent measures that cause the construct under study (Bollen, 1989). Changes in the construct are therefore not expected to cause any changes in the indicators (for an overview of indicator specification, see (Jarvis, Mackenzie, & Podsakoff, 2003)). As a result, items within a formative scale are not expected to correlate. Tests of convergent and discriminant validity based on the inter-correlations between items are therefore not relevant for evaluating the psychometric properties of formative items. Instead, item weights and their significance are used to indicate how relevant each item is in measuring its latent con-

Table 1. Descriptive statistics, weights and t-statistics for formative indicators measuring competence

	Mean	*Std. dev.*	*Weight*	*t-stat.*
Competence (Formative)				
Q10	4.11	1.73	0.16	1.82
Q11	4.25	1.71	0.04	0.34
Q14	3.65	1.64	0.11	1.10
Q16	4.38	1.74	0.13	1.80
Q22	4.08	1.53	0.55	6.39
Q25	4.31	1.61	0.10	1.09
Q26	4.55	1.60	0.11	1.41
Q27	3.63	1.83	0.13	1.40
Training (Formative)				
V8	3.98	1.06	0.18	2.02
V9-28	4.80	0.33	0.14	5.62

struct. These results are reported in Table 2. After examining the indicator weights and t-statistics, several indicators in the e-business competence scale were deleted because of negative weights indicating problems with multicollinearity. A new analysis of the reduced model showed no further problems. Of the eight remaining indicators three were found to have significant t-values (p≤ .05). These indicators were related to competences in e-business strategy and vision, sourcing of competence, and IT business process integration. This empirically suggests that the overall e-business related competence is primarily formed by competence in IT business process integration (Q22), knowledge of the value of e-business technologies in relation to business (Q10), and knowledge of outsourcing (Q16).

We found that the two indicators measuring training, V8 (financial resources of SMEs of different size to invest in training) and the index of V9-28 (competence areas represented in the training content offered) had both positive and significant weights (p≤.05). The other two indicators included in the measurement model of training had negative weights, indicating a problem with multi-collinearity and were therefore removed. The resulting measure of training consists of the SMEs' ability to invest in training, and the content of the training offered by the provider.

We assessed the reliability of the dependent variable constructs using Cronbach's alpha. Hair et al. (Hair, Anderson, Tatham, & Black, 1992) suggest that an alpha of 0.60 is acceptable for exploratory research and 0.80 for confirmatory research. Reliability analysis for the multi-item

Table 2. Results of the reliability test

Variable	**Reliability of scale**
E-business performance: efficiency (v11-13)	0.86
E-bus. performance: complementarities (v14-16)	0.88
E-business performance: lock-in (v17-18)	0.70
E-business performance: novelty (v19-20)	0.72

Table 3. Descriptive statistics: e-business performance, reflective indicators

E-business efficiency (Reflective)				
Composite Reliability 0.86; AVE 0.67	**Mean**	**Std. dev.**	**Loading**	**t-stat.**
Q28	3.66	1.90	0.84	49.20
Q29	3.84	1.91	0.85	62.36
Q30	4.20	1.76	0.76	22.77
E-business complementarities (Reflective)				
Composite Reliability 0.90; AVE 0.75				
Q31	3.78	1.76	0.84	35.37
Q32	3.98	1.75	0.90	81.06
Q33	3.60	1.78	0.86	59.06
E-business Lock-in (Reflective)				
Composite Reliability 0.85; AVE 0.74				
Q34	2.97	1.73	0.84	33.26
Q35	3.76	1.81	0.88	47.79
E-business Novelty (Reflective)				
Composite Reliability 0.87; AVE 0.77				
Q36	2.93	1.85	0.88	46.59
Q37	3.75	1.76	0.87	45.12

scales showed the following coefficient alphas: e-business efficiency 0.86, e-business complementarities 0.88, e-business lock-in 0.70, and e-business novelty 0.72. These results show that all concepts had sufficient reliability for exploratory research.

The reflective items are believed to be caused by the latent constructs they intend to measure (Bollen, 1989). Inter-correlations between the items are therefore expected. The psychometric properties of the reflective items were examined by analyzing their internal consistency in terms of their convergent and discriminant validity. Convergent validity was estimated based on the item loadings, and a loading of above .70 is recommended, which indicates that at least half of the variance in each item is accounted for by the latent construct (Nunnally, 1978). For all dimensions of e-business performance the items had sufficient convergent validity in terms of their squared loadings (see Table 2). In addition, average variance extracted (AVE) was calculated. AVE

indicated that the set of indicators as a whole was sufficient of explaining the latent construct. All constructs with reflective items had AVE above the recommended level of 0.5 (Fornell & Larcker, 1981), as shown in Table 3.

Test of Hypotheses

We tested the structural model with the estimated path coefficients and their standard errors, along with the R^2 value, which reflects the predictive ability of the model including the dependent variables' ability to explain the dependent variable. We used PLS-graph version 3.0 (W.W. Chin, 2001) for the structural analyses and hypotheses tests. The significance of each path in the structural model was estimated using the bootstrap re-sampling method with 200 re-samples. Our sample size of 339 exceeds the minimum recommended sample size of the greater of either 1) ten times the number of indicators in the scale with the largest number of formative indicators, or 2) ten times the largest number of structural paths directed at a particular dependent construct in the structural model (W. W. Chin, Marcolin, & Newsted, 1996).

Hypotheses H1a states a positive association between training and e-business performance in terms of efficiency, and this was not supported. Hypothesis H1b holds that training will be positively related to e-business performance in terms of complementarities, which was supported (.15, p≤.01). Hypothesis H1c states a positive relationship between training and lock-in, which was supported (.15; p≤.01), and finally hypothesis H1d states that training will be positively related to e-business performance in terms of novelty, which was also supported (.20, p≤.01). Hypothesis H2 states a positive relationship between training and the e-business related competence in the SMEs, which was supported (.26, p≤.01, R^2=.07). Finally, hypothesis H3a states a positive relationship between e-business competence and e-business performance in terms of efficiency, which received strong support (.58, p≤.01). Hypothesis H3b suggest that e-business competence is positively related to e-business performance in terms of complementarities, which was strongly supported (.61, p≤.01). Hypothesis H3c states that e-business competence is positively related to e-business performance in terms of lock-in, which received strong support (.49, p≤.01). The last hypothesis, H3d, holds that e-business competence will be positively related to e-business performance in terms of novelty, which was also strongly supported (.55, p≤.01). As a whole the structural model explained a substantial amount of variance in e-business performance. Competence and training explained 36%, 45%, 30% and 40% of the variance in e-business efficiency, complementarities, lock-in, and novelty, respectively. Figure 2 summarizes the significant findings of the structural model.

DISCUSSION

A number of recent studies have identified a positive relationship between training and performance (Edelman, Brush, & Manolova, 2002; Gray, 2004; Huang, 2001; Moore, Blake, Phillips, & McConaughty, 2003). However, the literature on the relationship between training and performance in SMEs is still ambiguous. The same is true for the relationships between e-business related training, e-business competence and business performance, and between e-business training and competence. This confusion is most likely a result of the partial focus in most of these studies where few have included both the effect of training and competence in understanding how e-business applications can influence e-business performance. This exploratory study examined the factors that affect e-business performance in SMEs by combining a research model developed from a review of the IT competence literature and the small business literature, with interviews and survey data from both SMEs and training providers. We have three contributions.

First, we have developed a conceptualization of e-business related training that both include the supply side as well as the demand side of training as suggested by Patton et al (2000). This conceptualization combines factors identified in the IS literature with factors identified in the small business literature.

Second, our empirical results from the context of e-business demonstrate a relationship between training, competence, and performance in SMEs. In addition to the direct relationship between e-business competence and performance, training was found both to influence competence levels and performance both direct and indirectly. These findings add to and support the small business literature which suggests that a positive relationship exists between SME training and performance (e.g. Cosh, Duncan, & Hughes, 1998). The findings

Figure 2. Structural model with significant paths and path coefficients

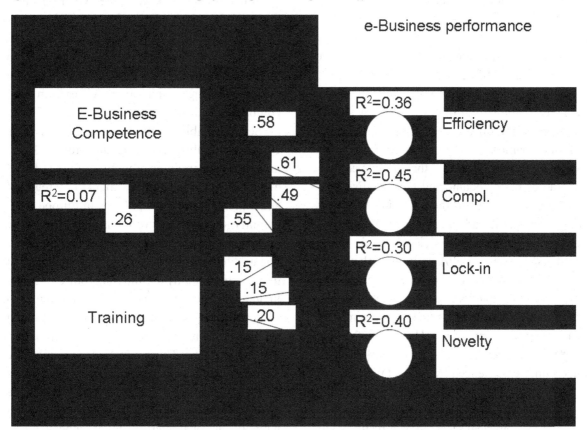

also support the proposition of Patton et al.(2000) that empirical studies should focus more on specific contexts when investigating the relationship between training and performance. Indeed, after implementing methodological improvements suggested by several authors our findings support the views that the ambiguities in the literature to a large extent are caused by methodological weaknesses in many empirical studies, thus hindering or obscuring the documentation of these relationships (e.g. Fuller-Love, 2006; Patton et al., 2000; Wade & Hulland, 2004).

Third, we have demonstrated that value creation in e-business can be explained by a limited set of e-business related competences as well as the demand and supply side of training. The competences which explained a substantial amount of e-business performance were competence in

e-business strategy and vision, competence in sourcing, and competence in process integration between IT and business. These competences explain a substantial amount of the variance in performance and should be considered by the SMEs in evaluating their e-business related competence level.

Public stimulation programs targeting SMEs would benefit from these results. Training providers should evaluate whether the content of their training programs sufficiently cover the competences identified in this study. Both public programs and training suppliers should be aware of the fact that the SMEs' lack of awareness and inability to invest in these training programs could represent significant barriers to developing e-business related competence and hence e-business performance.

Implications for SME Stimulation Programs

The crucial issue for agencies charged with the development of SME ICT capabilities is how they should best convey competence and skills to SMEs. Stimulation of SME training should be aware of the differences between SMEs and other companies, as well as the differences between SMEs. We have seen that various empirical studies have documented how SMEs differ from big companies in their training behavior. Bigger companies adopt more formal and proactive training than SMEs (Forth et al., 2006; Westhead & Storey, 1996). Current explanations for this difference include reduced awareness of new technology and its strategic potential among SME managers, as well as lack of awareness of available training programs (Harindranath et al., 2008), higher degree of external, market-based uncertainty experienced by SMEs (Westhead & Storey, 1996), as well as methodological explanations that informal training is more difficult to observe by empirical research as a result of the systematic nature of measurement rather than training (Barron, Berger, & Black, 1997; Forth et al., 2006).

We believe an obvious alternative explanation is financial risk. SMEs have limited financial resources and must be sensitive to their investments, including training programs. By being reactive rather than proactive, SMEs can start training "after the fact" when the need for competence is clear and backed up by their network or by direct market observations. This is risk reducing behavior which may be rational in a small business. If SMEs have more market-based, external uncertainties, then being reactive and waiting will most likely save financial resources. Being reactive will increase the likelihood of being made aware of training that is relevant for their specific industry, documented by the experiences made by other, trusted companies in their network. Training initiatives that comes early, e.g. from a public stimulation program, will most likely be met with reluctance due to the lack of validation from trusted partners in SMEs' network. It may be rational for SMEs to delay in adopting training that is perceived to be too risky, when direct evidence from the own market is lacking as well as experiences from other companies in the company's network.

Several public stimulation programs have experienced substantial reluctance from SMEs to take part in their training programs. In an EU-based evaluation and impact assessment of 10 regional and national e-business policies in Europe (EU-commission, 2005) recruitment of SMEs to the program is highlighted as one of the most problematic challenges. The evaluation concludes that the best stimulation programs targeting e-business included use of local networks for promotion and/or delivery of training services coupled with training content that was in line with SME needs and expectations. These experiences support the hypothesis that the local networks serve as lenses through which SMEs view and evaluate initiatives prior to their decision to participate. The local networks are characterized by an understanding of the nature of the SMEs, including their external market risks and need for competence. When the local network is included in the stimulation program uncertainties regarding the rigor, relevance and costs of the stimulation program are reduced. Thus, local networks create awareness and induce trust that reduces financial risk when SMEs decide on their behavior regarding training.

The importance of the network surrounding the SMEs has been highlighted by several researchers. In a study of supply chains in SMEs, low integration of networks was forwarded as a barrier to SME performance (Kim, Ow, & Jun, 2008). Bharati and Chaudhury (2006) studied the adoption of technologies by SMEs and found that the strongest influencing force to adoption were top management and customers in the business network. They found that the smallest SMEs had very low connections with their networks. These studies highlight the important role of business networks as well as the role of public-sector support agencies in providing training and support when SMEs lack an active business network.

We argue that future development programs targeting e-business training in SMEs should focus on the interplay between finance, awareness and trust (FAT) and design training strategies that take advantage of and use local networks as an important mechanism for creating sufficient levels of FAT in order to stimulate participation. We believe that FAT represents a mechanism that makes it rational for SMEs to delay their participation when FAT is not sufficient. Otherwise, the risks involved would be too high. Conversely, when the initiative is forwarded through the local network, FAT is most likely higher implying that the content can be trusted and not be a waste of time and money, which increases SME awareness and willingness to invest in the associated costs of training.

Awareness and trust are necessary but not sufficient for an SME to invest in training programs. Lack of financial ability could still hinder training. Our own empirical data presented in this chapter shows that the financial ability to invest in training programs increases with SME size in Finland, Norway and Spain (Figure 3). Figure 3 shows that the financial ability to invest in training is higher in the smallest SMEs in Spain and Norway than in Finland. As one can expect, the supply of training (Figure 4) to the smallest SMEs is also higher in Spain and Norway than in Finland. Figure 4 shows that providing training through the local network will not help when there is a shortage of funding. Public e-business stimulation programs in Spain were aware of this shortage of funding and targeted specific funding towards this SME-segment, making it possible for training providers to offer services to this segment. As a result, the training supply in Spain was more diverse than in

Figure 3. Ability to invest in training in different SME size segments

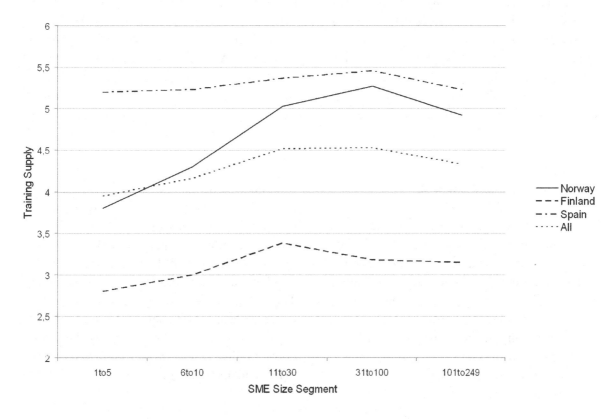

Figure 4. Training supply in different SME size segments

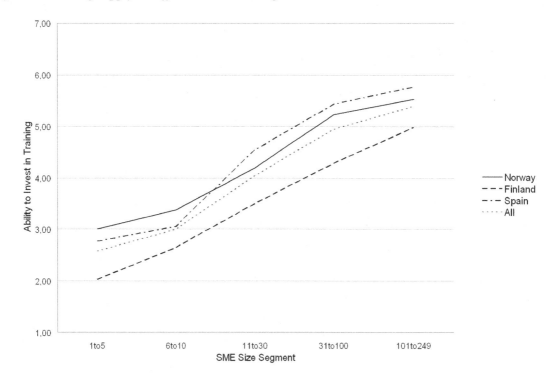

Scandinavia and contained consultancy as well as training available for all SME size segments. As we can see from Figure 4, Spain has almost an equal amount of training supply in all the SME size segments. It is likely that this is an important reason behind the higher level of e-business success that we observed among SMEs in Spain compared to Finland and Norway.

Implications for Future Research and Limitations

There is a need for more research into the nature of SMEs in general and into why training behavior and attitudes towards public stimulation programs seem to be different as a function of size. Future studies could explore why many international stimulation programs experience similar problems in recruiting SMEs to their programs. We believe that focusing on the role and importance of the local network in relation to the importance

of financial risk, awareness and trust in SMEs could provide answers as to why initiatives that utilize such networks seem to have a higher rate of success. As documented by (Harindranath et al., 2008), awareness of training programs among SME managers is necessary but not sufficient for utilizing the training, as documented by the review of European e-business policies (EU-commission, 2005).

Further research should also study the effects of public financing strategies targeting training in SMEs. The experiences from stimulating e-business in Spain, described above, points to an interesting effect of specific funding targeting the smallest of the SMEs in that the supply of training was more diverse than in Scandinavia. This could indicate that by introducing funds to cover the lack of financial ability, the market for training became more interesting for the suppliers of training, and hence they improved both the extent and diversity in their training supply. This implies that the local network may be overlooked and underutilized in public stimulation programs targeting SME development.

There is need for more studies on the issue of training and e-business competence, particularly in the context of SMEs. The lack of theoretical and empirical work on this topic and the results from our exploratory study, suggest that future research should devote more resources to further explore the importance of training, competence and performance in SMEs and investigate how improvements could influence the economy. Our findings suggest that context specificity is necessary to document effects of training and competence. Future studies should explore other contexts and investigate whether it is possible to generalize findings to other contexts or to SMEs in general.

Finally, development in important enterprise systems technologies such as "cloud computing" and "Software-as-a-Service" may alleviate some of the e-Business adoption problems for SMEs. These technologies may give SMEs an easy and inexpensive way to adopt e-Business by subscribing to e-Business services. What SME owners/ managers will need is competence on the strategic potential of the e-Business services.

This exploratory study has several limitations. Our data consist of subjective evaluations of e-business managers and training providers and are not necessarily reflecting objective facts. Future studies should include less subjective information about e-business performance and its antecedents. An interesting approach would be to follow e-business training programs over time with more in depth research methods focusing on how several characteristics of the training offered could influence the competence build up and the SME performance over time. Such studies should be followed by quantitative research methods that could test the hypotheses developed with the ability to generalize the results.

REFERENCES

Amit, R., & Zott, C. (2001). Value creation in e-business. *Strategic Management Journal*, *22*(6-7), 493–520. doi:10.1002/smj.187

Ballantine, J., Levy, M., & Powell, P. (1998). Evaluating information systems in small and medium-sized enterprises: issues and evidence. *European Journal of Information Systems*, *7*(4), 241–251. doi:10.1057/palgrave.ejis.3000307

Barron, J. M., Berger, M. C., & Black, D. A. (1997). How well do we measure training? *Journal of Labor Economics*, *15*(3), 507–528. doi:10.1086/209870

Bassellier, G., Reich, B. H., & Benbasat, I. (2001). Information technology competence of business managers: A definition and research model. *Journal of Management Information Systems*, *17*(4), 159–182.

Bharadwaj, A. S., Sambamurthy, V., & Zmud, R. W. (2000). *IT capabilities: theoretical perspectives and empirical operalization.* Paper presented at the 21st International Conference on Information Systems, Brisbane, Australia.

Bharati, P., & Chaudhury, A. (2006). Studying the Current Status of Technology Adoption. *Communications of the ACM*, *49*(10), 88–93. doi:10.1145/1164394.1164400

Bharati, P., & Chaudhury, A. (2009). SMEs and Competitiveness: The Role of Information Systems. *International Journal of E-Business Research*, *5*(1), i–ix.

Bollen, K. A. (1989). Structural equations with latent variables: Wiley-Interscience.

Boulay, D. A. (2008). An exploration of the relationships among organizational size, flexible work practices, training, and organizational performance using the 2002 national organizations survey. The Ohio State University.

Bryan, J. (2006). Training and Performance in Small Firms. *International Small Business Journal, 24*(6), 635–660. doi:10.1177/0266242606069270

Brynjolfsson, E., & Hitt, L. M. (1998). Beyond the productivity paradox. *Communications of the ACM, 41*(8), 49–55. doi:10.1145/280324.280332

Burke Jarvis, C., Mackenzie, S. B., & Podsakoff, P. M. (2003). A Critical Review of Construct Indicators and Measurement Model Misspecification in Marketing and Consumer Research. *The Journal of Consumer Research, 30*(September), 199–218. doi:10.1086/376806

Chin, W. W. (1998). The Partial Least Squares Approach for Structural Equation Modelling. In G. A. Marcoulides (Ed.), Modern Methods for Business Research. Hillsdale, NJ: Lawrence Erlbaum Associates.

Chin, W. W. (2001). PLS-Graph User's Guide, Version 3.0. Unpublished.

Chin, W. W., Marcolin, B. L., & Newsted, P. R. (1996). *A Partial Least Squares Latent Variable Modeling Approach for Measuring Interaction Effects: Results from a Monte Carlo Simulation Study and Voice Mail Emotion/Adoption Study.* Paper presented at the Seventeenth International Conference on Information Systems.

Clarke, R. (2003). If e-business is different, then so is reseach in e-business. In K. Viborg Andersen, S. Elliott, P. Swatman, E. M. Trauth & N. Bjørn-Andersen (Eds.), Seeking success in e-business. Boston, MA: Kluwer Academic Publishers.

Cosh, A., Duncan, J., & Hughes, A. (1998). *Investment in Training and Small Firm Growth and Survival: An Empirical Analysis for the UK 1987-95.* Dfee Publivations Research Report No. 36.

Dans, E. (2001). IT investment in small and medium enterprises: paradoxically productive? *The Electronic Journal of Information Systems Evaluation, 4*(1).

Davenport, T. H. (1993). Process Innovation: Re-engineering Work Through Information Technology. Boston: Harvard Business School Press.

Dean, J., Holmes, S., & Smith, S. (1997). Understanding Business Networks: Evidence from Manufacturing and Service Sectors in Australia. *Journal of Small Business Management, 35*(1), 79–84.

Debreceny, R., Putterill, M., Tung, L. L., & Gilbert, A. L. (2002). New tools for the determination of e-commerce inhibitors. *Decision Support Systems, 34*(2), 177–195. doi:10.1016/S0167-9236(02)00080-5

DeLone, W. H. (1988). Determinants of Success for Computer Usage in Small Business. *MIS Quarterly, 12*(1), 51–61. doi:10.2307/248803

Devins, J., & Johanson, S. (2003). Training and Development Activities in SMEs: Some Findings from an Evaluation of the OSF Objective 4 Programme in Britain. *International Small Business Journal, 22*(2), 205–218.

Edelman, L. F., Brush, C. G., & Manolova, T. S. (2002). The impact of human and organizational resources on small organizations strategy. *Journal of Small Business and Enterprise Development, 9*(3), 236–244. doi:10.1108/14626000210438562

Eikebrokk, T. R., & Olsen, D. H. (2007). An empirical investigation of competency factors affecting e-business success in European SMEs. *Information & Management, 44*(4). doi:10.1016/j.im.2007.02.004

European Commission. (2002a). *eEurope Go Digital - Benchmarking national and regional e-business policies for SMEs.*

European Commission. (2002b). *Synthesis Report - Benchmarking National and Regional e-Business Policies.*

European Commission. (2004). *SME definitions*. Retrieved Marsh 23, 2004, from http://europa.eu.int/comm/enterprise/enterprise_policy/sme_definition/index_en.htm

Feeny, D. F., & Willcocks, L. P. (1998). Core IS capabilities for exploiting information technology. *Sloan Management Review, 39*(3), 9–21.

Fillis, I., Johannson, U., & Wagner, B. (2003). A conceptualisation of the opportunities and barriers to e-business developemnt in the smaller firm. *Journal of Small Business and Enterprise Development, 10*(3), 336–341. doi:10.1108/14626000310489808

Fornell, C. (1982). A Second generation of multivariate analysis. New York: Praeger.

Fornell, C., & Larcker, D. F. (1981). Evaluating Structural Equation Models with Unobservable Variables and Measurement Error. *JMR, Journal of Marketing Research, 28*, 39–50. doi:10.2307/3151312

Forth, J., Bewley, H., & Bryson, A. (2006). Small and medium-sized enterprises: findings from the 2004 Workplace Employee Relations Survey. University of Westminster.

Fuller-Love, N. (2006). Management development in small firms. *International Journal of Management Reviews, 8*(3), 175–190. doi:10.1111/j.1468-2370.2006.00125.x

Golden, P. A., & Dollinger, M. (1993). Cooperative Alliances and Competitive Strategies in Small Manufacturing Firms. *Entrepreneurship Theory and Practice*, 43-56.

Grandon, E. E., & Pearson, J. M. (2004). Electronic commerce adoption: an empirical study of small and medium US businesses. *Information & Management, 42*, 197–216.

Gray, C. (2004). Management development in small and medium enterprises. *Advances in Developing Human Resources, 6*(4), 451–469. doi:10.1177/1523422304268381

Hair, J. F., Anderson, R. E., Tatham, R. L., & Black, W. C. (1992). Multivariate Data Analysis. New York: Macmillan Publishing Company.

Hammer, M. (1990). Reengineering work: Don't Automate, Obliterate. *Harvard Business Review, 68*(4).

Harindranath, G., Dyerson, R., & Barnes, D. (2008). ICT Adoption and Use in UK SMEs: a Failure of Initiatives? *The Electronic Journal of Information Systems Evaluation, 11*(2), 91–96.

Heijden, H. d. (2000). *Measuring IT core capabilities for electronic commerce: results from a confirmatory analysis*. Paper presented at the 21st International Conference on Information Systems, Brisbane, Australia.

Hill, R., & Stewart, J. (1999). Human resource development in small organizations. *Human Resource Development International, 2*(2), 103–123. doi:10.1080/13678869900000013

Huang, T. (2001). The relation of training practices and organizational performance on small and medium size enterprises. *Education + Training, 43*(8/9), 437-444.

Ihlström, C., & Nilsson, M. (2003). E-business adoption by SMEs - Prerequisites and attitudes of SMEs in a Swedish network. *Journal of Organizational Computing and Electronic Commerce, 13*(3-4), 211–223. doi:10.1207/S15327744JOCE133&4_04

Ivis, M. (2001). Analysis of barriers impeding e-business adoption among Canadian SMEs: Canadian E-Business Opportunities Roundtable.

Jarratt, D. G. (1998). A Strategic Classification of Business Alliances: A Qualitative Perspective Built from a Study of Small and Medium-sized Enterprises. *Qualitative Market Research: An International Journal, 1*(1), 39–49. doi:10.1108/13522759810368442

Jarvis, C. B., Mackenzie, S. B., & Podsakoff, P. M. (2003). A critical review of construct indicators and measurement model misspecification in marketing and consumer research. *The Journal of Consumer Research, 30*(september), 199–218. doi:10.1086/376806

Johansson, N., & Mollstedt, U. (2006). Revisiting Amit and Zott's model of value creation sources: The SymBelt Customer Center case. *Journal of Theoretical and Applied Electronic Commerce Research, 1*(3), 16–27.

Johnson, S. (2002). Lifelong learning and SMEs: Issues and research for policy. *Journal of Small Business and Enterprise Development, 9*(3), 285–295. doi:10.1108/14626000210438607

Johnston, K., Shi, J., Dann, Z., & Barcay, I. (2006). Knowledge, power and trust in SME e-based virtual organisations. *International Journal of Networking & Virtual Organizations, 3*(1), 42–59. doi:10.1504/IJNVO.2006.008784

Jöreskog, K. G., & Wold, H. (1982). Systems under indirect observation: Causality, structure, prediction: North-Holland.

Keen, P. G. W. (1991). Redesigning the organization through Information Technology. *Planning Review, 19*(3).

Kim, D., Ow, T. T., & Jun, M. (2008). SME Strategies: An Assessment Of High vs. Low Performers. *Communications of the ACM, 51*(11), 113–117. doi:10.1145/1400214.1400237

Kinkaide, P. (2000). The New Frontier: SME's Enterprise and E-Business in Western Canada. Edmonton.

Kitching, J., & Blackburn, R. (2002). *The nature of training and motivation to train in small firms*: Kingston University: Small Business Research Centre.

Lawrence, K. L. (1997). *Factors Inhibiting the Utilisation of Electronic Commerce Facilities in Tasmanian Small-to-Medium Sized Enterprises.* Paper presented at the 8th Australasian Conference on Information Systems.

Lee, C. S. (2001). An analytical Framework for Evaluting E-commerce Business Models and Strategies. *Internet Research: Electronic Network Applications and Policy, 11*(4), 349–359. doi:10.1108/10662240110402803

Lee, D. M. S., Trauth, E. M., & Farwell, D. (1995). Critical Skills and Knowledge Requirements of Is Professionals - a Joint Academic-Industry Investigation. *MIS Quarterly, 19*(3), 313–340. doi:10.2307/249598

Lee, J.-N. (2001). The impact of knowledge sharing, organizational capability and partnership quality on IS outsourcing success. *Information & Management, 38*, 323–335. doi:10.1016/S0378-7206(00)00074-4

Lee, S., & Lim, G. G. (2005). The impact of partnership attributes on EDI implementation success. *Information & Management, 42*, 503–516. doi:10.1016/S0378-7206(03)00153-8

Lewis, R., & Cockrill, A. (2002). Going global-remaining local: the impact of e-commerce on small retail firms in Wales. *International Journal of Information Management, 22*(3), 195–209. doi:10.1016/S0268-4012(02)00005-1

Love, P. E. D., & Irani, Z. (2004). An exploratory study of information technology evaluation and benefits management practices of SMEs in the construction industry. *Information & Management, 42*, 227–242.

Lynch, L. M., & Black, S. E. (1998). Beyond the incidence of employer-provided training. *Industrial & Labor Relations Review*, *52*(1), 64–81. doi:10.2307/2525243

MacGregor, R. C. (2004). The Role of Strategic Alliances in the Ongoing Use of Electronic Commerce Technology in Regional Small Business. *Journal of Electronic Commerce in Organizations*, *2*(1), 1–14.

Marlow, S. (1998). So Much Opportunity -- So Little Take-up: The Case of Training in Small Firms. *Small Business and Enterprise Development*, *5*(1), 38–47. doi:10.1108/EUM0000000006729

Maton, K. (1999). Evaluation of Small Firms Training Loans: UK Research Partnerships Ltd., Dfee Publications.

Mehrtens, J., Cragg, P. B., & Mills, A. B. (2001). A model of Internet adoption by SMEs. *Information & Management*, *39*, 165–176. doi:10.1016/S0378-7206(01)00086-6

Moore, R., Blake, D., Phillips, G., & McConaughty, D. (2003). Training that works: Lessons from California's Employment Training Panel program. Kalamazoo, MI: W.E. Upjohn Institute.

Mowshowitz, A. (1997). Virtual Organization. *Communications of the ACM*, *40*(9). doi:10.1145/260750.260759

Nunnally, J. C. (1978). Psychometric theory (2nd ed.). New York: McGraw-Hill.

Patton, D., Marlow, S., & Hannon, P. (2000). The Relationship Between Training and Small Firm Performance, Research Frameworks and Lost Quests. *International Small Business Journal*, *19*(1), 11–27. doi:10.1177/0266242600191001

Peppard, J., Lambert, R., & Edwards, C. (2000). Whose job is it anyway? organizational information competencies for value creation. *Information Systems Journal*, *10*, 291–322. doi:10.1046/j.1365-2575.2000.00089.x

Premaratne, S. P. (2001). Networks, Resources and Small Business Growth: The Experience in Sri Lanka. *Journal of Small Business Management*, *39*(4), 363–371. doi:10.1111/0447-2778.00033

Rayport, J. F., & Sviokla, J. J. (1995, November-December). Exploiting the Virtual Value Chain. *Harvard Business Review*, •••, 75–85.

Rosenfeld, S. (1996). Does Cooperation Enhance Competitiveness? Assessing the Impacts of Inter-firm Collaboration. *Research Policy*, *25*(2), 247–263. doi:10.1016/0048-7333(95)00835-7

Rowden, R. (2002). The relationship between workplace learning and job satisfaction in U.S. smal to midsize businesses. *Human Resource Development Quarterly*, *13*(4), 407–425. doi:10.1002/hrdq.1041

Saeed, K. A., Grover, V., & Hwang, Y. (2005). The relationship of e-commerce to customer value and firm performance: an empirical investigation. *Journal of Management Information Systems*, *22*(1), 223–256.

Sambamurthy, V., Bharadwaj, A., & Grover, V. (2003). Shaping agility through digital options: Reconceptualizing the role of information technology in contemporary firms. *MIS Quarterly*, *27*(2), 237–263.

Sambamurthy, V., & Zmud, R. W. (1994). IT management competency assessment: a tool for creating business value through IT. Morristown, New Jersey: Financial Executives Research Foundation.

Shi, Z., Kunnathur, A. S., & Ragu-Nathan, T. S. (2005). IS outsourcing management competence dimensions: instrument development and relationship exploration. *Information & Management*, *42*(6), 901–919. doi:10.1016/j.im.2004.10.001

Storey, D. (2004). Exploring the link, among small firms, between management training and firm performance: a comparison between the UK and other OECD countries. *International Journal of Human Resource Management, 15*(1), 112–130. doi:10.1080/0958519032000157375

Tetteh, E., & Burn, J. (2001). Global Strategies for SME-business: Applying the SMALL Framework. *Logistics Information Management, 14*(1/2), 171–180. doi:10.1108/09576050110363202

Timmers, P. (1999). Electronic commerce: strategies and models for business-to-business trading. West Sussex, UK: John Wiley & Sons Ltd.

Troshani, I., & Rao, S. (2007). Enabling e-business competitive advantage: perspectives from the Australian Financial Services Industry. *International Journal of Business and Information, 2*(1), 80–103.

United States Department of Education. (2004). *National household education surveys of successful small manufacturing and processing companies*: National Center forEducations Statistics.

Wade, M. R., & Hulland, J. (2004). Review: The resource-based view and information systems research: review, extension, and suggestions for future research. *MIS Quarterly, 28*(1), 107–142.

Westhead, P., & Storey, D. (1996). Management Training and Small Firm Performance: Why is the Link so Weak? *International Small Business Journal, 14*(4), 13–25. doi:10.1177/0266242696144001

Westhead, P., & Storey, D. (1997). Training Provision and the Development of Small and Medium-sized Enterprises. London: Dfee.

APPENDIX 1. DESCRIPTIVE STATISTICS (FIGURE 5, FIGURE 6)

Figure 5. SME sample

Item	n	Mean	Std. Deviation
Q1	339	29,52	34,84
Q2	339	1,00	,00
Q3	339	2,06	,80
Q5	321	4,38	1,74
Q6	327	4,43	1,42
Q7	309	4,72	1,55
Q8	299	4,34	1,72
Q9	330	4,74	1,45
Q10	325	4,32	1,42
Q11	261	3,66	1,90
Q12	258	3,84	1,91
Q13	303	4,20	1,76
Q14	274	3,78	1,76
Q15	283	3,98	1,75
Q16	286	3,60	1,78
Q17	287	2,97	1,73
Q18	299	3,76	1,81
Q19	309	2,93	1,85
Q20	307	3,75	1,76
E-bus. Efficiency	234	3,89	1,64
E-bus. Complem.	255	3,79	1,59
E-bus. Lock-in	276	3,34	1,55
E-bus. Novelty	299	3,36	1,59
Valid N (listwise)	172		

Figure 6. E-business systems used in the SME sample

E-business systems	# SMEs	Per cent
Web pages with information to individual customers about products and services (V4a)	256	75,5
Web pages where individual customers can make orders (V4b)	134	39,5
Web pages where companies can find information about products and services (V4c)	270	79,6
Systems for electronic sales of products and services to other companies (V4d)	51	15
EDI solutions on the Internet (V4e)	73	21,5
Systems where suppliers can find information about our demand and supply (V4f)	62	18,3
Systems that integrate supply chains (V4g)	36	10,6
Other (V4h)	102	30,1

APPENDIX 2. THE SURVEY INSTRUMENT FOR SMES

Country: O Finland O Norway O Spain

Introduction to Respondent

This interview is part of a project that investigates the use of e-commerce or e-business in small and medium-sized companies in Europe. In this interview you will be presented with questions about e-business, which can be defined as utilizing technologies for conducting business over the Internet. This implies all types of business interactions over the Internet with suppliers, customers and other business partners.

We ask you to answer as correct as possible based on the knowledge you have of your company. This survey is anonymous and we guarantee that it will not be possible to trace any of the answers back to you and your company.

Background information (Table 4)

Table 4.

Q1.	Approximately how many employees are there in your company? _____ **employees**								
Q2.	In what type of industry is your company? O **Tourism** O **Transport** O **Food & Beverages**								
Q3.	Does your company use web pages, e-mail or e-commerce systems for business purposes?O **Yes** O **No**								
Q4.	What types of e-business systems does your company use? (multiple responses possible)								
	O web pages whith information to individual customers about products or services								
	O web pages where individual customers can make orders								
	O web pages where companies can find information about products or services								
	O systems for electronic sales of products and services to other companies								
	O EDI solutions on the Internet								
	O systems that enables your suppliers to see information about your demand or production								
	O systems that integrates supply chains								
	O other								
Q5.	To what extent are IT activities in your company outsourced to external providers?	a very low extent	1　2　3　4　5　6　7						a very high extent
Q6.	To what extent is your company informed about commercially available e-business systems?	a very low extent	1　2　3　4　5　6　7						a very high extent
Q7.	To what extent is your company informed about providers of e-business related training?	a very low extent	1　2　3　4　5　6　7						a very high extent
Q8.	To what extent has your company implemented its e-business intentions?	a very low extent	1　2　3　4　5　6　7						a very high extent

In the next section we would like you to assess your company's level of competence in various topics related to e-business. The questions are in the form of propositions. We ask you to give your evaluation of how accurately you feel that these propositions describe the situation in your company. If you find that any of the propositions are irrelevant, please indicate so by answering "not applicable". Please indicate how well you agree with the proposition by answering a number between 1: totally disagree and up to 7: totally agree.

Strategy and Vision

The Concept of E-Business (Table 5)

Table 5.

		totally disagree						*totally agree*	*N/A*
Q10.	Our company has a high level of knowledge of how e-business technologies can be of value to our business	1	2	3	4	5	6	7	☐
Q11.	Our company has a high level of knowledge of how our main competitor(s) use IT to support similar business areas	1	2	3	4	5	6	7	☐
Q12.	In general, e-business is well understood by my company	1	2	3	4	5	6	7	☐

Strategic Planning (Table 6)

Table 6.

		totally disagree						totally agree	N/A
Q13.	Our company has a high level of knowledge of strategic planning	1	2	3	4	5	6	7	☐
Q14.	Our company has a well developed set of strategic planning techniques	1	2	3	4	5	6	7	☐
Q15.	In general, strategic planning is well understood by our company	1	2	3	4	5	6	7	☐

Sourcing and Alignment

Sourcing Competencies (Table 7)

Table 7.

		totally disagree						totally agree	N/A
Q16.	Our company has a high level of knowledge on outsourcing of activities to other companies	1	2	3	4	5	6	7	☐
Q17.	Our company has a high level of knowledge on how to use competencies in our business partners	1	2	3	4	5	6	7	☐

Alignment Competencies (Table 8)

Table 8.

		totally disagree						totally agree	N/A
Q18.	In my company business and IT managers very much agree on how IT contributes to business value	1	2	3	4	5	6	7	☐
Q19.	In my company there is effective exchange of ideas between business people and IT people	1	2	3	4	5	6	7	☐
Q20.	In general, my company is good at using the competencies it already has	1	2	3	4	5	6	7	☐
Q21.	In general, my company is good at using competencies represented in our business partners	1	2	3	4	5	6	7	☐

IT-Business Process Integration

Competence in Process Integration (Table 9)
Table 9.

		totally disagree						totally agree	N/A
Q22.	My company is actively working with the impact of e-business on its business processes	1	2	3	4	5	6	7	☐
Q23.	In general, my company is good at reorganizing work to utilize new information technology	1	2	3	4	5	6	7	☐

Management of IT (Table 10)
Table 10.

		totally disagree						totally agree	N/A
Q24.	My company's IT resources are effectively managed	1	2	3	4	5	6	7	☐
Q25.	My company is good at achieving the anticipated benefits from IT investments	1	2	3	4	5	6	7	☐

Systems and Infrastructure (Table 11)
Table 11.

		totally disagree						totally agree	N/A
Q26.	The systems infrastructure is very flexible in relation to my company's future needs	1	2	3	4	5	6	7	☐
Q27.	The IT systems make it possible for my company to effectively cooperate electronically with business partners	1	2	3	4	5	6	7	☐

In the last section we would like you to assess your company's experiences with the effects of its e-business efforts. We ask you to give your evaluation of what you feel has come out of your company's e-business efforts.

E-Business Success

Efficiency (Table 12)
Table 12.

		totally disagree						totally agree	N/A
Q28.	Our e-business efforts have reduced costs by electronic order taking over the Internet	1	2	3	4	5	6	7	☐
Q29.	Our e-business efforts have made us able to deliver faster	1	2	3	4	5	6	7	☐
Q30.	Our e-business efforts have reduced costs in communication with suppliers and customers	1	2	3	4	5	6	7	☐

Complementarities (Table 13)

Table 13.

		totally disagree						totally agree	N/A
Q31.	As a result of our e-business efforts our products or services complement products or services from other suppliers	1	2	3	4	5	6	7	☐
Q32.	Our business efforts make it possible for other suppliers to complement our products or services	1	2	3	4	5	6	7	☐
Q33.	Our e-business efforts have made our supply chain strongly integrated to our partners' supply chains	1	2	3	4	5	6	7	☐

Lock-In (Table 14)

Table 14.

		totally disagree						totally agree	N/A
Q34.	Our e-business efforts make it more expensive for our customers or suppliers to replace us	1	2	3	4	5	6	7	☐
Q35.	Our e-business efforts have made our products and services more tailored to our customers' needs	1	2	3	4	5	6	7	☐

Novelty (Table 15)

Table 15.

		totally disagree						totally agree	N/A
Q36.	Our e-business efforts have made our company a pioneer in utilizing e-commerce solutions	1	2	3	4	5	6	7	☐
Q37.	Our e-business efforts have made us cooperating with our customers or suppliers in new and innovative ways	1	2	3	4	5	6	7	☐

General (Table 16)

Table 16.

		totally disagree						totally agree	N/A
Q38.	In general, my company has experienced very positive effects from its e-business efforts	1	2	3	4	5	6	7	☐

Other/Control

Leader vs. Follower (Table 17)
Table 17.

		totally disagree						totally agree	N/A
Q39.	There is a dominating customer or supplier who dictates our e-business efforts	1	2	3	4	5	6	7	☐
Q40.	Our company is good at implementing changes in its organization	1	2	3	4	5	6	7	☐
Q41.	Overall, my company has a high level of competence for utilizing e-business technology	1	2	3	4	5	6	7	☐

APPENDIX 3. THE SURVEY INSTRUMENT FOR TRAINING SUPPLIERS (TABLE 18)
Table 18.

V1.	Approximately, how many employees are there in your company? _____ employees						
V2.	Does your company off e-business-related training and courses?: ☐ Yes, ☐ No						
V3.	Does your company off software related to e-business solutions to SMEs?: ☐ Yes, ☐ No						
V4.	Does your company offer training and courses, which assist SMEs in utilizing web pages or e-commerce systems? ☐ Yes, ☐ No						
V5.	To what extent do you supply training and courses to these categories of SMEs						
		Not at all					Very large extent
	1-5 employees	1	2	3	4	5	6	7
	6-10 employees	1	2	3	4	5	6	7
	11-30 employees	1	2	3	4	5	6	7
	31-100 employees	1	2	3	4	5	6	7
	101-250 employees	1	2	3	4	5	6	7
V6.	To what extent are SMEs informed about providers of e-business related training?	a very low extent 1 2 3 4 5 6 7 a very high extent
V7.	In your view, to what extent are SMEs successfully implementing e-business efforts?	a very low extent 1 2 3 4 5 6 7 a very high extent
V8.	In your view, to what extent do the following types of SMEs have sufficient financial resources to invest in training programs?						
		Not at all					*Very large extent*
	1-5 employees	1	2	3	4	5	6	7
	6-10 employees	1	2	3	4	5	6	7
	11-30 employees	1	2	3	4	5	6	7
	31-100 employees	1	2	3	4	5	6	7
	101-250 employees	1	2	3	4	5	6	7
In this section we would like you to focus on the building of competencies in SMEs. As a provider of training and courses to what extent do you stimulate building of competence in the following areas?							

		Not at all					Very large extent	
V9.	The value of e-business solutions for SMEs	1	2	3	4	5	6	7
V10.	The utilization of e-business solutions in the customer's industry	1	2	3	4	5	6	7
V11.	General understanding of e-business	1	2	3	4	5	6	7
V12.	Strategic planning in general	1	2	3	4	5	6	7
V13.	The use of strategic planning techniques	1	2	3	4	5	6	7
V14.	Outsourcing in general	1	2	3	4	5	6	7
V15.	Sourcing of e-business related competencies	1	2	3	4	5	6	7
V16.	Alignment of IT and business	1	2	3	4	5	6	7
V17.	Consensus building between IT and business people	1	2	3	4	5	6	7
V18.	Utilizing competencies in the organization	1	2	3	4	5	6	7
V19.	Utilizing competencies in business partners	1	2	3	4	5	6	7
V20.	The improvement of business processes	1	2	3	4	5	6	7
V21.	Process integration between IT and business	1	2	3	4	5	6	7
V22.	Reengineering work to utilize new information technology	1	2	3	4	5	6	7
V23.	Change management in general	1	2	3	4	5	6	7
V24.	Change management in relation to IT-investments	1	2	3	4	5	6	7
V25.	IT management	1	2	3	4	5	6	7
V26.	The ability to realize benefits of IT-investments	1	2	3	4	5	6	7
V27.	IT systems infrastructure	1	2	3	4	5	6	7
V28.	Effective electronic cooperation between business partners	1	2	3	4	5	6	7

Chapter 13
Deploying the Internet for Leveraging Strategic Assets

Frank Schlemmer
Optik Schlemmer, Germany

Brian Webb
Queen's University Belfast, UK

ABSTRACT

SMEs frequently suffer from resource poverty. The authors suggest that the Internet can be used to leverage their strategic assets and propose a theoretical framework with the independent variables business resources, dynamic capabilities and IT assets. Survey data of 146 small firms suggest that the Internet is complementary with business resources and dynamic capabilities but not with IT assets. This research may enable small firm managers to create competitive advantage by identifying strategic assets that are complementary with the Internet. Furthermore, the authors highlight the threat of an over-investment in IT assets at SMEs[i].

INTRODUCTION

In contrast to large companies small and medium-sized enterprises (SMEs) frequently suffer from 'resource poverty' (Welsh and White, 1981; Bharati and Chaudhury, 2009), which often affects strategy development and creates perceptual and physical barriers to growth (Fillis, Johansson and Wagner, 2004). For example, small companies usually have fewer financial and human resources (Chow, Haddad and Williamson, 1997; Ihlstrom and Nilsson, 2003; Gribbins and King, 2004, Montazemi,

2006). However, according to the resource-based view of the firm (RBV) the value of strategic assets can be increased if they are combined with other strategic assets, which is called complementarity. Complementarity can be defined as "an enhancement of resource value, [which] arises when a resource produces greater returns in the presence of another resource than it does alone" (Powell and Dent-Micallef 1997, p.379). Teece (1986, p.301) suggests that complementary assets are especially important for small companies because, in contrast to their larger competitors, they "are less likely to have the relevant specialized and cospecialized assets within their boundaries and so will either have

DOI: 10.4018/978-1-61520-627-8.ch013

to incur the expense of trying to build them, or of trying to develop coalitions with competitors/owners of the specialized assets". However, the complementarity of strategic assets is typically taken for granted but has hardly been empirically scrutinised, and non-anecdotal studies analyzing the interaction effects of strategic assets within a firm are frequently inconclusive (Powell and Dent-Micallef 1997; Song, Droge, Hanvanich and Calantone 2005; Zhu and Kraemer 2002)[ii]. Therefore, Song et al. (p.271) conclude "clearly, resource combinations do not always lead to synergistic performance impact."

This chapter seeks to analyze whether strategic assets are complementary with the Internet. It contributes to the underdeveloped research on complementarity by introducing the Internet as a complementary resource. The authors argue that the Internet can be extremely important for SMEs, and that it can be used to "level the playing field" (Wigand, Steinfeld and Markus, 2005). This research aims at providing SME managers with information about which strategic assets can be leveraged by the Internet. Based on the literature review and survey data the authors suggest that researchers should examine complementarity at research settings in which a clear distinction of strategic assets is feasible. This chapter is organized as follows. In the next section the literature on the resource-based view and complementarity is briefly reviewed and the hypotheses are presented. After that, the research methodology is described; followed by the results. And then the discussion, the conclusions, the limitations, and some suggestions for future research are offered.

The Internet as a Complementary Resource

According to the resource-based view of the firm (RBV), firms perform differently because they differ in terms of the strategic assets they control (Barney 1991; Penrose 1959; Wernerfelt 1984). The founding idea of viewing a firm as a bundle of

strategic assets was pioneered in 1959 by Penrose in her theory of the growth of the firm. This research focuses especially on the complementarity of the Internet. Under the resource-based view, a complementary interaction typically enhances the value for both (or all) strategic assets, although the causality may be ambiguous (Barney, 1991). Yet, researchers have only started to analyze complementarity of strategic assets. Current empirical work can be divided in the following two research streams.

One stream of research focuses on complementarity of strategic assets that are not controlled by a single firm, for example at strategic alliances or at mergers and acquisitions. For example, Rothaermel (2001) found that firms focusing on complementarity outperform those firms that limit their focus on the exploration of new technologies. Stuart (2000) suggested that the reputation of a larger firm is a complementary resource for a smaller firm. In particular, an alliance with a larger firm can help a smaller firm build confidence and attract customers, which then drives financial performance for both partners. Chung, Singh, and Lee (2000) suggest that banks tend to ally with other banks which can complement their weaknesses. Krishnan, Miller, and Judge (1997) suggest that complementary top management teams (defined as differences in functional backgrounds between acquiring and acquired firm managers) drive post-acquisition firm performance. In the same vein, Capron and Pistre (2002) argue that acquirers only earn abnormal returns when their strategic assets are complementary with the target and not if they only receive strategic assets from the target.

The second research stream focuses on complementarity within a company. Powell and Dent-Micallef (1997) examined complementarity of IT assets with business resources and human resources and came to inconclusive results. Similarly, Song et al. (2005) found complementarity between marketing-related capabilities and technology-related capabilities only in high, but not in low technology turbulent environments. Zhu and Kraemer (2002) examined the relationship of dynamic capabilities and firm performance and came to inconsistent results for traditional versus technology companies. In contrast, Zhu (2004) empirically demonstrated complementarity between IT infrastructure and e-Commerce capability.

In conclusion, research on complementarity can be divided into two research streams. The first one is about complementarity of both, internal strategic assets (those that are controlled by a firm) and external strategic assets (those that are controlled by other firms), and the second research stream is about complementarity of internal strategic assets (assets within a single firm). Whereas research of the first category yielded convincing results (for example Rothaermel 2001; Capron and Pistre 2002) the inconclusiveness of research of the second category suggests that further work in this area is necessary (Powell and Dent-Micallef 1997; Song et al. 2005). A possible explanation for researchers' problems in evaluating the complementarity of internal strategic assets is that this would require a clear distinction between the different strategic assets (the independent variables). In other words it would be necessary to "unbundle" the performance-driving strategic assets, which appears to be impossible, considering that every firm's bundle of strategic assets is unique (Penrose, 1959). The authors therefore suggest searching for research settings in which an evaluation of separated strategic assets is more feasible, because this frequently yielded valuable insights, for example at strategic alliances (Rothaermel 2001; Stuart, 2000) or at mergers and acquisitions (Krishnan et al. 1997; Carpon and Pistre, 2002).

The authors suggest that the Internet itself can be a complementary resource, and analyze if the Internet is complementary with strategic assets. In particular, the authors analyze if there is an interaction effect between a construct labelled Internet performance and the relationship between strategic assets and financial performance.

Research Model

The authors believe that the Internet can be seen as a complementary resource. For example it may enable a firm to enhance its supplier relationships, while the pre-existing supplier relationships maximize the Internet's inherent information-sharing capabilities. The ubiquitous Internet would be a commodity resource, yet it may be combined with supplier trust to an embedded, mutually reinforcing, advantage producing resource bundle (Barua et al. 2004; Powell and Dent-Micallef 1997). Zhu (2004) demonstrated complementarity of IT infrastructure and e-Commerce capability. However, this research focuses especially on the attributes of the Internet as opposed to Zhu's e-Commerce capability. In particular, the authors argue that the Internet can be seen as an external strategic asset that can be used by any competing firm (further discussed below), and use the Powell and Dent-Micallef (1997) framework for examining complementarity of business resources, dynamic capabilities, and IT assets with the Internet (see Figure 1).

Powell and Dent-Micallef's (1997) model for analyzing the relationships of business resources, human resources, and IT resources with performance is based on the work of Walton (1989) and Keen (1993). Powell and Dent-Micallef's measures were especially designed for large enterprises with human resources departments and cross-sectional teams. These measures appeared to be inappropriate for small companies, which perform activities with less expertise, because they don't have functional specialists. In contrast to large firms, small firms' capabilities are mainly determined by the owner manager and not by department managers (Verhees and Meulenberg 2004; Jones 2004). Furthermore, Powell and Dent-Micallef used human resources as an independent variable. In this study the newer concept of dynamic capabilities will be used instead, because it appeared to be more appropriate for small firms, because it evaluates the skills on an organiza-

Figure 1. Research model

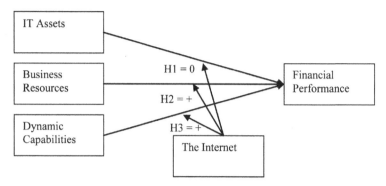

tional rather than a department-level, and it puts a high emphasis on flexibility (in contrast to most human resources measures), and flexibility is a typical strength of small firms (Dean et al. 1998; Verdu-Jover et al. 2006). Furthermore, the theoretical concept of dynamic capabilities is deeply embedded in the resource-based view, whereas most theories on human resources appeared to have other theoretical groundings.

Definitions of resources, capabilities, and strategic assets are shown in Table 1.[iii] They are all taken out of the literature. A description of the independent variables (strategic assets) and the hypotheses follows.

IT Assets

Tippins and Sohi's (2003) model was used for this study. They define IT assets as "the extent to which a firm is knowledgeable about and effectively utilizes IT to manage information within the firm." (Tippins and Sohi 2003, p.748). Their

construct consists of IT knowledge, IT operations, and IT objects. *IT knowledge* is the extent to which a firm possesses a body of technical knowledge about objects such as computer based systems. *IT operations* are conceptualized as the extent to which a firm utilizes IT to manage market and customer information. *IT objects* represent computer-based hardware, software and support personnel.

Mata et al. (1995) analyzed the relationship between IT assets and competitive advantage. They focus especially on two underlying assertions of the RBV: (1) strategic assets differ between competing firms (resource heterogeneity) and (2) these differences are long lasting (resource immobility). [iv] They conclude that those IT systems that are used by several competing firms can't be a source of competitive advantage because the assertion of resource heterogeneity is not met. Furthermore, IT could only be a source of sustainable competitive advantage if firms without it are at competitive disadvantage acquiring, developing, and using it

Table 1. Definitions

	Authors	Definition
Resources	Amit and Schoemaker, 1993	Stocks of available factors that are owned or controlled by the firm.
Dynamic capabilities	Teece et al., 1997	The firm's ability to integrate, build, and reconfigure internal and external strategic assets.
Strategic assets	Amit and Schoemaker, 1993	A set of difficult to trade and imitate, scarce, appropriable, and specialized resources and capabilities that bestow the firm's competitive advantage

(resource immobility). The majority of IT assets may be easily copied by competing firms, and subsequently research on the relationship of IT assets with financial performance is frequently inconclusive, and most studies fail to demonstrate IT's direct performance impacts (see Wade and Hulland 2004 for a review). However, Clemons and Row (1991) suggested that even if IT per se can't create sustainable competitive advantage, it can be used to leverage other strategic assets.

The authors argue that the same logic applies analogously to the Internet. The Internet does not fulfill any of the two criteria: It can be used by any company, and does therefore not fulfill the assertion of resource heterogeneity. Furthermore it is ubiquitous, and therefore doesn't fulfill the assertion of resource immobility. Subsequently, deploying the Internet can't be a source of competitive advantage. However, it may be possible to use the Internet for leveraging strategic assets (like for example dynamic capabilities and business resources) (Fernandez and Nieto, 2006). In this section a set of hypotheses will be offered which suggest complementarity of strategic assets (business resources and dynamic capabilities) with the Internet. However, this does *not* apply to IT assets. The authors argue that both IT assets and the Internet don't fulfill the requirements of resource heterogeneity and resource immobility, and therefore can be used by any competing firm. Combining strategic assets that are ubiquitous can't be a source of competitive advantage. It is therefore suggested that:

Hypothesis 1: *IT assets are not complementary to the Internet.*

(Please note that this is the only hypothesis that does not imply complementarity.)

Business Resources

In addition to the IT assets the authors also included strategic assets that might be complementary with the Internet. Following Powell and Dent-Micallef's (1997), business resources were defined as a set of strategic assets that can be used in combination with the Internet for creating competitive advantage. Business resources were divided into five sub-resources: relationships with customers and suppliers; external-driven e-business; benchmarking; strategic use of the Internet; and financial resources. Each of them are now considered in turn.

Supplier relationships are becoming increasingly essential and strategic (Quayle, 2002, Cousins and Spekman 2003), and they play an important role for integrating processes via the Internet (Porter 2001, Tanner et al., 2008). The capacity to craft and maintain trusting and economically viable supplier relationships, and then to leverage these relationships with the Internet, requires tacit, complex coordination and communication skills that competitors may find difficult to imitate (Hall 1993; Winter, 1987, Pollard and Diggles, 2006). This is especially important for SMEs that participate in supply chains (Kim et al., 2008).

Customer relationships are a critical success factor in e-business (Schroder and Madeja, 2004), especially for SMEs (Manley, 2008). Keller Johnson (2002) argued that companies that already excel in managing customer relationships can use the Internet for further improving them. Su, Chen and Sha (2007) highlight the importance of technology for managing customer knowledge in the digital economy, and Letaifa and Perrien (2007) suggest that successful implementation of e-CRM tools requires an innovative and customer-driven culture. Winter, Gaglio and Rajagopalan (2009) suggested that SMEs which lack at adopting IT can face difficulties in acquiring customers. Zhu et al. (2002) and Xu, Rohatgi and Duan (2007) found that a lack of trading partner readiness to adopt e-Business is a significant e-business adoption inhibitor. Within the RBV-logic, *supplier driven e-business* can be seen as a resource for companies that are deploying the Internet. Consumer readiness is an Internet adoption driver (Zhu et al. 2002), and like the above described supplier-driven e-business *customer-driven e-business* can be seen as a resource for companies that are deploying the Internet. *Benchmarking* is important for small companies (Barclay, 2006; Chan, Bhargava, and Street 2006) and it is a widespread practice for the development of IT systems (Whitley 1992). Teo and Choo (2001) found out that using the Internet has a positive impact on the quality of competitive intelligence information. Furthermore they found a positive link between the quality of competitive intelligence and firm performance. Porter (2001) argues that integrating the Internet with traditional competitive advantages and ways for competing win in many industries. *Strategic use of the Internet* can lead to competitive advantage, because production and procurement can be more effective and buyers will value a combination of on- and off-line services. Small companies usually have fewer *financial resources* than larger ones, which often limits their opportunities (Caldeira and Ward 2003; Chow et al. 1997; Van Auken 2005).

It is therefore proposed that (in contrast to IT assets) business resources differ between competing firms and that these differences are long lasting. Therefore the assertions of resource heterogeneity and resource immobility are met, and business resources are complementary with the Internet. It is therefore suggested that:

> **Hypothesis 2:** *Business resources are complementary to the Internet.*

Dynamic Capabilities

Dynamic capabilities have the following three characteristics (Teece et al. 1997): (1) coordination/integration, (2) learning, and (3) reconfiguration:

1. The effective and efficient internal **coordination or integration** of strategic assets determines a firm's performance. Increasingly, competitive advantage also requires the integration of external activities and technologies, for example in the form of alliances and the virtual corporation. Internet technologies play an important role in the integration of collaborative activities and knowledge management in the product development process (Lee et al., 2006). Soo, Devinney and Midgley (2007) highlight the importance of integrating external knowledge into the organization.

2. **Learning** is the process by which repetition and experimentation enable tasks to be performed better and quicker. It also enables new production opportunities to be identified. Collaborations and partnerships can be a source for new organizational learning, helping firms to recognize dysfunctional routines, and preventing strategic blind spots. Bierly and Daly (2007) highlight the importance of external learning sources and dynamic capabilities at SMEs. They suggest that learning from customers is a predictor of innovation speed, learning from suppliers is a predictor of operational efficiency, and learning from other industries is a predictor of superior process technologies. However, learning from competitors is negatively associated with the development of product technologies and basic research. Additionally, smaller firms learn more from suppliers and the scientific community than larger firms, while larger firms learn more from partnerships and consultants. Furthermore, SMEs are more

nimble and flexible in adapting their systems and structures for Knowledge Management purposes, with fewer problems of communication, implementation, and replacement costs (Chan and Chao, 2008).

3. Fast changing markets require the ability to **reconfigure** the firm's asset structure, and to accomplish the necessary internal and external **transformation** (Amit and Schoemaker 1993). Change is costly and therefore firms have to develop processes to minimize low pay-off change. The capability to change depends on the ability to scan the environment, to evaluate markets, and to quickly accomplish reconfiguration and transformation ahead of competition. This can be supported by decentralization and local autonomy (Teece et al., 1997).

Schlemmer and Webb (2008) highlight the importance of dynamic capabilities for the creation of competitive advantages at SMEs. Rindova and Kotha (2001) conducted case studies on Yahoo! and Excite and suggested that the fast changing virtual markets require dynamic capabilities. Ma and Loeh (2007) show that the dynamic capabilities approach can provide a holistic perspective to understand enterprise system driven process innovation at Chinese companies, which are facing a dynamic external environment. Wu, Lin and Hsu's (2007) survey of 100 Taiwan companies related to the electronic IT industries suggests that dynamic capabilities are related to innovative performance. They further found moderating effects between dynamic capabilities and relationship capital. Zhu and Kraemer (2002) found a positive relationship between e-commerce capability (a set of measures based on the dynamic capabilities framework) and some measures of financial performance. In his later work, Zhu (2004) then found complementarity between e-Commerce capability and IT-infrastructure and a positive relationship to financial performance. It is therefore suggested that:

Hypothesis 3: *Dynamic capabilities are complementary to the Internet.*

METHODOLOGY

The Sample

This research aims at examining complementarity that is widely generalizable for small firms in different industries, and therefore it did not focus on one single industry. Thus this study complies with the resource-based view, which is grounded in the assumption that performance differences are mainly caused by firm and not by industry effects (Barney 1991; Hawawini et al. 2003). Yeoh and Roth (1999) argue that strategic assets are unique for each industry. In contrast, the authors believe that for example the quality of customer relationships, which has already been applied to retailers (Powell and Dent-Micallef 1997), or the capabilities of coordination, which has been used for manufacturing companies (Caloghirou et al., 2004), can be valuable for all profit-organizations. Similarly, Chan et al. (2006) suggest that the key-organizational challenges of small firms are not influenced by the type of industry. In addition, the Internet blurs and shifts existing market boundaries (Amit and Zott 2001) and therefore the differentiation in different industries appears to be less important.

The "First Stop Shop" (an organization funded by the European Union and the Belfast City Council) database was used, because it was the only database that the authors were aware of that also included a large number of local companies' (Belfast/Northern Ireland/UK) websites. The authors focused especially on local companies because this study is part of a bigger research project, which also required interview data. Those companies that provided their Internet address in the database were selected and a paper-based questionnaire was sent to them. Only small firms with less than 250 employees were examined.

The original database contained 7600 companies; the authors only those companies that provided their Internet address in the database (2377) were included, because the authors wanted to ensure that the surveyed firms deploy the Internet to some extent. After separating the non-profit organizations and companies with more than 250 employees, 1963 addresses remained. 50 companies were used for the pilot.[v] A questionnaire was sent to the remaining 1913 subjects. 44 questionnaires were returned because the companies have gone away or closed, and 11 answered that they would not complete the questionnaire because it was not appropriate for their organization. This led to a sample of 1858 companies. 228 questionnaires were returned therefore the response rate was 12.3 percent (228/1858). After eliminating the remaining non-profit organizations, non-independent and too large companies, 146 companies remained. The response rate of 12.3 percent is not great; however, it may be satisfactory considering the requirement of CEO's direct involvement (Lee, Lee, and Pennings 2001), and similar response rates are common in SME research (e.g. Voordeckers, Gils and Heuvel (2007) had 9.2% and Cooper, Upton and Seaman (2005) had 11.3%).

The Measures

As described in the previous section, the constructs were taken out of the literature. However, some modifications were necessary, this also applies to some variables: One variable of the set for business resources about cross sectional teams and one variable of the set for IT assets about a formal IT department were dropped, because the authors believe that small companies typically neither have cross-sectional teams nor a formal MIS department. 10 new questions were included, the vast majority of them in the dynamic capabilities section according to the suggestions of Caloghirou et al. (2004). The reason for the modifications of the original dynamic capabilities construct was that they were used as a set of dependent variables

and that section appeared therefore quite short. Details of the modifications can be obtained from the first author. The questionnaire is presented as Appendix 1.

The financial performance measures consisted of revenues, sales growth and return on assets. Revenues indicate the company's success in its market transactions, sales growth indicates increasing customer acceptance, and return on assets indicates the management's effectiveness in deploying their assets. Managers were asked if their performance over the last three years was outstanding and if they have exceeded their competitors. Internet performance (a modification of Powell and Dent-Micallef's IT-performance), defined as the degree to which firm performance has been improved by the Internet, was also measured. Similar to Zhuang and Lederer (2003), the Powell and Dent-Micallef measures were modified by replacing the impact of IT by the impact of the Internet. Therefore, managers were asked about the impact of the Internet on their productivity, competitive position, sales, profitability and overall performance. A 5-point Likert-type measurement scale was deployed.

By using subjective measures it is assumed, given the senior executives involved, that respondents had sufficient perspective and information to assess their firm performance relative to competitors. It is broadly accepted that objective performance measures are highly correlated with the subjective ones, and can be used if objective data is not available (Dess 1987; Dess and Robinson 1984; Powell and Dent-Micallef 1997). Some researchers even prefer subjective measures, because it could reduce the problems of varying accounting conventions in areas such as inventory valuation, depreciation, and officers' salaries (Powell and Dent-Micallef 1997). The authors ideally would have preferred to triangulate the perceived performance with accounting-based data, but small firms are usually held privately and would not provide confidential information as a matter of policy. The authors have also been unable to find valid secondary data.[vi] But even where secondary data is available, small firm organizational form (sole proprietorship, partnership, corporation, etc.) can cause artificial differences. Also, owner compensation can affect the performance of small, privately-held firms (Dess and Robinson 1984).

Tanriverdi and Venkatraman's (2005) suggest that most studies on complementarity only capture potential complementarity, which is limited to a firm's potential for improving financial performance by synergy effects of strategic assets. Most researchers assume that the potential for the complementarity of strategic assets will automatically translate into actual complementarity and improved performance. In practice however, firms are not always able to exploit potential synergies of strategic assets. This is evident in many unsuccessful mergers, acquisitions, and joint ventures that actually destroy value (Tanriverdi and Venkatraman, 2005). The interchangeable usage of potential complementarity and actual complementarity doesn't take into account that firms may not be able to create complementarity. In this study this problem was approached by asking the managers directly about the performance impacts of the complementary resource (the Internet).

RESULTS

Strategic Assets and Financial Performance

On average 14.4 percent of company revenues were generated online, 22.7 percent of products and services were procured on the Internet, and 22.9 staff were employed. Only four companies were pure dotcoms, creating 100 percent of their revenues online.

Following Powell and Dent-Micallef (1997) the following linear regression model was estimated:

$$Z_Y = \alpha + \beta_B Z_B + \beta_D Z_D + \beta_I Z_I + \varepsilon$$

Z_Y stands for financial performance, α for the intercept B for the variable set of business resources, D for dynamic capabilities, and I for IT assets. β_X are the standardized partial regression coefficients for estimating performance Z_Y. The authors assume that β_B, and β_D will be positive and significant and β_I about zero (Powell and Dent-Micallef 1997). ε is the residual term that captures the net effect of all unspecified factors.

In Table 2 Cronbach alphas, which are a measure for scale reliability, are presented. The dependent variables were quite high with 0.90 for financial performance and 0.95 for Internet performance. Cronbach alphas of all variables exceeded the recommended minimum of 0.6 (Bagozzi and Yi 1988), with a range from 0.66 to 0.88 for business resources (overall 0.74), 0.64 to 0.84 for dynamic capabilities (overall 0.87), and 0.61 to 0.92 for IT assets (overall 0.90). All variable sets correlate statistically significant with financial performance (see Table 2).

Table 3 shows the results from multiple regression for the independent variable sets (business resources, dynamic capabilities, and IT assets), the control variable (firm size "ln emp" measured as the natural logarithm of employees), and for the dependent variables. The variables combined explain 22.4 percent of financial performance variance, and an estimated 20.2 percent of variance in population (using adjusted R^2, which estimates population effects based on sample degrees of freedom).

The significant intercorrelations between some of the sub-variables in the model led us to resolve multicollinearity problems by dropping variables (Gujarati 1995). Therefore, in addition to the analysis with the constructs, variables were dropped and the results after dropping variables were compared to the results of the original construct. It was then checked if dropping variables changes the conclusions of the study. Those variables, that had correlations higher than 0.5 with

Table 2. Descriptive statistics

N=146	Alpha	Mean	S.D.	Financial Performance
Relationships	0.69	3,97	0,67	0,07
Extern Driven e-Business	0.66	2,46	0,99	0,17*
Benchmarking	n.a.	2,72	1,22	0,14
Strategic Internet	0.88	3,43	1,14	0,04
Financial Resources	n.a.	3,00	1,11	0,51***
BUSINESS RESOURCES	0.74	3,12	0,65	0,31***
IT Knowledge	0.92	3,33	1,08	0,16*
IT Operations	0.87	2,55	0,93	0,25**
IT Objects	0.61	3,21	1,01	0,14
IT ASSETS	0.90	3,03	0,85	0,22**
Integration	0.64	3,69	0,59	0,27***
Learning	0.84	3,63	0,73	0,33***
Reconfiguration	0.68	3,38	0,63	0,38***
DYNAMIC CAPABILITIES	0.87	3,57	0,56	0,38***
Internet Performance	0.95	2,74	1,10	0,21**
Financial Performance	0.90	2,92	0,81	1

*** Correlation is significant at the 0.001 level (2-tailed).
** Correlation is significant at the 0.01 level (2-tailed).
* Correlation is significant at the 0.05 level (2-tailed).

an included variable (benchmarking, integration, reconfiguration, IT knowledge, and IT objects), were dropped. The regression analysis with the remaining variables yielded insignificant results

Table 3. Regression

	Internet Performance	Financial Performance
Business Resources	.424***	.190*
Dynamic Capabilities	-.059	.336***
IT Assets	.312***	-.114
ln emp	-.250***	.263***
R	.720***	.473***
R^2	.518	.224
Adjusted R^2	.505	.202

*** Correlation is significant at the 0.001 level (2-tailed).
** Correlation is significant at the 0.01 level (2-tailed).
* Correlation is significant at the 0.05 level (2-tailed).

for the variables relationships, external driven e-Business, strategic Internet and IT operations. They were therefore also excluded. Thus, in this additional test, business resources were only measured by financial resources, dynamic capabilities by learning, and IT assets were excluded. The results of the regression analysis after dropping variables would not have changed any of the conclusions. The authors therefore suggest that multicollinearity is not a problem.[vii] Please note that this was just an additional test for multicollinearity issues; the authors used the constructs and not single variables for our regression. Furthermore, the assumptions of multiple regression (normality, linearity, homoscedasticity, and independence of residuals) were examined according to the suggestions of Pallant (2002) and the results analysis indicates a direct relationship between business resources and dynamic capabilities and financial performance; and no affect of IT assets on financial performance. Furthermore, business resources and IT assets are related to Internet performance and dynamic capabilities are not.

Complementarity of the Internet and Strategic Assets

Powell and Dent-Micallef (1997) used a median split for analyzing complementarity of IT assets with other firm assets. All companies were ranked according to their IT assets and divided into IT-leading and IT-lagging companies. The authors modified their methodology and ranked the companies according to their Internet performance. The median was at 2.8 with 74 companies that achieved 2.8 or less at Internet performance. They were labeled as Internet-lagging and 72 companies that achieved more than 2.8, and they were labeled as Internet-leading.

Powell and Dent-Micallef (1997) used three steps for examining complementarity. First, they compared the means of the independent variables (the strategic assets) between IT-leading and lagging companies. Second, they expected that the

correlation between strategic assets and financial performance was stronger for IT-leading companies than for IT-lagging companies. And finally, they expected that financial performance would be better for IT-leading companies, compared to IT-lagging companies.

Our results are shown in Table 4. As expected, the means of all independent variable sets (the strategic assets) are higher at Internet-leading companies. Furthermore, financial performance of Internet-leading companies is better than financial performance of Internet-lagging companies. Independent samples t-test showed that the differences between Internet-leading and Internet lagging companies were statistically significant for all variables. Table 5 indicates that the relationship between strategic assets and financial performance differs between Internet-leading and Internet-lagging companies. Whereas performance is strongly related to firm size (measured as the logarithm of employees) at Internet-lagging companies, strategic assets are strongly related to financial performance at Internet-leading companies. Furthermore, the explanatory power of the model is much higher for the Internet-leading companies (adjusted $R^2 = 0.276$) than for Internet-lagging companies (adjusted $R^2 = 0.175$).

Hypothesis 1 which suggested no complementarity of IT assets and the Internet was not supported. The authors would have expected that the relationship between IT assets and financial performance to be non-significant and about zero, like it is for the complete sample (including Internet-lagging and leading companies) and for Internet-lagging companies. Surprisingly, the relationship between IT assets and financial performance is *significantly negative* (-.283*) for Internet-leading companies. Possible reasons could be that Internet-leading companies overinvested in IT assets or that the investments have not paid off yet (further discussed in the next section). Hypotheses 2 and 3, which suggested complementarity between the Internet and busi-

Table 4. Internet-leading and internet-lagging companies

	Internet-lagging (n=74)		Internet-leading (n=72)		Δ
	Mean	**Std. Deviation**	**Mean**	**Std. Deviation**	**T-Test**
Business Resources	2,8	0,5	3,4	0,6	6.49***
IT Assets	2,6	0,8	3,4	0,7	6.08***
Dynamic Capabilities	3,3	0,6	3,8	0,4	5,56***
Internet Performance	1,9	0,6	3,7	0,7	17,44***
Financial Performance	2,8	0,8	3,1	0,7	2,31*

*** T-Test is significant at the 0.001 level (2-tailed).

** T-Test is significant at the 0.01 level (2-tailed).

* T-Test is significant at the 0.05 level (2-tailed).

ness resources and the Internet and dynamic capabilities, were supported.

In appendix 2 hierarchical regression analysis was used for evaluating complementarity of the Internet. The results strongly supported the findings above. However, no significant interaction effect between IT assets and the Internet was found. The authors believe that this could be a problem of the relatively small sample size.

DISCUSSION

This study aimed at examining complementarity between strategic assets and the Internet, and started with the examination of the main effect of strategic assets on financial performance. Our data suggests that business resources and dynamic capabilities are related to financial performance of small firms, and as expected IT assets didn't have a direct relationship to financial performance.

In the next step complementarity of the Internet with strategic assets was examined. Therefore the sample was divided into Internet-leading and Internet-lagging companies, and the results suggest that the Internet is complementary with business resources and dynamic capabilities. Surprisingly the interaction effect between the Internet and IT assets was significantly negative at Internet-leading companies. As already suggested in the literature review, research on the relationship between IT assets and financial

Table 5. Regression results

		Internet-lagging	Internet-leading
ln emp		.421***	.121
Business Resources		.012	.304*
Dynamic Capabilities		.206†	.460**
IT Assets		-.071	-.283*
R		.469**	.562***
R^2		.220	.316
Adjusted R^2		.175	.276

*** Correlation is significant at the 0.001 level (2-tailed).

** Correlation is significant at the 0.01 level (2-tailed).

* Correlation is significant at the 0.05 level (2-tailed).

† Correlation is significant at the 0.1 level (2-tailed).

performance is frequently inconclusive, however negative relationships are quite untypical (Wade and Hulland 2004), and according to the resource-based logic, the authors would have expected no direct relationship between IT assets and financial performance (Mata et al., 1995). However, these results are similar to the original study which suggested that financial performance of IT-leading companies was lower than financial performance of IT-lagging companies (Powell and Dent-Micallef 1997). The authors propose two possible reasons for this phenomenon: First, the Internet-leading companies may have over-invested in IT assets. Song et al. (2005, p.271) suggested "Clearly, resource combinations do not always lead to synergistic performance impact and managers should avoid over-investing in contexts where resources can not be leveraged through configuration, complementarity and/or integration. In terms of resource-based theory, synergistic rents cannot always be obtained". In the literature review the authors suggested that, according to the resource-based logic, IT assets and the Internet can not be complementary because they both don't fulfill the criteria of resource heterogeneity and resource immobility. However, this relatively sophisticated resource-based logic may be difficult to understand for managers of small firms, who perform some activities with less expertise because they do not have functional specialists, compared to larger companies (Verhees and Meulenberg 2004). Therefore, there appears to be a threat for managers of small firms to over-invest in IT assets. A second possible reason for the negative relationship could be that the IT investments haven't paid off yet. Performance was evaluated over the past three years. However, the Internet and e-Business are still relatively young areas, and many companies may be in an early stage, and it may take more time until the investments pay off, and Oh and Pinsonneault's (2007) research on SMEs suggested that that extracting benefits from strategic IS resources designed to help firms grow is very difficult.

CONCLUSIONS AND IMPLICATIONS

This chapter suggests that small firms can use the Internet to leverage their business resources and dynamic capabilities, but that IT-assets cannot be leveraged by the Internet. The chapter contributes to the still underdeveloped research on complementarity by discussing the role of the Internet as a complementary resource for small firms. Based on the literature review and the empirical findings the authors suggest that researchers should look out for research settings in which a clear distinction of the strategic assets, that are expected to be complementary, is feasible. The authors further believe that a strategic asset that neither meets the requirement of resource heterogeneity nor the requirement of resource immobility (like for example the Internet and IT assets) can still be used to leverage other strategic assets, if the other strategic assets fulfill those requirements.

This study has the following managerial implications. The complementarity of the Internet with business resources and dynamic capabilities suggests that companies controlling those strategic assets should seriously consider conducting e-Business. Furthermore, this research is a warning for mangers not to over-invest in strategic assets that have no rent-creating potential. If strategic assets are generic and mobile they can neither be a source of competitive advantage nor can they be complementary with other strategic assets that don't have rent-creating potential. In particular, this research poses the threat of an over-investment in IT assets to managers of small firms.[viii]

LIMITATIONS AND FUTURE RESEARCH

Some limitations of this research should be noted. First, the subjective measures for firm-performance have not been validated by secondary data. Second, there is a threat of common method bias because the data was only collected from a single questionnaire. These limitations are a typical problem that arises when small firms are examined because they frequently don't publish their performance data as a matter of policy (Dess and Robinson 1984). However, the authors believe that analyzing small firms yields the advantage of relatively simple organizational structures. Furthermore, the owner manager of a small company may be more involved in the actual working processes and be better informed about the impact of the Internet on the processes than the CEO of a large company, who may never even have visited entire departments of his/her firm. In addition, the analysis represents only a snapshot in time, and there are no guarantees that the conditions under which the data is collected will remain the same, this applies especially to the fast changing virtual markets. And finally, it was not controlled for industry effects.

The limitations suggest avenues for future research. Additional research could aim at identifying research settings in which an evaluation of separated strategic assets is feasible, like for example at strategic alliances (Rothaermel 2001) and mergers and acquisitions (Carpon and Pistre 2002), which has barely been researched at SMEs (Kollmann and Häsel, 2008). Furthermore, little is known about complementarity of strategic assets that don't have rent-creating potential by themselves, like for example the Internet or generic IT assets. In addition, the findings could be supplemented by longitudinal research, for example using panel data or time series to examine the development of strategic assets and their complementarity. Furthermore, whereas the research on small companies yields some advantages, it would also be interesting to compare this study with research on large companies. And finally, our data does not yield an explanation for the negative interaction effect of the Internet on the relationship between IT assets and financial performance. The authors suggested that it could

be due to the companies' early Internet adoption stage or due to over-investments in IT. However, these suggestions await empirical verification.

REFERENCES

Amit, R., & Schoemaker, P. J. H. (1993). Strategic assets and organizational rent. *Strategic Management Journal, 14*(1), 33–46. doi:10.1002/smj.4250140105

Amit, R., & Zott, C. (2001). Value creation in e-business. *Strategic Management Journal, 22*(6/7), 453–520.

Bagozzi, R. P., & Yi, Y. (1988). On the evaluation of structural equation models. *Journal of the Academy of Marketing Science, 16*(1), 74–94. doi:10.1007/BF02723327

Barclay, I. (2006). Benchmarking best practice in SMEs for growth. *International Journal of Technology Management, 33*(2-3), 234–254. doi:10.1504/IJTM.2006.008313

Barney, J. (1991). Firm resources and sustained competitive advantage. *Journal of Management, 17*(1), 99–120. doi:10.1177/014920639101700108

Barua, A., Konana, P., Whinston, A. B., & Yin, F. (2004). An Empirical investigation of net-enabled business value. *MIS Quarterly, 28*(4), 585–620.

Bharati, P., & Chaudhury, A. (2009). SMEs and Competiveness: The Role of Information Systems. *International Journal of E-Business Research, 5*(1), 1–9.

Bierly, P. E., & Daly, P. S. (2007). Sources of external organisational learning in small manufacturing firms. *International Journal of Technology Management, 38*(1/2), 45–68. doi:10.1504/IJTM.2007.012429

Caldeira, M. M., & Ward, J. M. (2003). Using resource-based theory to interpret the successful adoption and use of information systems and technology in manufacturing small and medium-sized enterprises. *European Journal of Information Systems, 12*, 127–141. doi:10.1057/palgrave. ejis.3000454

Caloghirou, Y., Protogerou, A., Spanos, Y., & Papagiannakis, L. (2004). Industry- versus firm-specific effects on performance: Contrasting SMEs and large-sized firms. *European Management Journal, 22*(2), 231–243. doi:10.1016/j. emj.2004.01.017

Capron, L., & Pistre, N. (2002). When do acquirers earn abnormal returns? *Strategic Management Journal, 23*(9), 781–794. doi:10.1002/smj.262

Chan, I., & Chao, C. K. (2008). Knowledge Management in Small and Medium-Sized Enterprises. *Communications of the ACM, 51*(4), 83–88. doi:10.1145/1330311.1330328

Chan, Y. E., Bhargava, N., & Street, C. T. (2006). Having arrived: The homogeneity of high-growth small firms. *Journal of Small Business Management, 44*(3), 426–440. doi:10.1111/j.1540-627-X.2006.00180.x

Chow, C. W., Haddad, K. M., & Williamson, J. E. (1997). Applying the Balanced Scorecard to small companies. *Strategic Finance, 79*(2), 21–28.

Chung, S., Singh, H., & Lee, K. (2000). Complementarity, status similarity and social capital as drivers of alliance formation. *Strategic Management Journal, 21*(1), 1–22. doi:10.1002/(SICI)1097-0266(200001)21:1<1::AID-SMJ63>3.0.CO;2-P

Clemons, E. K., & Row, M. C. (1991). Sustaining IT advantage: The role of structural differences. *MIS Quarterly, 15*(3), 275–292. doi:10.2307/249639

Cooper, M. J., Upton, N., & Seaman, S. (2005). Customer relationship management: A comparative ananlysis of family and nonfamily business practices. *Journal of Small Business Management, 43*(3), 242–257.

Cousins, P. D., & Spekman, R. (2003). Strategic supply and the management of inter- and intra-organisational relationships. *Journal of Purchasing and Supply Management, 9*, 19–29. doi:10.1016/S1478-4092(02)00036-5

Dean, T. J., Brown, R. L., & Bamford, C. E. (1998). Differences in large and small firm responses to environmental context: Strategic implications from a comparative analysis of business formations. *Strategic Management Journal, 19*(8), 709–728. doi:10.1002/(SICI)1097-0266-(199808)19:8<709::AID-SMJ966>3.0.CO;2-9

Dess, G. G. (1987). Consensus on strategy formulation and organizational performance: Competitors in a fragmented industry. *Strategic Management Journal, 8*(3), 259–277. doi:10.1002/smj.4250080305

Dess, G. G., & Davis, P. S. (1984). Porter's (1980). generic strategies as determinants of strategic group membership and organizational performance. *Academy of Management Journal, 27*(3), 467–488. doi:10.2307/256040

Fernandez, Z., & Nieto, A. J. (2006). The internet: competitive strategy and boundaries of the firm. *International Journal of Technology Management, 35*(1-4), 182–195. doi:10.1504/IJTM.2006.009234

Fillis, I., Johansson, U., & Wagner, B. (2004). A qualitative investigation of smaller firm e-business development. *Journal of Small Business and Enterprise Development, 11*(3), 349–361. doi:10.1108/14626000410551609

Gribbins, M. L., & King, R. C. (2004). Electronic retailing strategies: A case study of small businesses in the gifts and collectibles industry. *Electronic Markets, 14*(2), 138–152. doi:10.1080/10196780410001675086

Gujarati, D. N. (1995). Basic Econometrics (3rd ed.). New York: McGraw-Hill.

Hall, R. (1993). A framework linking intangible resources and capabilities to sustainable competitive advantage. *Strategic Management Journal, 14*(8), 607–618. doi:10.1002/smj.4250140804

Hawawini, G., Subramanian, V., & Verdin, P. (2003). Is performance driven by industry- or firm-specific factors? New look at the old evidence. *Strategic Management Journal, 24*(1), 1–16. doi:10.1002/smj.278

Ihlstrom, C., & Nilsson, M. (2003). E-business adoption by SMEs - prerequisites and attitudes of SMEs in a Swedish network. *Journal of Organizational Computing and Electronic Commerce, 13*(3/4), 211–223. doi:10.1207/S15327744JOCE133&4_04

Jones, C. (2004). An alternative view of small firm adoption. *Journal of Small Business and Enterprise Development, 11*(3), 362–370. doi:10.1108/14626000410551618

Keen, P. (1993). Information technology and the management difference: A fusion map. *IBM Systems Journal, 32*(1), 17–39.

Keller Johnson, L. (2002). New views on digital CRM. *MIT Sloan Management Review, 44*(1), 10–27.

Kim, D., Ow, T. T., & Junc, M. (2008). SME Strategies: An Assessment of High vs. Low Performers. *Communications of the ACM, 51*(11), 113–117. doi:10.1145/1400214.1400237

Kollmann, T., & Häsel, M. (2008). Cross-channel cooperation: on the collaborative integration of online and offline business models of e-entrepreneurs and traditional SMEs. *International Journal of Entrepreneurship and Small Business, 6*(2), 212–229. doi:10.1504/IJESB.2008.018629

Krishnan, H. A., Miller, A., & Judge, W. Q. (1997). Diversification and top management complementarity: Is performance improved by merging similar or dissimilar teams? *Strategic Management Journal, 18*(5), 361–374. doi:10.1002/(SICI)1097-0266(199705)18:5<361::AID-SMJ866>3.0.CO;2-L

Lee, C., Lee, K., & Pennings, J. M. (2001). Internal capabilities, external networks, and performance: A study on technology-based ventures. *Strategic Management Journal, 22*(6/7), 615–640. doi:10.1002/smj.181

Lee, H. J., Ahn, H. J., Kim, J. W., & Park, S. J. (2006). Capturing and reusing knowledge in engineering change management: A case of automobile development. *Information Systems Frontiers, 8*(5), 375–395. doi:10.1007/s10796-006-9009-0

Letaifa, S., & Perrien, J. (2007). The impact of E-CRM on organisational and individual behavior: The effect of the remuneration and reward system. *International Journal of E-Business Research,* (3): 2–13.

Ma, X., & Loeh, H. (2007). Closing the gap: How should Chinese companies build the capabilities to implement ERP-driven process innovation? *International Journal of Technology Management, 39*(3/4), 380–395. doi:10.1504/IJTM.2007.013501

Manley, K. (2008). Against the odds: Small firms in Australia successfully introducing new technology on construction projects. *Research Policy, 37*(10), 1751–1764. doi:10.1016/j.respol.2008.07.013

Mata, F. J., Fuerst, W. L., & Barney, J. B. (1995). Information Technology and sustained competitive advantage: A resource-based analysis. *MIS Quarterly*, *19*(4), 487–495. doi:10.2307/249630

Montazemi, A. R. (2006). SMEs in Canada and the U.S. *Communications of the ACM*, *49*(12), 109–112. doi:10.1145/1183236.1183240

Newbert, S. L. (2007). Empirical research on the resource-based view of the firm: An assessment and suggestions for future research. *Strategic Management Journal*, *28*(2), 121–146. doi:10.1002/smj.573

Oh, W., & Pinsonneault, A. (2007). On the Assessment of the Strategic Value of Information Technologies: Conceptual and Analytical Approaches. *MIS Quarterly*, *31*(2), 239–265.

Pallant, J. (2002). SPSS Survival manual. Buckingham: Open University Press.

Penrose, E. (1959). The Theory of Growth of the Firm. London: Basil Blackwell.

Pollard, C., & Diggles, A. (2006). The role of trust in Business-to-Business e-Commerce collaboration in a unique environment in Australia. *International Journal of E-Business Research*, *2*(3), 71–88.

Porter, M. E. (2001, March). Strategy and the internet. *Harvard Business Review*, 63–78.

Powell, T. C., & Dent-Micallef, A. (1997). Information technology as competitive advantage: The role of human, business and technology resources. *Strategic Management Journal*, *18*(5), 375–405. doi:10.1002/(SICI)1097-0266-(199705)18:5<375::AID-SMJ876>3.0.CO;2-7

Quayle, M. (2002). Supplier development and supply chain management in small and medium size enterprises. *International Journal of Technology Management*, *23*(1/2/3), 172–188. doi:10.1504/IJTM.2002.003004

Rindova, V. P., & Kotha, S. (2001). Continuous morphing: competing through dynamic capabilities form and function. *Academy of Management Journal*, *44*(6), 1263–1280. doi:10.2307/3069400

Rothaermel, F. T. (2001). Incumbent's advantage through exploiting complementary assets via interfirm cooperation. *Strategic Management Journal*, *22*(6/7), 687–699. doi:10.1002/smj.180

Schlemmer, F., & Webb, B. (2008). The managing director and the development of dynamic capabilities: An application of enactment theory. *The International Journal of Organizational Analysis*, *16*(1/2), 109–137. doi:10.1108/19348830810915523

Schroder, D., & Madeja, N. (2004). Is customer relationship management a success factor in electronic commerce? *Journal of Electronic Commerce Research*, *5*(1), 38–52.

Sher, P. J., & Lee, V. C. (2004). Information technology as a facilitator for enhancing dynamic capabilities through knowledge management. *Information & Management*, *41*(8), 933–945. doi:10.1016/j.im.2003.06.004

Song, M., Droge, C., Hanvanich, S., & Calantone, R. (2005). Marketing and technology resource complementarity: An analysis of their interaction effect in two environmental contexts. *Strategic Management Journal*, *26*(3), 259–276. doi:10.1002/smj.450

Soo, C. W., Devinney, T. M., & Midgley, D. F. (2007). External knowledge acquisition, creativity and learning in organisational problem solving. *International Journal of Technology Management*, *38*(1/2), 137–159. doi:10.1504/IJTM.2007.012433

Stuart, T. E. (2000). Interorganizational alliances and the performance of firms: A study of growth and innovation rates in a high-technology industry. *Strategic Management Journal, 21*(8), 791–811. doi:10.1002/1097-0266(200008)21:8<791::AID-SMJ121>3.0.CO;2-K

Su, C., Chen, Y., & Sha, D. Y. (2007). Managing product and customer knowledge in innovative new product development. *International Journal of Technology Management, 39*(1/2), 105–130. doi:10.1504/IJTM.2007.013443

Tanner, C., Wölfle, R., Schubert, R., & Quade, M.. Current Trends and Challenges in Electronic Procurement: An Empirical Study. *Electronic Markets, 18*(1), 16–18.

Tanriverdi, H., & Venkatraman, N. (2005). Knowledge relatedness and the performance of multibusiness firms. *Strategic Management Journal, 26*(2), 97–119. doi:10.1002/smj.435

Teece, D. J. (1986). Profiting from technological innovation: Implications for integration, collaboration, licensing and public policy. *Research Policy, 15*(6), 285–305. doi:10.1016/0048-7333-(86)90027-2

Teece, D. J., Pisano, G., & Shuen, A. (1997). Dynamic capabilities and strategic management. *Strategic Management Journal, 18*(7), 509–533. doi:10.1002/(SICI)1097-0266-(199708)18:7<509::AID-SMJ882>3.0.CO;2-Z

Teo, T. S. H., & Choo, W. Y. (2001). Assessing the impact of using the internet for competitive intelligence. *Information & Management, 39*(1), 67–83. doi:10.1016/S0378-7206(01)00080-5

Tippins, M. J., & Sohi, R. (2003). IT competency and firm performance: Is organizational learning the missing link? *Strategic Management Journal, 24*(8), 745–761. doi:10.1002/smj.337

Van Auken, H. (2005). Differences in the usage of bootstrap financing among technology-based versus nontechnology-based firms. *Journal of Small Business Management, 43*(1), 93–103. doi:10.1111/j.1540-627X.2004.00127.x

Verdu-Jover, A., Llorens-Montes, F. J., & Garcia-Morales, V. J. (2006). Environment-flexibility coalignment and performance: An analysis in large versus small firms. *Journal of Small Business Management, 44*(3), 334–349. doi:10.1111/j.1540-627X.2006.00175.x

Verhees, F. J. H. M., & Meulenberg, M. T. G. (2004). Market orientation, innovativeness, product innovation, and performance in small firms. *Journal of Small Business Management, 42*(2), 134–154. doi:10.1111/j.1540-627X.2004.00102.x

Voordeckers, W., & Gils, A.V., & Heuvel, Jeron Van Den. (2007). Board Composition in small and medium-sized family firms. *Journal of Small Business Management, 45*(1), 137–157. doi:10.1111/j.1540-627X.2007.00204.x

Wade, M., & Hulland, J. (2004). Review: The resource-based view and information systems research: Review, extension, and suggestions for future research. *MIS Quarterly, 28*(1), 107–142.

Walton, R. (1989). Up and Running: Integrating Information Technology and the Organization. Boston, MA: Harvard Business School Press.

Welsh, J. A., & White, J. F. (1981). A small business is not a little big business. *Harvard Business Review, 59*(4), 18–32.

Wernerfelt, B. (1984). A resource-based view of the firm. *Strategic Management Journal, 5*(2), 171–180. doi:10.1002/smj.4250050207

Whitley, R. (1992). The Customer Driven Company. Reading, MA: Addison-Wesley.

Wigand, R. T., Steinfeld, C. W., & Markus, M. L. (2005). Information Technology Standards Choices and Industry Structure Outcomes: The Case of the U.S. Home Mortgage Industry. *Journal of Management Information Systems*, *22*(2), 165–191.

Winter, S. G. (1987). Knowledge and competence as strategic assets. In D. Teece (Ed.), The Competitive Challenge (pp. 159-184). Berkeley, CA: Center for Research in Management

Winter, S. G., Gaglio, C. M., & Rajagopalan, H. K. (2009). The Value of Information Systems to Small and Medium-Sized Enterprises: Information and Communications Technologies as Signal and Symbol of Legitimacy and Competitiveness. *International Journal of E-Business Research*, *5*(1), 65–91.

Wu, S., Lin, L., & Hsu, M. (2007). Intellectual capital, dynamic capabilities and innovative performance of organisations. *International Journal of Technology Management*, *39*(3/4), 279–296. doi:10.1504/IJTM.2007.013496

Xu, M., Rohatgi, R., & Duan, Y. (2007). E-Business adoption in SMEs: Some preliminary findings from electronic components industry. *International Journal of E-Business Research*, *3*(1), 74–90.

Yeoh, P., & Roth, K. (1999). An empirical analysis of sustained advantage in the U.S. pharmaceutical industry: Impact of firm resources and capabilities. *Strategic Management Journal*, *20*(7), 637–653. doi:10.1002/(SICI)1097-0266-(199907)20:7<637::AID-SMJ42>3.0.CO;2-Z

Zhu, K. (2004). The complementarity of information technology infrastructure and e-Commerce capability: A resource-based assessment of their business value. *Journal of Management Information Systems*, *21*(1), 167–202.

Zhu, K., & Kraemer, K. L. (2002). e-commerce metrics for Net-enhanced organizations: Assessing the value of e-commerce to firm-performance in the manufacturing sector. *Information Systems Research*, *13*(3), 275–295. doi:10.1287/isre.13.3.275.82

Zhu, K., Kraemer, K. L., & Xu, S. (2002). A cross-country study of electronic business adoption using the Technology-Organization-Environment Framework, *Twenty Third International Conference on Information Systems*, 2002, pp337-348.

Zhuang, Y., & Lederer, A. L. (2003). An instrument for measuring the business benefits of e-commerce retailing. *International Journal of Electronic Commerce*, *7*(3), 65–99.

ENDNOTES

[i] This is a modified version of a study that was previously published in the International Journal of e-Business research and in the book "Information Technology and Competitive Advantage in Small Firms".

[ii] There were also studies that examined complementarity at strategic alliances (Rothaermel, 2001; Stuart, 2000) and mergers and acquisitions (Krishnan, Miller and Judge, 1997; Capron and Pistre, 2002). However, it may be difficult to apply the findings to this research setting (further discussed in the literature review).

[iii] For a more detailed discussion of different definitions see McGrath et al. (1995) and Caldeira and Ward (2003).

[iv] This is based on Barney's (1991) earlier work, which suggests that resources can only lead to competitive advantage if they are valuable, rare, imperfectly imitable, and not strategically substitutable by other resources (the VRIN-attributes).

v   Following the suggestions of Dillman (1978) a pilot test was used to identify possible problems with the questionnaire. Therefore managers were asked to complete the questionnaire and then they were asked to identify problems, like for example unclear questions or questions that were difficult to answer. They were furthermore asked, if they believe that any important variables are missing. However, only some minor points were raised, and subsequently the result of the pilot was only some minor changes in the wording of a few questions.

vi   The following two attempts were made for triangulating the survey's performance data. First, this research was part of a bigger research project, which also required the collection of qualitative data. The authors therefore visited 17 companies and conducted interviews with the owner managers, and they were asked about their performance. 9 of the 17 managers refused to offer any performance information as a matter of firm policy, and only 8 managers gave us some performance information. It is of course not possible to triangulate this information with the survey data and to get statistically significant results with a sample size of 8. However, the qualitative analysis of the interviews and of the information that was offered on the firms' websites strongly supported the survey data. Second, a literature review of the leading strategic management journals was conducted to identify suitable databases for this research. Databases that were frequently used in strategic manage-

ment research were, for example, Dun & Bradstreet, Standard and Poor and Kompass. In addition, the authors went to the local city council, which provides some basic performance data. However, this data did not appear to be valid. First, the authors would have expected to find relatively "irregular" numbers with a variety of digits, like for example £123,456. However, all numbers were suspiciously regular, which typically started with the digit 1 and ended with zeros, like for example £100,000. Therefore, the data appeared to be very imprecise. In addition, the performance data appeared to be completely outdated. For example, the authors couldn't find data on young companies at all, and when data from secondary sources were triangulated with current information from our survey, the interviews and the companies' websites the data appeared too old. Similar problems are frequently reported in small firm research, because they frequently don't publish and performance data (Dess and Robinson, 1984).

vii   The VIF values for the construct were between 1.1 and 1.7. The VIF values for the single variables (after dropping variables) were between 1.1 and 1.4 which also suggests that multicollinearity is not a problem.

viii   Please note that the authors don't suggest that managers should stop all investments in IT, it is just suggested that managers should monitor their IT budgets carefully and try to increase value for money in terms of IT spending.

APPENDIX 1 (TABLE 6)
Table 6.

Business Resources	strongly disagree				strongly agree
Relationships					
1. We have very open, trusting relationships with our suppliers	1	2	3	4	5
2. We have very open, trusting relationships with our customers	1	2	3	4	5
External driven e-Business					
3. Our suppliers strongly urged us to adopt e-business	1	2	3	4	5
4. Our customers strongly urged us to adopt e-business	1	2	3	4	5
Benchmarking					
5. We actively research the best e-business practices of our competitors	1	2	3	4	5
Strategic use of the Internet					
6. The internet has a strategic meaning for our company	1	2	3	4	5
7. We use the internet actively to reach strategic aims	1	2	3	4	5
Availability of financial resources					
8. Overall, we have enough financial resources	1	2	3	4	5
IT Assets	strongly disagree				strongly agree
IT knowledge					
9. Overall, our technical support staff is knowledgeable, when it comes to computer-based systems	1	2	3	4	5
10. Our firm possesses a high degree of computer-based technical expertise	1	2	3	4	5
11. We are very knowledgeable about new computer-based innovations	1	2	3	4	5
12. We have the knowledge to develop and maintain computer-based communication links with our customers	1	2	3	4	5

IT operations

13. Our firm is skilled at collecting and analyzing market information about our customers via computer-based systems

| 1 | 2 | 3 | 4 | 5 |

14. We routinely utilize computer-based systems to access market information from outside databases

| 1 | 2 | 3 | 4 | 5 |

15. We have set procedures for collecting customer information from online sources

| 1 | 2 | 3 | 4 | 5 |

16. We use computer-based systems to analyze customer and market information

| 1 | 2 | 3 | 4 | 5 |

17. We utilize decision-support systems frequently when it comes to managing customer information

| 1 | 2 | 3 | 4 | 5 |

18. We rely on computer-based systems to acquire, store, and process information about our customers

| 1 | 2 | 3 | 4 | 5 |

IT objects

19. Every year we budget a significant amount of funds for new information technology hardware and software

| 1 | 2 | 3 | 4 | 5 |

20. Our firm creates customized software applications when the need arises

| 1 | 2 | 3 | 4 | 5 |

21. Our firm's members are linked by a computer network

| 1 | 2 | 3 | 4 | 5 |

Dynamic Capabilities   strongly disagree   strongly agree

Integration

22. Overall, our management has expertise to conduct the major strategic moves

| 1 | 2 | 3 | 4 | 5 |

23. Overall, our employees have very good communication skills

| 1 | 2 | 3 | 4 | 5 |

24. Our management has expertise in coordinating internal processes and operations

| 1 | 2 | 3 | 4 | 5 |

25. The feedback of our customers helps us to improve our products and/ or services

| 1 | 2 | 3 | 4 | 5 |

26. The internet has changed our processes significantly

| 1 | 2 | 3 | 4 | 5 |

27. We have had problems integrating e-business applications in previous IT (reversed)

| 1 | 2 | 3 | 4 | 5 |

Learning

28. Overall, our company acquires new knowledge effectively [1] [2] [3] [4] [5]

29. Overall, our company reacts quickly to market changes [1] [2] [3] [4] [5]

30. Overall, our company accumulates knowledge effectively [1] [2] [3] [4] [5]

31. Our company recognizes how customers can benefit from new technologies [1] [2] [3] [4] [5]

Reconfiguration

32. We continuously adapt to customers shifting needs. [1] [2] [3] [4] [5]

33. We quickly respond to competitive strategic moves [1] [2] [3] [4] [5]

34. We easily get rid of assets that have no more value [1] [2] [3] [4] [5]

Performance

Internet Performance   strongly disagree   strongly agree

35. The internet has dramatically increased our productivity [1] [2] [3] [4] [5]

36. The internet has improved our competitive position [1] [2] [3] [4] [5]

37. The internet has dramatically increased our sales [1] [2] [3] [4] [5]

38. The internet has dramatically increased our profitability [1] [2] [3] [4] [5]

39. The internet has dramatically improved our overall performance [1] [2] [3] [4] [5]

Financial Performance   strongly disagree   strongly agree

40. Over the past 3 years, our revenues have been outstanding [1] [2] [3] [4] [5]

41. Over the past 3 years, our revenues have exceeded our competitors [1] [2] [3] [4] [5]

42. Over the past 3 years, our sales growth has been outstanding [1] [2] [3] [4] [5]

43. Over the past 3 years, our sales growth has exceeded our competitors [1] [2] [3] [4] [5]

44. Over the past three years, our return on assets has been outstanding	1	2	3	4	5

45. Over the past 3 years, our return on assets has exceeded our competitors	1	2	3	4	5

General Questions

46. How many full-time employees work in your company? [____]

47. What percentage of your revenue is created by e-commerce? [____]

48. What percentage of the goods and services you buy are ordered via the internet? [____]

49. What is your SIC-code? [____]

50. Are you a for-profit or a non-profit organization?   [For-profit]   [Non-profit]

51. Is your company independent? (This means you have e.g. no parent company or you are not part of a franchising system).   [Yes]   [No]

APPENDIX 2

There are two dominant methods for analysing the interaction effect (in this case, the complementarity of strategic assets with the Internet) in social sciences (Jaccard, Turrisi and Wan, 1990). First, the dichotomising approach is based on median splits. This procedure was used by Powell and Dent-Micallef (1997), when they ranked all companies according to their IT assets and divided them into IT-leading and IT-lagging companies. The authors used this approach in the study. Second, complementarity can be evaluated by deploying hierarchical regression. This approach was chosen by Zhu (2004) and Song et al. (2005). In the appendix this approach was also deployed for demonstrating the validity of our method.

The term without the interaction effect is compared with a term including the interaction effect (the interaction effect is the statistical term for complementarity). At term 1:

$$Z_Y = \alpha + \beta_I Z_I + \beta_B Z_B + \beta_D Z_D + \beta_{IP} Z_{IP} + \varepsilon$$

Z_Y stands again for financial performance, α for the intercept I for the variable set of IT assets, B for business resources, and D for dynamic capabilities. The authors now also introduce IP for Internet performance. β_X are the standardized partial regression coefficients for estimating performance Z_Y. ε is the residual term that captures the net effect of all unspecified factors. Term 1 is supplemented by an interaction effect (term 2):

Whereas term 2a is the interaction effect of IT and the Internet:

$$Z_Y = \alpha + \beta_B Z_B + \beta_D Z_D + \beta_I Z_I + \beta_{IP} Z_{IP} + \beta_{ITIP} Z_{IT*} Z_{IP} + \varepsilon$$

and term 2b is the interaction effect of business resources and the Internet:

$$Z_Y = \alpha + \beta_B Z_B + \beta_D Z_D + \beta_I Z_I + \beta_{IP} Z_{IP} + \beta_{BRIP} Z_{BR*} Z_{IP} + \varepsilon$$

and term 2c is the interaction effect of dynamic capabilities and the Internet:

$$Z_Y = \alpha + \beta_B Z_B + \beta_D Z_D + \beta_I Z_I + \beta_{IP} Z_{IP} + \beta_{DCIP} Z_{DC*} Z_{IP} + \varepsilon$$

ITIP stands for the interaction effect of IT assets and the Internet, BRIP for the interaction of business resources and the Internet and DCIP for dynamic capabilities and the Internet (Jaccard et al., 1990; Zhu, 2004; Song et al., 2005). If an interaction effect is present, then the R^2 of term 2 must be higher than at term 1. A hierarchical regression analysis was conducted. The first level were the control variable (ln emp), the second level was term 1, and the third level term 2. The results are shown Table 7 below.
Table 7.

	Adjusted R^2		
Term 1	0.203***		
Term 2	Term 2a IT-IP	Term 2b BR-IP	Term 2c DC-IT
	0.201***	0.226***	0.225***

As described above, complementarity can be demonstrated by comparing the term without the interaction effect (term 1) with the term with the interaction effect (term 2). A higher adjusted R^2 of term 2 would indicate complementarity. As expected adjusted R^2 was lower at term 2a, because the Internet is not complementary with IT assets. However, terms 2b and 2c were higher than term 1, which suggests that the Internet is complementary with business resources and dynamic capabilities. This suggests that hypotheses 2 and 3 were also supported with this method.

The dichotomising approach showed a negative interaction effect of the Internet on the relationship between IT assets and financial performance. At the hierarchical regression analysis the interaction effect was not statistically significant. The authors believe that this could be due to the relatively small sample size (n=146). The hierarchical regression approach appears to be difficult at small sample sizes because it requires the consideration of additional constructs; which would require larger samples (Jaccard, Turrisi, and Wan, 1990).

Chapter 14

Business Process Digitalization and New Product Development:
An Empirical Study of Small and Medium-Sized Manufacturers

Jun Li
University of New Hampshire, USA

Michael Merenda
University of New Hampshire, USA

A.R. (Venky) Venkatachalam
University of New Hampshire, USA

ABSTRACT

Previous research has largely ignored how business process digitalization across the value chain enhances firm innovation. This chapter examines the relationship between the extensiveness of business process digitalization (BPD) and new product development (NPD) in a sample of 85 small U.S. manufacturers. Scores of extensiveness were derived from the number of adopted e-business practices regarding inter and intra-firm activities such as: customer and supplier services (computer-aided design and manufacturing), employee services (education/training), and industry scanning (technology sourcing). The authors found that (1) NPD is positively related to the extensive use of BPD, and (2) the relationship between NPD and the extensiveness of BPD is stronger in more mature firms than that in younger firms. The authors conclude that small and medium-sized enterprise (SME) production innovation strategies are positively associated with the strategic use of BPD and span spatial, temporal, organizational, and industry boundaries thus aiding SME global competitiveness.

INTRODUCTION

Over the past decades, the rapid developments of the Internet and the information technologies have profoundly impacted every aspect of organizational and social activities. Many business organizations, including small and medium-sized enterprises (SMEs), have started to adopt business process digitalization (hereafter "BPD") as a tool to gain market and operational efficiency (e.g., BarNir, Gallaugher & Auger, 2003; Bharadwaj & Soni, 2007; Johnston, Wade & McClean, 2007). Business process digitalization, in this study, is defined as

DOI: 10.4018/978-1-61520-627-8.ch014

an enterprise-wide information system based on the technological foundation of the Internet. To date, the majority of research on SME's BPD has focused on the antecedents of SMEs engaging in one or few specific types of e-business practice or process (Wymer & Regan, 2005). For example, scholars have examined factors at the organizational level (e.g., Burke, 2005; Dholakia & Kshetri, 2004; Nielson, Host & Mols, 2005; Xu, Rohatgi & Duan, 2007); the industrial level (e.g., Dholakia & Kshetri, 2004; Lee, 2004); and the institutional level (e.g., Kshetri, 2007) that influence the SME's decision to adopt BPD. Less in quantities, studies also have looked at the role of BPD in influencing SMEs' market and operational performance (e.g., Johnston et al., 2007; Merono-Cerdan & Soto-Acosta, 2006; Rajendran & Vivekanandan, 2008; Zhu, Kraemer, Xu & Dedrick, 2004).

While these studies provide good understanding of the antecedents and the financial consequences of BPD, how BPD affects SME's new product development is still unclear. As a key indicator of firm innovation, new product development is crucial to the survival and success of business and enterprise, including SMEs (Huang, Soutar & Brown, 2002). This study aims to understand how SMEs can enhance new product development through use of BPD. Building upon insights from the knowledge-based view (Conner, 1991; Grant, 1996; Kogut & Zander, 1992) and the organizational learning theory (Argyris & Schon, 1978; Cyert & March, 1963), the central thesis of this study is that the extensive use of BPD enhances the firm's knowledge-base resources and improves its organizational learning, therefore contributing to SME's new product development.

This study has several contributions. First, it complements current research on the consequences of SME e-business practices and processes. The existing studies on the impact of SME BPD have largely focused on operational outcomes such as financial or market performance (e.g., Johnston et al., 2007; Servais, Madsen & Rasmussen, 2007). Our study enriches this research stream

by looking at the impact of BPD on new product development, one of the important measures for firm competitiveness. Second, we attempt to conceptualize BPD as a strategic process employed by SMEs to leverage information technologies as rent seeking and value creation initiatives. We posit that BPD not only enhances operational effectiveness of the firm (Porter, 1991), but also is conducive to entrepreneurial decision-making and innovation (von Hippel, 2005). Third, the existing studies typically examine BPD independent of other possible moderating variables. The contingency theory (Donaldson, 2001) suggests that the impacts of BPD may vary, depending on certain types of organizational characteristics. We explored the potential moderating effects of organizational characteristics (firm age and type of products) on the effect of BPD on new product development.

THEORY AND HYPOTHESES

The Knowledge-Based View

Extending from the resource-based view of the firm (Barney, 1991; Wernerfelt, 1984), the knowledge-based view (Conner, 1991; Grant, 1996; Kogut & Zander, 1992) considers knowledge as the most strategically significant resource of the firm. Organizational knowledge is embedded and carried through multiple entities including organizational culture and identity, policies, routines, documents, systems, and employees (Nonaka, 1994). Because knowledge-based resources are heterogeneous and difficult to imitate and transfer across organizations, the knowledge bases and capabilities among firms are the major determinants of sustained competitive advantage and superior firm performance (Barney, 1991).

Scholars have argued that information technologies[1] can play an important role in the knowledge-base of the firm in that information systems can be used to synthesize, enhance, and expedite large-scale intra- and inter-firm knowledge management (Alavi & Leidner, 2001). Furthermore, scholars have argued that information technology *capability* is one of the critical firm capabilities that may contribute to firm superior performance (e.g., Mata, Fuerst & Barney, 1995; Wade & Hulland, 2004). Bharadwaj (2000) proposed and empirically tested three types of IT-based resources that generally contribute to firm superior performance. They are (1) tangible IT infrastructure, which includes physical IT assets and systems; (2) human IT resources, the IT employees and managers; and (3) IT enabled intangible resources, which includes customer orientation, knowledge-base assets and synergy. Bharadwaj further argued that IT *capability* as an important organizational capability, does not come from any specific set of IT functionalities, rather it comes from the *integration* of the three IT-based resources. This capability can serve as a form of isolation mechanism, which is hard for rivals to imitate due to its social complexity, path dependence, and causal ambiguity (Bharadwaj, 2000).

Organizational Learning

Early theorists in organization learning (e.g., Argyris & Schon, 1978; Cyert & March, 1963; Daft & Weick, 1984) view organizations as open systems in which insights and knowledge can be developed though the interaction between the organization and its environment. Although different models/terms have been used to describe the process of organization learning, scholars tend to agree that an organizational learning process consists of four basic components: information acquisition, information dissemination, shared interpretation, and development of organizational memory (c.f., Tippins & Sohi, 2003). According to Tippins and Sohi's summary, information acquisition refers to the process in which firms seek and gather useful information. Dissemination of information refers to the distribution of information among organi-

zational units and people. Shared interpretation is organization's consensus among organization members with regard to the meaning of information. And organizational memory refers to the stored information or experience the organization has about a particular phenomenon.

A general finding of research on the relationship between information technologies and organizational learning is that information systems facilitate the process of organizational learning by enabling and supporting knowledge acquisition, information distribution, information interpretation, and organizational memory (e.g., Kane & Alavi, 2007). The information system flattens the structure of the organization and promotes greater dissemination of information throughout the organization. This makes the organization more open, informed, flexible, and organic. Increased availability of information helps members share information thereby increasing learning. For example, market intelligence systems help the firm acquire critical competitive and market information; and the internal IT system (E-mails, forums, and bulletin boards, etc.) facilitates internal information distribution and interpretation process. Furthermore, information technology helps expand the scale and/scope of organization learning in that the firm can access, acquire, absorb, and utilize external information and/or knowledge by overcoming spatial and temporal distances (Boudreau, Loch, Robey & Straud, 1998).

The Extensiveness of BPD and New Product Development

As mentioned earlier, we define business process digitalization as an enterprise-wide information system based on the technological foundation of the Internet. Specifically, we refer to enterprise-wide Internet/Intranet applications which compass various aspects of organizational activities and processes. This includes B2C (business to customers), B2S (business to suppliers), B2E (business to employees) and B2O (business to others) IT applications that cover various inter and intra-firm activities, such as customer and supplier services (computer-aided design and manufacturing), employee services (education/training), and industry scanning (technology sourcing) and so on[2]. The focus of this study is not the *intensity* of BPD in any specific category. Instead, we are interested in how *extensive* use of BPD, i.e., the *scope* of Internet and Intranet applications applied across both horizontal and vertical value chains influences SME product innovation.

The scope of BPD and its relationship with firm innovation has received increasing attention among scholars in this field recently. Zwass (2003) identified five domains of e-business and proposed a "5-C framework", which includes (1) commerce (for example marketplace and universal supply chain linkage), (2) collaboration (the network and collaborative relationships between the firm and external parties); (3) communication (such as forum, interactive medium, and delivery vehicle); (4) connection (the connectivity, development platform, as well as universal telecommunication network), and (5) computation (computing utility). In each of these domains, e-business practices lead to specific innovational opportunities. For example, e-marketplace allows for the opportunities for customization, price discovery, and new business models. e-collaboration helps expand the boundary of organizational knowledge and enhance the firm's overall innovation ability. Zwass finally emphasizes that it is the combination of these aspects, not isolation, leads the firm to be more innovative in terms of opportunity seeking and capturing. In an empirical study, Beck and his colleagues found that firms with an all-embracing approach utilizing e-commerce applications are often more efficient than others with lower e-commerce diffusions (Beck, Wigand & Konig, 2005).

We argue that the scope of BPD (i.e., the extensiveness of Internet use through B2C, B2S, B2E and B2O models) will have positive impact on SME new product development. A fully-embraced approach of BPD not only enhances the knowledge base for the firm, but also enhances the firm's competency in learning through the systems. From the knowledge-based view, applying Internet technology in various business practices and processes enhances the firm's IT infrastructure as well as human IT resources (Bharadwaj, 2000). The extensive use of BPD enables the firm to collect and analyze large amount of information at relatively lower cost. Further, firms with a full spectrum of e-business system are able to build up a set of complementary resources (technological and/or organizational) that are unique to the venture (Bharadwaj, 2000). In a recent study, Devaraj, Krajewski, and Wei found that while firms using e-business for customer integration does not have direct impact on firm performance, firms using e-business for *both* customer integration *and* supplier integration significantly outperform the others (Devaraj, Krajewski & Wei, 2007). It is the enterprise-wide information system, rather than any particular IT system, leads to competitive advantage of the firm (Henderson & Venkatraman, 1993).

Taking an organization learning perspective, extensive BPD enhances firm's ability to generate product innovations as well. First, as discussed earlier, extensive Internet and Intranet applications enhance the firm's ability to acquire information; Second, the wide use of Internet improves communication efficiently and effectiveness within the organization which will enhance the process of knowledge dissimilation and sharing within the organization. For example, Ortega, Marinez, and Hoyos found that for firms using different information technologies (Internet, EDI, etc.) on e-customer relationship management (E-CRM), there is a direct and positive transmission of knowledge from E-CRM to B2B development (Ortega, Marinez & Hoyos, 2008). Third, extensive use of BPD expands organization boundary in terms of technology transfer and knowledge creation. Research has demonstrated that firms' ability to generate product innovations increasingly relies on the effective acquisition of new product knowledge through external linkages (Bierly & Chakrabarti, 1996; Rothwell & Dodgson, 1991). The more extensive a SME uses BPD for its business and organizational activities, the more the firm builds up links with external entities (such as suppliers, customers, trade associations, industry research institutes and/or universities), which increases the firm's learning base for knowledge creation (Nonaka, 1994).

Therefore we predict,

> **Hypothesis 1:** *The extensiveness (the scope) of business process digitalization is positively associated with SME new product development.*

Moderating Effects of Firm Age and Product Type

Contingency theory posits that the effects of organizational characteristics on effectiveness and/or performance are often influenced by third variable such as organization size and environmental uncertainty (Donaldson, 2001). In this study we considered two important contingencies: firm age and type of products. Firm age is one of the central constructs studied by organizational ecologists and has been demonstrated to have important implications to venture success (Freeman, Carroll & Hannan, 1983; Henderson, 1999). Research has shown that compared to older firms, younger (or newer) firms have higher liabilities of newness (Stinchcombe, 1965), less financial and personal resources, and have not yet developed organizational routines or systems (Nelson & Winter, 1982). We argue that these limitations will weaken the impact of BPD on new product development. From a knowledge-based view, the lack of IT infrastructure, less developed human IT resources, and immature organizational systems makes it difficult for younger firms to fully exploit the values of BPD. Indeed, younger firms may not have strong incentives to apply a fully integrated

information system, as there is less need for it until the business is growing. Researchers have found that younger firms tend to have less formal market research an environmental scanning behaviors (Mohan-Neill, 1995). Also, with limited linkages to external partners, younger firms will have less chance to expand their knowledge bases across organization boundaries. Therefore we predict,

> **Hypothesis 2.1:** *Firm age positively moderates the relationship between the extensiveness (the scope) of business process digitalization and SME new product development.*

Another moderator we examined is the firm's type of products. Specifically we categorized the products of the sample firms into two categories, one is the *"off-the-shelf"* products which are standardized products targeting the mass market, the other is customer-collaborated products, which involves customer designing, testing, and collaborations. We argue that in firms that have higher percentage of customer-collaborated products in their product lines, the relationship between the extensiveness of BPD and new product development would be stronger than that in firms that have higher percentage of *"off-the-shelf"* products. Firms producing higher percentage of customer-collaborated products have both incentives and the needs to have more frequent interactions with customers, suppliers, designers as well as producers than those producing lower percentage of such products. In many cases, small and medium-sized firms produce customer-collaborated products required by large corporations outsourcing programs through increased collaboration and development of advanced information technologies (Chan & Chung, 2002). From the knowledge-based view and organizational learning perspectives, a higher percentage of customer-collaborated products suggests a higher level of information exchange, knowledge sharing and integration, which ultimately lead to a higher level of product innovation.

Therefore we predict,

Hypothesis 2.2: *The percentage of customer-collaborated products in total sales positively moderates the relationship between business process digitalization and SME new product development.*

METHODOLOGY

Sample and Data Collection

The initial sample consists of 414 small and medium-sized manufacturers in engineering, electronics, computer and software industries that were identified from Reference USA and Mass High Tech Databases. We selected small manufacturers in these industries of their capacity for innovation and intensive and extensive use of electronic and non-electronic environments to link with customers, suppliers, employees and others in the value chain. To be qualified to be included in the sample, a firm must (1) have less than 500 employees, and (2) annual sales are between $5 million and $1 billion. These criteria are consistent with previous research (BarNir et al., 2003).

Telephone survey was made to the CEO or the President of the company to collect data about the firm and their e-business strategies. In addition to providing background information on the company and themselves, respondents were asked to evaluate their use of the Internet with customers, suppliers, employees and others. Out of 414 firms, 50 firms didn't have correct contact information, giving a pool of 364 firms to contact. 85 firms responded the telephone survey for a response rate of 23.3%. The telephone survey was administered by the University's survey center during 2005.

Measures

New product development. In the questionnaire, we asked the respondent what percentage of the company's sales was generated from new prod-

ucts introduced in the past 3 years, compared to its top 3 competitors. Answers range from (1) "Substantially below top 3 competitors"; (2) " Somewhat below top 3 competitors"; (3) "Average of top 3 competitors"; (4) "Somewhat above top 3 competitors"; to (5) "Substantially above top 3 competitors". Therefore this variable was measured by an index, with 1 as the lowest level and 5 as the highest.

Extensiveness of BPD. Adopting the measures used by Theyel, Merenda and Venkatachalam (2001), we identified and categorized 19 distinct e-business practices encompassing areas of B2C, B2S, B2E and B2O to measure the firm's extensiveness (the scope) of business process digitalization. A detailed list of these 19 activities is listed in Appendix A. For each activity, if the SME has implemented in its organization, the firm will be scored 1. If the firm has never conducted the specific e-business practice, the firm will be scored 0. The extensiveness of business process digitalization then is operationalized as: [(the firm's total score)/19].

Firm age. Firm age is measured by the difference between the founding year of the firm and the year when the survey was completed (2005).

Customer-collaborated products. This is a ratio variable, measuring the percentage of products that were manufactured through customer cooperation in total sales.

The following variables were included as controls. The first one is *IT expenditure.* We asked the respondent to evaluate their annual spending on information technology compared to their top 3 competitors in choosing one of the followings: (1) Substantially below top 3 competitors; (2) Somewhat below top 3 competitors; (3). Average of top 3 competitors; (4) Somewhat above top 3 competitors; and (5) Substantially above top 3 competitors. Therefore IT expenditure was scaled from 1 (the lowest) to 5 (the highest). *IT manager* was included to control whether or not a senior manager was assigned to be in charge of IT system in the firm. Finally we included a dummy variable, *Using Internet as management tool,* to control how important the management team utilizes the Internet as an administrative or management tool for firm activities (with lowest as 0, and highest as 5).

Analysis and Results

We employed a hierarchical approach in analyzing both the main and interaction effects. First we created a base model of OLS regression, which includes all our control variables. We subsequently added independent variables and moderating variables in full models. We then tested for the significance of the difference between the full models and the nested base model by using Chi-square tests. A significant Chi-square test means additional variance of probability of persistence explained by the added-on predictors.

Despite overall statistical significance, the original model (the normal model) suffered from reduced sample caused by missing values. To address this, we employed multiple imputation method (Robin, 1977; Rubin, 1987). Multiple imputation involves three steps. First, the missing data are filled in *m* times to generate *m* complete data sets; second, the *m* complete data sets are analyzed using standard procedures; third, the results from the *m* complete data sets are combined for the inference. It is noted that the imputed values produced from an imputation model are not intended to be "guesses" as to what a particular missing value might be; rather, this procedure is intended to create an imputed data set which maintains the overall variability in the population while preserving relationships with other variables. For this paper we reported results from both the normal model and the imputed model.

Means, standard deviations, and correlation matrix are reported in Table 1. Table 2 and Table 3 report the results obtained from the hierarchical OLS regressions for the normal model and the imputed model respectively. In Table 2, Model 1 only included control variables. Model 2 test

the impact of extensiveness of business process digitalization on new product development. Models 3-4 included moderating variables (firm age and product type). Since including different interaction variable requires different imputed data sets, we did two sets of hierarchical regressions for imputed model in Table 3. Similar with Table 1, in Table 3, Model 1 and Model 4 only included control variables. Model 2 and Model 5 included independent variable. Model 3 and Model 6 included the interaction term of firm age and the interaction term of product type respectively. In most cases, positive change of Chi-square values and their significance levels confirm that adding the independent variables as well as the moderating variables help improve the overall explanatory power of the model of new product development.

Hypothesis 1 predicts that the extensiveness of business process digitalization is positively related with new product development. Results from the normal model (Table 2) support this hypothesis. The coefficients for this independent variable are consistently positive and significant (b=1.769, p<.05; b=2.649, p<.01; and b=2.178, p<.05 in Model 2, 3 and 4 respectively). Results from the imputed model (Table 3) reported partial support (b=.775, p<.05 in Model 5). Overall the results from both models suggest that the extensiveness of business process digitalization has a positive influence on new product development. Therefore Hypothesis 1 is supported.

Hypothesis 2.1 predicts that firm age has a positive moderating effect on the relationship between the extensiveness of business process digitalization and new product development. Results from both the normal model (Table 2) and the imputed model (Table 3) provide strong evidence for this hypothesis. The coefficients for this variable are positive and significant (b=.135, p<.05 in Model 3 of Table 2, b=.077, p<.001 in Model 3 of Table 3). To facilitate interpretation, we conducted the following analysis to plot this interaction effect. First, variable means in Model 3 of Table 3 were

Table 1. Means, standard deviations and correlation matrix (normal model)

Variable	N	Mean	S.D.	1	2	3	4	5	6
1. New product development	62	3.58	.86						
2. IT expenditure	55	2.85	1.13	.62 ***					
3. IT manager	84	.44	.50	.26 *	.44 ***				
4. Internet as management tool	73	1.82	1.05	.21	.20	.09			
5. Customer-collaborated products (%)	71	25.86	30.45	-.14	-.11	-.07	-.09		
6. Firm age	81	34.84	22.67	.09	-.15	.11	-.23†	-.05	
7. Extensiveness of BPD	85	.85	.23	.30 *	.31 *	.18†	.09	-.12	.27 *

*** p<.001, **p<.01, *p<.05, †p<.1;

substituted for all predictors except firm age and extensiveness of business process digitalization. The result was a reduced equation with two predictors and their cross product. Second, we followed the procedure of Cohen and Levinthal (1990). The values for firm age were taken one standard deviation above zero point and one standard deviation below zero point respectively. Substituting each of these values into the reduced equation yielded two linear equations, which are depicted in Figure

Table 2. Results of hierarchical regressions on new product development (normal model) *

Variable	Model 1	Model 2	Model 3	Model 4
IT expenditure	.434 **	.402 **	.374 **	.399 **
IT manager	.423	.450	.475	.506
Internet as management tool	.201	.123	.109	.078
Customer-collaborated products	.002	.007 †	.007 †	.006
Firm age	.006	.003	-.011	.002
Extensiveness of BPD		1.769 *	2.649 **	2.178 *
Extensiveness of BPD × Firm age			.135 *	
Extensiveness of BPD ×				
Customer-collaborated products				-.027
F-value	5.75 **	7.19 **	9.71 ***	7.02 ***
R-Squared	.43	.51	.60	.53
Δ F		4.56 *	5.76 *	.90
Δ R-Squared		.09 *	.09 *	.02
N	33	33	33	33

***p<.001, **p<.01, *p<.05, †p<.1
* OLS regression with robust errors on centered variables.

*Table 3. Results of hierarchical regressions on new product development (imputed model) ***

Variable	Model 1	Model 2	Model 3	Model 4	Model 5	Model 6
IT expenditure	.518 ***	.508 ***	.502 ***	.558 **	.506 ***	.511 ***
IT manager	.164	.164	.138	.115	.111	.090
Internet as management tool	.078	.073	.081	.104	.066	.085
Customer-collaborated products	.005 *	.005 *	.005 *	.003	.003	.003 †
Firm age	.007	.006	-.000	.009 **	.007 †	.007 †
Extensiveness of BPD		.169	1.139		.775 *	.694
Extensiveness of BPD × Firm age			.077 **			
Extensiveness of BPD × Customer-collaborated products						.008
F-value	15.64 ***	13.46 ***	12.78 ***	19.50 ***	15.50 ***	21.49 ***
R-Squared	.44	.45	.54	.50	.53	.54
Δ F		.26	15.28 ***		5.90 *	.51
Δ R-Squared		.01	.09 ***		.04 *	.01
N	85	85	85	85	85	85

***p<.001, **p<.01, *p<.05, †p<.1
* OLS regression with robust errors on centered variables.

1. As shown in Figure 1, when firm age is higher (+1 standard deviation), the effect of extensiveness of business process digitalization on new product development is stronger than when firm age is lower (-1 standard deviation). Therefore, Hypothesis 2.1 is supported.

Hypothesis 2.2 predicts that customer-collaborated products moderate the relationship between business process digitalization and new product development. We predict that business process digitalization has greater impact on new product development in firms with higher percentage of customer-collaborated products in sales than that in firms with lower percentage of customer-collaborated products in sales (higher percentage of "off-the-shelf" type products in sales). Results from Table 2 and Table 3 didn't provide supportive evidences (b=-.027 n.s. in Model 4 of Table 2;

b=.008, n.s. in Model 6 of Table 3). Therefore we didn't find evidence supporting Hypothesis 2.2.

DISCUSSION, LIMITATIONS, AND CONCLUSION

This study investigates the relationship between the extensiveness of business process digitalization (the extensive use of e-business practices across value chains) and SME new product development. Driven by the interest of how small and medium-sized firms achieve enhanced innovation capability, we performed a quantitative study on 85 SMEs. We found that the extensiveness of business process digitalization has a significantly positive impact on SME new product development. Furthermore, this impact is greater in more

Figure 1. Moderating effect of firm age

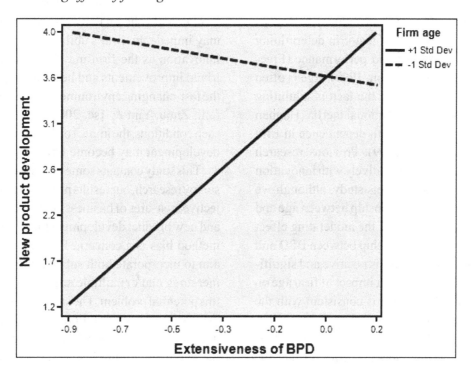

mature firms than in younger firms. We did not find evidence that firms with higher percentage of customer-collaborated products in total sales benefited more from business process digitalization with regard new product development.

We believe our study is one of the first empirical studies examining the impact of extensiveness of business process digitalization on SME new product development. Previous literature has mostly focused on either the antecedents of BPD or the financial consequences of using one or more specific types of e-business practice or process, leaving the impact of using an enterprise-wide BPD on firm product innovation largely unexplored (e.g., Nielson et al., 2005; Xu et al., 2007). By adopting insights from the knowledge-based view of the firm and organization learning theory, this study found a linkage between BPD and new product development. This is a critical finding for small and medium-sized enterprise competitiveness. The positive relationship between BPD and new product development suggests that SMEs can

achieve competitive advantages by embracing and exploiting an enterprise-wide information system. The advantages are created through the enhanced efficiency and effectiveness in information and/or knowledge acquisition, absorption, interpretation, and dissemination process. The extensiveness of BPD also allows the firm to develop unique, hard-to-imitate IT capability and IT enabled knowledge base through synergy and learning effects. More importantly, our study echoes recent research on strategic use of Internet (e.g., Lumpkin & Dess, 2004; Sadowski, Maitland & van Dongen, 2002). Most organizations and their CEOs have failed to comprehend that the Internet is both a new technology and a strategic innovation, particularly when SMEs are constrained by technological, financial and human resources. The results from this study imply that despite these constraints and limitations, SMEs have the opportunity to enhance its firm competency by applying BPD throughout the organization.

The moderating effect of firm age on the relationship between BPD and new product development is interesting. Organizational ecologists argue that age is a critical factor in determining organizational survival and performance (Freeman et al., 1983; Henderson, 1999). Age is often been considered as one of the factors inhibiting innovation due to organizational inertia (Hannan & Freeman, 1984) and path dependence in firm strategy (Henderson, 1999). Previous research tends to relate firm age negatively with innovation (e.g., Hansen, 1992). In this study, although we did not find a direct relationship between age and new product development, the moderating effect of firm age on the relationship between BPD and new product development is positive and significant, suggesting an indirect impact of firm age on innovation in SMEs. This is consistent with the structural view of the organization (Churchill & Lewis, 1983; Miller, 1982). Mature small firms are more stable than younger firms so that the enterprise-wide information system can be fully exploited and integrated with business and organization processes. Further, the strategic use of the Internet across the organization requires adoption and implementation of Internet/IT systems, and leadership and an organizational culture for support and reinforcement (Claver, Llopis, Garcia & Molina, 1998). Mature small businesses have advantages in this regard because they are more stable than younger firms.

The failure to observe a positive moderating effect of customer-collaborated products deserves our explanation. One plausible explanation might be that for many small and medium-sized manufacturers, customer-collaborated products are often designed and manufactured collaboratively with larger OEMs (Wood, Kaufman & Merenda, 1996). As a major platform, the business to customer system in SME serves to strengthen the relationships between the focal SME and providing innovative products and services to the OEMs. Although the e-system enhances the efficiencies and effectiveness in knowledge sharing between the SME and their larger customers, there are limitations. Research has shown that customer concentration may impede the firm's ability to conduct radical innovation as the firm may become focused on trivial improvements and become insulated from the fast-changing environment and/or technology (c.f., Zhou, Yim & Tse, 2005). Therefore under such conditions, the impact of BPD on new product development may become limited.

This study contains some limitations. Like most survey research, our results primarily relied on subjective measures of business process digitalization and new product development therefore common method bias is a concern. Future studies should aim to incorporate both subjective and objective measures, and/or multiple respondents to alleviate this potential problem. The study's cross-sectional design is also a limitation. The current model does not allow for causal interpretations among the variables. Future research could investigate the dynamic relationship between changes in the firm's extensive use of new product development and innovation by using longitudinal data. Finally, although the results from the imputed model are mostly consistent with that of the normal model and has legitimate statistical significance, this method has its own limitations. Future studies should aim to enhance the dataset to deal with the missing values, for example, expanding the sample size.

In summary, with a sample of 85 small and medium-sized U.S. manufacturers, this paper examines the role of business process digitalization in new product development. We found that it is the *extensiveness* of business process digitalization that contributes to new product development in SMEs. We demonstrated that this positive relationship was moderated by firm age. It is our hope that this study will facilitate further discussion and provide meaningful implications for SMEs on the value of business process digitalization in fostering new product development and long-term competitiveness.

REFERENCES

Alavi, M., & Leidner, D. E. (2001). Review: Knowledge management and knowledge management systems: Conceptual foundations and research issues. *MIS Quarterly, 25*(1), 107–136. doi:10.2307/3250961

Argyris, C., & Schon, D. (1978). Organizational learning: A theory of action perspective. Reading, MA: Addison-Wesley.

Barney, J. (1991). Firm resources and sustained competitive advantage. *Journal of Management, 17*(1), 99–120. doi:10.1177/014920639101700108

BarNir, A., Gallaugher, J. M., & Auger, P. (2003). Business process digitization, strategy, and the impact of firm age and size: The case of the magazine publishing industry. *Journal of Business Venturing, 18*(6), 789–814. doi:10.1016/S0883-9026(03)00030-2

Beck, R., Wigand, R. T., & Konig, W. (2005). The diffusion and efficient use of electronic commerce among small and medium sized enterprises: An international three industry survey. *Electronic Markets, 15*(1), 38–52. doi:10.1080/10196780500035282

Bharadwaj, A. S. (2000). A resource-based perspective on information technology capability and firm performance: An empirical investigation. *MIS Quarterly, 24*(1), 169–196. doi:10.2307/3250983

Bharadwaj, P. N., & Soni, R. G. (2007). E-commerce usage and perception of e-commerce issues among small firms: Results and implications from an empirical study. *Journal of Small Business Management, 45*(4), 501–521. doi:10.1111/j.1540-627X.2007.00225.x

Bierly, P., & Chakrabarti, A. (1996). Generic knowledge strategies in the us pharmaceutical industry. *Strategic Management Journal, 17,* 123–135.

Boudreau, M.-C., Loch, K. D., Robey, D., & Straud, D. (1998). Going global: Using information technology to advance the competitiveness of the virtual transnational organization. *The Academy of Management Executive, 12*(4), 120–128.

Burke, K. (2005). The impact of firm size on Internet use in small businesses. *Electronic Markets, 15*(2), 79–93. doi:10.1080/10196780500083738

Chan, M. F. S., & Chung, W. W. C. (2002). A framework to development an enterprise information portal for contract manufacturing. *International Journal of Production Economics, 75*(1/2), 113–126. doi:10.1016/S0925-5273(01)00185-2

Churchill, N. C., & Lewis, V. L. (1983). The five stages of small business growth. *Harvard Business Review, 61*(3), 30–39.

Claver, E., Llopis, J., Garcia, D., & Molina, H. (1998). Organizational culture for innovation and new technological behavior. *The Journal of High Technology Management Research, 9*(1), 55. doi:10.1016/1047-8310(88)90005-3

Cohen, W. M., & Levinthal, D. A. (1990). Absorptive-capacity - a new perspective on learning and innovation. *Administrative Science Quarterly, 35*(1), 128–152. doi:10.2307/2393553

Conner, K. R. (1991). A historical comparison of resource-based theory and 5 schools of thought within industrial-organization economics - do we have a new theory of the firm. *Journal of Management, 17*(1), 121–154. doi:10.1177/014920639101700109

Cyert, R. M., & March, J. G. (1963). A behavioral theory of the firm. Englewood Cliffs, NJ: Prentice-Hall.

Daft, R. L., & Weick, K. E. (1984). Toward a model of organizations as interpretation systems. *Academy of Management Review, 9*(2), 284–295. doi:10.2307/258441

Devaraj, S., Krajewski, L., & Wei, J. C. (2007). Impact of e-business technologies on operational performance: The role of production information integration in the supply chain. *Journal of Operations Management*, *25*(6), 1199–1216. doi:10.1016/j.jom.2007.01.002

Dholakia, R. R., & Kshetri, N. (2004). Factors impacting the adoption of the Internet among SMEs. *Small Business Economics*, *23*(4), 311–322. doi:10.1023/B:SBEJ.0000032036.90353.1f

Donaldson, L. (2001). The contingency theory of organizations. Thousand Oaks, CA: Sage Publications.

Freeman, J., Carroll, G. R., & Hannan, M. T. (1983). The liability of newness: Age dependence in organizational death rates. *American Sociological Review*, *48*(5), 692–710. doi:10.2307/2094928

Grant, R. M. (1996). Toward a knowledge-based theory of the firm. *Strategic Management Journal*, *17*, 109–122. doi:10.1002/(SICI)1097-0266-(199602)17:2<109::AID-SMJ796>3.0.CO;2-P

Hannan, M. T., & Freeman, J. (1984). Structural inertia and organizational change. *American Sociological Review*, *49*(2), 149–164. doi:10.2307/2095567

Hansen, J. A. (1992). Innovation, firm size, and firm age. *Small Business Economics*, *4*(1), 37–44.

Henderson, A. D. (1999). Firm strategy and age dependence: A contingent view of the liabilities of newness, adolescence, and obsolescence. *Administrative Science Quarterly*, *44*(2), 281–314. doi:10.2307/2666997

Henderson, J. C., & Venkatraman, N. (1993). Strategic alignment: Leveraging information technology for transforming organizations. *IBM Systems Journal*, *32*(1), 4–16.

Huang, X., Soutar, G. N., & Brown, A. (2002). New product development processes in small and medium-sized enterprises: Some Australian evidence. *Journal of Small Business Management*, *40*(1), 27–42. doi:10.1111/1540-627X.00036

Johnston, D. A., Wade, M., & McClean, R. (2007). Does e-business matter to SMEs? A comparison of the financial impacts of Internet business solutions on European and North American SMEs. *Journal of Small Business Management*, *45*(3), 354–361. doi:10.1111/j.1540-627X.2007.00217.x

Kane, G. C., & Alavi, M. (2007). Information technology and organizational learning: An investigation of exploration and exploitation processes. *Organization Science*, *18*(5), 796–812. doi:10.1287/orsc.1070.0286

Kogut, B., & Zander, U. (1992). Knowledge of the firm, combinative capabilities, and the replication of technology. *Organization Science*, *3*(3), 383–397. doi:10.1287/orsc.3.3.383

Kshetri, N. (2007). The adoption of e-business by organizations in china: An institutional perspective. *Electronic Markets*, *17*(2), 113–125. doi:10.1080/10196780701296022

Lee, J. (2004). Discriminant analysis of technology adoption behavior: A case of Internet technologies in small businesses. *Journal of Computer Information Systems*, *44*(4), 57–66.

Lumpkin, G. T., & Dess, G. G. (2004). E-business strategies and Internet business models: How the Internet adds value. *Organizational Dynamics*, *33*(2), 161–173. doi:10.1016/j.orgdyn.2004.01.004

Mata, F. J., Fuerst, W. L., & Barney, J. B. (1995). Information technology and sustained competitive advantage: A resource-based analysis. *MIS Quarterly*, *19*(4), 487–505. doi:10.2307/249630

Merono-Cerdan, A. L., & Soto-Acosta, P. (2006). Examining e-business impact on firm performance through website analysis. *International Journal of Electronic Business, 3*(6), 1–1.

Miller, D. (1982). Evolution and revolution - a quantum view of structural-change in organizations. *Journal of Management Studies, 19*(2), 131–151. doi:10.1111/j.1467-6486.1982.tb00064.x

Mohan-Neill, S. I. (1995). The influence of firm's age and size on its environmental scanning activities. *Journal of Small Business Management, 33*(4), 10–21.

Nelson, R. R., & Winter, S. G. (1982). An evolutionary theory of economic change. Cambridge, MA: Harvard University Press.

Nielson, J. F., Host, V., & Mols, N. P. (2005). Adoption of internet-based marketing channels by small- and medium-sized manufacturers. *International Journal of E-Business Research, 1*(2), 1–23.

Nonaka, I. (1994). A dynamic theory of organizational knowledge creation. *Organization Science, 5*(1), 14–37. doi:10.1287/orsc.5.1.14

Ortega, B. H., Marinez, J. J., & Hoyos, M. (2008). The role of information technology knowledge in b2b development. *International Journal of E-Business Research, 4*(1), 40–54.

Porter, M. E. (1991). Towards a dynamic theory of strategy. *Strategic Management Journal, 12*, 95–117. doi:10.1002/smj.4250121008

Rajendran, R., & Vivekanandan, K. (2008). Exploring relationship between information systems strategic orientation and small business performance. *International Journal of E-Business Research, 4*(2), 14–28.

Robin, D. B. (1977). Formalizing subjective notions about the effect of nonrespondents in sample surveys. *Journal of the American Statistical Association, 72*, 538–543. doi:10.2307/2286214

Rothwell, R., & Dodgson, M. (1991). External linkages and innovation in small and medium-sized enterprises. *R & D Management, 21*(2), 125–138. doi:10.1111/j.1467-9310.1991.tb00742.x

Rubin, D. B. (1987). Multiple imputation for nonresponse in surveys. New York: John Wiley.

Sadowski, B. M., Maitland, C., & van Dongen, J. (2002). Strategic use of the internet by small- and medium-sized companies: An exploratory study. *Information Economics and Policy, 14*(1), 75–93. doi:10.1016/S0167-6245(01)00054-3

Servais, P., Madsen, T. K., & Rasmussen, E. S. (2007). Small manufacturing firms' involvement in international e-business activities. *Advances in International Marketing(17)*, 297-317.

Stinchcombe, A. L. (1965). Social structure and organizations. In J. G. March (Ed.), Handbook of organizations (pp. 142-193). Chicago: Rand McNally & Company.

Theyel, G., Merenda, M., & Venkatachalam, A. R. (2001 October). How small and medium size manufacturers use the internet for technology development. *Journal of Business and Entrepreneurship,* 83-106.

Tippins, M. J., & Sohi, R. S. (2003). It competency and firm performance: Is organizational learning a missing link? *Strategic Management Journal, 24*(8), 745–761. doi:10.1002/smj.337

von Hippel, E. (2005). Democritizing innovation. Cambridge, MA: MIT Press.

Wade, M., & Hulland, J. (2004). Review: The resource-based view and information systems research: Review, extension, and suggestions for future research [1]. *MIS Quarterly, 28*(1), 107–142.

Wernerfelt, B. (1984). A resource-based view of the firm. *Strategic Management Journal, 5*(2), 171–180. doi:10.1002/smj.4250050207

Wood, C. H., Kaufman, A., & Merenda, M. (1996). How Hadco became a problem solving supplier. *Sloan Management Review, 37*(2), 77–88.

Wymer, S., & Regan, E. (2005). Factors influencing e-commerce adoption and use by small and medium businesses. *Electronic Markets, 15*(4), 438–453. doi:10.1080/10196780500303151

Xu, M., Rohatgi, R., & Duan, Y. (2007). E-business adoption in SMEs: Some preliminary findings from electronic components industry. *International Journal of E-Business Research, 3*(1), 74–90.

Zhou, K., Yim, C. K., & Tse, D. K. (2005). The effects of strategic orientations on technology- and market-based breakthrough innovations. *Journal of Marketing, 69*(2), 42–60. doi:10.1509/jmkg.69.2.42.60756

Zhu, K., Kraemer, K. L., Xu, S., & Dedrick, J. (2004). Information technology payoff in e-business environments: An international perspective on value creation of e-business in the financial services industry. *Journal of Management Information Systems, 21*(1), 17–54.

Zwass, V. (2003). Electronic commerce and organizational innovation: Aspects and opportunities. *International Journal of Electronic Commerce, 7*(3), 7–37.

ENDNOTES

[1] Although in theory part we use information technologies in general sense, we used it as a synonym of BPD in the hypothesis development section.

[2] For a detailed list of applications, see Appendix A.

APPENDIX A

Survey questions on the extensiveness of BPD:

1. Please indicate the extent of use the following Internet applications when dealing with your major customers (B2C):
   (1) Storefronts
   (2) Customer services
   (3) E-payments
   (4) E-collaboration in product design and development
   (5) E-collaboration in manufacturing
2. Please indicate the extent of use the following Internet applications when dealing with your major suppliers (B2S):
   (1) Storefronts
   (2) Customer services
   (3) E-payments
   (4) E-collaboration in product design and development
   (5) E-collaboration in manufacturing
3. Please indicate the extent of use the following Internet applications when dealing with your major employees (B2E):
   (1) Training and education
   (2) Human resource applications (benefits, job postings)
   (3) Product design and development
   (4) Product manufacturing
4. Please indicate the extent to use the following Internet applications when dealing with other external entities (i.e., Government, Consultants, Industry Associations, Educational Institutions) (B2O):
   (1) Technology sourcing
   (2) Competitive intelligence
   (3) Market research/ industry analysis
   (4) Government compliance
   (5) New business development

Chapter 15
Information Technology Interventions for Growth and Competitiveness in Micro-Enterprises

Sajda Qureshi
University of Nebraska at Omaha, USA

Mehruz Kamal
University of Nebraska at Omaha, USA

Peter Wolcott
University of Nebraska at Omaha, USA

ABSTRACT

The use of Information and Communication Technologies (ICTs) by Small and Medium Sized Enterprises (SMEs) have the potential to enable these businesses to grow through access to new markets and administrative efficiencies. However, the growth of the smallest of these SMEs which are micro-enterprises is hindered by their inability to adopt ICTs effectively to achieve competitive advantage. This chapter investigates how micro-enterprises can adopt ICTs to grow and achieve competitiveness. This investigation of a set of seven micro-enterprises took place through an interpretive field study in which action research was used to diagnose and treat the micro-enterprises with interventions through a process of "Information Technology (IT) Therapy." This process involved providing individualized IT solutions to pressing problems and opportunities and the development of a longer-term IT project plan, customized for each of the businesses. The increase in competitiveness of these micro-enterprises was assessed using the Focus Dominance Model and their growth through a modified model of micro-enterprise growth based on the resource based view of the firm. This research also contributes with a unique set of skills and experiences that ITD innovators can bring in helping micro-enterprises achieve sustained growth and competitive advantage.

DOI: 10.4018/978-1-61520-627-8.ch015

INTRODUCTION

There is evidence to suggest that use of Information and Communications Technology (ICT) can play an important role on the growth of small businesses (Matthews 2007, Sullivan 1985, Qiang et al 2006, Raymond et al 2005). In this sense, IT can be employed to bring about increased competitiveness if it enables businesses to create new jobs, increase productivity and sales through access to new markets and administrative efficiencies (Qureshi 2005, Matthews 2007). These outcomes can be achieved through measurable improvements in the lives of people living with limited resources to sustain themselves. Duncombe and Heeks (2003) suggest that there is a role for the ICT intermediary in providing the needed information on markets, customers and suppliers. In their study of 1000 small business enterprises in the US, Riemenschneider et al (2003) found that businesses were prepared to overcome obstacles to IT adoption to achieve web presence. This is because pressures to keep with the competition and promote services to customers are greater than the obstacles to setting up websites. There is a sense that small and medium enterprises hold the promise of growing incrementally on existing capabilities, and providing a seedbed for the emergence of dynamic and efficient larger national firms (Levy 2001, Mathews 2007, Servon and Doshna 2000).

It also appears that the promise of eBusiness adoption by micro-enterprises can potentially provide these businesses with the ability to access new markets and reduce costs through administrative efficiencies (Brown and Lockett 2004, Pateli and Giaglis 2004). However, the use of ICT by Small and medium Sized Enterprises (SMEs) remains a challenge in both developed as well as developing countries (Schreiner and Woller 2003, Sanders 2002, Lichtenstein and Lyons 2001, Hyman and Dearden 1998, Honig 1998, Piscitello and Sgobbi 2004). In particular the opportunities opened up

by the internet are limited in SMEs especially due to the challenges faced by globalization (Piscitello and Sgobbi 2004). Small and medium sized businesses are seen to be organizations that employ less than 500 people and typically have problems adopting IT due to competitive pressures and underestimation of time taken to implement IT (Riemenschneider et al 2003). A form of small business being investigated in this paper is the micro-enterprise. Micro-enterprises are tiny businesses with fewer than 10 employees - often just one. The micro-enterprises studied in this paper are part of a Micro-enterprise development program. Such programs make loans and or provide classes to poor people to help them start or strengthen their businesses (Schreiner and Woller 2003).

The challenges faced by micro-enterprises make it even more difficult for them to adopt ICTs for competitiveness. In particular, Piscitello and Sgobbi (2004) suggest that the key barrier to the adoption of ICTs is not size but the learning processes followed by the firms and access to networks of similar internet enabled business services. While a great deal has been written about the challenges faced by micro-enterprise adoption of ICTs, little has been done to provide business models that enable micro-enterprises to use ICTs competitively. According to Grosh and Somolekae (1996), barriers to growth of micro-enterprises are access to capital, educational level of the entrepreneur, legal barriers and start-up financing. In their study of information systems for rural micro-enterprise in Botswana, Duncombe and Heeks (2003) suggest that the role of ICT in enabling information and knowledge is important for both social and economic development. They found that there was a reliance on localized, informal social networks for their information for rural micro-enterprise. Information from these networks was of poor quality and not readily available; it appeared to fail the poorest and most disadvantaged entrepreneurs. In this sense, ICTs can represent an unaffordable addition to costs and the benefits of using them are not always apparent (Duncombe and Heeks 2003, Matthews 2007, Southwood 2004).

This paper investigates how micro-enterprises can adopt ICTs to grow and achieve competitiveness. The question investigated in this paper is: How can micro-enterprises adopt ICTs to achieve competitiveness? In order to answer this question, this paper investigates a set of seven micro-enterprises in the underserved communities of Omaha, Nebraska. The micro-enterprises had received hardware and software through a grant from the eBay Foundation administered by a micro-enterprise development program called the New Community Development Corporation. Through a series of action research steps carried out by the researchers, the ICT challenges faced by the micro-enterprises were diagnosed and treated with interventions through a process of "Information Technology (IT) Therapy" (Wolcott et al, 2007; Qureshi et al, 2008). This process involved providing individualized IT solutions to pressing problems and opportunities and the development of a longer-term IT project plan, customized for each of the businesses. In addition to the IT therapy process, the researchers were able to analyze the potential use of the awarded technology to help achieve operational efficiency and competitive advantage. This was done by mapping each of the micro-enterprises' current IT use combined with increase in IT awareness (on the part of the micro-entrepreneur) and transferred IT skills (to the micro-entrepreneur) – both as a result of the IT therapy process - to a theoretical model.

THEORETICAL BACKGROUND

Small Businesses and Information Technology

Past studies have shown that the use of ICT can play an important role on the growth of small businesses (Matthews 2007, Sullivan 1985, Qiang

et al 2006, Raymond et al 2005). Cragg and King (1993) have shown that there is a gradual increase in the number of small firms that either adopt various new technologies or take steps to upgrade what they currently possess. The studies suggest that IT can be employed to bring about increased competitiveness if it enables businesses to create new jobs, increase productivity and sales through access to new markets and administrative efficiencies (Qureshi 2005, Matthews 2007). Small and medium sized businesses that have adopted and used ICTs have seen positive outcomes related to operational efficiencies, increased revenues, and are able to better position themselves within their market niche. Qiang et al. (2006) observed that businesses that utilized e-mail to communicate with their customers experienced sales growth 3.4 per cent greater than those which did not. Similar outcomes were also observed for productivity and reinvestment. Both these components were found to be greater for more intensive users of IT (Qiang et al., 2006). Other research in this area also highlights the positive impact of IT use within small businesses. A 4% increase in sales as well as 5% increase in export performance was obtained when e-business techniques were adopted by SMEs in the manufacturing sector in Canada (Raymond *et al.,* 2005). Specifically, Raymond et al. (2005) mention that by using technologies such as websites, email and telephones to communicate with customers, SMEs can provide better customer service as well as expand their customer base to help reach out to both local as well as international consumers for their products. In another study Southwood (2004) found that ICT investments by SMEs in South Africa resulted in profitability gains from cost savings rather than from increase in sales.

In addition, studies have established that Information Systems play a significant role in small firms (Harrison et al. 1997, Igbaria et al. 1997). In particular, Street and Meister (2004) conducted a study that showed that improved internal transparency is a key component for small business development. The study concluded that Information Systems play a major role in enhancing communication and that the need for an appropriate IS occurs at a very early stage, even before many of the other structural or organizational changes are required. There also exist a number of studies that take the focus away from the direct impacts of IT in small businesses and instead look into various other angles of IT adoption and use in such types of businesses: Raymond (1988) studied the effect of computer training on attitudes and usage behavior; Montazemi (1988) investigated the relationship between computing issues and satisfaction of end-users; DeLone (1988) examined the link between CEO involvement and computer use effectiveness. While developing upon current research, this paper focuses on the adoption of ICTs by micro-enterprises to achieve competitiveness.

Although current literature supporting adoption of technology by small businesses exists, in practice, this is not the scenario – particularly in the case of micro enterprises. In a study of a set of micro enterprises in North Omaha, many entrepreneurs who had received state-of-the-art technology to assist them with their businesses had not even opened the packaging within which these technologies were contained six months after they had received them (Wolcott *et al.* 2007)! In another study by Qiang *et al* (2006), among the *micro firms*, only 27 percent use e-mail and 22 percent use Web sites to interact with clients and suppliers. The study suggests that if computer use affects firm productivity and ICT expands networking within sectors and industries, the micro firms may not be benefiting from these externalities – benefits from ICTs. In addition, Bharati and Chaudhury (2006) surveyed micro, small and medium manufacturing firms within the Boston metropolitan area and found that most of the micro firms were using simple technologies such as basic e-mail, and simple software packages as compared to more complex technologies that

were being used by the medium sized firms. Their survey results showed that the micro firms were not aware of most technologies that could be used for improving their business performance.

Challenges Facing Small Businesses

In order for micro-enterprises to benefit from ICTs and reach a level where they may be competitive, they need to overcome some of the barriers that are holding them back. Relevant literature in this area has identified a number of different challenges facing these small businesses.

- *Affordability* (Mansell & When, 1998; Hazan, 2002): This is a major issue with small businesses as they operate on very restricted budgets and do not have sufficient capital to invest towards state-of-the-art technologies.
- *Awareness about IT* (Owen & Darkwa, 1999): Most micro-entrepreneurs do not possess any technical skills and are oblivious to the capabilities that ICT has to offer. As a result, their ignorance on the power of IT may inhibit small businesses from growing and flourishing.
- *Infrastructure* (Baark & Heeks, 1998; Latchem & Walker, 2001; O'Farrell, Norrish, & Scott, 1999; Barton & Bear, 1999): A core requirements for any form of ICT implementation is to have a basic infrastructure in place that will support the new form of technology that is being introduced into that environment. Lack of such infrastructure will be a major barrier to the adoption and use of ICT.
- *Private/Government sectors* (Lefebvre and Lefebvre, 1996): These two agencies in any community play an important role in either facilitating or inhibiting the development of IT infrastructures to promote increased ICT adoption and use.

• *Management's capacity* (Lefebvre and Lefebvre, 1996): Management's capacity to incorporate IT into small business environments are also a crucial aspect in successful IT adoption and use; and lack of such capacity could become a major hindrance.

In other studies by Duncombe & Heeks (2002) as well as Moyi (2003), obstacles faced by rural micro-enterprises were highlighted. The challenges related to issues of remote locations, lack of education and literacy on the part of the business owner, poor business skills, poverty and lack of affordability, and lack of transportation.

Information Technology and Competitiveness

Despite these limitations, the competitive advantages of using ICT by the micro-enterprises outweigh the challenges. The relationship between IT and competitive advantage was first researched by McFarlan and McKenney (1983) who came up with a grid to place organizations based on the strategic impact of existing IT applications and the strategic impact of current IT applications development within the firm. The grid was helpful to the extent that management could utilize it to consider the right alternatives to pursue for improved competitiveness. Information technology can add economic value to an organization through 1) the reduction in the costs incurred by the organization, and 2) by differentiating the organization's products or services (Bakos and Treacy, 1986; McFarlan, 1984; Wiseman, 1988). Taking this notion that IT can add value to a firm, Porter and Millar (1985) moves the discussion further by analyzing how advances in information technology have changed the way organizations conduct business and how it may serve to provide a competitive advantage. They explain three core ways in which IT may impact competitiveness: 1. by changing the industry structure, 2. by sup-

porting cost and differentiation strategies, and 3. by creating opportunities to generate new businesses from within existing businesses. Ives and Learmonth (1984) narrow down the focus of a firm to emphasize customer relationships, and they show how information system technology can enhance relationships with the company's customers. They outline a 13-step customer resource lifecycle highlighting potential uses of IT at the various stages to enable competitive advantage for the firm providing the product or service to the customer (Ives and Learmonth, 1984).

Sethi and King (1994) have attempted to measure the extent to which IT applications may provide competitive advantage. They referred to the construct measuring this notion as "CAPITA" (competitive advantage provided by an information technology application) and operationalized it through five main dimensions – efficiency (degree to which an IT application enables a company to produce lower priced products than competing products), functionality (degree to which an IT application provides users with the functionality they desire), threat (impact of the IT application on the bargaining power of customers and suppliers), preemptiveness (early and successful penetration of the IT application into the market), and synergy (the degree to which the IT application is tightly integrated with the business goals, and strategies of the organization). In summarizing the early notions of how IT may impact an organization's competitive advantage, see four distinct strategies emerge: 1) Low-cost leadership – using information systems and technology to produce products and services at a lower price than competitors while enhancing quality and level of service; 2) Product differentiation – using information systems and technology to differentiate products, and enable new services and products; 3) Focus on market niche – using information systems and technology to enable a focused strategy on a single market niche; and 4) Customer and supplier intimacy – using information systems to develop strong ties and loyalty with customers and suppliers.

Figure 1. Resource-based view of the firm

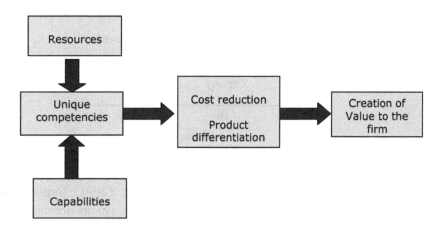

Due to rapid changes in markets, customer expectations, as well as technologies and most importantly globalization, has made competitive advantages short lived. Along those lines, Mata, Fuerst, and Barney (1995) talk about how IT may provide not only competitive advantage but also *sustained* competitive advantage using a resource-based analysis. They emphasize that the "create-capture-keep" paradigm (Clemons and Kimbrough, 1986; Clemons and Row, 1987, 1991b; Feeny and Ives, 1990) whereby customers make certain investments (switching costs) specific to a particular supplier of IT, enabling those suppliers of IT to achieve competitive advantage does not truly hold when it comes to the sustainability of the competitive advantage. Instead, Mata et al (1995) takes the resource-based view of the firm (Clemons, 1991; Barney, 1991; Conner, 1991). In the resource-based view of the firm, resources and capabilities may provide a unique set of competencies that may serve to address either cost reduction or product differentiation strategies to eventually create value for the organization. This is summarized in Figure 1.

Using the resource-based perspective, Mata et al (1995) put forward two major notions to explain sustained competitive advantage. The first concept is that of resource heterogeneity which states that competing firms may vary in their resources and capabilities. The second concept is that of resource immobility which says that the differences in resources and capabilities between competing firms may be long lasting. Their argument is that if a firm's IT resources are distributed heterogeneously among competing firms and if the firms without the resources find it more costly to develop, acquire and implement the same strategy as the firms that already have the resources, then those resources can serve to be a source of sustained competitive advantage. Mata et al (1995) develop a framework using the concepts of resource heterogeneity and resource immobility to depict how these two notions relate to competitive advantage. They then apply this model to four characteristics of IT – access to capital (McFarlan, 1984), proprietary technology, technical IT skills (Copeland and McKenney, 1988), and managerial IT skills (Capon and Glazer, 1987) – that prior literature has suggested to be sources of sustained competitive advantage. Their findings imply that organizing and managing IT within a firm, or in other words, managerial IT skills are the only source of sustained IT competitive advantage and that less focus should be made on the information technology itself.

Figure 2. The focus-dominance model (Source: Levy et al., 2001)

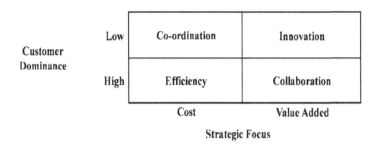

In order to be able to achieve competitive advantage through its adoption of ICTs, what should a micro-enterprise facing multiple challenges do? Prior research has shown that there are two distinct routes by which small businesses incorporate ICTs. One route is to enhance day-to-day operational support and transaction processing activities (Blili and Raymond, 1993; Foong, 1999; Levy and Powell, 1998; Poon and Swatman, 1999). These studies have shown that small businesses adopt and use simple ICTs without any form of planned strategy to integrate other aspects of the business. And so any form of IT-based competitive advantage is accidental rather than planned (Hashmi and Cuddy, 1990). The second route that is typically taken is to use ICTs to improve interaction and relationships with customers. SMEs, and in particular micro-enterprises are strongly influenced by customer needs. Porter (1980) states, that in many small businesses, customer power is very high. It has been seen that a majority of SMEs depend on a small number of customers who purchase large amounts of goods and services. These major customers are then in a position to influence the price of goods and services that are being produced by the small businesses (Reid and Jacobsen, 1988). Close relationships among SMEs and their customers enable these businesses to respond quickly to customers' changed requirements. Lefebvre and Lefebvre (1993) have shown that there is a link between the innovative efforts of an SME and its competitive position.

Levy et al. (2001) formulated an analytical framework (focus-dominance model), that incorporates both forms of strategic focus - the issue of cost reduction versus value added and the second one being customer dominance i.e. few versus many customers - that emerged from prior research described above. The model examines the potential for SMEs to realize value from IS capabilities. The framework shows where SMEs would fit in terms of the trend they show in IT investments and market strategies. The model is shown in Figure 2. The framework may be viewed as providing four different approaches to ICT adoption as a result of integrating the two dimensions of strategic focus. The *efficiency* quadrant may comprise SMEs that exploit simple systems such as word processing and trivial accounting processes (Naylor and Williams, 1994). The *co-ordination* quadrant is composed of those SMEs that have a need to increase market share and their customer base. The *collaboration* segment then attracts SMEs that attempt to incorporate emerging technologies to manage relationships with the businesses' major customers. And finally the *innovation* quadrant comprises of those SMEs that actively seek to adopt new information and communication technologies to help achieve competitive advantage. In a follow-up study, Levy *et al.* (2002) investigated 43 SMEs to observe their positions in the focus-dominance model. The results revealed that most of the 43 SMEs make only one move, from *efficiency* to *co-ordination*, or from *efficiency* to *collaboration*. SMEs taking either one these routes tend to avoid losing control and so opt to stay within their current markets. It was also seen that only 17 of the 43 SMEs wanted to move to the *innovation* quadrant possibly due to an environment scan whereby they become aware of "best practices" and strategies that would assist them to manage business growth.

This focus-dominance model was chosen to investigate how micro-enterprises can adopt ICTs to achieve competitiveness. This model is seen to be a valuable means for the analysis of each of the micro-enterprises in the study because it enables us to: 1) Identify the strategic position of each micro-enterprise at the time the study was conducted; 2) Predict the strategic position the micro-enterprise will be in a few years based on the context-specific business goals of each micro-enterprise; 3) Identify the information systems that will support the micro-enterprise in its current strategic position and 4) Map what information systems will be needed to support the micro-enterprise in its projected strategic position.

Moreover, the four quadrants of the focus-dominance model is an outcome of the true conditions encountered by SMEs highlighted through prior research. The unique contribution of the research taken up by the authors of this paper is to apply this model to the context of micro-enterprises (as noted earlier, these are the smallest form of businesses) – which has not yet been studied in the realm of this or any other theoretical model. The results will show that micro-enterprises do indeed fall into distinct categories and we provide support for our results by using the established notion of resource-based view of the firm to illustrate competitive advantage (Clemons, 1991; Barney, 1991; Conner, 1991; Mata et al., 1995). Our analysis reveals that through the micro-enterprises' current IT resources – combined with capabilities provided through the IT therapy process, produce unique competencies to position these small businesses to be competitive.

METHODOLOGY

In order to investigate how the micro-enterprises can use ICTs to increase their competitiveness, an interpretive field study was carried out. According to Klein and Myers (1999), Information Systems research can be classified as interpretive if it is assumed that our knowledge of reality is gained only through social constructions. Interpretive methods in IS are aimed at producing an understanding of the context of the information system and the process by which the information system influences and is influenced by the context (Walsham 1993). This research follows an interpretive field study approach in which seven case studies are carried out. These case studies are carried out using Klein and Myers (1999) principles of the hermeneutic circle, contextualization, interaction between researchers and subjects, abstraction and generalization, dialogical reasoning, the principle of multiple interpretations, and the principle of suspicion. Within each case study, the data was collected and analyzed in iterative cycles of action research. Action research involves the application of tools and methods from the social and behavioral sciences to practical problems with the intention both of improving the practice and of contributing to theory and knowledge in the area studied. Action researchers participate directly or intervene in a situation or phenomenon in order to apply a theory and evaluate the value and usefulness of that theory (Checkland, 1981, 1991; Galliers, 1991). This conforms to Klein and Myers (1999) third principle which requires that there is critical reflection on how the data are socially constructed through interaction between researchers and participants. Action research is a change oriented research methodology that seeks to introduce changes with positive social values, the key focus being on a problem and its solution (Elden and Chisholm 1993). Action research is typically carried out as part of an attempt to solve problems by allowing the researcher to become a participant in the action, the process of change itself becoming the subject of research (Checkland 1981).

Research Setting

This study investigated seven micro-enterprises undergoing change through the adoption of ICTs for competitiveness. Each business has been given an arbitrary name for the purpose of this study and to maintain confidentiality of the businesses. All of the businesses are located in Omaha, Nebraska. Following are brief descriptions of each of the micro-enterprises studied:

1. LD specializes in high quality soups and sandwiches. During the period of this study LD moved its deli from its original location to a better one that could serve local businesses and students.
2. FD specializes in the design of elegant, conservative women's clothing. The owner has aspirations of being a player in the global fashion market.
3. CZ is a franchise that pairs individuals of all ages who need tutoring in any subject with tutors who can provide the service.
4. HH offers a structured residence with treatment and support services to individuals who are transitioning from a treatment program back to society.
5. HE offers massage therapy services. The owner is seeking to diversify into the retail sale of a variety of natural health products.
6. EP is a modeling agency that provides models who reflect the diversity of "normal" (nonglamorous) Americans.
7. HC This on-line business sells wedding cake toppers that reflect the ethnic diversity of customers.

The micro-enterprise owners were all recipients of small technology grants from eBay Foundation's Techquity Grant Program. The Techquity Grant Program offers small grants, typically around $2000, to be used for purchasing hardware, software, and training that would promote the development of micro-enterprises. The grant program was locally administered by the New Community Development Corporation (NCDC), a non-profit that provides affordable housing and business development services in the greater Omaha area. The anticipated benefit to the micro-enterprises would be more effective utilization of technology, improved thinking about technology and the role of information, and, in general, economic and human development.

Research Design

The design of the research involved seven case studies in which action research was carried out to diagnose the problem in each case, intervene to solve the problem, collect data through interviews and observations of the effects of the interventions and analyze the results in preparation for the next cycle. Action research used in this way was an iterative cycle in which the researcher begins with a **plan** of how to carry out the activity, then **act** to intervene to solve the immediate problem, **observe** the results of the intervention and **reflect** on the impact and next steps (Zuber-Skerrit, 1991, Avison et al. 1999). Carried out as part of an academic service-learning course – *Information Technology for Development* (IT4D), the action research was supplemented by the **absorb**ing of knowledge through classroom lectures and discussion. The participative learning process took place in the form of group discussions in which problems were discussed and solutions arrived at collectively.

In this study, the plan was to assist the micro-enterprises through partnership with New Community Development Corporation (NCDC). The cycle continued to action or intervention, to solve

Table 1. Data collection steps

Action Research	Case 1: LD	Case 2: FD	Case 3: CZ	Case 4: HH	Case 5: HE	Case 6: EP	Case 7: HC
Plan	Researchers' and the micro-entrepreneurs share initial understandings in Hermeneutic dialogue. Contextualization of the social and historical background of the micro-enterprise and diagnosis of the problem to arrive at the current state of the micro-enterprise on the focus-dominance model.						
Act	IT Therapy interventions through interactions between the researchers and participants to solve the problem. Principle of abstraction and generalization adhered to through the use of two theoretical models to frame and interpret findings from this study.						
Observe	Collection of data through interviews and observations. The principle of multiple interpretations was achieved through class discussions when the ITD innovators implementing the IT interventions discussed the results in class and the second form of interpretation came from the subjects, or in other words, the micro-entrepreneurs						
Reflect	Analysis of the data and interpretation to reveal future state on the focus-dominance model.. Principle of dialogical reasoning used to analyze how context-sensitive assistance (IT therapy) may enable micro-entrepreneur to overcome some of the technical and social barriers that they face.						

the problem or manage the change process; this is where the researcher collected the data. On location at the micro-businesses, the ITD innovators worked with business owners to understand the business and existing technology, implement technology-based projects, and train business owners as appropriate. This process was referred to as "IT therapy" in which assistance was given to the micro-business owner to solve their immediate IT needs.

These steps were carried out within each case study using Klein and Myers (1999) principles. These principles guide our assessment of the action research steps taken to understand the current situation and map it on to Levy et al's (2001) focus-dominance model. Then diagnose the problem, carry out the IT therapy interventions, collect the data and map the future state of each micro-enterprise using Levy et al (2001)'s model. This iterative data collection and analysis process was designed to enable each micro-enterprise's ability to adopt ICTs to achieve competitiveness to be investigated. This is illustrated in Table 1.

The design of this field study conforms to the principles that guide the evaluation of interpretive field studies model by Klein and Myers (1999). The *Principle of the Hermeneutic Circle* states that an understanding of a complex whole is obtained from preconceptions regarding the meanings of its parts and their interrelationships. Applying this principle to the current study, the *parts* are the researchers' and the micro-entrepreneurs initial understandings and the *whole* are the shared meanings (e.g. increased awareness and acceptance of the utility that the awarded technology can help the micro-entrepreneurs in their business) that arise from the close interactions between them. The multiple interventions in the IT therapy process is supported by the view that in a number of iterations of the hermeneutic circle, a complex whole of shared meanings emerges. *The Principle of Contextualization*: is addressed by treating the micro-entrepreneurs as active actors (e.g. learning new IT skills, gaining trust over technology, working together with the ITD innovators to develop technology plans, etc.) and through the action research steps that were used to collect data for this research, they served as producers of history. *The Principle of Interaction between the Researcher and the Subjects was* addressed by the close and continuous interaction of the researchers with the microentrepreneurs as described in the action research steps utilized for the data collection phase of the study (Klein and Myers, 1999).

In developing the theoretical contributions of this research, *the Principle of Abstraction and Generalization* guided our use of the focus-dominance model (Levy et al., 2001) which was used to provide a systematic means for understanding the historical, current as well as the future predicted IS-based positions of each of the micro-enterprises. The resource-based view of the firm helped us tie in the concept of IT therapy as a *capability* that when integrated with IT resources within each of the micro-enterprises may help bring about competitiveness. *The Principle of Dialogical Reasoning* formed the basis of the context-sensitive assistance (IT therapy) may assist small businesses to overcome some of the technical and social barriers that they face (Klein and Myers, 1999).

Data on each case being studied was gathered through observation while implementing the IT therapy. The reflection entailed interpretation of the data, and consequences of action that then fed into the planning stage to modify the methodology or model that then determine what action would be taken in the next cycle. On their own time, the ITD innovators maintained a reflective journal, worked on assigned class exercises and readings, and prepared a technology plan for the micro-businesses. Using the techniques provided to them, the ITD innovators implemented the IT interventions by interacting closely with the micro-entrepreneurs. In this way they interacted as *IT for Development (ITD) innovators* as they implemented the IT and training interventions that enabled the technology to be adopted in innovative ways. The IT4D class sessions served as a sounding board for issues and proposed solutions, offered advice or relevant information, and offered constructive criticism of proposed courses of action to address any IS/ICT adoption/implementation issues specific to any of the micro-businesses. Further cycles of activities continued until a desired end-state is achieved (Zuber-Skerrit, 1991, Avison et al. (1999, p.96).

RESULTS

The current and the future trends in how each of the micro-enterprises use their IS have been mapped onto the focus-dominance model (Levy et al., 2001) after the researchers in the study had an opportunity to discuss and observe the manner in which these small businesses carry out their activities following the action research steps outlined in the methodology section. The IT therapy phase involved the ITD innovators working with business owners to understand the business and existing technology, implementing technology-based projects, and training business owners is also mentioned. This process of "IT therapy", or in other words, assistance given to the micro-business owner to solve their immediate IT needs, is important to the extent that it supports a major resource capability that is lacking and in much needed demand on the part of the micro-enterprises. The future IS trends for each of the businesses were based on the researchers' understanding of the micro-enterprise's future strategic growth plans and their IS requirements. The results were discussed with the business partners (the micro-enterprises) in the study. Following are the individual mappings for each of the micro-enterprises in the study.

LD: LD specializes in high quality soups and sandwiches. During the period of this study LD moved its deli from its original location to a better one that could serve local businesses and students (See Figure 3).

Current state: LD has high customer dominance because it is currently dependent on a specific client group. The owner of LD typically uses a PDA, Cell phone, email and a simple software package such as, QuickBookas for the business operations. The old register system is merely a calculator. It does not provide any data to the owner on trends, sandwich purchases, inventory usage, or payroll. Although, the owner is aware

Figure 3. Focus-dominance model mapping for LD

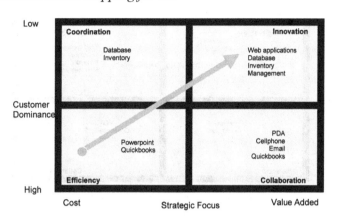

of the benefits of the technology the business currently possesses might bring, due to lack of skills and IT knowledge, the business is yet to exploit the technology for competitive advantage. LD's current state of affairs makes it position itself in the *efficiency* quadrant of the focus-dominance model since according to Levy et al. (2001), the main focus of IS use in the *efficiency* quadrant is for control of the business, primarily financial control. The information systems in this context are concerned with improving the efficiency of internal processes.

IT therapy: The ITD innovators helped the owner select a register system that will not only handle ideal usage issues (ideal usage is the total amount of use of a particular item that is an ingredient for various menu items) but also maintain payroll information – thus eliminating the problems of previously manually calculating payroll at the end of each pay period. The Internet café implementation is a work in progress. A wireless communication network through a local Internet Service provider was set up. For a small fee per month, LD will have enough bandwidth to operate 20-25 computers on the same network.

Future state: LD's biggest struggle is going to be integrating a logical inventory and database system into the business. The owner is really working hard to be innovative with the move to

the new location. The owner knows what it will take for the business to be successful at this new location and part of that will be incorporating a better inventory system and a customer database. The new location will have free wireless access for customers. Eventually, the business web site will have a customer information database that will be used as an advertising and marketing tool for LD for improved customer service. Since LD is looking to grow and build its customer base, it will eventually have low customer dominance (many customers i.e. few customers will not be able to dominate the business) and moreover the owner's intention of integrating the heart of the business which is the inventory management system with the other aspects of the business makes it position itself distinctly within the *innovation* quadrant. Levy et al. (2001) state that in this quadrant, the IS are a tightly woven part of the business strategy.

CZ: CZ is a franchise that pairs individuals of all ages who need tutoring in any subject with tutors who can provide the service (See Figure 4).

Current state: The current state of CZ can be classified as residing in both the *coordination* as well as in the *collaboration* quadrants. CZ's presence in the coordination quadrant arises from the fact that CZ has to deal with a large number of students and tutors and so customer dominance is

Figure 4. Focus-dominance model mapping for CZ

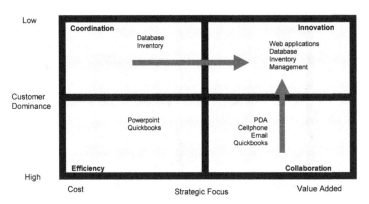

low. CZ already has its own coordination components such as infrastructure, database, accounting system and marketing means from the franchiser to help it maintain its relationships with its customers (Levy et al., 2001). Additionally, CZ is viewed to reside in the collaboration quadrant since they have collaborative systems such as internal work processes using manual and automatic tools.

IT therapy: The owners of CZ would like to have the process of matching tutors with students automated through online means. In addition they would like to have a software package that can take care of scheduling issues. In response to the needs of CZ, the following IT therapy interventions were carried out: creation of a decision-making framework to resolve whether it would make more sense to build the matching and scheduling system in-house versus purchasing an off-the-shelf application and customizing it to fit the needs of the micro-enterprise.

Future state: CZ is heading to a possible *innovation* state from both the *coordination* and *collaboration* quadrants for its business. Once the owner invests money to develop their own application or purchase an existing off-the-shelf one, the business will generate exponential growth based on their current footing. Once they confirm their decision in investing capital on IT development, they will get more customers and tutors online. It will bring them financial freedom exponentially.

The owner is clear as to what needs to be done to align the business strategy with the needed IS requirements to be a competitive force in the market (Levy et al., 2001).

HH: HH offers a structured residence with treatment and support services to individuals who are transitioning from a treatment program back to society (See Figure 5).

Current state: HH had an office management system which included a desktop and a laptop computer. Both computers were used for normal operations such as writing assessment reports, working on Power Point, internet research and e-mail communications. The desktop was the main repository for historical records including past guest records and financial information. The desktop was used for writing standard forms used in operations such as rules violation notices. The laptop was mainly used by the owner and is used in the same way as the desktop except in the case of the financial information. This redundancy in operations increased the ability for all employees to work on separate assignments simultaneously. Some of the functions of the laptop system were that the owner is managing progress and evaluative data in an Excel spreadsheet and used offsite for presentations and guest evaluations. In addition HH had a guest computer lab consisting of one desktop computer located in a common area. The intent of this system was to give guests a resource

Figure 5. Focus-dominance model mapping for HH

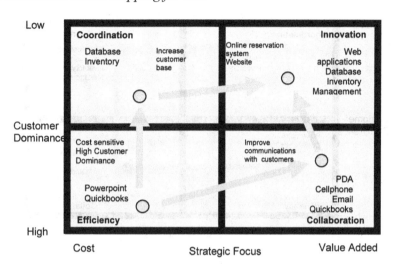

for looking for jobs and staying in contact with family and friends. The computers could be used for resume writing and for enhancing computer skills as well computer based training. The computer lab accessed the internet from the same wireless connection as the management system. WiFi capability in the house made the guest computer systems expandable with relative ease and low cost. The state of HH was purely in the *efficiency* quadrant of the focus-dominance chart since the focus was on low-cost IS to maintain operational effectiveness (Levy et al., 2001).

IT therapy: In responding to the immediate IT needs of HH, the following IT therapy interventions were carried out: Streamlined business practices including system maintenance and backup of standard procedures; financial data updated and used for making proposals to prospective lenders; business input, output and outcome data updated for display to potential donors and stake holders as well as referral services; data prepared for a database on resident statistics.

Future state: HH is looking to take a phased incremental approach via *coordination* and *collaboration* to reach its desired spot in the *innovation* quadrant. The owners of HH realize that there

is a need for better data management as well as improved communication with donors and guests and stakeholders. In attempting to move to the *co-ordination* and *collaboration* quadrants from their current state, HH is aware that the business will need to 1. Develop a website to get more exposure in the community and provide URL address to key stakeholders (increase customer base by reducing customer dominance and moving into the *coordination* quadrant); 2. Network with local education providers to allow guests to obtain needed training for the future (improve relationships with few customers i.e. local educational institutes through increased customer dominance by moving into the *collaboration* quadrant); 3. Work with local businesses to develop a community and a pool of potential job opportunities (improve relationships with few customers i.e. local businesses through increased customer dominance by moving into the *collaboration* quadrant); and 4. Present successful outcomes either in person through presentations or online through their website to stakeholders. In addition, the owners of HH want to go a step farther and maintain a strategic focus to drive them into the *innovation* quadrant. They would like to have innovative web-based applications that will

Figure 6. Focus-dominance model mapping for HE

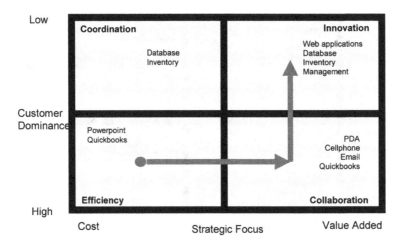

enable online reservation capability. The website should also offer capabilities to allow referral services to contact HH and eventually develop a treatment and payment plan online through a range of treatment options and payment types. Such an IS will tie in all of their business strategies to show relevant outcomes to stakeholders – thus moving them towards the *innovation* quadrant as a result of aligning IS with their overall business strategies (Levy et al., 2001).

HE: HE offers massage therapy services. The owner is seeking to diversify into the retail sale of a variety of natural health products (See Figure 6).

Current state: The owner has technology already available to her, but needs help utilizing it. There was an unopened PDA, a laptop, and a desktop. The owner would like to get things organized between the two computers and the PDA. The owner wanted help learning QuickBooks and possibly setting up a company website. She needed security on her laptop and Microsoft Office 2003 installed on both computers. This business lies in the *efficiency* quadrant as it is only beginning to set-up the technology for the business and the primary focus of the IS will be for controlling the business by improving the efficiency of internal processes (Levy et al., 2001)

IT therapy: The ITD Innovators provided the following IT therapy interventions: installing Microsoft Office 2003; setting up security on the laptop computer; connecting the PDA to both the laptop and desktop; installing a CD-backup system; helping the owner learn how to organize her contact information in Microsoft Outlook.

Future state: Since HE is only at the very early stages of incorporating technology into the business, the owner did not have a well thought out plan as to how the business would want to grow using the technology. The owner did express the intent to have a company website to eventually sell the company's products.

EP: EP is a modeling agency that provides models who reflect the diversity of "normal" (non-glamorous) Americans (See Figure 7).

Current state: EP has two dimension of the concept of customer. There are the models who sign up online that can be seen as customers and EP as the agency. The companies who require models for shoots are also customers of EP. EP has low customer dominance since it deals with a large number of models as well as agencies and so very few customers can dominate EP. EP's current

Figure 7. Focus-dominance model mapping for EP

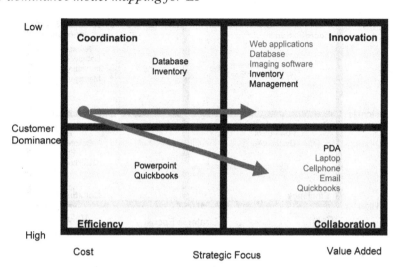

state makes it reside in the *coordination* quadrant of the focus-dominance model since according to Levy et al. (2001), the primary use of IS in the *coordination* quadrant is to maintain customer relationships – which is a function of the larger customer base. Typically, information systems in this context hold basic customer data.

IT therapy: A major task for the ITD innovators in this case was training the business owner to help her understand the strategic importance of technology in the business. Remote desktop was installed and demonstrated to show how greater mobility and convenience could be achieved through technology. Basic workstation maintenance such as ensuring critical patches and updates were current. The differences between critical and non-critical updates were explained. Desktop security and wireless security were explained to the users. Using QuickBooks to cut down on time spent on non-value added services was explained. Website ranking and place was also explained with possible solutions. It is important to mention here that an ITD innovators role was to increase the owner's comfort level with the technology.

Future state: EP is heading towards both the *collaboration* as well as the *innovation* quadrants.

It is heading to the *collaborative* quadrant since the owner has to maintain close contact with current clients as in photographers, ad agencies and also the listed models. Laptop and cell phone use allow the owner to have a mobile office when the owner travels, in addition to keeping in touch with clients that need models. This mode of operation is consistent with Levy et al.'s (2001) description whereby they state that businesses in the *collaboration* quadrant need to communicate and exchange information with major customers in a cost-efficient manner. In addition, EP is also heading to the *innovation* quadrant since the business model of EP relies on a web presence and is looking to be ahead of its competitors by enabling models to sign up online and get scheduled for photo shoots which will enable it to align its core business strategy with its online presence (Levy et al., 2001).

HC: HC is an on-line business that sells wedding cake toppers that reflect the ethnic diversity of customers (See Figure 8).

Current state: The business started in the *efficiency* quadrant. The customer dominance is currently quite high as the business has only had a few sales and relies on a small number of

Figure 8. Focus-dominance model mapping for HC

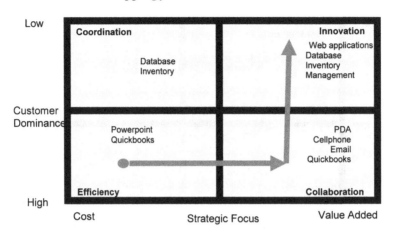

customers. Although HC is an online business, the owner has minimal interaction with the business website and uses minimal ICT for day-to-day business operations. In addition, HC's current state can be considered to reside in the *collaboration* quadrant since the owner of HC interacts with a small number of suppliers to obtain the cake toppers. And this trend is consistent with Levy et al.'s (2001) description since in this quadrant, the businesses need to communicate with major customers (in the case of HC, its major customers are its suppliers).

IT therapy: Some of the significant IT therapy interventions that were carried out for HC are as follows: *New website* – A completely new website was developed. The new website has a more organized and efficient layout comparable to other leading online competitors of similar products. *Training* - Training for the owner has come in the form of providing her with a manual to help add/delete products on the website so that customers will always have the new and updated product list. And most importantly, the owner will not have to depend on someone else to change the products for her – she will be able to perform the changes herself by following the steps outlined in the manual. A couple of hands-on sessions were done with the ITD innovator so that

any confusion could be cleared. *Perceptions and attitude changes* - One of the owner's needs is to have the business website look more "crisp" and professional. On doing some preliminary research as to the look and feel of other comparable businesses, we had to suggest to the owner to change the colors and layout of her current site to help attract more customers. We had to persuade the owner to shift away from her inefficient current layout and existing bold colors (red and black) to a more "crisper" organized layout and softer colors to help attract more customers.

Future state: HC is primarily an internet business which entails web applications. The owner understands that in order to be competitive, the business will need to take a strategic focus to carrying out business online by selling its products through a professional looking website. The owner is looking to take the necessary steps to align HC's business strategy to its IS needs and the design and implementation of the newly developed website was the first step towards achieving that goal.

FD: FD specializes in the design of elegant, conservative women's clothing. The owner has aspirations of being a player in the global fashion market (See Figure 9).

Current state: FD has a laptop and an electronic cash register with some back-office software. FD

Figure 9. Focus-dominance model mapping for FD

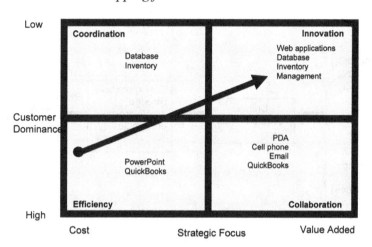

currently resides in the *efficiency* quadrant since the owner has been using the technology available to the business for primarily basic day-to-day operational activities (Levy et al., 2001).

IT therapy: On meeting with the owner of FD and analyzing the technology needs of the business, The ITD innovators came up with the following list of items to be carried out to assist in the growth of the business: develop a website to promote its products, a developer to update and to do maintenance, and training and technical support for FD's staff to be able to update the website regularly; FD may benefit from online free technical assistance programs.

Future state: FD's main objective is to grow and attract new customers. The owner realizes that the only way to effectively achieve that goal is to have a web presence on the internet through a business website. The owner would like the following goals to be accomplished through the website: 1. To use it as a place to target new customers by advertising the owner's fashion designs; 2. To sell and promote the business on the web; 3. To advertise and provide information about FD. Achieving these three goals will enable it to align its core business strategy with its IS (Levy et. al, 2001).

ANALYSIS

The results from the analysis indicate that five out of the seven micro-enterprises in this study start off in the *efficiency* quadrant in the focus-dominance model. According to Levy et al. (2001), this implies that the focus of the IS was to help reduce costs and achieve simple administrative efficiencies. On initial meetings with the microentrepreneurs, the researchers found that the business owners had no clear business strategy and was not aware of how they could derive the maximum benefit from the IS or technology that they had been awarded through the e-bay Techquity grant. Through the action research steps described in the methodology section, the researchers were able to instill an awareness and understanding of how the microentrepreneurs needed to align the goals of their business and how the available technology could help them reach that end state. The IT therapy process used with each of the micro-enterprises helped to address some of the immediate IT needs of the business. The immediate visible and measurable outcomes were in the area of improved day-to-day business administrative activities mainly through automation of many of the tedious manual activities. This form of outcome seems to support the view

Figure 10. Model of micro-enterprise growth

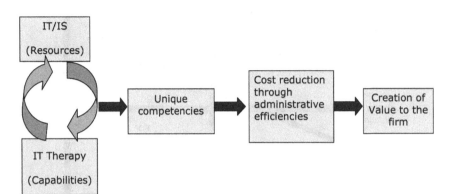

coming out from the strategic IT literature which states that one of the core ways in which IT may add value to a firm is by reducing costs incurred by the organization (Bakos and Treacy, 1986; McFarlan, 1984; Wiseman, 1988).

It can be seen that in all the micro-enterprises in this study, the final strategic position that resulted lay in the *innovation* quadrant of the focus-dominance model. The path to the *innovation* quadrant was different for each of the micro-enterprises. Depending on their context, some showed a tendency for a direct shift from the *efficiency* quadrant to the *innovation* quadrant. Whereas, others tended to take routes via either the *coordination* quadrant, or the *collaboration* quadrant, or via both. This implies that all the micro-enterprise owners are looking to integrate their IS with their business strategies by taking into consideration both internal (improving operational efficiency) as well as external (improved relationships with suppliers and customers) aspects of the business (Levy et al., 2001). This form of alignment of IS with business strategy will enable the micro-enterprises to reach a state whereby they will have a strong platform to be competitive with other businesses in their market.

The resource-based view of the firm (Clemons, 1991; Barney, 1991; Conner, 1991; Mata et al., 1995) to explain competitive advantage provides support for not only the outcomes from this study,

but also for the *process* by which IT therapy was used to assist the microeneterprises to have the potential to be competitive. In the resource-based view of the firm, resources and capabilities may provide a unique set of competencies that may serve to address either cost reduction or product differentiation strategies to eventually create value for the organization. Applying this perspective to the context of our study, the term *resources*, refers to the technology that was awarded to each of the micro-enterprises through the e-bay techquity grant program. The term, *capabilities,* refers to the context-sensitive technical assistance or the IT therapy that was provided by the ITD innovators in the case of each of the micro-enterprises.

Integrating the awarded IT (resources) with the IT therapy process (capabilities) produces certain context-sensitive competencies (for some of the micro-enterprises these were in the form of improved awareness of IT and for some others these were in the form of immediate solutions to technical problems that helped them clear the bottleneck that they were facing) for each of the micro-enterprises that as our results show, addressed cost reduction strategies through improved administrative efficiencies. Figure 10 shows a modified version of the resource-based view of the firm that incorporates the process of IT therapy. It shows how the integration of the IT therapy process with existing IT resources within the micro-enterprises creates added value to the firm – supporting and providing a means for competitiveness with other organizations. The effect of aligning the resources with the capabilities is illustrated in Figure 10.

This model illustrates how the IT therapy interventions bring about unique competencies that enable value to be created in the firm through cost reduction and administrative efficiencies. More specifically, the IT Therapy component of the work was focused on the entrepreneurs' strongly perceived issues and problems: LD's Internet connection was very unreliable; HH needed to provide better statistics to stakeholders; FD wanted to be able to show potential customers a PowerPoint show of her fashions; HE had customer information scattered in many different places; EP was frustrated by having to maintain duplicate accounting systems at work and at home; HC had ideas for enhancing her web site; CZ needed a more effective means of tracking tutors. In addition, the ITD innovators applied their skills and experiences to identify solutions to problems the entrepreneurs may not have been aware of.

The resource based view of the firm suggests that sustaining the growth of these micro-enterprises would require sustaining the skills and experience developed through the IT therapy process. Competitive advantages that these micro-enterprises gain from the direction of their growth can be stimulated through additional interventions guided by the focus-dominance model. This research has also brought to light a unique set of skills and experiences that ITD innovators can bring to bear in helping micro-enterprises achieve sustained growth and competitive advantage.

CONCLUSION

This research suggests that while micro-enterprises have the potential to serve as the seedbed for economic development, they must overcome a number of challenges that obstruct their path.

Very few micro-enterprise entrepreneurs possess the technical skills or information systems necessary to streamline their business operations and help them compete and expand into new markets. This is why they need interventions by ITD innovators who can give them the skills that enable the micro-entrepreneurs to diagnose business problems, design IT and training interventions and implement processes to support IT adoption. An innovative approach was developed by integrating context-sensitive technical assistance, or in other words, "IT therapy" with existing IT resources in micro-enterprises to show how these small businesses may become competitive. This research has investigated how through the process of context-sensitive IT assistance has the potential to enable micro-enterprises to achieve competitiveness. This research is based on an interpretive field study method of inquiry as outlined by Klein and Myers (1999) with data collection being carried out using action research steps (Zuber-Skerrit, 1991; Avison et al., 1999). This paper used the Focus-Dominance model to investigate the adoption of ICT for competitive advantage by a set of seven micro-enterprises and the resource based view of the firm to develop a model of micro-enterprise growth. Further research needs to consider the effect of multiple interventions across a broader range of micro-enterprises over time through a longitudinal design.

REFERENCES

Avison, D. E., Lau, F., Myers, M., & Nielsen, P. A. (1999). Action Research. *Communications of the ACM, 42*(1), 94–97. doi:10.1145/291469.291479

Baark, E., & Heeks, R. (1998). *Evaluation of Donor-Funded Information Technology Transfer Projects in China: A Life-Cycle Approach.* Retrieved Dec 12, 2007, from http://idpm.man. ac.uk/wp/di/di_wp01.htm

Bakos, J.Y., & Treacy, M.E. (1986 June). Information Technology and Corporate Strategy: A Research Perspective. *MIS Quarterly, 1*(2), 107-1 19.

Barney, J. B. (1991). Firm Resources and Sustained Competitive Advantage. *Journal of Management, 17*(1), 99–120. doi:10.1177/014920639101700108

Barton, C., & Bear, M. (1999). *Information and Communications Technologies: Are they the Key to Viable Business Development Services for Micro and Small Enterprises?* Report for USAID as part of the Microenterprise Best Practices Project. Retrieved December 12, 2007, from http://www.mip.org/PUBS/MBP/ict.htm

Bharati, P., & Chaudhury, A. (2006). Current Status of Technology Adoption: Micro, Small and Medium Manufacturing Firms in Boston. *Communications of the ACM, 49*(10), 88–93. doi:10.1145/1164394.1164400

Blili, S., & Raymond, L. (1993). Information technology: threats and opportunities for small and medium-sized enterprises. *International Journal of Information Management, 13*, 439–448. doi:10.1016/0268-4012(93)90060-H

Brown, D. H., & Lockett, N. (2004). Potential of critical e-applications for engaging SMEs in e-business: a provider perspective. *European Journal of Information Systems, 13*, 21–34. doi:10.1057/palgrave.ejis.3000480

Capon, N., & Glazer, R. (1987 July). Marketing and Technology: A Strategic Coalignment. *Journal of Marketing, 51*(3), 1-1 4.

Checkland, P. (1981). Systems Thinking, Systems Practice. New York: John Wiley & Sons.

Checkland, P. (1991). From Framework through Experience to Learning: The Essential Nature of Action Research. In H.-E. Nissen, H. Klein, & R. Hirschheim (Eds.), Information Systems Research: Contemporary Approaches and Emergent Traditions (pp. 397-403). North Holland: Elsevier Publishers.

Clemons, E. K. (1991, November). Corporate Strategies for Information Technology: A Resource-Based Approach. *Computer, 24*(11), 23–32. doi:10.1109/2.116848

Clemons, E. K., & Row, M. C. (1991a, September). Sustaining IT Advantage: The Role of Structural Differences. *MIS Quarterly, 15*(3), 275–292. doi:10.2307/249639

Clemons, E.K., & Row, M.K. (1991b). Information Technology at Rosenbluth Travel: Competitive Advantage in a Rapidly Growing Service Company. *Journal of Management Information Systems, 8*(2), 53-79.

Conner, K. R. (1991, March). A Historical Comparison of Resource-Based Theory and Five Schools of thought Within Industrial Organization Economics: Do We Have a New Theory of the Firm? *Journal of Management, 17*(1), 121–154. doi:10.1177/014920639101700109

Copeland, D. G., & McKenney, J. L. (1988, September). Airline Reservation Systems: Lessons from History. *MIS Quarterly, 12*(3), 353–370. doi:10.2307/249202

Cragg, P. B., & King, M. (1993). Small-Firm Computing: Motivators and Inhibitors. *MIS Quarterly, 17*(1), 47–60. doi:10.2307/249509

DeLone, W. H. (1988). Determinants of Success for Computer Usage in Small Business. *MIS Quarterly, 12*(1), 51–61. doi:10.2307/248803

Duncombe, R., & Heeks, R. (2003). An information systems perspective on ethical trade and self-regulation. *Information Technology for Development, 10*(2), 123–139. doi:10.1002/itdj.1590100206

Feeny, D. F., & Ives, B. (1990). In Search of Sustainability: Reaping Long-Term Advantage from Investments in Information Technology. Journal of Management Information Systems, 7(1), 27-46.

Foong, S.-Y. (1999). Effect of end user personal and systems attributes on computer based information systems success in Malaysian SMEs. *Journal of Small Business Management, 37*(3), 81–87.

Galliers, R. D. (1992). Choosing Information Systems Research Approaches. In R. D. Galliers (Ed.), Information Systems Research: Issues, Methods and Practical Guidelines (pp. 144-162). Henley-on-Thames, UK: Alfred Waller.

Grosh, B., & Somolekae, G. (1996). Mighty oaks from little acorns: Can micro-enterprise serve as the seedbed of industrialization? *World Development, 24*(12), 1879–1890. doi:10.1016/S0305-750X(96)00082-4

Harrison, D. A., Mykytyn, P. P. Jr, & Riemenschneider, C. K. (1997). Executive Decisions About Adoption of Information Technology in Small Business: Theory and Empirical Tests. *Information Systems Research, 8*(2), 171–195. doi:10.1287/isre.8.2.171

Hashmi, M. S., & Cuddy, J. (1990). Strategic initiatives for introducing CIM technologies in Irish SMEs. In L. Faria & W. van Puymbroeck (Eds.), *Computer Integrated Manufacturing – Proceedings of the Sixth CIM-Europe Annual Conference.* Lisbon: Springer Verlag.

Hazan, M. (2002). *Virtual South: E-Commerce for unprivileged artisans.* Retrieved Dec 12, 2007, from http://www.iicd.org/stories/

Honig, B. (1998). What determines success? Examining the human, financial, and social capital of Jamaican microentrepreneurs. *Journal of Business Venturing, 13*(5), 371–394. doi:10.1016/S0883-9026(97)00036-0

Hyman, E. L., & Dearden, K. (1998). (n.d.). Comprehensive impact assessment systems for NGO microenterprise development programs. *World Development, 26*(2), 261–276. doi:10.1016/S0305-750X(97)10022-5

Igbaria, M., Zinatelli, N., Cragg, P. B., & Cavaye, A. L. M. (1997). Personal Computing Acceptance Factors in Small Firms: A Structural Equation Model. *MIS Quarterly, 21*(3), 279–305. doi:10.2307/249498

Ives, B., & Learmonth, G. P. (1984). The Information Systems as a Competitive weapon. *Communications of the ACM, 27*(12), 1193–1201. doi:10.1145/2135.2137

Klein, H. K., & Myers, M. D. (1999, March). A Set of Principles for Conducting and Evaluating Interpretive Field Studies in Information Systems. *MIS Quarterly, 23*(1), 67–94. doi:10.2307/249410

Latchem, C., & Walker, D. (2001). Telecentres: Case Studies and Key Issues. Vancouver: The Commonwealth of Learning.

Lefebvre, L., & Lefebvre, E. (1993). Competitive positioning and innovative efforts in SMEs. *Small Business Economics, 5*, 297–305. doi:10.1007/BF01516250

Lefebvre, L., & Lefebvre, L. A. (1996). *Information and Telecommunication Technologies: The Impact of their Adoption on Small and Medium-sized Enterprises.* Retrieved Dec, 12, 2007, from http://web.idrc.ca/en/ev-9303-201-1-DO_TOPIC.html

Levy, M., & Powell, P. (1998). SME flexibility and the role of information systems. *Journal of Small Business Economics, 11*, 183–196. doi:10.1023/A:1007912714741

Levy, M., Powell, P., & Yetton, P. (2001). (forthcoming). SMEs: Aligning IS and the Strategic Context. *Journal of Information Technology*.

Levy, M., Powell, P., & Yetton, P. (2002). The Dynamics of SME Information Systems. *Small Business Economics, 19*, 341–354. doi:10.1023/A:1019654030019

Lichtenstein, G. A., & Lyons, T. S. (2001). The entrepreneurial development system: Transforming business talent and community economies. *Economic Development Quarterly, 15*(1), 3–20. doi:10.1177/089124240101500101

Mansell, R., & Wehn, U. (1998). Knowledge Societies: Information Technology for Sustainable Development. Oxford: Oxford University Press.

Matthews, P. (2007). ICT Assimilation and SME Expansion. *Journal of International Development, 19*(6): 817–827. doi:10.1002/jid.1401

McFarlan, F.W. (1984). Information Technology Changes the Way You Compete. *Harvard Business Review, 62*(3), 98-1 03.

McFarlan, F. W., & McKenney, J. L. (1983). Corporate Information Systems Management. Homewood, IL: Richard D. Irwin.

Montazemi, A. R. (1988). Factors Affecting Information Satisfaction in the Context of the Small Business Environment. *MIS Quarterly, 12*(2), 239–256. doi:10.2307/248849

Moyi, E. D. (2003). Networks, information and small enterprises: New Technologies and the ambiguity of empowerment. In Information Technology for Development (Vol. 10, pp. 221-232).

Naylor, J., & Williams, J. (1994). Successful Use of IT in SMEs. *European Journal of IS, 3*(1), 48–56.

O'Farrell, C., Norrish, P., & Scott, A. (1999). *Information and Communication Technologies (ICTs) for Sustainable Livelihoods*. Burton Hall: Intermediate Technology Development Group.

Owen, W., & Darkwa, O. (1999). Role of Multipurpose Community Telecentres in Accelerating National Development in Ghana. *First Monday, 5*(1), 1–23.

Pateli, A. G., & Giaglis, G. M. (2004). A research framework for analyzing eBusiness models. *European Journal of Information Systems, 13*, 302–314. doi:10.1057/palgrave.ejis.3000513

Piscitello, L., & Sgobbi, F. (2004, June). Globalisation, E-Business and SMEs: Evidence from the Italian District of Prato. *Small Business Economics, 22*(5), 333. doi:10.1023/B:SBEJ.0000022208.34741.55

Poon, S., & Swatman, P. (1999). An exploratory study of small business Internet commerce issues. *Information & Management, 35*, 9–18. doi:10.1016/S0378-7206(98)00079-2

Porter, M. E. (1980). Competitive Strategy: Techniques for Analyzing Industries and Competitors. New York: Free Press.

Porter, M.E., & Millar, V.E. (1985 July-August). How Information Gives You Competitive Advantage. *Harvard Business Review, 63*(4), 149-1 60.

Qiang, C. Z., Clarke, G. R., & Halewood, N. (2006). The Role of ICT. In World Bank (Ed.), Doing Business: Information and Communications for Development—Global Trends and Policies. Washington, DC: World Bank.

Qureshi, S. (2005). How does Information technology effect Development? Integrating Theory and Practice into a Process Model. In *Proceedings of the eleventh Americas Conference on Information Systems*, Omaha, NE.

Qureshi, S., Kamal, M., & Wolcott, P. (2008). Sustainability of Information Technology Therapy on Micro-enterprise Development. HICSS.

Raymond, L. (1988). The Impact of Computer Training on the Attitudes and Usage Behaviour of Small Business Managers. *Journal of Small Business Management, 26*(3), 9–13.

Raymond, L., Bergeron, F., & Blili, S. (2005). The assimilation of E-business in manufacturing SMEs: determinants and effects on growth and internationalization. *Electronic Markets, 15*(2), 106–118. doi:10.1080/10196780500083761

Reid, G., & Jacobsen, C. (1988). The Small Entrepreneurial Firm. Aberdeen, Scotland: Aberdeen University Press.

Riemenschneider, C., Harrison, D., & Mykytyn, P. (2003). Understanding IT Adoption Decisions in Small Business: Integrating Current Theories. *Information & Management*, 40.

Sanders, C. K. (2002). The impact of micro-enterprise assistance programs: A comparative study of program participants, non participants, and other low-wage workers. *The Social Service Review, 76*(2), 321–340. doi:10.1086/339664

Schreiner, M., & Woller, G. (2003). Micro-enterprise Development Programs in the United States and in the Developing World. *World Development, 31*(9), 1567–1580. doi:10.1016/S0305-750X(03)00112-8

Servon, L. J., & Doshna, J. P. (2000). Microenterprise and the economic development toolkit: A small part of the big picture. *Journal of Developmental Entrepreneurship, 5*(3), 183.

Sethi, V., & King, W. R. (1994, December). Development of Measures to Assess the Extent to Which an Information Technology Application Provides Competitive Advantage. *Management Science, 40*(12). doi:10.1287/mnsc.40.12.1601

Southwood, R. (2004). ICTs and Small Enterprise: A Motor of Economic Development in Africa. IICD Research Briefs, 9. The Hague: IICD.

Street, C. T., & Meister, D. B. (2004). Small Business Growth and Internal Transparency: The Role of Information Systems. *MIS Quarterly, 28*(3), 473–506.

Sullivan, B. C. (1985). Economics of Information Technology. *International Journal of Social Economics, 12*(1), 37. doi:10.1108/eb013983

Thong, J., Yap, C., & Rahman, K. (1996). Top management support, external expertise and information systems implementation in small businesses. *Information Systems Research, 7*(2), 248–267. doi:10.1287/isre.7.2.248

Wiseman, C. (1988). Strategic Information Systems. Homewood, IL: Irwin.

Wolcott, P., Qureshi, S., & Kamal, M. (2007). An Information Technology Therapy Approach to Micro-enterprise Adoption of ICTs. In *Americas Conference on Information Systems (AMCIS)*.

Yap, C. (1989). Computerization problems facing small and medium enterprises: the experience of Singapore. In *Proceedings of the 20th Annual Meeting of the Midwest Decision Sciences Institute*, Miami University, Oxford, OH (pp. 19-21, 128-134).

Zuber-Skerrit, O. (1991). Action Research for Change and Development. Aldershot, UK: Gower Publishing.

Compilation of References

Abdullah, M. A., & Bakar, M. I. H. (2000). Small and medium enterprises in Asian Pacific countries. Huntington, NY: Nova Science Publishers.

Abell, W., & Lim, L. (1996). Business use of the internet in New Zealand. Retrieved August 2004 from http://ausweb.scu.edu.au/aw96/business/abell/index.htm

Aberdeen Group. (2009). The ROI of Social Media Marketing: Why it pays to drive word of Mouth. Retrieved from http://www.adberdeen.com

Abernethy, M. (2002). SMEs: Small World Order. The Bulletin, 120(34).

Abuhamdieh, A., Kendall, J. E., & Kendall, K. E. (2002). An Evaluation of the Web presence of a nonprofit organization: Using the balanced scorecard approach in ecommerce. In R. Traunmüller (Ed.), Information systems: The e-business challenge (pp. 210-222). Boston: Kluwer Academic Publishers.

Abuhamdieh, A., Kendall, J.E., & Kendall, K.E. (2007). E-commerce Opportunities in the Nonprofit Sector: The case of New York Theatre Group. International journal of cases on electronic commerce, 3(1), 29-48.

Adam, F., & O'Doherty, P. (2000). Lessons from Enterprise Resource Planning Implementations in Ireland - Towards Smaller and Shorter ERP projects. Journal of Information Technology, 15(4), 305–316. doi:10.1080/02683960010008953

Agell, J. (2004). Why are small firms different? Managers' views. The Scandinavian Journal of Economics, 106(3), 437–452. doi:10.1111/j.0347-0520.2004.00371.x

Agilemanifesto. (2001). Manifesto for agile software development. Retrieved on February 20, 2007, from http://www.agilemanifesto.org/

Agrawal, A. (2001). University-to-industry knowledge transfer: literature review and unanswered questions. International Journal of Management Reviews, 3, 285–302. doi:10.1111/1468-2370.00069

Agrawal, A., & Henderson, R. (2002). Putting patents in context: Exploring knowledge transfer from MIT. Management Science, 48(1), 44–60. doi:10.1287/mnsc.48.1.44.14279

Aiken, L. S., & West, S. G. (1991). Multiple Regression: Testing and Interpreting Interactions. Thousand Oaks, CA: Sage Publications.

Ajzen, I. (1991). The theory of planned behavior. Organizational Behavior and Human Decision Processes, 50(2), 179–211. doi:10.1016/0749-5978(91)90020-T

Akkeren, J. K., & Cavaye, A. L. (2000). Why Australian Car Retailers do not Adopt E-Commerce Technologies. In Americas Conference in Information Systems (AMCIS) (pp. 72-81).

Alam, S. S., & Ahsan, N. (2007). ICT adoption in Malaysian SMEs from services sectors: Preliminary findings. Journal of Internet Banking and Commerce, 12(3), 1–11.

Alavi, M., & Leidner, D. E. (2001). Review: Knowledge management and knowledge management systems: Conceptual foundations and research issues. MIS Quarterly, 25(1), 107–136. doi:10.2307/3250961

Albert, S., & Whetten, D. (1985). Organizational identity. In L.L. Cummings & B. Staw (Eds.), Research in organizational behavior, 7 (pp. 263-295). Greenwich, CT: JAI Press.

Aldrich, H. E., & Fiol, C. M. (1994). Fools rush in? The institutional context of industry creation. Academy of Management Review, 19(4), 645–670. doi:10.2307/258740

Allen, M. W., & Caillouet, R. H. (1994). Legitimation endeavors: Impression management strategies used by an organization in crisis. Communication Monographs, 61, 44–62. doi:10.1080/03637759409376322

Allred, A., Addams, H. L., & Chakraborty, G. (2007). Is Informal Planning the Key to the Success of the INC 500? Journal of Small Business Strategy, 18(1), 95–104.

Al-Qirim, N. (2006). Personas of E-Commerce Adoption in Small Businesses in New Zealand. Journal of Electronic Commerce in Organizations, 4(3), 18–45.

Al-Qirim, N. A. Y. (2004). Electronic commerce in small to medium-sized enterprise: Frameworks, issues, and implications. Hershey, PA: Idea Group Publishing.

Alter, S., & Sherer, S. A. (2004). A General, But Readily Adaptable Model Of Information System Risk. Communications of AIS, 2004(14), 1-28.

Amit, R., & Schoemaker, P. J. H. (1993). Strategic assets and organizational rent. Strategic Management Journal, 14(1), 33–46. doi:10.1002/smj.4250140105

Amit, R., & Zott, C. (2001). Value creation in e-business. Strategic Management Journal, 22(6/7), 453–520.

Andersen, O. J. (2008). A bottom-up perspective on innovations: Mobilizing knowledge and social capital through innovative processes of bricolage. Administration & Society, 40(1), 54–81. doi:10.1177/0095399707311775

Anderson, C., & Andersson, M. (2006). The long tail: Hyperion New York.

Anderson, P. (2007 February). What is Web 2.0? Ideas, technologies and implications for education. JISC Technology and Standards Watch, 1-64.

Ang, J. S. (1992). On the theory of finance for privately held firms. Journal of Small Business Finance, 1(3), 185–203.

Ang, J. S., Cole, R. A., & Lin, J. W. (2000). Agency costs and ownership structure. The Journal of Finance, 55(1), 81–106. doi:10.1111/0022-1082.00201

Aragon-Sanchez, A., & Sanchez-Marin, G. (2005). Strategic orientation, management characteristics, and performance: A study of Spanish SMEs. Journal of Small Business Management, 43(3), 287–308.

Archer, N., Wang, S., & Kang, C. (2008). Barriers to the adoption of online supply chain solutions in small and medium enterprises. Supply Chain Management, 13(1), 73–82. doi:10.1108/13598540810850337

Argyris, C., & Schon, D. (1978). Organizational learning: A theory of action perspective. Reading, MA: Addison-Wesley.

Armstrong, J. S., & Overton, T. S. (1977). Estimating Nonresponse Bias in Mail Surveys. JMR, Journal of Marketing Research, 14(3), 396–402. doi:10.2307/3150783

Arnold, S. J., Handelman, J., & Tigert, D. J. (1996). Organizational legitimacy and retail store patronage. Journal of Business Research, 35, 229–239. doi:10.1016/0148-2963(95)00128-X

Asian Development Bank. (2003). Private sector development and finance. Asian Development Bank. Retrieved August 2009, from http://www.adb.org/PrivateSector/default.asp

Au, N., Ngai, E. W. T., & Cheng, T. C. E. (2008). Extending the Understanding of End User Information Systems Satisfaction Formation: An Equitable Needs Fulfillment Model Approach. MIS Quarterly, 32(1), 43–66.

Audretsch, D., & Feldman, M. (1996). R&D Spillovers and the Geography of Innovation and Production. The American Economic Review, 630–640.

Auh, S., Bell, S., McLeod, C., & Shih, E. (2007). co-Production and customer loyalty in financial services. Journal of Retailing, 83(3), 359–370. doi:10.1016/j.jretai.2007.03.001

Australian Bureau of Statistics. (2000). Small business in Australia 1999. Retrieved from http://www.ausstats. abs.gov.au/ausstats/subscriber.nsf/0/F64FDF829D4BE5 0BCA2568E80004BADB/$File/13210_1999.pdf

Australian Bureau of Statistics. (ABS 2006). 8127.0 Australian Small Business Operators - Findings from the 2005 and 2006 Characteristics of Small Business Surveys, 2005-06. Retrieved June 2009 from http:// www.abs.gov.au

Australian Government Information Management Office. (2005). E-Government: Australia's Approach. Keynote Address, Special Minister of State Senator The Hon Eric Abetz, Commonwealth of Australia, Nikkei Fifth Strategic Conference on e-Government, 28th – 29th July, Tokyo, Japan.

Avison, D. E., Lau, F., Myers, M., & Nielsen, P. A. (1999). Action Research. Communications of the ACM, 42(1), 94–97. doi:10.1145/291469.291479

Avison, D., Jones, J., Powell, P., & Wilson, D. (2004). Using and validating the strategic alignment model. The Journal of Strategic Information Systems, 13, 223–246. doi:10.1016/j.jsis.2004.08.002

Aydin, M. N., Harmsen, F., Slooten, K. v., & Stegwee, R. A. (2005). On the adaptation of an agile information systems development method. Journal of Database Management, 16(4), 24–40.

Baark, E., & Heeks, R. (1998). Evaluation of Donor-Funded Information Technology Transfer Projects in China: A Life-Cycle Approach. Retrieved Dec 12, 2007, from http://idpm.man.ac.uk/wp/di/di_wp01.htm

Bagozzi, R. P., & Yi, Y. (1988). On the evaluation of structural equation models. Journal of the Academy of Marketing Science, 16(1), 74–94. doi:10.1007/BF02723327

Bailey, J. E., & Pearson, S. W. (1983). Development of a tool for measuring and analysing computer user satisfaction. Management Science, 29(5), 530–545. doi:10.1287/mnsc.29.5.530

Bajaj, K. K., & Nag, D. (1999). E-commerce: The cutting edge of business. New Delhi: Tata McGraw-Hill.

Baker, T., & Nelson, R. E. (2005). Creating something from nothing: Resource construction through entrepreneurial bricolage. Administrative Science Quarterly, 50(3), 329–366. doi:10.2189/asqu.2005.50.3.329

Baki, B., & Çakar, K. (2005). Determining the ERP package-selecting criteria: The case of Turkish manufacturing companies. Business Process Management Journal, 11(1), 75–86. doi:10.1108/14637150510578746

Bakos, J.Y., & Treacy, M.E. (1986 June). Information Technology and Corporate Strategy: A Research Perspective. MIS Quarterly, 1(2), 107-1 19.

Bakos, Y. (1998 August). The Emerging Role of Electronic Marketplaces on the Internet. Communications of the ACM.

Bala, H., & Venkatesh, V. (2007). Assimilation of Interorganizational Business Process Standards. Information Systems Research, 18(3), 340–362. doi:10.1287/isre.1070.0134

Baldoni, J. (2009). What executives can learn from Obama's BlackBerry. Harvard Business Publishing. Retrieved from http://blogs.harvardbusiness.org/baldoni/2009/01/a_virtual_leadership_lesson_ob.html?loomia_ow=t0:a38:g26:r2:c0.031242:b20799 989

Ballantine, J., Levy, M., & Powell, P. (1998). Evaluating information systems in small and medium-sized enterprises: issues and evidence. European Journal of Information Systems, 7(4), 241–251. doi:10.1057/palgrave.ejis.3000307

Balmer, J. M. T. (1998). Corporate identity and advent of corporate marketing. Journal of Marketing Management, 14, 963–996. doi:10.1362/026725798784867536

Barclay, I. (2006). Benchmarking best practice in SMEs for growth. International Journal of Technology Management, 33(2-3), 234–254. doi:10.1504/IJTM.2006.008313

Bargh, J. A. 1984. Automatic and conscious processing of social information. In R.S. Wyer, Jr., & T.K. Srull (Eds.), Handbook of social cognition (pp. 1-43). Hillsdale, NJ: Erlbaum.

Barley, S. R., & Tolbert, P. S. (1997). Institutionalization and structuration: Studying the links between action and institution. *Organization Studies*, 18(1), 93–117. doi:10.1177/017084069701800106

Barney, J. (1991). Firm resources and sustained competitive advantage. *Journal of Management*, 17(1), 99–120. doi:10.1177/014920639101700108

BarNir, A., Gallaugher, J. M., & Auger, P. (2003). Business process digitization, strategy, and the impact of firm age and size: The case of the magazine publishing industry. *Journal of Business Venturing*, 18(6), 789–814. doi:10.1016/S0883-9026(03)00030-2

Barrett, R., & Burgess, J. (2008). Small firms and the challenge of equality, diversity and difference Equal Opportunities International, 27(3), 213 - 220.

Barron, J. M., Berger, M. C., & Black, D. A. (1997). How well do we measure training? *Journal of Labor Economics*, 15(3), 507–528. doi:10.1086/209870

Barry, H., & Milner, B. (2002). SME's and Electronic Commerce: A Departure from the Traditional Prioritisation of Training? *Journal of European Industrial Training*, 26(7), 316–326. doi:10.1108/03090590210432660

Barton, C., & Bear, M. (1999). Information and Communications Technologies: Are they the Key to Viable Business Development Services for Micro and Small Enterprises? Report for USAID as part of the Microenterprise Best Practices Project. Retrieved December 12, 2007, from http://www.mip.org/PUBS/MBP/ict.htm

Bartunek, J. M. (2007). Academic-Practitioner Collaboration Need Not Require Joint Or Relevant Research: Toward A Relational Scholarship Of Integration. *Academy of Management Journal*, 50(6), 1323–1333.

Barua, A., Konana, P., Whinston, A. B., & Yin, F. (2004). An Empirical investigation of net-enabled business value. *MIS Quarterly*, 28(4), 585–620.

Baskerville, R., & Myers, M. D. (2004). Special Issue On Action Research In Information Systems: Making Is Research Relevant To Practice--Foreword. *MIS Quarterly*, 28(3), 329–335.

Bassellier, G., Reich, B. H., & Benbasat, I. (2001). Information technology competence of business managers: A definition and research model. *Journal of Management Information Systems*, 17(4), 159–182.

Bauer, M. (2004). FDD and project management. *Cutter IT Journal*, 17(6), 38–44.

Baum, J. A., & Oliver, C. (1991). Institutional linkages and organizational mortality. *Administrative Science Quarterly*, 36(2), 187–219. doi:10.2307/2393353

Baumol, W. J. (2002). Entrepreneruship, innovation and growth: The David-Goliath Symbiosis. *Journal of Entrepreneurial Finance and Business Ventures*, 7(2), 1–10.

Beatty, R., Shim, J., & Jones, M. (2001). Factors Influencing Corporate Web Site Adoption: A Time-based Assessment. *Information & Management*, 38(6), 337–354. doi:10.1016/S0378-7206(00)00064-1

Beaver, G., & Prince, C. (2004). Management, strategy and policy in the UK small business sector: A critical review. *Journal of Small Business and Enterprise Development*, 11, 34–49. doi:10.1108/14626000410519083

Beaver, G., & Ross, C. (2000). Enterprise in recession: The role and context of strategy. *International Journal of Entrepreneurship and Innovation*, 1(1), 23–31.

Beck, K., & Andres, C. (2005). Extreme programming explained: Embrace change (2nd ed.). Boston: Addison-Wesley.

Beck, R., Wigand, R. T., & Konig, W. (2005). The diffusion and efficient use of electronic commerce among small and medium sized enterprises: An international three industry survey. *Electronic Markets*, 15(1), 38–52. doi:10.1080/10196780500035282

Beckinsale, M., Levy, M., & Powell, P. (2006). Exploring internet adoption drivers in SMEs. *Electronic Markets*, 16(4), 361–370. doi:10.1080/10196780600999841

Beckinsdale, M., Levy, M., & Powell, P. (2006). Exploring Internet adoption drivers in SMEs. *Electronic Markets*, 16(4), 137–188.

Beer, D., & Burrows, R. (2007). Sociology and, of and in Web 2.0: some initial considerations. *Sociological*

Research, 12(5). Retrieved from http://www.socresonline.org.uk/12/5/17.html

Beheshti, H. M. (2004). The impact of IT on SMEs in the United States. Information Management & Computer Security, 12(4), 318–327. doi:10.1108/09685220410553532

Bell, D. (1973). The Coming of Post-Industrial Society. Business & Society Review/Innovation(5).

Benbasat, I., & Zmud, R. W. (1999). Empirical Research In Information Systems: The Practice Of Relevance. MIS Quarterly, 23(1), 3–16. doi:10.2307/249403

Benbasat, I., Bergeron, M., & Dexter, A. (1993). Development and Adoption of Electronic Data Interchange Systems: A Case Study of the Liquor Distribution Branch of British Columbia. In Proceedings of Administrative Science Association of Canada Twenty First Annual Conference, Lake Louise, Alberta, Canada, May (pp.153-163).

Berg, P. O. (1985). Organization change as a symbolic transformation process. In P. Frost, L. Moore, M.R. Louis, C. Lundberg, & J. Martin (Eds.), Reframing organizational culture (pp. 281-300). Beverly Hills, CA: Sage.

Berger, A. N., Frame, W. S., & Miller, N. H. (2005). Credit scoring and the availability, price, and risk of small business credit. Journal of Money. Credit and Banking, 37(2), 191–222. doi:10.1353/mcb.2005.0019

Berger, P. L., & Luckmann, T. (1967). The social construction of reality. NY: Anchor Books.

Bergeron, F., & Raymond, L. (1992). Planning of information systems to gain a competitive advantage. Journal of Small Business Management, 30, 21–26.

Bernoff, J., & Li, C. (2008). Harnessing the Power of the Oh-So-Social Web. MIT Sloan Management Review, 49(3), 36–42.

Bernroider, E. (2008). IT governance for enterprise resource planning supported by the DeLone-McLean model of information system success. Information & Management, 45(5), 257–269. doi:10.1016/j.im.2007.11.004

Bernroider, E. W. N., & Leseure, M. J. (2005). Enterprise resource planning (ERP) diffusion and characteristics according to the system's lifecycle: A comparative view of small-to-medium-sized and large enterprises. Working papers on information processing and Information Management. Wien, Austria: Vienna University of Economics and Business Administration, Institute of Information Processing and Information Management.

Berry, M. (1998). Strategic planning in small high tech companies. Long Range Planning, 31(3), 455–466. doi:10.1016/S0024-6301(98)80012-5

Berthon, P., Pitt, L. F., & Campbell, C. (2008). Ad Lib: When customers create an ad. California Management Review, 50(4), 6–30.

Bhabha, H. K. (1996). Cultures in between. In S. Hall & P. du Gay (Eds.), Questions of cultural identity (pp. 53-60). London & Thousand Oaks, CA, Sage.

Bhabha, H. K. (2008). The Location of culture. New York: Routledge Classics. (Original work published in 1994.).

Bharadwaj, A. S. (2000). A resource-based perspective on information technology capability and firm performance: An empirical investigation. MIS Quarterly, 24(1), 169–196. doi:10.2307/3250983

Bharadwaj, A. S., Sambamurthy, V., & Zmud, R. W. (2000). IT capabilities: theoretical perspectives and empirical operalization. Paper presented at the 21st International Conference on Information Systems, Brisbane, Australia.

Bharadwaj, P. N., & Soni, R. G. (2007). E-commerce usage and perception of e-commerce issues among small firms: Results and implications from an empirical study. Journal of Small Business Management, 45(4), 501–521. doi:10.1111/j.1540-627X.2007.00225.x

Bharati, P., & Chaudary, A. (2009). SMEs and Competitiveness: The Role of Information Systems. International Journal of E-Business Research, 5(1).

Bharati, P., & Chaudhury, A. (2002). Assimilation of Internet-based technologies in small and medium sized manufacturers. Proceedings of 2002 IRMA International Conference.

Bharati, P., & Chaudhury, A. (2006). Studying the current status: Examining the extent and nature of adoption of technologies by micro, small, and medium-sized manufacturing firms in the greater Boston area. Communications of the ACM, 49(10), 88–93. doi:10.1145/1164394.1164400

Bharati, P., & Chaudhury, A. (2008). IT Outsourcing Adoption by Small and Medium Enterprises: A Diffusion Innovation Approach. In Proceedings of the Americas Conference on Information Systems (AMCIS), August 14-17.

Bharati, P., & Chaudhury, A. (2009). SMEs and competitiveness - The role of information systems. International Journal of E-Business Research, 5(1), 1–9.

Bierly, P. E., & Daly, P. S. (2007). Sources of external organisational learning in small manufacturing firms. International Journal of Technology Management, 38(1/2), 45–68. doi:10.1504/IJTM.2007.012429

Bierly, P., & Chakrabarti, A. (1996). Generic knowledge strategies in the us pharmaceutical industry. Strategic Management Journal, 17, 123–135.

Biernacki, P., & Waldorf, D. (1981). Snowball sampling: Problems and techniques of chain referral sampling. Sociological Methods & Research, 10(2), 141–163.

Biever, C. (2006, December 23). Web 2.0 is all about the feel-good factor. New Scientist, 192, 30.

Birdsall, W. F. (2007). Web 2.0 as a social movement. Webology, 4(2). Retrieved from http://www.webology.ir/2007/v4n2/a40.html

Bleistein, S. J., Cox, K., Verner, J., & Phalp, K. T. (2006). B-SCP: A requirements analysis framework for validating strategic alignment of organisational IT based on strategy, context, and process. Information and Software Technology, 48, 846–868. doi:10.1016/j.infsof.2005.12.001

Blili, S., & Raymond, L. (1993). Information technology: Threats and opportunities for small and medium sized enterprises. International Journal of Information

Management, 13(6), 439–448. doi:10.1016/0268-4012-(93)90060-H

Bodnar, G. H. (2003). IT governance. Internal Auditing, 18(3), 27–32.

Boll, S. (2007). MultiTube—Where Web 2.0 and Multimedia Could Meet. IEEE MultiMedia, 14(1), 9–13. doi:10.1109/MMUL.2007.17

Bollen, K. A. (1989). Structural equations with latent variables: Wiley-Interscience.

Boohalis, D. (1996). Enhancing the competitiveness of small and medium sized tourism enterprise at the destination level. Electronic Markets, 6(1).

Boston Consulting Group. (1999). E-tail of the Tiger: Retail E-Commerce in the Asia Pacific. Boston, MA: Boston Consulting Group.

Boter, H., & Lundström, A. (2005). SME perspectives on business support services. Journal of Small Business and Enterprise Development, 12(2), 244–258. doi:10.1108/14626000510594638

Botta-Genoulaz, V., Millet, P.-A., & Grabot, B. (2005). A survey on the recent reserach literature on ERP systems. Computers in Industry, 56(6), 510–522. doi:10.1016/j.compind.2005.02.004

Boudreau, M.-C., Loch, K. D., Robey, D., & Straud, D. (1998). Going global: Using information technology to advance the competitiveness of the virtual transnational organization. The Academy of Management Executive, 12(4), 120–128.

Boulay, D. A. (2008). An exploration of the relationships among organizational size, flexible work practices, training, and organizational performance using the 2002 national organizations survey. The Ohio State University.

Bourgeois, L. J. (1981). On the measurement of organizational slack. Academy of Management Review, 6, 29–39. doi:10.2307/257138

Bourgeois, L. J., & Singh, J. V. (1983). Organizational slack and political behavior within top management teams. Academy of Management Proceedings, 43-47.

Brabham, D. (2008). Crowdsourcing as a model for problem solving: an introduction and cases. Convergence. Retrieved from http://con.sagepub.com/cgi/content/abstract/14/1/75

Bracker, J. S., & Pearson, J. N. (1986). Planning and financial performance of small mature firms. Strategic Management Journal, 7(6), 503–522.

Bracker, J. S., Keats, B. W., & Pearson, J. N. (1988). Planning and financial performance among small firms in a growth industry. Strategic Management Journal, 9(6), 591–603. doi:10.1002/smj.4250090606

Brancheau, J. C., & Wetherbe, J. C. (1990). The adoption of spreadsheet software: Testing innovation diffusion theory in the context of end-user computing. Information Systems Research, 1(2), 115–143. doi:10.1287/isre.1.2.115

Brigham, E. F., & Smith, K. V. (1967). The cost of capital to small firm. The Engineering Economist, 13(1), 1–26. doi:10.1080/00137916708928761

Bromiley, P. (1991). Testing a causal model of corporate risk taking and performance. Academy of Management Journal, 34(1), 37–59. doi:10.2307/256301

Brown, D. H., & Lockett, N. (2004). Potential of critical e-applications for engaging SMEs in e-business: a provider perspective. European Journal of Information Systems, 13, 21–34. doi:10.1057/palgrave.ejis.3000480

Bryan, J. (2006). Training and Performance in Small Firms. International Small Business Journal, 24(6), 635–660. doi:10.1177/0266242606069270

Brynjolfsson, E., & Hitt, L. M. (1998). Beyond the productivity paradox. Communications of the ACM, 41(8), 49–55. doi:10.1145/280324.280332

Bunker, D., & MacGregor, R. C. (2000). Successful generation of Information Technology (IT) requirements for Small/Medium Enterprises (SMEs). - Cases from regional Australia. In Proceedings of SMEs in Global Economy. Wollongong, Australia (pp. 72-84).

Buonanno, G., Faverio, P., Pigni, F., & Ravarini, A. (2005). Factors affecting ERP system adoption: A comparative analysis between SMEs and large companies. Journal of Enterprise Information Management, 18(4), 384–426. doi:10.1108/17410390510609572

Burke Jarvis, C., Mackenzie, S. B., & Podsakoff, P. M. (2003). A Critical Review of Construct Indicators and Measurement Model Misspecification in Marketing and Consumer Research. The Journal of Consumer Research, 30(September), 199–218. doi:10.1086/376806

Burke, G., & Jarratt, D. (2004). The influence of information and advice on competitive strategy definition in small-and medium-sized enterprises. Qualitative Market Research, 7, 126–138. doi:10.1108/13522750410530039

Burke, K. (2005). The impact of firm size on Internet use in small businesses. Electronic Markets, 15(2), 79–93. doi:10.1080/10196780500083738

Caldeira, M., & Ward, J. (2003). Using resource-based theory to interpret the successful adoption and use of information systems and technology in manufacturing small and medium-sized enterprises. European Journal of Information Systems, 12(2), 127–141. doi:10.1057/palgrave.ejis.3000454

Caloghirou, Y., Protogerou, A., Spanos, Y., & Papagiannakis, L. (2004). Industry- versus firm-specific effects on performance: Contrasting SMEs and large-sized firms. European Management Journal, 22(2), 231–243. doi:10.1016/j.emj.2004.01.017

Capon, N., & Glazer, R. (1987 July). Marketing and Technology: A Strategic Coalignment. Journal of Marketing, 51(3), 1-1 4.

Capron, L., & Pistre, N. (2002). When do acquirers earn abnormal returns? Strategic Management Journal, 23(9), 781–794. doi:10.1002/smj.262

Carnaghan, C., Downer, P., Klassen, D., & Pittman, J. (2004). CAP Forum on E-Business: E-Commerce and Tax Planning: Canadian Experiences. Canadian Accounting Perspectives, 3(2), 261–287. doi:10.1506/V82X-X152-PND1-ABHE

Cavalluzzo, K., & Wolken, J. (2005). Small business loan turndowns, personal wealth, and discrimination. The Journal of Business, 78(6), 2153–2177. doi:10.1086/497045

CBS. (2004). Survey usaha terintegrasi 2004. Central Bureau of Statistics (CBS).

Celuch, K., Murphy, G. B., & Callaway, S. K. (2007). More bang for your buck: Small firms and the importance of aligned information technology capabilities and strategic flexibility. The Journal of High Technology Management Research, 17(2), 187–197. doi:10.1016/j.hitech.2006.11.006

Chaffey, D., Mayer, R., Johnston, K., & Ellis-Chadwick, F. (2000). Internet Marketing, Strategy, Implementation and Practice. Reading, MA: FT/Pretnice Hall.

Chahine, S., & Filatotev, I. (2008). The Effects of Information Disclosure and Board Independence on IPO Discount. Journal of Small Business Management, 46(2), 219–241. doi:10.1111/j.1540-627X.2008.00241.x

Chan, I., & Chao, C. (2008). Knowledge management in small and medium-sized enterprises. Communications of the ACM, 51(4), 83–88. doi:10.1145/1330311.1330328

Chan, M. F. S., & Chung, W. W. C. (2002). A framework to development an enterprise information portal for contract manufacturing. International Journal of Production Economics, 75(1/2), 113–126. doi:10.1016/S0925-5273(01)00185-2

Chan, Y. E., & Huff, S. L. (1992). Strategy: An information systems research perspective. The Journal of Strategic Information Systems, 1(4), 191–204. doi:10.1016/0963-8687(92)90035-U

Chan, Y. E., & Huff, S. L. (1993). Strategic information systems alignment. Business Quarterly, 58(1), 51–55.

Chan, Y. E., Bhargava, N., & Street, C. T. (2006). Having arrived: The homogeneity of high-growth small firms. Journal of Small Business Management, 44(3), 426–440. doi:10.1111/j.1540-627X.2006.00180.x

Chan, Y. E., Huff, S. L., Barclay, D. W., & Copeland, D. G. (1997). Business strategic orientation, information systems strategic orientation, and strategic align-

ment. Information Systems Research, 8(2), 125–150. doi:10.1287/isre.8.2.125

Chau, P. Y. K., & Tam, K. Y. (1997). Factors Affecting the Adoption of Open Systems: An Exploratory Study. MIS Quarterly, 21(1), 1–24. doi:10.2307/249740

Chau, S. B., & Turner, P. (2001). A Four Phase Model of EC Business Transformation Amongst Small to Medium Sized Enterprises. In Proceedings of the 12th Australasian Conference on Information Systems, Coffs Harbour, Australia.

Checkland, P. (1981). Systems Thinking, Systems Practice. New York: John Wiley & Sons.

Checkland, P. (1991). From Framework through Experience to Learning: The Essential Nature of Action Research. In H.-E. Nissen, H. Klein, & R. Hirschheim (Eds.), Information Systems Research: Contemporary Approaches and Emergent Traditions (pp. 397-403). North Holland: Elsevier Publishers.

Chell, E., Hawarth, J., & Brearley, S. (1991). The entrepreneurial personality. London: Routledge.

Chen, J., & McQueen, R. J. (2008). Factors Affecting E-Commerce Stages of Growth in Small Chinese Firms in New Zealand: An Analysis of Adoption Motivators and Inhibitors. Journal of Global Information Management, 16(1), 26–61.

Cheng, J., & Kesner, I. (1997). Organizational slack and response to environmental shifts: The impact of resource allocation patterns. Journal of Management, 23, 1–18. doi:10.1177/014920639702300101

Chepaitis, E. V. (2002). E-commerce and the information environment in an emerging economy: Russia at the turn of the century. In P. C. Palvia, S. C. J. Palvia, & E. M. Roche (Eds.), Global Information Technology and Electronic Commerce: Issues for the new millennium (pp. 53 - 72).

Chesbrough, H. (2003). The Era of Open Innovation. MIT Sloan Management Review, 44(3), 45–41.

Chin, W. W. (1998). The Partial Least Squares Approach for Structural Equation Modelling. In G. A. Marcoulides

(Ed.), Modern Methods for Business Research. Hillsdale, NJ: Lawrence Erlbaum Associates.

Chin, W. W. (2001). PLS-Graph User's Guide, Version 3.0. Unpublished.

Chin, W. W., Johnson, M., & Schwarz, A. (2008). A Fast Form Approach to Measuring Technology Acceptance and Other Constructs. MIS Quarterly, 32(4), 687–703.

Chin, W. W., Marcolin, B. L., & Newsted, P. R. (1996). A Partial Least Squares Latent Variable Modeling Approach for Measuring Interaction Effects: Results from a Monte Carlo Simulation Study and Voice Mail Emotion/Adoption Study. Paper presented at the Seventeenth International Conference on Information Systems.

Chirico, F. (2008). The Creation, Sharing and Transfer of Knowledge in Family Business. Journal of Small Business and Entrepreneurship, 21(4), 413–434.

Chitura, T., & Mupemhi, S., Dube & Bolongkikit, T. (2008). Barriers to Electronic Commerce Adoption in Small and Medium Enterprises: A Critical Literature Review. Journal of Internet Banking and Commerce, 13(2), 1–13.

Chiware, E. R. T., & Dick, A. L. (2008). The use of ICTs in Namibia's SME sector to access business information services. The Electronic Library, 26(2), 145–157. doi:10.1108/02640470810864055

Chong, S. (2005). Electronic Commerce adoption by Small- and Medium-sized Enterprises in Australia: An Empirical Study of Influencing Factors. Journal of Contemporary Issues in Business and Government, 11(1), 49–70.

Chong, S. (2006, August). An Empirical Study of Factors that Influence the Extent of Deployment of Electronic Commerce for Small- and Medium-sized Enterprises in Australia. Journal of Theoretical and Applied Electronic Commerce Research, 1(2), 45–57.

Chow, C. W., Haddad, K. M., & Williamson, J. E. (1997). Applying the Balanced Scorecard to small companies. Strategic Finance, 79(2), 21–28.

Christian, R. C. (1959). Industrial marketing. Journal of Marketing, 79–80. doi:10.2307/1248856

Chung, S., Singh, H., & Lee, K. (2000). Complementarity, status similarity and social capital as drivers of alliance formation. Strategic Management Journal, 21(1), 1–22. doi:10.1002/(SICI)1097-0266(200001)21:1<1::AID-SMJ63>3.0.CO;2-P

Churchill, G. A. (1991). Marketing research: Methodological foundations (5th Ed.). Chicago: Dryden Press.

Churchill, N. C., & Lewis, V. L. (1983). The five stages of small business growth. Harvard Business Review, 61(3), 30–39.

Churchill, N., & Lewis, V. (2000). The five stages of small business growth. Small Business: Critical Perspectives on Business and Management, 291.

Chwelos, P., Benbasat, I., & Dexter, A. S. (2001). Research report: Empirical test of an EDI adoption model. Information Systems Research, 12(3), 304–321. doi:10.1287/isre.12.3.304.9708

Clarke, R. (2003). If e-business is different, then so is reseach in e-business. In K. Viborg Andersen, S. Elliott, P. Swatman, E. M. Trauth & N. Bjørn-Andersen (Eds.), Seeking success in e-business. Boston, MA: Kluwer Academic Publishers.

Claver, E., Llopis, J., Garcia, D., & Molina, H. (1998). Organizational culture for innovation and new technological behavior. The Journal of High Technology Management Research, 9(1), 55. doi:10.1016/1047-8310(88)90005-3

Clemons, E. K. (1991, November). Corporate Strategies for Information Technology: A Resource-Based Approach. Computer, 24(11), 23–32. doi:10.1109/2.116848

Clemons, E. K., & McFarlan, F. W. (1986). Telecom: Hook Up Or Lose Out. Harvard Business Review, 64, 91–97.

Clemons, E. K., & Row, M. C. (1991). Sustaining IT advantage: The role of structural differences. MIS Quarterly, 15(3), 275–292. doi:10.2307/249639

Clemons, E.K., & Row, M.K. (1991b). Information Technology at Rosenbluth Travel: Competitive Advantage in a Rapidly Growing Service Company. *Journal of Management Information Systems, 8*(2), 53-79.

Cloete, E., Courtney, S., & Fintz, J. (2002). Small Businesses' Acceptance and Adoption of E-commerce in the Western Cape Province of South Africa. *Electronic Journal of Information Systems in Developing Countries, 10*(4), 1–13.

Cochran, A. B. (1981). Small business mortality rates: A review of the literature. *Journal of Small Business Management, 19*(4), 50–59.

Cockburn, I., & Henderson, R. (1998). Absorptive capacity, coauthoring behavior, and the organization of research in drug discovery. *The Journal of Industrial Economics,* 157–182.

Cohen, W. M., & Levinthal, D. A. (1990). Absorptive-capacity - a new perspective on learning and innovation. *Administrative Science Quarterly, 35*(1), 128–152. doi:10.2307/2393553

Colyvas, J., Crow, M., Gelijns, A., Mazzoleni, R., Nelson, R., & Rosenberg, N. (2002). How do university inventions get into practice? *Management Science, 48*(1), 61–72. doi:10.1287/mnsc.48.1.61.14272

Compeau, D. R., Higgins, C. A., & Huff, S. (1999). Social cognitive theory and individual reactions to computing technology: A longitudinal study. *MIS Quarterly, 23*(2), 145–158. doi:10.2307/249749

Conner, K. R. (1991, March). A Historical Comparison of Resource-Based Theory and Five Schools of thought Within Industrial Organization Economics: Do We Have a New Theory of the Firm? *Journal of Management, 17*(1), 121–154. doi:10.1177/014920639101700109

Constantinides, E. (2004). Influencing The Online Consumer's Behaviour: The Web Experience. *Journal of Internet Research, 14*(2), 111–126. doi:10.1108/10662240410530835

Constantinides, E. (2006). The Marketing Mix Revisited: Towards the 21st Century Marketing. *Journal of Marketing Management, 22*(3 -4), 407 – 438.

Constantinides, E., & Fountain, S. (2008). Web 2.0: Conceptual Foundations and Marketing Issues. *Journal of Direct, Data and Digital Marketing Practice, 9*(3).

Constantinides, E., Lorenzo, C., & Gómez, M.A. (2008). Social Media: A new frontier for retailers? *European Retail Research, 22*(1).

Conte, D. M., & Langley, S. (2007). *Theatre management: Producing and managing the performing arts.* Hollywood, CA: Entertainment Pro.

Cooper, M. J., Upton, N., & Seaman, S. (2005). Customer relationship management: A comparative ananlysis of family and nonfamily business practices. *Journal of Small Business Management, 43*(3), 242–257.

Cooper, R., & Zmud, R. (1990). Information technology implementation research: A technological diffusion approach. *Management Science, 36*(2), 123–139. doi:10.1287/mnsc.36.2.123

Copeland, D. G., & McKenney, J. L. (1988, September). Airline Reservation Systems: Lessons from History. *MIS Quarterly, 12*(3), 353–370. doi:10.2307/249202

Corbitt, B., Behrendorf, G., & Brown-Parker, J. (1997). SMEs and Electronic Commerce. *The Australian Institute of Management, 14,* 204–222.

Cormican, K., & O'Sullivan, D. (2004). Auditing best practice for effective product innovation management. *Technovation, 24,* 819–829. doi:10.1016/S0166-4972-(03)00013-0

Corrocher, N., & Fontana, R. (2008). Expectations, network effects and timing of technology adoption: Some empirical evidence from a sample of SMEs in italy. *Small Business Economics, 31*(4), 425–441. doi:10.1007/s11187-007-9062-1

Cortés, M., & Rafter, K. M. (2007). *Nonprofits & Technology.* Chicago: Lyceum Books, Inc.

Cosh, A., Duncan, J., & Hughes, A. (1998). Investment in Training and Small Firm Growth and Survival: An Empirical Analysis for the UK 1987-95. Dfee Publivations Research Report No. 36.

Costa, G., & Gianecchini, M. (2006). Tecnologia, cambiamento organizzativo e competitività. Il ruolo dei sistemi informativi integrati. Paper presented at the workshop WOA 2006: Organizzazione, Regolazione e Competitività, Fisciano, Salerno.

Cousins, P. D., & Spekman, R. (2003). Strategic supply and the management of inter- and intra-organisational relationships. Journal of Purchasing and Supply Management, 9, 19–29. doi:10.1016/S1478-4092(02)00036-5

Coviello, N. E., & Brodie, R. J. (2001). Contemporary Marketing practices of consumer and business-to-business firms: how different are they? Journal of Business and Industrial Marketing, 16(5), 382–400. doi:10.1108/08858620110400223

Cox, L. W., Camp, S. M., & Sexton, D. L. (2000). The Kauffman Financial Statements Database. In J.A. Katz (Ed.), Databases for the Study of Entrepreneurship. Advances in Entrepreneurship Research, 4, 305-334.

Coyle, K. (2007). The Library Catalog in a 2.0 World. Journal of Academic Librarianship, 33(2), 289–291. doi:10.1016/j.acalib.2007.02.003

Cragg, P. B., & Zinatelli, N. (1995). The Evolution of information systems in small firms. Information & Management, 29(1), 1–8. doi:10.1016/0378-7206(95)00012-L

Cragg, P., & King, M. (1993). Small-firm computing: motivators and inhibitors. MIS Quarterly, 17(1), 47–60. doi:10.2307/249509

Craig, E. (2007). Changing paradigms: managed learning environments and Web 2.0. Campus-Wide Information Systems, 24(3), 152–161. doi:10.1108/10650740710762185

Cronbach, L. J. (1951, September). Coefficient alpha and internal structure of tests. Psychometrika, 16, 297–334. doi:10.1007/BF02310555

Croteau, A.-M., & Bergeron, F. (2001). An information technology trilogy: business strategy, technological deployment and organisational performance. The Journal of Strategic Information Systems, 10, 77–99. doi:10.1016/S0963-8687(01)00044-0

Culkin, N., & Smith, D. (2000). An emotional business: A guide to understanding the motivations of small business decision takers. International Journal of Qualitative Marketing Research, 3(3), 145–157. doi:10.1108/13522750010333898

Cummings, M. F. (2003). Understanding Enterprise, Entrepreneurship and Small Business (Book). Irish Journal of Management, 24(1), 229–230.

Cyert, R. M., & March, J. G. (1963). A behavioral theory of the firm. Englewood Cliffs, NJ: Prentice-Hall, Inc.

Cymfony. (2006). Making the case for a Social MediaStrategy [White paper]. Retrieved from http://www.cymfony.com

Da Silveira, G., Borenstein, D., & Fogliatto, F. S. (2001). Mass customization: Literature review and research directions. International Journal of Production Economics, 72(1), 1–13. doi:10.1016/S0925-5273(00)00079-7

Daft, R. L., & Weick, K. E. (1984). Toward a model of organizations as interpretation systems. Academy of Management Review, 9(2), 284–295. doi:10.2307/258441

Damanpour, F. (1991). Organizational innovation: A meta-analysis of effects of determinants and moderators. Academy of Management Journal, 34(3), 555–590. doi:10.2307/256406

Damanpour, F., & Wischnevsky, J. D. (2006). Research on innovation in organizations: Distinguishing innovation-generating from innovation-adopting organizations. Journal of Engineering and Technology Management, 23(4), 269–291. doi:10.1016/j.jengtecman.2006.08.002

Damanpour, F., Szabat, K. A., & Evan, W. M. (1989). The relationship between types of innovation and organizational performance. Journal of Management Studies, 26(6), 587–601. doi:10.1111/j.1467-6486.1989.tb00746.x

Damsgaard, J., & Lyytinen, K. (1998). Contours of Diffusion of Electronic Data Interchange in Finland: Overcoming Technological Barriers and Collaborating to Make it Happen. The Journal of Strategic Information Systems, 7, 275–297. doi:10.1016/S0963-8687(98)00032-8

Dandridge, T. C. (1979). Children are not little grown-ups: Small business needs its own Organizational Theory. *Journal of Small Business Management, 17*(April), 53–57.

Daniel, E. M., & Grimshaw, D. J. (2002). An exploratory comparison of electronic commerce adoption in large and small enterprises. *Journal of Information Technology, 17*(3), 133–147. doi:10.1080/0268396022000018409

Daniel, E., Wilson, H., & Myers, A. (2002). Adoption of e-commerce by SMEs in the UK. *International Small Business Journal, 20*(3), 253–270. doi:10.1177/0266242602203002

Daniel, F., Lohrke, F. T., Fornaciari, C. J., & Turner, R. A. (2004). Slack resources and firm performance: a meta-analysis. *Journal of Business Research, 57*, 565–574. doi:10.1016/S0148-2963(02)00439-3

Dans, E. (2001). IT investment in small and medium enterprises: paradoxically productive? *The Electronic Journal of Information Systems Evaluation, 4*(1).

Darwell, C., Sahlman, W. A., & Roberts, M. J. (1998). DigitalThink: Startup (Case # 9-898-186). Cambridge, MA: Harvard Business School Publishing.

Das, S. R., Zahra, S. A., & Warkentin, M. E. (1991). Integrating the content and process of strategic MIS planning with competitive strategy. *Decision Sciences, 22*(5), 953–984.

Davenport, T. (1998). Putting the Enterprise into the Enterprise System. *Harvard Business Review, 76*(4), 121–131.

Davenport, T. H. (1993). Process Innovation: Reengineering Work Through Information Technology. Boston: Harvard Business School Press.

Davenport, T. H., & Markus, M. L. (1999). Rigor Vs. Relevance Revisited: Response To Benbasat And Zmud. *MIS Quarterly, 23*(1), 19–23. doi:10.2307/249405

Davies, A. J., & Garcia-Sierra, A. J. (1999). Implementing electronic commerce in SMEs – three case studies. *BT Technology Journal, 17*(3), 97–111. doi:10.1023/A:1009684605872

Davis, D. (1996). Business Research for Decision Making (4th Ed.). Pacific Grove, CA: Duxbury Press.

Davis, F. D. (1989). Perceived usefulness, perceived ease of use, and user acceptance of information technology. *MIS Quarterly, 13*, 319–339. doi:10.2307/249008

Davis, R. (2001). Business process modelling with ARIS: A practical guide. London: Springer Verlag.

De Saulles, M. (2007). Information literacy amongst UK SMEs: An information policy gap. *Aslib Proceedings: New Information Perspectives, 59*(1), 68–79.

Dean, J., Holmes, S., & Smith, S. (1997). Understanding Business Networks: Evidence from Manufacturing and Service Sectors in Australia. *Journal of Small Business Management, 35*(1), 79–84.

Dean, T. J., Brown, R. L., & Bamford, C. E. (1998). Differences in large and small firm responses to environmental context: Strategic implications from a comparative analysis of business formations. *Strategic Management Journal, 19*(8), 709–728. doi:10.1002/(SICI)1097-0266-(199808)19:8<709::AID-SMJ966>3.0.CO;2-9

Debreceny, R., Putterill, M., Tung, L. L., & Gilbert, A. L. (2002). New tools for the determination of e-commerce inhibitors. *Decision Support Systems, 34*(2), 177–195. doi:10.1016/S0167-9236(02)00080-5

Dedrick, J., & Kraemer, K. L. (2001). China IT Report. *Electronic Journal of Information Systems in Developing Countries, 6*(2), 1–10.

DeFelice, A. (2006, January 1). A new Marketing Medium. CRM.com.

DeLone, W. H. (1988). Determinants of Success for Computer Usage in Small Business. *MIS Quarterly, 12*(1), 51–61. doi:10.2307/248803

DeLone, W. H., & McLean, E. R. (1992). Information Systems success: The quest for the dependent variable. *Information Systems Research, 3*(1), 60–95. doi:10.1287/isre.3.1.60

Dembla, P., Palvia, P., & Brooks, L. (2007). Organizational adoption of web-enabled services for information dissemination. Journal of Information Science and Technology, 3(3), 24–49.

Dennis, C. (2000). Networking for marketing advantage. Management Decision, 38(4), 287–292. doi:10.1108/00251740010371757

Denzin, N. K. (1989). The research act: A theoretical introduction to sociological methods. Englewood Cliffs, NJ: Prentice Hall.

DEPKOP. (2005a). Peran Koperasi dan Usaha Kecil Menengah Dalam Pembangunan Nasional. Kementrian Koperasi dan Usaha Kecil Menengah.

DEPKOP. (2005b). Statistik Usaha Kecil Menengah. 2005. Kementrian Koperasi dan Usaha Kecil Menengah.

Deshpande, A., & Jadad, A. (2006). Web 2.0: Could it help move the health system into the 21st century? Journal of Men's Health & Gender, 3(4), 332–336. doi:10.1016/j.jmhg.2006.09.004

Desouza, K., & Awazu, Y. (2006). Knowledge management at SMEs: five peculiarities. Journal of Knowledge Management, 10(1), 32–43. doi:10.1108/13673270610650085

Dess, G. G. (1987). Consensus on strategy formulation and organizational performance: Competitors in a fragmented industry. Strategic Management Journal, 8(3), 259–277. doi:10.1002/smj.4250080305

Dess, G. G., & Davis, P. S. (1984). Porter's (1980). generic strategies as determinants of strategic group membership and organizational performance. Academy of Management Journal, 27(3), 467–488. doi:10.2307/256040

Devaraj, S., Krajewski, L., & Wei, J. C. (2007). Impact of e-business technologies on operational performance: The role of production information integration in the supply chain. Journal of Operations Management, 25(6), 1199–1216. doi:10.1016/j.jom.2007.01.002

Devins, J., & Johanson, S. (2003). Training and Development Activities in SMEs: Some Findings from an Evaluation of the OSF Objective 4 Programme in Britain. International Small Business Journal, 22(2), 205–218.

Dholakia, R. R., & Kshetri, N. (2004). Factors impacting the adoption of the Internet among SMEs. Small Business Economics, 23(4), 311–322. doi:10.1023/B:SBEJ.0000032036.90353.1f

Dholakia, R., Johnson, J., Della Bitta, A., & Dholakia, N. (1993). Decision-making Time in Organizational Buying Behavior: An Investigation of Its Antecedents. Journal of the Academy of Marketing Science, 21(4), 281–292. doi:10.1007/BF02894521

Dickerson, M. D., & Gentry, J. W. (1983). Characteristics of adopters and non-adopters of home computers. The Journal of Consumer Research, 10, 225–235. doi:10.1086/208961

DiMaggio, P. J., & Powell, W. W. (1983). The iron cage revisited: Institutional isomorphism and collective rationality in organizational fields. American Sociological Review, 48, 147–160. doi:10.2307/2095101

Dixon, D. F., & Blois, K. J. (1983). Some Limitations of the 4 P's as a Paradigm for Marketing. In Back to Basics, Proceedings of the Marketing Education Group, Cranfield School of Management (pp. 92-107).

Donaldson, L. (2001). The contingency theory of organizations. Thousand Oaks, CA: Sage Publications.

Donnellon, A., Gray, B., & Bougon, M. G. (1986). Communication, meaning, and organized action. Administrative Science Quarterly, 31(1), 43–55. doi:10.2307/2392765

Dos Santos, B., & Peffers, K. (1998). Competitor and vendor influence on the adoption of innovative applications of electronic commerce. Information & Management, 34, 175–184. doi:10.1016/S0378-7206(98)00053-6

Dougherty, D., & Hardy, C. (1996). Sustained product innovation in large, mature organizations: Overcoming innovation-to-organization problems. Academy of Management Journal, 39(5), 1120–1153. doi:10.2307/256994

Doukidis, G. I., Lybereas, P., & Galliers, R. D. (1996). Information systems planning in small business: A stages of growth analysis. Journal of Systems and Software, 33, 189–201. doi:10.1016/0164-1212(95)00183-2

Drakopoulou-Dodd, S., Jack, S., & Anderson, A. R. (2002). Scottish Entrepreneurial Networks in the International Context. *International Small Business Journal*, 20(2), 213–219. doi:10.1177/0266242602202005

Drazin, R., & Schoonhoven, C. B. (1996). Community, population, and organization effects on innovation: A multilevel perspective. *Academy of Management Journal*, 39(5), 1065–1083. doi:10.2307/256992

Drejer, I., & Jørgensen, B. (2002). The generation and application of knowledge in public-private collaborations. *Knowledge Creation and the Learning Economy*.

Du, H., & Wagner, C. (2006). Weblog success: Exploring the role of Technology. *International Journal of Human-Computer Studies*, 64, 789–798. doi:10.1016/j.ijhcs.2006.04.002

Duhan, S., Levy, M., & Powell, P. (2005). IS strategy in SMEs using organizational capabilities: The CPX framework. In *Thirteenth European Conference on Information Systems*, 26th to 28th May, Regensburg, Germany.

Duncombe, R., & Heeks, R. (2003). An information systems perspective on ethical trade and self-regulation. *Information Technology for Development*, 10(2), 123–139. doi:10.1002/itdj.1590100206

Dutton, J., & Dukerich, J. (1991). Keeping an eye on the mirror: Image and identity in organizational adaptation. *Academy of Management Review*, 34, 517–554. doi:10.2307/256405

Dytche, J., & Warren, A. (2007a). I99 Corridor Innovation Portal – Summary. Farrell Center for Corporate Innovation and Entrepreneurship, Smeal College of Business, The Pennsylvania State University.

Dytche, J., & Warren, A. (2007b). Penn State KIZ Innovation Grant Team I-99 Innovation Network Portal. Farrell Center for Corporate Innovation and Entrepreneurship, Smeal College of Business, The Pennsylvania State University.

Earl, M. J. (1993). Experiences in strategic information systems planning. *MIS Quarterly*, 17(1), 1–24. doi:10.2307/249507

Easton, A. (1966). Corporate style versus corporate image. *JMR, Journal of Marketing Research*, 3, 68–174. doi:10.2307/3150206

E-Commerce Times. (2008). B2B in a Web 2.0 World, Part 2: Social Media Marketing. Retrieved from http://www.ecommercetimes.com/story/B2B-in-a-Web-20-World-Part-2-Social-Media-Marketing-62988.html

Edelman, L. F., Brush, C. G., & Manolova, T. S. (2002). The impact of human and organizational resources on small organizations strategy. *Journal of Small Business and Enterprise Development*, 9(3), 236–244. doi:10.1108/14626000210438562

Edelman, L. F., Brush, C., & Manolova, T. (2005). Co-alignment in the resource--performance relationship: Strategy as mediator. *Journal of Business Venturing*, 20(3).

Eikebrokk, T. R., & Olsen, D. H. (2007). An empirical investigation of competency factors affecting e-business success in European SMEs. *Information & Management*, 44(4). doi:10.1016/j.im.2007.02.004

Eikelmann, S., Hajj, J., & Peterson, M. (2008). Opinion piece: Web 2.0: Profiting from the threat. *Journal of Direct. Data and Digital Marketing Practice*, 9, 293–295. doi:10.1057/palgrave.dddmp.4350094

EIRO. (2006). Industrial relations in SMEs. Retrieved March 2006, from http://www.eiro.eurofound.eu.int/1999/05/study/tn9905201s.html

Eisenhardt, K. M. (1989). Building theories from case study research. *Academy of Management Review*, 14(4), 532–550. doi:10.2307/258557

Ekanem, I. (2005). 'Bootstrapping': The investment decision-making process in small firms. *The British Accounting Review*, 37(3), 299–318. doi:10.1016/j.bar.2005.04.004

Eleftheriadou, D. (2008). Small- and Medium-Sized Enterprises Hold the Key to European Competitiveness: How to Help Them Innovate through ICT and E-business. *The Global Information Technology Report 2007-2008*. World Economic Forum.

Elliot, R., & Boshoff, C. (2007). The influence of the owner-manager of small tourism businesses on the success of internet marketing. South African Journal of Business Management, 38(3), 15–27.

Elsbach, K. D. (1994). Managing organizational legitimacy in the California cattle industry: The construction and effectiveness of verbal accounts. Administrative Science Quarterly, 39, 57–88. doi:10.2307/2393494

Elsbach, K. D., & Sutton, R. I. (1992). Acquiring organizational legitimacy through illegitimate actions: A marriage of institutional and impression management theories. Academy of Management Journal, 35(4), 699–738. doi:10.2307/256313

Elsbach, K. D., Sutton, R. I., & Principe, K. E. (1998). Averting expected challenges through anticipatory impression management: A Study of hospital billing. Organization Science, 9(1), 68–86. doi:10.1287/orsc.9.1.68

Esteves, J. (2009). A benefits realization road-map framework for ERP usage in small and medium-sized enterprises. Journal of Enterprise Information Management, 22(1/2), 25–35. doi:10.1108/17410390910922804

European Commission, & DG Enterprise and Industry. (2008). A comprehensive policy to support SMEs. Retrived April 18, 2009, from http://ec.europa.eu/enterprise/entrepreneurship/sme_policy.htm

European Commission. (2002). Benchmarking National and Regional E-business Policies for SMEs. Final report of the E-business Policy Group of the European Union, Brussels.

European Commission. (2002a). eEurope Go Digital - Benchmarking national and regional e-business policies for SMEs.

European Commission. (2002b). Synthesis Report - Benchmarking National and Regional e-Business Policies.

European Commission. (2004). SME definitions. Retrieved Marsh 23, 2004, from http://europa.eu.int/comm/enterprise/enterprise_policy/sme_definition/index_en.htm

European Commission. (2008). The European e-Business Report 2008. The impact of ICT and e-business on firms, sectors and the economy. 6th Synthesis Report of the Sectoral e-Business Watch.

European Commission. (n.d.). Definition of SME. Retrieved March 31, 2009 from http://ec.europa.eu/enterprise/enterprise_policy/SME_definition/index_en.htm

EuropeanCommision. (2005). SME definition. Retrieved on March 25, 2008, from http://ec.europa.eu/enterprise/enterprise_policy/sme_definition/index_en.htm

Faberman, R. (2002). Job flows and labor dynamics in the US Rust Belt. Monthly Labor Review, 125(9), 3–10.

Feeny, D. F., & Ives, B. (1990). In Search of Sustainability: Reaping Long-Term Advantage from Investments in Information Technology. Journal of Management Information Systems, 7(1), 27-46.

Feeny, D. F., & Willcocks, L. P. (1998). Core IS capabilities for exploiting information technology. Sloan Management Review, 39(3), 9–21.

Feitzinger, E., & Lee, H. L. (1997). Mass Customization at Hewlett-Packard, The Power of Postponement. Harvard Business Review, (January –February): 116–121.

Feldman, M. S. (1989). Order without design: Information production and policy making. Stanford, CA: Stanford University Press.

Feldman, M. S., & March, J. G. (1981). Information in organizations as signal and symbol. Administrative Science Quarterly, 26(2), 171–186. doi:10.2307/2392467

Feldman, M., Feller, I., Bercovitz, J., & Burton, R. (2002). Equity and the technology transfer strategies of American research universities. Management Science, 48(1), 105–121. doi:10.1287/mnsc.48.1.105.14276

Fernandez, Z., & Nieto, A. J. (2006). The internet: competitive strategy and boundaries of the firm. International Journal of Technology Management, 35(1-4), 182–195. doi:10.1504/IJTM.2006.009234

Fichman, R. (2000). The diffusion and assimilation of information technology innovations. In R. Zmud (Ed.),

Framing the Domains of IT Management: Projecting the Future Through the Past (pp. 105-104). Cincinnati, OH: R. Pinnaflex Educational Resources.

Fillis, I., & Wagner, B. (2005). E-business Development: An Exploratory Investigation of the Small Firm. *International Small Business Journal*, 23(6), 604–634. doi:10.1177/0266242605057655

Fillis, I., Johannson, U., & Wagner, B. (2003). A conceptualisation of the opportunities and barriers to e-business developemnt in the smaller firm. *Journal of Small Business and Enterprise Development*, 10(3), 336–341. doi:10.1108/14626000310489808

Fillis, I., Johansson, U., & Wagner, B. (2004). A qualitative investigation of smaller firm e-business development. *Journal of Small Business and Enterprise Development*, 11(3), 349–361. doi:10.1108/14626000410551609

Fink, D. (1998). Adoption of information technology in small and medium enterprises. *International Journal of Information Management*, 18(4), 243–253. doi:10.1016/S0268-4012(98)00013-9

Fiol, C. M. (1996). Squeezing harder doesn't always work: Continuing the search for consistency in innovation research. *Academy of Management Review*, 21(4), 1012–1021.

Fishbein, M., & Ajzen, I. (1975). Belief, attitude, intention, and behavior: An introduction to theory and research. Reading, MA: Addison-Wesley.

Fisher, D. M., Fisher, S. A., & Kiang, M. Y. (2004). Evaluating mid-level ERP software. *Journal of Computer Information Systems*, 45(1), 38–46.

Fiske, S. T., & Taylor, S. E. (1991). Social cognition (2nd ed.). New York: McGraw Hill.

Flynn, D. J., & Arce, E. A. (1995). Theoretical and practical issues in the use of strategic information systems planning (SISP) approaches to integrating business and IT in organisations. *International Journal of Computer Applications in Technology*, 8(1/2), 61–68.

Foong, S.-Y. (1999). Effect of end user personal and systems attributes on computer based information systems

success in Malaysian SMEs. *Journal of Small Business Management*, 37(3), 81–87.

Fornell, C. (1982). A Second generation of multivariate analysis. New York: Praeger.

Fornell, C., & Larcker, D. F. (1981). Evaluating Structural Equation Models with Unobservable Variables and Measurement Error. *JMR, Journal of Marketing Research*, 28, 39–50. doi:10.2307/3151312

Forrester Research. (2002). E-Commerce Next Wave: Productivity and Innovation. Presented by J. Meringer in a seminar on Revenue Implications of E-commerce: Trends in E-commerce, WTO Committee on Trade and Development, April.

Forrester Research. (2005, September 14). US eCommerce Forecast: Online Retail Sales To Reach $329 Billion By 2010. Forrester Research Inc. Retrieved September 2005, from http://www.forrester.com/Research/Document/Excerpt/0,7211,37626,00.html

Forth, J., Bewley, H., & Bryson, A. (2006). Small and medium-sized enterprises: findings from the 2004 Workplace Employee Relations Survey. University of Westminster.

Frame, W. S., Srinivasan, A., & Woosley, L. (2001). The effect of credit scoring on small-business lending. *Journal of Money. Credit & Banking*, 33(3), 813–825. doi:10.2307/2673896

Franke, N., & Piller, F. (2004). Value creation by toolkits for user innovation and design: the case of the watch market. *Journal of Product Innovation Management*, 21, 401–415. doi:10.1111/j.0737-6782.2004.00094.x

Franquesa, J., & Brandyberry. Organizational slack and information technology innovation adoption in SMEs. *International journal of e-business research*, 5(1), 25-48.

Freeman, J., Caroll, G. R., & Hannan, M. T. (1983). The liability of newness: Age dependence in organizational death rates. *American Sociological Review*, 48, 692–710. doi:10.2307/2094928

Frenkel, M. (2008). The multinational corporation as a third space: Rethinking international management discourse on knowledge transfer through Homi Bhaba. Academy of Management Review, 33(4), 924–942.

Frielink, A. B. (1961). Auditing Automatic Data Processing. Amsterdam, Netherlands: Elsevier.

Frost, F. A. (2003). The Use of Strategic Tools by Small and Medium-sized Enterprises: An Australian Study. Strategic Change, 12, 49–62. doi:10.1002/jsc.607

Fuller-Love, N., & Street, K. (2006). Management development in small firms. International Journal of Management Reviews, 8(3), 175–190. doi:10.1111/j.1468-2370.2006.00125.x

Gable, G., & Stewart, G. (1999). SAP R/3 implementation issues for small to medium enterprises. Americas Conference on Information Systems. Milwaukee, WI: Association for Information Systems, 779-781.

Gaglio, C. M., Cecchini, M., & Winter, S. (1998). Gaining legitimacy: The symbolic use of technology by new ventures. In Frontiers of Entrepreneurship Research (pp. 208-215). Wellesley, MA: Babson College.

Galliers, R. D. (1992). Choosing Information Systems Research Approaches. In R. D. Galliers (Ed.), Information Systems Research: Issues, Methods and Practical Guidelines (pp. 144-162). Henley-on-Thames, UK: Alfred Waller.

Garelli, S. (2001 June). The World Competitiveness Yearbook 2001. International Institute for Management Development.

Garg, A., Goyal, D., & Lather, A. (2008). Information systems success factors in software SMEs: a research agenda. International Journal of Business Information Systems, 3(4), 410–430. doi:10.1504/IJBIS.2008.018041

Gaskill, L. R., & Gibbs, R. M. (1994). Going away to college and wider urban job opportunities take highly educated away from rural areas. Rural Development Perspectives, 10(3), 35–44.

Gaskill, L. R., Van Auken, H. E., & Kim, H. (1993). The Impact of Operational Planning on Small Business Retail Performance. Journal of Small Business Strategy, 5(1), 21–35.

Gatignon, H., & Robertson, T. (1989). Technology Diffusion: An Empirical Test of Competitive Effects. Journal of Marketing, 53(1), 35–49. doi:10.2307/1251523

Gefen, D., & Heart, T. (2006). On the Need to Include National Culture as a Central Issue in E-commerce Trust Belief. Journal of Global Information Management, 14(4), 1–30.

Gefen, D., Rose, G., Warkentin, M., & Pavlou, P. (2005). Cultural Diversity and Trust in IT Adoption: A Comparison of Potential E-voter in the USA and South Africa. Journal of Global Information Systems, 13(1), 54–78.

Geiger, S. W., & Cashen, L. H. (2002). A multidimensional examination of slack and its impact on innovation. Journal of Managerial Issues, 14(1), 68–85.

George, G. (2005). Slack resources and the performance of privately held firms. Academy of Management Journal, 48(4), 661–676.

Germain, R., Droge, C., & Daugherty, P. (1994). A Cost and Impact Typology of Logistics Technology and the Effect of its Adoption on Organisational Practice. Journal of Business Logistics, 15(2), 227–248.

Gibbs, J., Kraemer, L., & Dedrick, J. (2003). Environment and Policy Factors Shaping Global E-commerce Diffusion: A Cross-Country Comparison, The Information Society. Special Issue: Globalization of Electronic Commerce, 19(1), 5–18.

Gillin, P. (2007). The New Influencers, a marketer's guide to the New Social media. Fresno, CA: Quill Driver Books.

Gillin, P. (2009). Secrets of the Social Media Marketing. Fresno, CA: Quill Driver Books.

Gioia, D. A. (1986). Symbols, scripts, and sensemaking: creating meaning in the organizational experience. In H.P. Sims, Jr., & D.A. Gioia (Eds.), The thinking organization: Dynamics of organization cognition (pp. 49-74). San Francisco: Jossey Bass.

Gioia, D. A., Shultz, M., & Corley, K. G. (2000). Organizational identity, image, and adaptive instability. Academy of Management Review, 25(1), 63–81. doi:10.2307/259263

Glaser, B. G., & Strauss, A. L. (1967). The discovery of grounded theory. Chicago, IL: Aldine.

Golden, P. A., & Dollinger, M. (1993). Cooperative Alliances and Competitive Strategies in Small Manufacturing Firms. Entrepreneurship Theory and Practice, 43-56.

Grandon, E., & Michael, J. (2004). Electronic commerce adoption an empirical study of small and medium US business. Information & Management, 42, 197–216.

Grandon, E., & Pearson, J. M. (2003). Strategic Value and Adoption of Electronic Commerce: An Empirical Study of Chilean Small and Medium Businesses. Journal of Global Information Technology Management, 6(3), 22–43.

Grandon, E., & Pearson, J. M. (2004). Electronic commerce adoption: an empirical study of small and medium US business. Information & Management, 42, 197–216.

Grant, R. M. (1996). Toward a knowledge-based theory of the firm. Strategic Management Journal, 17, 109–122. doi:10.1002/(SICI)1097-0266(199602)17:2<109::AID-SMJ796>3.0.CO;2-P

Gray, C. (2004). Management development in small and medium enterprises. Advances in Developing Human Resources, 6(4), 451–469. doi:10.1177/1523422304268381

Gregor, S., Martin, M., Fernandez, W., Stern, S., & Vitale, M. (2006). The transformational dimension in the realization of business value from information technology. The Journal of Strategic Information Systems, 15, 249–270. doi:10.1016/j.jsis.2006.04.001

Greve, H. R. (2003). A behavioral theory of R&D expenditures and innovations: Evidence from shipbuilding. Academy of Management Journal, 46(6), 685–702.

Gribbins, M. L., & King, R. C. (2004). Electronic retailing strategies: A case study of small businesses in the gifts and collectibles industry. Electronic Markets, 14(2), 138–152. doi:10.1080/10196780410001675086

Griffy-Browne, C., & Chun, M. (2007). Aligning businesses and IS resources in Japanese SMEs: A resource based view. Journal of Global Information Technology Management, 10(3), 28–51.

Grosh, B., & Somolekae, G. (1996). Mighty oaks from little acorns: Can micro-enterprise serve as the seedbed of industrialization? World Development, 24(12), 1879–1890. doi:10.1016/S0305-750X(96)00082-4

Grove, S. J., & Fisk, R. P. (1989). Impression management in services marketing: A dramaturgical perspective. In R.A. Giacalone and P. Rosenfeld (Eds.), Impression management in the organization (pp. 427-438). Hillsdale, NJ: Lawrence Erlbaum.

Guimaraes, T. (2000). The impact of competitive intelligence and IS support in changing small business organisations. Logistics Information Management, 13, 117–125. doi:10.1108/09576050010326510

Gujarati, D. N. (1995). Basic Econometrics (3rd ed.). New York: McGraw-Hill.

Hadjimanolis, A. (1999). Barriers to Innovation for SMEs in a Small Less Developed Country (Cyprus). Technovation, 19(9), 561–570. doi:10.1016/S0166-4972-(99)00034-6

Hadjimanolis, A. (2006). A case study of SME-university research collaboration in the context of a small peripheral country (Cyprus). International Journal of Innovation Management, 10(1), 65. doi:10.1142/S1363919606001405

Hagmann, C., & McCahon, C. S. (1993). Strategic information systems and competitiveness. Information & Management, 25, 183–192. doi:10.1016/0378-7206-(93)90067-4

Hair, J. F., Anderson, R. E., Tatham, R. L., & Black, W. C. (1992). Multivariate Data Analysis. New York: Macmillan Publishing Company.

Hair, J. F., Anderson, R. E., Tatham, R. L., & Black, W. C. (1998). Multivariate Data Analysis with Readings (5th Ed.). Englewood Cliffs, NJ: Prentice-Hall.

Hall, C. (2002). Profile of SMEs and SME issues 1990-2000. Asia-Pacific Economic Cooperation, Singapore.

Hall, R. (1993). A framework linking intangible resources and capabilities to sustainable competitive advantage. Strategic Management Journal, 14(8), 607–618. doi:10.1002/smj.4250140804

Hammer, M. (1990). Reengineering work: Don't Automate, Obliterate. Harvard Business Review, 68(4).

Han, S. W. (2004). ERP - Enterprise resource planning: A cost-based business case and implementation assessment. Human Factors and Ergonomics in Manufacturing, 14(3), 239–256. doi:10.1002/hfm.10066

Hanks, S. H., Watson, C. J., Jansen, E., & Chandler, G. N. (1993). Tightening the Life-Cycle Construct: A Taxonomic Study of Growth Stage Configurations in High-Technology Organizations. Entrepreneurship: Theory & Practice, 18(2), 5–30.

Hannan, M. T., & Carroll, G. R. (1992). Dynamics of organizational populations: Density, legitimation, and competition. New York: Oxford University Press.

Hannan, M. T., & Freeman, J. (1984). Structural inertia and organizational change. American Sociological Review, 49(2), 149–164. doi:10.2307/2095567

Hansen, J. A. (1992). Innovation, firm size, and firm age. Small Business Economics, 4(1), 37–44.

Harindranath, G., Dyerson, R., & Barnes, D. (2008). ICT Adoption and Use in UK SMEs: a Failure of Initiatives? The Electronic Journal of Information Systems Evaluation, 11(2), 91–96.

Harrison, D. A., Mykytyn, P. P. Jr, & Riemenschneider, C. K. (1997). Executive Decisions About Adoption of Information Technology in Small Business: Theory and Empirical Tests. Information Systems Research, 8(2), 171–195. doi:10.1287/isre.8.2.171

Harrison, R. T., Dibben, M. R., & Mason, C. M. (1997). The role of trust in the informal investor's investment decision: An exploratory analysis. Entrepreneurship Theory and Practice, 21(4), 63–81.

Hashmi, M. S., & Cuddy, J. (1990). Strategic initiatives for introducing CIM technologies in Irish SMEs. In L. Faria & W. van Puymbroeck (Eds.), Computer Integrated Manufacturing – Proceedings of the Sixth CIM-Europe Annual Conference. Lisbon: Springer Verlag.

Hatch, M. J., & Schultz, M. (1997). Relations between organizational culture, identity, and image. European Journal of Marketing, 5(6), 356–365.

Haugh, H., & McKee, L. (2004). The Cultural Paradigm of the Smaller Firm. Journal of Small Business Management, 42(4), 377–394. doi:10.1111/j.1540-627X.2004.00118.x

Hawawini, G., Subramanian, V., & Verdin, P. (2003). Is performance driven by industry- or firm-specific factors? New look at the old evidence. Strategic Management Journal, 24(1), 1–16. doi:10.1002/smj.278

Hazan, M. (2002). Virtual South: E-Commerce for unprivileged artisans. Retrieved Dec 12, 2007, from http://www.iicd.org/stories/

Heijden, H. d. (2000). Measuring IT core capabilities for electronic commerce: results from a confirmatory analysis. Paper presented at the 21st International Conference on Information Systems, Brisbane, Australia.

Henderson, A. D. (1999). Firm strategy and age dependence: A contingent view of the liabilities of newness, adolescence, and obsolescence. Administrative Science Quarterly, 44(2), 281–314. doi:10.2307/2666997

Henderson, J. C., & Venkatraman, N. (1993). Strategic alignment: Leveraging information technology for transforming organizations. IBM Systems Journal, 32(1), 4–16.

Henderson, J., & Smith, J. (2002). Academia, Industry, and the Bayh-Dole Act: An Implied Duty to Commercialize. Center for the Integration of Medicine and Innovative Technology (CIMIT), Cambridge, MA. Retrieved from http://www.cimit.org/coi_part3. pdf

Hendry, C., Brown, J., & Defillippi, R. (2000). Understanding Relationships between Universities and SMEs in Emerging High Technology Industries: The Case of Opto-Electronics. International Journal of Innovation Management, 4(1), 51.

Hermana, B., Sugiharto, T., & Margianti, E.S. (2006). Determinants of Internet Adoption by Indonesian Small Business Owners: Reliability and validity of Research Instrument. E-LIS, 1- 14

Herold, D. M., Jayaraman, N., & Narayanaswamy, C. R. (2006). What is the relationship between organizational slack and innovation? Journal of Managerial Issues, 18(3), 372–392.

Heugens, P. P. M. A. R., & Lander, M. W. (2009). Structure! Agency! (and other quarrels), A meta-analysis of institutional theories of organization. Academy of Management Journal, 52(1), 61–85.

Highsmith, J. (2002). Agile software development ecosystems. Boston: Pearson Education, Inc.

Hill, R., & Stewart, J. (1999). Human resource development in small organizations. Human Resource Development International, 2(2), 103–123. doi:10.1080/13678869900000013

Hill, R., & Stewart, J. (2000). Human Resource Development in Small Organisations. Journal of European Industrial Training, 24(2/3/4), 105 - 117.

Hillman, A. J., Shropshire, C., & Cannella, A. A. (2007). Organizational predictors of women on corporate boards. Academy of Management Journal, 50(4), 941–952.

Hirschheim, R., & Newman, R. (1991). Symbolism and information systems development: Myth, metaphor and magic. Information Systems Research, 2, 29–62. doi:10.1287/isre.2.1.29

Hirschheim, R., & Sabherwal, R. (2001). Detours in the Path toward strategic information systems alignment. California Management Review, 44(1), 87–108.

Hitt, L. M., Wu, D. J., & Zhou, X. (2002). Investment in enterprise resource planning: business impact and productivity measures. Journal of Management Information Systems, 19(1), 71–98. doi:10.1201/1078/43199.19.1.20020101/31479.10

Hitwise, U. S. (n.d.). Research note: Measuring Web 2.0 consumer participation.

Hofer, C. W., & Schendel, D. (1978). Strategy formulation: Analytical concepts. Minneapolis, MN: West Publishing CO.

Holmes, S., & Gibson, B. (2001). Definition of small business: final report. The University of Newcastle, NSW, Australia.

Holmes, T. P., Vlosky, R. P., & Carlson, J. (2004). An exploratory comparison of Internet use by small wood products manufacturers in the North Adirondack Region of New York and the State of Louisiana. Forest Products Journal, 54(12), 277–282.

Holtz-Eakin, D., Joulfaian, D., & Rosen, H. S. (1994a). Entrepreneurial decisions and liquidity constraints. The Rand Journal of Economics, 25(2), 334–347. doi:10.2307/2555834

Holtz-Eakin, D., Joulfaian, D., & Rosen, H. S. (1994b). Sticking it out: Entrepreneurial survival and liquidity constraints. The Journal of Political Economy, 102(1), 53–75. doi:10.1086/261921

Honig, B. (1998). What determines success? Examining the human, financial, and social capital of Jamaican microentrepreneurs. Journal of Business Venturing, 13(5), 371–394. doi:10.1016/S0883-9026(97)00036-0

Horton, R. B. (1991). The Corporation of the 1990s: Information Technology and Organizational Transformation. Sloan Management Review, 32(4), 85–86.

Hua, G. B. (2007). Applying the strategic alignment model to business and ICT strategies of Singapore's small and medium-sized architecture, engineering and construction enterprises. Construction Management and Economics, 25(2), 157–169. doi:10.1080/01446190600827041

Huang, T. (2001). The relation of training practices and organizational performance on small and medium size enterprises. Education + Training, 43(8/9), 437-444.

Huang, X., Soutar, G. N., & Brown, A. (2002). New product development processes in small and medium-sized enterprises: Some Australian evidence. Journal of Small Business Management, 40(1), 27–42. doi:10.1111/1540-627X.00036

Human, S. E., & Provan, K. G. (2000). Legitimacy building in the evolution of small firm multilateral networks: A comparative study of success and demise. Administrative

Science Quarterly, 45, 327–365. doi:10.2307/2667074

Hussin, H., King, M., & Cragg, P. (2002). IT alignment in small firms. *European Journal of Information Systems*, 11(2), 108–127. doi:10.1057/palgrave/ejis/3000422

Hussin, H., King, M., & Cragg, P. (2002). IT alignment in small firms. *European Journal of Information Systems*, 11, 108–127. doi:10.1057/palgrave/ejis/3000422

Hyman, E. L., & Dearden, K. (1998). (n.d.). Comprehensive impact assessment systems for NGO microenterprise development programs. *World Development*, 26(2), 261–276. doi:10.1016/S0305-750X(97)10022-5

Iacovou, A. L., Benbasat, I., & Dexter, A. (1995). Electronic data interchange and small organizations: adoption and impact of technology. *MIS Quarterly*, 19(4), 465–485. doi:10.2307/249629

IBM. (1984). Business systems planning – information systems planning guide (4th Ed.). IBM Publication #GE20-0527-4.

IDC. (2004, August 6). IDC Predicts Double Digit Growth of Asia/Pacific Internet Buyers from 2003 to 2008. IDC Australia. Retrieved September 2005, from http://www.idc.com.au/newsletters/idcpulse/detail.asp?intID=43

IEI. (2003). Facts & Figures: The Internet and Business. The Internet Economy Indicators. Retrieved June 4, 2003, from http://www.internetindicators.com/facts.html

Igbaria, M., Zinatelli, N., Cragg, P. B., & Cavaye, A. L. M. (1997). Personal Computing Acceptance Factors in Small Firms: A Structural Equation Model. *MIS Quarterly*, 21(3), 279–305. doi:10.2307/249498

Igbaria, M., Zinatelli, N., Cragg, P., & Cavaye, A. (1997). Personal computing acceptance factors in small firms: a structural equation model. *MIS Quarterly*, 21(3), 279–302. doi:10.2307/249498

Ihlström, C., & Nilsson, M. (2003). E-business adoption by SMEs - Prerequisites and attitudes of SMEs in a Swedish network. *Journal of Organizational Computing and Electronic Commerce*, 13(3-4), 211–223. doi:10.1207/S15327744JOCE133&4_04

INC. Magazine. (1995 August). Started with $1,000 or less. 27-38.

Ind, N. (1992). The corporate image. London: Kogan Page.

Ismail, N. A., & King, M. (2007). Factors influencing the alignment of accounting information systems in small and medium sized Malaysian manufacturing firms. *Journal of Information Systems and Small Business*, 1(1-2), 1–20.

Ives, B., & Learmonth, G. P. (1984). The Information Systems as a Competitive weapon. *Communications of the ACM*, 27(12), 1193–1201. doi:10.1145/2135.2137

Ivis, M. (2001). Analysis of barriers impeding e-business adoption among Canadian SMEs: Canadian E-Business Opportunities Roundtable.

Izushi, H. (2003). Impact of the length of relationships upon the use of research institutes by SMEs. *Research Policy*, 32(5), 771–788. doi:10.1016/S0048-7333-(02)00085-9

Jackson, M. H., Poole, M. S., & Kuhn, T. (2002). The social construction of technology in studies of the workplace. In L. Lievrouw & S. Livingstone (Eds.), Handbook of new media: Social shaping and consequences of ICTs (pp. 236-253).

Jacob, C. (2000). Advanced Data Analysis. Lecture Series, Curtin University of Technology, Western Australia.

Jafari, S. M., Osman, M. R., Yusuff, R. M., & Tang, S. H. (2006). ERP Systems Implementation in Malaysia: The Importance of Critical Success Factors. *International Journal of Engineering and Technology*, 3(1), 125–131.

Jaffe, A., Trajtenberg, M., & Henderson, R. (1993). Geographic localization of knowledge spillovers as evidenced by patent citations. *The Quarterly Journal of Economics*, 577–598. doi:10.2307/2118401

Jarratt, D. G. (1998). A Strategic Classification of Business Alliances: A Qualitative Perspective Built from a Study of Small and Medium-sized Enterprises. *Qualitative Market Research: An International Journal*, 1(1), 39–49. doi:10.1108/13522759810368442

Jarvis, C. B., Mackenzie, S. B., & Podsakoff, P. M. (2003). A critical review of construct indicators and measurement model misspecification in marketing and consumer research. *The Journal of Consumer Research, 30*(september), 199–218. doi:10.1086/376806

Jennex, M. E., Amoroso, D., & Adelakun, O. (2004). E-Commerce Infrastructure Success Factors for Small Companies in Developing Economies. *Electronic Commerce Research, 4*(3), 263–286. doi:10.1023/B:ELEC.0000027983.36409.d4

Jensen, M. C. (1986). Agency costs of free cash flow, corporate finance, and takeovers. *The American Economic Review, 76*, 323–329.

Jensen, M. C., & Meckling, W. H. (1976). Theory of the firm: Managerial behavior, agency costs, and ownership structure. *Journal of Financial Economics, 3*, 305–360. doi:10.1016/0304-405X(76)90026-X

Jeyaraj, A., Rottman, J., & Lacity, M. J. (2006). A review of the predictors, linkages, and biases in IT innovation adoption research. *Journal of Information Technology, 21*(1), 1–23. doi:10.1057/palgrave.jit.2000056

Jocumsen, G. (2004). How do small Business Managers make strategic marketing decisions? *European Journal of Marketing, 38*(5/6): 659–674. doi:10.1108/03090560410529277

Johansson, N., & Mollstedt, U. (2006). Revisiting Amit and Zott's model of value creation sources: The SymBelt Customer Center case. *Journal of Theoretical and Applied Electronic Commerce Research, 1*(3), 16–27.

Johnson, S. (2002). Lifelong learning and SMEs: Issues and research for policy. *Journal of Small Business and Enterprise Development, 9*(3), 285–295. doi:10.1108/14626000210438607

Johnson, S. (2007, January 1). It's all about us. *Time*, 55.

Johnston, D. A., Wade, M., & McClean, R. (2007). Does e-business matter to SMEs? A comparison of the financial impacts of Internet business solutions on European and North American SMEs. *Journal of Small Business Management, 45*(3), 354–361. doi:10.1111/j.1540-627-X.2007.00217.x

Johnston, H. R., & Carrico, S. R. (1988). Developing capabilities to use information strategically. *MIS Quarterly, 12*(1), 37–48. doi:10.2307/248801

Johnston, K., Shi, J., Dann, Z., & Barcay, I. (2006). Knowledge, power and trust in SME e-based virtual organisations. *International Journal of Networking & Virtual Organizations, 3*(1), 42–59. doi:10.1504/IJNVO.2006.008784

Johnston, W. A., & Dark, V. J. (1986). Selective attention. *Annual Review of Psychology, 37*, 43–75. doi:10.1146/annurev.ps.37.020186.000355

Jones, C. (2004). An alternative view of small firm adoption. *Journal of Small Business and Enterprise Development, 11*(3), 362–370. doi:10.1108/14626000410551618

Jöreskog, K. G., & Wold, H. (1982). *Systems under indirect observation: Causality, structure, prediction:* North-Holland.

Joslin, E. O. (1968). *Computer Selection*. London: Addison-Wesley.

Kaewkitipong, L., & Brown, D. (2008). Adoption and Evaluation of E-business in Thai SMEs: A Process Perspective. *AMCIS 2008 Proceedings*, 1-13.

Kahn, M. (1999). The silver lining of Rust Belt manufacturing decline. *Journal of Urban Economics, 46*(3), 360–376. doi:10.1006/juec.1998.2127

Kalakota, R., & Whinston, A. B. (1997). *Electronic commerce: A manager's guide*. Reading, MA: Addison-Wesley.

Kane, G. C., & Alavi, M. (2007). Information technology and organizational learning: An investigation of exploration and exploitation processes. *Organization Science, 18*(5), 796–812. doi:10.1287/orsc.1070.0286

Kapurubandara, M., & Lawson, R. (2006). Barriers to Adopting ICT and e-commerce with SMEs in Developing Countries: An Exploratory study in Sri Lanka. *CollECTeR, 2006*, 1–13.

Karger, D., & Quan, D. (2004). What Would It Mean to Blog on the Semantic Web? Berlin Heidelberg: Springer.

Karin, I., & Eiferman, R. (2006). Technology-Based Marketing (TBM), A new competitive approach for High-Tech Industries. International Journal of Global Business and Competitiveness, 2(1), 19–25.

Kartiwi, M. (2006). Case Studies of E-commerce Adoption in Indonesian SMEs: The Evaluation of Strategic Use. Australasian Journal of Information Systems, 14(1), 69–80. doi:10.3127/ajis.v14i1.8

Kartiwi, M. (2008). Electronic Commerce Adoption in Urban and Rural Indonesian SMEs. PhD Dissertation, University of Wollongong, Australia.

Kartiwi, M., & MacGregor, R. C. (2007). Electronic Commerce Adoption Barriers in Small to Medium-sized Enterprises (SMEs) in Developed and Developing Countries: A Cross-country Comparisons. Journal of E-commerce in Organizations, 5(3), 35–51.

Katila, R., & Shane, S. (2005). When does lack of resources make new firms innovative? Academy of Management Journal, 48(5), 814–829.

Kaynak, E., Tatoglu, E., & Kula, V. (2005). An analysis of the factors affecting the adoption of electronic commerce by SMEs: Evidence from an emerging market. International Marketing Review, 22(6), 623–640. doi:10.1108/02651330510630258

Kearns, G. S., & Lederer, A. L. (2000). The effect of strategic alignment on the use of IS-based resources for competitive advantage. The Journal of Strategic Information Systems, 9(4), 265–293. doi:10.1016/S0963-8687(00)00049-4

Keegan, V. (2007, July 5). Amateurs can be good and bad news. The Guardian.

Keen, A. (2007). The Cult of the Amateur: How today's Internet is killing our culture. New York: Doubleday / Random House.

Keen, P. (1993). Information technology and the management difference: A fusion map. IBM Systems Journal, 32(1), 17–39.

Keen, P. G. W. (1991). Redesigning the organization through Information Technology. Planning Review, 19(3).

Keil, M., & Tiwana, A. (2006). Relative importance of evaluation criteria for enterprise systems: a conjoint study. Information Systems Journal, 16(3), 237–262. doi:10.1111/j.1365-2575.2006.00218.x

Keller Johnson, L. (2002). New views on digital CRM. MIT Sloan Management Review, 44(1), 10–27.

Kendall, J. E. (2008). Metaphors for e-collaboration: A study of nonprofit theatre Web presence. In N. Kock (Ed.), E-collaboration in modern organizations: Initiating and managing distributed projects (pp. 14-30). Hershey, PA: Information Science Reference.

Kendall, J. E., & Kendall, K. E. (1999). Web pull and push technologies: The emergence and future of information delivery systems. In K. E. Kendall, (Ed.), Emerging information technologies: Improving decisions, cooperation, and infrastructure (pp.265-288). Thousand Oaks, CA: SAGE Publications, Inc.

Kendall, J. E., & Kendall, K. E. (2001). A Paradoxically Peaceful Coexistence Between Commerce and Ecommerce. Journal of Information Technology. Theory and Application, 3(4), 1–6.

Kendall, J. E., & Kendall, K. E. (2009). SMEs, IT, and the third space: Colonization and creativity in the theatre industry. In B. Stahl, G. Dhillon, & R. Baskerville, (Eds.), The role of IS in leveraging the intelligence and creativity of SMEs. New York: Springer.

Kendall, J., Tung, L., Chua, K. H., Ng, C. H., & Tan, S. M. (2001). Receptivity of Singapore's SMEs to electronic commerce adoption. The Journal of Strategic Information Systems, 10(3), 223–242. doi:10.1016/S0963-8687-(01)00048-8

Kendall, K. E. (1999). Emerging information technologies. In K. E. Kendall (Ed.), Emerging information technologies: Improving decisions, cooperation, and infrastructure (pp. 1-18). Thousand Oaks, CA: SAGE Publications, Inc.

Kendall, K. E., Kendall, J. E., & Lee, K. C. (2005). Understanding disaster recovery planning through a theatre metaphor: Rehearsing for a show that might never open. Communications of AIS, 16, 1001–1012.

Keniry, J., Blums, A., Notter, E., Radford, E., & Thomson, S. (2003). Regional business - A plan for action. Department of Transport and Regional Services. Retrieved December 13, 2003, from http://www.rbda.gov.au/action_plan

Kettinger, W. J. (1994). National infrastructure diffusion and the U.S. information super highway. Information & Management, 27(6), 357–368. doi:10.1016/0378-7206-(94)90016-7

Khiang, A. L. B., & Chye, G. N. K. (2002). Information technology and e-commerce for successful SMEs. Malaysian Management Review, 37(2), 5–19.

Kim, D. J. (2008). An OBTG (Organisational - Business - Technological - Governmental) E-business Adoption Model for Small and Medium Sized Enterprises. AMCIS 2008 Proceedings, 1-8.

Kim, D., Ow, T. T., & Jun, M. (2008). SME Strategies: An Assessment Of High vs. Low Performers. Communications of the ACM, 51(11), 113–117. doi:10.1145/1400214.1400237

King, J., Gurbaxani, V., & Kraemer, K. (1994). The institutional factors in Information Technology innovation. Information Systems Research, 5(2), 139–169. doi:10.1287/isre.5.2.139

King, W. R. (1988). Strategic planning for information resources: The evolution of concepts and practice. Information Resources Management Journal, 1(4), 1–8.

Kinkaide, P. (2000). The New Frontier: SME's Enterprise and E-Business in Western Canada. Edmonton.

Kishore, R., & McLean, E. R. (2007). Reconceptualizing innovation compatibility as organizational alignment in secondary IT adoption contexts: An investigation of software reuse infusion. IEEE Transactions on Engineering Management, 54(4), 756–775. doi:10.1109/TEM.2007.906849

Kitching, J., & Blackburn, R. (2002). The nature of training and motivation to train in small firms: Kingston University: Small Business Research Centre.

Kivimaki, M., & Lansisalmi, H. (2000). Communication as a determinant of organizational innovation. R & D Management, 30(1), 33–42. doi:10.1111/1467-9310.00155

Klein, H. K., & Myers, M. D. (1999, March). A Set of Principles for Conducting and Evaluating Interpretive Field Studies in Information Systems. MIS Quarterly, 23(1), 67–94. doi:10.2307/249410

Kling, R., & Iacono, S. (1984). The control of information systems after implementation. Communications of the ACM, 27(12), 1218–1226. doi:10.1145/2135.358307

Kling, R., & Iacono, S. (1988). The mobilization of support for computerization: the role of computerization movements. Social Problems, 35(3), 226–243. doi:10.1525/sp.1988.35.3.03a00030

Kogut, B., & Zander, U. (1992). Knowledge of the firm, combinative capabilities, and the replication of technology. Organization Science, 3(3), 383–397. doi:10.1287/orsc.3.3.383

Kohler, T., Matzler, K., & Fuller, J. (2009). Avatar-based innovation: Using virtual worlds for real-world innovation. Technovation, 29, 395–407. doi:10.1016/j.technovation.2008.11.004

Kollmann, T., & Häsel, M. (2008). Cross-channel cooperation: on the collaborative integration of online and offline business models of e-entrepreneurs and traditional SMEs. International Journal of Entrepreneurship and Small Business, 6(2), 212–229. doi:10.1504/IJESB.2008.018629

Korica, P., Mauer, H., & Schinagl, W. (2006). The growing importance of E-Communities on the Web. In Proceedings IADIS International Conference, Web Based Communities 2006, Spain.

Kotha, S. (1989). Generic manufacturing strategies: A conceptual synthesis. Strategic Management Journal, 10(3), 211–231. doi:10.1002/smj.4250100303

Kracaw, W. A., Lewellen, W. G., & Woo, C. Y. (1992). Corporate growth, corporate strategy, and the choice of capital structure. Managerial and Decision Economics, 13, 515–526. doi:10.1002/mde.4090130607

Krishnan, H. A., Miller, A., & Judge, W. Q. (1997). Diversification and top management complementarity: Is performance improved by merging similar or dissimilar teams? Strategic Management Journal, 18(5), 361–374. doi:10.1002/(SICI)1097-0266(199705)18:5<361::AID-SMJ866>3.0.CO;2-L

Kshetri, N. (2007). The adoption of e-business by organizations in china: An institutional perspective. Electronic Markets, 17(2), 113–125. doi:10.1080/10196780701296022

Kuan, K. K. Y., & Chau, P. Y. K. (2001). A perception-based model for EDI adoption in small businesses using a technology-organization-environment framework. Information & Management, 38, 507–521. doi:10.1016/S0378-7206(01)00073-8

Kumar, K., & Hillegersberg, J. V. (2000). ERP experiences and evolution. Communications of the ACM, 43(4), 22–26. doi:10.1145/332051.332063

Kumar, V., Maheshwari, B., & Kumar, U. (2002). Enterprise resource planning systems adoption process: a survey of Canadian organizations. International Journal of Production Research, 40(3), 509–523. doi:10.1080/00207540110092414

Kumar, V., Maheshwari, B., & Kumar, U. (2003). An investigation of critical management issues in ERP implementation: empirical evidence from Canadian organizations. Technovation, 23(10), 793–807. doi:10.1016/S0166-4972(02)00015-9

Kurnia, S., & Johnston, R. B. (2000). The need for a processual view of inter-organizational systems adoption. The Journal of Strategic Information Systems, 9(4), 295–319. doi:10.1016/S0963-8687(00)00050-0

Kwon, T., & Zmud, R. (1987). Unifying the fragmented models of Information System implementation. In R. Boland and R. Hirschheim (Eds.), Critical Issues in Information System Research. New York: John Wiley.

Kyobe, M. (2008). The Impact of Entrepreneur Behaviours on the Quality of e-Commerce Security: A Comparison of Urban and Rural Findings. Journal of Global Information Technology Management, 11(2), 58–79.

Kyobe, M. (2008). The influence of strategy-making types on IT alignment in SMEs. Journal of Systems and Information Technology, 10(1), 22–38. doi:10.1108/13287260810876876

Kyobe, M. E. (2004). Investigating the strategic utilization of IT resources in the small and medium-sized firms of the eastern Free State province. International Small Business Journal, 22(2), 131–158. doi:10.1177/0266242604041311

Lal, K. (2002). E-business and manufacturing sector: A study of small and medium-sized enterprises in India. Research Policy, 31, 1199–1211. doi:10.1016/S0048-7333-(01)00191-3

Lall, V., & Teyarachakul, S. (2006). Enterprise Resource Planning (ERP) System selection: A Data Envelopment Analysis (DEA) approach. Journal of Computer Information Systems, 47(1), 123–127.

Larsson, E., Hedelin, L., & Gärling, T. (2003). Influence of expert advice on expansion goals of small businesses in rural Sweden. Journal of Small Business Management, 41(2), 205–212. doi:10.1111/1540-627X.00076

Latchem, C., & Walker, D. (2001). Telecentres: Case Studies and Key Issues. Vancouver: The Commonwealth of Learning.

Laukkanen, S., Sarpola, S., & Hallikainen, P. (2007). Enterprise size matters: objectives and constraints of ERP adoption. Journal of Enterprise Information Management, 20(3), 319–334. doi:10.1108/17410390710740763

Law, C. C. H., & Ngai, E. W. T. (2007). ERP system adoption: An exploratory study of the organizational factors and impacts of ERP success. Information & Management, 44(4), 418–432. doi:10.1016/j.im.2007.03.004

Lawrence, K. L. (1997). Factors Inhibiting the Utilisation of Electronic Commerce Facilities in Tasmanian Small-to-Medium Sized Enterprises. In Proceedings of

8th Australasian Conference on Information Systems (pp. 587-597).

Lawrence, W. W. (2007). Small Business Operation Strategy: Aligning Priorities and Resources. *Journal of Small Business Strategy, 18*(2), 89–103.

Lederer, A. L., & Gardiner, V. (1992). Strategic information systems planning: The method/1 approach. *Information Systems Management, 9*(3/4), 13–20. doi:10.1080/10580539208906877

Lee, C. S. (2001). An analytical Framework for Evaluting E-commerce Business Models and Strategies. *Internet Research: Electronic Network Applications and Policy, 11*(4), 349–359. doi:10.1108/10662240110402803

Lee, C., Lee, K., & Pennings, J. M. (2001). Internal capabilities, external networks, and performance: A study on technology-based ventures. *Strategic Management Journal, 22*(6/7), 615–640. doi:10.1002/smj.181

Lee, D. M. S., Trauth, E. M., & Farwell, D. (1995). Critical Skills and Knowledge Requirements of Is Professionals - a Joint Academic-Industry Investigation. *MIS Quarterly, 19*(3), 313–340. doi:10.2307/249598

Lee, H. J., Ahn, H. J., Kim, J. W., & Park, S. J. (2006). Capturing and reusing knowledge in engineering change management: A case of automobile development. *Information Systems Frontiers, 8*(5), 375–395. doi:10.1007/s10796-006-9009-0

Lee, J. (2004). Discriminant analysis of technology adoption behavior: A case of Internet technologies in small businesses. *Journal of Computer Information Systems, 44*(4), 57–66.

Lee, J.-N. (2001). The impact of knowledge sharing, organizational capability and partnership quality on IS outsourcing success. *Information & Management, 38*, 323–335. doi:10.1016/S0378-7206(00)00074-4

Lee, R. P., & Grewal, R. (2004). Strategic responses to new technologies and their impact on firm performance. *Journal of Marketing, 68*, 157–171. doi:10.1509/jmkg.68.4.157.42730

Lee, S., & Lim, G. G. (2005). The impact of partnership attributes on EDI implementation success. *Information & Management, 42*, 503–516. doi:10.1016/S0378-7206-(03)00153-8

Lee, Y. (1996). 'Technology transfer'and the research university: a search for the boundaries of university-industry collaboration. *Research Policy, 25*(6), 843–863. doi:10.1016/0048-7333(95)00857-8

Lees, J. D. (1987). Successful development of small business information systems. *Journal of Systems Management, 25*(3), 32–39.

Lefebvre, E., & Lefebvre, L. A. (1992). Firm innovativeness and CEO characteristics in small manufacturing firms. *Journal of Engineering and Technology Management, 9*(3), 243–277. doi:10.1016/0923-4748-(92)90018-Z

Lefebvre, L. A., Mason, R., & Lefebvre, E. (1997). The influence Prism in SMEs: The power of CEOs perceptions on technology policy and its organisational impacts. *Management Science, 43*(6), 856–878. doi:10.1287/mnsc.43.6.856

Lefebvre, L., & Lefebvre, E. (1993). Competitive positioning and innovative efforts in SMEs. *Small Business Economics, 5*, 297–305. doi:10.1007/BF01516250

Lefebvre, L., & Lefebvre, L. A. (1996). Information and Telecommunication Technologies: The Impact of their Adoption on Small and Medium-sized Enterprises. Retrieved Dec, 12, 2007, from http://web.idrc.ca/en/ev-9303-201-1-DO_TOPIC.html

Lertwongsatien, C., & Wongpinunwatana, N. (2003). E-commerce adoption in Thailand: An empirical study of Small and Medium Enterprises (SMEs). *Journal of Global Information Technology Management, 6*(3), 67–83.

Letaifa, S., & Perrien, J. (2007). The impact of E-CRM on organisational and individual behavior: The effect of the remuneration and reward system. *International Journal of E-Business Research, (3)*: 2–13.

Levenburg, N. M., Schwarz, T. V., & Motwani, J. (2005). Understanding Adoption of Internet Technologies Among SMEs. Journal of Small Business Strategy, 16(1), 51–69.

Levy, M., & Powell, P. (1997). Assessing the value of information systems planning at Heath Springs. International Journal of Technology Management, 13(4), 426–442. doi:10.1504/IJTM.1997.001673

Levy, M., & Powell, P. (1998). SME flexibility and the role of information systems. Journal of Small Business Economics, 11, 183–196. doi:10.1023/A:1007912714741

Levy, M., & Powell, P. (2000). Information systems strategy for small and medium sized enterprises: an organisational perspective. The Journal of Strategic Information Systems, 9(1), 63–84. doi:10.1016/S0963-8687(00)00028-7

Levy, M., & Powell, P. (2000). Information systems strategy for small and medium sized enterprises: An organisational perspective. Strategic Information Systems, 9, 63–84. doi:10.1016/S0963-8687(00)00028-7

Levy, M., & Powell, P. (2003). Exploring SME Internet Adoption: Towards a Contingent Model. Electronic Markets, 13(2), 173–181. doi:10.1080/1019678032000067163

Levy, M., & Powell, P. (2005). Strategies for growth in SMEs: The role of information and information systems. Oxford, UK: Elsevier Butterworth-Heinemann.

Levy, M., Loebbecke, C., & Powell, P. (2003). SMEs, co-opetition and knowledge sharing: the role of information systems. European Journal of Information Systems, 12(1), 3–17. doi:10.1057/palgrave.ejis.3000439

Levy, M., Powell, P., & Galliers, R. (1999). Assessing information systems strategy development frameworks in SMEs. Information & Management, 36(5), 247–261. doi:10.1016/S0378-7206(99)00020-8

Levy, M., Powell, P., & Worrall, L. (2005). Strategic intent and e-business in SMEs: Enablers and inhibitors. Information Resources Management Journal, 18(4), 1–20.

Levy, M., Powell, P., & Yetton, P. (1998). SMEs and the gains from IS: from cost reduction to value added.

Levy, M., Powell, P., & Yetton, P. (2001). SMEs: Aligning IS and the Strategic Context. Journal of Information Technology, 16(2), 133–144. doi:10.1080/02683960110063672

Levy, M., Powell, P., & Yetton, P. (2001). SMEs: Aligning IS and the strategic context. Journal of Information Technology, 16(3), 133–144. doi:10.1080/02683960110063672

Levy, M., Powell, P., & Yetton, P. (2002). The dynamics of SME information systems. Small Business Economics, 19(4), 341–354. doi:10.1023/A:1019654030019

Levy, M., Powell, P., & Yetton, P. (2003). IS alignment in small firms: New paths through the maze. Paper presented at the Proceedings of the 11th European Conference on Information Systems, ECIS 2003, Naples, Italy.

Lewis, R., & Cockrill, A. (2002). Going global-remaining local: the impact of e-commerce on small retail firms in Wales. International Journal of Information Management, 22(3), 195–209. doi:10.1016/S0268-4012(02)00005-1

Li, C., Bernoff, J., Feffer, K. A., & Pflaum, C. N. (2007). Marketing On Social Sites. Forrester. Retrieved from http://www.forrester.com/Research/Document/Excerpt/0,7211,41662,00.html

Li, E. Y., & Chen, H. G. (2001). Output-driven information system planning: A case study. Information & Management, 38, 185–199. doi:10.1016/S0378-7206-(00)00066-5

Liao, X. W., Li, Y., & Lu, B. (2007). A model for selecting an ERP system based on linguistic information processing. Information Systems, 32(7), 1005–1017. doi:10.1016/j.is.2006.10.005

Lichtenstein, G. A., & Lyons, T. S. (2001). The entrepreneurial development system: Transforming business talent and community economies. Economic Development Quarterly, 15(1), 3–20. doi:10.1177/089124240101500101

Lindermann, N., & Valcárel, S. Schaarschmidt, & von Kortzfleisch, H. (2009). SME 2.0: Roadmap towards Web 2.0-based open innovation in SME-Networks—A case study based research framework. In G. Dhillon, B.C.

Stahl, and R. Baskerville (Eds.), CreativeSME2009, IFIP Advances in information and communication technology, 301 (pp. 28-41). Berlin: Springer.

Lockett, N., & Brown, D. H. (2006). Aggregation and the Role of Trusted Third Parties in SME E-Business Engagement. International Small Business Journal, 24(4), 379–404. doi:10.1177/0266242606065509

Lomerson, W. L., McGrath, L. C., & Schwager, P. H. (2004). An examination of the benefits of e-business to small and medium size businesses. In Proceedings of the 7th Annual conference of the Southern Association for Information System, Southern Association for Information Systems.

Lord, R. G., & Foti, R. J. (1986). Schema theories, information processing and organizational behavior. In H.P. Sims, Jr., & D.A. Gioia (Eds.), The thinking organization: Dynamics of organization cognition (pp. 20-48). San Francisco: Jossey Bass.

Love, P. E. D., & Irani, Z. (2004). An exploratory study of information technology evaluation and benefits management practices of SMEs in the construction industry. Information & Management, 42, 227–242.

Luftman, J. N. (1996). Applying the strategic alignment model. New York: Oxford University Press.

Luftmann, J. N. (2005). Key issues for IT executives 2004. MIS Quarterly Executive, 4(2), 269–285.

Lumpkin, G. T., & Dess, G. G. (2004). E-business strategies and Internet business models: How the Internet adds value. Organizational Dynamics, 33(2), 161–173. doi:10.1016/j.orgdyn.2004.01.004

Lundström, A., & Stevenson, L. (2002). On the road to Entrepreneurship Policy: The Entrepreneurship Policy for the Future Series. In Forum för Småföretagsforskning (FSF 2002) (Vol. 2).

Lynch, L. M., & Black, S. E. (1998). Beyond the incidence of employer-provided training. Industrial & Labor Relations Review, 52(1), 64–81. doi:10.2307/2525243

Lyytinen, K., & King, J. L. (2004). Nothing At The Center?: Academic Legitimacy in the Information Systems

Field 12. Journal of the Association for Information Systems, 5(6), 220–246.

Ma, X., & Loeh, H. (2007). Closing the gap: How should Chinese companies build the capabilities to implement ERP-driven process innovation? International Journal of Technology Management, 39(3/4), 380–395. doi:10.1504/IJTM.2007.013501

Mac Gregor, R., & Vrazalic, L. (2005). The Role of Small Business Clusters in Prioritising Barriers to E-commerce Adoption: A Study of Swedish Regional SMEs. CRIC Cluster conference. Beyond Cluster-Current Practices & Future Strategies, Ballarat, Victoria.

MacGregor, R. C. (2004). The Role of Strategic Alliances in the Ongoing Use of Electronic Commerce Technology in Regional Small Business. Journal of Electronic Commerce in Organizations, 2(1), 1–14.

MacGregor, R. C., & Bunker, D. (1996). The effect of priorities introduced during computer acquisition on continuing success with IT in small business environments. In Proceedings of Information Resource Management Association International Conference, Washington (pp. 271-227).

MacGregor, R. C., & Vrazalic, L. (2005). A Basic Model of Electronic Commerce Adoption Barriers: A Study of Regional Small Businesses in Sweden and Australia. Journal of Small Business and Enterprise Development, 12(4), 510–527. doi:10.1108/14626000510628199

MacGregor, R. C., & Vrazalic, L. (2007). E-commerce in Regional Small to Medium Enterprises. Hershey, PA: IGI Global.

MacGregor, R. C., Bunker, D., & Waugh, P. (1998). Electronic commerce and small/medium enterprises in Australia: An EDI pilot study. In Proceedings of Proceedings of 11th International Bled E-commerce Conference, 8th-10th June, Bled, Slovenia (pp. 331-345).

Mach, T.L., & Wolken, J.D. (2006 October). Financial services used by small businesses: Evidence from the 2003 Survey of Small Business Finances. Federal Reserve Bulletin, A167-A195.

Magnusson, M. (2001). E-commerce in small businesses - focusing on adoption and implementation. In Proceedings of Proceedings of the 1st Nordic Workshop on Electronic Commerce, May 28-29, Halmstad, Sweden.

Malie, M., Duffy, N., & van Rensburg, A. C. J. (2008). Enterprise resource planning solution selection criteria in medium-sized South African companies. South African Journal of Industrial Engineering, 19(1), 17–41.

Manley, K. (2008). Against the odds: Small firms in Australia successfully introducing new technology on construction projects. Research Policy, 37(10), 1751–1764. doi:10.1016/j.respol.2008.07.013

Mansell, R., & Wehn, U. (1998). Knowledge Societies: Information Technology for Sustainable Development. Oxford: Oxford University Press.

March, J. G. (1991). Exploration and exploitation in organizational learning. Organization Science, 2, 71–87. doi:10.1287/orsc.2.1.71

Markland, R. E. (1974). The role of the computer in small business management. Journal of Small Business Management, 12(1), 21–26.

Markus, H., & Zajonc, R. B. (1985). The cognitive perspective in social psychology. In G. Lindzey & E. Aronson (Eds.), Handbook of social psychology (Vol. 1, 3rd ed., pp. 137-230). New York: Random House.

Markus, M. L., & Tanis, C. (2000). The Enterprise System Experience: From Adoption to Success. In R. W. Zmud (Ed.), Framing the Domains of IT Management: Projecting the Future through the Past (pp. 173-207). Cincinnati, OH: Pinnaflex Educational Resources Inc.

Marlow, S. (1998). So Much Opportunity -- So Little Take-up: The Case of Training in Small Firms. Small Business and Enterprise Development, 5(1), 38–47. doi:10.1108/EUM0000000006729

Marshall, P., & McKay, J. (2004). Strategic IT planning, evaluation and benefits management: The basis for effective IT governance. Australasian Journal of Information Systems, 11(2), 14–26.

Marshall, P., Sor, R., & McKay, J. (2000). The Impacts of Electronic Commerce in the Automobile Industry: An Empirical Study in Western Australia. In B. Wangler & L. Bergman (Eds.), CAiSE 2000 (pp. 509-521). Berlin Heidelberg: Springer Verlag.

Martin, C. J. (1989). Information management in the smaller business: The role of the top manager. International Journal of Information Management, 9(3), 187–197. doi:10.1016/0268-4012(89)90006-6

Martin, J. (1982). Strategic Data Planning Methodologies. Upper Saddle River, NJ: Prentice Hall.

Martin, J. SJ. (2007). A Jesuit Off-Broadway. Chicago, IL: Loyola Press.

Martin, L., & Matlay, H. (2001). 'Blanket approaches to promoting ICT in small firms: some lessons from DTI ladder adoption model in the UK'. Internet Research: Electronic Networking Applications and Policy, 11(5), 399–410. doi:10.1108/EUM0000000006118

Martin, P. Y., & Turner, B. A. (1986). Grounded theory and organizational research. The Journal of Applied Behavioral Science, 22(2), 141–157. doi:10.1177/002188638602200207

Massey, T. (1986). Computers in Small Business: A Case of Under-Utilisation. American Journal of Small Business, 11(2), 51–60.

Masuda, Y. (1980). The information society as post-industrial society, The information society as post-industrial society.

Mata, F. J., Fuerst, W. L., & Barney, J. B. (1995). Information Technology and sustained competitive advantage: A resource-based analysis. MIS Quarterly, 19(4), 487–495. doi:10.2307/249630

Maton, K. (1999). Evaluation of Small Firms Training Loans: UK Research Partnerships Ltd., Dfee Publications.

Matthews, P. (2007). ICT Assimilation and SME Expansion. Journal of International Development, 19(6): 817–827. doi:10.1002/jid.1401

Matzler, K., Schwarz, E., Deutlinger, N., & Harms, R. (2008). The Relation between Transformational Leadership, Product Innovation and Performance in SMEs. Journal of Small Business and Entrepreneurship, 21(2), 139–152.

McAfee, A. (2006). Enterprise 2.0: The Dawn of Emergent Collaboration. MIT Sloan Management Review, 47(3), 21–28.

McCole, P., & Ramsey, E. (2005). A Profile of Adopters and Non-adopters of eCommerce in SME Professional Service Firms. Australasian Marketing Journal, 13(1), 36–48.

McFarlan, F. W. (1981). Portfolio approach to information systems. Harvard Business Review, 59(5), 142–150.

McFarlan, F. W., & McKenney, J. L. (1983). Corporate Information Systems Management. Homewood, IL: Richard D. Irwin.

McFarlan, F.W. (1984). Information Technology Changes the Way You Compete. Harvard Business Review, 62(3), 98-1 03.

McKelvey, B. (2006). Response - Van de Ven and Johnson's engaged scholarship: Nice try, but. Academy of Management Review, 31(4), 822–829.

McKinsey. (2007). How businesses are using Web 2.0: A McKinsey global survey. The McKinsey Quarterly.

McKinsey. (2008a, July). Building the Web 2.0 Enterprise: McKinsey Global Survey Results. The McKinsey Quarterly.

McKinsey. (2008b, June). The next step in Open Innovation. The McKinsey Quarterly.

McLuhan, M. (1994). Understanding media: The extensions of man. New York, NY: Mentor. (Original work published in 1964). Reissued in 1994. Cambridge, MA: MIT Press.

Meers, K. A., & Robertson, C. (2007). Strategic Planning Practices in Profitable Small Firms in the United States. Business Review (Federal Reserve Bank of Philadelphia), 7(1), 302–307.

Mehrtens, J., Cragg, P., & Mills, A. (2001). A model of Internet adoption by SMEs. Information & Management, 39(3), 165–176. doi:10.1016/S0378-7206(01)00086-6

Mekelburg, D. (2003). Project Expectations: The boundaries for agile development. Crosstalk: The Journal of Defense Software Engineering, April, 28-30.

Melewar, T. C., & Karaosmanoglu, E. (2006). Seven dimensions of corporate identity: A categorisation from the practitioners' perspectives. European Journal of Marketing, 40(7/8), 846–869. doi:10.1108/03090560610670025

Melville, N., Kraemer, K. L., & Gurbaxani, V. (2004). Information technology and organizational performance: An integrative model of IT business value. MIS Quarterly, 28(2), 283–322.

Meredith, G. G. (1994). Small Business Management in Australia (4th Ed.). New York: McGraw Hill.

Merhrtans, J., Cragg, P., & Mills, A. (2001). A model of internet adoption by SMEs. Information & Management, 39.

Merono-Cerdan, A. L., & Soto-Acosta, P. (2006). Examining e-business impact on firm performance through website analysis. International Journal of Electronic Business, 3(6), 1–1.

Meso, P., & Jain, R. (2006). Agile software development: Adaptive systems principles and best practice. Information Systems Management, 23(3), 19–30. doi:10.1201/10 78.10580530/46108.23.3.20060601/93704.3

Metaxiotis, K. (2009). Exploring the rationales for ERP and knowledge management integration in SMEs. Journal of Enterprise Information Management., 22(1/2), 51–62. doi:10.1108/17410390910922822

Meyer, J., & Rowan, B. (1977). Institutionalized organizations: Formal structure as myth and ceremony. American Journal of Sociology, 83, 340–363. doi:10.1086/226550

Microsoft. (2006). Microsoft's Definition of Small and Medium Business. Retrieved September 20, 2008, from http://www.microsoft.com/technet/solutionaccelerators/smbiz/smbprgovw/progovrw_1.mspx#ETAAC

Miles, M. B., & Huberman, A. M. (1994). Qualitative Data Analysis (2nd Ed.). Thousand Oaks, CA: Sage Publications.

Miles, R. E., Snow, C. C., Meyer, A. D., Henry, J., & Coleman, J. (1978). Organizational strategy, structure, and process. Academy of Management Review, 3(3), 546–562. doi:10.2307/257544

Miller, D. (1982). Evolution and revolution - a quantum view of structural-change in organizations. Journal of Management Studies, 19(2), 131–151. doi:10.1111/j.1467-6486.1982.tb00064.x

Miller, N. J., & Besser, T. L. (2000). The importance of community values in small business strategy formation: Evidence from rural Iowa. Journal of Small Business Management, 38(1), 68–85.

Min, S. K., Suh, E. H., & Kim, S. Y. (1999). An integrated approach toward strategic information systems planning. The Journal of Strategic Information Systems, 8, 373–394. doi:10.1016/S0963-8687(00)00029-9

Miner, J. B., & Raju, N. S. (2004). Risk Propensity Differences Between Managers and Entrepreneurs and Between Low- and High-Growth Entrepreneurs: A Reply in a More Conservative Vein. The Journal of Applied Psychology, 89(1), 3–13. doi:10.1037/0021-9010.89.1.3

Mir, D. F., & Feitelson, E. (2007). Factors Affecting Environmental Behavior in Micro-enterprises. International Small Business Journal, 25(4), 383–415. doi:10.1177/0266242607078583

Mirchandani, A. A., & Motwani, J. (2001). Understanding small business electronic commerce adoption: an empirical analysis. Journal of Computer Information Systems, 41(3), 70–73.

Mirza, A. A. (in press). International journal of technology in small and medium enterprises (IJTSME). Announcement available at http://www.igi-global.com/journals/. Last accessed on April 7, 2009.

Moch, M. K., & Morse, E. V. (1977). Size, centralization, and organizational adoption of innovations. American Sociological Review, 42(5), 716–725. doi:10.2307/2094861

Mohan-Neill, S. I. (1995). The influence of firm's age and size on its environmental scanning activities. Journal of Small Business Management, 33(4), 10–21.

Mohr, J., Fisher, R., & Nevin, J. (1996, July). Collaborative communication in interfirm relationships: Moderating effects of integration and control. Journal of Marketing, 60, 349–370. doi:10.2307/1251844

Mole, K. F. (2007). Tacit knowledge, heuristics, consistency and error signals, How do business advisers diagnose their SME clients? Journal of Small Business and Enterprise Development, 14(4), 582–601. doi:10.1108/14626000710832712

Molla, A., & Heeks, R. (2007). Exploring E-commerce Benefits for Businesses in a Developing Country. The Information Society, 23, 95–108. doi:10.1080/01972240701224028

Montazemi, A. R. (1988). Factors affecting information satisfaction in the context of the small business environment. MIS Quarterly, 12(2), 239–256. doi:10.2307/248849

Montazemi, A. R. (2006). How they manage IT: SMEs in Canada and the U.S. Communications of the ACM, 49(12), 109–112. doi:10.1145/1183236.1183240

Moore, G. C., & Benbasat, I. (1991). Development of an instrument to measure the perceptions of adopting an information technology innovation. Information Systems Research, 2(3), 192–222. doi:10.1287/isre.2.3.192

Moore, G., & Benbasat, J. (1991). Development of an instrument to measure the perceptions of adopting an Information Technology innovation. Information Systems Research, 2(3), 192–222. doi:10.1287/isre.2.3.192

Moore, R., Blake, D., Phillips, G., & McConaughty, D. (2003). Training that works: Lessons from California's Employment Training Panel program. Kalamazoo, MI: W.E. Upjohn Institute.

Morabito, V., Pace, S., & Previtali, P. (2005). ERP Marketing and Italian SMEs. European Management Journal, 23(5), 590–598. doi:10.1016/j.emj.2005.09.014

Morgan, G., Frost, P. J., & Pondy, L. R. (1983). Organizational symbolism. In L.R. Pondy, P.G. Frost, G. Morgan & T.C. Dandridge (Eds.), Organizational symbolism. Greenwich, CT: JAI Press.

Morgan, K. (1997). The learning region: Institutions, innovations and regional renewal, regional studies. The Journal of Regional Studies Association, 31(5), 491–503. doi:10.1080/00343409750132289

Mowshowitz, A. (1997). Virtual Organization. Communications of the ACM, 40(9). doi:10.1145/260750.260759

Moyi, E. D. (2003). Networks, information and small enterprises: New Technologies and the ambiguity of empowerment. In Information Technology for Development (Vol. 10, pp. 221-232).

Mukti, N. A. (2000). Barriers to putting businesses on the Internet in Malaysia. Electronic Journal of Information Systems in Developing Countries, 2(6), 1–6.

Murphy, J. (1996). Small Business Management. London: Pitman.

Murphy, K. E., & Simon, S. J. (2002). Intangible benefits valuation in ERP projects. Information Systems Journal, 12, 301–320. doi:10.1046/j.1365-2575.2002.00131.x

Musser, J., & O'Reilly, T. (2006). Web 2.0 principles and Best Practices. O'Reilly Radar Report.

Nah, F. F. H., & Delgado, S. (2006). Critical success factors for enterprise resource planning implementation and upgrade. Journal of Computer Information Systems, 46(SI), 99-113.

Nakamura, M., Vertinsky, I., & Zietsma, C. (1997). Does culture matter in inter-firm cooperation? Research consortia in Japan and the USA. Managerial and Decision Economics, 18(2).

Nambisan, S., & Nambisan, P. (2008). How to Profit From a Better 'Virtual Customer Environment. MIT Sloan Management Review, 49(3), 53–61.

Naylor, J., & Williams, J. (1994). Successful Use of IT in SMEs. European Journal of IS, 3(1), 48–56.

Needleman, M. (2007). Web 2.0/Lib 2.0—What Is It? (If It's Anything at All). Serials Review, 33(3), 202–203. doi:10.1016/j.serrev.2007.05.001

Nelson, R. R., & Winter, S. G. (1982). An evolutionary theory of economic change. Cambridge, MA: Harvard University Press.

Nerur, S., & Mahapatra, R. (2005). Challenges of migrating to agile methodologies. Communications of the ACM, 48(5), 72–78. doi:10.1145/1060710.1060712

Neuman, L. W. (1999). Social research methods: Qualitative and Quantitative Approaches (4th Ed.). Upper Saddle River, NJ: Allyn & Bacon, U.S.A.

Newbert, S. L. (2007). Empirical research on the resource-based view of the firm: An assessment and suggestions for future research. Strategic Management Journal, 28(2), 121–146. doi:10.1002/smj.573

Newman, D. A. (2009). Missing data techniques and low response rates: the role of systematic nonresponse parameters. In C. E. Lance & R. J. Vandenberg (Eds.) Statistical and methodological myths and urban legends (pp. 7-36). New York: Routledge.

Nielson, J. F., Host, V., & Mols, N. P. (2005). Adoption of internet-based marketing channels by small- and medium-sized manufacturers. International Journal of E-Business Research, 1(2), 1–23.

Nilakanta, S., & Scamell, R. (1990). The effect of information sources and communication channels on the diffusion of innovation in a data base development environment. Management Science, 36(1), 24–40. doi:10.1287/mnsc.36.1.24

Nohria, N., & Gulati, R. (1996). Is slack good or bad for innovation? Academy of Management Journal, 39(5), 1245–1264. doi:10.2307/256998

NOIE. (2002). e-Business for Small Business. The National Office of Information Economy. Retrieved May 25, 2003, from http://www.noie.gov.au/projects/ebusiness/Advancing/SME/

Noir, C., & Walsham, G. (2007). The great legitimizer: ICT as myth and ceremony in the Indian healthcare sector. Information Technology & People, 20(4), 313–333. doi:10.1108/09593840710839770

Nonaka, I. (1994). A dynamic theory of organizational knowledge creation. Organization Science, 5(1), 14–37. doi:10.1287/orsc.5.1.14

Nonaka, I., & Konno, N. (1998). The concept of ba: Building a foundation for knowledge creation. California Management Review, 40(3), 40–54.

Nonaka, I., & Takeuchi, H. (1995). The knowledge-creating company: How Japanese companies create the dynamics of innovation. New York: Oxford University Press.

Nunnally, J. C. (1978). Psychometric theory (2nd ed.). New York: McGraw-Hill.

Nyden, P., & Wiewel, W. (1992). Collaborative research: Harnessing the tensions between researcher and practitioner. The American Sociologist, 23(4), 43–55. doi:10.1007/BF02691930

O'Farrell, C., Norrish, P., & Scott, A. (1999). Information and Communication Technologies (ICTs) for Sustainable Livelihoods. Burton Hall: Intermediate Technology Development Group.

O'Farrell, P., & Hitchens, D. (1988). Alternative theories of small-firm growth: a critical review. Environment and Planning, 20(10), 1365–1383. doi:10.1068/a201365

O'Regan, N., & Ghobadian, A. (2004). Short- and long-term performance in manufacturing SMEs: Different targets, different drivers. International Journal of Productivity and Performance Management, 53(5), 405–424. doi:10.1108/17410400410545888

O'Regan, N., & Ghobadian, A. (2005). Strategic planning - a comparison of high and low technology manufacturing small firms. Technovation, 25(10), 1107–1117. doi:10.1016/S0166-4972(03)00091-9

O'Regan, N., & Ghobadian, A. (2006). Perceptions of generic strategies of small and medium sized engineering and electronics manufacturers in the UK: The applicability of the Miles and Snow typology. Journal of Manufacturing Technology Management, 17(5), 603–620. doi:10.1108/17410380610668540

O'Regan, N., & Ghobadian, A. (2007). Formal strategic planning: Annual raindance or wheel of success? Strategic Change, 16(1-2), 11–22. doi:10.1002/jsc.777

O'Regan, N., Ghobadian, A., & Gallear, D. (2006). In search of the drivers of high growth in manufacturing SMEs. Technovation, 26(1), 30–41. doi:10.1016/j.technovation.2005.05.004

Ochara, N. M., Van Belle, J., & Brown, I. (2008). Global Diffusion of the Internet XIII: Internet Diffusion in Kenya and Its Determinants - A Longitudinal Analysis. CAIS, 23(7), 123-150.

OECD. (2002). Electronic commerce and SMEs, ICT and electronic commerce for SMEs: Progress Report. Working Party on Small and Medium-Sized Enterprises and Entrepreneurship, Geneva, DSTI/IND/PME (2002)7.

Ogawa, S., & Piller, F. (2006). Reducing the risks of new product development. MIT Sloan Management Review, 47(2), 65–71.

Oh, K., Cruickshank, D., & Anderson, A. R. (2009). The adoption of e-trade innovations by Korean small and medium sized firms. Technovation, 29(2), 110–121. doi:10.1016/j.technovation.2008.08.001

Oh, W., & Pinsonneault, A. (2007). On the Assessment of the Strategic Value of Information Technologies: Conceptual and Analytical Approaches. MIS Quarterly, 31(2), 239–265.

Orlikowski, W. J. (1991). Integrated information environment or matrix of control? The contradictory implications of information technology. Accounting. Management and Information Technologies, 1, 9–42. doi:10.1016/0959-8022(91)90011-3

Orlikowski, W. J., & Iacono, C. S. (2000). The truth is not out there: an enacted view of the 'digital economy. In E. Brynjolfsson & B. Kahin (Eds.), Understanding the Digital Economy: Data, Tools, and Research. Cambridge, MA: MIT Press.

Orlikowski, W. J., & Iacono, C. S. (2001). Research Commentary: Desperately seeking the IT in IT research – A call to theorizing the IT artifact. Information Systems Research, 12(2), 121–134. doi:10.1287/isre.12.2.121.9700

Ortega, B. H., Marinez, J. J., & Hoyos, M. (2008). The role of information technology knowledge in b2b development. International Journal of E-Business Research, 4(1), 40–54.

Oshikoya, T. W., & Hussain, M. N. (2007). Information technology and the challenge of economic development in Africa. In A. Opoku-mensah & M. M. A. Salih (Eds.), African E-markets: Information and Economic Development. Copenhagen: CODI.

Oviatt, B. M., & McDougall, P. P. (1994). Toward a theory of international new ventures. Journal of International Business Studies, 25(1), 45–64. doi:10.1057/palgrave.jibs.8490193

Owen, W., & Darkwa, O. (1999). Role of Multipurpose Community Telecentres in Accelerating National Development in Ghana. First Monday, 5(1), 1–23.

Pace, C. R. (1939). Factors Influencing Questionnaire Returns from Former University Students. The Journal of Applied Psychology, 23(3), 388–397. doi:10.1037/h0063286

Pallant, J. (2002). SPSS Survival manual. Buckingham: Open University Press.

Palvia, P. C., & Palvia, S. C. (1999). An examination of the IT satisfaction of small-business users. Information & Management, 35(3), 127–137. doi:10.1016/S0378-7206-(98)00086-X

Palvia, S. C. J., & Vemuri, V. K. (2002). Global E-commerce: An Examination of Issues Related to Advertising and Intermediation. In P.C. Palvia, S.C.J. Palvia, & E.M. Roche (Eds.), Global Information Technology and Electronic Commerce: Issues for the new millennium (pp. 215 - 254).

Panyasorn, J., Panteli, N., & Powell, P. (2009). Knowledge management in small firms. In G. Dhillon, B.C. Stahl, and R. Baskerville (Eds.), CreativeSME2009, Advances in information and communication technology, 301 (pp. 192-210). Berlin: Springer.

Papp, R. (1999). Business-IT alignment: Productivity paradox payoff? Industrial Management & Data Systems, 99(8), 367–373. doi:10.1108/02635579910301810

Pare, G. (2004). Investigating information systems with positivist case study research. Communications of the Association for Information Systems, 13, 233–264.

Parise, S., & Guinan, P. J. (2008). Marketing using Web 2.0. In Proceedings of the 41st Hawaii International Conference on System Sciences.

Parker, C. M., & Castleman, T. (2007). New directions for research on SME-eBusiness: insights from an analysis of journal articles from 2003 to 2006. Journal of Information Systems and Small Business, 1(1-2), 21–40.

Parker, C. M., & Castleman, T. (2007). New directions for research on SME-ebusiness: Insights from an analysis of journal articles from 2003-2006. Journal of Information Systems and Small Business, 1(1-2), 21–40.

Parnell, J. A. (2002). A business strategy typology for the new economy: Reconceptualization and synthesis. Journal of Behavioral and Applied Management, 3(3), 206–229.

Pateli, A. G., & Giaglis, G. M. (2004). A research framework for analyzing eBusiness models. European Journal of Information Systems, 13, 302–314. doi:10.1057/palgrave.ejis.3000513

Patton, D., Marlow, S., & Hannon, P. (2000). The Relationship Between Training and Small Firm Performance, Research Frameworks and Lost Quests. International Small Business Journal, 19(1), 11–27. doi:10.1177/0266242600191001

Pavitt, K., Robson, M., & Townsend, J. (1987). The size of distribution of innovating firms in the UK: 1945-1983. The Journal of Industrial Economics, 35, 297–316. doi:10.2307/2098636

Payton, F., & Glnzberg, M. (2001). Interorganisational health care systems Implementations: An exploratory study of early Electronic Commerce initiatives. Health Care Management Review, 26(2), 20–32.

Pedrycz, W. (2006). Quantitative logic-based framework for agile methodologies. Journal of Systems Architecture, 52, 700–707. doi:10.1016/j.sysarc.2006.06.014

Penrose, E. (1959). The Theory of Growth of the Firm. London: Basil Blackwell.

Peppard, J., Lambert, R., & Edwards, C. (2000). Whose job is it anyway? organizational information competencies for value creation. Information Systems Journal, 10, 291–322. doi:10.1046/j.1365-2575.2000.00089.x

Peppard, J., Ward, J., & Daniel, E. (2007). Managing the realization of business benefits from IT investments. MISQ Executive, 6(1), 1–11.

Peppers, D., & Rogers, M. (1995). A new Marketing paradigm: share of customer, not market share. Managing Service Quality, 5(3), 48–51. doi:10.1108/09604529510796412

Perry, S. C. (2001). The relationship between written business plans and the failure of small businesses in the US. Journal of Small Business Management, 39(3), 201–208. doi:10.1111/1540-627X.00019

Peters, S. C. A., Heng, M. S. H., & Vet, R. (2002). Formation of the information systems in a global financial services Company. Information and Organization, 12, 19–38. doi:10.1016/S1471-7727(01)00011-2

Petersen, M. A., & Rajan, R. G. (1994). The benefits of lending relationships: Evidence from small business data. The Journal of Finance, 49(1), 3–37. doi:10.2307/2329133

Pfeffer, J. (1981). Management as symbolic action: The creation and maintenance of organizational paradigms. In L.L. Cummings & B.M. Staw (Eds.), Research in organizational behavior (Vol. 13, pp. 1-52). Greenwich, CT: JAI Press.

Pfeffer, J., & Salancik, G. R. (1978). The external control of organizations: A resource dependence perspective. New York: Harper and Row.

Pflughoeft, K. A., & Ramamurthy, K., Soofi, Ehsan, Yasai-Ardekani, M., & Zahedi, F. (2003). Multiple conceptualizations of small business Web use and benefit. Decision Sciences, 34(3), 467–512. doi:10.1111/j.1540-5414.2003.02539.x

Pikkarainen, M., & Passoja, U. (2005). An approach for assessing suitability of agile solutions: A case study. Paper presented at the International conference of Extreme Programming and agile process in software engineering, UK.

Piscitello, L., & Sgobbi, F. (2004, June). Globalisation, E-Business and SMEs: Evidence from the Italian District of Prato. Small Business Economics, 22(5), 333. doi:10.1023/B:SBEJ.0000022208.34741.55

Pollard, C., & Diggles, A. (2006). The role of trust in Business-to-Business e-Commerce collaboration in a unique environment in Australia. International Journal of E-Business Research, 2(3), 71–88.

Poon, S. (2000). Business Environment and Internet Commerce Benefit-A Small business Perspective. European Journal of Information Systems, 9, 72–81.

Poon, S., & Swatman, P. (1999). An exploratory study of small business Internet commerce issues. Information & Management, 35, 9–18. doi:10.1016/S0378-7206-(98)00079-2

Poon, S., & Swatman, P. M. C. (1997). Small business use of Internet Findings from Australian case studies. International Marketing Review, 14.   .

Poon, S., & Swatman, P. M. C. (1998). Small Business Internet Commerce Experiences: A Longitudinal Study. In Proceedings of Proceedings of the 11th International Bled Electronic Commerce Conference, June 8-10. Bled, Slovenia (pp. 295-309).

Porter, M. E. (1980). Competitive Strategy: Techniques for Analyzing Industries and Competitors. New York: Free Press.

Porter, M. E. (1991). Towards a dynamic theory of strategy. Strategic Management Journal, 12, 95–117. doi:10.1002/smj.4250121008

Porter, M. E. (2001, March). Strategy and the internet. Harvard Business Review, 63–78.

Porter, M.E., & Millar, V.E. (1985 July-August). How Information Gives You Competitive Advantage. Harvard Business Review, 63(4), 149-1 60.

Potts, J., Hartley, J., Banks, J., Burgess, J., Cobcroft, R., Cunningham, S., & Montgomery, L. (2008). Consumer co-creation and situated creativity. Industry and Innovation, 15(5), 459–474. doi:10.1080/13662710802373783

Powell, T. C., & Dent-Micallef, A. (1997). Information technology as competitive advantage: The role of human, business and technology resources. Strategic Management Journal, 18(5), 375–405. doi:10.1002/(SICI)1097-0266(199705)18:5<375::AID-SMJ876>3.0.CO;2-7

Powell, W. W., & DiMaggio, P. J. (1991) Introduction. In W.W. Powell & P.J. DiMaggio (Eds.), The new institutionalism in organizational analysis. London: University of Chicago Press.

Prahalad, C. K., & Ramaswamy, V. (2004). Co-Creation experiences: the next practice in value creation. Journal of Interactive Marketing, 18(3), 5–14. doi:10.1002/dir.20015

Prananto, A., McKay, J., & Marshall, P. (2003). The spectrum of e-business maturity in Australian SMEs: A multiple case study approach to the applicability of the stages of growth for e-business model. Paper presented at the Proceeding of the 11th European conference on information systems (ECIS).

Prasad, P. (1993). Symbolic processes in the implementation of technological change: A symbolic interactionist study of work computerization. Academy of Management Journal, 36, 1400–1429. doi:10.2307/256817

Premaratne, S. P. (2001). Networks, Resources and Small Business Growth: The Experience in Sri Lanka. Journal of Small Business Management, 39(4), 363–371. doi:10.1111/0447-2778.00033

Premkumar, G. (2003). A meta-analysis of research on information technology implementation in small business. Journal of Organizational Computing and Electronic Commerce, 13(2), 91–121. doi:10.1207/S15327744JOCE1302_2

Premkumar, G., & Ramamurthy, K. (1995). The Role of Interorganisational and Organizational Factors on the Decision Mode for Adoption of Interorganisational Systems. Decision Sciences, 26(3), 303–336. doi:10.1111/j.1540-5915.1995.tb01431.x

Premkumar, G., & Roberts, M. (1998). Adoption of new Information Technologies in rural small businesses. The International Journal of Management Science, 27, 467–484.

Premkumar, G., & Roberts, M. (1999). Adoption of new information technologies in rural small businesses. OMEGA. The International Journal of Management Science, 27(4), 467–484.

Prospero Technologies, L. L. C. (2007). Social MediaSurvey. Retrieved from http://www.prospero.com/about_press_release_071016.asp

Proudlock, M. J., Phelps, B., & Gamble, P. R. (1998). IS decision-making: A study in information-intensive firms. Journal of Information Technology, 13(1), 55–66. doi:10.1080/026839698344954

Pucihar, A., Bogataj, K., & Lenart, G. (2009). Increasing SMEs' efficiency through the single European electronic market as a new business model. In B Paape, & D. Vuk (Ed.), Synthesized organization (pp. 347-368). Frankfurt am Main: P. Lang.

Purao, S., & Campbell, B. (1998). Critical Concerns for Small Business Electronic Commerce: Some Reflections Based on Interviews of Small Business Owners. In Proceedings of the Association for Information Systems Americas Conference, Baltimore, MD, 14 – 16 August (pp. 325 - 327).

Purcell, F., & Toland, J. (2004). Electronic Commerce for the South Pacific: A Review of E-Readiness. Electronic Commerce Research, 4, 241–262. doi:10.1023/B:ELEC.0000027982.96505.c6

Qiang, C. Z., Clarke, G. R., & Halewood, N. (2006). The Role of ICT. In World Bank (Ed.), Doing Business: Information and Communications for Development—Global Trends and Policies. Washington, DC: World Bank.

Quaddus, M., & Hofmeyer, G. (2007). An investigation into the factors influencing the adoption of B2B trading exchanges in small businesses. European Journal of Information Systems, 16(3), 202–215. doi:10.1057/palgrave.ejis.3000671

Quale, M., & Christiansen, J. (2004). Business issues in the 21st century. In N. A.-. Qirim (Ed.), Electronic commerce in small to medium-sized enterprises: Frameworks, issues and implications. Hershey, PA: Idea Group Publishing.

Quayle, M. (2002). Supplier development and supply chain management in small and medium size enterprises. International Journal of Technology Management, 23(1/2/3), 172–188. doi:10.1504/IJTM.2002.003004

Quayle, M. (2002). E-commerce: The challenge for UK SMEs in the twenty-first century. International Journal of Operations & Production Management, 22(10), 1148–1161. doi:10.1108/01443570210446351

Quelch, J. (2008). How Better Marketing Elected Barack Obama. Harvard Business Publishing. Retrieved from http://blogs.harvardbusiness.org/quelch/2008/11/how_better_marketing_elected_b.html

Qureshi, S. (2005). How does Information technology effect Development? Integrating Theory and Practice into a Process Model. In Proceedings of the eleventh Americas Conference on Information Systems, Omaha, NE.

Qureshi, S., Kamal, M., & Wolcott, P. (2008). Sustainability of Information Technology Therapy on Micro-enterprise Development. HICSS.

Rajendran, R., & Vivekanandan, K. (2008). Exploring relationship between information systems strategic orientation and small business performance. International Journal of E-Business Research, 4(2), 14–28.

Ramdani, B., & Kawalek, P. (2009). Predicting SMEs' adoption of enterprise systems. Journal of Enterprise Information Management, 22(1/2), 10–24. doi:10.1108/17410390910922796

Ramsey, E., Ibbotson, P., & McCole, P. (2008). Factors that impact technology innovation adoption among irish professional service sector SMEs. International Journal of Innovation Management, 12(4), 629–654. doi:10.1142/S1363919608002114

Ranganathan, C., & Brown, C. V. (2006). ERP investments and the market value of firms: toward an understanding of influential ERP project variables. Information Systems Research, 17(2), 145–161. doi:10.1287/isre.1060.0084

Ranger-Moore, J., Banaszak-Holland, J., & Hannan, M. T. (1991). Density-dependent dynamics in regulated industries: Founding rates of banks and life insurance companies. Administrative Science Quarterly, 36(1), 36–65. doi:10.2307/2393429

Rao, S. S. (2000). Enterprise resource planning: business needs and technologies. Industrial Management & Data Systems, 100(2), 81–88. doi:10.1108/02635570010286078

Rao, S. S., Metts, G., & Monge, C. A. M. (2003). Electronic commerce development in small and medium sized enterprises: A stage model and its implications. Business Process Management Journal, 9(1), 11–32. doi:10.1108/14637150310461378

Rathnam, R. G., Johnsen, J., & Wen, H. J. (2004/2005). Alignment of business strategy and IT strategy: A case study of a fortune 50 financial service company. Journal of Computer Information Systems, 45(2), 1–8.

Ray, G., Muhanna, W. A., & Barney, J. B. (2007). Competing With IT: The Role of Shared IT-Business Understanding. Communications of the ACM, 50(12), 87–91. doi:10.1145/1323688.1323700

Raymond, L. (1985). Organizational characteristics and MIS success in the context of small business. MIS Quarterly, 9(1), 37–52. doi:10.2307/249272

Raymond, L. (1988). The Impact of Computer Training on the Attitudes and Usage Behaviour of Small Business Managers. Journal of Small Business Management, 26(3), 9–13.

Raymond, L. (1990). End-User computing in the small business context - Foundations and directions for research. Database, 20(4), 20–26.

Raymond, L. (2001). Determinants of Web Site Implementation in Small Business. Internet Research: Electronic Network Applications and Policy, 11(5), 411–422. doi:10.1108/10662240110410363

Raymond, L., & Sylvestre, U. (2007). A profile of ERP adoption in manufacturing SMEs. Journal of Enterprise Information Management, 20(4), 487–502. doi:10.1108/17410390710772731

Raymond, L., Bergeron, F., & Blili, S. (2005). The assimilation of E-business in manufacturing SMEs: determinants and effects on growth and internationalization. Electronic Markets, 15(2), 106–118. doi:10.1080/10196780500083761

Rayport, J. F., & Sviokla, J. J. (1995, November-December). Exploiting the Virtual Value Chain. Harvard Business Review, •••, 75–85.

Reich, B. H., & Benbasat, I. (2000). Factors that influence the social dimension of alignment between business and information technology objectives. MIS Quarterly, 24(1), 81–113. doi:10.2307/3250980

Reid, G., & Jacobsen, C. (1988). The Small Entrepreneurial Firm. Aberdeen, Scotland: Aberdeen University Press.

Reynolds, J., Savage, W., & Williams, A. (1994). Your own business: A practical, guide to success. ITP.

Reynolds, P. (1994). Autonomous firm dynamics and economic growth in the United States, 1986-1990. Regional Studies, 28(4), 429–442. doi:10.1080/00343409412331348376

Rha, J.-Y., Widdows, R., Hooker, N. H., & Montalto, C. P. (2002). E-consumerism as a tool for empowerment. Journal of Consumer Education, 19(20), 61–69.

Riemenschneider, C. K., & McKinney, V. R. (2001). Assessing belief differences in small business adopters and non-adopters of web-based e-commerce. Journal of Computer Information Systems, 42(2), 101–107.

Riemenschneider, C., Harrison, D., & Mykytyn, P. Jr. (2003). Understanding IT adoption decisions in small business: Integrating current theories. Information &

Management, 40, 269–285. doi:10.1016/S0378-7206-(02)00010-1

Rindova, V. P., & Kotha, S. (2001). Continuous morphing: competing through dynamic capabilities form and function. Academy of Management Journal, 44(6), 1263–1280. doi:10.2307/3069400

Ring, P., & Van de Ven, A. (1994). Developmental processes of cooperative interorganizational relationships. Academy of Management Review, 90–118. doi:10.2307/258836

Riquelme, H. (2002). Commercial internet adoption in China: Comparing the experiences of small, medium and large businesses. Internet Research: Electronic Networking Applications and Policy, 12(3), 276–286. doi:10.1108/10662240210430946

Riquelme, H. (2002). Commercial Internet Adoption in China: Comparing the experiences of small, medium and large businesses. Internet Research: Electronic Networking Applications and Policy, 12(3), 276–286. doi:10.1108/10662240210430946

Robertson, T., & Gatignon, H. (1986). Competitive Effects on Technology Diffusion. Journal of Marketing, 50(3), 1–12. doi:10.2307/1251581

Robey, D., & Azevedo, A. (1994). Cultural analysis of the organizational consequences of information technology. Accounting, Management, and Information Technologies, 4, 23–37. doi:10.1016/0959-8022(94)90011-6

Robin, D. B. (1977). Formalizing subjective notions about the effect of nonrespondents in sample surveys. Journal of the American Statistical Association, 72, 538–543. doi:10.2307/2286214

Robinson, R. B., & Pearce, J. A. (1984). Research thrusts in small firm strategic planning. Academy of Management Review, 9(1), 128–137. doi:10.2307/258239

Rogers, E. M. (1962). Diffusion of innovations. New York: The Free Press.

Rogers, E. M. (1995). Diffusion of Innovations (4th Ed.). New York: The Free Press.

Rogers, E. S., Chamberlin, J., Ellison, M. L., & Crean, T. (1997). A consumer-constructed scale to measure empowerment among users of mental health services. Psychiatric Services (Washington, D.C.), 48(8), 1041–1047.

Rosenfeld, S. (1996). Does Cooperation Enhance Competitiveness? Assessing the Impacts of Inter-firm Collaboration. Research Policy, 25(2), 247–263. doi:10.1016/0048-7333(95)00835-7

Rosner, M. (1968). Economic determinants of organizational innovation. Administrative Science Quarterly, 12, 614–625. doi:10.2307/2391536

Rotch, W. (1967). Management of small enterprises: Cases and readings. Richmond, VA: University of Virginia Press.

Rothaermel, F. T. (2001). Incumbent's advantage through exploiting complementary assets via interfirm cooperation. Strategic Management Journal, 22(6/7), 687–699. doi:10.1002/smj.180

Rothwell, R., & Dodgson, M. (1991). External linkages and innovation in small and medium-sized enterprises. R & D Management, 21(2), 125–138. doi:10.1111/j.1467-9310.1991.tb00742.x

Rowden, R. (2002). The relationship between workplace learning and job satisfaction in U.S. smal to midsize businesses. Human Resource Development Quarterly, 13(4), 407–425. doi:10.1002/hrdq.1041

Rubin, D. B. (1987). Multiple imputation for nonresponse in surveys. New York: John Wiley.

Rubin, D. B. (1996). Multiple imputation after 18+ years. Journal of the American Statistical Association, 91, 473–489. doi:10.2307/2291635

Rue, L. W., & Ibrahim, N. A. (1998). The relationship between planning sophistication and performance in small businesses. Journal of Small Business Management, 36(4), 24–32.

Runyan, R. C., & Huddleston, P. (2006). Getting customers downtown: the role of branding in achieving success for central business districts. Journal of Product and Brand Management, 15(1), 48–63. doi:10.1108/10610420610650873

Sabherwal, R., Jeyaraj, A., & Chowa, C. (2006). Information System Success: Individual and Organizational Determinants. Management Science, 52(12), 1849–1864. doi:10.1287/mnsc.1060.0583

Sadowski, B. M., Maitland, C., & van Dongen, J. (2002). Strategic use of the internet by small- and medium-sized companies: An exploratory study. Information Economics and Policy, 14(1), 75–93. doi:10.1016/S0167-6245(01)00054-3

Saeed, K. A., Grover, V., & Hwang, Y. (2005). The relationship of e-commerce to customer value and firm performance: an empirical investigation. Journal of Management Information Systems, 22(1), 223–256.

Saffu, K., Walker, J. H., & Hinson, R. (2008). Strategic value and electronic commerce adoption among small and medium-sized enterprises in a transitional economy. Journal of Business and Industrial Marketing, 23(6), 395–404. doi:10.1108/08858620810894445

Saga, V. L., & Zmud, R. W. (1994). The nature and determinants of IT acceptance, routinization and infusion. In L. Levine (Ed.), Diffusion, transfer and implementation of information technology (pp. 67-86). North Holland: Elsevier Science.

Sambamurthy, V., & Zmud, R. W. (1994). IT management competency assessment: a tool for creating business value through IT. Morristown, New Jersey: Financial Executives Research Foundation.

Sampat, B., Mowery, D., & Ziedonis, A. (2003). Changes in university patent quality after the Bayh–Dole act: a re-examination. International Journal of Industrial Organization, 21(9), 1371–1390. doi:10.1016/S0167-7187-(03)00087-0

Sanders, C. K. (2002). The impact of micro-enterprise assistance programs: A comparative study of program participants, non participants, and other low-wage workers. The Social Service Review, 76(2), 321–340. doi:10.1086/339664

Santarelli, E., & D'Altri, S. (2003). The diffusion of e-commerce among SMEs: Theoretical implications and empirical evidence. Small Business Economics, 21, 273–283. doi:10.1023/A:1025757601345

SBA. (1998). The New American Evolution: The Role and Impact of Small Firms. Small Business Research Report. Retrieved September 12, 2008, from http://www.sba.gov/advo/

SBA. (2004a). Office of Size Standards. Starting Your Business. Retrieved September 12, 2008, from http://www.sba.gov

SBA. (2004b). Small Business Resources for Faculty, Student, and Researchers. Retrieved September 12, 2008, from http://www.sba.gov/advo/

SBA. (2004c). Small Firms and Technology: Acquisitions, Inventor Movement, and Technology Transfer. Small Business Research Summary No. 233. Retrieved September 12, 2008, from http://www.sba.gov/advo/

SBA. (2004d). Top Ten Reasons to Love Small Business. Small Business Administration News Release, SBA 04-06 ADVO. Retrieved September 12, 2008, from http://www.sba.gov/advo/

Scheer, A. W., Abolhassan, F., Jost, W., & Kirchmer, M. (Eds.). (2003). Business process change management: ARIS in Practice. Berlin: Springer.

Schein, E. H. (1985). Organizational culture and leadership. San Francisco, CA: Jossey-Bass.

Schlemmer, F. (2009). The Internet as a complementary resource for SMEs: The interaction effect of strategic assets and the Internet. International journal of e-business research issue, 5(1), 1-25.

Schlemmer, F., & Webb, B. (2008). The managing director and the development of dynamic capabilities: An application of enactment theory. The International Journal of Organizational Analysis, 16(1/2), 109–137. doi:10.1108/19348830810915523

Schmid, B., Stanoevska-Slabeva, K., & Tschammer, V. (2001). Towards the E-society: E-commerce, E-business,

E-government. Amsterdam: Kluwer Academic Publishers.

Schreiner, M., & Woller, G. (2003). Micro-enterprise Development Programs in the United States and in the Developing World. World Development, 31(9), 1567–1580. doi:10.1016/S0305-750X(03)00112-8

Schroder, D., & Madeja, N. (2004). Is customer relationship management a success factor in electronic commerce? Journal of Electronic Commerce Research, 5(1), 38–52.

Schwenk, C. R., & Shrader, C. B. (1993). Effects of formal strategic planning on financial performance in small firms: A meta-analysis. Entrepreneurship Theory and Practice, 17(3), 53–64.

Scott, J. E. (2008). Technology Acceptance and ERP Documentation Usability. Communications of the ACM, 51(11), 121–124. doi:10.1145/1400214.1400239

Scott, W. R. (2001). Institutions and organizations (2nd ed.). Thousand Oaks, CA: Sage.

Scupola, A. (2003). The Adoption of Internet Commerce by SMEs in the South of Italy: An Environmental, Technological and Organizational Perspective. Journal of Global Information Technology Management, 6(1), 51–71.

Scupola, A. (2003). The adoption of Internet commerce by SMEs in the south of Italy: An environmental, technological and organizational perspective. Journal of Global Information Technology Management, 6(1), 52–71.

Scupola, A. (2008). Conceptualizing Competences in E-Services Adoption and Assimilation in SMEs. Journal of Electronic Commerce in Organizations, 6(2).

Scupola, A. (2008a). E-Services: Definition, Characteristics and Taxonomy: Guest Editorial Preface, Special on E-Services. Journal of Electronic Commerce in Organizations, 6(2).

Scupola, A. (2009). SMEs' E-commerce Adoption: Perspectives from Denmark and Australia. Journal of Enterprise Information Management, 22(1-2).

Scupola, A., & Steinfield, C. (2008). The role of a network organization and Internet-based technologies in clusters-The Case of Medicon Valley. In L. Fuglsang (Ed.), Innovation and the Creative Process. Cheltenham, UK: Edward Elgar.

Senn, J. A., & Gibson, V. R. (1981). Risks of investment in microcomputers for small business management. Journal of Small Business Management, 19(3), 24–32.

Servais, P., Madsen, T. K., & Rasmussen, E. S. (2007). Small manufacturing firms' involvement in international e-business activities. Advances in International Marketing(17), 297-317.

Servon, L. J., & Doshna, J. P. (2000). Microenterprise and the economic development toolkit: A small part of the big picture. Journal of Developmental Entrepreneurship, 5(3), 183.

Sethi, V., & King, W. R. (1994, December). Development of Measures to Assess the Extent to Which an Information Technology Application Provides Competitive Advantage. Management Science, 40(12). doi:10.1287/mnsc.40.12.1601

Sharif, N. (1994). Technology change management: Imperatives for developing economies. Technological Forecasting and Social Change, 47, 103–114. doi:10.1016/0040-1625(94)90043-4

Sharma, M. K. (2009). Receptivity of india's small and medium-sized enterprises to information system adoption. Enterprise Information Systems, 3(1), 95–115. doi:10.1080/17517570802317901

Shepherd, D. A., & Zacharakis, A. (2003). A new venture's cognitive legitimacy: An assessment by customers. Journal of Small Business Management, 41(2), 148–167. doi:10.1111/1540-627X.00073

Sher, P. J., & Lee, V. C. (2004). Information technology as a facilitator for enhancing dynamic capabilities through knowledge management. Information & Management, 41(8), 933–945. doi:10.1016/j.im.2003.06.004

Shi, Z., Kunnathur, A. S., & Ragu-Nathan, T. S. (2005). IS outsourcing management competence dimensions:

instrument development and relationship exploration. Information & Management, 42(6), 901–919. doi:10.1016/j.im.2004.10.001

Siddharthan, N. (1992). Transaction costs, technological transfer and in-house R&D: A study of the Indian private corporate sector. Journal of Economic Behavior & Organization, 18, 265–271. doi:10.1016/0167-2681-(92)90031-6

Simon, H. A. (1957). Administrative Behavior. New York: Free Press.

Singh, J. V. (1986). Performance, slack, and risk taking in organizational decision making. Academy of Management Journal, 29(3), 562–585. doi:10.2307/256224

Singh, J. V., Tucker, D. J., & House, R. J. (1986). Organizational legitimacy and the liability of newness. Administrative Science Quarterly, 31(2), 171–193. doi:10.2307/2392787

Singh, J. V., Tucker, D., & Meinhard, A. G. (1991). Institutional change and ecological dynamics. In W.W. Powell & P.J. DiMaggio (Eds.), The new institutionalism in organizational analysis (pp. 390-422). Chicago, IL: University of Chicago Press.

Small Business Administration. (2003). Small Serial innovators: The small firm contribution to technical change. Small Business Research Summary, #225. Washington, DC. Retrieved from www.sba.gov/advo/

Small Business Administration. (2006). The Small Business Economy: For Data Year 2005. Washington, D.C.: www.sba.gov/advo/.

Smith, K. G., Guthrie, J. P., & Chen, M.-J. (1989). Strategy, size and performance. Organization Studies, 10(1), 63–81. doi:10.1177/017084068901000104

Snyder, M., & Stukas, A. (1999). Interpersonal processes: The interplay of cognitive, motivational and behavioral activities in social interaction. Annual Review of Psychology, 50, 273–303. doi:10.1146/annurev.psych.50.1.273

Soh, C., Mah, Q. Y., Gan, F. Y., Chew, D., & Reid, E. (1997). The use of the Internet for business: The experience of early adopters in Singapore. *Internet Research, 7*(3), 217–228. doi:10.1108/10662249710171869

Song, M., Droge, C., Hanvanich, S., & Calantone, R. (2005). Marketing and technology resource complementarity: An analysis of their interaction effect in two environmental contexts. *Strategic Management Journal, 26*(3), 259–276. doi:10.1002/smj.450

Soo, C. W., Devinney, T. M., & Midgley, D. F. (2007). External knowledge acquisition, creativity and learning in organisational problem solving. *International Journal of Technology Management, 38*(1/2), 137–159. doi:10.1504/IJTM.2007.012433

Southwood, R. (2004). ICTs and Small Enterprise: A Motor of Economic Development in Africa. *IICD Research Briefs, 9*. The Hague: IICD.

Spanos, Y. E., & Voudouris, I. (2009). Antecedents and trajectories of AMT adoption: The case of greek manufacturing SMEs. *Research Policy, 38*(1), 144–155. doi:10.1016/j.respol.2008.09.006

Spector, A. (1961). Basic dimensions of the corporate image. *Journal of Marketing*, 47–51. doi:10.2307/1248513

Speyer, M., Pohlmann, T., & Brown, K. (2006). IT spending in the SMB sector. Cambridge, MA: Forrester Research.

Starr, J. A., & MacMillan, I. C. (1990). Resource co-optation via social contracting: Resource acquisition strategies for new ventures. *Strategic Management Journal, 11*, 79–92. doi:10.1002/smj.4250110107

Steinfield, C., & Scupola, A. (2008). Understanding the Role of ICT Networks in a Biotechnology Cluster: An Exploratory Study of Medicon Valley. *The Information Society, 24*(5), 319–333. doi:10.1080/01972240802356091

Steinfield, C., Scupola, A., & Lopez-Nicolas, C. (2009). Social Capital, ICT Use and Company Performance: Findings from the Medicon Valley Biotech Cluster. In *Proceedings of the International Conference on Organizational Learning, Knowledge and Capabilities (OLKC), Amsterdam, The Netherlands, April 26-28, 2009*.

Stelzner, M. (2009). How marketers are using social Media to grow their business. *Social Media Marketing Industry Report*. Retrieved from http://www.Whitepapersource.com

Stevenson, M. K., Busemeyer, J. R., & Naylor, J. C. (1990). Judgment and decision-making theory. In M.D. Dunnette & L.M. Hough (Eds.) *Handbook of industrial and organizational psychology* (Vol. 1, pp. 283-374). Palo Alto, CA: Consulting Psychologists Press.

Stewart, D. W., & Shamdasani, P. N. (1990). *Focus groups: Theory and practice*. Newbury Park, CA: Sage.

Stinchcombe, A. (1968). *Constructing social theories*. New York: Harcourt Brace.

Stinchcombe, A. L. (1965). Social structure and organizations. In J. G. March (Ed.), *Handbook of organizations* (pp. 142-193). Chicago: Rand McNally & Company.

Stockdale, R., & Standing, C. (2004). Benefits and barriers of electronic marketplace participation: an SME perspective. *Journal of Enterprise Information Management, 17*(4), 301–311. doi:10.1108/17410390410548715

Stokes, D. (1997). *Pasteur's quadrant: Basic science and technological innovation*: Washington, DC: Brookings Institution Press.

Stoneburner, G., Feringa, A., & Goguen, A. (2002). *Risk management guide for information technology systems*. Washington, DC: US Gov. Print. Off.

Storey, D. (1998). *Understanding the small business sector*. Stamford, CT: International Thomson Business Press.

Storey, D. (2004). Exploring the link, among small firms, between management training and firm performance: a comparison between the UK and other OECD countries. *International Journal of Human Resource Management, 15*(1), 112–130. doi:10.1080/0958519032000157375

Stotey, D. (1994). *Understanding the Small Business Sector*. New York: Routledge.

St-Pierre, J., & Raymond, L. (2004). Short-term effects of benchmarking on the manufacturing practices and performance of SMEs. International Journal of Productivity and Performance Management, 53(8), 681–699. doi:10.1108/17410400410569107

Strauss, A. L., & Corbin, J. (1998). Basics of qualitative research: Technique and procedure for developing grounded theory. Thousand Oaks, CA: Sage.

Street, C. T., & Meister, D. B. (2004). Small Business Growth And Internal Transparency: The Role Of Information Systems. MIS Quarterly, 28(3), 473–506.

Street, C. T., & Meister, D. B. (2004, September). Small business growth and internal transparency: The role of information systems. MIS Quarterly, 28(3), 473–506.

Stuart, T. E. (2000). Interorganizational alliances and the performance of firms: A study of growth and innovation rates in a high-technology industry. Strategic Management Journal, 21(8), 791–811. doi:10.1002/1097-0266-(200008)21:8<791::AID-SMJ121>3.0.CO;2-K

Su, C., Chen, Y., & Sha, D. Y. (2007). Managing product and customer knowledge in innovative new product development. International Journal of Technology Management, 39(1/2), 105–130. doi:10.1504/IJTM.2007.013443

Suchman, M. C. (1995). Managing legitimacy: Strategic and institutional approaches. Academy of Management Review, 20(3), 571–610. doi:10.2307/258788

Sudzina, F. (2007). Importance of EPR selection criteria in Slovak companies. Manažment v teórii a praxi, 3(4), 4-20.

Sulčič, V. (2008). E-poslovanje v Slovenskih malih in srednje velikih podjetjih. Management, 3(3), 347–361.

Sullivan, B. C. (1985). Economics of Information Technology. International Journal of Social Economics, 12(1), 37. doi:10.1108/eb013983

SURS – Statistični urad RS. (2007). Uporaba informacijsko-komunikacijske tehnologije v podjetjih z 10 in več zaposlenimi osebami. 1. Četrtletje 2007. Retrieved February 17, 2008, from http://www.stat.si/novica_prikazi.aspx?id=1284

Swaine, M. (2007). Web 2.0 and the engineering of trust. Dr. Dobb's Journal, 32(1), 16–18.

Swanson, E. B. (1994). Information systems innovation among organizations. Management Science, 40(9), 1069–1092. doi:10.1287/mnsc.40.9.1069

Swanson, E. B., & Ramiller, N. C. (1997). The organizing vision in information systems innovation. Organization Science, 8(5), 458–474. doi:10.1287/orsc.8.5.458

Swisher, P. S. (2007). The managed web: A look at the impact of Web 2.0 on media asset management for the enterprise. Journal of Digital Asset Management, 3(1), 32–42. doi:10.1057/palgrave.dam.3650061

Tan, J., & Peng, M. W. (2003). Organizational slack and firm performance during economic transitions: Two studies from an emerging economy. Strategic Management Journal, 24(13), 1249–1263. doi:10.1002/smj.351

Tan, J., Tyler, K., & Manica, A. (2007). Business-to-Business Adoption of eCommerce in China. Information & Management, 44, 332–351. doi:10.1016/j.im.2007.04.001

Tan, M. (1998). Creating the digital economy: perspectives from Singapore, Electronic Commerce in the Information Society. In Proceedings from the 11th International Bled Electronic Commerce Conference, Bled, Slovenia, June 8 – 10.

Tan, M., & Teo, T. S. H. (2000). Factors Influencing the Adoption of Internet Banking. Journal of the AIS, 1(5), 1–42.

Tanner, C., Wölfle, R., Schubert, R., & Quade, M.. Current Trends and Challenges in Electronic Procurement: An Empirical Study. Electronic Markets, 18(1), 16–18.

Tanriverdi, H., & Venkatraman, N. (2005). Knowledge relatedness and the performance of multibusiness firms. Strategic Management Journal, 26(2), 97–119. doi:10.1002/smj.435

Taylor, M., & Murphy, A. (2004). SMEs and e-business. Journal of Small Business and Enterprise Development, 11(3), 280–289. doi:10.1108/14626000410551546

Te'eni, D., & Kendall, J. E. (2004). Internet commerce and fundraising. In D.R. Young (Ed.), Effective economic decision-making by nonprofit organizations (pp. 167-189). New York, NY: The Foundation Center. U.S. Small Business Administration. (n.d.). Retrieved March 31, 2009, from http://web.sba.gov/faqs/faqIndexAll.cfm?areaid=15

Teece, D. J. (1986). Profiting from technological innovation: Implications for integration, collaboration, licensing and public policy. Research Policy, 15(6), 285–305. doi:10.1016/0048-7333(86)90027-2

Teece, D. J., Pisano, G., & Shuen, A. (1997). Dynamic capabilities and strategic management. Strategic Management Journal, 18(7), 509–533. doi:10.1002/(SICI)1097-0266(199708)18:7<509::AID-SMJ882>3.0.CO;2-Z

Templerley, N. C., Galloway, J., & Liston, J. (2004). SMEs in Australia's Higher technology Sector: Challenges and Opportunities. AEEMA.

Teo, T. S. H., & Choo, W. Y. (2001). Assessing the impact of using the internet for competitive intelligence. Information & Management, 39(1), 67–83. doi:10.1016/S0378-7206(01)00080-5

Tetteh, E., & Burn, J. (2001). Global Strategies for SME-business: Applying the SMALL Framework. Logistics Information Management, 14(1/2), 171–180. doi:10.1108/09576050110363202

Teubner, R. A. (2007). Strategic information systems planning: A case study from the financial services industry. The Journal of Strategic Information Systems, 16, 105–125. doi:10.1016/j.jsis.2007.01.002

Teubner, R. A., & Mocker, M. (2005). Strategic information planning – Insights from an action research project in the financial services industry. Working Paper No. 3, ECRIS - European Center for Information Systems.

Theyel, G., Merenda, M., & Venkatachalam, A. R. (2001 October). How small and medium size manufacturers use the internet for technology development. Journal of Business and Entrepreneurship, 83-106.

Thomas, A. R. (2007). The end of mass Marketing: or, why all successful Marketing is now direct Marketing. Direct Marketing: An International Journal, 1(1), 6–16. doi:10.1108/17505930710734107

Thompson, S., & Brown, D. (2008). Change Agents Intervention in E-business Adoption by SMEs: Evidence from a Developing Country. AMCIS 2008 Proceedings, 1-7.

Thong, J. (2001). Resource constraints and information systems implementation in Singaporean small businesses. OMEGA International Journal of Management Science, 29, 143–156. doi:10.1016/S0305-0483(00)00035-9

Thong, J. Y. L. (1999). An integrated model of information systems adoption in small businesses. Journal of Management Information Systems, 15(4), 187–214.

Thong, J. Y. L. (2001). Resource constraints and information systems implementation in Singaporean small business. Omega, 29(2), 143–156. doi:10.1016/S0305-0483(00)00035-9

Thong, J. Y. L., Yap, C., & Raman, K. S. (1996). Top management support, external expertise and information systems implementation in small business. Information Systems Research, 7(2), 248–267. doi:10.1287/isre.7.2.248

Thong, J., Yap, C., & Rahman, K. (1996). Top management support, external expertise and information systems implementation in small businesses. Information Systems Research, 7(2), 248–267. doi:10.1287/isre.7.2.248

Throp, J. (1998). The information paradox: Realizing the business benefits of information technology. Toronto: McGraw-Hill Ryerson.

Thursby, J., Jensen, R., & Thursby, M. (2001). Objectives, characteristics and outcomes of university licensing: A survey of major US universities. The Journal of Technology Transfer, 26(1/2), 59–72. doi:10.1023/A:1007884111883

Timmers, P. (1999). Electronic commerce: strategies and models for business-to-business trading. West Sussex, UK: John Wiley & Sons Ltd.

Timmons, J. (1999). New venture creation: Entrepreneurship for the 21st century. Boston, MA: Irwin McGraw-Hill.

Tippins, M. J., & Sohi, R. (2003). IT competency and firm performance: Is organizational learning the missing link? Strategic Management Journal, 24(8), 745–761. doi:10.1002/smj.337

Tornatzky, L. G., & Fleischer, M. (1990). The Processes of Technological Innovation, Lexington, MA: Lexington Books.

Tornatzky, L., & Klein, K. (1982). Innovation characteristics and innovation adoption-implementation: A meta analysis of findings. IEEE Transactions on Engineering Management, 29(11), 28–45.

Tozer, E. E. (1996). Strategic IS/IT Planning. Boston, MA: Butterworth-Heinemann.

Troshani, I., & Rao, S. (2007). Enabling e-business competitive advantage: perspectives from the Australian Financial Services Industry. International Journal of Business and Information, 2(1), 80–103.

Truex, D. P., Baskerville, R., & Klein, H. (1999). Growing systems in emergent organizations. Communications of the ACM, 42(8), 117–123. doi:10.1145/310930.310984

Tse, T., & Soufani, K. (2003). Business strategies for small firms in the new economy. Journal of Small Business and Enterprise Development, 10, 306–320. doi:10.1108/14626000310489781

Tsikriktsis, N., Lanzolla, G., & Frohlich, M. (2004). Adoption of e-processes by service firms: An empirical study of antecedents. Production and Operations Management, 13(3), 216–229.

Tsui, F. F., & Karam, O. (2006). Essentials of software engineering. Sudbury, MA: Jones & Bartlett Publishers.

Tucker, D., & Lafferty, A. (2004). Implementing Electronic Commerce in SMEs: Processes and Barriers. Journal of Electronic Commerce in Organizations, 2(4), 20–29.

Tung, L., & Rieck, O. (2005). Adoption of electronic government services among business organizations in Singapore. The Journal of Strategic Information Systems, 14, 417–440. doi:10.1016/j.jsis.2005.06.001

Turk, D., France, R., & Bernhard Rumpe, B. (2005). Assumptions underlying agile software-development processes. Journal of Database Management, 16(4), 62–87.

Tushman, M., & O'Reilly, C. (2007). Research and relevance: implications of Pasteur's quadrant for doctoral programs and faculty development. [AMJ]. Academy of Management Journal, 50(4), 769–774.

Tuunainen, V. K. (1998). Opportunities of Effective Integration of EDI for Small Businesses in the Automotive Industry. Information & Management, 34(6), 361–375. doi:10.1016/S0378-7206(98)00070-6

Ueda, K., Takenaka, T., & Fujita, K. (2008). Toward value co-creation in manufacturing and servicing. CIRP Journal of Manufacturing Science and Technology, 1, 53–58. doi:10.1016/j.cirpj.2008.06.007

Umble, E. J., Haft, R. R., & Umble, M. M. (2003). Enterprise resource planning: implementation procedures and critical success factors. European Journal of Operational Research, 146(2), 241–257. doi:10.1016/S0377-2217(02)00547-7

United States Department of Education. (2004). National household education surveys of successful small manufacturing and processing companies: National Center for Educations Statistics.

Urata, S. (2000). Outline of Tentative Policy Recommendation for SME Promotion in Indonesia. JICA. Retrieved November 2003, from http://www.jica.or.id/FOCI_urata.html

Urban, G. (2005). Don't Just Relate - Advocate!: A Blueprint for Profit in the Era of Customer Power. Philadelphia, PA: Wharton School Publishing.

Van Akkeren, J., & Cavaye, A. L. M. (1999). Factors Affecting Entry-Level Internet Technology Adoption by Small Business in Australia: An Empirical Study.

In Proceedings of Proceedings of the 10th Australasian Conference on Information Systems, 1-3 December. Wellington, New Zealand.

Van Auken, H. (2005). Differences in the usage of bootstrap financing among technology-based versus nontechnology-based firms. Journal of Small Business Management, 43(1), 93–103. doi:10.1111/j.1540-627-X.2004.00127.x

Van Beveren, J. V., & Thomson, H. (2002). The use of electronic commerce by SMEs in Victoria, Australia. Journal of Small Business Management, 40(3), 250–253. doi:10.1111/1540-627X.00054

Van de Ven, A. H. (2007). Engaged scholarship: a guide for organizational and social research. Oxford, UK: Oxford University Press.

Van De Ven, A. H., & Johnson, P. E. (2006). Nice Try, Bill, But... There You Go Again. Academy of Management Review, 31(4), 830–832.

van den Hoonaard, W. C. (1997). Working with sensitizing concepts: Analytical field research. Thousand Oaks, CA: Sage.

van der Veen, M. (2004). Explaining E-Business adoption, Innovation and Entrepreneurship in Dutch SMEs. Doctoral Thesis, University of Twente.

Van Everdingen, Y., van Hillegersberg, J., & Waarts, E. (2000). ERP adoption by European mid-size companies. Communications of the ACM, 43(4), 27–31. doi:10.1145/332051.332064

van Grembergen, W., De Haes, S., & Guldentops, E. (2004). Structures, processes and relational mechanisms for IT governance. In W. van Grembergen (Ed.), Strategies for Information Technology Governance. Hershey, PA: Idea Group Publishing.

van Riel, C. B. M. (1997). Research in corporate communications: An overview of an emerging field. Management Communication Quarterly, 11(2), 288–309. doi:10.1177/0893318997112005

Varadarajan, R., & Yadav, M. (2002). Marketing Strategy and the Internet: An Organizing Framework. Journal of the Academy of Marketing Science, 30(4), 296–312. doi:10.1177/009207002236907

Venkatesan, V. S., & Fink, D. (2002). Adoption of Internet Technologies and E-Commerce by Small and Medium Enterprises (SMEs) in Western Australia. In Proceedings of the Information Resource Management Association International Conference (pp. 1136-1137).

Venkatesh, V., Morris, M. G., Davis, G. B., & Davis, F. D. (2003). User acceptance of information technology: Toward a unified view. MIS Quarterly, 27(3), 425–478.

Verdu-Jover, A., Llorens-Montes, F. J., & Garcia-Morales, V. J. (2006). Environment-flexibility coalignment and performance: An analysis in large versus small firms. Journal of Small Business Management, 44(3), 334–349. doi:10.1111/j.1540-627X.2006.00175.x

Verhees, F. J. H. M., & Meulenberg, M. T. G. (2004). Market orientation, innovativeness, product innovation, and performance in small firms. Journal of Small Business Management, 42(2), 134–154. doi:10.1111/j.1540-627X.2004.00102.x

Verville, J., & Halingten, A. (2003). A six-stage model of the buying process for ERP software. Industrial Marketing Management, 32(7), 585–594. doi:10.1016/S0019-8501(03)00007-5

Vesper, K. H. (1996). New venture experience. Seattle, WA: Vector Books.

Viagas, R. (1998). How To Tell Broadway from Off-Broadway. Retrieved July 31, 2009, from http://www.playbill.com/features/article/76751-How_To_Tell_Broadway_from_Off-Broadway_from_._._.

Vijayasarathy, L. R., & Turk, D. (2008). Agile software development: A survey of early adopters. Journal of Information Technology Management, 19, 1–8.

Volz, J. (2004). How to run a theater. New York: Back Stage Books.

von Hippel, E. (2004). Democratizing innovation: the evolving phenomenon of user innovation. Journal für Betriebswirtschaft, 55(1), 63–78. doi:10.1007/s11301-004-0002-8 von Hippel, E. (2005). Democritizing innovation. Cambridge, MA: MIT Press.

Voordeckers, W., & Gils, A.V., & Heuvel, Jeron Van Den. (2007). Board Composition in small and medium-sized family firms. Journal of Small Business Management, 45(1), 137–157. doi:10.1111/j.1540-627X.2007.00204.x

Wade, M., & Hulland, J. (2004). Review: The resource-based view and information systems research: Review, extension, and suggestions for future research. MIS Quarterly, 28(1), 107–142.

Wagner, B. A., Fillis, I., & Johansson, U. (2003). E-business and e-supply strategy in small and medium sized businesses (SMEs). Supply Chain Management, 8(4), 343–354. doi:10.1108/13598540310490107

Wainwright, D., Green, G., Mitchell, E., & Yarrow, D. (2005). Towards a framework for benchmarking ICT practice, competence and performance in small firms. Performance Measurement and Metrics, 6(1), 39–52. doi:10.1108/14678040510588580

Walczuch, R., Van Braven, G., & Lundgren, H. (2000). Internet adoption barriers for small firms in the Netherlands. European Management Journal, 18(5), 561–572. doi:10.1016/S0263-2373(00)00045-1

Walker, E. W. (1975). Investment and Capital Structure Decision Making in Small Business. In E.W. Walker (Ed.), The Dynamic Small Firm: Selected Readings. Austin, TX: Austin Press.

Walton, R. (1989). Up and Running: Integrating Information Technology and the Organization. Boston, MA: Harvard Business School Press.

Wang, S., & Cheung, W. (2004). E-business adoption by travel agencies: Prime candidates for mobile e-business. International Journal of Electronic Commerce, 8(3), 43–63.

Ward, J., & Peppard, J. (2002). Strategic planning for information systems. West Sussex, UK: John Wiley & Sons.

Warren, A., Hanke, R., & Trotzer, D. (2008). Models for university technology transfer: resolving conflicts between mission and methods and the dependency on geographic location. Cambridge Journal of Regions. Economy and Society, 1(2), 219.

Warren, M. (2004). Farmers online: drivers and impediments in adoption of Internet in UK agricultural businesses. Journal of Small Business and Enterprise Development, 11(3), 371–381. doi:10.1108/14626000410551627

Webb, B., & Sayer, R. (1998). Benchmarking small companies on the Internet. Long Range Planning, 31(6), 815–827. doi:10.1016/S0024-6301(98)80018-6

Webb, D. M. (2004). Running theaters: Best practices for leaders and managers. New York: Allworth Press.

Wei, C. C., Chien, C. F., & Wang, M. J. J. (2005). An AHP-based approach to ERP system selection. International Journal of Production Economics, 96(1), 47–62. doi:10.1016/j.ijpe.2004.03.004

Weick, K. E. (1983). Managerial thought in the context of action. In S. Srivasta & Associates (Eds.), The executive mind (pp. 221-242). San Francisco, CA: Jossey-Bass.

Welsh, J. A., & White, J. F. (1981). A small business is not a little big business. Harvard Business Review, 59(4), 18–32.

Wernerfelt, B. (1984). A resource-based view of the firm. Strategic Management Journal, 5(2), 171–180. doi:10.1002/smj.4250050207

Westhead, P., & Storey, D. (1996). Management Training and Small Firm Performance: Why is the Link so Weak? International Small Business Journal, 14(4), 13–25. doi:10.1177/0266242696144001

Westhead, P., & Storey, D. (1997). Training Provision and the Development of Small and Medium-sized Enterprises. London: Dfee.

Wheelwright, S. C. (1984). Strategy, Management, and Strategic planning approaches. Interfaces, 14(1), 19–33. doi:10.1287/inte.14.1.19

Whiteley, D. (2000). E-Commerce - Strategy, Technologies and Applications. Berkshire, UK: McGraw-Hill Publishing Company.

Whitley, R. (1992). The Customer Driven Company. Reading, MA: Addison-Wesley.

Wier, B., & Hunton, J., & HassabElnaby, H. R. (2007). Enterprise resource planning systems and non-financial performance incentives: The joint impact on corporate performance. International Journal of Accounting Information Systems, 8(3), 165–190. doi:10.1016/j.accinf.2007.05.001

Wiewel, W., & Hunter, A. (1985). The interorganizational network as a resource: A comparative case study on organizational genesis. Administrative Science Quarterly, 30(4), 482–499. doi:10.2307/2392693

Wigand, R. T., Steinfeld, C. W., & Markus, M. L. (2005). Information Technology Standards Choices and Industry Structure Outcomes: The Case of the U.S. Home Mortgage Industry. Journal of Management Information Systems, 22(2), 165–191.

Will, M. (2008). Talking about the future within an SME? Corporate foresight and the potential contributions to sustainable development. Management of Environmental Quality, 19(2), 234–242. doi:10.1108/14777830810856618

Wilson, A. N. (2007, June 8). The Internet is destroying the world as we know it. Daily Mail Online.

Winborg, J., & Landstrom, H. (2001). Financial bootstrapping in small businesses: Examining small business managers' resource acquisition behaviors. Journal of Business Venturing, 16, 235–254. doi:10.1016/S0883-9026(99)00055-5

Wind, J., & Mahajan, V. (2001). The Challenge of Digital Marketing. In J. Wind & V. Mahajan (Eds.), Digital Marketing: Global Strategies from the world's leading experts (pp. 3-25). New York: John Wiley & Sons.

Winston, E. R., & Dologite, D. (2002). How does attitude impact IT implementation: A study of small business owners. Journal of End User Computing, 14(2), 16–29.

Winter, S. G. (1987). Knowledge and competence as strategic assets. In D. Teece (Ed.), The Competitive Challenge (pp. 159-184). Berkeley, CA: Center for Research in Management

Winter, S. G., Gaglio, C. M., & Rajagopalan, H. K. (2009). The Value of Information Systems to Small and Medium-Sized Enterprises: Information and Communications Technologies as Signal and Symbol of Legitimacy and Competitiveness. International Journal of E-Business Research, 5(1), 65–91.

Winter, S. J. (1996). The symbolic value of computers: Expanding analyses of organizational computing. In J.W. Beard (Ed.), Impression management and information technology (pp. 21-38). Westport, CT: Quorum Books.

Wiseman, C. (1988). Strategic Information Systems. Homewood, IL: Irwin.

Wiseman, R. M., & Bromiley, P. (1996). Toward a model of risk in declining organizations: An empirical examination of risk, performance and decline. Organization Science, 7(5), 524–543. doi:10.1287/orsc.7.5.524

Wolcott, P., Qureshi, S., & Kamal, M. (2007). An Information Technology Therapy Approach to Micro-enterprise Adoption of ICTs. In Americas Conference on Information Systems (AMCIS).

Wolff, J. A., & Pett, T. L. (2006). Small-Firm Performance: Modelling the Role of Product and Process Improvements. Journal of Small Business Management, 44(2), 268–284. doi:10.1111/j.1540-627X.2006.00167.x

Wong, K. Y., & Aspinwall, E. (2005). An empirical study of the important factors for knowledge-management adoption in the SME sector. Journal of Knowledge Management, 9(3), 64–82. doi:10.1108/13673270510602773

Wong, S., & Chin, K. (2007). Organizational innovation management: An organization-wide perspective. Industrial Management & Data Systems, 107(9), 1290–1315. doi:10.1108/02635570710833974

Wood, C. H., Kaufman, A., & Merenda, M. (1996). How Hadco became a problem solving supplier. Sloan Management Review, 37(2), 77–88.

Woolgar, S., Vaux, J., Gomes, P., Ezingeard, J., & Grieve, R. (1998). Abilities and competencies required, particularly by small firms, to identify and acquire new technology. Technovation, 18(8-9), 575–592. doi:10.1016/S0166-4972(98)00049-2

World Bank Group. (2006). Country groups. Retrieved March 2006 from http://web.worldbank.org/

Woznica, J., & Healy, K. (2009). The level of information systems integration in SMEs in Irish manufacturing sector. Journal of Small Business and Enterprise Development, 16(1), 115–130. doi:10.1108/14626000910932917

Wu, S., Lin, L., & Hsu, M. (2007). Intellectual capital, dynamic capabilities and innovative performance of organisations. International Journal of Technology Management, 39(3/4), 279–296. doi:10.1504/IJTM.2007.013496

Wymer, S., & Regan, E. (2005). Factors influencing e-commerce adoption and use by small and medium businesses. Electronic Markets, 15(4), 438–453. doi:10.1080/10196780500303151

Wynn, M. (2009). Information systems strategy development and implementation in SMEs. Management Research News, 32(1), 78–90. doi:10.1108/01409170910922041

O'Reilly, T. (2005). What is Web 2.0? Retrieved from http://www.oreillynet.com/pub/a/oreilly/tim/news/2005/09/30/what-is-web-20.html

Xu, M., Rohatgi, R., & Duan, Y. (2007). E-business adoption in SMEs: Some preliminary findings from electronic components industry. International Journal of E-Business Research, 3(1), 74–90.

Xu, S., Zhu, K., & Gibbs, J. (2004). Global technology, local adoption: A cross-country investigation of internet adoption by companies in the United States and China. Electronic Markets, 14(1), 13–24. doi:10.1080/1019678042000175261

Yakel, E. (2006). Inviting the user into the virtual archives. OCLC Systems & Services, 22(3), 159–163. doi:10.1108/10650750610686207

Yang, K. H., Lee, S. M., & Lee, S. (2007). Adoption of information and communication technology: Impact of technology types, organization resources and management style. Industrial Management & Data Systems, 107(9), 1257–1275. doi:10.1108/02635570710833956

Yap, C. (1989). Computerization problems facing small and medium enterprises: the experience of Singapore. In Proceedings of the 20th Annual Meeting of the Midwest Decision Sciences Institute, Miami University, Oxford, OH (pp. 19-21, 128-134).

Yeoh, P., & Roth, K. (1999). An empirical analysis of sustained advantage in the U.S. pharmaceutical industry: Impact of firm resources and capabilities. Strategic Management Journal, 20(7), 637–653. doi:10.1002/(SICI)1097-0266(199907)20:7<637::AID-SMJ42>3.0.CO;2-Z

Yeung, J. H. Y., Shim, J. P., & Lai, A. Y. K. (2003). Current progress of e-commerce adoption: Small and medium enterprises in Hong Kong. Communications of the ACM, 46(9), 226–232. doi:10.1145/903893.903941

Yin, R. K. (1989). Case study research: Design and methods. Newbury Park, CA: SAGE Publications, Inc.

Yin, R. K. (1994). Case Study Research - Design and Methods (2nd Ed.). Thousand Oaks, CA: Sage Publications. Retrieved from http://www.abs.gov.au

Young, G. O., et al. (2009, January 6). Can enterprise Web 2.0 survive the recession? Forrester.

Zhang, X., & Chen, R. (2008). Examining the mechanism of the value co-creation with customers. International Journal of Production Economics, 116, 242–250. doi:10.1016/j.ijpe.2008.09.004

Zhou, K., Yim, C. K., & Tse, D. K. (2005). The effects of strategic orientations on technology- and market-based breakthrough innovations. Journal of Marketing, 69(2), 42–60. doi:10.1509/jmkg.69.2.42.60756

Zhu, K. (2004). The complementarity of information technology infrastructure and e-Commerce capability: A resource-based assessment of their business value. Journal of Management Information Systems, 21(1), 167–202.

Zhu, K., & Kraemer, K. L. (2002). e-commerce metrics for Net-enhanced organizations: Assessing the value of e-commerce to firm-performance in the manufacturing sector. Information Systems Research, 13(3), 275–295. doi:10.1287/isre.13.3.275.82

Zhu, K., Kraemer, K. L., & Xu, S. (2002). A cross-country study of electronic business adoption using the Technology-Organization-Environment Framework, Twenty Third International Conference on Information Systems, 2002, pp337-348.

Zhu, K., Kraemer, K. L., Xu, S., & Dedrick, J. (2004). Information technology payoff in e-business environments: An international perspective on value creation of e-business in the financial services industry. Journal of Management Information Systems, 21(1), 17–54.

Zhu, K., Kraemer, K., & Xu, S. (2003). E-Business adoption by European firms: A cross-country assessment of the facilitators and inhibitors. European Journal of Information Systems, 12(4), 251–268. doi:10.1057/palgrave.ejis.3000475

Zhuang, Y., & Lederer, A. L. (2003). An instrument for measuring the business benefits of e-commerce retailing. International Journal of Electronic Commerce, 7(3), 65–99.

Zimmerman, M. A. (1997). New venture legitimacy—A review. Paper presented at the annual meeting of the Academy of Management, Boston, MA.

Zimmerman, M. A., & Zeitz, G. J. (2002). Beyond survival: Achieving new venture growth by building legitimacy. Academy of Management Review, 27(3), 414–431. doi:10.2307/4134387

Zinatelli, N., Cragg, P. B., & Cavaye, A. L. M. (1996). End user computing sophistication and success in small firms. European Journal of Information Systems, 5(3), 172–181. doi:10.1057/ejis.1996.23

Zolkos, R. (2005). Striking a balance between business and IT. Business Insurance, 7, 20–21.

Zuber-Skerrit, O. (1991). Action Research for Change and Development. Aldershot, UK: Gower Publishing.

Zwass, V. (1996). Electronic Commerce: Structures and Issues. International Journal of Electronic Commerce, 1(1), 3–23.

Zwass, V. (2003). Electronic commerce and organizational innovation: Aspects and opportunities. International Journal of Electronic Commerce, 7(3), 7–37.

About the Contributors

Pratyush Bharati is an Associate Professor in the Management Science and Information Systems department of College of Management at the University of Massachusetts. He received his Ph. D. from Rensselaer. His present research interests are in: diffusion of information technologies in small and medium sized enterprises (SMEs), international software services industry, web-based decision support systems and service quality. His research has been published or is forthcoming in several international journals including Communications of the ACM, Decision Support Systems, IEEE Computer and IT and People.

In Lee is a professor in the Department of Information Management and Decision Sciences in the College of Business and Technology at Western Illinois University. He received his MBA from the University of Texas at Austin and Ph.D. from University of Illinois at Urbana-Champaign. He is a founding editor-in-chief of the International Journal of E-Business Research. He has published his research in such journals as *Communications of the ACM, IEEE Transactions on Systems, Man, and Cybernetics, IEEE Transactions on Engineering Management, International Journal of Production Research, Computers and Education, Computers and Operations Research, Computers and Industrial Engineering, Business Process Management Journal, Journal of E-Commerce in Organizations, International Journal of Simulation and Process Modeling,* and others. His current research interests include e-commerce technology development and management, investment strategies for computing technologies, and intelligent simulation systems.

Professor Abhijit Chaudhury has a bachelors and masters degree in engineering. He obtained in PhD is Management from Purdue University. He has over a decade of industrial experience in oil and energy sector working for European Multinationals such as BP and CFP. He has previously published in MISQ, ISR, JMIS, CACM and various transactions of IEEE. His current interest is in the area of SMEs and Global Competition.

* * *

Jocelyn Armarego worked for 10 years in industry before joining the academic staff of first Curtin and then Murdoch Universities. This chapter reflects her interests in the management of software development methodologies within an organisational context, in particular non-traditional methodologies, including formal methods, and agile methodologies. She has been involved in several projects that address the alignment of industry perspectives of ICT with formal education.

Alan A. Brandyberry is an associate professor of information systems at Kent State University. His research interests include the adoption, diffusion, and valuation of technologies; decision modeling utilizing artificial intelligence techniques; advanced database systems; and behavioral issues related to IT usage. He has previously published in a variety of journals including Decision Sciences, the DATA-BASE for Advancement of Information Systems, the European Journal of Operational Research, the International Journal of Technology Management, and the Journal of Information Systems Education. He holds a DBA from Southern Illinois University, an MS in decision and information systems from Arizona State University, an MBA from Eastern Illinois University, and a BS in engineering mechanics from the University of Illinois.

Deborah Bunker is a Senior Lecturer in the Discipline of Business Information Systems at the University of Sydney in Australia. She holds a Ph.D. in Information Systems Management. Her research interests are in IS philosophy, IS management, IS adoption, diffusion, and e-Commerce/e-Business and she has published widely in these areas. Deborah is President of the Australasian Association of IS (AAIS) and is a founding member and the Vice Chair of IFIP TC 8 WG 8.6 on the adoption and diffusion of IT.

Brian Cameron (email: bcameron@ist.psu.edu) is a Professor of Practice at the College of Information Sciences and Technology in The Pennsylvania State University. He has received his PhD from the Pennsylvania State University. He has strong technical research and teaching experiences including enterprise architecture, enterprise integration, information systems design and development, IT project/portfolio management, and service-oriented architecture and has conducted several studies, including a study on the Impact of Personality Type and Learning Style on Virtual IT Project Team Effectiveness.

Sandy Chong, first class Honors in Marketing, PhD in Information Systems, is a Senior Research Fellow of Curtin Business School at the Curtin University of Technology. She is an active participant of industry-linked research projects in Australia, the Chair of an industry BPM roundtable in Western Australia, a Senior Research Fellow of the Asia-Pacific Procurement Research Group, and the R&D Chair for the School of Marketing at Curtin University of Technology. She conducts research in the area of innovative business and technology adoption, internet marketing, business process management (BPM), corporate communication, corporate governance, online environmental sustainability reporting, strategic alliances, supply chain intelligence, as well as IT procurement. She has presented papers at major conferences, and her work is evident in her publications which appear in information systems, marketing, supply management and global business management journals. Her industry experience includes training and consultancy, international marketing, strategic marketing management, advertising, and quantitative market research.

Efthymios Constantinides studied Economics in Athens and followed post graduate studies in Economics of European Integration in Amsterdam. He received his PhD on Marketing in Virtual Environments. After a corporate career of ten years he worked for 10 years as senior lecturer Marketing for the International Agricultural College Larenstein, (The Netherlands); since 2001 he works as Assistant Professor E-Commerce at the Faculty of Management and Governance of the University of Twente (Enschede, The Netherlands). His research interests are focused on consumer behaviour and marketing strategy in virtual environments; in particular on utilizing the Social Web environment as source of market intelligence and as active marketing instrument.

Kristy de Salas is a Senior Lecturer in the School of Computing and Information Systems at the University of Tasmania. Kristy has a research and practical interest in Information Systems Strategy in Small and Medium-sized Enterprises. Given the resource limitations of the SME, Kristy has been working with local businesses to develop tools and techniques to aid in the design and deployment of IS strategies in these businesses.

Tom R. Eikebrokk is Associate Professor of Information Systems in the Department of Information Systems, University of Agder, Norway. Dr. Eikebrokk received his PhD in Information Systems from the Norwegian School of Economics and Business Administration. He has published in journals such as Information & Management, Journal of Research and Practice in Information Technology, International journal of E-Business Research and at conferences like HICSS and ECIS. His main research interests are IT in SMEs, business process management, Evaluation of IT, IT and inter-organizational cooperation.

Jaume Franquesa is an assistant professor of management at Kent State University. He obtained his PhD in strategic management from Purdue University. His research interests are in the areas of entrepreneurship and small business management, as well as in corporate governance and the management of the diversified firm. Dr. Franquesa has published articles in Frontiers of Entrepreneurship Research, and Advances in Entrepreneurship Research, as well as in edited books and various national and international conference proceedings.

Connie Marie Gaglio is an Associate Professor of Management and Co-Director of the Ohrenschall Center for Entrepreneurship at San Francisco State University. She received her Ph.D. from the University of Chicago, her BA from SUNY-Brockport and has over 18 years of business experience in marketing and marketing research for startup companies, Fortune 500 companies and her own businesses. Her research in entrepreneurship includes entrepreneurial decision making, how new firms gain legitimacy, the role of the entrepreneur in economic theory, marketing strategies and tactics for new firms, and the impact of entrepreneurial education on a firm's success.

Paula Goulding is an adjunct academic with the School of IT at Murdoch University. She was previously a member of the Murdoch academic staff for fifteen years, after ten years in the IT industry. Her areas of interest include IT strategy and innovative practice.

Mehruz Kamal is currently pursuing her PhD in Information Technology in the College of Information Science and Technology at the University of Nebraska at Omaha. Her current research interests include IT adoption in small businesses and knowledge networking. Her research work has been presented at various peer-reviewed conferences and workshops such as AMCIS, HICSS, and MWAIS. She holds a Masters and a Bachelors of Science degree in Computer Science from Illinois Institute of Technology. Mehruz currently serves as the Editorial Assistant for the Journal of Information Technology for Development.

Pattama Kanavittaya is currently a doctoral student in the School of IT at Murdoch University. Prior to completing a Master of Commerce at Curtin University of Technology she worked in ICT positions within organisations in Thailand and Western Australia.

Mira Kartiwi is a PhD candidate at University of Wollongong in Australia. Her dissertation is concerned with the uptake of e-commerce by urban and rural SMEs in Indonesia. She has published a number of recent articles in journals and international conference proceedings. Her research interests include e-commerce in SMEs, women in IT, and IT and e-commerce in developing economies.

Arvind Karunakaran (email: axk969@ist.psu.edu) is a Research Assistant and a Graduate Student at the College of Information Sciences and Technology in The Pennsylvania State University. He has received his Bachelors in Computer Science and Engineering from Anna University, India. His research interest is at the intersection of collaborative sensemaking, organizational design and identity.

Julie E. Kendall, Ph. D., is a Professor of Management in the School of Business-Camden, Rutgers University. Dr. Kendall is a fellow of the Decision Sciences Institute and a Past Chair of IFIP Working Group 8.2. She was awarded the Silver Core from IFIP. Professor Kendall has published in MIS Quarterly, Decision Sciences, Information & Management, CAIS, EJIS, Organization Studies, JITTA and many other journals. Additionally, Dr. Kendall has co-authored the forthcoming text, Systems Analysis and Design, 8th edition. She co-edited the volume Human, Organizational, and Social Dimensions of Information Systems Development and is on the Senior Advisory Board for JITTA and is on the editorial boards of the Decision Sciences Journal of Innovative Education, Journal of Database Management, and IRMJ. Dr. Kendall is currently an Associate Editor for CAIS, and served as an Associate Editor for MIS Quarterly. She was honored as a member of the inaugural Circle of Compadres for the PhD Project begun by the KPMG Foundation, which helps minority doctoral students. She has served as a nominator for the Drama League in New York City, is a member of the council for the Rutgers Camden Center for the Arts and continues to publish research on ecommerce and nonprofit theatres.

Kenneth E. Kendall, Ph. D. is a Distinguished Professor of Management in the School of Business-Camden, Rutgers University. He is one of the founders of the International Conference on Information Systems (ICIS) and a Fellow of the Decision Sciences Institute (DSI). He served as the President of DSI and as a Program Chair for both DSI and AMCIS. Dr. Kendall was named as one of the top 60 most productive MIS researchers in the world, and he was awarded the Silver Core from IFIP. Dr. Kendall served as Associate Editor for Decision Sciences. He is on the editorial boards of ISJ, JITD, and Decision Sciences Journal of Innovative Education. He co-authored Systems Analysis and Design, forthcoming in its 8th edition. Ken edited Emerging Information Technologies: Improving Decisions, Cooperation, and Infrastructure and co-edited The Impact of Computer Supported Technologies on Information Systems Development. He was honored as a member of the inaugural Circle of Compadres for the PhD Project, which helps minority doctoral students. He is Chairman of the Board of the nonprofit EgoPo Theatre of Philadelphia. Ken has served as a nominator for the Drama League in New York City and continues to publish research on opera and IT, as well as ecommerce and theatres.

Gregor Lenart is a teaching assistant and senior researcher at the Faculty of Organizational Science, University of Maribor. He received his PhD in the MIS field from Faculty of Organizational Sciences at University of Maribor, Slovenia in 2003. He is a member of eCenter and head of the eCollaboration Laboratory. His current research includes computer supported collaborative work, group support systems and knowledge management. He is also actively involved in several EU research projects focusing on mobile commerce and e-business. He has published over 50 papers in journals and conference proceedings.

Jun Li is an Assistant Professor of Strategic Management and Entrepreneurship in the Department of Management at the University of New Hampshire. His research interests include strategic leadership in entrepreneurial teams, high-technology IPO firms, SME strategies and international strategy in emerging markets. Dr. Li received his B.A. and M.A. degrees from Beijing University, P.R. China and his Ph.D. from Texas A&M University at College Station.

Robert MacGregor is an Associate Professor in the School of Information Systems and Technology at the University of Wollongong in Australia. He is also the former Head of Discipline in Information Systems. His research expertise is in the area of information technology/electronic commerce in SMEs. He has authored over 80 journal and conference publications examining the use and adoption of IT in SMEs. Rob was the recipient of the 2004 Australian Prime Minister's Award for Excellence in Business Community Partnerships (NSW). Rob is also the founding Editor of the Australasian Journal of Information Systems and was Conference Chair of the Australian Conference of Information Systems in 1992. In his spare time, Rob writes music and has written several film scores.

Peter Marshall is the Woolworth's Chair of IT and Systems and Deputy Head of School of the School of Information Systems at the University of Tasmania. He is dedicated and committed to interesting, relevant and useful Information Systems (IS) research informed by a social constructionist perspective. His major research areas are information systems strategy, IT governance and business process management. Other research interests include qualitative research methods, the philosophical basis of IS research and systems analysis/organisational problem solving. Peter's research has been published in IT and People, the Australasian Journal of Information Systems, the Canadian Journal of Operational Research and Information Processing and The Qualitative Report. Peter has co-authored three textbooks in Information Systems.

Michael Merenda is a Professor of Strategic Management and Entrepreneurship and Chair of the Management and Marketing Departments at the University of New Hampshire. His most recent publications have been on SME competitiveness through the strategic use of information technology and the Internet. His research has appeared in: International Journal of Case Method Research & Application, Journal of Excellence in College Teaching, The Case Research Journal, Telecommunication Policy, The Sloan Management Review, Journal of Business & Entrepreneurship, Journal of Industrial and Corporate Change, and the New England Journal of Higher Education and Economic Development. Mike received his B.S. and M.B.A. degrees from Northeastern University and his Ph.D. from the University of Massachusetts in Amherst.

Dag H. Olsen is Associate Professor of Information Systems in the Department of Information Systems, University of Agder, Norway. Dr. Olsen received his PhD in Industrial economics from the Norwegian University of Science and Technology. He has published in journals such as Information & Management, European Journal of Information Systems, IEEE Transactions on Engineering Management, International journal of E-Business Research and Scandinavian Journal of Information Systems. His main research interests are e-business, enterprise systems, IT and business development, business process management, IT and inter-organizational cooperation and IT competency.

Andreja Pucihar is an Assistant Professor of e-business and management of information systems (MIS) at the Faculty of Organizational Sciences, University of Maribor. She received her PhD in the MIS field from Faculty of Organizational Sciences at University of Maribor, Slovenia in 2002. Since 1995, she has been involved in eCenter and its several research and e-commerce activities. She is a head of eMarkets Laboratory and contact person for Living laboratory for research fields of eMarkets, eSMEs and eGovernment. She is involved into several EU projects focusing on e-business and e-government and intensively cooperates with industry. Her current research includes: e-marketplaces, e-business, supply chain management, e-government and new e-business models. She has published over 100 papers in journals and conference proceedings. She is a conference chair of annual international conference Bled eConference (http://BledConference.org).

Sandeep Purao (email: spurao@ist.psu.edu) is an Associate Professor of Information Sciences and Technology in The Pennsylvania State University. He has the following experience: He has received his PhD from the University of Wisconsin-Milwaukee. His research focuses on various aspects of information system design and development. His current research projects include risk management for small and medium business, integrating workflow patterns into design, reuse-based design, flexible information system design, empirical investigations of individual design behaviors, and design theory.

Sajda Qureshi is an Associate Professor at the Information Systems and Quantitative Analysis Department at the College of Information Science and Technology at the University of Nebraska at Omaha. She holds a Ph.D. in Information Systems from the London School of Economics. She has over 100 publications in journals such as Group Decision and Negotiation, Information Infrastructure and Policy, IEEE Transactions in Professional Communications and Communications of the ACM, books published by Prentice Hall, Springer-Verlag, Chapman and Hall and North-Holland and conferences such as the ICIS and HICSS. She is currently the Editor-in-Chief of the Journal of Information and Technology for Development.

Hari K. Rajagopalan is an Assistant Professor of Management at Francis Marion University. He received his Ph.D. and MS from the University of North Carolina at Charlotte, his B.E. from Guindy, Anna University, Madras India, and his MBA from Delhi University, Delhi, India. Previously he worked in the IT industry in research and development of Web-enabled ERP products. Dr. Rajagopalan's research interests include complex adaptive systems, meta-heuristic search methods, pricing of digital goods and location of emergency medical systems. He has published papers in European Journal of Operational Research, Computers and Operations Research, and Decision Support Systems.

Frank Schlemmer is the owner and manager of a medium-sized retail company based in Germany and holds a doctorate from Queen's University Management School, Belfast. He has published a number of articles, book chapters and books in the area of SME Research, Strategic Management Research and E-Business Research.

Ada Scupola is an associate professor at the Department of Communication, Business and Information Technologies, Roskilde University, Denmark. She holds a Ph.D in social sciences from Roskilde University, an MBA from the University of Maryland at College Park, USA and a M.Sc. from the University of Bari, Italy. She is the editor-in-chief of The International Journal of E-Services and Mobile Applications. Her main research interests are e-services, outsourcing, open and user driven innovation, ICT in supply chain, adoption and diffusion of e-commerce and e-services in SMEs, ICTs in clusters of companies. She is collaborating and has collaborated to several national and international research projects on the above subjects. Her research has been published in several international journals among which International Journal of E-Services and Mobile Applications, The Information Society, Journal of Enterprise Information Management, Journal of Electronic Commerce in Organizations, The Journal of Information Science, The Journal of Global Information Technology Management, Scandinavian Journal of Information Systems, The Journal of Electronic Commerce in Developing Countries and in numerous book chapters and international conferences.

Frantisek Sudzina is an assistant professor in information systems at Copenhagen Business School, Denmark. He received his master degree in economics and business management and PhD in sectoral and intersectoral economies from the University of Economics Bratislava, Slovakia in 2000 and 2003, respectively. He received his bachelor and master degrees in mathematics from Safarik University Kosice, Slovakia in 2002 and 2004 respectively. He received his bachelor and master degrees in computer science from Safarik University Kosice, Slovakia in 2005 and 2006 respectively. Currently, he pursues his master degree in bioinformatics at Copenhagen University, Denmark. His research interests include information systems (enterprise systems, business intelligence, Web 2.0 applications, information strategy, open source software, data mining), and quantitative methods (econometrics, operations research, statistics). Dr. Sudzina has published over 100 papers in journals and conference proceedings.

A.R. (Venky) Venkatachalam is Professor of Information Systems, Chairperson of the Decision Sciences department, and Director of Enterprise Integration Research Center in the Whittemore School of Business and Economics at the University of New Hampshire. He received his bachelors degree with honors in mechanical engineering from the University of Madras, India, MBA from the Indian Institute of Management Calcutta, and Ph.D. from the University of Alabama. Dr. Venkatachalam is an Associate Editor for the Journal of Information Technology Cases and Applications Research and serves on the editorial review boards of several research journals in the information systems area. He is also a consultant to the industry in the areas of Electronic Commerce and intelligent information systems. Dr. Venkatachalam has received several awards and honors including the 2006 University of New Hampshire's Faculty Excellence in Research Award.

Brian Webb is Senior Lecturer at Queen's University Management School, Belfast, and at the Open University Business School. He is a former Distinguished Erskine Fellow in the Department of Accounting, Finance, and Information Systems, Faculty of Commerce, University of Canterbury, New Zealand. He holds a Bachelor's degree from Queen's, an MBA from the University of Ulster and a PhD from University College London. In 1999 he was Visiting Scholar in the Department of Computer Science, University of British Columbia.

Phyl Willson completed her PhD at the University of Tasmania in June 2008. Dr. Willson's PhD topic was IT Governance in Theory and Practice. She is now working on research across a range of areas including wireless networks, broadband, with the Tasmanian Electronic Commerce Centre (TECC) and in the areas of ICT and SMEs, IT governance, business process management, business process outsourcing and qualitative research methods. Dr. Willson's research has previously been published in Information Systems Management (ISM), the Australasian Journal of Information Systems (AJIS), Journal of Research and Practice in Information Technology (JRPIT) and at international conferences.

Susan J. Winter is a Program Director at the National Science Foundation's Office of Cyberinfrastructure and a Visiting Associate Professor of Management Information Systems at Portland State University. She received her Ph.D. from the University of Arizona, her MA from Claremont Graduate University and her BS from the University of California at Berkeley. Her work investigates the interplay between information technology, individuals and the social environment. Recent research interests include the symbolic aspects of ICT, its impact on employees and the organization of work. Dr. Winter has published papers in such journals as Information Systems Research, the European Journal of Information Systems, Information and Management, and the Journal of Business Ethics, and contributed chapters to scholarly books.

Peter Wolcott obtained his Ph.D. in 1993 from the Department of Management Information Systems at the University of Arizona, where he pursued interests in the international dimensions of information technology. Dr. Wolcott has long-standing interests in the international dimensions of information technologies. His most active research at present focuses on the role of information technology for development (ITD). He teaches students to apply ITD concepts and practices to promote economic, social, and human development in micro-enterprises.

Judy Young is a lecturer within the School of Computing and Information Systems at the University of Tasmania. Her main interests are in the supervision of PhD candidates and researching in a wide range of information systems (IS) areas including gender, virtual organisations, business modelling, culture and enterprise research planning, and enterprise architecture. Along with her two co-authors listed above, Judy is an active member of the Interpretivist Research in Information Systems (IRIS) research group.

Index

Symbols

5-C framework 293

A

accounting 147, 151, 158
action research 23, 203, 210, 214, 306, 308,
        313, 314, 315, 316, 323, 325
action research (AR) 197
actual complementarity 273
adaptive software development (ASD) 219
ad hoc 198, 199, 200, 235
adoption 110, 111, 112, 113, 114, 115, 116,
        117, 120, 121, 122, 123, 124, 125, 126,
        127, 128, 129, 130, 132, 133, 134, 135,
        136, 137, 138, 139, 140, 141, 142, 143,
        169, 170, 171, 172, 173, 174, 175, 176,
        177, 178, 179, 180, 181, 183, 184, 185,
        186, 187, 188, 189, 190, 191, 192, 193,
        234, 237, 238, 239, 240, 248, 251, 253,
        255
adoption process 112
advanced technology 61, 66, 69, 70, 75
affordability 309
agile methodologies 215, 217, 219, 231, 232
agile software development 215, 216, 217,
        218, 219, 220, 225, 228, 229
alignment 239, 240
alliance 222, 224, 226
analyser 218, 220, 222, 224, 226, 227
ANOVA 62, 65, 66, 71, 74
antecedent factors 135
applied theory research 23
ARIS modelling approach 206, 211, 214

Australia 109, 110, 111, 117, 121, 122, 124,
        126, 127, 128, 130, 131, 132, 133, 136,
        140, 141, 142, 143, 145, 147, 155, 156,
        157, 158, 159, 160, 162, 164, 165, 167,
        168
Australian Bureau of Statistics (ABS) 132,
        147, 161, 197, 203
average variance extracted (AVE) 245

B

black markets 151
blogging 50, 51, 53
blogs 2, 4, 8, 10, 13, 21
bricolage 169, 176, 184, 185, 187
Broadway 41, 42, 44, 45, 46, 47, 48, 49, 51,
        52, 53, 55, 56
bulletin boards 292
business domain 235, 238
business-IT synergies 26
business process digitalization (BPD) 290,
        291, 292, 293, 294, 295, 297, 298, 299,
        300, 304, 305
business sectors 136, 237
business strategy 195, 196, 201, 203, 204, 208,
        209, 210, 215, 216, 217, 218, 220, 221,
        222, 223, 224, 225, 226, 227, 228, 229,
        230, 231, 232, 233, 239
business sustainability 237
business systems planning 198
business-to-business 112, 118
business to customers (B2C) 290, 292, 293,
        295, 305
business to employees (B2E) 292, 293, 295,
        305

business to others (B2O) 292, 293, 295, 305
business to suppliers (B2S) 292

C

capability 292, 298, 299, 301
catch-22 86
centralised 222, 227
chief information officer (CIO) 62, 63, 64, 66,
    67, 68, 69, 70, 71, 73, 74, 75
client companies 137
cloud computing 251
communication factors 119
competitive advantage provided by an informa-
    tion technology application (CAPITA)
    310
Competitive Potential 221, 224, 227, 228
computerized core 171, 172, 176, 177, 178,
    179, 181, 183
computer networks 146
computer training 309
connectivity 61, 66, 70, 73
contractual arrangements 240
corporate communication mix 2
corporate image 83, 84, 87, 92, 94, 95, 98, 99,
    101, 102, 104, 106, 107
corporate subsidiaries 178
critical success factors 198
CRM 62, 66, 72, 74
cross-country awareness 111
crowdsourcing 4, 11, 13
customer-collaborated products 294, 295, 297,
    298, 299, 300
customer-driven e-business 270
customer pressure 122, 124, 125
customer relationships 269

D

decentralised 222, 227
defender 217, 218, 220, 222, 223, 226
determinant factor 140
developed economies 145, 146, 151, 152, 154,
    156, 158
developing economies 145, 146, 147, 151, 152,
    154, 155, 156, 158, 159, 160
digitalization 290, 292, 294, 295, 296, 297,
    298, 299, 300

dot.com boom 1
"dot-com" bubble 109
DSS capability 50, 51, 53
Dual Lens Approach 203, 204, 205, 207, 208,
    209, 210
dynamic capabilities 265, 267, 268, 269, 270,
    271, 272, 273, 275, 276, 277, 281, 283,
    288, 289
dynamic systems development method
    (DSDM) 219, 224

E

eBay Foundation 308, 314
e-business 58, 59, 61, 62, 66, 70, 73, 74, 75,
    77, 78, 205, 207, 208, 234, 235, 236,
    237, 238, 239, 240, 241, 242, 243, 244,
    245, 246, 247, 249, 72, 250, 251, 252,
    253, 254, 256, 258, 259, 260, 261, 262,
    263, 264, 270, 274, 275, 277, 283, 285,
    290, 291, 293, 295, 298, 299, 302, 303,
    304, 307, 308, 326, 328
e-business enablement 61, 66, 70, 73, 75
e-business techniques 308
EC applications 111, 120
e-commerce 132, 133, 134, 135, 136, 137, 138,
    139, 140, 141, 142, 144, 145, 146, 148,
    151, 152, 153, 154, 155, 156, 157, 158,
    159, 160, 161, 162, 163, 164, 165, 166,
    167, 169, 171, 172, 173, 176, 177, 178,
    179, 181, 183, 184, 185, 186, 188, 191,
    193, 267, 271, 281, 283
e-commerce adoption 132, 133, 134, 135, 137,
    139, 140, 141, 142, 145, 146, 151, 152,
    153, 154, 155, 157, 158, 159, 160, 161,
    164, 172, 178, 190, 191
economic development associations 24
e-customer relationship management (E-CRM)
    293
EDB department 139, 141
educational level 136
efficiency 222, 223
electronic commerce (EC) 109, 110, 111, 112,
    113, 114, 115, 116, 117, 118, 120, 121,
    122, 123, 124, 125, 126, 131
electronic data interchange (EDI) 112, 133,
    142, 172, 188, 190

electronic transactions 138, 139

e-mail 139, 292, 308, 309, 316, 318

empirical evidence 237, 238

end-users 309

enterprise resource planning (ERP) system 57,
    58, 59, 60, 61, 62, 63, 64, 65, 66, 67, 68,
    69, 70, 71, 72, 73, 74, 75, 76, 77, 78, 79,
    80

enterprise scale 148

enterprise-wide systems 58

entrepreneur 307, 308, 309, 315, 316, 325

entrepreneurship 151, 155

environmental factors 133, 135, 136, 141

e-procurement 178

European Commission 147, 155

European Union (EU) 236, 238, 248, 250

evaluation research 23

extent of deployment 112, 113, 126, 127

external consultants 237

external environmental context 134

external environmental factors 114, 115, 117,
    119

external linkages 239

external validity 136

extreme programming (XP) 219

F

Facebook 51

factor analysis 147, 157

feature driven development (FDD) 219, 224,
    229

Federal Reserve Board 177

finance 147, 150, 152, 161

finance, awareness and trust (FAT) 249

financial incentives 139, 140

financial resources 269, 270, 275, 285

financing 82, 86, 101

firm age 294, 295, 297, 298

focus dominance model 306

Fortune 500 companies 239

forums 292

F-value 122

G

GDP 146, 170, 234

global environment 111

globalization 139, 140, 307, 311

global markets 146

H

hands-on experience 124

healthy private sectors 146

homoscedasticity 275

human resource management 137

human resources 58, 64, 265, 266, 267, 268

hybridity 41, 42, 44, 49, 50, 53

I

I-99 corridor 22, 23, 24, 30, 31, 32, 33, 34, 36

ICT adoption 82, 83, 84, 93, 94, 98, 237

ICT champions 237

ICT consulting services 134

ICT expectations 81

ICT investments 237, 239

ICT technology 237

implementation success 109, 112, 117

industry identity 84

industry pressure 140

informal management practices 198

information engineering 198

information strategy 57, 62, 63, 66, 67, 68, 69,
    71, 73, 75

information systems (IS) 22, 23, 25, 26, 28, 32,
    33, 35, 36, 37, 38, 39, 40, 112, 133, 134,
    135, 136, 141, 161, 170, 195, 196, 197,
    198, 199, 200, 201, 202, 203, 204, 206,
    207, 208, 209, 210, 211, 212, 213, 214,
    215, 216, 218, 229, 230, 231, 232, 233,
    291, 292, 293, 294, 299, 300, 308, 309,
    313, 326, 327, 328, 329

Information Systems Planning 198

information technology and information sys-
    tems (IT/IS) 215, 216, 217, 218, 219,
    220, 221, 222, 223, 224, 225, 226, 227,
    228, 229

information technology for development
    (IT4D) 314, 316

information technology (IT) therapy 306, 308,
    313, 315, 316, 317, 318, 319, 320, 321,
    322, 323, 324, 325

infrastructure 111, 116, 126, 128, 131, 239,
    240, 261, 264, 309

infusion 222, 225, 226
innovation adoption 169, 170, 171, 173, 174, 176, 179, 180, 183, 184, 185, 186, 187, 191
innovation factors 114, 115, 119
insourcing 222
institutional theory 84, 99
Internal barriers 152
internal (employed) specialists 147
internal environmental factors 114, 115
internal transparency 308
international consumers 308
Internet 146, 153, 163, 164, 165, 166, 167, 168, 172, 173, 178, 179, 187, 190, 192, 238, 240, 254, 255, 258, 259, 261, 265, 266, 267, 269, 270, 271, 272, 273, 274, 275, 276, 277, 278, 285, 287, 288, 289, 290, 291, 292, 293, 295, 296, 297, 298, 299, 300, 301, 302, 305
Internet applications 1, 15, 21
Internet-based EC 111, 113
Internet-based software 215
Internet infrastructure 151
Internet penetration 110
Internet-related technologies 141
Internet service providers 137, 140
inter-organisational system (IOS) 112, 133
Intranet 136, 137
inventory 147
inverted U-shaped relationship 170, 176, 183
IS application delivery 239
IS assets 161
IS field 238
IS literature 238, 246
IS phenomenon 82
IS portfolio 203, 208, 210
IS strategy 63, 195, 196, 197, 198, 199, 200, 201, 202, 203, 204, 208, 209, 210, 211
IS strategy formulation method 195, 196
IT adoption 307, 309, 310, 325
IT application 178, 310
IT applications 310
IT assets 265, 266, 267, 268, 269, 270, 272, 273, 275, 276, 277, 278, 288, 289, 292
IT-based resources 292
IT-based utilities 196

IT budget 239
IT-business partnership 240
IT-business partnerships 239
IT department 57, 62, 63, 66, 67, 68, 69, 73, 74, 75, 200, 201, 204
IT expenditure 295, 297, 298
IT for development (ITD) 306, 315, 316, 317, 320, 321, 322, 323, 324, 325
IT for Development (ITD) innovators 306, 315, 316, 317, 321, 323, 324, 325
IT functionalities 292
IT infrastructure 217, 220, 221, 225, 226, 267, 271, 292, 293, 294, 309
IT innovations 170, 175, 185, 187
IT knowledge 138, 139, 268, 274, 285
IT-lagging companies 275, 277, 288
IT-leading companies 275, 277
IT management 239, 255, 264
IT manager 295, 297, 298
IT managers 63
IT maturity 215, 218, 228
IT objects 268, 274, 286
IT operations 268, 275, 286
IT project management 239
IT project plan 306, 308
IT related services 140
IT resources 292, 293, 294, 311, 313, 316, 324, 325
IT satisfaction 134, 142
IT service providers 25, 26
IT services 132, 137, 138, 140
IT skills 308, 311, 315
IT solutions 306, 308
IT strategy 215, 216, 218, 221, 224, 225, 226, 229, 232
IT system 292, 293, 295

J

junk mail 139

K

knowledge-based view 291, 293, 294, 299
knowledge bases 291, 294
knowledge networks 22, 24, 25, 29, 31, 35

L

lack of time 152, 158, 160
legacy industrial era regions 22, 24, 25, 30, 31, 33, 34, 35, 36
legitimacy 81, 82, 83, 84, 85, 86, 87, 88, 89, 90, 91, 92, 93, 94, 95, 96, 97, 98, 99, 100, 101, 102, 103, 104, 105, 106, 107
level of usage 112, 113, 126
leveraging advanced IT research (LAIR) 22, 24, 33, 35
Likert scale 62, 65
localisation 151, 159
local market 137
low risk propensity 198
low technology turbulent environments 266
loyalty 310

M

management of information systems (MIS) 112, 127, 128, 129, 272, 278, 279, 281, 282
management's capacity 310
management style 148
management support 119
marketing 147, 162, 163
market intelligence 1
market niche 308, 310
medium business 27, 28, 39, 197
medium sized firms 309
micro businesses 197
micro-enterprises 306, 307, 308, 309, 310, 312, 313, 314, 315, 316, 318, 323, 324, 325, 327, 329
micro-entrepreneur 308, 315
micro firms 309
mimicry 41, 42, 44, 46, 47, 48, 49, 53
MS Dynamics NAV 64

N

New Community Development Corporation (NCDC) 314
new jobs 307, 308
new product development 295, 297, 302
new product development (NPD) 290
non-financial measurements 147

nonprofit 41, 42, 43, 44, 45, 46, 47, 48, 49, 50, 51, 52, 53, 55, 56
nonprofit theatre 41, 42, 43, 44, 45, 46, 47, 49, 50, 51, 52, 53
non-respondents 118

O

observability 109, 115, 119, 122, 124, 126
OECD countries 236, 256
Off-Broadway 42, 45, 51, 52, 55, 56
"off-the-shelf" products 294
online customer support 136, 137, 138, 140
online forums 2, 9, 11, 14
on-line store-front 179
online training 136, 137, 140
on-the-job-training 124
opportunistic 222, 226
O'Reilly, Tim 5, 6, 11, 18, 49
organisational factors 152, 160
organisational readiness 119
organizational factors 134
organizational learning 291, 292, 293, 294, 299, 302, 303
organizational readiness 133
organizational size 134
organizational slack 169, 170, 171, 172, 173, 174, 176, 183, 184, 185, 186, 187, 188, 189, 192
organizational structure 134
outsourcing 222, 227, 240, 244, 254, 255, 260
overall satisfaction 109, 111, 112, 113, 114, 116, 117, 122, 123, 124, 125, 126

P

paradigm model 83, 91, 94
partial least squares analysis (PLS) 243, 245, 252
payment obligations 151
Peer-to-Peer applications 2
perceived financial cost 134
perceived governmental support 122
perceived readiness 119, 122, 123
perceived technical competence 134
personnel 147
podcasts 50, 51, 53
policy research 23

positive assets 178
positive sales 178
potential complementarity 273
potential slack 169, 170, 174, 175, 176, 177,
    179, 180, 181, 183, 184, 185, 186
poverty 310
private/government sectors 309
Product differentiation 310
production 147
productivity 307, 308, 309
prospector 218, 220, 222, 225, 226, 227

R

relevance 22, 23, 30, 34, 35, 40
rent-creating potential 277, 278
resource-based view 291, 303
resource-based view of the firm (RBV) 265,
    266, 268, 270
resource heterogeneity 311
resource immobility 311
resource poverty 148, 265
rigor 22, 23, 30, 35
'rigor-relevance' gap 22
RSS feeds 50, 51, 53
Rust Belt 24, 38

S

schema theory 97
schematic processing 88
SCM 62, 66, 72, 74
security 152, 154, 160
selective sourcing 222
Service Level 221
service range 148, 150
servicing 147
shared responsibility 222
short message service (SMS) 51
Singapore 109, 110, 111, 117, 120, 121, 122,
    126, 128, 130, 131
small and medium businesses (SMB) 24, 27,
    34, 40, 43, 47, 132
small business 24, 26, 27, 28, 36, 37, 39, 40,
    111, 113, 129, 130, 131, 197, 213, 214,
    235, 236, 252, 253, 254, 255, 256, 307,
    308, 309, 310, 312, 313, 316, 325, 328,
    329

small-business users 134, 142
small firms 110, 265, 267, 268, 271, 272, 276,
    277, 278, 279, 282, 308
small to medium enterprises (SME) 1, 3, 4, 5,
    7, 12, 13, 14, 15, 18, 19, 22, 23, 24, 25,
    26, 27, 28, 29, 30, 31, 32, 33, 34, 35,
    36, 37, 38, 39, 40, 41, 42, 43, 46, 47,
    48, 49, 50, 51, 104, 105, 107, 110, 111,
    113, 114, 115, 116, 117, 121, 122, 123,
    124, 125, 126, 127, 128, 129, 130, 131,
    132, 133, 134, 135, 158, 159, 160, 161,
    162, 163, 164, 165, 166, 167, 168, 169,
    170, 171, 172, 173, 174, 175, 176, 177,
    178, 179, 180, 181, 183, 184, 185, 186,
    187, 188, 190, 191, 192, 193, 195, 196,
    197, 198, 199, 215, 216, 217, 218, 220,
    221, 227, 228, 229, 230, 231, 232, 234,
    235, 236, 237, 238, 239, 241, 242, 243,
    244, 246, 247, 293, 294, 295, 298, 299,
    300, 302, 304, 306, 307, 308, 312, 313,
    326, 327, 328, 329
Smartphone 50, 53
social bookmarking 50, 51, 53
social Internet 1
social media 1, 2, 3, 4, 5, 6, 7, 8, 9, 10, 11, 12,
    13, 14, 15, 16, 17, 19
social networking 51
social networking sites 50
social networks 2, 11, 12, 14, 307
social relationships 1
software-as-a-service 251
software components 136
sourcing 239, 240, 244, 247, 290, 293, 305
special interest groups 82
stakeholders 81, 82, 83, 84, 85, 86, 87, 88, 95,
    99, 101
strategic alignment model (SAM) 218, 221,
    224, 227
strategic assets 265, 266, 267, 268, 269, 270,
    271, 273, 275, 276, 277, 278, 283, 288
strategic information systems planning (SISP)
    198, 199, 210, 211
Strategic Integration 221
strategic IS planning 82
strategic planning for information resources
    198

strategic positioning 84
strategy set transformation 198
supplier contracts 86
supplier driven e-business 270
supplier pressure 122, 125
supplier relationships 269
survey of small business finances (SSBF) 177, 178, 179, 180, 181, 185, 186, 187, 193
synergistic 266, 277
synergy 292, 299

T

tax breaks 139
technological infrastructure 111
technology acceptance model (TAM) 172
technology-organization-environment (TOE) 172, 173, 185
technology support infrastructure 134
technology transformation 221
telecommunication 235
telecommunications-based tools 235
telecommunications networks 132
the third space 41, 42, 43, 44, 49, 50, 51, 52, 53, 55
turnover growth 57, 62, 69, 70, 73
twitter 51

U

United States Small Business Administration (SBA) 147
user generated content (UGC) 5, 21

V

variety of communication channels 122, 124
vendor-related criteria 57, 60, 61, 66, 71
venture capital (VC) 31
venture success 294
video camera 138, 140
virtual markets 271, 278
virtual worlds 50, 51, 52, 53

W

Web 2.0 1, 2, 3, 4, 5, 6, 7, 8, 9, 10, 11, 12, 13, 14, 15, 16, 17, 18, 19, 20, 21, 41, 49, 50, 51, 52, 53, 55
Web 2.0-based applications 1, 10, 11
Web-base collaboration 50
web-based auctions 241
Web-based technology 217
web presence 307, 321, 323
World Wide Web (WWW) 109

X

XML 76

Y

YouTube 50, 51, 52, 53